UNDERDEVELOPMENT TO DEVELOPING ECONOMIES

Underdevelopment
to
Developing Economies

Edited by S. P. SINGH

1978

OXFORD UNIVERSITY PRESS

BOMBAY OXFORD NEW YORK

Oxford University Press

OXFORD LONDON GLASGOW
NEW YORK TORONTO MELBOURNE WELLINGTON
IBADAN NAIROBI DAR ES SALAAM CAPE TOWN
KUALA LUMPUR SINGAPORE JAKARTA HONG KONG TOKYO
DELHI BOMBAY CALCUTTA MADRAS KARACHI

Printed by K. P. Puthran at the Tata Press Limited, 414, Veer Savarkar Marg, Bombay 400 025 and published by R. Dayal, Oxford University Press, Oxford House, Apollo Bunder, Bombay 400 039

INTRODUCTION

In the introduction to *The Economics of Underdevelopment* which appeared nineteen years ago, we indicated that it would be followed by two further volumes of selected readings covering the remaining aspects of the subject. The second volume in the series, *Accelerating Investment in Developing Economies*,* was published eight years ago. The present volume is the third in the series. The first volume comprised articles which deal with the economics of underdevelopment in an overall manner. The focus is on underdevelopment as a total problem, not the parts of the problem. They represent the formative years of the subject when separate articles on specific aspects were rarely written. In subsequent years specialized treatment of the problems of investment was in vogue. This is reflected in the selections for the second volume. The remaining problem areas are covered in the present volume: dualism, agriculture, industrialization, wages, employment, trade and foreign exchange.

Nearly twenty-five years ago we were attracted by the early signs of the emergence of a new branch of study: economics of underdevelopment. It was seen as a subject deep and broad enough to be treated as a separate branch of economics. Moreover, it had both continuity and rigour entitling it to be a legitimate part of the future history of economic analysis. But most of the contributions were scattered in journals. It was not possible for a serious beginner to go quickly to those pieces which contained ideas that were likely to influence thought and reality for many more years to come. We, therefore, planned for these three volumes of selected readings.

Today the situation is somewhat different. The initial flood of ideas is no longer there. As it happens with other innovations, we seem to be settling down to 'normalcy'. Moreover, the important new ideas are now in most cases not coming forth only in the journals, but explored in a large number of monographs. There has also been a dissection of underdevelopment into its various 'components': poverty, regional planning, appropriate technology, inequality, neo-colonialism, etc. Such developments mark the end of a phase and the beginning of another.

We hope these three volumes contain most of the important contributions to thought on the subject during the first phase of about twenty-five years. Our eyes were always set for such pieces

* Both Volumes, Oxford University Press, 1958 and 1969, respectively.

which aimed at developing new concepts, tools and models; or, which made a new use of existing concepts, tools and models for a better understanding of the problem of underdevelopment. In other words, we were attracted more by the finer aspects of economics 'as a tool of analysis' than by the conclusions in respect of an immediate or pressing policy issue. The former have not only more longevity, but also greater value as inputs in the training of the coming generations of students of economics, particularly in the developing societies. They must master the rigours of the methodology of economic science, so that they are better equipped to deal with the changing policy issues. We see great merit in interdisciplinary studies on problems of development. That represents the latest in policy research. But the new trend, if it has to go a long way, must of necessity assume the best of rigour from each participating discipline and the development of each discipline in its own right.

It is admitted that the three volumes put together leave out some important areas altogether. We regret, for instance, the exclusion of planning. But that would have meant one more volume. The choice was really difficult, and we thought it expedient not to extend the series by one more volume. Perhaps, the totality of the new context as it obtains today does not justify such an extension of the series. It is also admitted that even within the areas selected for inclusion many important pieces have not been included. The response in respect of permission to reprint in case of second and third volumes was not as spontaneous and encouraging as it was in case of the first volume. This also explains largely the long delays in the publication of subsequent volumes.

The present volume contains twenty-two articles selected from various journals and monographs. Four of them have appeared earlier in other anthologies. All these pieces have been arranged under seven sections.

The first section entitled 'Agrarianism, Dualism and Development' contains three contributions. The first two by G. Ranis and J. C. H. Fei and D. W. Jorgenson, present two widely-known models of dualistic economies. The distinctions between classical and neo-classical assumptions are clearly spelt out and relationships between population growth, surplus labour, agricultural and industrial sectors and employment have been brought out meaningfully. The third piece by C. H. C. Kao, K. R. Anschel and C. K. Eicher is a short but highly useful lookback at the development of the concept of disguised unemployment.

Six contributions are included in the second section which focuses on problems of labour in models of developing economies. They deal with wages and employment in labour surplus economies, labour migration in the two-sector model, labour absorption in the industrial sector, and, urban unemployment in developing economies. These studies are based on neat and compact models which in most cases are also supported by recent empirical evidence.

The Third section contains two papers on development of agriculture. K. N. Raj discusses the role of input improvements: irrigation, fertilizers and the high-yielding variety of seeds. The other paper by V. M. Dandekar discusses the basics of the debate on agrarian reform.

One major controversy of fifties and sixties, particularly in the context of the Latin American developing societies, had been between monetarists and structuralists. In much broader context, import-substituting industrialization had been the dominant development philosophy of most developing societies during this period. Both helped in the generation of analytical economic thought and literature. It is represented appropriately and adequately by three excellent papers in the fourth section by D. Felix, J. H. Power and A. O. Hirschman.

The fifth section includes five papers on problems of international trade in the context of the developing countries. There are several excellent papers of the fifties, particularly those written by H. W. Singer, H. Myint, H. G. Johnson, R. Prebisch, R. Baldwin and others. We have preferred the papers of the later years because we found them incorporating the earlier thinking and yet moving several steps ahead. M. H. Watkins covers the famous staple theory of growth, the concept of the leading sector of growth and the gains from trade. H. B. Chenery reviews the literature of about twenty-five years on the place of the doctrine of comparative advantage in development policy; and he presents his own thinking, particularly in the area of programming models of growth. J. Vanek's is a succinct but neat and compact presentation, ideal for the student of international trade aspects of economic growth in less-developed countries. P. Bardhan deals with application of the concept of external economies to theories of economic development and protection. The paper by B. Balassa discusses policy issues relating to trade from the viewpoint of the developing countries in today's context and covers the important theme: from import substitution to export promotion.

The late sixties witnessed an important debate on the two-gap theory of constraints to development in less-developed countries, more particularly the foreign exchange constraint. We have selected from this literature two useful papers by H. J. Bruton and R. R. Nelson, to comprise the sixth section.

The last paper by A. O. Hirschman and M. Rothschild is included to represent new directions in thinking and the attempts at sophisticated model building in an area which still remains woolly for the social scientists.

We take this opportunity to state that articles in this volume, like the earlier two volumes, have been reproduced as originally published (retaining the American or British spellings as in the original). In other words, nothing has been left out. Only a few modifications have been made so as to conform to the general style of the book. Once again we feel sorry to have had to leave out many articles which we would have very much liked to include. The reasons are the same as were stated in the Introduction to the first volume. That, however, is neither meant to explain or justify any blemishes or shortcomings in the selections for this volume. The responsibility is clearly the editor's.

We may add that several articles included in the first and second volumes also discuss some important aspects of problems covered by the present volume. These can be reached with the help of indexes to those volumes.

We have great pleasure in acknowledging a debt of gratitude to all the authors whose contributions comprise this volume and who so readily and generously allowed us to reprint them. We are also indebted to the original publishers who co-operated with us in a similar manner. Particular assistance was extended by Professor Albert O. Hirschman and the Secretary to the Delegates of the Clarendon Press, to whom our thanks are due.

The first two volumes were jointly edited by my teacher and colleague for over two decades, Professor A. N. Agarwala, and myself. Before we could meet and discuss the selection, he died in an air crash in May 1973. I wish he could have shared the responsibility for the shortcomings of this volume as well.

Bombay S.P.S.

CONTENTS

IV Import-Substituting Industrialization

V Trade and Development

VI Foreign Exchange Constraint

VII Inequality and Development

ACKNOWLEDGEMENTS

Johns Hopkins Press for 'Agrarianism, Dualism and Economic Development' by John C. H. Fei and Gustav Ranis from *The Theory and Design of Economic Development*, (eds) I. Adelman and E. Thorbecke, 1966.

Oxford Economic Papers for 'Surplus Agricultural Labour and the Development of a Dual Economy' by Dale W. Jorgenson, November 1967; for 'Urban Unemployment and Economic Growth in Africa' by C.R. Frank Jr., July 1968; for 'Employment and Wages in Dual Agriculture' by Robert Mabro, November 1971; for 'Economic Theory and Agrarian Reform' by V.M. Dandekar, February 1962; for 'External Economies, Economic Development and the Theory of Protection' by Pranab Bardhan.

McGraw Hill Book Co., New York, for 'Disguised Unemployment in Agriculture: A Survey' by Charles H. C. Kao, Kurt R. Anschel and Carl K. Eicher from *Agriculture in Economic Development* (eds) C. K. Eicher and K. W. Witt, 1964.

Quarterly Journal of Economics for 'Employment and Industrialization in Developing Economies' by Werner Baer and Michel E.A. Hervé, February 1966; for 'Economic Growth and International Trade in Pure Theory' by Jaroslav Vanek, August 1971; for 'The Changing Tolerance for Income Inequality in the Course of Economic Development' by Albert O. Hirschman, November 1973.

American Economic Review for 'Wages and Employment in a Labor-Surplus Economy' by Lloyd G. Reynolds, September 1965; for 'Migration, Unemployment and Development: A Two-Sector Analysis' by John R. Harris and Michael P. Todaro, March 1970; for 'Comparative Advantage and Development Policy' by Hollis B. Chenery, March 1961; for 'Trade Policies in Developing Countries by Bela Balassa, May 1971; for 'The Two-Gap Approach to Aid and Development: Comment' by Henry J. Bruton, June 1969.

Economic Development and Cultural Change for 'Industrial Sector Labor Absorption' by Gustav Ranis, April 1973.

Macmillan, London, for 'Some Questions Concerning Growth, Transformation and Planning of Agriculture in Developing Countries' by K.N. Raj from *Economic Development in South Asia*, (eds) E.A.G. Robinson and M. Kidron, 1970.

Studies in Comparative International Development for 'Monetarists, Structuralists and Import-Substituting Industrialization: A Critical Appraisal', 1965.

Philippine Journal of Economics for 'Import Substitution as an Industrialization Policy' by John H. Power, second semester 1966.

Yale University Press for 'The Political Economy of Import-Substituting Industrialization in Latin America' by A. O. Hirschman from *A Bias for Hope*, (ed) A. O. Hirschman, 1971.

The Canadian Journal of Economic and Political Science for 'A Staple Theory of Economic Growth' by Melville H. Watkins, May 1963.

Journal of Political Economy for 'The Effective Exchange Rate Employment and Growth in a Foreign Exchange—Constrained Economy' by Richard R. Nelson, May/June 1970.

1

AGRARIANISM, DUALISM AND ECONOMIC DEVELOPMENT

John C. H. Fei and Gustav Ranis

I Introduction

FROM THE BEGINNINGS of our science, economists have been trying to gain a better understanding of the economy's growth performance. In the recent resurgence of interest in development, after the long neoclassical interregnum, there has been some effort to glean as much helpful information as possible from the analysis of earlier work. Both the old writers and the new increasingly seem to agree that the real world essence of a developing system cannot be meaningfully 'captured' by conventional aggregative analysis and that the search for significant intersectoral relations and intersectoral asymmetries may well provide the key to the enhanced understanding we seek.

Nevertheless, when endeavoring to extract the maximum transferable knowledge from the writings of the physiocrats and the classicists, for example, we must be painfully aware that each such formulation is inevitably the product of its own particular historical conditions and circumstances. The transferability of any particular set of concepts is circumscribed by differences in the social issues faced, in the tools available, and, consequently, in the vision of the future presented. Therefore the usefulness of past theories is limited for examining the problems facing us now in the less developed world.

In this general context we think it useful to distinguish among three major types of economic systems—agrarianism, dualism, and economic maturity. Economic maturity has been exhaustively treated by post-Keynesian growth theorists[1] and is not our major concern here, but we believe the distinction between agrarian and

1 See, for example, R. M. Solow, 'A Contribution to the Theory of Economic Growth,' *Quarterly Journal of Economics*, LXX (February, 1956), pp. 65–90; T. W. Swan, 'Economic Growth and Capital Accumulation,' *Economic Record*, XXXII (November, 1956), pp. 334-61.

dualistic economies to be of considerable importance for a fuller understanding of the relevance of earlier writers to our present concern with growth in the less-developed economy.

The central feature of agrarianism is the overwhelming preponderance of traditional agricultural pursuits. While other economic activities may be in evidence, they are of distinctly secondary importance in both a quantitative and qualitative sense. Those nonagricultural pursuits which exist are characterized by a modest use of capital. The agrarian economy is essentially stagnant, with nature and population pressure vying for supremacy over long periods of recorded history. Moreover, the prognosis for the future is likely to be 'more of the same.'

The central feature of dualism, on the other hand, is the coexistence of a large agricultural sector with an active and dynamic industrial sector. Industry uses capital, and both sectors undergo continuous technological change as they 'interact' during the growth process. The dualistic economy strives to adjust the historical preponderance of agriculture by gradually shifting its center of gravity toward industry through factor reallocation. Its inherent condition is thus one of change, and its vision of the future is the ultimate graduation into economic maturity.

It is our view that both the eighteenth-century physiocrats and the later classicists were really addressing themselves to the problem of growth in an agrarian economy. The physiocrats' major contribution undoubtedly lay in the recognition—for the first time—that the growth of the economy must be viewed basically as an interrelated system of intersectoral flows. In their world, only the preponderant agricultural sector is capable of producing a surplus, as agricultural workers exploit the fundamental bounty of nature. Nonagriculture is peopled by the so-called 'sterile classes' which cannot produce a surplus, but can only transform value created in agriculture. The owners of the land, the landlord, the nobility, or the church 'own' whatever 'slack' there may be in the system, whether in the form of the emerging agricultural surplus or of redundant manpower available for personal services, feudal wars, and the like. These slacks are largely consumed by the propertied classes, either directly, in the form of food, or indirectly, in the form of the output of the sterile classes, as services and handicraft products, which are delivered in exchange for the wage goods provided. It is at least implicitly assumed that no marked changes in agricultural production techniques can occur and that the artisan and service sectors remain completely stagnant. Thus, to the physiocrats, growth was tantamount to the perpetuation of the cultural life of the ruling classes made possible by the assumed regularity of the circular flow mechanism described in their 'tableau économique.'

The classical school of economists was heavily influenced by its physiocratic predecessors and also turned its attention primarily to analysis of the agrarian economy. As Schumpeter points out, before 1790 'all countries—even England—were predominantly agrarian.'[2] Thus, while the classicists referred to the growth of industry, their analytical attention was concentrated on distribution on the long-run growth prospects of an undifferentiated, monolithic economy dominated by agriculture. The tripartite division of income, perhaps their major analytical contribution, is analyzed in a setting in which 'the typical capitalist... was the "farmer" in the British sense, who rented land [from the absentee landlord] and hired laborers, received the product at the end of the year and turned over to the two other claimants their respective shares.'[3] There is occasional reference to nonagricultural activities now viewed as capable of producing a surplus along with agriculture,[4] but as Schumpeter put it, 'the manufacturing industry that economists beheld and reasoned about was all along the manufacturing industry of the artisan.'[5]

In the agrarian system there is still no clearly discernible industrial capital in the form of reproducible plant and equipment, but only the extension of production advances in the form of wage goods to industrial workers for the support of further production.[6] Technological change is once again either ignored or considered to be of only secondary interest. The classicists made a considerable advance in presenting a fully deterministic system capable of dynamic analysis, but they saw their problem in physiocratic terms and their prediction of the ultimate stationary state was one of continued agrarian stagnation. 'Both groups [the classicists

2 Joseph A. Schumpeter, *History of Economic Analysis* (New York, 1954), p. 565.

3 Frank H. Knight, 'Capital and Interest,' reprinted in *Readings in the Theory of Income Distribution* (Philadelphia, 1946), p. 385.

4 Even though Smith still exempted services as nonproductive and sterile.

5 'No author' Schumpeter went on to say, 'not even A. Smith had any very clear ideas of what the processes really meant that led to.... the Industrial Revolution.' Schumpeter, *History*, p. 150.

6 Knight, 'Capital and Interest,' p. 386.

and physiocrats] viewed production as the creation of a "surplus" of tangible wealth . . . available for such "unproductive" uses as the support of government and the cultural life. [And both] shared the popular belief that agriculture is the only activity which is really productive.'[7]

In sharp contrast to the essentially agrarian view of both the physiocrats and the classicists, modern writers, returning to a concern with growth in the underdeveloped world after the Second World War, have made dualism the central focus of their analysis.[8] This emphasis is primarily borne of the fact that while analyzing poor and largely agricultural economies, they see before them the vision of the wealthy and industrialized mature economy. Regardless of analytical differences among them, they are implicitly or explicitly interested in the process of transformation from an overwhelmingly agricultural dualistic economy to a mature industrial economy.

This dualistic outlook is characterized by the incorporation of a set of new analytical facets of growth which are largely absent in the earlier agrarian way of thinking. While economic events involving the nonagricultural sector represent a diversion from the main stream of agrarian thought, they occupy center stage in the dualistic framework of analysis. The postulation of two major production sectors (agriculture and industry) and the formal analysis of the asymmetrical structural relations between them may be said to constitute the heart of modern growth theory. The nonagricultural parasitic sector of agrarianism now becomes a bona fide industrial sector characterized by the use and the constant augmentation of a stock of real capital. Another major change in emphasis consists of the introduction of technological change in both the agricultural and industrial sectors and the major role assigned to it in the analysis of the growth process. The classical problem of population pressures on the land is now handled in conjunction with the problem of labor reallocation from the agricultural to the industrial sector. Economic surpluses can now be generated in the industrial sector

7 *Ibid.*, p. 385.

8 See R. Nurkse, *Problems of Capital Formation in Underdeveloped Countries* (Oxford; 1957); W. A. Lewis, 'Economic Development with Unlimited Supplies of Labour,' *Manchester School*, XXII (May, 1954), pp 139–91; J.C. H. Fei and G. Ranis, *Development of the Labour Surplus Economy: Theory and Policy* (Homewood, Ill., 1964); B. Higgins, *Economic Development* (New York, 1959); P. N. Rosenstein-Rodan, 'Problems of Industrialization of Eastern and South-Eastern Europe,' *Economic Journal*, LIII (June-September, 1943), pp 202-11.

as profits as well as in the agricultural sector; the intersectoral channelization of this savings fund constitutes an essential ingredient of the dualistic framework of thinking. Finally, the agrarian economy is isolated from the rest of the world and impervious to stimuli from abroad, but the dualistic economy enjoys the advantage of an international division of labor and the borrowing of technology from abroad.

Thus while agrarianism is primarily concerned with the maintenance and survival of a monolithic production structure, dualism strives for the demise of the agrarian system through a radical change in the production structure. The agrarian view is one of resignation and fatalistic acceptance of the restraining hand of 'natural law' while dualistic writers wish to attain a better future through a fuller understanding of the growth process and the application of relevant growth promotion policies. In summary, from the viewpoint of the technical equipment brought to bear, the assessment of the most pressing social problem of the day, and the vision of the future prospects of the society as a whole, agrarian and dualistic thinkers diverge in a fundamental sense.

Each system is characterized by its own internal rules of growth, the analysis of which is the major purpose of this paper. However, we believe that a fuller understanding of the total growth phenomenon will be achieved by viewing these separate regimes as occurring in a natural historical sequence. Ultimately, we must consider the transition from one phase to another, in which context such research into growth-promoting policies is likely to be most relevant and fruitful.

It is our view that at least one important type of growth proceeds via the natural sequence from agrarianism to dualism to maturity. For example, the agrarian pattern should by no means be viewed simply as a historical curiosity; in fact, much of the present-day underdeveloped world, particularly in Africa, finds itself in an essentially agrarian condition, with non-agriculture either totally absent or restricted to artisan handicraft and service activities. A relevant theory of development must be able to analyze not only the workings of the dualistic economy and the conditions for a successful transition from dualism to maturity,[9] but also the

9 We shall not be concerned with this transition in the present paper. For a treatment of growth under dualism and the transition to maturity see Fei and Ranis, *Labour Surplus Economy*.

workings of the agrarian economy and the transition from agrarian stagnation to rigorous growth under dualism. We hope that this paper will contribute to this undertaking. Section II will explain the workings of the agrarian economy. In Section III we present a preliminary view of the dualistic economy, which provides the guidelines for the construction of a formally deterministic growth model for such an economy in Section IV. Some conclusions are presented in Section V.

II Development of the Agrarian Economy

The predominant form of economic activity in the agrarian economy is the production of agricultural goods by the application of labor (*L*) to land (*T*). In Figure 1a, labor (land) is measured on the horizontal (vertical) axis, and the curve, indexed by *Y*, is a typical production contour for agricultural goods. Following the classical tradition, we assume that land is fixed (at *T*). For this amount of land, the total productivity of labor is represented by the curve TPP_0 in Figure 1b. As the figure indicates, at some labor input point (at $\bar{A}$) the TPP of labor levels off and becomes constant (the MPP*L* approaches zero). Thus $0\bar{A}$ units of workers represent the nonredundant agricultural labor force. Any workers in excess of this amount do not make a positive contribution to output and thus represent the redundant labor force.[10] As long periods of time elapse and crop practices improve due to technological change, the *TPPL* curve may shift upward to the position *TPPt* (Figure 1b) at time *t* (from the initial position).[11] This summarizes the basic production conditions encountered in the agrarian economy.

10 The controversial assumption of a zero marginal product of labor (*MPPL*) is not essential to the argument and is made only to facilitate exposition of our analysis of the 'slack' phenomenon in the agrarian economy. Some writers (such as Theodore Schultz, *Transforming Traditional Agriculture* [New Haven, 1964]) object to the notion of a zero marginal product on regional peak demand and other grounds. We do not insist on an *MPPL* of precisely zero, but we have little understanding for those who deny that there is considerable redundancy of full-time equivalent agricultural workers in many parts of the contemporary underdeveloped world, as well as in the agrarian past of other regions. If a man is needed only for the two-month harvest period, he can be considered five-sixths redundant.

11 In Figure 1a, the ridge line O*R* passes through point *X* vertically lined up with point *A*. The technological change depicted is assumed to be of the neutral variety (i.e., the output index in Figure 1a is simply 'blown up' and the *TPPL* curve in Figure 1b shifts up proportionally).

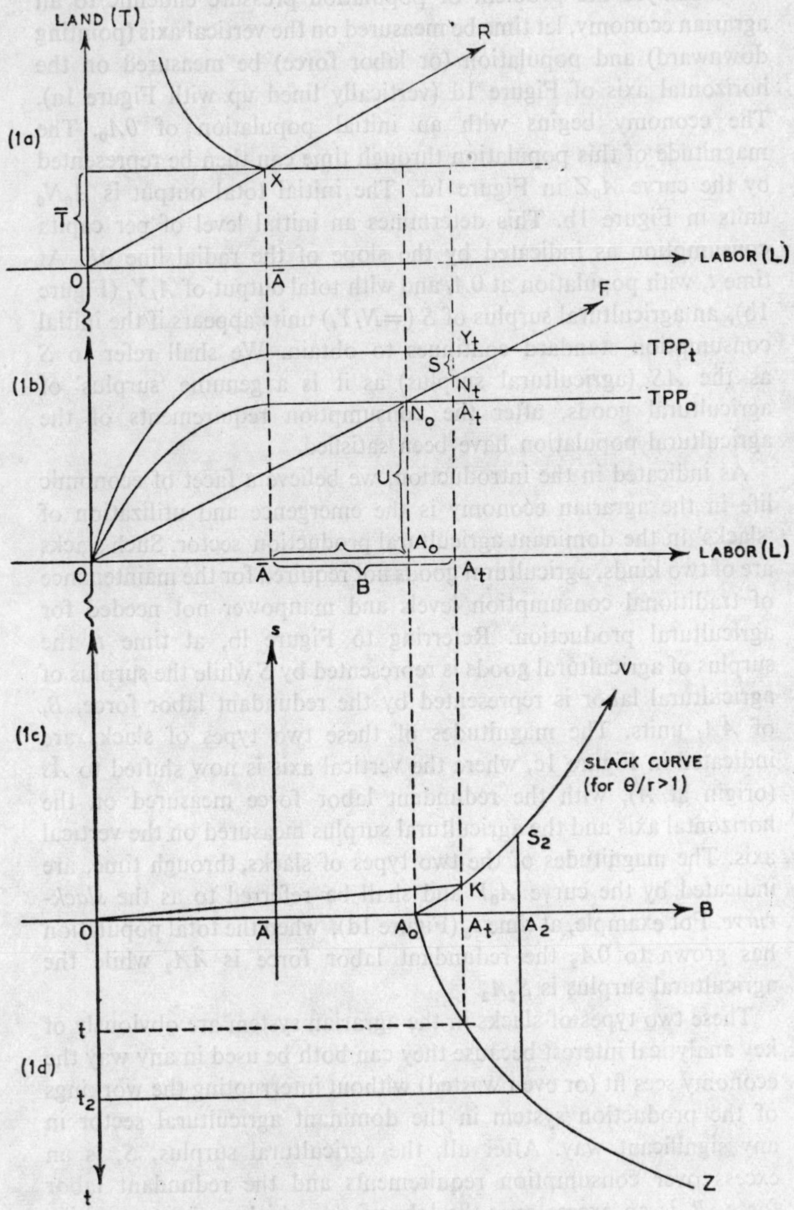

Figure 1. The Agrarian Economy

To analyze the problem of population pressure endemic to an agrarian economy, let time be measured on the vertical axis (pointing downward) and population (or labor force) be measured on the horizontal axis of Figure 1d (vertically lined up with Figure 1a). The economy begins with an initial population of $0A_0$. The magnitude of this population through time can then be represented by the curve A_0Z in Figure 1d. The initial total output is A_0N_0 units in Figure 1b. This determines an initial level of per capita consumption as indicated by the slope of the radial line $0F$. At time t, with population at $0A_t$ and with total output of A_tY_t (Figure 1b), an agricultural surplus of S ($=N_tY_t$) units appears if the initial consumption standard continues to obtain. We shall refer to S as the *AS* (agricultural surplus) as it is a genuine 'surplus' of agricultural goods, after the consumption requirements of the agricultural population have been satisfied.

As indicated in the introduction, we believe a facet of economic life in the agrarian economy is the emergence and utilization of 'slacks' in the dominant agricultural production sector. Such slacks are of two kinds, agricultural goods not required for the maintenance of traditional consumption levels and manpower not needed for agricultural production. Referring to Figure 1b, at time t, the surplus of agricultural goods is represented by S while the surplus of agricultural labor is represented by the redundant labor force, B, of $\bar{A}A_t$ units. The magnitudes of these two types of slacks are indicated in Figure 1c, where the vertical axis is now shifted to $\bar{A}s$ (origin at $\bar{A}$), with the redundant labor force measured on the horizontal axis and the agricultural surplus measured on the vertical axis. The magnitudes of the two types of slacks, through time, are indicated by the curve A_0V and shall be referred to as the *slack-curve*. For example, at time t_2 (Figure 1d), when the total population has grown to $0A_2$ the redundant labor force is $\bar{A}A_2$ while the agricultural surplus is S_2A_2.

These two types of slacks in the agrarian system are obviously of key analytical interest because they can both be used in any way the economy sees fit (or even wasted) without interrupting the workings of the production system in the dominant agricultural sector in any significant way. After all, the agricultural surplus, S, is an excess over consumption requirements and the redundant labor force, B, is an excess over the labor force which makes a positive contribution to agricultural production. The emergence and utilization of these slacks over long periods of time determines to a large extent the ultimate fate of the agrarian system.

The Emergence of Slack

We have depicted the case of slack emergence in Figure 1c in which both B and S increase through time. To investigate the conditions leading to this result, let us make the simplifying assumption that the production function in the agricultural sector is of the Cobb-Douglas type, that is, $Y=e^{\theta t}T^{\alpha}A^{1-\alpha}$. With T constant, we can define the unit of measurement of output (Y) and obtain a production function of the type

$$Y=\begin{cases} e^{\theta t}A^{1-\alpha} \textit{ for } A>A \\ e^{\theta t}U \text{ for } A<A \end{cases} \quad (1.1)$$

where θ is the rate of technological change, A is the nonredundant labor force, and U is the initial total agricultural output ($U=A_0\ N_0$ in Figure 1b). We assume here that the initial population $0A_0$ is greater than the non-redundant labor force ($0\bar{A}$), that is, there are some disguised unemployed or redundant workers in existence initially. Moreover, assuming the population to be growing at a constant rate, r, we have

$$A=A_0e^{rt}. \quad (1.2)$$

The initial per capita consumption standard, C^*, is then defined by

$$C^*=U/A_0. \quad (1.3)$$

The magnitude of the redundant labor force, B, is given by

$$B=A-\bar{A} \quad (1.4)$$

and the agricultural surplus is

$$S=Y-AC^*=e^{\theta t}U-A_0e^{rt}U/A_0=U(e^{\theta t}-e^{rt}). \quad (1.5)$$

Using the population growth equation ($A/A_0=e^{rt}$) to eliminate 't' from the above expression, we have

$$S=U[(A/A_0)^{\theta/r}-A/A_0] \quad (1.6)$$

expressing a functional relation between A (size of population) and S (size of agricultural surplus). This expression can be simplified when we define

$A_0=1$ (the initial population A_0 is defined as one unit)[12] (1.7a)

and

12 Under this convention, the magnitude $\acute{A}$ is the fraction of the initial population which is non-redundant.

$s = S/U$ (the unit of measurement of the surplus S is conveniently defined in terms of the constant U). (1.7b)

Under the above simplifications, (1.6) becomes

$$s = A^{\theta/r} - A. \tag{1.8}$$

This curve passes through the point A_0 (now assumed to be "1") on the horizontal axis since $s=0$ when $A=1$ (Figure 1c). Finally we can derive the slack curve itself with the aid of relation (1.4):

$$s = (A+B)^{\theta/r} - (A+B). \tag{1.9}$$

Thus we see that the slack curve of Figure 1c is derived under the assumption that both technological change and population growth proceed at an exogenously given constant rate with $\theta > r$. We shall assume that this inequality holds[13] and a slack emerges.

There exist a series of possible alternatives for the disposition of the emerging slack with major significance for the future prospects of the agrarian system. We shall deal in this paper with only two major alternatives, the consumption-population adjustment and the technological adjustment.

Consumption–Population Adjustment

The most obvious method of utilizing the surplus is to devote all of it to increases in per capita consumption. This, in turn, may have repercussions on the (no longer exogenous) population growth rate To see this in greater detail, the possible increment in per capita consumption at time t (the amount of increase in per capita consumption possible over the 'traditional' base year level) is given by the slope of the straight line $0K$ ($KA_t / 0A_t$) in Figure 1c. As the point K moves upward on the slack-curve, the per capita consumption level increases.

In order to rigorously deduce the magnitude of this increase, we can easily, using (1.1), calculate the rate of increase of per capita output (ηy^*) as follows:

$$\eta_Y = \begin{pmatrix} \theta + (1-\alpha)\eta_A & \text{for } A \leq \bar{A} \\ \theta & \text{for } A \geq \bar{A} \end{pmatrix} \text{ rate of increase of } Y \tag{1.10a}$$

13 If θ is less than r the slack-curve is negative and decreasing through time. The economy is not capable of generating either type of slack and hence the analysis of such an economy which cannot even maintain its initial consumption standard is not very interesting from the long run point of view—though at times undoubtedly of historical relevance.

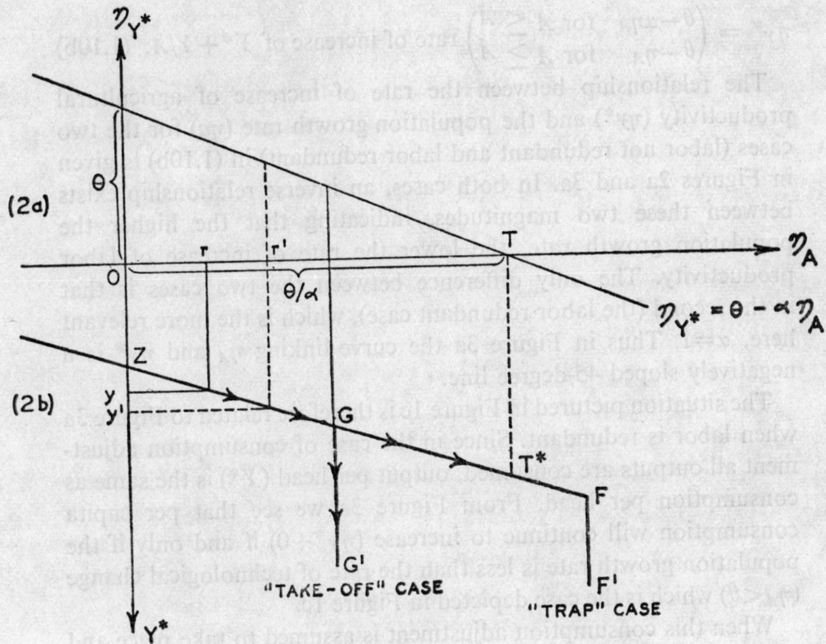

Figure 2. Long Term Prospects: Labor Non-Redundant Case

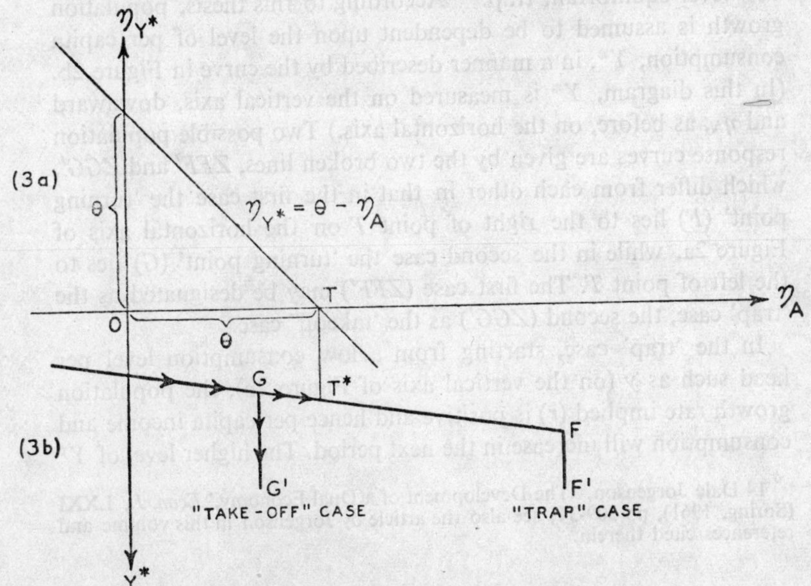

Figure 3. Long Term Prospects: Labour Redundant Case

$$\eta_Y{}^* = \begin{pmatrix} \theta - \alpha\eta_A & \text{for } A \leq \bar{A} \\ \theta - \eta_A & \text{for } A \geq \bar{A} \end{pmatrix} \text{ rate of increase of } Y^* + Y/A. \quad (1.10b)$$

The relationship between the rate of increase of agricultural productivity (ηy^*) and the population growth rate (ηa) for the two cases (labor not redundant and labor redundant) in (1.10b) is given in Figures 2a and 3a. In both cases, an inverse relationship exists between these two magnitudes, indicating that the higher the population growth rate, the lower the rate of increase of labor productivity. The only difference between the two cases is that in the second (the labor redundant case), which is the more relevant here, $\alpha=1$. Thus in Figure 3a the curve linking η_A and $\eta_Y{}^*$ is a negatively sloped 45-degree line.

The situation pictured in Figure 1c is therefore related to Figure 3a when labor is redundant. Since in the case of consumption adjustment all outputs are consumed, output per head (Y^*) is the same as consumption per head. From Figure 3a we see that per capita consumption will continue to increase ($\eta_Y{}^*+0$) if and only if the population growth rate is less than the rate of technological change ($\eta_A<\theta$) which is the case depicted in Figure 1c.

When this consumption adjustment is assumed to take place and when the classical endogenous population growth theory is also accepted, we obtain what may be called the Jorgenson thesis of the 'low level equilibrium trap.'[14] According to this thesis, population growth is assumed to be dependent upon the level of per capita consumption, Y^*, in a manner described by the curve in Figure 2b. (In this diagram, Y^* is measured on the vertical axis, downward and η_A, as before, on the horizontal axis.) Two possible population response curves are given by the two broken lines, ZFF' and ZGG', which differ from each other in that in the first case the 'turning point' (F) lies to the right of point T on the horizontal axis of Figure 2a, while in the second case the 'turning point' (G) lies to the left of point T. The first case (ZFF') may be designated as the 'trap' case, the second (ZGG') as the 'takeoff' case.

In the 'trap' case, starting from a low consumption level per head such as y (on the vertical axis of Figure 2b), the population growth rate implied (r) is positive and hence per capita income and consumption will increase in the next period. The higher level of Y^*

14 Dale Jorgenson, 'The Development of a Dual Economy,' *Econ. J.*, LXXI (Spring, 1961), pp 309-34; see also the article by Jorgenson in this volume and references cited therein.

or C^* leads to a still higher population growth rate (r'), a lower, but still positive rate of increase of Y^* (or C^*), and so on. This process continues with the time path indicated by the arrows until point T^* (and T) is reached, when (simultaneously) per capita income (and consumption) increases cease ($\eta_Y{}^*=0$) and the population growth rate reaches a stationary equilibrium. At this level of population growth rate, θ/α, technological change and diminishing returns to labor just offset each other, keeping per capita output at a constant level. The economy is thus caught in a low-level equilibrium 'trap.'

In the 'takeoff' case, starting again from such a point as 'y' and the population growth rate implied thereby, the rate of growth of income (and consumption) per head is seen to be *positive* and hence the value of income (and consumption) per head will be higher in the next period. In Figure 2b, the time path will be as before, toward point T^*. However, at point G before T^* is realized, population is no longer responsive to increased per capita income (and consumption) because there exists a maximum rate of population growth.[15] In Figure 2b, the growth path will follow the arrows toward G' once the turning point G has been reached. This constancy of the population growth rate implies a constancy henceforth in the rate of increase of per capita income (and consumption). The agrarian economy has thrown off its Malthusian shackles and continues to increase its per capita consumption level; it may be said to have reached a 'takeoff.'

Although the Jorgenson formulation is independent of the question of redundancy or nonredundancy of the labor force in the typical agricultural production situation, it is easily adapted to the case where this phenomenon is accepted. For this case a diagram similar to Figure 2ab, that is, Figure 3ab can be constructed. The

15 Dale Jorgenson, 'Dual Economy,' makes unnecessarily restrictive and unrealistic assumptions concerning this 'turning point,' namely that a saturation point for the per capita consumption of agricultural goods is reached at *precisely* the same point at which population growth becomes nonresponsive to further increases in Y^*. He utilizes this consideration to show the necessity of the ultimate evolution of an industrial sector, a subject to which we shall return later. Moreover, Jorgenson stipulates a constant death rate and a birth rate which rises with per capita income. What little we know about these matters indicates that the birth rate behaves unpredictably and that it is the decline in the death rate—related to preventive and public health expenditures (and not per capita income)—which causes the rise in population growth. Though Jorgenson claims to be neoclassical, his acceptance of the consumption adjustment and Malthusian population thesis gives his framework a distinctly classical cast, especially when θ is 0 or negligible.

explanation of the latter diagram follows exactly the same lines as the analysis just presented for 2ab. The only difference is that 'the critical turning point,' T (or T^*), occurs where the rate of population growth (η_A) is equal to the rate of technological change (θ) on the horizontal axis. Thus if the point at which population becomes nonresponsive to further increases in per capita income (and consumption) is to the left of T^* (for example, at G) we again have takeoff; otherwise the economy is 'trapped'.

The above analysis may be used to interpret Jorgenson's theory of the agrarian economy. Jorgenson's approach is important; his rigorously formulated dynamic model permits us to distinguish precisely between the trap and nontrap cases in the monolithic agrarian economy and thus between continued stagnation and takeoff. Nevertheless, the analysis is based on unrealistic or unduly restrictive assumptions. First, the assumption is made that the entire increase in the agricultural surplus is used for consumption by farm labor. This may occasionally be true in a completely freeholder economy but is highly unrealistic given most land ownership and tenure arrangements in the agrarian economy. Secondly, the acceptance of the Malthusian population theory is, at least according to much modern demographic testimony, subject to considerable doubt. Thirdly, and most important, in the Jorgenson world the rate of technological change in agriculture is mysteriously fixed and constant, which offends our sense of the real world. It rules out an important and perhaps more realistic alternative to the consumption-population adjustment mechanism as a method of disposing of the economy's agricultural slack. We shall call this alternative the 'technology adjustment mechanism' and explore it at greater length.

Technology Adjustment

Any alternative adjustment mechanism is most conveniently discussed when, given a rate of population growth (r) and a rate of technological change (θ), per capita income is rising and two kinds of slacks are being generated. Both common sense and the lessons of the physiocrats and historical experience imply that a full consumption adjustment is unlikely to occur. Moreover, alternative and more realistic ways to dispose of the surplus may have an important feed-back effect on agricultural productivity increase itself.

As noted earlier, the physiocrats clearly saw the possibility of using the emerging agricultural slack for nonproductive purposes, that is, for an expansion of so-called sterile activities. Thus, in terms of Figure 1c, as a particular quantity of redundant workers (B) and agricultural surplus (S) is generated, those who own the slack, the landlords, the nobility, the church, may utilize it to expand their consumption of services, handicrafts, and other luxury products. Alternatively, as the income of the ruling classes rises they may choose to enlarge the military establishment, wage war with their neighbors, build pyramids, construct churches, or enhance the general 'cultural attainments' of the society in some other way. There are an unlimited variety of uses to which the economy's slack can be put by those who have control over its disposition.

We contend that the choice of alternative uses of an economy's agricultural slack may have a considerable impact on the productive performance of agriculture through its effect on the rate of technological change, θ. In other words, as long as the economy is basically agrarian and not dualistic, when its nonagricultural activities are stagnant and parasitic, the rate of agricultural productivity increase may be adversely affected.

We should recall that technological change in the agrarian economy involves long-term, sometimes hardly perceptible changes in the state of the arts. The agrarian economy represents essentially a struggle between nature and numbers, with slight improvements in crop practices over the centuries. According to the testimony of agricultural economists, this slow improvement trend of agricultural labor productivity, θ, can be sustained only if the agricultural infrastructure is kept in decent repair and improved upon. Irrigation, for example, has been one of the oldest concerns of man. Without proper irrigation and drainage facilities or where such networks have fallen into disrepair it is very difficult, if not impossible, to translate the slow but persistent accumulation of human experience on the soil into secular, if slow, increases in productivity.

The human resource inputs of one period required to elicit such productivity increases in the next may thus be very important to technological change. While a portion of the agrarian economy's labor force may, for example, be redundant in contributing to this year's output (using this year's state of the arts), it is instead required for a variety of activities which may render agriculture more productive in the future. The unemployed and underemployed in agriculture can and do play a major historical role in digging irrigation ditches, constructing levees and dams, terracing, and in simply keeping existing facilities from falling into disrepair. The magnitude of θ is thus, at least in considerable part, a function of the extent to which the underemployed agricultural labor force is engaged in long gestation-period productivity-enhancing activities.

This is why determination of how the agrarian economy's slack is utilized is so crucial. Clearly, it is up to the owners of the agricultural surplus and those who control the human resources available whether the slack is to be deployed in θ-enhancing directions or dissipated in high living and conspicuous consumption. But it is almost typical of the agrarian economy that the owning classes do not have a clear vision of the future and do not associate productivity increases with current allocation decisions about the work and leisure of their resources. More likely, they respond to their rising income by increasing their demand for the products of the sterile classes, and the surplus of agricultural goods is used to hire away the surplus in manpower from agriculture-enhancing activities and provide more personal services, more luxury goods, more pomp and circumstance, larger armies, and more wars. In the Middle Ages the tithe was extracted for the support of the church and the plethora of feudal payments to support both the military and civilian manpower demands of king and baron. In Tokugawa, Japan, a high tax on land went almost exclusively for the support of the court and the warrior classes.[16] As surplus manpower is thus bid away the rate of agricultural productivity increase is likely to suffer. Thus, once we reject the rather untenable notion of a fixed, exogenously given, long-term rate of agricultural advance, we can see that in the typical agrarian economy there are forces at work tending toward a secular decline in θ. We believe that this technology adjustment is based on a realistic view of the long-run problem of the agrarian society. Ultimately this downward pull can bring the system to a halt, quite aside from the danger of the demographic trap of the Jorgenson consumption-population-adjustment school.

This hypothesis concerning 'economic stagnation' brought about via 'technology adjustment' may now be presented in a more rigorous formal fashion—not for the sake of precise model construction but because only in this way can the 'logical consistency' of the

16 Thomas Smith, *The Agrarian Origins of Modern Japan* (Stanford, 1959).

above ideas be put to the test. In Figure 4, we reproduce the slack curve $\bar{A}FS$ of Figure 1c. Let 'd' denote a wage premium, the amount of excess over the prevailing per capita consumption standard, C^*, which must be paid to the sterile worker if he is to be wooed away from agricultural pursuits. The number of sterile workers is T; then the consumption per head of these workers is C^*+d, and the consumption per head of the nonsterile workers is C^*. The postulation of a positive wage premium, 'd,' is due to the fact that it generally takes a positive real social cost to mobilize, convert, and sustain each sterile worker (soldier, priest, artisan, feudal servant) who has been induced (or forced) to leave his dependent life in agriculture. Since agricultural surplus, S, is the amount of surplus after allowing for consumption by the entire population at level C^*, S represents the 'fund' out of which the wage premium to the sterile workers can be paid. Thus if all the surplus food is used to draw off workers for a variety of parasitic activities, we have

$$S = Td \tag{1.11}$$

which is described by the straight line $\bar{A}X$ in Figure 4.

This line now permits us to determine the allocation of the economy's total labor force, A, at any point into three categories, nonredundant or productive labor, $\bar{A}$, sterile redundant labor, T, and nonsterile redundant labor, M:

$$A = A + T + M. \tag{1.12}$$

For example, point F represents a typical point on the slack curve (Figure 4). At F the entire population, EF, is divided into three portions: the nonredundant labor force, $\bar{A}$, the sterile redundant labor force, T, and the nonsterile redundant labor force, M. The latter (composed of M units of labor) represents redundant workers only from the *static* point of view; at any point in time they can be withdrawn from the agricultural sector without adversely affecting the total agricultural output of that year. However, from the dynamic point of view, they are productive in the sense that their removal from the agricultural sector will adversely affect future agricultural productivity by causing θ to turn down as a consequence of a relative neglect of agricultural overheads. The basic notion here is that the gradual, nonspectacular spread of new agricultural techniques is inhibited by the failure to maintain and improve irrigation and drainage facilities. feeder roads, and the like. These activities are bound to be heavily labor-using in the agrarian economy and once they are neglected, the long-run processes of slowly accumulating knowledge and passing it on from generation to generation are impaired.

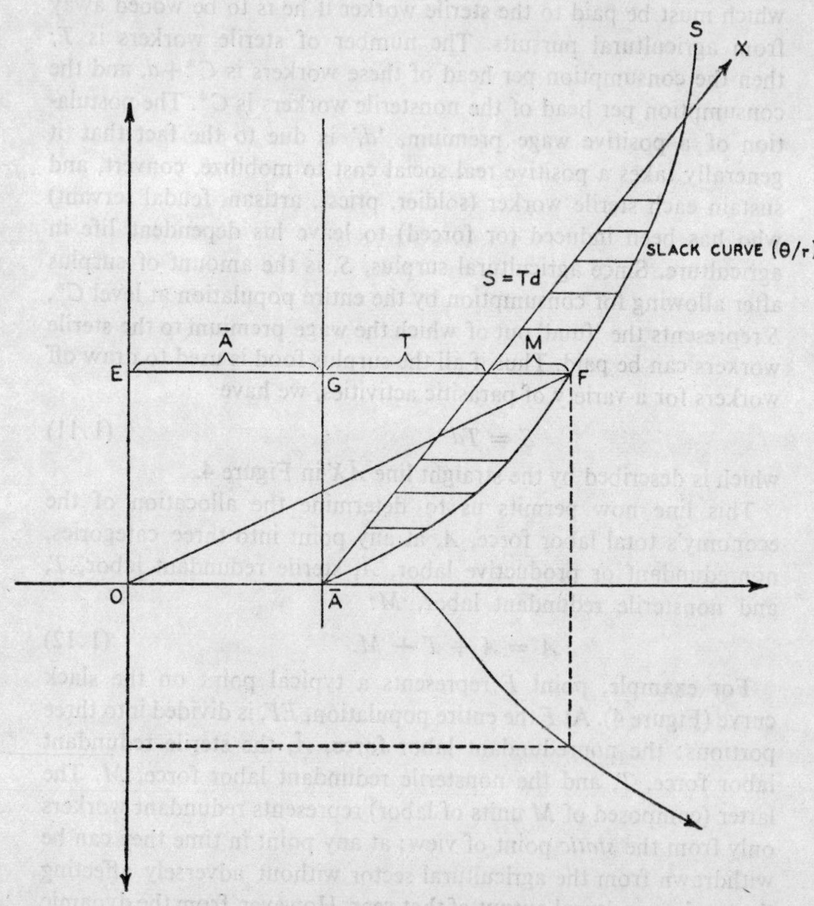

Figure 4. Slack Curve

In Figure 4, the shaded horizontal distances between the slack curve ($\bar{A}FS$) and the straight line ($\bar{A}X$) (1.11) represent various possible magnitudes of such redundant nonsterile workers. From the concavity of the slack curve (as previously derived) we know that, given a fixed value of both innovation intensity (θ) and population growth rate (r), the magnitude of the nonsterile redundant classes (M) will eventually decrease to zero as the absolute size of the economy's population continues to expand and the economy continues to move 'upward' along the slack curve. This means that, sooner or later, the agricultural sector will begin to suffer from a 'shortage' of this θ-maintaining type of labor, and the 'dynamic efficiency' of agricultural activities cannot be maintained at the level of θ once M dips below a certain critical minimum level.

The above idea can be described rigorously by a behavioristic relation between θ and the labor force needed to sustain θ. For this purpose, let us denote $(\bar{A}+M)/L$ by 'q'; 'q' is the total nonsterile labor force as a fraction of the total labour force, L. For simplicity, we can postulate an increasing functional relation between θ and q:

$$q=Q(\theta) \quad \text{with } Q'>0 \tag{1.13a}$$

where

$$q=(\bar{A}+M)/L=(L-T)/L \tag{1.13b}$$

which states that a higher level of θ necessitates the application of a higher fraction of the total labor force as nonsterile labor.

Given fixed per capita consumption, C^*, the total consumption demand of the nonsterile workers is $C^*(\bar{A}+M)$ or $C^*(L-T)$ and that of the sterile workers is $(C^*+d)T$. Since total output is LY^*, we have

$$C^*(L-T)+(C^*+d)T=LY^* \tag{1.14a}$$

which applies

$$T/L=(Y^*-C^*)/d \tag{1.14b}$$

and hence (by 1.13b)

$$q=1+(C^*-Y^*)/d=\phi(Y^*) \text{ with } \phi'<0. \tag{1.14c}$$

The last equation states that the value of q is uniquely determined by Y^*, as indicated by the notation $\phi(Y^*)$. The value of q is inversely related to Y^*. Together with (1.13a) we see that θ is a function of Y^* and is, in fact, inversely related to Y^* (as per capita output increases, the value of θ decreases). This may be written as:

$$\theta=h(Y^*) \quad \text{with } h'<0. \tag{1.15}$$

We shall refer to equation (1.15) as the innovation response curve since it specifies the level of innovational intensity in response to per capita income changes. This relationship (which may seem contrary to common sense) is due to the fact that increases in the well-being of the propertied classes, as reflected in higher per capita incomes and surpluses, lead to an increase in demand for the services of the sterile classes to the point that agricultural productivity increases sooner or later begin to suffer. While there are good reasons to assume that such a relationship is not inevitable in every agrarian society, it seems reasonable. In both Tokugawa, Japan, and medieval Europe the evidence indicates that the ruling classes did not concern themselves with maintaining agricultural progress but rather devoted their energies to the 'good life' and/or making war on their neighbors—both activities making substantial demands on redundant labor resources.

Turning now to Figure 5a, equation (1.10b) is written as $\eta_Y^* = \theta - r$ and represented by the positively sloped straight line. While η_Y^* is plotted on the vertical axis, the magnitude of θ is indicated on the horizontal axis. Moreover, since in our analysis, the population growth rate is assumed to be constant ($\eta_A = r$), the straight line is a 45-degree line which intersects both axes at distance r from the

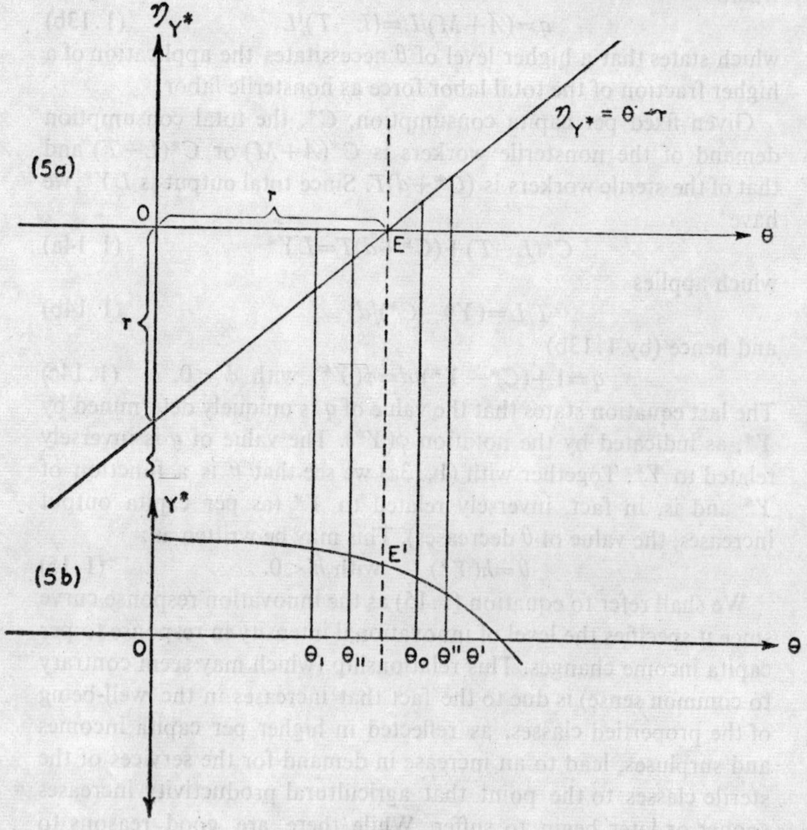

Figure 5. Technology Adjustment

origin. In Figure 5b, vertically lined up with Figure 5a, Y^* is measured on the vertical and θ on the horizontal axis, and the innovation response curve (1.15) is represented by the negatively sloped curve. Moreover, a vertical dotted line is drawn from point E to obtain point E' on the innovation response curve.

Our theory of stagnation via the technology adjustment mechanism can now be summarized with the help of Figure 5b. Starting from a point such as θ' greater than r, for example, the value of θ necessarily decreases (from θ' to θ'') because the value of ηY^* is positive (see Figure 5a). During this process, output per head (Y^*) increases but as a decreasing rate (see Figure 5b). Eventually, the value of θ decreases to a stationary value (θ_0) at E, equal in magnitude to the population growth rate (r).[17] The economy will then be expanding in a stationary equilibrium state characterized by the constancy of Y^*. In this fashion, the phenomenon of long-term stagnation results from the workings of the technology adjustment mechanism.

Up to this point, our analysis of the agrarian economy has focused entirely on understanding the internal workings of that system and examining the plausibility of alternative mechanisms by which it either escapes from its low-level equilibrium trap or faces the prospect of long-run stagnation. This has entailed a view of growth within a fixed regime, defined by a given set of rules. The focal point of the analysis has been in terms of real resource behavior patterns in the agrarian regime.

In this context, the consumption-population adjustment mechanism was found to be unrealistic. Similar objections could undoubtedly be raised against the alternative technology-adjustment mechanism, presented here, but we find it more reasonable since it includes in the explanatory model certain historical features characteristic of the agrarian economy neglected in the Jorgenson approach. This includes the existence of a nonconsumed agricultural surplus and of nonagricultural production activities and the importance of the forces which determine the rate of technological change. What is perhaps indicated for the future is a partial synthesis of the consumption-population adjustment and the technology-adjustment mechanisms in exploring the long-run behavior of the agrarian system; both mechanisms may be at work to some extent in yielding

17 Similarly, in the unlikely case that the initial θ is less than the population growth rate, r (e.g., at θ_1), θ will be increasing to the same stationary value.

the observed "trap" outcome. In the real world undoubtedly all the potential surpluses are not consumed by the agricultural working population, nor are they likely to be entirely diverted to support the luxury life of the propertied classes. The extent to which increases in per capita income lead to increases in per capita consumption, or to surpluses available for other purposes, will depend on such institutional factors as the existing class structure, tenure arrangements, and the relative power of the landlord to adjust rental charges. Clearly, considerably more inquiry into such organizational characteristics of the agrarian economy is needed before we can be sure of the more precise causation of the observed long-run quasi-equilibrium in the system.

There is, however, a second issue to be addressed—the nature of the transition from agrarianism to dualism. This is no longer a largely quantitative or real resource question, but one relating to an institutional transformation affecting the rules of growth themselves. The analysis of such a transition, for the nontrapped agrarian economy is much more complicated than any real resources calculus. If the regime of agrarianism is to be transformed into one of dualism, institutional arrangements must first be constructed so that the various economic functions endemic to dualism (bound to be vastly more complicated than those of agrarianism) can be performed. It is clear that we cannot even hope to analyze the transformation without a full understanding of the dualistic regime which follows.[18]

III The Dualistic Economy: A Bird's-eye View

The dualistic economy exhibits structural characteristics which are markedly different from those of the agrarian economy—even though both are underdeveloped and heavily agricultural. A major distinguishing feature of the dualistic economy is the coexistence of a subsistence agricultural sector and a commercialized industrial sector. In contrast with the subsidiary and "sterile" handicrafts and services of the agrarian economy, using virtually no real capital, the industrial production sector is dynamic and vigorous (if initially small), and real capital formation plays an important role. The basic

18 Jorgenson's view varies from ours on this point. He says that as the agrarian economy ceases to be trapped by Malthusian pressures (phenomenon completely determined by real resources calculation) the transition to dualism is easy and automatic. Jorgenson does not differentiate the problems

problem in this economy is not one of how to satisfy the growing luxury tastes of the leisure classes in the presence of diminishing returns in agriculture, but of how to shift the economy's center of gravity from agriculture to industry until agriculture becomes a mere appendage.

Specifically, the importance of real fixed capital in the industrial sector of the dualistic economy cannot be overstated. This is true because with the advent of real capital, we introduce important new analytical facets; a new source of income (capitalist profits) and a new source of surplus (capitalist savings), both absent in the agrarian economy. Associated with this new source of income is a new propertied class, the industrial capitalist, with ownership of the industrial capital stock being created out of the savings of the industrial sector. This emerging capitalist class is anxious to increase its ownership of the industrial capital stock as much and as quickly as possible. It wishes not only to siphon off the new surplus for reinvestment in industry but also to enhance the productive power of the new capital through the incorporation with it of as much technological change as possible. The owners of the industrial capital—unlike the sterile classes in the agrarian society—thus have an incentive to innovate or to adopt and adapt the innovations of others along the economy's industrial production functions.

It should be clear that the dualistic economy's total saving fund is composed of two kinds of surpluses, industrial profits and agricultural surplus. This total saving fund must then be allocated to the two sectors—along with entrepreneurial activity—to increase agricultural labor productivity in one sector, thus freeing labor, and to increase industrial labor productivity in the other, thus creating a demand for the allocated labor force. At the same time, given the consumer preferences of the typical worker, the output generated in the two sectors must be such as to prevent a 'shortage' of food or of industrial goods, as indicated by a marked change in the intersectoral terms of trade. Thus allocation decisions, taking into account both capital accumulation and technological change in each sector, must proceed in a balanced fashion so as to avoid the overexpansion of either sector in the course of the reallocation process. With the economy's saving and entrepreneurial energies expended so as to insure the synchronized forward movement of both sectors, the prospects for success are heightened.

While it is, of course, true that capital accumulation (as well as technological change) may enhance agricultural productivity in the dualistic economy, we accept the evidence of such successful agricultural revolutions as those in Japan, Taiwan and Greece to the effect that physical capital plays a relatively less important role in agriculture; the labor-intensive adoption of new techniques, the application of fertilizer, and the like are considerably more important. Thus the net flow of capital resources (as well as labor resources) in the course of dualistic growth is out of agriculture and into industry.

Acceptance of this notion of a balanced intersectoral allocation process in the dualistic economy leads us directly to the idea that the ownership of industrial capital goods may be viewed as a possible reward for the generation of an agricultural surplus. Moreover, once the agricultural propertied classes, the landlords and nobility, begin to view the acquisition of industrial assets as more desirable than the making of war and the good life in the agrarian context, the transition to dualism is assisted directly and there is an important feed-back on the incentive toward further increases of agricultural productivity. The landlord views agriculture as a direct means of participating, along with the original industrial capitalist, in the ownership of the productive assets in the growing industrial sector.

These claims against the industrial sector are established in the course of facilitating the net flow of surplus (or savings) from agriculture to the rest of the economy. Surplus food is sold by the landlord in the intersectoral commodity market and the proceeds invested in the industrial sector. This is accomplished most easily by the dualistic landlord[19] who has one foot in each sector and directly owns and manages the newly created industrial production structure. Alternatively, the claims against the industrial sector can be acquired by the owner of the agricultural surplus through a system of financial intermediation, such as the purchase of savings certificates, bonds, and stocks, implying the more customary separation between ownership and control. But institutions of this type are difficult to establish in the typical underdeveloped economy and, once established, they may not be accepted. The most trusted financial intermediary is obviously oneself or one's close relatives, which is why the dualistic landlord (as encountered in Japan) or

19 For a fuller analysis, see Fei and Ranis, *Labor Surplus Economy*, Chapter 5.

his counter part are so important for the transition from agrarianism to dualism as well as for dualism's continued growth. The dualistic landlord as agricultural entrepreneur has an increasing interest in innovating in that sector as the potentialities of industrialization become apparent to him; similarly, as industrial entrepreneur he is anxious to innovate or to adapt the industrial innovation of others to the fullest extent possible. Technological change in both sectors is thus bound to yield increasing surpluses for the owning class and a more rapid accumulation of the desired industrial capital stock. In juxtaposition to the technology adjustment mechanism of the agrarian economy, which has a negative effect on θ, the dualistic economy is characterized by a technology adjustment mechanism which has a positive effect on θ. No longer are human resources and entrepreneurial attention pulled away from agriculture and squandered on luxuries and frills, but increasing agricultural productivity is viewed as a major engine for the balanced forward motion of the entire dualistic system. We may call this a positive technology adjustment mechanism.

One other facet of the emerging dualistic economy deserves further consideration—the determination of the nature and rate of technological change in the industrial sector. As long as the economy is basically agrarian it is relatively insulated from change domestically and from the rest of the world. Once the transition to dualism is under way, however, the economy becomes more fully exposed to the rest of the world, both through the exchange of primary products for imported consumer and capital goods and through the accompanying transfer of technology. As we have already pointed out, the incentive for the entrepreneurs to adopt new and more efficient production functions clearly exists; but the prior preoccupation of the propertied classes and their limited experience with industrial production causes them to turn for help, at least initially, to the outside.

As Veblen pointed out long ago,[20] considerable advantages attach to the 'latecomer nation' attempting to industrialize. Such an economy is in a position to survey the technological shelf already perfected by others and to pick and choose that which seems most suitable—without itself incurring the considerable cost of trial and

20 Thorstein J. Veblen, 'The Opportunity of Japan,' *Essays in Our Changing Order* (New York, 1934) pp. 248-66.

experimentation. But, while innovations with the highest payoff or yield are likely, at least initially, to emanate from abroad, this does not necessarily imply the adoption of the latest, most up-to-date techniques known, nor the mere transplantation of processes from one country to another. As the nineteenth-century Japanese experience illustrates,[21] technological transfers from the more advanced to the latecomer country are most effective when handled selectively, in some cases via adoption of methods already obsolete abroad and in others the transfer of the latest ('most modern') methods. The heavy borrowing of industrial technology from abroad in the early decades of the dualistic economy does not, moreover, preclude a considerable dosage of domestic innovational activity. Such activity will, however, be directed more toward the adaptation of imported techniques to different local conditions (such as the greater relative availability of cheap labor) than to the creation, from scratch, of new methods of production.

The role of technological change, both in its intensity or strength and in its slantedness or bias, can thus be of great importance in the early industrialization process. T. Watanabe concludes that "the most important causes for Japan's rapid industrialization can be found in the nature and growth of technological change."[22] Innovations, for example, were responsible for as much as 80 per cent of the absorption of industrial labor during the early period.[23]

It is also a fact of life, as Veblen points out, that the early advantage of the latecomer is ultimately dissipated. As the technological shelf of the more advanced countries is cleared of relevant techniques, the annual rate of technological advance of the industrial sector of the dualistic economy is likely to slow down. As the dualistic economy becomes more and more industrialized, however, in the course of a successful labor reallocation process its domestic skill and ingenuity levels will be rising; increasingly as the importance of borrowed industrial technology declines, the economy will be in a position to produce its own technological advances domestically. In fact, it may be the capacity to generate a sustained flow

21 See G. Ranis, 'Factor Proportions in Japanese Economic Development,' *American Economic Review*, XLVII (September, 1957), pp. 594-607, for a fuller statement on the subject of this paragraph.

22 'Ecnomic Aspects of Dualism in the Industrial Development of Japan,' *Economic Development and Cultural Change*, XIII (April, 1965), pp 293-312.

23 Fei and Ranis, *Labor Surplus Economy*, pp. 125-31.

of indigenous technological change in a routinized fashion which separates the mature from the underdeveloped society.

IV. Development of the Dualistic Economy

The above discussion has emphasized the essential characteristics of development in a dualistic economy. Now, with a rigorously formulated growth model, we can explain how the time path of an interrelated system of economic magnitudes is determined. Such a dynamic system must, in addition, be capable of emphasizing all the essential growth-related phenomena in a dualistic economy outlined in the last section.

Although there are only two production sectors, the growth process in the dualistic economy is by nature very complicated. This process involves production-centered phenomena (such as the use of capital and labor and the generation of innovational activities) in two separate production sectors. Therefore, one must take account of such crucial intersectoral relations as the transfer of labor from the agricultural to the industrial sector, the intersectoral channelization of savings, and the possibilities of the intrasectoral and intersectoral stimulation of technological change. Central to this process are not only the forces of production (the production functions of the two sectors) and consumption (the consumer preference function), but also the impact of such 'exogenous' forces as population growth and the substantial possibility of importing technology. Finally, we should recall that all these real production, allocation, consumption, and distribution decisions must be made within the context of a set of organizational devices to handle and coordinate the various disparate economic activities. For example, with respect to the particular institutional milieu of capitalism or the 'mixed economy,' this involves the use of wages and prices as instruments of stimulation and harmonization. When the workings of this entire system are to be understood, satisfying all the major conditions imposed by the real world, the dynamic general equilibrium model which emerges is, by necessity, complicated and cumbersome.

In order to introduce the model in its entirely, let us first present the following system of growth equations; our immediate task is to explain the economic significance of these equations individually and then to show that, collectively, they determine the entire growth process in an orderly fashion. (To facilitate our exposition a brief description of each variable and of the relationship in which it is involved is presented after each equation.)

$$Y = \begin{cases} e^{\int \theta dt} A^{\alpha} & \text{for } A < \check{A} \\ e^{\int \theta dt} V & \text{for } \check{A} \leq A \end{cases}$$ (production function in the agricultural sector where $Y =$ agricultural output; $A =$ agricultural labor force; $\theta =$ innovation intensity in agricultural sector). (2.1a)

$$P = A + L$$ (labor allocation equation; $P =$ total population; $L =$ labor force in the industrial sector). (2.1b)

$$S = Y - Aw$$ (definition of total agricultural surplus (TAS); $S = TAS$; $w =$ institutional real wage in terms of agricultural goods). (2.1c)

$$V = S/L$$ (definition of average agricultural surplus (AAS); $V = AAS$). (2.1d)

$$\tau = gL/S$$ (definition of terms of trade; $\tau =$ terms of trade [units of industrial goods exchanged per unit of agricultural goods]). (2.1e)

$$w = \phi(V)$$ (determination of industrial real wage; $w =$ real wage in terms of industrial goods). (2.1f)

$$g = \lambda w$$ (determination of surplus coefficient; $g =$ surplus coefficient; $\lambda =$ proportionality factor between g and w). (2.1g)

$$\theta = f(\tau) \qquad \theta' \geq 0$$ (intensity of agricultural innovation function). (2.1h)

$$\eta_P = r$$ (population growth function; $r =$ population growth rate). (2.1i)

$X = F(t)\, K^B L^{1-B}$	(production function in the industrial sector; X = industrial output; K and L= real capital and labor force in the industrial sector).	(2.1j)
$J = \eta_F = b + ae^{-ut}$ $a \geqslant 0, b \geqslant 0, u \geqslant 0$	(innovation intensity in industrial sector).	(2.1k)
$\pi_1 = BX$	(profits in the industrial sector: π_1).	(2.1l)
$\pi_2 = Lg$	(savings of the agricultural sector used in the industrial sector: π_2).	(2.1m)
$\eta_K = (\pi_1 + \pi_2)/K$	(rate of growth of capital in the industrial sector).	(2.1n)
$\eta_L = \eta_K + J/B - \eta_w/B$	labor absorption equation in industrial sector).	(2.1o)

The basic production conditions for the dualistic economy are given by (2.1a) for the agricultural sector and by (2.1j) for the industrial sector. For the latter, we have postulated a Cobb-Douglas function with neutral innovation in the Hicksian sense. The *intensity of innovation*[24], denoted by J, is defined by

$$J = (\partial x / \partial t)/x \qquad (2.2a)$$

which, when applied to (2.1j), leads to

$$J = \eta_F = (\partial F / \partial t)/F. \qquad (2.2b)$$

Furthermore, for the production function in (2.1j), we have assumed that the innovation behavior (in the industrial sector) takes on a special form as depicted by the curve indicated in Figure 6 (the curve J, labeled 'innovation intensity'). This assumption is due to the fact that, for a contemporary dualistic economy, arriving on the scene as a latecomer anxious to borrow technology from abroad, it is reasonable to postulate that J initially takes on this shape, monotonically decreasing to a stationary level 'b,' as the advantages of the initial latecomer status are gradually exhausted (as innovations become increasingly 'domestically' generated rather than imported). This innovation behavior in the industrial sector

24 'In words, J is the fractional increase of output due to the passage of time', only holding both K and L constant. See Fei and Ranis, *Labor Surplus Economy*, Chapter 3.

is approximated by equation (2.1k). From this equation, we easily have

$\eta_J = -u/(1 + (b/a)e^{ut})$ (rate of increase of innovation intensity). (2.3a)

$F = F(0)e^{\int J dt} = F(0)e^{bt-(a/u)e^{-ut}+au}$ (level of innovation). (2.3b)

In Figure 6, η_J, the rate of increase of innovation intensity, is represented by the monotonically increasing curve below the horizontal axis. Thus the underlying assumption is 'deceleration' of innovation intensity. The curve for $F(t)$ in (2.3b) is plotted in the same diagram and represents the cumulative output-raising effect of innovation. Figure 6 thus helps us to visualize the innovation

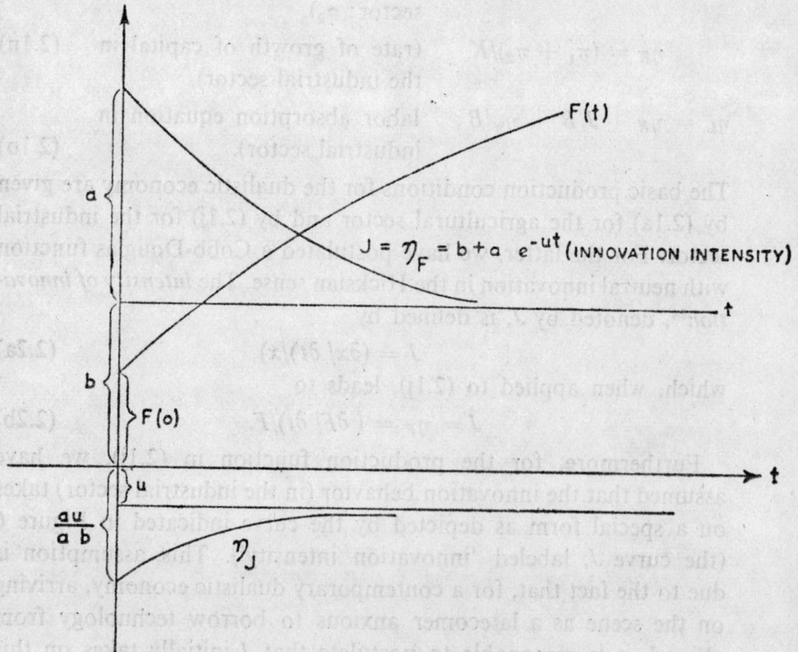

Figure 6. Industrial Sector Innovation Intensity

behavior postulated for the industrial sector of the dualistic economy. Finally, using (2.3b), the production function (2.1j) takes on the following form through a redefinition of the unit of measurement of output:

$$X = e^{bt-(a/u)e^{-ut}+au}K^{B}L^{1-B}. \quad (2.4)$$

Next comes (2.1a), the production function for the agricultural sector of the dualistic economy, which is seen to be similar to (1.1), the production function postulated for the agrarian economy. For example, when labor is not redundant, it is deduced from a Cobb-Douglas function with neutral innovations.:

$$Y = F(t)A^{\alpha}T^{1-\alpha} \tag{2.5}$$

where T stands for land and $F(t)$ is the 'innovation level' factor similar to $F(t)$ in (2.1j) for the industrial sector. Denoting the innovational intensity in the agricultural sector by θ,

$$\theta = \eta_F \quad \text{by (2.2a) applied to (2.5),} \tag{2.6a}$$

hence

$$F = F(0)e^{\theta\int dt}. \tag{2.6b}$$

When (2.6b) is substituted in (2.5), we obtain (2.1a) after redefining the unit of measurement of output and assuming land to be fixed. The intensity of agricultural innovation, θ, is formally introduced into the production function because of our conviction, previously stated, that the analysis of changing innovational behavior in the agricultural sector is central to the performance of the dualistic economy. In this sense, the treatment given to agricultural innovations is completely symmetrical to that given to industrial innovations, J. Nevertheless, the symmetry in treatment ceases when we proceed beyond this formal level. The basic difference between J in the industrial sector and θ in the agricultural sector is that while J is assumed to be determined exogenously, the value of θ is determined endogenously.

Equation (2.1b) simply states that the total labor force (P) is to be allocated, at all times, either to the agricultural sector (A) or to the industrial sector (L) while equation (2.1i) states that the total population is growing at a constant rate, r. Together, these equations emphasize that the dualistic economy is subject to population pressure and that the reallocation of labor (from the agricultural to the industrial sector) is a crucial aspect of growth in the dualistic economy. In fact, *all* the remaining equations in (2.1), in one way or another, are related to the process of labor reallocation.

Equations (2.1c) and (2.1d) present definitions of *TAS* (*total agricultural surplus*, denoted by S) and *AAS* (*average agricultural surplus* denoted by V) respectively. In order to deduce these concepts we assume that a fixed level of real wage, in terms of agricultural goods $\bar{w}$, is given exogenously as the *IRW* (*institutional real wage*), as determined institutionally in the agricultural sector. In a poor, underdeveloped economy, the *IRW* may be close to the level of subsistence wage and remains fixed at this level as long as there are redundant workers in the agricultural sector. The total agricultural surplus, *S*, is the surplus of agricultural goods after the entire agricultural labor force has been fed at *w* (see 2.1c). The measure of the availability of agricultural goods per unit of worker already allocated to the industrial sector is *AAS* (see 2.1d.)[25]

The economic significance of the *AAS* is as a measurement of the extent of commodity support that the agricultural sector furnishes to the industrial sector. The magnitude of the *AAS* directly determines the terms of trade when we know consumer preferences as well as the level of the institutional wage in terms of agricultural goods. This relation is fully analyzed elsewhere,[26] so we shall only present a brief summary here.

Let us assume that regardless of the ownership of *TAS*, the entire amount (*S*) will be exchanged for industrial goods in the intersectoral commodity market. On the other side of this transaction are industrial workers who, after receiving their wage in industrial goods, seek to acquire agricultural goods for consumption. Assume that the real wage (in terms of industrial goods) which prevails in the industrial sector is 'tied' to the agricultural real wage (the $\bar{w}$) as they have the same exchange value.

In Figure 7, agricultural (industrial) goods are measured on the vertical (horizontal) axis and the indifference map of a typical worker in the industrial sector is given. The constant institutional level of the real wage, $\bar{w}$, in agriculture is marked off on the vertical axis and the price-consumption curve from point $\bar{w}$ is constructed. In case the amount *AAS* is known, its magnitude can be indicated by a point such as *A* on the vertical axis. This permits us to obtain point *D* on the price-consumption curve. It is then obvious that the slope of the straight line, $\bar{w}D$, represents the terms of trade (τ) between the two production sectors—for only at these terms of trade will the intersectoral commodity market be cleared and will the *AAS* be purchased by the typical industrial worker. This holds true under the assumption that the industrial wage *in terms of agricultural goods* is pinned at $\bar{w}$ units of food (the institutional real

25 *TAS* and *AAS* are defined in this same fashion in Fei and Ranis, *Labor Surplus Economy*.

26 Fei and Ranis, *Labor Surplus Economy*, Chapter 5.

wage in terms of agricultural goods prevailing in the industrial sector not only is tied to the value of the agricultural real wage but—for simplicity's sake—is equal to it). The value of the real wage in industrial goods then is $0B$ and the distance g as noted on the horizontal axis is called the *surplus coefficient* (g). Specifically, the economic interpretation of g is the amount of industrial goods which the typical industrial worker gives up in exchange for the surplus of agricultural wage goods he has acquired. Since the total expenditure of all industrial workers is gL units of industrial goods, the *terms of trade* (τ) between the two sectors is gL/S as in equation (2.1e).

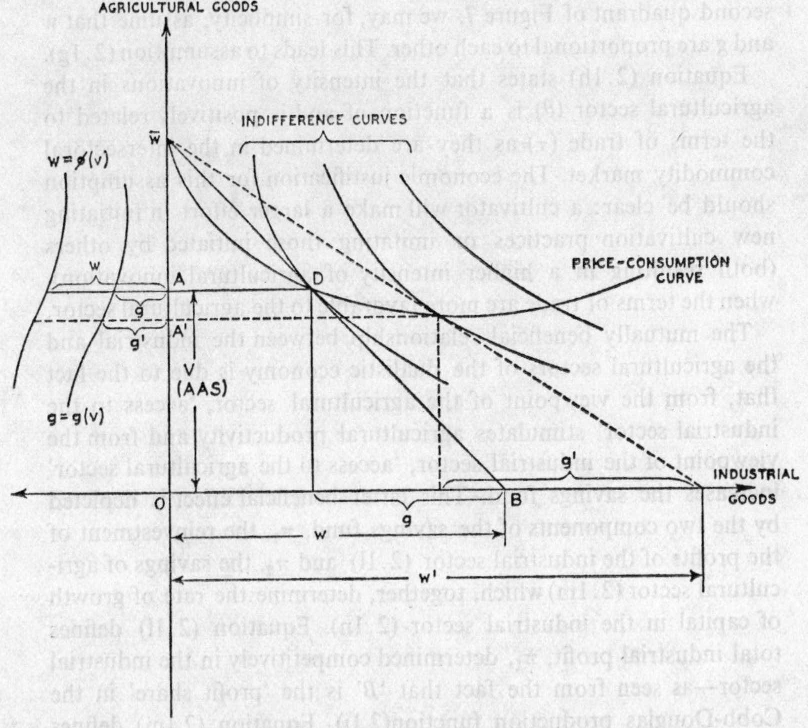

Figure 7. Intersectoral Relations

The above analysis shows that the industrial real wage in terms of industrial goods is controlled by the relative availability of agricultural surplus through a mechanism operating in the intersectoral commodity market. This functional relationship between the *AAS* and w (the real wage in terms of *industrial* goods) is given by equation (2.1f) and is represented by the curve in the second quadrant of Figure 7. As indicated in this diagram, any increase in *AAS* will depress the real industrial wage through a cheapening of food (a deterioration of agriculture's terms of trade). When this occurs, the value of the surplus coefficient (g) also decreases as the expenditure (in *industrial* goods) of a typical industrial worker declines. Thus, there is an inverse functional relationship between *AAS* (i.e., V) and the surplus coefficient (g) as is indicated by the curve (denoted by $g = g(V)$) in the second quadrant of Figure 7. From these two curves ($w = \phi(V)$) and ($g = g(V)$) indicated in the second quadrant of Figure 7, we may, for simplicity, assume that w and g are proportional to each other. This leads to assumption (2.1g).

Equation (2.1h) states that the intensity of innovations in the agricultural sector (θ) is a function of and is positively related to the terms of trade (τ) as they are determined in the intersectoral commodity market. The economic justification for this assumption should be clear: a cultivator will make a larger effort in initiating new cultivation practices or imitating those initiated by others (both resulting in a higher intensity of agricultural innovation), when the terms of trade are more favorable to the agricultural sector.

The mutually beneficial relationship between the industrial and the agricultural sectors of the dualistic economy is due to the fact that, from the viewpoint of the agricultural sector, 'access to the industrial sector' stimulates agricultural productivity and from the viewpoint of the industrial sector, 'access to the agricultural sector' increases the savings fund. This latter beneficial effect is depicted by the two components of the savings fund, π_1, the reinvestment of the profits of the industrial sector (2.1l) and π_2, the savings of agricultural sector (2.1m) which, together, determine the rate of growth of capital in the industrial sector (2.1n). Equation (2.1l) defines total industrial profit, π_1, determined competitively in the industrial sector—as seen from the fact that 'B' is the 'profit share' in the Cobb-Douglas production function(2.1j). Equation (2.1m) defines agricultural savings, π_2 since Lg is the total amount of industrial goods which the owners of the agricultural surplus acquired through the intersectoral commodity market—as described in (2.1e).

Equation (2.1o) is the labor absorption equation which states that the rate of increase of employment of labor in the industrial sector is positively related to the rate of capital accumulation (2.1n) and innovation intensity, J (2.1k) and is negatively related to the rate of increase of the real wage (2.1f). This equation is obtained directly by computing the marginal productivity of labor (the competitive level of real wage) and its rate of increase through time from the production function in (2.1j):

(2.7a) $w = MPP_L = \partial X/\partial L = F(t)\,(1-B)\,(K/L)^B$ (competitive real wage)

(2.7b) $\eta_w = (dw/dt)/w = J + B\eta_K - B\eta_L.$

The rate of labor absorption (2.1o) is, of course, crucial in the development of the dualistic economy—as, when compared with the population growth rate (2.1i) we can determine whether an increasing fraction of the total population is gradually being employed in the industrial sector, that is, whether or not the center of gravity can be gradually shifted from the agricultural to the industrial sector.

Having explained the above fifteen equations individually, we now turn to the problem of the dynamic determinism of the growth process through the interaction of the forces summarized with the help of these equations. To assist us in achieving a firmer grasp of the workings of the dualistic economy as an organic analytical whole, a fuller understanding of the proposed causal order of the economic forces at work may be helpful. In Figure 8 a causal order chart is presented. The heavy horizontal line marks off two adjacent periods, such as $t=0$ (above the line) and $t=1$ (below the line). In each period, we find three large circles including three clusters of economic concepts: agricultural sector concepts (circle on the left), industrial sector concepts (circle on the right), and intersectoral concepts (circle in the center). Although this grouping is not exact, it may help us to develop a sense of order for the growing system as a whole. The various arrows indicate the assumed direction of causation (or the order of determination of the system). For convenience we use the notation (x, y) to refer to an arrow which initiates from concept 'x' and points to concept 'y'. Finally, numbers (1, 2, 3....) are attached to the various concepts to identify their order of presentation in our discussion.

The initial values, at $t=0$, are given of population $P(0)$, innovational intensity in agriculture $\theta(0)$, industrial labor force $L(0)$, industrial capital stock $K(0)$, level of innovation in the industrial sector $F(0)$, and constant institutional wage in agriculture, $\bar{w}$. The initial values of these six variables (and of only these) are assumed to be given. To determine the other economic magnitudes within the agricultural sector, given the size of the total population, $P(0)$, and the total industrial labor force, $L(0)$, we can immediately determine the size of the agricultural labor force, $A(0)$, by using (2.1b). Since the initial intensity of agricultural innovation, $\theta(0)$, is given, this, together with $A(0)$, determines total agricultural output, $Y(0)$, by using the production function (2.1a). We can then determine the size of the agricultural surplus by using $Y(0)$, $A(0)$, and the

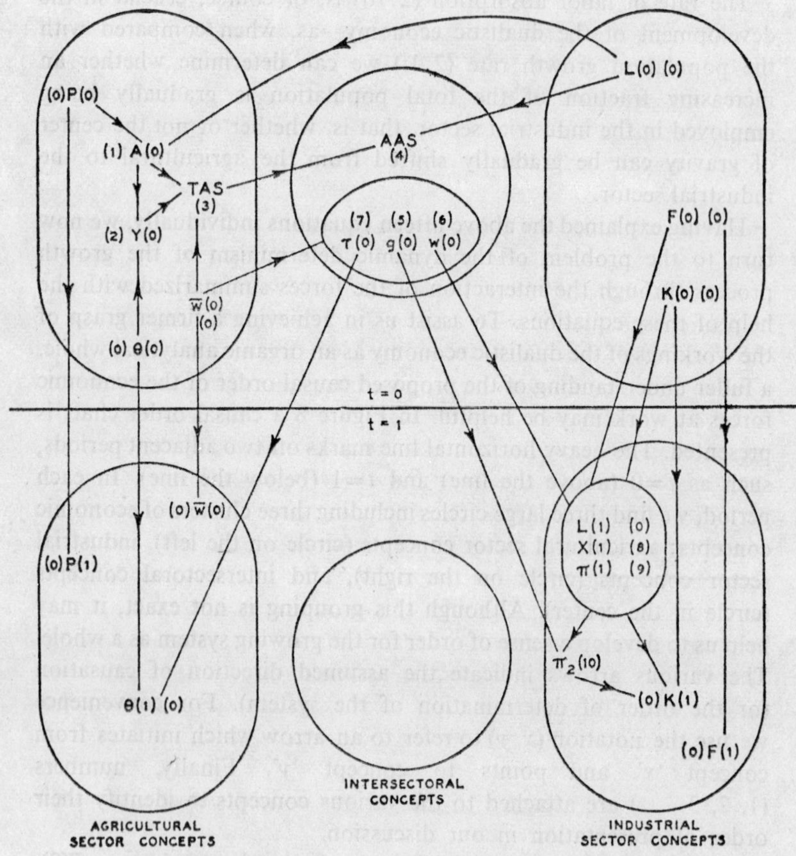

Figure 8. Causal Order Chart

institutional wage, $\overline{w}$, according to (2.1c). In this way all the concepts in the agricultural circle at time $t = 0$ can be determined.

Next, given total agricultural surplus, *TAS*, and the size of the industrial labor force, we can, by using (2.1d), determine the magnitude of the average agricultural surplus, *AAS*. The *AAS* concept represents a crucial link between the two sectors of the dualistic economy since, together with the institutional wage, $\bar{w}$, it determines a set of three important economic magnitudes, the industrial real wage, $w(0)$ (by 2.1f), the surplus coefficient $g(0)$ (by 2.1g), and the intersectoral terms of trade, $\tau(0)$ (by 2.1e). This completes the determination of all the concepts in the intersectoral concept circle at $t=0$.

The industrial sector circle at $t=1$ indicates that the size of the previous period's industrial capital stock, $K(0)$, the level of innovation, $F(0)$, and the wage rate, $w(0)$, determine the amount of industrial labor absorbed in this period, $L(1)$, as per equation (2.1o). This, in turn, determines industrial output, $X(1)$, and industrial profits, $\tau_1(1)$, by use of the industrial production function (2.1j) and the distribution equation (2.1l). Furthermore, the surplus coefficient, $g(0)$, and the industrial labor force, $L(1)$, together determine the agricultural surplus contribution to the total savings fund, $\pi_2(1)$, in accordance with equation (2.1m). Once we know the total savings $(\pi_1+\pi_2)$ we can determine the capital stock in the next period, $K(1)$. The level of innovation in the next period, $F(1)$, is then determined as we have assumed that innovation in the industrial sector is exogenously given according to (2.1k). In this fashion all the concepts in the industrial circle at $t=1$ are determined.

To complete this discussion of determinism, we see that the total population at $t=1$ is given by (2.1i). However, more significantly we can determine the level of innovational intensity, $\theta(1)$, as a phenomenon directly related to the activities in the intersectoral commodity market; the terms of trade, $\tau(0)$, and the innovation intensity in the previous period, $\theta(0)$, determine the innovation intensity, $\theta(1)$, and hence the level of technology in this period according to (2.1h).

There are altogether fifteen variables (P, A, L, Y, S, θ V, g, w, T, X, π_1, π_2, K, F) to be determined by the fifteen equations in (2.1). Furthermore, the five variables ($P(0)$, $L(0)$, $Q(0)$, $F(0)$, and $K(0)$) whose initital values are assumed to be given at $t=0$ (which are indexed by causal order '0') are again determined at $t=1$. This means that the whole cycle can start once again and determine all the magnitudes in the next round ($t=2$). Finally, there are seven variables in Figure 8 (numbers 1–7) which appear in $t=0$ but not in $t=1$; and there are three variables (numbers 8—10) which appear in $t=1$ but not in $t=0$. This means that there can be no problem of inconsistency through overdeterminacy in any subsystem of the above equation system.

V. Conclusion

The main purpose of this paper has been to contrast two definable regimes—of agrarianism and dualism—relevant to the problem of development and to explore the rules of growth peculiar to each. We have endeavored to draw as much as possible on the growth-theoretic implications of the work of both the physiocratic and classical schools as well as the more modern writers concerned with development in the less-developed world.

The reasons for this inquiry are clear. On the one hand, we believe that agrarianism represents not only an important, if neglected, state of economic organization in the historical past but also accurately describes the modus vivendi of substantial portions of the contemporary underdeveloped world. On the other hand, we firmly believe that the growing interest in the analysis of growth under conditions of economic dualism constitutes a big step forward in our understanding of the essential facets of the growth process. Finally, we are convinced that in the idealized life cycle of historical development, a successfully evolving economic system is likely to proceed from agrarianism through dualism to economic maturity.

To bring our over-all framework somewhat closer to the real world and to the possibilities of empirical verification we have endeavored to move toward the evolution of a fully deterministic system to explain long-term agrarian behavior as well as a deterministic model to describe the dynamic interaction of both sectors in the growing dualistic economy. This attempt to describe the dynamic rules of growth of the agrarian and dualistic systems must be viewed as representing our best, and undoubtedly inadequate, thinking in the present state of our knowledge.

We have been even less definitive about the problem of the transition from one regime to the other. The reasons for this should be equally clear, namely, while the task of explaining the 'machinery' which moves the system under conditions of agrarianism or dualism is challenging enough in and of itself, an adequate explanation of the transition from one regime to the other is considerably more complicated. An analysis of what permits an economy to graduate from agrarianism to dualism requires a change in the method of traditional analysis. It requires proceeding beyond the resources framework, in which the economist is at home, to the mutual interaction between the economy's human agents, the instituational framework within which they organize themselves, and these economic functions proper. As an illustration of the difficulty in analyzing this 'transitional' problem, we can mention of the most basic differences between dualism and agrarianism, the *causation of agricultural innovations*. This issue deserves a prominent place because it is likely to be the most critical issue in a contemporary underdeveloped economy. Stagnation in agricultural technique represents a development bottleneck which, to the present time, few underdeveloped countries have succeeded in overcoming.

In our view, in a dualistic economy, the motivation for an increase in the annual flow of agricultural innovations is directly tied up with the opportunities perceived, on the part of the decision-making units in agriculture, for acquiring ownership of the industrial sector capital stock or industrial consumer goods. The incentive to increase agricultural productivity is enhanced if it becomes clear that the proceeds from such increases can be utilized to obtain assets in the industrial sector—either directly or through financial intermediaries—or to obtain industrial consumer goods previously imported or not within the consumer's horizon. Once the relationship between either or both of these objectives and the human effort and toil involved in applying fertilizer and water, using better seeds, pesticides, crop rotations, and so forth becomes clear, marked changes in agricultural productivity can be realized. Historical experience in such diverse areas as Japan, Greece, and Mexico indicates that the dynamic outwardlooking agricultural sector of the dualistic economy, in which activities on the soil are not hermetically sealed off from the rest of the system, can yield increases in θ over a decade larger than those achieved through centuries of inner-oriented agrarian isolation.

The importance of contiguity or 'connectedness' between the agricultural and industrial sectors of the dualistic economy has been much neglected. If the owner of the surplus can invest directly in an extension of the industrial sector close to the soil and in familiar surroundings, he is much more likely to choose the productivity out of which further savings can be channelized. The experience of nineteenth-century Japan indicates that such intersectoral 'connectedness' is much enhanced by the growth of decentralized rural industry, often linked with large-scale urban production stages via a putting-out system. The Japanese government's role, using the famous land tax, was undoubtedly of considerable importance in financing social and economic overheads in the early Meiji period. But it was really the flow of private voluntary savings through a large number of small hands which was responsible—increasingly throughout the nineteenth century—for financing of the prodigious Japanese industrialization effort. It was, in fact, mainly the medium-sized landlord, with one foot in the agricultural and one in the industrial sector, reacting to the intersectoral terms of trade and the changing relative returns to investments of his time and ingenuity, who propelled the dualistic system forward. As late as 1883, 80 per cent of all Japanese factories were located rurally, with 30 per cent of the still agricultural labor force engaged in rural industrial 'side jobs.'

A dualistic landlord, or his counterpart in another context, not only eases the difficulties of the required intersectoral financial intermediation but reduces problems attending the immobility of traditional rural labor, increases the potentialities of using efficient labor-intensive production function, and avoids the over-expansion of capital-hungry urban centers.[27] We do not wish to deprecate the conventional wisdom about the importance of government experimentation and research, of education and extension activities, all of which undoubtedly facilitate the propagation of technological change; but we do want to emphasize the importance of a motivational dimension without which the chances of a really dynamic, balanced growth performance in the dualistic economy are considerably dimmed.

Herein, in fact, lies the essence of the difference between agrarianism and dualism. In agrarianism no active innovational inducement mechanism is at play, no entrepreneurial group exists sensitive to surplus-generating opportunities within and outside of agriculture. In the dualistic setting, on the other hand, there is an entrepreneurial class with decision-making power and access to land which associates its personal well-being—either as industrial

27 For a fuller discussion of the role of the dualistic landlord in nineteenth-century Japan, see Fei and Ranis, *Labor Surplus Economy*, Chapter 5.

consumer goods or ownership of industrial capital goods—in a clear and direct fashion with the continuous improvement of agricultural practices. Such a group is unlikely either to be very large in number or to exhibit conventional Schumpeterian characteristics, but it is composed of leaders who are followed and imitated by the large mass of dispersed cultivators and make it possible for the dualistic economy to progress and ultimately graduate into economic maturity.

The above association obtained by deductive reasoning and buttressed by inductive evidence for nineteenth-century Japan must undoubtedly be subjected to fuller empirical testing. There seems to be little doubt about the general relevance of industrial proximity for agricultural productivity change in the United States.[28] With respect to less-developed countries, Nicholls has carried on some as yet unpublished work on Brazil which points in the same direction. The importance of the decentralized rural-oriented character of the Japanese industrialization effort has been documented elsewhere at considerable length.[29] Schultz acknowledges that 'the process of development appears to have its mainspring in the industrialization complex,'[30] that divergences in the pattern of agricultural productivity are related to the proximity of an industrial-urban complex.

At the present state of our knowledge, we have barely scratched the surface in understanding the full workings and changing nature of the crucial innovations inducement mechanism in agriculture or elsewhere without which our progress is bound to remain limited.[31] We must learn more about tenure and other institutional aspects in agriculture which make it more likely for θ-enhancing activities to replace θ-obstructing activities as a routine matter. What is ultimately needed is a new deterministic transition theory to go along with any satisfactory deterministic theory of agrarianism and dualism, taken separately.

Our paper frankly espouses the notion that development is likely

28 See, for example, W. Nicholls, 'Industrialization, Factor Markets and Agricultural Development,' *Journal of Political Economy*, LXIX (1961), p. 340; W. Nicholls and A. M. Tang, *Economic Development in the South Piedmont, 1860-1950: Its Importance For Agriculture*, (Nashville, 1958).

29 See Fei and Ranis, *Labor Surplus Economy*, and John P. Lewis, *Quiet Crisis in India: Economic Development and American Policy* (Washington, 1962).

30 Theodore Schultz, *The Economic Organization of Agriculture* (New York, 1953).

31 This is still, lamentably, the case even for the mature industrial system.

to proceed via the transition first, from agrarianism to dualism and, then, from dualism to maturity.[32] Yet we think we differ from the stages theorists in that we proceed from a fairly well-defined analytical framework within which precise questions can be asked concerning the functions that need to be performed within each stage as well as to effect the transition between any two stages. Parts of our framework may well be inadequate and will need to be modified or replaced as more evidence is accumulated and better theorizing becomes possible. But retention of such an analytical framework is essential if a satisfactory refutable theory (or set of theories) of development is someday to emerge.

32 The conditions for success in the latter transition have been elaborated earlier (Fei and Ranis, *Labor Surplus Economy*, Chapter 7).

2

SURPLUS AGRICULTURAL LABOUR AND THE DEVELOPMENT OF A DUAL ECONOMY

Dale W. Jorgenson

I. Introduction

THE POINT OF DEPARTURE for this paper is the well-established empirical association between the degree of industrialization and the level of economic development. This association characterizes both time series data for individual countries and international cross-sections at a given point of time. High income per head is associated with a relatively large proportion of the total population engaged in industry. Low income per head is associated with a predominance of employment in the agricultural sector. The process of economic development may be studied as an increase in income per head or as an increase in the role of industrial activity relative to that in agriculture. Quantitatively speaking, gross domestic product *per capita* for the world excluding centrally planned economies increased from \$334 to \$534 in U.S. dollars of 1958 between 1938 and 1961. In the same period value added in industrial activity increased from \$117 to \$223. Similarly, in 1961 gross domestic product *per capita* for industrialized countries was \$1,486 U.S. dollars of 1958; the corresponding figure for less industrialized countries was \$132 *per capita*. Value added in industry *per capita* was \$666 for industrialized countries and \$36 for less industrialized countries.[1] For both time series and cross-sections high levels of output are associated with a high degree of industrialization.

1 Statistical Office of the United Nations, Department of Economic and Social Affairs, *The Growth of World Industry, 1938-1961, International Analyses and Tables*, New York, United Nations, 1965, pp. 194-5. For more detailed support of the association between degree of industrialization and the level of economic development for time series, the following may be consulted: F. Dovring, 'The share of agriculture in a growing population', *Monthly Bulletin of Agricultural Economics and Statistics*, 8 (1959), pp. 1-11, reprinted in Carl K. Eicher and Lawrence W. Witt (eds.), *Agriculture in Economic Development*. New York: McGraw-Hill, 1964, pp. 78-98; S. Kuznets, 'Quantitative aspects of the economic growth of nations, II. Industrial distribution of national product

The great disparity in degree of industrialization in developed and less developed countries is mirrored by a bifurcation in theories of economic growth. In models of a developed economy the analysis is concentrated on the allocation of national product between consumption and investment. Technology may be characterized by fixed factor proportions, as in Harrod's model of economic growth, or by variable factor proportions, as in Tinbergen's model.[2] Technological change may be embodied or disembodied, neutral or biased. Similarly, the model may be closed by assuming that investment is a constant fraction of national output or that investment depends on the distribution of income as in Kaldor's theory of economic growth.[3] For present purposes the similarities of theories of growth for an advanced economic system are more important than the differences. The industrial composition of output, that is, the proportion of output generated by industry, by agriculture, and by the remaining sectors of the economy, is entirely ignored. The central feature of the process of increasing income *per capita*, namely, an increase in the role of industry relative to that of agriculture, is left entirely out of account.

By contrast, in models of a less developed economy the analysis is concentrated on the relationship between the growth of income and the growth of population. One branch of the modern literature on theories of development originated with the paper 'Economic Development with Unlimited Supplies of Labour', by W. A. Lewis.[4]

---

and labor force', *Economic Development and Cultural Change*, 5, Supplement (1957). Similar support for the association on international cross-sections may be obtained from: C. Clark, *The Conditions of Economic Progress*, 3rd ed. London: Macmillan, 1957; H. B. Chenery, 'Patterns of industrial growth', *American Economic Review*, 50 (1960), pp. 624-54; Centre for Industrial Development, Department of Social and Economic Affairs, *A Study of Industrial Growth*, New York, United Nations, 1965.

2 R. F. Harrod, 'An essay in dynamic theory', *Economic Journal*, 49 (1939), pp. 14-33; J. Tinbergen, 'Zur Theorie der langfristigen Wirtschaftsentwicklung', *Weltwirtschaftliches Archiv*, 55 Band (1942), pp. 511-49, translated and reprinted as 'On the theory of trend movements', in L. H. Klaasen, L. M. Koyck, and H. J. Witteveen (eds.), *Jan Tinbergen Selected Papers*, Amsterdam, North Holland, 1959, pp. 182-221.

3 N. Kaldor, 'A model of economic growth', *Economic Journal*, 67 (1957), pp. 591-624, reprinted in *Essays in Economic Stability and Growth*. Glencoe: Free Press, 1960, pp. 259-300; N. Kaldor, 'Capital accumulation and economic growth', in F. A. Lutz and D. C. Hague (eds.), *The Theory of Capital*. London: Macmillan, 1961, pp. 177-222; N. Kaldor and J. Mirrlees, 'A new model of economic growth', *Review of Economic Studies*, 29 (1962), pp. 172-92.

4 W. A. Lewis, 'Economic development with unlimited supplies of labour', *The Manchester School*, 22 (1954), pp. 139-91; W. A. Lewis, 'Unlimited labour: further notes', *The Manchester School*, 26 (1958), pp. 1-32.

Lewis postulates that the fundamental characteristic of certain less developed economies is the existence of disguised unemployment. Lewis's analysis of the role of the unemployed in the determination of wages during economic development is strictly analogous to that of Marx. Wages are tied to a subsistence level so that agricultural output *per capita* remains constant so long as disguised unemployment persists. A second branch of the modern theory of development originates with Harvey Leibenstein's book of 1954.[5] The central result of Leibenstein's theory is the existence of a low-level equilibrium trap, a kind of Malthusian equilibrium of population and sustenance. The Malthusian equilibrium level of income is stable for small changes in income; to achieve sustained economic growth something like a massive infusion of capital is required. As in theories of economic growth, the industrial composition of output is entirely ignored in theories of economic development.

It is widely recognized that under contemporary conditions many less developed countries have important relations with developed countries either through international trade or through the establishment of a modern 'enclave' in an otherwise purely traditional social and economic setting.[6] Either relationship gives rise to economic and social 'dualism' in which a given economic or social system consists of two component parts—an advanced or modern sector and a less advanced or traditional sector. To capture the essence of dualistic development it is necessary to focus on the association between the degree of industrialization and the level of economic development. A theory of development of a dual economy requires a theory of the industrial composition of output and its relationship to the level of economic development. The process of economic development must be studied as an increase in the role of industrial activity relative to that in agriculture. In the development of a dual economy these two developments are intimately related.

5 H. Leibenstein, *A Theory of Economic-Demographic Development*, Princeton: Princeton University Press, 1954; see also: H. Leibenstein, *Economic Backwardness and Economic Growth*. New York: Wiley, 1957.

6 This point of view is elaborated in my paper, 'The development of a dual economy', *Economic Journal*, 71 (1961), especially pp. 309-11 The same point of view is expressed by Luigi Spaventa, 'Dualism in economic growth', *Banca Nazionale Del Lavoro, Quarterly Review*, 51 (1959), especially pp. 386-90. An excellent review of the literature on economic dualism through 1960 is given by Howard S. Ellis, 'Las economias duales y el progreso', *Revista de Economia Latinoamericana* (1961), pp. 3-17.

The purpose of this paper is to present a theory of development of a dual economy, focusing on the relationship between the degree of industrialization and the level of economic development. The theory of development of a dual economy has been approached within both classical and neo-classical frameworks. The chief difference between these two approaches to the development of a dual economy is in conditions governing the supply of labour to the industrial sector. In the classical approach to the theory, the real-wage rate is assumed to be fixed in terms of agricultural goods; from the point of view of industry labour is available in unlimited amounts at a fixed real wage. In the neo-classical approach labour is never available to the industrial sector without sacrificing agricultural output. From the point of view of the industrial sector the real-wage rate rises steadily over time, depending on the rates of technological progress in both sectors and the rate of capital accumulation. Disguised unemployment is assumed to be non-existent. As Lewis points out, a phase of development characterized by disguised unemployment may be followed by a phase without unemployment: 'When the labour surplus disappears our model of the closed economy no longer holds. Wages are no longer tied to a subsistence level.'[7] Within both frameworks it is possible to examine aspects of industrialization of strategic importance for developing countries such as changes in the structure of output and employment and changes in the rate of investment, capital intensity, and factor substitution.

II Development of a Dual Economy: A Classical Approach

In presenting the classical approach to the theory of development of a dual economy the essential assumption proposed by Lewis, unlimited supplies of labour at a fixed real-wage rate, will be retained. In the theory of development of a dual economy, the economic system may be divided into two sectors—the advanced or modern sector, which we will call, somewhat inaccurately, the industrial sector or manufacturing, and the backward or traditional sector, which may be suggestively denoted agriculture. This terminology has been used by Lewis and by Fei and Ranis as well as by the present author.[8] It is clear that industry includes a good many

7 Lewis, 1954, p. 176.

8 Lewis, 1954, pp. 146-8; Jorgenson, 1961, p. 311; J. C. H. Fei and G. Ranis, 'A theory of economic development', *American Economic Review*, 51 (1961), pp. 533-4.

traditional activities and that these activities have many of the characteristics of the backward sector; similarly, the agricultural sector may include a relatively advanced sub-sector. Examples of the former would include small-scale industry in Japan; examples of the latter would include plantation agriculture in Asia and agriculture in areas of European settlement in parts of Africa. Nevertheless, it is useful to regard the backward sector as mainly agricultural and the advanced sector as primarily industrial.

Productive activity in each sector may be characterized by a function relating output to each of the factors of production—land, labour, and capital. The special character of the theory of development of a dual economy is an asymmetry in the productive relations. The output of the traditional sector is a function of land and labour alone; there is no accumulation of capital except in the form of land reclamation. This assumption is made by the present author and also by Lewis and by Fei and Ranis.[9] Of course, other assumptions are possible. Even in relatively primitive societies, there are important uses of capital in agricultural production.[10] Capital is accumulated in the form of land reclamation and in the form of equipment for agriculture, fishing, and hunting. In the study of primitive societies, saving and investment, ownership of property, and even credit cannot be ignored. For present purposes, the assumption of no capital in agriculture is useful. The essential distinction is between agriculture which uses capital produced in the advanced or modern sector and agriculture which uses only traditional forms of capital. We will refer to an agricultural sector utilizing modern forms of capital as commercialized agriculture. For present purposes the special role of commercialized agriculture will be ignored. The resulting theory of development of a dual economy is of special relevance to the less developed countries.

It will be assumed that land is fixed in supply. Further, it is assumed that agricultural activity is characterized by constant returns to scale with all factors variable. These assumptions are made by the present author and by Fei and Ranis.[11] Although there are many ways to account for diminishing returns, e.g. declining quality of

9 Lewis, 1954, p. 146; Jorgenson, 1961, p. 311; J. C. H. Fei and G. Ranis, *Development of the Labor Surplus Economy*. Homewood: Irwin, 1964, p. 16.

10 See, for example, the essays in R. Firth and B. S. Yames (eds.), *Capital, Saving and Credit in Peasant Societies*. Chicago: Aldine, 1964.

11 Jorgenson, 1961, p. 311; Fei and Ranis, 1964, pp. 15-16.

land as more and more is put under cultivation as in Ricardo's extensive margin—the initial assumption that land is fixed in supply implies that the diminishing returns arise at the intensive margin of the Ricardian scheme. In the neo-classical theory of development of a dual economy it is assumed that the marginal productivity of labour in agriculture is always positive. In the classical theory it is assumed that there is some point at which the marginal productivity of labour becomes zero. If population exceeds the quantity at which the marginal productivity of labour becomes zero, labour is available to the manufacturing sector without loss of agricultural output. This assumption, made by Lewis and by Fei and Ranis,[12] will be retained in the present version of the classical theory of development of a dual economy.

Land does not appear as a factor of production in the manufacturing sector; the level of manufacturing output is a function of capital and labour alone. In manufacturing, expansion of productive activity proceeds with constant returns to scale. This appears to be a reasonable assumption, at least on the basis of evidence from the manufacturing industries of advanced economies.[13] A second feature of the production functions for agriculture and manufacturing is that each function will shift over time so that a given bundle of factors will generate a higher level of output at one date than at an earlier date. In short, technological change will be assumed to take place in the manner indicated by Tinbergen and other contributors to the neo-classical theory of economic growth. A special problem arises in applying this assumption to the classical theory of development of a dual economy. For simplicity, it will be assumed that the size of labour force for which the marginal productivity of labour becomes zero remains the same for all technological changes. Of course, the output of the agricultural sector at this point increases over time as the agricultural production function shifts upward.

In the classical approach to the theory of development of a dual economy population growth is ignored or shunted aside as a qualification to the main argument. Lewis discusses a demographic theory quite similar to that of Leibenstein, as outline above. However, this demographic theory is not integrated into the theory of

12 Lewis, 1954, p. 141; J. C. H. Fei and G. Ranis, 'Unlimited supply of labour and the concept of balanced growth', *Pakistan Development Review*, 1(1961), p. 30.

13 See Jorgenson, 1961, p. 311, and the references given there.

economic development in a satisfactory way. For Lewis's main line of argument is suffices to assume that unlimited quantities of labour are available to the industrial sector at a fixed real wage; an unlimited supply of labour may have its origin in population growth, but population growth is not affected by activity in either the agricultural or industrial sectors until the phase of disguised unemployment is completed. A similar assumption is made by Fei and Ranis: 'Population growth will be treated as a known phenomenon exogenous to our model.'[14] This assumption must be qualified in that so long as the real wage remains fixed, the consumption of workers consists entirely of products of the agricultural sector. In the words of Fei and Ranis: "... as a consequence of the natural austerity condition arising from the same unlimited supply of labor situation, much industrial output must take the form of capital goods due to the absence of a domestic market for consumer goods."[15] For simplicity, it will be assumed that so long as there is disguised unemployment, population expands at the same rate as the growth of agricultural output. This is the only assumption which is consistent with the view of Lewis and of Fei and Ranis that the real-wage remains fixed and equal to the initial level of real income in the agricultural sector. At this level of income all of the income of workers in either sector is used for consumption of agricultural products.

The chief difference between the classical approach to the development of a dual economy and the neo-classical approach is in the conditions governing the supply of labor. In the classical theory, labour is available to the industrial sector in unlimited quantities at a fixed real-wage rate, measured in agricultural goods. Lewis suggests that it is immaterial to his argument whether the marginal productivity of labour in agriculture is zero or simply less than the real-wage rate.[16] Fei and Ranis distinguish between phases of development in which the marginal productivity of labour is zero and in which the marginal productivity of labour is positive but less than the real wage.[17] In the first of these phases labour may be supplied to the industrial sector at no loss in agricultural output; in the second of these phases, labour may be supplied to the industrial

14 Fei and Ranis, 'A theory of economic development', 1961, p. 550.
15 Fei and Ranis, *Development of a Labor Surplus Economy*, 1964, p. 118.
16 Lewis, 1954, p. 142.
17 Fei and Ranis, 'A theory of economic development', 1961, p. 537.

sector only at some sacrifice in agricultural output. In both phases labour is available to the industrial sector at a fixed real-wage rate only if the terms of trade between agriculture and industry remain fixed and if population growth is precisely equal to the growth of agricultural output. If the terms of trade should turn against industry, a constant real wage (measured in agricultural goods) will imply a rising price of labour relative to the price of industrial goods.

Finally, in the present version of the classical approach to the development of a dual economy, it will be assumed that saving is equal to total profits in the industrial sector. This assumption is consistent with Lewis's observation that: 'We have seen that if unlimited labour is available at a constant real wage, the capitalist surplus will rise continuously, and annual investment will be a rising proportion of the national income.'[18] As Lewis emphasizes: 'Practically all saving is done by people who receive profits or rents. Workers' savings are very small.'[19] The present assumption implies that agricultural rents, in so far as they exist at all, are exchanged for goods produced by the industrial sector. The agricultural products represented by these rents are then provided to the industrial workers. The institutional mechanism by which this transaction takes place may vary from one economy to another. For example, agricultural rents may be taxed away and the proceeds spent on governmentally financed investment; alternatively, landlords may themselves invest in the industrial sector, becoming industrial capitalists; finally, landlords may consume goods produced by the industrial sector so that all investment is done by the owners of industrial capital. For present purposes it suffices to assume that saving is equal to total profits in the industrial sector without specifying whether the resulting accumulation of capital is owned by the government, the landlords, or the industrial capitalists.

We are now in a position to lay out a more concrete version of the classical approach to the development of a dual economy. To begin the analysis we consider an economic system in which no development of manufacturing activity has taken place; all productive activity is concentrated in the traditional or backward sector. We will assume that there is some maximum quantity of labour which may be employed in the agricultural sector with

18 Lewis, 1954, p. 171.
19 Lewis, 1954, p. 157.

positive marginal productivity; the agricultural labour force, say A, is always less than this maximum quantity of labour. If we let Y be the level of agricultural output and L the fixed quantity of land available to the economy, then a simple version of the production function for agriculture, characterized by constant returns to scale with all factors variable, is given by the Cobb-Douglas function:

$$Y = e^{\alpha t} L^{\beta} A^{1-\beta},$$

where $e^{\alpha t}$ represents the shift factor corresponding to technological progress. Changes in techniques are assumed to take place at a constant percentage rate, α. The constant β represents the elasticity of output with respect to an increase in the supply of land; if the supply of land is fixed it is possible to choose the origin for measuring the passage of time so that the production function can be rewritten in the simpler form:

$$Y = e^{\alpha t} A^{1-\beta}.$$

For a total population in excess of the maximum quantity which may be employed at positive marginal productivity, we may distinguish between the labour force employed at positive marginal productivity, say A, the agricultural labour force, and the labour force which is redundant, say R. Then total population is the sum of the agricultural labour force and redundant labour:

$$P = A + R.$$

If we represent the maximum labour force which may be employed at positive marginal productivity by A^+, then the agricultural labour force is the minimum of total population and this maximum labour force:

$$A = \min \begin{cases} P \\ A^+ \end{cases}.$$

Of course, if the agricultural labour force is equal to total population, disguised unemployment is zero: if the agricultural labour force is equal to the maximum level, A^+, redundant labour is equal to the difference between total population and this maximum level.

Under the assumptions that the rate of technological progress in agriculture is positive and that the maximum quantity of labour which may be employed with positive marginal productivity is fixed over time, the development of an economy in which all productive activity is concentrated in the traditional or backward sector is simple to describe. At a constant real-wage rate, measured in agricultural goods, population increases at the same rate as agricultural output. In the presence of redundant labour, the rate of growth of agricultural output and population is constant and equal to the rate of technological progress in agriculture, α. In the absence of redundant labour, population growth can exceed the rate of technological progress since the rate of growth of output is equal to the rate of technological progress, α, plus the elasticity of output with respect to labour, $1-\beta$, multiplied by the rate of growth of population. With a constant real-wage rate the rate of growth of population is simply α/β, a positive quantity. Hence, in an economy in which there is no redundant labour initially, population will grow at a positive rate until the maximum quantity of labour which can be employed with positive marginal productivity is reached. After this point the rate of population growth will slow to the rate of technological progress, α, and all increments in population will become part of the redundant labour force.

We next consider an economic system in which development of manufacturing activity has taken place. Conditions of production in the manufacturing sector must be described. We have assumed that the production function in manufacturing exhibits constant returns to scale. We have also assumed that the output of manufactured goods for a given bundle of capital and labour increases over time. If we denote the quantity of manufacturing output by X, the manufacturing labour force by M, and the quantity of capital by K, then a simple version of the production function for manufacturing is given by the Cobb-Douglas function:

$$X = e^{\lambda t} K^{\sigma} M^{1-\sigma},$$

where $e^{\lambda t}$ represents technological change, as before, and the constant σ represents the elasticity of manufacturing output with respect to an increase in the supply of land.

With respect to the supply of labour to the manufacturing sector, we have assumed that redundant labour is available to the industrial sector at a fixed real wage, measured in agricultural goods. We may also assume that the terms of trade between agriculture and manufacturing are fixed. If we assume further that competitive conditions prevail in manufacturing, the marginal product of labour is equal to the fixed real wage, measured in either agricultural or manufacturing goods. This assumption is made by Lewis and by

Fei and Ranis.[20] If we denote the fixed real wage measured in manufactured goods by w, the marginal product of labour in the manufacturing sector is then:

$$\frac{\partial X}{\partial M} = (1 - \sigma)\frac{X}{M} = w.$$

If there is no redundant labour, the marginal productivity of labour in the agricultural sector may still be below the real-wage rate, measured in agricultural goods. However, labour may be transferred from the agricultural sector to the industrial sector only by sacrificing agricultural output. Under these conditions it may still be assumed that the terms of trade between agriculture and manufacturing are fixed. This assumption is made by Lewis.[21] Alternatively, it may be assumed that the terms of trade turn against manufacturing, so that the wage rate measured in manufactured goods increases. This assumption is made by Fei and Ranis.[22] In the present version of the classical approach to the theory of development of a dual economy, the terms of trade between agriculture and manufacturing cannot be determined endogenously. For simplicity, we will begin with Lewis's assumption that the terms of trade are fixed; under this assumption the marginal product of labour in manufacturing is fixed. Using the marginal productivity relationship given above to eliminate the manufacturing labour force from the production function for manufacturing, we may write:

$$X = \left(\frac{1-\sigma}{w}\right)^{(1-\sigma)/\sigma} e^{(\lambda/\sigma)t}K.$$

If we assume that saving is equal to the share of profits in the industrial sector, ignoring depreciation we may set the rate of change of capital equal to the share of profits in manufacturing output:

$$\dot{K} = \sigma X,$$

so that the rate of growth of capital may be written:

$$\frac{\dot{K}}{K} = \sigma\left(\frac{1-\sigma}{w}\right)^{(1-\sigma)/\sigma} e^{(\lambda/\sigma)t}.$$

20 Lewis, 1954, pp. 146-9; Fei and Ranis, 1964, pp. 16-19.

21 Lewis, 1954, p. 142.

22 Fei and Ranis, 1964, p. 209.

Using the production function and the fact that the output per man remains constant, the rate of growth of manufacturing output may be written:

$$\frac{\dot{X}}{X} = \frac{\lambda}{\sigma} + \sigma \left(\frac{1-\sigma}{w}\right)^{(1-\sigma)/\sigma} e^{(\lambda/\sigma)t}.$$

The rate of growth of manufacturing employment is, of course, equal to the rate of growth of manufacturing output.

For an economy with total population in excess of the maximum quantity which may be employed at a positive marginal productivity in agriculture plus the manufacturing labour force, there is redundant labour. Total population is the sum of the agricultural labour force, the industrial labour force, and redundant labour:

$$P = A + M + R.$$

The agricultural labour force is the minimum of total population less the manufacturing labour force and the maximum labour force which may be employed at positive marginal productivity:

$$A = \min \begin{cases} P - M \\ A^{+} \end{cases}.$$

So long as there is redundant labour in the agricultural sector, manufacturing output and manufacturing employment grow at a rate which is positive and increasing. Capital in manufacturing also grows at a rate which is positive and increasing, but always less than the rate of growth of output. This implies that the capital-output ratio is always falling; a similar result is obtained by Fei and Ranis.[23] Since agricultural output is increasing at a constant rate, to the rate of technological progress in agriculture, population is increasing at this same rate. Whatever the initial value of the rate of growth of manufacturing output, this rate of growth eventually exceeds any fixed rate of growth. The sum of redundant labour and manufacturing employment grows at a rate which exceeds the rate of growth of population; but this rate must be fall to the rate of growth of population. Hence, the rate of growth of manufacturing employment eventually becomes so large as to force the rate of growth of redundant labour to become negative and decreasing. Under these conditions redundant labour eventually disappears altogether. This concludes the description of the first phase of development with unlimited supplies of labour. The point at which redundant

23 J. C. H. Fei and G. Ranis, 'Capital accumulation and economic development', *American Economic Review*, 53 (1963), p. 288.

labour disappears is called the 'Lewis turning-point' by Fei and Ranis.[24]

After the Lewis turning-point is reached the marginal productivity of labour in the agricultural sector is positive but less than the real-wage rate, measured in agricultural goods. Under the assumption that the real-wage rate remains fixed when measured in agricultural goods, the rate of growth of population is equal to the rate of technological change in the agricultural sector less the elasticity of agricultural output with respect to labour multiplied by the rate of decline of the agricultural labour force. Where w_A is the proportion of the agricultural labour force in total population and w_M the proportion of the manufacturing labour force, this condition on the rate of population growth implies:

$$\alpha + (1-\beta)\frac{\mathring{A}}{A} = w_A\frac{\mathring{A}}{A} + w_M\frac{\dot{M}}{M},$$

or, simply:

$$\alpha + (w_M-\beta)\frac{\mathring{A}}{A} = w_M\frac{\dot{M}}{M}.$$

For this condition to be satisfied, the manufacturing proportion, w_M, must be such that the rate of growth of the agricultural labour force is negative at the Lewis turning-point. Furthermore, the rate of growth of the agricultural labour force must remain negative until the labour force itself reaches the level at which the marginal product of labour in agriculture, measured in agricultural goods, is equal to the real wage. For this it suffices to assume that the share of manufacturing in the total labour force exceeds the elasticity of agricultural output with respect to land. Under this condition the agricultural labour force declines at an increasing rate until the marginal product of labour is equal to the real wage. At this point a third phase of the development of dual economy is reached. In this phase the wage rate of labour is the same in agriculture and in manufacturing.

The third phase of development of a dual economy under the classical approach is described by Lewis as follows: 'When capital catches up with labour supply, an economy enters upon the [third] phase of development. Classical economics ceases to apply; we are in the world of neo-classical economics, where all the factors of production are scarce, in the sense that their supply is inelastic. Wages are no longer constant as accumulation proceeds; the

24 Fei and Ranis, 'A theory of economic development', 1961, p. 540.

benefits of improved technology do not all accrue to profits; and the profit margin does not necessarily increase all the time....'[25] Fei and Ranis describe the third phase as follows: 'The transition into phase [three] constitutes a major landmark in the developmental process. With the completion of the transfer of the disguisedly unemployed, there will occur a switch, forced by circumstance in employer behaviour, i.e., the advent of a fully commercialized agricultural sector. This landmark may be defined as the end of the take-off process. We know of no other way to establish a nonarbitrary criterion for an economy reaching the threshold of so-called self-sustaining growth.'[26] The basic point made by Lewis and by Fei and Ranis is that a neo-classical theory of growth for an advanced economy applies after the third phase of development has been reached. Hence, further discussion of this phase will be postponed until the neo-classical theory of development for a dual economy has been discussed.

Parenthetically, it should be remarked that Fei and Ranis attempt to combine Lewis's notion of disguised unemployment with the critical minimum effort hypothesis of Leibenstein. Their criterion for a critical minimum effort is that the rate of growth of population must be less than the rate of growth of the industrial labour force. In the presence of disguised unemployment, this condition is always satisfied, provided only that the rate of technological change in the industrial sector is positive. With a positive rate of technological change the rate of growth of the industrial labour force eventually exceeds any fixed rate of growth; with a fixed real wage, measured in agricultural goods, the growth of population is limited by the rate of technological change in the agricultural sector. In the absence of disguised unemployment, the critical minimum effort criterion is satisfied only under a somewhat different set of conditions. We will return to the discussion of this problem after our review of the neo-classical theory.

III Development of a Dual Economy: a Neo-classical Approach[27].

The distinguishing characteristics of the neo-classical theory of the development of a dual economy are the technology of the agricultural sector and the conditions governing the supply of

25 Lewis, 1954, pp. 26-27.
26 Fei and Ranis, 'A theory of economic development', 1961, p. 537.
27 This section is based on my paper 'The development of a dual economy'.

labour. First, in the neo-classical approach it is assumed that the productivity of labour in agriculture is always positive so that labour is never redundant. Secondly it is assumed that the real-wage rate is variable rather than fixed; wage rates in the backward sector are assumed to be proportional to those in the advanced sector. The interpretation of this relationship will be discussed below, Except for the possibility that labour may be redundant, the description of technology for the agricultural sector is the same for both classical and neo-classical theories. In the neo-classical approach there is no level of the agricultural labour force at which the marginal productivity of labour is zero. It is assumed that the agricultural production function for any level of the agricultural labour force may be characterized by the Cobb Douglas production function:

$$Y = e^{\alpha t} L^{\beta} A^{1-\beta},$$

where variables and parameters have the same interpretation as in the classical approach. Assuming that the supply of land is fixed, this production function may be rewritten in the form:

$$y = e^{\alpha t} A^{-\beta},$$

where $y = Y/A$ is agricultural output per head.

Conditions of production in the manufacturing sector are the same as those of the classical theory. We have assumed that the manufacturing production function may be characterized by constant returns to scale and that the output of manufactured goods for a given quantity of capital and labour increases over time; a simple version of the manufacturing production function is the Cobb-Douglas function:

$$X = e^{\lambda t} K^{\sigma} M^{1-\sigma}$$

where variables and parameters have the same interpretation as in the classical theory. Second, we assume that saving is equal to the share of profits in the manufacturing sector; as before, we ignore depreciation so that the rate of change of capital may be set equal to the share of profits in manufacturing output:

$$\dot{K} = \sigma X.$$

This assumption is identical to that made in the classical approach.

To close the model for the neo-classical theory of the development of a dual economy it is necessary to describe the allocation of labour between the backward and advanced sectors of the economy. To simplify the discussion we will assume that as agricultural output per head increases, all output is consumed up to a level of agricultural output per head equal to the critical value, y^+. We assume that once the critical value is attained all further increases in consumption per head take the form of manufactured goods. Under these assumptions agricultural output per head in excess of the critical value, y^+, constitutes a surplus; we may define the agricultural surplus per head, say s, as the difference between agricultural output per head and the critical value, y^+:

$$s = y - y^+.$$

If agricultural output per head exceeds the critical level, part of the labour force may be released from the land to produce manufactured goods with no reduction in the rate of growth of total population.[28]

As before, we denote agricultural population by A and manufacturing population by M; total population, say P, is the sum of these two components:

$$P = A + M.$$

The demographic theory for the development of a dual economy is as follows: The net rate of reproduction is the minimum of the rate corresponding to the minimum force of mortality ϵ and a rate which corresponds to output of food per head; the basic demographic relationship may be written:

$$\frac{\dot{P}}{P} = \min \begin{cases} \gamma y \dfrac{A}{P} - \delta \\ \epsilon \end{cases}$$

where yA/P is output of food per head for the whole economy and δ is the minimum net reproduction rate equal to the maximum possible force of mortality (mass starvation) and ϵ is a fixed birth-rate that depends on medical technique and social institutions. For an economy with an agricultural surplus, total food consumption is the critical level y^+, multiplied by total population; the proportion of the total labour force employed in agriculture is the ratio of this critical level of agricultural production per head to the actual level of output per head:

28 The relationship between the existence of an agricultural surplus and development of the advanced sector has been discussed by Lewis and by Fei and Ranis. This relationship is also discussed by N. Kaldor in his paper, 'Characteristics of economic development', in *Essays on Economic Stability and Growth*. Glencoe: Free Press, 1960, pp. 233-42. The necessity of an agricultural surplus has been emphasized by William H. Nicholls in his papers, 'The place of agriculture in economic development', in Eicher and Witt (eds.), *Agriculture in Economic Development*, pp. 11-44, and 'An agricultural surplus as a factor in economic development, *Journal of Political Economy*, 71 (1963), pp. 12-9.

$$\frac{y^+}{y}=\frac{A}{P}\,.$$

Of course, this relationship holds only when an agricultural surplus exists, that is, if $y > y^+$. Under these assumptions, the relationship governing the distribution of labour between the backward sector and the advanced sector may be represented by:

$$\frac{A}{P}=\min\begin{cases}1\\ y^+/y\end{cases}$$

To study the development of a dual economy for the case in which the advanced sector is economically viable, we must assume at the outset that an agricultural surplus eventually emerges, that is, that $\alpha-\beta\epsilon>0$, which is both necessary and sufficient for the emergence of an agricultural surplus. The case in which the advanced sector is not economically viable will be treated subsequently. We assume first that the initial level of agricultural output per head is below the critical level, y^+. An industrial labour force comes into being when agricultural output per head attains the critical value, y^+, that is, when agricultural output attains the minimum level necessary for population to grow at its maximum rate. From this point forward population grows at the maximum rate of net reproduction, ϵ.

From the fact that population is growing at a constant rate and that consumption of food per head is stationary, we obtain the following expression for the growth of the agricultural labour force:

$$A=P(0)e^{(\epsilon-\alpha/1-\beta)t}=A(0)e^{(\epsilon-\alpha/1-\beta)t}.$$

Agricultural population may grow, decline, or remain constant, depending on the magnitude of the parameters ϵ, the rate of growth of total population, and α, the rate of technological progress in agriculture.

The manufacturing population is equal to total population less agricultural population; hence the growth of the manufacturing labour force is governed by the following expression:

$$M=P(0)[e^{\epsilon t}-e^{(\epsilon-\alpha/1-\beta)t}].$$

which is zero at time $t=0$ and grows at a rate which is always more rapid than the rate of growth of total population. To show this we begin with the assumption that an agricultural surplus eventually emerges, namely:

$$\alpha-\beta\epsilon>0,$$

which implies: $$\epsilon-\alpha < \epsilon(1-\beta),$$

so that: $$\epsilon > \frac{\epsilon-\alpha}{1-\beta}.$$

The rate of growth of population is greater than that of the agricultural population alone; hence the manufacturing labour force is growing at a rate which exceeds that of total population. The rate of growth of the manufacturing labour force is always declining and approaches, as a limit, the rate of growth of population, ϵ.

To study the growth of manufacturing output, it is necessary to characterize the process of capital accumulation in the advanced sector of the economy. The fundamental relationships include the expression given above for the growth of the manufacturing labour force, the production function for the manufacturing sector, and the savings function. Combining these relationships we may eliminate the output of the manufacturing sector and the manufacturing labour force to obtain a differential equation in capital alone:

$$K = \sigma K^{\sigma} P(0)^{1-\sigma} e^{\lambda t} [e^{\epsilon t} - e^{(\epsilon-\alpha/1-\beta)t}]^{1-\sigma}$$

which is the fundamental differential equation for the neo-classical theory of development of a dual economy. From this fundamental equation it may be deduced immediately that there is no stationary situation for any economy in which the advanced sector is economically viable; that is, provided that there is a positive and growing agricultural surplus, the advanced sector must continue to grow. The pattern of growth of the advanced sector is determined by two initial conditions, the size of total population at the time that the growth of the advanced sector begins and the size of the initial capital stock. Only the initial size of the population has any effect on the long-run pattern of growth of the economy; the influence of the initial size of capital stock eventually dies out.[29] Secondly, it may be shown that there is no critical minimum level of the initial capital stock required for sustained economic growth. Given any positive initial capital stock, no matter how small, the existence of a positive and growing agricultural surplus generates sustained economic growth.

For the neo-classical theory of the development of a dual economy capital and output grow at the same rate in the long run, namely, $\lambda/(1-\sigma)+\epsilon$, where λ is the rate of technological progress in industry,

29 A proof of this proposition is given in 'The development of a dual economy', pp. 330-3.

$1-\sigma$ is the share of labour in manufacturing output, and ϵ is the rate of growth of population. Population grows at the rate ϵ; since the share of labour in manufacturing output is constant, the wage rate of the manufacturing labour force eventually grows at the rate $\lambda/1-\sigma$. In the short run the beginning of the growth of the advanced sector is always characterized by a 'big push', that is, an extraordinarily high rate of growth of manufacturing output. From the viewpoint of the neo-classical theory of the development of a dual economy, such a high initial rate of growth may be interpreted as a statistical artifact. Using the production function for the advanced sector, we may derive the relation:

$$\frac{\dot{X}}{X}=\lambda+\sigma\frac{\dot{K}}{K}+(1-\sigma)\frac{\dot{M}}{M}$$

so that the rate of growth of manufacturing output is equal to the rate of technological progress plus a weighted average of the rates of growth of capital stock and of the manufacturing labour force. But the initial rate of growth of the manufacturing labour force is essentially unbounded; this rate of growth declines gradually, approaching a long-run equilibrium value equal to the rate of growth of total population. The existence of a statistically observable 'big push' is no evidence for the necessity of a massive infusion of capital from outside the system for a 'take-off' into sustained growth; sustained growth depends on the economic viability of the advanced sector and not on the initial level of capital stock. The advanced sector is economically viable if and only if there is a positive and growing agricultural surplus.

We have assumed that wage rates in the backward sector of a dual economy are proportional to those in the advanced sector. Using this relationship and the saving function it is possible to determine the terms of trade between agriculture and industry. The balance of trade between agriculture and industry requires that the value of labour income in both sectors is equal to the value of manufacturing output not used for additions to capital together with the value of total agricultural output. This balance relation may be written:

$$wM+\mu wA=(1-\sigma)X+qY,$$

where q is the terms of trade between agriculture and industry and μ is the constant of proportionality between wage rates in the agricultural sector and wage rates in the industrial sector.

The constant of proportionality may be interpreted in a number of different ways. First, in a 'strict' neo-classical theory wage rates in the two sectors must be equal. In this case the constant of proportionality, μ, is unity. Alternatively, if the process of development of a dual economy is characterized by a steady flow of labour from agriculture to industry, a differential between agricultural and industrial wages may be required to sustain this flow.[30] As a third alternative, if land is owned by the cultivators but the full value of the land cannot be realized by outright sale, the industrial wage rate must be sufficiently high to cover both labour and property income for a member of the agricultural labour force.[31] If nothing can be realized by the sale of land, the industrial wage rate would have to be equal to unity divided by the share of labour in total agricultural output. Other interpretations of the constant of proportionality could doubtless be given. Provided that μ is a fixed constant the balance relation may be rewritten in the form:

$$\mu w A = q Y,$$

so that:

$$\frac{\dot{w}}{w} + \frac{\dot{A}}{A} \qquad \frac{\dot{Y}}{}$$

and:

$$\frac{\dot{q}}{q} = \left[\frac{\epsilon - \alpha}{1 - \beta} - \epsilon \right] \quad \bar{w}.$$

In the long run the rate of growth of the wage rate in manufacturing is equal to $\lambda/\!-\!\sigma$, so that the rate of growth of the terms of trade is the sum of a negative and a positive quantity; hence the terms of trade may turn in favour of agriculture or industry, depending on the relative magnitude of the two quantities.

IV Beyond Disguised Unemployment

Where the advanced sector is already in existence, wage rates in the advanced and backward sectors may be taken to be equal, as in the 'strict' neo-classical approach. Then the neo-classical theory of the development of a dual economy may be reinterpreted as a theory of the neo-classical phase of Lewis's theory of economic development. The growth of the manufacturing labour force and manufacturing output and the accumulation of capital are described by the relations given above for the neo-classical theory. However, the initial phases of the development of the advanced sector are

30 See, for example, 'The development of a dual economy', pp. 322–3.
31 Lewis, 1954, pp. 148-9.

not the same as in the neo-classical theory. In the classical theory the phase of redundant labour initiates the development of manufacturing. This sector develops further in the phase of disguised unemployment, where there is no redundant labour but the marginal product of labour in the agricultural sector is below the real wage rate, measured in agricultural goods. Finally, the marginal products of labour in both sectors are brought into equality with the fixed real-wage rate. By this time a certain amount of capital has been accumulated in the manufacturing sector. Given the manufacturing labour force, the second initial condition for the fundamental relations of the neo-classical theory of development of a dual economy, namely, the size of total population when agricultural output per head reaches its critical value, y^{+}, can be computed by inserting the manufacturing labour force into the equation:

$$M(t) = P(0)[e^{\epsilon t} - e^{[\epsilon - \alpha/1-\beta]t}],$$

by inserting total population into the equation:

$$P(t) = P(0)e^{\epsilon t},$$

and by computing $P(0)$ and the origin for the measurement of time. These constants may then be used to determine the course of economic growth in the neo-classical phase of the classical theory of the development of a dual economy. Of course, the fundamental relations of the neo-classical theory are valid for the classical theory only *after* the beginning of the neo-classical phase.

Up to this point we have considered only the case in which the advanced sector is economically viable. A necessary and sufficient condition for the economic viability of the advanced sector is the eventual emergence of a positive and growing agricultural surplus. Provided that an agricultural surplus eventually emerges, the development of a dual economy may be characterized in two ways. If there is disguised unemployment as in the classical approach, the manufacturing sector develops in three separate phases. First, manufacturing output and employment grow at a rate which is positive and increasing. Capital in manufacturing also grows at a rate which is positive and increasing, but always less than the rate of growth of manufacturing output. Redundant labour eventually disappears. Secondly, provided that the share of manufacturing in the total labour force exceeds the elasticity of agricultural output with respect to land, the agricultural labour force declines at an increasing rate until the marginal product of labour is equal to the real wage in both sectors. The realization of this condition marks the end of disguised unemployment. Finally, the manufacturing sector enters on to the neo-classical phase. This phase is the same as the phase of 'dualistic' development in the neo-classical theory, provided that the initial conditions of the fundamental relations of the neo-classical theory are properly reinterpreted. If there is no disguised unemployment as in the neo-classical approach, the backward sector develops according to the fundamental relations describing an increase in agricultural output per head until the critical level, y^+, is reached. At this level the force of mortality reaches its minimum and the net reproduction rate for total population reaches its maximum. From this point forward the development of the manufacturing sector is described by the fundamental relations for capital accumulation and for the growth of manufacturing output and employment. These relations are the same as those describing the neo-classical phase of development of a dual economy in the classical approach.

We may now consider the case in which the advanced sector is not economically viable. First, we will describe the neo-classical theory of development for this case. If capital for the advanced sector is already in existence, the condition for economic viability of this sector, $\alpha - \beta\epsilon > 0$, is not satisfied. There are two possibilities. First, suppose that $\alpha = \beta\epsilon$; then the manufacturing labour force is equal to zero and there is no manufacturing production. Secondly, suppose that $\alpha < \beta\epsilon$ and the initial value of the manufacturing labour force is positive. Then this labour force declines to zero after which there is no further manufacturing production. Total population becomes entirely concentrated in the agricultural sector and agricultural output per head eventually declines to that associated with the low-level equilibrium trap.

The classical theory of development where the advanced sector is not economically viable at the maximum net reproduction rate is somewhat more complex. We consider development only in the third or neo-classical phase. In this phase the development of a dual economy is characterized by the same fundamental relations as in the neo-classical approach. If the advanced sector is not economically viable, two possibilities exist. First, if $\alpha = \beta\epsilon$, the existence of a positive manufacturing labour force contradicts the fundamental differential equation for the neo-classical theory of development of a dual economy. Hence, for the classical approach this condition must be ruled out by assumption. Secondly, if $\alpha < \beta\epsilon$, the manufacturing labour force begins to decline as soon as disgused unemployment is eliminated. This decline continues until the agricultural labour force reaches its maximum level, so that further increases in the agricultural labour force are redundant. Throughout the decline of the manufacturing labour force the real wage in both sectors remains constant with no disguised unemployment.

With a fixed real wage, measured in agriucltural goods, the rate of population growth must decline to the rate of technological progress in agriculture when the agricultural labour force reaches its maximum, so that $\epsilon=\alpha$ from this point forward. At this lower rate of population growth the advanced sector is always economically viable. The labour force in manufacturing begins to grow at a rate exceeding that of population growth but eventually declines to this rate of growth. The renewed growth of the manufacturing labour force is characterized by a 'big push', that is, an extraordinarily high rate of growth of the manufacturing labour force. As in the neo-classical theory of the development of a dual economy, this high initial rate of growth may be interpreted as statistical artifact. The existence of such a statistically observable 'big push' is no evidence for the necessity of a massive infusion of capital from outside the system for a 'take-off'. Sustained growth depends on the economic viability of the advanced sector at the new rate of population growth and not on the initial level of capital stock.

In the second phase of growth in the manufacturing labour force the labour force in agriculture remains constant at its maximum level, while agricultural output grows at the same rate as population. Manufacturing output and capital stock eventually increase at the rate $\lambda(1—\alpha)+\alpha$ and the real wage, measured in manufacturing goods, grows at the rate $\lambda/1—\sigma$. Throughout the second phase of growth in the manufacturing labour force, the real wage, measured in agricultural goods, is increasing at the rate of technological progress in agriculture, α. The terms of trade between agriculture and industry eventually grows at the rate $\lambda/(1—\sigma)—\alpha$. This rate may be positive or negative, depending on the relative rates of technological progress in the two sectors.

In the classical theory of the development of a dual economy the phase of development beginning with no manufacturing production but with redundant agricultural labour or disguised unemployment is characterized by a rate of growth of the manufacturing labour force that exceeds the rate of growth of population. This characterization is a necessary consequence of the classical theory whether or not the advanced sector is economically viable at the maximum rate of net reproduction. If the advanced sector is not economically viable at this rate of population growth, the initial phase of disguised unemployment is followed by a phase of absolute decline in the manufacturing labour force that terminates with the agricultural labour force at its maximum level and with a reduced rate of population growth. This phase is followed by a second phase of growth in the manufacturing labour force. Again, the rate of growth of the manufacturing labour force exceeds the rate of growth of population.

We conclude that the criterion for a critical minimum effort proposed by Fei and Ranis, that the rate of growth of population must be less than the rate of growth of the industrial labour force, provides no indication whatever concerning the economic viability of the advanced sector. The advanced sector is economically viable if and only if there is a positive and growing agricultural surplus, that is $\alpha > \beta\epsilon$. During the phase of disguised unemployment, the critical minimum effort criterion of Fei and Ranis is satisfied whether or not the advanced sector is economically viable. Where their criterion is satisfied, the elimination of disguised unemployment may be followed by sustained economic growth or by a period of absolute decline in the manufacturing labour force. Only the existence of a positive and growing agricultural surplus assures that growth will be sustained.

V Summary and Conclusion

In the preceding sections we have described two alternative approaches to the theory of development of a dual economy. In order to facilitate comparison of the two approaches, we have attempted to develop both within the same framework. Within this framework the basic differences between the two approaches are in assumptions made about the technology of the agricultural sector and about conditions governing the supply of labour. In the classical approach it is assumed that there is some level of the agricultural labour force beyond which further increments in this labour force are redundant. In the neo-classical approach the marginal productivity of labour in agriculture is assumed to be always positive so that labour is never redundant. In the classical approach the real-wage rate, measured in agricultural goods, is assumed to be fixed 'institutionally' so long as there is disguised unemployment in the agricultural sector. In the neo-classical approach the real-wage rate is assumed to be variable rather than fixed; it is further assumed that at very low levels of income the rate of growth of population depends on the level of income. These are the basic differences between the neo-classical and classical approaches to the theory of development of a dual economy.

The neo-classical and classical theories differ in the characterization of the backward or traditional sector of the economy. These differences have implications for the behaviour of the backward sector. Among the implications we may note that according to the classical approach, the agricultural labour force must decline absolutely before the end of the phase of disguised unemployment; in the neo-classical approach the agricultural labour force may rise, fall, or remain constant. The differences between the two approaches also have implications for the behaviour of the advanced sector; unfortunately, these implications depend on the actual behaviour of the terms of trade between the backward and advanced sectors. In the neo-classical approach the terms of trade may rise or fall. In the classical approach the terms of trade cannot be determined endogenously. Alternative assumptions about the course of the terms of trade may be made. Corresponding to each assumption about the terms of trade, there is an alternative theory for the behaviour of the advanced sector. Since any assumption about the course of the terms of trade is consistent with the classical approach, the behaviour of the terms of trade cannot provide a test of this approach. The classical approach may be tested only by deriving the implications of this approach for the advanced sector, given the observed behaviour of the terms of trade, and confronting these implications with empirical evidence.

We have developed the classical theory in detail only on the assumption that the terms of trade between the backward and advanced sectors remain constant. Proceeding on this assumption, we have derived the following implications of the classical approach: (1) output and employment in the advanced sector grow at the same rate so long as there is disguised unemployment in the backward sector; that is, labour productivity in the advanced sector remains constant; (2) capital grows at a slower rate than output and labour so that capital-output ratio falls; this result corresponds to that of Fei and Ranis;[32] (3) the rates of growth of manufacturing output, employment, and capital increase during the phase of disguised unemployment. For the neo-classical approach, the corresponding results are: (1) output and capital in the advanced sector grow at the same rate, asymptotically, so that the capital-output ratio remains constant; (2) manufacturing employment grows more slowly than either output or capital so that labour productivity in the advanced sector rises; (3) the rates of growth of manufacturing output and employment decrease throughout the development process. Since the classical approach reduces to the neo-classical approach after the phase of disguised unemployment is completed, the two approaches have different implications only for situations where it is alleged that disguised unemployment exists.

In view of the similarities between classical and neo-classical approaches to the development of dual economy it is not surprising that many implications of one model are also implications of the other. For example, both models imply that if the proportion of manufacturing output to agricultural output increases, the share of saving in total income also increases. Thus either model suffices to explain an increase in the fraction of income saved in the course of economic development. The fact that the implications of the two approaches for the share of saving are identical is of considerable significance. According to Lewis: 'The central problem in the theory of economic development is to understand the process by which a community which was previously saving and investing [four or five per cent.] of its national income or less, converts itself into an economy where voluntary saving is running at about [twelve to fifteen per cent.] of national income or more. This is the central problem because the central fact of economic development is rapid capital accumulation (including knowledge and skills with capital).'[33] Both classical and neo-classical theories of the development of a dual economy provide an explanation of an increase in the share of saving. In each case the explanation is based on the relationship between saving and industrial profits. Disguised unemployment is neither necessary nor sufficient to generate a sustained rise in the share of saving. Ultimately, a sustained increase in the saving share depends on a positive and growing agricultural surplus and not on the presence or absence of disguised unemployment.

32 Fei and Ranis, 1963, p. 288.
33 Lewis, 1954, p. 155.

The role of the industrial sector in economic development is critical for the elimination of disguised unemployment. In the absence of industrialization an economy with redundant labour is characterized by population growth at a rate equal to the rate of growth of agricultural output. Agricultural output grows at the rate of technological progress in agriculture. All increments in population become part of the redundant labour force. In the presence of industrialization the rate of growth of manufacturing employment eventually becomes so large as to force the rate of growth of redundant labour to become negative; redundant labour eventually disappears altogether. The disappearance of disguised unemployment is, however, no indication that the industrial sector is economically viable. If the condition for persistence of an agricultural surplus is not satisfied, the initial phase of disguised unemployment is followed by a phase of absolute decline in the manufacturing labour force that terminates with the agricultural labour force at its maximum level and with a reduced rate of population growth. The condition that population grows more slowly than the manufacturing labour force provides no indication of the economic viability of the advanced sector at a given rate of population growth.

In the theory of development of a dual economy, there is no critical minimum level of initial capital stock required for sustained economic growth. Given any positive initial capital stock, no matter how small, the existence of a positive and growing agricultural surplus generates sustained growth of the industrial sector. In the long run the development of a dual economy is characterized by a growth in industrial output at a rate equal to the sum of the rate of growth of population and the ratio of the rate of technological progress in industry to the share of labour in that sector. Agricultural output grows at a rate equal to the rate of growth of population; hence the ratio of industrial output to agricultural output is always increasing. Similarly, the rate of growth of the industrial labour force is equal to the rate of growth of population in the long run. The rate of growth of the agricultural labour force is equal to the difference between the rate of growth of total population and the rate of technological progress in agriculture divided by the share of labour in agriculture. The existence of a positive and growing agricultural surplus assures that this rate of growth is less than that of population; accordingly, the ratio of industrial labour force to agricultural labour force is always increasing.

Finally, capital and output in the industrial sector eventually grow at the same rate so that capital per man increases at a rate equal to the rate of growth of output per man, namely, the rate of technological progress in industry divided by labour's share in industry. The share of capital formation in national product is always increasing, ultimately approaching the share of property in the product of the industrial sector.

We conclude that the industrial sector plays a strategic role in the development of a dual economy with or without disguised unemployment. Industrial output and industrial labour force ultimately come to dominate a developed economy as a consequence of the shift in a consumer demand from agricultural to industrial products and as a result of the rising proportion of investment demand in total output as income *per capita* increases. However, supply conditions for the agricultural sector must not be neglected in any analysis of prospects for industrialization. Unless technological progress in agriculture is sufficiently rapid to outpace the growth of population and the force of diminishing returns, the industrial sector may not be economically viable.

In the absence of a growing agricultural surplus, forced industrialization at fixed real wages may result in a phase of growth in the relative importance of industry with no improvement in levels of living, followed by an absolute reduction in the size of the industrial sector as population growth is forced down to the Malthusian level consistent with the increase of sustenance. Since the criterion for the persistence of an agricultural surplus depends on the rate of growth of population, the rate of advance of agricultural technology required for improvement in levels of living is larger the larger the rate of population growth. The recent increase of rates of population growth in low-income countries has increased the threshold for rates of improvement in agricultural technology required to sustain industrial development. Where the condition for viability of the industrial sector is not met, any policy for industrialization must be accompanied by policies for population control and for the introduction of non-traditional factors into the agricultural sector.[34]

34 T. W. Schultz, *Transforming Traditional Agriculture*, New Haven: Yale University Press, 1964. The importance of policies of this type for low-income countries has been emphasized by Schultz in this book.

3

DISGUISED UNEMPLOYMENT IN AGRICULTURE : A SURVEY

Charles H. C. Kao, Kurt R. Anschel, and Carl K. Eicher

Introduction

One of the recurring concepts in the postwar economic development literature is that of disguised unemployment—that is, the case in which the marginal product of labor is zero or negative. Although much has been written about this topic, the literature is widely scattered and often inaccessible. Moreover, the articles and papers reprinted in this Part assume an implicit knowledge about the evolution of the concept of disguised unemployment, the theoretical underpinnings of the concept, and the present status of empirical studies of the issue. Therefore, the modest objective of this survey paper is to review the literature on disguised unemployment as background for understanding the articles reprinted as Selections 8, 9, 10, and 11.*

This paper is divided into three sections. In the first, disguised unemployment is discussed in historical perspective. The second examines the theoretical foundation of disguised unemployment with special references to contributions by Nurkse,[33] Lewis,[24] Eckaus,[7] Leibenstein,[21 22] and Mellor.[29] Since the presence or absence of disguised unemployment is an empirical issue, the final section examines recent empirical studies to appraise methodological advances in measuring disguised unemployment in less developed countries.

Disguised Unemployment In Historical Perspective

Joan Robinson coined the words 'disguised unemployment' in 1936 to describe workers in developed countries who accepted inferior occupations as a result of being laid off from industries suffering from a lack of effective demand.[43 44] She was referring to workers having a low rather than a zero marginal product of labor.

* Articles refer to those in the original monograph where this perhaps first appeared (ed.)

Studies by Buck[2], Warriner[55] and Rosenstein-Rodan[45] in the 1930s and 1940s in less developed countries presented statistical data for China and Southeastern Europe to suggest that a large percentage of agricultural labor was idle for substantial periods of the year. In fact Buck collected data on over 15,000 farms in China during the years 1929-33 which revealed that only 35 per cent of the men between fifteen and sixty years of age had full-time jobs. Buck's labor utilization approach, of course, did not reveal anything about the marginal product of labor. Doreen Warriner followed in 1939 with a widely quoted study[55] which revealed that before World War II in 'Eastern Europe as a whole, one-quarter to one-third of the farm population is surplus. . .' (p. 68). Next, in 1943 Rosenstein-Rodan[45] wrote that twenty to twenty-five million of the 100 to 110 million people in Eastern and Southeastern Europe were either wholly or partially unemployed (p. 202). In 1945, Mandelbaum[26] estimated that from 20 to 27 per cent of the active rural workers in Greece, Yugoslavia, Poland, Hungary, Rumania, and Bulgaria were redundant; he presented a 'mechanical' model of planned industrialization to absorb the surplus labor within one generation. The studies cited so far all measured labor utilization in agriculture in many countries in the 1930s and 1940s and are widely cited as support for the existence of disguised unemployment in agriculture. In fact, the widely quoted 1951 United Nations report[53] by a group of experts including W. Arthur Lewis, T. W. Schultz, and D. R. Gadgil cited these studies and added that it seems 'safe to assume that for many regions of India and Pakistan, and for certain parts of the Philippines and Indonesia, the surplus [rural population] cannot be less than the pre-war average for the East European Region' (p. 9). The experts advanced this definition of disguised unemployment: zero marginal product of agricultural labor and the condition of *ceteris paribus*, which has been adopted by Leibenstein,[21] [22] Viner[54] Rosenstein-Rodan,[46] and many others.

The presence or absence of disguised unemployment is partly an issue of definition. While the writers mentioned above accept a zero marginal product of labor and the condition of *ceteris paribus*, Navarrete and Navarrete in a 1951 article[32] relaxed the *ceteris paribus* assumption and included the introduction of some capital into the production function in their definition of underemployment. Obviously the greater the reorganization of agriculture and the greater the introduction of capital, the larger the volume of workers who can be transferred out of agriculture without affecting agricultural output.

In 1953, Nurkse[33] introduced a theory of economic development on the assumption that disguised unemployment was present over a wide portion of UDCs. Nurkse stated that development could be initiated and accelerated in these countries by forming capital through the employment of redundant rural labor, and output does not fall, in the Nurkse schema, when workers are shifted to nonfarm works because he relaxes the static assumptions slightly to permit better organization through 'consolidation of scattered strips and plots of land' (p. 33). The Egyptian economist Koestner was among the first to criticize the disguised unemployment doctrine when, in an article written in 1953,[20] he strongly criticized Nurkse's position. Lewis presented another version of disguised unemployment in 1954, when he introduced a model of capital formation and development in which the capitalist sector grew by drawing on cheap rural labor without any significant reduction in agricultural output.[24] [25] This is discussed in more detail in the next section of this paper. Next, Eckaus explained the existence of disguised unemployment by limited technical substitutability of factors of production in agriculture.[7]

Concentrated opposition to disguised unemployment came from Warriner in 1955[57] and Schultz in 1955 and 1956.[47] [48] Warriner reversed her earlier position in *Land and Poverty in the Middle East*[56] in which she showed that 50 per cent of the Egyptian rural population was surplus by noting that she had omitted the labor requirement for capital maintenance in agriculture (p. 26). Schultz[47] wrote that 'all too much attention is being directed to taking up the existing slack in countries that now have a poor collection of resources on the assumption that there are many underemployed resources readily available for economic growth' (p. 373). While Schultz cited examples in Latin American countries where the removal of agricultural labor resulted in a decline in agricultural output,[47] he argued on a broader scale and wrote, 'I know of no evidence for any poor country anywhere that would even suggest that a transfer of some small fraction, say, 5 per cent of the existing labor force out of agriculture, with other things equal, could be made without reducing its (agricultural) production' (p. 375). Viner was the next strong opponent of disguised unemployment.[54] Writing in 1957, he criticized writers such as Eckaus[7] who contended that disguised unemployment could exist in agriculture because of limited technical substitutability of factors of production by noting:[54]

> In an unpublished dissertation in 1957, Kenadjian reviewed a wide range of studies of disguised unemployment and concluded:[18] . . . that almost invariably the estimates of surplus labor have been inflated and the opinions about the extent of redundance in a particular country have contained elements of gross exaggeration in all the countries about which quantitative information can be found to any significant extent. In particular, assertions that disguised unemployment exists in proportions as high as 25 to 30 percent of the labor force in any sector of the economy of even the most overpopulated countries of the world appear to be entirely without foundation (p 259).

Haberler joined the attack in 1957[12] and 1959[13] and criticized disguised unemployment, basing his reasoning on the propositions earlier advanced by Schultz and Viner.

Our discussion so far has summarized the important literature in the disguised unemployment debate, with the exception of theoretical developments by Eckaus, Leibenstein, Lewis, Nurkse, Georgescu-Roegen and Mellor, which are inspected more fully in the next section. Five empirical studies will be discussed in detail in the final section.

The Theoretical Foundation of Disguised Unemployment

This section will examine the assumptions and theoretical foundation underlying the concept of disguised unemployment. Almost all economists define disguised unemployment as the existence of a portion of the labor force which can be removed without reducing output. Most also assume that no other changes occur (*ceteris paribus*). The theoreticians must suggest answers to the following questions if they are to explain why disguised unemployment exists contrary to the expectations of orthodox theory. First, if labor is unemployed or otherwise wasted, why are techniques not introduced which use less land and capital relative to labor? Second, with given technology (fixed capital-land-labor ratios), why is labor used to the point where no returns are forthcoming? Employers of hired labor lose money when they pay a wage to labor whose product is zero or negligible. The self-employed who produce nothing would do better to hire out their surplus labor for a wage. Third, why are wages higher than the marginal product? If large numbers of people produce nothing or very little, wages normally would be bid down to the marginal product of labor.

We will attempt to outline how several economists deal with one or more of the above questions. Eckaus[7] discusses only the first; Lewis,[24] Georgescu-Roegen,[11] Leibenstein,[21 22] and Nurkse[33] propose solutions to the second and third. Mellor,[29] on the other hand pursues a different path by arguing that unemployment may be related to a deficiency of demand.

Eckaus, writing in 1955, is the only one who systematically analyzes the technological restraints which might lead to disguised unemployment. He says that 'disguised unemployment exists when with agricultural techniques remaining unchanged, withdrawal of farm labor would not reduce output' (p. 545). He then asks why, if labor is in surplus, more labor-intensive techniques are not in use. He believes that even the most labor-intensive agricultural process requires some minimum amount of capital per unit of labor; there is some minimum ratio of capital to labor, but many underdeveloped nations have less capital than is required to utilize their whole labor force. Hence, a portion of the available labor supply is unused. Eckaus left it to others to explain why labor is used until its marginal product is zero, but continues to be paid a positive wage.

Lewis, in his well-known article[24] 'Economic Development with Unlimited Supplies of Labor,' analyzes the relationship between the subsistence and capitalist sectors of an underdeveloped country. In his model, surplus labor is available in both rural and urban areas. The rural labor surplus is disguised in the sense that everyone is working, but if some portion is withdrawn output will not fall; the remaining workers will just work harder. The urban surplus labor is openly unemployed; porters waiting for the next ship to come in, retail traders waiting for a customer, messengers sitting in the courtyard. Workers, rural and urban, do not receive their marginal product, but a higher traditional wage. Lewis suggests that the average product per worker in agriculture determines the traditional wage. Labor employed in the capitalist sector will also be paid the traditional wage as long as there is a surplus of labor in the subsistence sector. The low and constant wages permit large profits for potential reinvestment in the capitalist sector. The economy grows at a faster rate, because profits grow relative to the size of the capitalist sector and an increasing proportion of national income is reinvested.

In this article, Lewis's chief contribution to the concept of disguised unemployment is his explanation of the existence of a greater than zero wage when the marginal product of labor is zero. He explains by tradition and lack of alternatives the existence of self-employed labor which receives a positive wage, but whose marginal product is negligible. In a peasant agriculture, each family member receives the family's average product regardless of contribution. Since there are no opportunities for receiving a wage higher than the average product on the family's farm, there is no motivation to leave the farm and the average product will be greater than the marginal product.

Georgescu-Roegen, in Selection 8 of this book, provides an alternative explanation of zero marginal product of agricultural labor.[11] Georgescu-Roegen contends that neither capitalism nor socialism is an efficient form of organizing agriculture in an overpopulated country. Under capitalism, labor will not be employed beyond the point where its marginal product equals the wage rate and, as a result, a portion of the labor force will remain idle and the total agricultural output will not be maximized. Feudalism, as Georgescu points out, provided such an institutional framework because the family maximized employment beyond the point where its marginal product equaled wages. Today feudalism has been replaced by individual peasant holdings and the total agricultural output is still maximized because the employment of the peasant family is governed by maximizing total family output rather than by the principle of marginal productivity. Hence, marginal product is zero when the total output of the family farm is maximized.*

Leibenstein provides another explanation of a greater than zero wage rate. When labor is unemployed and the labor market is competitive, wages would be bid down to very low levels. He explains the phenomenon of greater than zero wages through an interaction between labor productivity and wage rates. Since output per man increases due to improved nutrition when wage rates increase, landlords find it profitable to hire all available labor to prevent wage rates being bid down, poor nutrition, and the resulting small output per man. Although net revenue would be

*Dandekar (Selection 9) disagrees with Georgescu-Roegen's analysis.

higher if only a portion of the labor force were utilized, wages would fall, causing productivity to decline.†

Nurkse defines disguised unemployment as zero marginal product of labor when some organizational changes are introduced. If minor changes such as consolidation of landholdings are permitted, then a substantial amount of agricultural labor can be used in other pursuits, such as building dams and rural roads, without reducing agricultural output. Nurkse explains that labor is used until no more output is forthcoming, because family labor is not paid. He assumes a freeholding peasant agriculture in which food is shared among all family members. Nurkse does not believe that significant savings of labor can be made through the reduction of leisure time or through the exertion of greater effort by the remaining workers, but must be obtained through better use of labor time. Owing to poor organization, much time is spent on essentially inefficient tasks, such as walking from place to place, transporting materials and products, and organizing and supervising other workers. He suggests that through reorganization enough labor time can be saved to make feasible the utilization of labor in other capacities.

Nurkse's early optimism for releasing surplus labor through changes in agricultural organization was qualified somewhat in 1958 when he wrote that such changes in agricultural organization 'are a major undertaking and cannot be lightly taken for granted' (p. 262).

The last approach to disguised unemployment to be discussed assumes a deficiency of demand. Mellor[29] is the chief proponent of this position. He argues that the peasant in the underdeveloped country works hard to achieve some traditionally determined minimum standard of living, but has no motivation for increasing his income above that level because of tradition-bound consumption patterns.

Mellor's deficient demand approach is similar to the concept of unemployment advanced by Joan Robinson in her demand deficiency theory. There are few empirical data to support Mellor's position. For a survey of literature rejecting the notion of tradition-bound peasant consumption patterns in Africa, for example, see the recent article by Jones.[17]

†Criticisms and amendments to Leibenstein's propositions are found in References 36, 9, 27 and 58.

Empirical Studies of Disguised Unemployment

Five empirical studies of disguised unemployment in Thailand, India, Italy, and Greece are examined in this section (References 30, 31, 40, 46 and 49).* Three are on the micro level. Two are on the macro level. Discussion will center on two aspects: the methodology adopted in these studies and their empirical results.

Generally speaking, two methods are available to measure disguised unemployment. The first is the direct method, which is based upon a sample survey. This method uses the labor utilization and the labor productivity approaches. The labor utilization approach presents an inventory of what labor is used in the field or in other farm tasks as a percentage of the available supply. The labor productivity approach goes a step further and examines the relationship between the quantity of labor used and/or available and the level of production.[29]

The indirect method, which relies on secondary data, is the second method of measuring disguised unemployment. The three variants of this method measure (1) the difference between the number of labor hours required to produce a given output and the number of labor hours available from the active agrarian population, (2) the difference between the density of population deemed adequate for a given type of cultivation and the actual density of population and (3) the difference between the number of acres or hectares required under a given type of cultivation to provide one person with a 'standard income,' in contrast to the number of available acres or hectares and available agrarian population. (See Reference 46, p. 2.)

Mellor and Stevens's Study in Thailand

Mellor and Stevens undertook a study of the average and marginal product of farm labor in Thailand, which was based on labor income records obtained by personal interviews in 104 rice farms at Bang Chan, Thailand, and published in 1956.[30] All farms were assumed to have a similar rice production function. The total output of rice was estimated with a high degree of accuracy because most of the rice was taken to the local miller for polishing. Labor inputs were measured in terms of man equivalents on the basis of interviews

*Other empirical studies of disguised unemployment are in References 4 18, 38 and 39. Oshima also mentions some additional empirical studies in Reference 36.

concerning the number of persons available for farm work on each farm. In their analysis, Mellor and Stevens[30] said: '. . . labor that is available for farm work but is doing no work is counted as part of labor input. Labor that is actually on the field but contributing no increment in output through its efforts is not treated differently from labor that is not working but is available for such work' (p. 785). To estimate the productivity of labor they used a least-square linear regression equation. The equation is $Y=30.4+13.5X$ (Y = total product, X = man equivalent). The b (slope) value in the equation of 13.5 tang (which is equal to approximately 24 pounds or 0.54 bushel) is not significantly different from zero at the 5 per cent level of significance. They write,[30] 'This is consistent with the hypothesis that in this type of area, the marginal product of labor will be zero or close to zero' (p. 987). Thus, disguised unemployment existed in this area. More recently, Mellor[29] commented on this village study and stated that the data were inadequate for more than a rough approximation of disguised unemployment (p. 3). Given the assumptions of labor homogeneity and a uniform production function, this study represents a valid method of measuring marginal labor productivity.

Harry T. Oshima, commenting recently on the Mellor and Stevens's study, stated:[37]

> There is one empirical study, . . . of 104 farms in one Thai village. In this pioneer study, the conclusion is reached that there is substantial zero MPP farm workers. I feel it is hazardous to regard this study as conclusive for either theoretical or policy use. The spread of the data in the scatter diagram relating rice yields to labor input for each of the 104 farms suggests to me, not a linear regression line as it does to the authors, but inadequate data and/or dubious assumptions. For example, they assume that rice production functions for each of the 104 farms were the same. In estimating labor input, the authors exclude working children under 15 years old and include all persons 15 years and above, whether working or not (p. 450).

Mujumdar's Study in India

In a recent book, Mujumdar studies two facets of underemployment in agriculture, namely disguised and seasonal unemployment.[31] Attention here is given to the empirical results of disguised unemployment.

Field investigation covering three months in 1954-55 was conducted in nine selected villages of the Bombay-Karnatak region to measure the degree of disguised unemployment. The author interviewed village officers and studied village records to determine the population, occupations, land use, number of livestock, labor movements, work schedule, and standard cultivated holdings in each village. Also, twenty-five families in each village were intensively interviewed to determine family size, occupation, sources of income, size of holdings, and annual work schedule.

The author uses the standard cultivated holding as his most important tool in estimating underemployment. He defines it as 'the area of land which is sufficient to absorb, in given conditions of techniques and type of farming, the labour of an average farm family working with a pair of bullocks' (pp. 83-84). Unfortunately, Mujumdar does not tell us how he determined the standard holding. He simply states: 'When once the standard holding is defined for a village or area, the intensity of employment can be measured against the standard so determined. The ideal case being that of full employment when the cultivated holding is of the size of the standard unit or above. All other cases come under disguised unemployment . . .' (p. 202).

Mujumdar finds in his nine-village study of small farmers that 'roughly about 71 per cent of the farmers are affected by disguised unemployment' (p. 208). Thus, this figure, 'in spite of all the limitation, present[s] in concrete terms the alarming proportions which the phenomenon of disguised unemployment has assumed' (p. 208).

There are at least three shortcomings of Mujumdar's methodology. First, the standard holding is essentially an arbitrary unit. It assumes that bullocks are used in producing all crops and allows no alternative production techniques. Nor does it recognize the possibility that bullocks may be labor-replacing, and hence uneconomical, on farms with large amounts of available family labor relative to land. In addition, Mujumdar makes no adjustments for differences in capital, land fertility, and irrigation on each farm. Second, Mujumdar makes no special attempt to quantify the labor input and include it in his analysis. He assumes that all farms are using the most labor-intensive techniques available. Yet, this, he admits, is not true of India. Third, Mujumdar, like many other economists, fails to relate his empirical definition to his theoretical definition of disguised unemployment which is defined as 'taking the size of labor force as given, disguised unemployment may be described as a situation in which the withdrawal of a certain quantity of the factor labor to other uses, will not diminish the total output of the sector from which it is withdrawn, given a measure of reorganization in the sector' (p. 39).

Mujumdar's empirical definition classifies any worker on a farm of less than the standard holding as underemployed; he sees no need to estimate his productivity or the productivity of the group. Using the standard holding rather than the marginal productivity technique, Mujumdar arrives at the dubious conclusion that more than 70 per cent of the agricultural population could be removed from the region without lowering production.

Rosenstein-Rodan's Study in Southern Italy

In 1957, Rosenstein-Rodan[46] wrote that it was his firm belief that disguised unemployment of more than 5 per cent exists in many—though not all—underdeveloped countries; he supported this belief by measuring disguised unemployment in southern Italy (p. 1). He used the static concept of disguised unemployment.*

The following major assumptions and criteria were used:† (1) Only agricultural small holdings of peasant owners and tenants were included. (2) The active population was assumed to be between fourteen and sixty-five years of age. Coefficients of labor efficiency of men, women, and children were used for each type of cultivation. (3) Surplus workers were assumed to be involuntarily unemployed. (4) Labor hours required for each type of cultivation over the whole year, month by month, were counted and compared with available labor hours. An average of 270 available workdays per year was assumed. (5) A distinction was made between (*a*) removable disguised underemployment or disguised unemployment, (*b*) disguised fractional underemployment, that is, labor hours not used throughout the whole year which do not add up to an entire labor unit (persons in this category cannot be moved out of agriculture), and (*c*) seasonal underemployment due to climatic factors. These distinctions were taken into account in calculating the number of

*The static concept refers to the amount of population in agriculture which can be removed without any change in the method of cultivation and without leading to any reduction in output. Hence, the marginal product of labor is zero. See Reference 46, p. 1.

†Only the six most relevant considerations are listed here.

laborers, affected by disguised unemployment. (6) A slight deviation from the static concept was allowed in the analysis. The author used the direct method of questionnaires to distinguish different types of cultivation, different sizes and forms of property, the composition of the labor force, and the number of labor hours required and supplied.

Rosenstein-Rodan[46] found that 'more than 10 per cent of the active labor force in southern Italian agriculture is surplus . . .' (p. 4). Later, however, Kenadjian[48] discussed this matter with Rosenstein-Rodan and reported: 'When Rosenstein-Rodan observes that in southern Italy around 10 to 12 per cent of the actual population in agriculture are removable, he is including among the removable surplus the individuals who are needed for 50 days or less. If the more rigid definition, which is also the more sensible one, is adopted, the removable surplus is reduced to 5 per cent' (p. 250).

This clearly illustrates that a careful appraisal of the definition is necessary before one so blindly accepts an author's statement that 10, 20, or 70 per cent of the labor is redundant in agriculture.

Schultz's Study in India

As was pointed out earlier, T. W. Schultz supported the validity of the disguised unemployment concept in the United Nations report[53] in 1951 (p. 9) and later rejected the existence of disguised unemployment in publications in 1956.[47,48] In his recently published book, he reinforced this position by turning to the influenza epidemic of 1918—1919 in India to test the hypothesis that the marginal product of a part of the labor force in agriculture was zero.[49] This incident was used because the epidemic struck suddenly; the death rate reached a peak within weeks and then diminished rapidly. Those who survived were not debilitated for very long. Schultz estimated the existence of disguised unemployment by comparing the reduction in acreage sown with the reduction in the labor force. Such a comparison assumes that if any disguised unemployment exists, the acreage sown will not be reduced as a result of a sudden reduction in the labor force. The rationale for such a comparison is[49] "where there are many people relative to land and much land is cultivated intensively, the expectation would be that acreage sown would be less sensitive to a decrease in the labor force than total yield" (p. 11). Therefore, the acreage sown 'would be a more decisive test than ....a reduction of the same percentage in agricultural production' (p. 11). Schultz found that the agricultural labor force in India was reduced by about 9 per cent, while:[49]

> The area in 1919-20 was, 10 million acres below, or 3.8 percent less than that of the base year 1916-17. In general, the provinces of India that had the highest death rates attributed to the epidemic also had the largest percentage decline in acreage sown to crops. It would be hard to find any support in these data for the doctrine that a part of the labor force in agriculture in India at the time of the epidemic had a marginal product of zero (p. 67).

The influenza epidemic test was a unique laboratory technique to use in measuring disguised unemployment. An advantage of this approach was that the influenza epidemic did not directly affect animals, and therefore the only change in the factors of production was in the number of workers. Since India's population grew 44 per cent from 1921 to 1951 as compared with 5 per cent from 1894 to 1921* the population pressures in India today are much different from those of the period studied by Schultz. Therefore, one wonders whether Schultz needs more observations from India in the post-1920 period and from other countries in the 1960s before he can conclude 'a part of the labor working in agriculture in poor countries (today) has a marginal productivity of zero. . . is a false doctrine' (p. 70).

Pepelasis and Yotopoulos' Study in Greece

Pepelasis and Yotopoulos[40] recently published a macro level study which was designed to measure the volume of removable surplus labor as well as that seasonal surplus labor in Greek agriculture for the period from 1953 to 1960. Removable (chronic) surplus labor was defined as the amount of labor which could be removed for at least one year without any change in the quantities of other factors of production and without leading to any reduction in output (p. 86). The authors measured surplus labor by comparing the labor available with the labor required for a given volume of output within the agriculture sector. The indirect method, using

*See A. Coale and E. Hoover, *Population Growth and Economic Development in Low-income Countries: A Case Study of India's Prospects*, Princeton University Press, Princeton, N.J., 1958.

secondary data, was employed to derive estimates of labor availability and labor requirements.

The labor available was calculated from the total size of the agricultural population from fifteen to sixty-nine years old, as measured by the Census. This estimate was converted into a labor potential and into homogeneous Man Productive Units on the basis of conversion coefficients measuring the workday of an adult male farm worker. Finally the Man Productive Units were converted into Man Productive Days available during the period from 1953 to 1960 (Chapter Four).

Separate estimates of the annual agricultural labor requirements for farming, husbandry, fishing, forestry, fishing and agricultural transport were computed. Given each year's agricultural activities, Pepelasis and Yotopoulos derived annual labor requirements by product by applying a 'labor-intensity coefficient', that is, a labor/land and/or a capital output ratio. The labor coefficients were 'expressed in terms of man and supplementary . . . nine-hour workdays estimated to be used per stremma of animal or unit of output to produce the given volume of agricultural output of the year' (p. 108). The authors found that 'chronic surplus labor in Greek agriculture is virtually nonexistent. From the eight year of our series, it existed only in 1953 and 1954 to a degree of 3.5 and 2.3 respectively. The other years of the period are marked by a seasonal shortage of labor' (p. 136). The authors commented on the feasibility of removing the chronically unemployed by noting 'if in one village of 100 working agricultural population the surplus labor is 2 per cent, this does not imply that we can remove for a whole year two workers without decreasing the total output of the village' (p. 138). This is so because that labor is not divisible, for both physical and institutional reasons. The 2 per cent, for example, may consist of fractions of labor in surplus spread among a number of families; therefore, "we cannot exactly determine how much chronic surplus labor it is feasible to remove . . . . Its size can only be determined through a *disaggregative microeconomic investigation based on the direct method of studying a sample of farm households*" (p. 138). The important point of this study is the nonexistence of disguised unemployment in Greek agriculture since 1954.

Summary

We have pointed out that the existence of disguised unemployment is largely a matter of definition and the assumptions about the institutional forces involved. Nevertheless, some writers agreed upon the zero product of labor definition in the early 1950s, and it is an understatement to say that the development literature in this period was optimistic about development through the transfer of redundant agricultural labor to other occupations. We have shown that the empirical studies supporting this optimism were often poorly conceived. In addition, we have noted that by considering temporary rather than permanent labor transfers and by allowing some reorganization of production, various writers have arrived at a high percentage of disguised unemployment. To date, there is little reliable empirical evidence to support the existence of more than token—5 per cent—disguised unemployment in underdeveloped countries as defined by a zero marginal product of labor and the condition of *ceteris paribus*.

REFERENCES

1. Barber, William J.: 'Disguised Unemployment in Underdeveloped Economies,' *Oxford Economic Papers*, vol. 13, pp. 103-115.
2. Buck, John Lossings: *Chinese Farm Economy*, The University of Chicago Press, Chicago, 1930.
3. ———: *Land Utilization in China*, The University of Chicago Press, Chicago, 1937.
4. Cho, Yong Sam: *Disguised Unemployment in South Korean Agriculture*, University of California Press, Berkeley, 1963.
5. Dandekar, V. N.; 'Economic Theory and Agrarian Reform,' *Oxford Economic Papers*, vol. 14, pp. 69-80, February, 1962.
6. Enke, S.: 'Economic Development with Unlimited and Limited Supplies of Labor,' *Oxford Economic Papers*, Vol. 14, pp 158-172, June 1962.
7. Eckaus, R. S.: 'Factor Proportions in Underdeveloped Countries,' *American Economic Review*, vol. 45, pp. 539-565, September, 1955
8. Ezekiel, Hannan: 'An Application of Leibenstein's Theory of Underemployment,' *Journal of Political Economy*, vol. 68, pp. 511. 517, October, 1960.
9. Fei, J. C. H. and Gustav Ranis: 'Capital Accumulation and Economic Development,' *American Economic Review*, vol. 53, pp. 283-313, June, 1963.
10. Frankel, S. Herbert: *The Economic Impact on Underdeveloped Societies*, Basil Blackwell, E. Mott, Ltd., Oxford, 1953.
11. Georgescu-Roegen, N.: 'Economic Theory and Agrarian Economics,' *Oxford Economic Papers*, vol. 12, pp. 1-40, February, 1963.
12. Haberler, Gottfried: 'Critical Observations on Some Current

Notions in the Theory of Economic Development,' *L'Industria*, no. 2, pp. 3-13, 1957.

13. ———: 'International Trade and Economic Development,' Fiftieth Anniversary Commemoration Lectures, Lecture III, National Bank of Egypt, Cairo, 1959.
14. Hsieh, Chiang: 'Underemployment in Asia: Nature and Extent,' *International Labor Review*, vol. 55, pp. 703-725, January-June, 1952.
15. ———: 'Underemployment in Asia: Its Relation to Investment Policy,' *International Labor Review*, vol. 56, pp. 30-39, July-December, 1952.
16 International Labor Office: *Measurement of Underemployment*, Geneva, 1957.
17. Jones, William O.: 'Economic Man in Africa,' *Food Research Institute Studies*, vol. 1, pp. 107-134, May, 1960.
18. Kenadjian, Berdj: 'Disguised Unemployment in Underdeveloped Countries,' unpublished doctoral dissertation, Harvard University, 1957.
19. Khan, Nasir Ahmad: *Problems of Growth of an Underdeveloped Economy—India*, Asia Publishing House, New York, 1961, Chap. VII.
20. Koestner, N.: 'Comments on Professor Nurkse's Capital Accumulation in Underdeveloped Countries,' *L'Egypte Contemporaine*, col. 44, pp. 1-8, Cairo, April, 1953.
21. Leibenstein, Harvey: 'The Theory of Underemployment in Backward Economies,' *Journal of Political Economy*, vol. 65, pp. 91-103, April, 1957.
22. ———: *Economic Backwardness and Economic Growth*, John Wiley and Sons, Inc., New York, 1957.
23. ———: 'Underemployment in Backward Economies: Some Additional Notes,' *Journal of Political Economy*, vol. 66, pp. 256-258, June, 1958.
24. Lewis, W. Arthur: 'Economic Development with Unlimited Supplies of Labor,' *Manchester School of Economic and Social Studies*, pp. 139-192, May, 1954.
25. ———: *The Theory of Economic Growth*, George Allen & Unwin, Ltd., London, 1955.
26. Mandelbaum, K.: *The Industrialization of Backward Areas*, Basil Blackwell & Mott, Ltd., Oxford, 1945.
27. Mazumdar, Dipak: 'The Marginal Productivity Theory of Wages and Disguised Unemployment,' *Review of Economic Studies*, vol. 26, pp. 190-7, June, 1959.
28. ———: 'Underemployment in Agriculture and the Industrial Wage Rate,' *Economica*, vol. 26, pp. 328-340, November, 1959.
29. Mellor, John W.: 'The Use and Productivity of Farm Family Labor in Early Stages of Agricultural Development,' *Journal of Farm Economics*, vol. 45, pp. 517-534, August, 1963.
30. Mellor, John W. and Robert D. Stevens: 'The Average and Marginal Product of Farm Labor in Underdeveloped Economies,' *Journal of Farm Economics*, vol. 38. pp. 780-791, August, 1956.

31. Mujumdar, N. A.: *Some Problems of Underemployment*, Popular Book Depot, Bombay, 1961.

32. Navarrete, Alfredo, Jr. and Ifigenia M. Navarrete: 'Underemployment in Underdeveloped Economies,' *International Economic Papers* no. 3. pp. 235-239, London, 1953, translated from *El Trimestre Economico*, vol. 17, no. 4, October-December, 1951.

33. Nurkse, Ragnar: *Problems of Capital Formation in Underdeveloped Countries*, Oxford University Press, Fair Lawn, N. J., 1953.

34. ———: 'Excess Population and Capital Construction,' *Malayan Economic Review*, vol. 2, pp. 1-11, October, 1957.

35. ———: 'Epilogue: 'The Quest for a Stabilization Policy in Primary Producing Countries,' *KYKLOS*, vol. 11, fasc. 2, pp. 261-262, 1958

36. Oshima, Harry T.: 'Underemployment in Backward Economies: An Empirical Comment,' *Journal of Political Economy*, vol. 66, pp. 259-264, June, 1958.

37. ———: 'The Ranis-Fei Model of Economic Development: Comment,' *American Economic Review*, vol. 53, pp. 448-452, June, 1963.

38 Parthasarathy, Gogula: 'Underemployment and Indian Agriculture'. unpublished doctoral dissertation, University of Wisconsin, 1957.

39. Patel, K. R.: 'The Nature and Extent of Under-Employment of the Self-Employed Cultivators,' unpublished doctoral dissertation, Unversity of Bombay, India, 1962.

40. Pepelasis, Adam A. and Pan A. Yotopoulos: *Surplus Labor in Greek Agriculture*, 1953-1960, Center of Economic Research, Research Monograph Series 2, Athens, Greece, 1962.

41. Ranis, Gustav and John C. H. Fei: 'A Theory of Economic Develop ment,' *American Economic Review*, vol. 51, pp. 553-558, September 1961.

42. ———: 'The Ranis-Fei Model of Economic Development: Reply,' *American Economic Review*, vol. 53, pp. 452-454, June, 1963.

43. Robinson, Joan: 'Disguised Unemployment,' *Economic Journal* vol. 46, pp. 225-237, June, 1936.

44. ———: *Essays in the Theory of Employment*, Oxford University Press, London, 1947.

45. Rosenstein-Rodan, P. N.: 'Problems of Industrialization of Eastern and South-Eastern Europe,' *Economic Journal*, vol. 53, pp. 202-211, June-September, 1943.

46. ———: 'Disguised Unemployment and Underemployment in Agriculture,' *Monthly Bulletin of Agricultural Economics and Statistics*, vol. 6, pp. 1-7, FAO, Rome, July-August, 1957.

47. Schultz, Theodore W.: 'The Role of Government in Promoting Economic Growth,' in Leonard D. White (ed)., *The State of the Social Sciences*, University of Chicago Press, Chicago, 1956, pp. 372-383.

48. ———: *The Economic Test in Latin America*, New York State School of Industrial and Labor Relations Bulletin 85, Cornell University, Ithaca, pp. 14-15, August, 1956.

49. ———: 'The Doctrine of Agricultural Labor of Zero Value,' *Transforming Traditional Agriculture*, Yale University Press, New Haven, Conn., 1964.

50. Sen, A. K.: *Choice of Techniques*, Basil Blackwell & Mott, Ltd., Oxford, 1960.

51. Singh, Tarlok: *Poverty and Social Change*, Longmans, Green & Co., Ltd., London, 1945.

52. Sovani, N. V.: 'Underemployment, Micro and Macro, and Development Planning,' *Indian Economic Journal*, vol. 2, no. 4, pp. 301-310, April 1955.

53. United Nations, *Measures for the Economic Development of Underdeveloped Countries*, Department of Economic and Social Affairs, New York, 1951.

54. Viner, Jacob: 'Some Reflections on the Concept of Disguised Unemployment,' *Contribucoes a Analise do Desenvolvimento Economico*, Livraria Ager Editora, Rio de Janeiro, 1957. Reprinted under the same title in *Indian Journal of Economics*, vol. 38, pp. 17-23, July, 1957.

55. Warriner, Doreen: *Economics of Peasant Farming*, Oxford University Press, London, 1939.

56. ———: *Land and Poverty in the Middle East*, Royal Institute of International Affairs, London, 1948.

57. ———: 'Land Reform and Economic Development,' Fiftieth Anniversary Commemoration Lectures, National Bank of Egypt, Cairo, 1955.

58. Wonnacott, Paul: 'Disguised and Overt Unemployment in Underdeveloped Economies,' *Quarterly Journal of Economics*, vol. 76, pp. 279-297, May, 1962.

4

EMPLOYMENT AND INDUSTRIALIZATION IN DEVELOPING COUNTRIES*

Werner Baer and Michel E. A. Hervé

I

SINCE WORLD WAR II a number of countries in the economically less-developed world have adopted a strategy of rapid industrialization in order to speed up their growth. Thus, for Latin Amerca as a whole, the pace setting sector has been manufacturing, growing at a rate of 5.9 per cent in the period 1945-49 to 1956-61, while the gross domestic product grew at 4.8 per cent.[1] Although in some countries the overall growth rate was far from satisfactory, there can be no doubt that in almost all countries where substantial industrialization was attempted, manufacturing was the most dynamic sector, being responsible for the simultaneous high growth rates in complementary activities, such as construction. The policy-makers who were responsible for industrialization policies were convinced that alternative development strategies, e.g., emphasizing agriculture, would have led to extremely low growth rates, especially due to weak world market conditions for such products.[2]

In the first half of the 1960's a note of concern, often bordering on disillusionment, could be observed among the most ardent industrialization advocates. The dynamic sector of the economy was not absorbing labor at a satisfactory rate. Not only did the industrial

*We should like to thank Peter Kilby and Peter Schran for helpful suggestions. This paper was written while the authors were members of the Economic Growth Center at Yale University.

1 This total hides the more startling cases, such as Brazil where the manufacturing growth rate for this period was 9.4 per cent and the overall growth rate was 5.7 per cent, or Colombia where the former was 7.2 per cent and the latter 4.3 per cent. The revised figures for Argentina show an overall growth rate of 3.2 per cent and a manufacturing growth rate of 4.1 per cent in the 1950-61 period.

2 There are, of course, many exceptions. Thus, a number of West African countries have greatly benefited from a development policy based on the export of a number of primary commodities, often to markets in Western Europe where they had a preferential position.

sector's rate of labor absorption fall behind the growth rate of the urban population in many countries, but it even fell behind the general growth rate of the population. For all of Latin America the yearly growth rate of the urban population in the period 1945-60 was 4.3 per cent, the growth rate of the economically active population in the nonagricultural sector was 3.9 per cent, and the growth rate of employment in manufacturing was 2.8 per cent. In Brazil, in the years 1950-60, while the urban population grew at 5.4 per cent, the employment growth rate in manufacturing was only 2.6 per cent. In other parts of the world the situation was similar. A recent analysis of employment in the modern sector of Asian countries stated that '. . . In India the share of the modern sector in total employment, which was over 6 per cent in 1951, increased by barely 1 percentage point over the decade 1951-61 despite, as noted, an annual growth rate of 4 per cent of modern sector employment. In the Philippines the corresponding share, which was about 22 per cent in 1956, moved up by a mere 2 percentage points by 1961.'[3]

This tendency has led the Economic Commission for Latin America to the following grim conclusions:[4]

'. . An appreciable proportion of the increase in the active population is not properly absorbed in the production process; economic development passes it by. This is mainly true of the population that moves from the country areas to the towns . . . Far from achieving integration in city life, and sharing better patterns of living, they put up their wretched shanty towns and eke out a hand-to-mouth existence in a whole wide range of ill-paid personal services, with periods of out-and-out unemployment.

Thus poverty, frustration and resentment surge in from the country to the towns, where the symptoms of the concentration of income are already so conspicuous. This is clear proof of the explosive social polarization of development, imputable to its dynamic weakness and distributional shortcomings.'

It is our purpose to examine these developments, to discern how inevitable they were, and to assess their implications for future development strategies.

3 Kailas C. Doctor and Hans Gallis. 'Modern Sector Employment in Asian Countries: Some Empirical Estimates,' *International Labour Review*, LXXXIX (Dec. 1964), p. 558.

4 United Nations, *Towards a Dynamic Development Policy for Latin America* (New York, 1963), p. 23.

II

Let us examine the extent of the employment lag in the manufacturing industries which manifested itself in a number of Latin American countries, Egypt, and India, all of which relied on industrialization to generate their economic growth in the postwar period. In Table I we have compared the rate of growth of output in various industries with the rate of growth of employment. In most countries the rate of growth of employment in the total manufacturing sector was substantially less than half the growth rate of output. In Argentina there was actually a fall of employment and in Mexico it was practically static.

An examination of individual industries reveals an interesting pattern. One not only finds a lag in employment in more advanced industries such as fabricated metal products, transportation equipment, chemicals, etc., but it is also noticeable in the more traditional industries such as textiles, clothing and shoes. In some of the countries (Argentina, Brazil) the production of the latter dates back for a few decades. These are also the industries which are often recommended in the earlier industrialization stages due to their greater simplicity and their supposed greater capacity to absorb labor. It will be observed that not only did labor absorption substantially lag behind output, but in some cases, such as in that of textiles in Argentina, Brazil, and Chile, the total amount of labor employed actually declined. This can be attributed both to the expansion of capacity by the adoption of relatively capital-intensive techniques and also to the modernization of old capacity in a more capital-intensive way.

A part of the explanation of this low labor absorption rate lies in a substantial natural increase in labor efficiency. It seems, however, that most of the explanation lies in the adoption of more capital-intensive techniques of production. As rough indicators of the degree of capital intensity in various industries we have taken installed power capacity per person employed, or, when this measure was not available, per capita electricity consumption by industry groups. In Table II we first examine the increase of this datum between the most recent census years available in various countries. The tentative conclusion one could derive from these data is that mechanization has taken place across the board. Not only was there an increase in industries which by their very nature are fairly

TABLE

GROWTH OF MANUFACTURING PRODUCTION AND

(yearly growth

Industrial Groups	Argentina O	Argentina E	Brazil O	Brazil E	Chile O	Chile E	Peru O	Peru E
Nonmetallic Minerals	2.7	−3.0	10.1	2.6	2.1	−2.7	6.6	5.6
Machinery (excluding electrical)	..	..	6.1	8.4	..	..	..	..
Fabricated Metal Products	12.6	0.0	12.1	5.0	0.0	2.9	..	..
Electrical Machinery	..	..	38.0	13.0	..	..	..	..
Transportation Equipment	..	..	55.0	15.4	..	..	..	..
Furniture	..	..	3.6	7.1	..	..	..	..
Paper & paper Products	4.8	2.8	8.4	4.7	7.2	2.9	18.1	3.3
Rubber	10.2	4.0	8.4	4.9	0.0	−0.7	9.4	7.3
Leather Goods	0.1	−4.9	4.1	2.4	0.0	−3.4	2.5	0.6
Chemicals	6.3	0.0	25.0	3.8	3.2	0.9	7.2	6.9
Textiles	0.6	−3.9	5.9	−2.5	0.7	−1.3	4.7	3.3
Clothing and Shoes	0.5	−2.9	8.9	2.9	3.4	−1.5	10.2	2.4
Food Products	..	..	7.2	0.7	..	..	..	..
Drinks	1.0	−2.0	5.1	neg.	4.0	2.7	5.1	6.8
Tobacco	..	..	10.2	−9.5	..	..	..	..
Printing and Publishing	0.9	−2.1	9.4	2.7	0.0	2.7	6.5	0.2
Basic Metals	8.4	0.2	..	..	5.0	1.1	11.3	3.7
Wood Products	..	..	..	..	..	..	5.5	3.4
Miscellaneous	..	..	..	..	..	..	..	..
Total	4.4	−2.0	9.8	2.6	5.4	1.7	6.6	4.4

Sources: United Nations, *The Growth of World Industry, 1938-1961* (New York 1963); *Revista Brasileira de Economica*, Mar. 1962.

Note: 0 = output; E = employment.

capital-intensive (such as chemicals, metal products, etc.), but the installed per capita power capacity or electricity consumption per capita has rapidly increased in the more traditional industries, which presumably are more labor-intensive in nature.

III

Concern about the employment effects of industrialization in underdeveloped countries has been expressed in the professional literature and in planning documents ever since the early postwar years. Although it was recognized that some degree of industrializa-

1
EMPLOYMENT IN SELECTED COUNTRIES
rates)

Colombia		Venezuela		Mexico		India		Egypt	
O	E	O	E	O	E	O	E	O	E
6.4	3.0	8.5	4.2	6.8	5.4	12.0	3.1	..	..
..	..	..	..	..	..	..	..	..	..
17.1	3.2	19.6	3.2	..	..	15.9	6.7	..	..
..	..	..	..	..	..	..	..	..	..
..	..	..	..	..	..	..	..	..	..
..	..	..	..	..	..	..	..	..	..
12.7	3.2	32.2	6.7	6.8	5.7	11.9	3.6	..	..
11.8	7.8	19.6	12.6	6.7	4.5	..	..	..	..
3.0	2.9	13.0	3.0	..	..	7.5	2.3	..	..
10.6	3.8	14.4	1.5	9.4	1.6	11.3	4.5	..	..
7.5	3.0	17.4	7.0	2.4	neg.	3.5	0.6	..	..
7.6	1.8	17.4	-1.1	..	..	6.7	5.8	..	..
..	..	..	..	..	..	..	..	..	..
} 5.0	} 1.1	} 11.4	} 4.7	} 5.5	} 1.8	} 4.1	} 2.8	..	..
..	..	..	..	..	..	..	..	..	..
..	..	14.5	6.8	..	..	..	..	..	..
28.6	3.2	..	..	5.3	neg.	7.8	4.4	..	..
6.8	2.4	3.0	2.3	..	..	18.3	8.6	..	..
..	..	29.4	16.9	..	..	..	..	..	..
7.6	2.5	13.0	2.1	6.5	0.4	6.8	3.3	5.5	3.9

Brazil: employment rates 1949-59; production-total 1947-60; all other 1947-58, except machinery (nonelectrical), electrical machinery, transportation equipment, furniture, clothing and shoes which are 1955-58.

Argentina: 1950-60; Chile: 1950-60; Peru: 1950-60; Colombia: 1950-60; Venezuela: 1950-60;

Mexico: 1950-61; India: 1950-60; Egypt: output 1956-60; employment 1947-57.

tion was necessary to attain growth rates which would raise the per capita income in a fairly short period of time in such countries as India or the major Latin American countries, it was also thought in most professional circles that new industries should as much as possible absorb the surplus labor which was streaming into urban centers. The strategies suggested were to develop industries which were by their very nature labor-intensive or to choose the most labor-intensive techniques possible in each industry promoted. This seemed a logical thing to do, not only from the point of view of coping with the surplus labor problem, but also from the point of

TABLE II

INSTALLED CAPACITY PER PERSON EMPLOYED

	Argentina (1939-1953)		Brazil (1950-60)		Chile* (1938-53)		Columbia (1953-58)		Mexico (1937-44)	UAR* (1948-58)
Nonmetallic Minerals	26	(2.82;3.55)	89	(1.52;2.88)	120	(6.1;13.4)	60	(3.55;5.69)	163	462
Fabricated Metal Products	101	(1.19;2.39)	6	(3.90;4.13)			1	(1.72;1.74)		
Electrical Machinery			54	(1.86;2.86)						
Transport Equipment			20	(2.14;2.57)						
Furniture			22	(3.46;4.22)						
Paper and Paper Products	58	(4.92;7.78)	47	(1.30;1.91)			–8	(4.40;4.03)		287
Rubber	10	(3.42;3.75)	17	(7.17;8.38)			17	(3.71;4.36)		
Leather Goods	71	(1.74;2.97)	51	(4.89;7.40)			1	(2.78;2.82)		150
Chemicals	99	(2.97;5.90)	28	(2.31;2.96)	18	(3.4;4.0)	152	(1.80;4.53)		189
Textiles	52	(1.35;2.05)	48	(1.65;2.44)	129	(1.4;3.2)	16	(2.48;2.88)	116	120
Clothing and Shoes	52	(.33; .50)	33	(.46; .61)	33	(.3; .4)	11	(.27; .30)		
Food Products }			58	(3.05;4.83)						
Drinks }	36	(3.00;4.09)	62	(2.31;3.74)	47	(1.9;2.8)	33	(2.21;2.95)	55	150
Tobacco }			4	(.52; .54)						
Printing and Publishing	107	(.82;1.70)	26	(.98;1.24)			7	(.91; .97)		
Basic Metals	156	(1.98;5.07)					87	(3.50;6.56)	–32	491
Wood Products	90	(1.58;3.00)	39	(2.88;3.99)	160	(.5;1.3)	43	(1.54;2.20)		
Miscellaneous	74	(1.04;1.81)	13	(1.27;1.44)			30	(.80;1.04)		
Total Manufacturing	62	(1.88;3.05)			109	(2.2;4.6)	38	(2.00;2.75)	56	167

Source: Same as for Table I; also for Brazil, *Recenseamento Geral do Brasil* 1960, *Censo Industrial*, IBGE, 1963.
Note: Parentheses: absolute numbers—HP per worker; electricity consumed in thousand KWH.
* Per capita electricity consumption in industry.

view of minimizing cost by using the relatively most abundant and cheapest factor of production.

From the very beginning Indian planners had intentions of stressing the promotion of industries which would maximize labor absorption, e.g., cottage industries.[5] However, in spite of these early efforts, Indian manufacturing development has taken place along fairly capital-intensive lines. Thus, after examining the data, Fei and Ranis concluded that '... from the outset India embarked on a policy of capital deepening in her industrial sector.'[6]

The difficulties encountered in effectively absorbing labor in newer industries in many industrializing countries were at first explained principally by the existence of a rigid factor proportion problem, in which the choices of techniques were few and of a relatively capital-intensive variety.[7] However, the mounting evidence accumulated in the 1950's and early 1960's suggests that even where a choice was possible, many developing countries were not adopting the most labor-intensive techniques possible or promoting only those industries which absorbed the highest amount of labor. A survey of the literature dealing with this problem reveals that gradually an explanation for these phenomena is emerging.

The situation in which developing countries find themselves has been most interestingly expressed by Singer when he said that '... In many respects the technology of a hundred years ago would be desirable for them (the developing countries), and would make their economic development easier. But that technology no longer exists. It has been scrapped, and rightly scrapped, in the industrialized countries—and the technology of the industrialized countries is the only existing technology.'[8]

The argument is not that older and more labor-intensive technologies are not available for given industries. They are indeed, in the sense that second-hand equipment can be bought. However, after acquiring an older plant, it will be found that the spare parts are not produced any more and that it would be considered a questionable use of capital to establish special spare parts industries to service

5 John P. Lewis, *Quiet Crisis in India* (Washington, D.C.: The Brookings Institution, 1962) p. 60.

6 John C. H. Fei, and Guster Ranis, *Development of the Labor Surplus Economy: Theory and Policy* (Homewood, Illinois: Irwin, 1964), p. 132.

7 R. S. Eckaus, 'The Factor-Proportions Problem in Underdeveloped Areas,' *American Economic Review*, XLV (Sept. 1955).

8 Hans W. Singer, *International Development: Growth and Change* (New York: McGraw-Hill, 1964), p. 59.

outmoded machinery. Furthermore, the technicians who are contracted to install new industries will usually be conversant mainly with the most up-to-date methods.

It is commonly held that countries like France and Germany benefited from advantages of being latecomers by not having to undergo the costly process of experimentation and trial and error, which Britain as the industrial leader had to undergo. The contemporary developing countries, however, find themselves at a distinct disadvantage since they are forced to use mainly the advanced technology of the industrialized countries which supposedly does not fit in efficiently with their factor endowments. They do not have an original technology of their own to conform to the latter or the resources to experiment widely with different types of production methods.[9]

Even in developing countries where older technologies have been in use for some time, the tendency is to scrap them and to adopt more modern methods. The trend towards the adoption of modern labor-saving technology has been especially supported by technical missions of international organizations. For example, in the early 1960's the Economic Commission for Latin America released two studies on the textile industry in Chile and Brazil, which recommended modernization of existing equipment.[10] Some of the reasons advanced, such as low labor productivity or high cost compared with other countries or low returns to investment, are open to doubt: low labor productivity is not unexpected in a labor-intensive industry; an international comparison of costs involves one in problems of exchange rates and other international comparison problems, and high costs are not necessarily to be avoided if one produces for a highly protected domestic market; and as far as low

[9] Singer *op. cit.*, p. 60.

[10] In the case of Chile, the study concluded that 'Without doubt, there exists an excess of personnel employed in practically all factories studied.' Much of this labor has extremely low productivity as revealed by the fact that to produce 100 yards of cotton textiles necessitates 2.33 hours of labor in the United States, 4.74 in Japan and 12.85 in Chile. The solution recommended is, among others, the installation of modern machinery, which presumably would be labor-saving and which would increase labor productivity substantially. See Naciones Unidas, Consejo Economico Y Social, 'La Industria Textile De Chile,' mimeo., April 1962 (trans. by authors), pp. 13-20. In the study of the Brazilian textile industry it was found that the lower wage level in Brazil as compared with that in the United States was not enough to compensate for the much lower productivity; thus, the labor cost per unit of fabric in Brazil was 31 per cent higher than in the United States. See, United Nations. *The Textile Industry in Latin America*, II (Brazil and New York, 1963), p. 90.

returns on investment are concerned, returns on already existing capital stocks should be viewed as quasi-rents. But the study found that in '. . . the cotton industry, 33 per cent of the over-all operational deficiency is due to the obsolescence of the machinery, the remaining 67 per cent being due to failure to make full use of the existing machinery; the latter relates to material factors such as the quality of the raw material, balanced output and plant layout, and human factors such as efficient management, the formation of a body of technicians and supervisors, and training of the workers.'[11] However, because of '. . . the impossibility of solving (the problem) . . . on a piecemeal basis . . . ,' the report concludes that re-equipment is the only solution. In other words, it is not possible to solve the 67 per cent deficiencies which are due to nonmachine problems in isolation of the 33 per cent deficiencies due to obsolete machinery. Re-equipment is also found to be 'by its very nature a dynamic element, which is closely linked with action in the other fields and would provide an impetus that would undoubtedly be lacking if action were confined to the administrative aspects.'[12]

These technical commissions made their recommendations appreciating the effects they would have on the employment picture. The report on Brazil specifically admits that new equipment will '. . . necessarily (involve) more automation, however modest the level of up-to-dateness aspired to . . .'[13] And further on it states that 'Any programme for the replacement of obsolete low yield equipment by modern machinery with a higher output will tend to reduce manpower absorption, and although the re-equipment considered here represents a level of productivity much lower than that in the textile industry in the United States, or even in Japan, it may well result in a considerable displacement of manpower.'[14] For Brazil the recommendations put forward implied a reduction of manpower of about 30 per cent in spinning mills and 45 per cent in weaving mills for each work shift.

It is clear that the institutional push is in the direction of adopting modern techniques of a labor-saving type both in new industries and in the modernization of older industries. Does this trend fly

[11] *The Textile Industry in Latin America*, *op. cit.*, p. 92.

[12] *Ibid.*, p. 92.

[13] *Ibid.*, p. 93.

[14] *Ibid.*, p. 104

in the face of a rational use of the most abundant factor of production? The dilemma that most developing countries seem to face is an abundant unskilled labor supply, on the one hand, and, on the other hand, the fact that older, more labor-intensive techniques of production are of an inefficient nature, i.e., producing a low return on capital invested in them. This conflict of interests was noted by a number of writers. Already in the mid-fifties, Galenson and Leibenstein remarked that 'One can easily visualize situations in which the maximum labor absorption criterion would not maximize the addition to total output.'[15] Commenting on the Indian experience, John P. Lewis says that:

> Any society, if it could rid itself of enough technique and capital, could keep every one of its ambulatory members fully employed grubbing for roots and berries. But that is not what is wanted — in India or elsewhere. The desire is for rising employment *with* rising per capita real income.[16]

In the same vein Galenson and Leibenstein suggested that should '. . . it be granted that the object of development is to attain a level of economic capacity which maximizes output *per capita* at a determined future time, then the correct criterion for allocating investment must be to choose for each unit of investment that alternative that will give each worker greater productive power than any other alternative.'[17]

A half a decade later, reviewing the experience of a number of countries, a group of experts from the ILO also came to the conclusion that '. . . as techniques are made less capital-intensive, more labour can, of course, be employed with any given volume of investment, but it does not appear to be the case that teehniques that employ more labour per unit of capital always yield a larger output per unit of capital. Indeed in a number of cases, it has been observed that some techniques that use much labour also use much capital per unit of output.'[18]

These claims are substantiated by studies of alternative techniques in the cotton weaving industry in India. The results are reproduced in Table III. The rates of profit per loom per year expressed as percentages of capital cost vary depending on the daily wage rate.

15 Walter Galenson and Harvey Leibenstein, 'Investment Criteria, Productivity, and Economic Development,' this *Journal*, LXIX (Aug. 1955), p. 348.

16 Lewis, *op. cit.*, p. 52.

17 Galenson and Leibenstein, *op. cit.*, p. 351.

18 International Labour Office, *Employment Objectives in Economic Development*, Report of a Meeting of Experts (Geneva, 1961), p. 67.

TABLE III

INDIA: SOME ECONOMIC CONSEQUENCES OF ALTERNATIVE TECHNIQUES IN THE COTTON-WEAVING INDUSTRY

Technique	Capital Cost per Loom (Rs)	Net Value Added per Loom per Year (Rs)	Worker Required per Loom per Day (no.)	Rates of Profit per Loom per Year (expressed as percentage of capital cost) at Daily Wages of				
				Rs 1	Rs 2	Rs 3	Rs 4	Rs 5
Fly-shuttle handloom	30-50	450	1	150	—*	—*	—*	—*
'Banaras' semi-automatic handloom	200	1,500	1	600	450	300	150	0
Cottage power loom	1,500	2,250	1	130	110	90	70	50
Factory nonautomatic power loom	4,000	6,000	1	143	135	128	120	113
Automatic power loom	10,000	6,000	$\frac{1}{8}$	60	59	59	59	58

Source: Raj, K. N., 'Employment and Unemployment in the Indian Economy: Problems of Classification, Measurement and Policy,' *Economic Development and Cultural Change*, VII (April 1959), 276.
* Negative percentage.

It can be seen that the most labor-intensive technique is never the one producing the highest return per unit of capital. At daily wages of Rs 1, Rs 2, Rs 3, and Rs 4, the semi-automatic handloom (still labor-intensive) produces the highest return per unit of capital. But at wages of Rs 5, the factory nonautomatic power loom becomes the most profitable. Theoretically speaking, the fly shuttle hand loom, the most labor-intensive combination of labor and capital, would lie on the outside of the ridge line in a production function.

The basic argument then is that given capital as the scarce factor in developing countries, the problem is not to save the use of it in the production process, but rather to maximize the output which can be gotten from it. In theory, if labor is a free factor, the production process chosen would correspond to a point on the ridge line of a production function. In this section we have examined the explanations given for deviations from this expected pattern. As convincing as these explanations are, the economist is bound to look for additional reasons of a more general, and perhaps fundamental, nature to account for the relatively capital-intensive production processes used in new industries in developing countries.

IV

Another, somewhat complementary, approach to the labor-absorption problem was made by Hirschman. He stressed that due to the shortage of managerial personnel and various types of skilled labor, 'machine paced' rather than 'operator paced' operations are advisable in order to prevent breakdowns, neglect of maintenance, etc., which would curtail productivity of capital.[19] In other words, given a shortage of skilled labor and managerial personnel, a capital-intensive technology will enable industry to economize these very scarce factors of production. More concretely, Hirschman claimed that modern and up-to-date technology '... perform(s) a crucial function in aiding management in the performance of new, unfamiliar, and perhaps somewhat uncongenial tasks. By predetermining to a considerable extent what is to be done where and at what point of time, the machines and the mechanical processes they perform reduce these difficulties immeasurably in comparison

19 Albert O. Hirschman, *The Strategy of Economic Development* (New Haven: Yale University Press, 1958), p. 145.

with a situation where work schedules depend exclusively on the convergence and coordination of many human wills and actions.'[20]

Myint analyzes the problem in a similar vein. He states that it is an error to examine the problem of choice of technique in a two-factor world, labor and capital. He states that in the real world '. . . the choice depends not only on two selected factors but on a variety of other things, notably the third main factor—skilled labor. Many underdeveloped countries suffer from a greater shortage of skills than of material capital, so that they sometimes prefer more expensive machinery, which reduces repairs and maintenance, to cheaper or second-hand machinery which, although it might reduce the ratio of capital to unskilled labor, requires a larger amount of the scarcest factor, skilled labor . . .'[21]

Is 'skilled labor' a separate factor of production? Or can it be considered as a combination of raw labor and capital? For an individual it is clear that the latter is the case. Generally, an unskilled person can be transformed into a skilled laborer after a certain amount of time, during which he is learning, though not producing and thus consuming capital. Should this reasoning be applied to the aggregate work force, one would fall into a fallacy of composition.[22]

At any given period, a certain proportion of the labor force will be skilled, usually a small proportion in a developing country. In the latter, the facilities for transforming raw into skilled labor are limited (e.g., possibilities for one-the-job training, vocational schools, etc.). Thus, in the short run, the supply of an increasing amount of skilled labor will be inelastic. This is true even if the country were prepared suddenly to channel a large proportion of investments into training facilities. Therefore, in the short run, the skilled labor supply is not likely to increase rapidly. Since when talking about development problems and their solutions we are

20 *Ibid.*, pp. 146-47. This hypothesis has yet to be fully tested. Some investigations have even come up with opposite conclusions. For example, Peter Kilby, in a forthcoming monograph on the Nigerian bread industry, found that capital-intensive projects actually require more highly skilled technicians for maintenance than labor-intensive alternatives require for supervision. However, it was also found that while the expatriate maintenance expert always is equal to his task, only about one-half of the expatriate supervisors prove equal to their much more difficult task.

21 H. Myint, *The Economic of the Developing Countries* (London: Hutchinson & Co. 1964), p. 137.

22 See Alfred Marshall, *Principles of Economics* (8th Ed.; New York: Macmillan. 1952), Book VI. Chap. IV, p. 561: Book VI, Chap. V, p. 570.

concerned about the short run, one will have to consider skilled labor as a separate production factor.

A skilled worker without either capital or unskilled labor is unproductive. However, capital and unskilled labor need to be combined with skilled labor to be productive.[23] Thus, a minimum of skilled labor is needed per unit of unskilled labor and per unit of capital.

Let us give an example. Suppose that for 10 unskilled workers we need 1 skilled worker. If we have 100 unskilled workers in the economy and 5 skilled workers, the effective supply of unskilled workers is not 100, but 50. On the other hand, if the number of skilled workers exceeded 10, the effective supply of unskilled workers would be 100. It follows that the effective supply of unskilled labor is determined by the amount which can be combined with the available supply of skilled labor. Should the supply of skilled labor be higher than the amount imposed by the ratio skilled/unskilled labor, the absolute supply of unskilled labor obviously would also be the effective supply. A similar reasoning can be applied to capital.

The effective supply of unskilled labor will probably be noticeably smaller than the absolute supply because of the scarcity of skilled labor. In the case of capital, the effective supply of capital will be little or no different from the absolute supply, because capital is also a scarce factor. If capital is scarce relative to skilled labor, the absolute supply is the effective supply. If capital is abundant relative to skilled labor, it is possible to import foreign technicians,[24] and to bring the effective capital supply to the level of the absolute capital supply.

The above reasoning should give us a framework within which to understand the tendency for adopting relatively capital-intensive techniques of production in the manufacturing sector of developing countries: Effective supply of labor is in fact much smaller than the absolute supply of labor.

23 It is evident that labor as a whole needs a minimum amount of capital, be it shovels or baskets, etc. And capital needs a minimum amount of unskilled labor.

24 Foreign technicians can be brought in to handle machines. It is more difficult, however, to import foreign skilled labor which is able or willing to work with local unskilled labor.

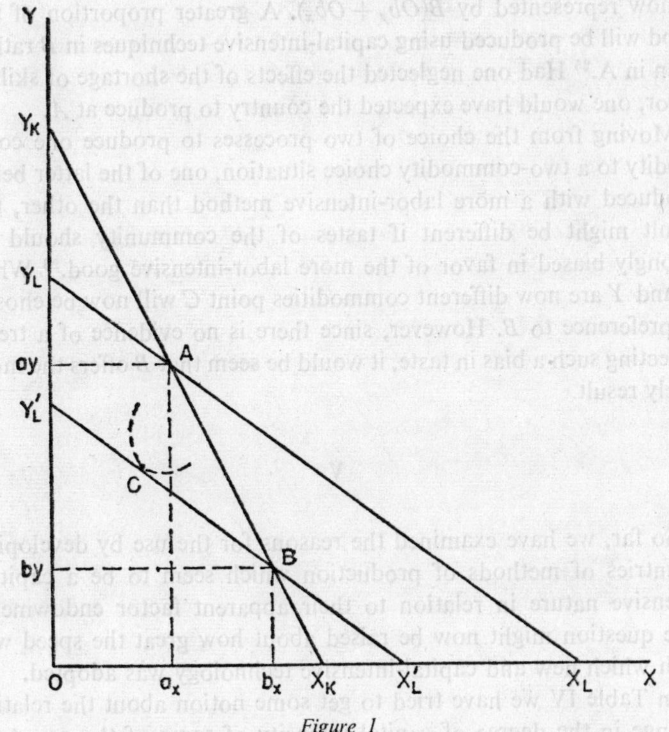

Figure 1

In Figure 1 we summarize our arguments. On the vertical and horizontal axes we measure the output of the same commodity. *Y* represents the commodity produced in a relatively labor-intensive way and *X* represents the commodity produced in a more capital-intensive way. Under the assumption that there is no shortage of skilled labor, line $Y_L — X_L$ represents the combinations of *X* and *Y* which could be produced with the available supply of labor, if capital were a free factor, and $Y_K — X_K$ represents the combinations of *X* and *Y* which could be produced with the available supply of capital, if labor were a free factor. Since *X* and *Y* are perfect substitutes, one would choose the maximum output represented by $A(Oa_y + Oa_x)$.

With the shortage of skilled labor the effective supply of unskilled labor will now determine a new production possibility line $Y^1{}_L — X^1{}_L$. As we have seen, this will have little influence on the supply of capital and $Y_K — X_K$ remains fixed. The new maximum output point is now represented by $B(Ob_y + Ob_x)$. A greater proportion of the good will be produced using capital-intensive techniques in *B* rather than in A.[25] Had one neglected the effects of the shortage of skilled labor, one would have expected the country to produce at *A*.

Moving from the choice of two processes to produce one commodity to a two-commodity choice situation, one of the latter being produced with a more labor-intensive method than the other, the result might be different if tastes of the community should be strongly biased in favor of the more labor-intensive good.[26] When *X* and *Y* are now different commodities point *C* will now be chosen in preference to *B*. However, since there is no evidence of a trend reflecting such a bias in taste, it would be seem that *B* offers the most likely result.

V

So far, we have examined the reasons for the use by developing countries of methods of production which seem to be a capital-intensive nature in relation to their apparent factor endowment. The question might now be raised about how great the speed was with which new and capital-intensive technology was adopted.

In Table IV we have tried to get some notion about the relative change in the degree of capital intensity of some of the countries when compared with the United States. This was done by dividing the measure of capital intensity in the initial year for each country by the relevant U.S. figure for 1939 and the second year by the 1954 U.S. figure.[27] It must be stressed that we are comparing trends and that we are assuming that these trends have remained the same into the 1960's.

It is obvious that in many industry groups not all the difference in installed power capacity per capita is due to the higher capital intensity of certain processes. The industry groups are at a very

25 Obviously the location of *B* will depend on the magnitude of the shift of the curve, i.e. on the required proportion of skilled to unskilled labor.

26 Because of what one would expect to be the slopes of the constraint lines, this bias would indeed be very strong. *Y*, being the labor-intensive good, can be assumed to be a more traditional good, while *X* would be a good increasingly used as a development proceeds. It is thus doubtful that the slope of an indifference curve would be such as drastically to favor the labor-intensive good. It is thus likely that the corner solution will be adopted.

27 Installed power capacity per capita is available only up to 1954 in the United States.

TABLE IV

INSTALLED CAPACITY PER PERSON: A COMPARISON
(ratios comparing selected countries with the United States)

	Argentina		Brazil		Chile*		Colombia	
	1939/1939	1953/1954	1950/1939	1960/1954	1948/1939	1953/1954	1953/1939	1958/1954
Nonmetallic Minerals	29	25	..	..	56	58	37	59
Machinery (excluding electrical)	..	..	38	46	..	..	..	..
Fabricated Metal Products	32	36	101	69	..	..	46	37
Electrical Machinery	..	..	52	74	..	..	..	..
Transportation Equipment	..	..	54	59	..	..	..	..
Furniture	..	..	43	58	..	..	..	..
Paper and Paper Products	39	40	62	44	..	..	34	26
Rubber	52	42	60	78	..	..	56	58
Leather Goods	64	73	..	..	..	..	102	101
Chemicals	26	18	..	..	36	5	16	20
Textiles	42	38	49	50	36	27	77	65
Clothing and Shoes	..	..	..	..	100	50	..	..
Food Products	..	..	43	73	..	..	..	..
Drinks	70	64	..	..	4	34	52	66
Tobacco	..	..	46	18	..	..	..	..
Printing and Publishing	61	87	41	64	..	..	67	82
Basic Metals	12	18	..	..	..	..	21	30
Wood Products	34	36	49	48	37	23	33	38
Miscellaneous	63	38	..	..	..	..	48	37
Total	36	28	..	..	42	29	39	36

Source: See Table II.
Note: These numbers represent the ratio of installed power capacity per capita in each country for the year indicated in the numerator to the same datum in the United States for the year indicated in the denominator.
* Per capita electricity consumption.

aggregative level and in many instances include products in the case of the United States of a highly capital-intensive nature which are not produced in any of the developing countries listed. We should also note that in the case of Brazil and Colombia, the comparison is with a technology in the United States which is ten to six years older in each comparison made. The general impression one has is that there was no drastic catching up with the United States. In many cases (e.g., Brazilian metal products, Colombian metal products, paper products, chemicals and textiles) the ratio fell, even though the per capita installed capacity was rising and the labor absorption was drastically lagging behind production in those same industries (compare with Tables I and II). Where the ratio rose, it should be remembered that the catching up was with the 1954 U.S. technology (e.g., Brazilian machinery and transport equipment, Colombian food products, etc.).

This evidence would suggest that although new industries developed were of a more capital-intensive type and older industries were changing technology in a more capital-using direction, there was no drastic rush to introduce the very latest labor-saving technology of the advanced industrial countries.

VI

Granted the necessity for continued development of industries along fairly capital-intensive lines, with the result that labor is not absorbed in sufficient quantities relative to the general population growth and especially the growth of urban areas, what implications are there from the point of view of the absorption of the growing labor force in developing countries?

As a starting point, one has a tendency to look towards the historical experience of the United States and Europe. Unfortunately, the early industrialization experience was along fairly labor-intensive lines. The trend in the twentieth century has been towards greater mechanization, with a growing proportion of the labor force employed in the service sector.

If modern industry requires a substantial service sector in order to function, such a requirement would eventually provide a major source for coping with the employment problem. Of course, by definition all workers not absorbed in industry or agriculture, unless listed as openly unemployed, are presumably in the service sector. We, however, are thinking of relatively productive services, as opposed to the more parasitic services one so frequently encounters in underdeveloped countries.

Galenson is fairly optimistic along those lines. He claims that '. . . too little attention has been paid to those sectors of the economy in which the bulk of the new jobs are likely to be located, namely commerce and services. This does not mean that manufacturing is unimportant; on the contrary, it is, in my estimation, the key sector for economic growth. Under conditions of modern technology, however, its role is not likely to be that of a major source of new employment. Rather, it will tend to generate the effective demand leading to employment expansion in other sectors. This multiplier effect is apt to be much more significant than any direct contributions that the manufacturing sector can make to the alleviation of mass unemployment.'[28] Taking data from a number of developed and some underdeveloped countries, he tried to establish a relationship through least squares method between employment in manufacturing and employment in tertiary activities. He found that employment in the latter was increasing a little over 1 per cent a year regardless of changes in employment in manufacturing, also that for a percentage increase in manufacturing employment there was an increase of ·6 per cent of employment in tertiary activities.[29]

We have tried to summarize and interpret the relatively optimistic view of Galenson in Figure 2. In the Northeast quadrant we have the relationship between new investment (I) and resulting changes in employment in manufacturing (N_m). N_L represents this relationship if a labor-intensive technique is used; N_K if a capital-intensive technique is used. The Northwest quadrant represents the relationship between changes in manufacturing employment and changes in total output. O_L represents this relationship assuming a labor-intensive technique is used; O_k assuming a capital-intensive technique is used. We are obviously assuming that the same amount of new investment will yield a larger increase in output when capital-intensive techniques are chosen. The Southwest quadrant represents the relationship between changes in output and changes of employment in the service sector. It can be seen that an investment

28 Walter Galenson, 'Economic Development and the Sectoral Expansion of Employment,' *International Labour Review*, LXXXVIII (June 1963), pp. 506-7.

29 *Ibid.*, p. 510.

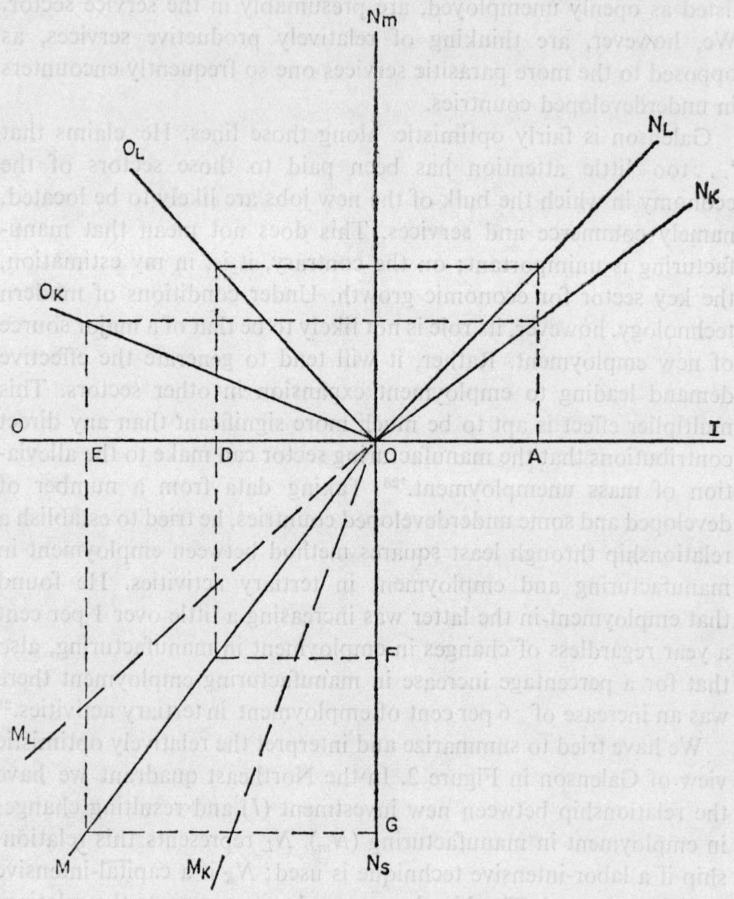

Figure 2

of OA can result in a creation of employment in manufacturing of AC, using labor-intensive techniques, and only AB, using capital-intensive techniques. However, the labor-intensive technique results in an output of only OD and service employment creation of only OF, while the capital-intensive technique creates output of OE and service employment of OG. As drawn in this diagram, the total employment creation is greater via the labor-saving technique. Whether such a favorable relationship exists remains to be seen.

Substantially more empirical research needs to be done on employment in the service sector and its relationship to other sectors. It is quite possible that the relationship between increased employment in the service sector and output depends on the technique of production used. More capital-intensive techniques might call forth a greater amount of service employment (OM_K); whereas labor-intensive techniques might have a much weaker service employment impact (OM_L). It could also be that the slope of the OM curves, which can be drawn as straight lines in the short run, will be influenced by the degree of development which the country had attained at the starting point of our analysis. For example, a fairly developed country might have a substantially expanded service sector; thus, additional investment in the manufacturing sector will call forth relatively small amounts of increased service employment.

In this analysis we have not explored dynamic elements; capital-intensive techniques supposedly lead to distribution of incomes more favorable to the saving classes, thus there is a greater potential for further investment expansion. On the other hand, it might be asked: if more capital-intensive techniques are used, which result in an uneven distribution of income, could this lead to a situation of increased production potential in the economy without the generation of effective demand to occupy the new capacity fully?

Our purpose in this essay has been to show that the lack of labor absorption in the manufacturing sector of developing countries is not necessarily due to conscious or wrong policy choices, but has several partial explanations which should be combined with the more general explanation of effective factor endowment.

5

WAGES AND EMPLOYMENT IN A LABOR-SURPLUS ECONOMY

*Lloyd G. Reynolds**

A DECADE AGO Arthur Lewis published the first of two pioneer articles on economic growth under conditions of labor surplus (5) (6).** While this problem has since been explored by other writers, particularly Gustav Ranis and John C. H. Fei (8) (9), it is appropriate to refer to a family of 'Lewis-type models' of economic development. These models depict the absorption of an initial labor surplus by transference of labor from the traditional to the modern sector of the economy. Thus far, however, there has been little effort to compare the development experience of specific countries with the predictions derived from Lewis-type models. The present essay is intended as a step in this direction, using data for the Puerto Rican economy from 1945 to date.

The salient features of the Lewis model are illustrated in Figure 1. The economy is divided into subsistence and capitalist sectors. The capitalist sector is 'that part of the economy which uses reproducible capital and pays capitalists for the use thereof' (5, p. 148). The subsistence sector includes everything else. While the subsistence sector is often identified empirically with traditiosal agriculture, Lewis notes that surplus labor may be found equally well in petty trade, domestic service, and other service occupations.

The subsistence sector contains surplus labor in the sense of workers whose marginal productivity is negligible, zero, or even negative.[1] These workers nevertheless receive an income, *OS* in

*The author is professor of economics and director of the Economic Growth Center at Yale University. He would like to acknowledge helpful comments by his colleagues Gustav Ranis and Werner Baer.

**See References at the end of the article.

1 The existence of zero marginal productivity as a common phenomenon has been disputed by some writers, including Theodore W. Schultz [10]. If I understand Schultz aright, he is arguing that, through generations of experimentation, traditional agriculture gets organized in a way which makes optimum use of whatever labor supply is available, and which leaves each member of the labor

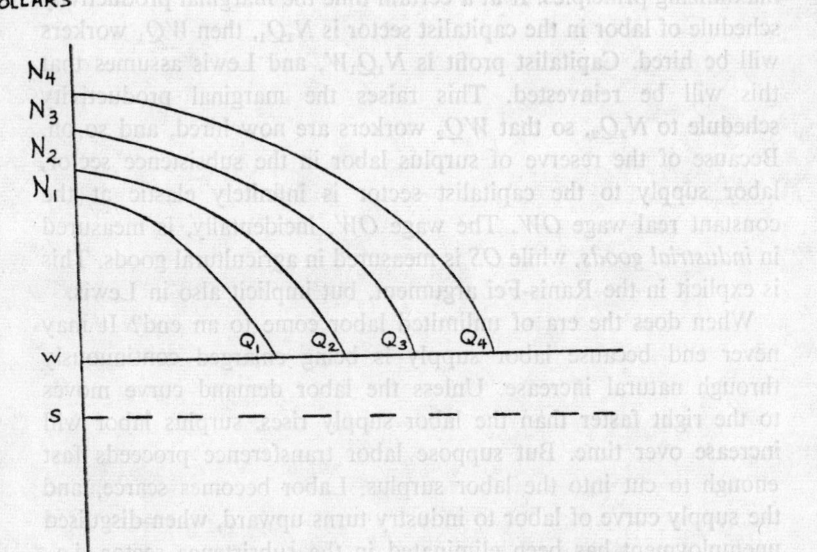

Figure 1

Figure 1, which enables them to live after a fashion. This situation can arise *inter alia* because the income of a family group is shared among family members regardless of their individual contribution.

The wage rate in the capitalist sector, *OW*, must be somewhat above average income in the subsistence sector. Lewis suggests that the margin is usually 30 per cent or more, though its exact size does not matter for his argument. The reasons for this wage gap include higher living costs in the towns, the psychological cost to workers of transferring from the leisurely pace of traditional activities to the tighter discipline of industry, and perhaps also higher conventional standards of living in urban areas.

Employment in the capitalist sector is determined on ordinary

force with a positive (though low) marginal product. If labor is withdrawn from agriculture *with no change in techniques*, output will fall. This may well be correct. But it does not contradict the possibility that, if techniques known and used in progressive agricultural economies can be transferred to a backward economy, labor can then be transferred out of agriculture with no loss of output. Withdrawal of labor may itself stimulate improvement of techniques. Moreover, nothing in the Schultz argument denies the possibility that the marginal productivity of labor, though positive, may be below the worker's income.

maximizing principles. If at a certain time the marginal productivity schedule of labor in the capitalist sector is N_1Q_1, then WQ_1 workers will be hired. Capitalist profit is N_1Q_1W, and Lewis assumes that this will be reinvested. This raises the marginal productivity schedule to N_2Q_2, so that WQ_2 workers are now hired, and so on. Because of the reserve of surplus labor in the subsistence sector, labor supply to the capitalist sector is infinitely elastic at the constant real wage OW. The wage OW, incidentally, is measured in *industrial goods,* while OS is measured in agricultural goods. This is explicit in the Ranis-Fei argument, but implicit also in Lewis.

When does the era of unlimited labor come to an end? It may never end because labor supply is being enlarged continuously through natural increase. Unless the labor demand curve moves to the right faster than the labor supply rises, surplus labor will increase over time. But suppose labor transference proceeds fast enough to cut into the labor surplus. Labor becomes scarce, and the supply curve of labor to industry turns upward, when disguised unemployment has been eliminated in the subsistence sector, i.e., when enough labor has been transferred to the modern sector so that the marginal productivity of those remaining in subsistence activity rises to the level of OS. Beyond this point, which Ranis and Fei term the *commercialization point,* the subsistence sector must pay workers the value of their (rising) marginal product and must compete with the industrial sector for scarce labor. The subsistence sector has vanished by becoming 'modern,' and both sectors now operate on commercial principles.

But the industrial wage rate may be forced up even before the commercialization point has been reached. Suppose, for example, that while labor productivity is rising in industry it remains unchanged in agriculture. When enough workers have been moved out of agriculture so that the marginal productivity of those remaining is no longer zero, further withdrawals of labor will reduce food output. Even without a drop in food output, expansion of incomes in the capitalist sector will raise the demand for food and, in a closed economy, turn the internal terms of trade in favor of agriculture. The industrial workers, whose wage is measured in industrial goods, will have to receive more of those goods to enable them to consume as much food as before.

The industrial wage level may also rise prematurely, that is, before the labor surplus is exhausted, for noneconomic reasons—a rise in conventional standards of life, voluntary increases granted by the capitalists on moral grounds, trade union pressure, or government regulation. This last possibility, which Lewis notes only in passing, has turned out to be quite important in Puerto Rico.

I *Aspects of the Puerto Rican Case*

Space does not permit an over-all review of the recent development of the Puerto Rican economy, but a few preliminary points must be made. Additional background material will be found in studies by Harvey Perloff [7], Werner Baer [1] [2], and others.

The growth rate of total and per capita output in Puerto Rico since 1940 has been one of the highest in the world. Real GNP per capita rose at an average rate of 4.1 per cent a year during the forties and 5.2 per cent a year during the 'fifties. In 1954 dollars, per capita GNP rose from $269 in 1940 to $673 in 1961, placing Puerto Rico almost above the range of 'underdeveloped' countries. GNP per employed worker, in 1954 dollars, rose from $932 in 1940 to $2,802 in 1961.

While the industrialization program has attracted the widest public attention, economic progress has been general. Food production has risen at a rate which has permitted Puerto Rico to maintain about the same degree of self-sufficiency despite much higher income levels. This degree is quite low, however, only about 40 per cent of Puerto Rican food consumption coming from domestic sources. Different sectors of the economy have expanded at different rates, and the industrial composition of output has changed materially. Manufacturing rose from 12 per cent of total output in 1940 to 23 per cent in 1962, while agriculture dropped from 32 per cent to 13 per cent. There were substantial increases in the contribution of the construction industry and the Commonwealth government to national product.

Manufacturing development has been stimulated by legislation granting manufacturers of products not produced in Puerto Rico (in 1947), full exemption from both income and property taxes for periods ranging from 10 to 17 years, depending on the part of the island in which the plant is located; by a wage level which in the late 'forties was only about one quarter of that in mainland manufacturing plants; and by an energetic and capable Economic Development Administration which provides a variety of market research, plant-construction, labor-training, financing, and technical advisory services. Since 1947 about thirteen hundred E.D.A.-sponsored manufacturing plants have been established in the island, the great majority being branch plants of mainland companies. The failure rate among these new establishments has been about one-third, but 910 of them were still in operation at the end of 1963, with a total employment of about seventy thousand workers, or one-tenth of the island's labor force. Manufacturing development has been primarily in light industry. Clothing, textiles, and food products provide about half of manufacturing employment. But in recent years there has been considerable development of oil refining, chemicals, paper, metal products, and other heavier types of industry.

The peculiarities of the Puerto Rican case are readily apparent. It is a small economy, with close ties to the United States, hence is a very open economy. Exports and imports run higher than 50 per cent of domestic output. Capital, labor, and commodities move freely between Puerto Rico and the mainland United States. Manufacturing investment has been financed mainly from the mainland rather than from domestic sources. Puerto Rico has autonomy in tax matters, but only limited autonomy in wage determination, and little control over product prices, which are dominated by price movements on the mainland.

In other respects, however, Puerto Rico appears as a labor-surplus economy in the early stages of industrialization, with the employment and wage problems common to such economies. From a research standpoint, the economic statistics available for Puerto Rico, which largely follow U.S. concepts and procedures, are of an unusually high quality. See in particular the sources cited in [11] [12] [13] [14] from which most of the data in this and subsequent sections were derived. We proceed, then, to examine the behavior of wages, productivity, profits, employment, and unemployment in Puerto Rico since World War II, and to compare this behavior with the predictions from Lewis-type models.[2]

2 The substantive sections of this paper draw heavily on the findings of the Manpower Resources Project, which the writer directed at the Social Science Research Center of the University of Puerto Rico. Many of the points made here will be documented more completely in a forthcoming volume by the writer and Professor Peter Gregory, of the University of Minnesota, who served as assistant director of the project. I would like to acknowledge Professor Gregory's contribution to our joint effort, both in terms of data accumulation and techniques of analysis. In particular, he developed the measures of elasticity of demand for manufacturing labor in Puerto Rico described in a later section. He should not

II *Employment and Unemployment*

Puerto Rico is one of the most densely populated areas on earth, with about 730 people per square mile in 1963. While birth rates have shown some tendency to fall since 1950, the rate of natural increase remains close to 2½ per cent a year. Total population is about 2½ million, the annual increment to population above 60,000. A major objective of the development program has been to provide jobs at a rate exceeding the rate of labor force growth, and thus to cut into the island's labor surplus.

Heavy emigration to the U.S. mainland, stimulated by good employment opportunities and cheap air travel, provided a respite from population pressure during the 'fifties. Net emigration from the island averaged 43,000 a year, or about three-quarters of the natural population increase, during the decade. Moreover, since migration was concentrated among young adults, the Puerto Rican labor force actually declined between 1950 and 1960. With a shrinking labor force and a booming island economy, one might have expected rapid strides toward elimination of unemployment.

When one looks at the data, however, one gets an unpleasant surprise. Total employment *fell* between 1950 and 1960. The extent of the decline in labor force and employment depends on whether one includes home needleworkers in the totals. If one excludes home needleworkers as being very part-time employees,[3] the labor force dropped by 35,000 and employment declined by 12,000 between 1950 and 1960. It follows that there was only modest progress in reducing unemployment.[4]

This impression is confirmed by Table 1. The percentage of full-time unemployed male workers was almost as high in 1963

be held accountable, however, for any defects in this interpretation of our findings. Professor Luz Torruellas, director of the department of economics at the University of Puerto Rico, who also served as assistant director of the project, was most helpful throughout, and her contribution is gratefully acknowledged.

3 The number of women doing needlework in their homes was 51,000 in 1950, only 10,000 in 1960, which is why their inclusion or exclusion makes a substantial difference in the behavior of employment. Net annual output per worker, however is estimated at only $143 for 1955 and $159 in 1960, which is suggestive of very part-time supplementary employment. On this ground it seems reasonable to set these workers aside as a separate category.

4 Since 1960, labor force and employment in Puerto Rico have begun to rise; and this has been accompanied by a sharp decline in net emigration to the mainland. So while part of the recent increase in employment is no doubt genuine, part may represent a 'backing up' of surplus labor and an increase in underemployment.

TABLE 1—EMPLOYMENT AND UNEMPLOYMENT IN PUERTO RICO, BY SEX
FISCAL YEARS 1951 AND 1963

Employment Status	Men 1951 No. (000)	Men 1951 Per cent	Men 1963 No. (000)	Men 1963 Per cent	Women 1951 No. (000)	Women 1951 Per cent	Women 1963 No. (000)	Women 1963 Per cent
Labor force	508	100.0	516	100.0	205	100.0	179	100.0
Employed	431	84.8	443	85.8	173	84.4	163	91.1
35 hours or more	255	50.2	300	58.1	71	34.6	91	50.8
less than 35 hours	162	31.9	117	22.7	93	45.4	55	30.7
employed but not working	14	2.8	26	5.0	9	4.4	17	9.5
Unemployed	78	15.3	73	14.1	32	15.6	16	8.9

Source: Puerto Rico Department of Labor, Bureau of Labor Statistics; 1963 figures are estimates based on extrapolation of data for the first three quarters; data *include* home needleworkers.

as it had been in 1951. The unemployment percentage for women, however, fell from 15.6 to 8.9 over this period. This reflects the fact that about 60 per cent of the jobs in the new E.D.A.-sponsored factories have been filled by women workers. Note also that the proportion of employed people working less than 35 hours a week dropped considerably for both sexes. In the case of men, this probably represents mainly a transference of underemployed workers out of agriculture. In the case of women, the figures reflect a decline of 40,000 in the number of home needleworkers, most of whom seem to have dropped out of the labor force instead of seeking other employment.

Why was there not more of a striking progress on the employment front? There are two lines of explanation that may be widely applicable to newly industrializing countries. First, economic development brings a shrinkage of employment in some sectors, so that total employment can rise only if this shrinkage is more than offset by expansion in other sectors. Second, manufacturing industries embodying modern production methods create relatively little employment; and part even of this employment involves drawing new people into the labor force rather than absorbing previously unemployed workers.

The most dramatic employment shrinkage in Puerto Rico has been in agriculture. In the single decade 1950-60, agricultural employment fell from 214,000 to 124,000. There was a drop of about 40,000 in sugar growing, 10,000 in tobacco cultivation, and 40,000 in food production for local consumption. This last decline is especially interesting, since the farm value of domestic food production on the island rose from about $70 million in 1949-50 to $130 million in 1960-61, indicating a substantial gain in real output. The implication is that the 1950 farm labor force was seriously underemployed.

This impression is confirmed by special studies of the Puerto Rico Department of Labor. Between 1955 and 1960, for example, the agricultural labor force dropped by 45,000. But the number of *fully employed agricultural workers* declined by only 12,000. The rest of the shrinkage came from a drop of 12,000 in the full-time unemployed, 8,000 in wage workers averaging less than 35 hours a week, and 12,000 in subsistence farmers.[5]

The decline of 41,000 in the number of home needleworkers between 1950 and 1960 has already been mentioned and in part discounted as representing a much smaller decline in equivalent full-time employment. It nevertheless represents a substantial decline in economic activity, due mainly to the fact that rising legal minimum wages have made it increasingly difficult for Puerto Rican producers to compete with products from the Philippines, Hong Kong, Japan, and other areas. Finally, economic development brought the usual rapid decline in the number of domestic servants, which fell from 31,000 in 1950 to 17,000 in 1960.

The declines in these sectors during the 'fifties were about balanced by expansion in others. Between 1950 and 1962 manufacturing added 36,000 workers, construction 24,000, government 12,000, and other service industries about 20,000. Together with smaller expansions in utilities, trade, and finance, about 115,000 jobs were added to the economy over these twelve years. Note that manufacturing provided less than one-third of the new jobs. It is significant also that, while manufacturing output tripled in real terms between 1950 and 1962, factory employment rose only 65 per cent. The source of these productivity gains will be explored in a later section.

5 Puerto Rico Department of Labor, Bureau of Labor Statistics, *Full Employment and Underemployment in Puerto Rico*, Special Reports Nos. 22, 27 31, and 34.

Today, about one-eighth of the Puerto Rican labor force is wholly unemployed. Another one-quarter work less than 35 hours a week.[6] There are doubtless others who could be withdrawn from agriculture, trade, and service with little loss of output. The unlimited supply of labor to industry remains a reality.

III *Wage Determination and Wage Behavior*

Despite this abundance of labor, Puerto Rican wages have risen at a startling rate. Between 1950 and 1963, the average hourly earnings of production workers in E.D.A.-sponsored manufacturing plants almost tripled (Table 2). The gap between Puerto Rican and mainland wages narrowed considerably. Because of substantial differences in the composition of manufacturing in the two areas,

TABLE 2—AVERAGE HOURLY EARNINGS OF PRODUCTION WORKERS IN E.D.A.-SPONSORED MANUFACTURING PLANTS AND IN U.S. MANUFACTURING, 1950-63

Year	E.D.A. Plants Puerto Rico	All Manufacturing United States	Ratio of E.D.A. Plants to U. S. Manufacturing
1950	$0.412	$1.501	.274
1951	.448	1.615	.277
1952	.453	1.705	.266
1953	.475	1.79	.265
1954	.505	1.81	.279
1955	.607	1.91	.318
1956	.720	2.02	.356
1957	.830	2.09	.397
1958	.884	2.14	.413
1959	.935	2.21	.423
1960	.983	2.30	.427
1961	1.031	2.34	.427
1962	1.091	2.39	.457
1963	1.159	2.47	.470

Sources: The Puerto Rican data for E.D.A.-sponsored plants are reported in E.D.A., *Annual Statistical Report*, 1960-62, pp. 27-31. The U.S. data derive from the U.S. Bureau of Labor Statistics. Data are for October of each year.

6 Only part of this group, of course, can be considered underemployed. Women workers in particular often prefer a part-time schedule. Special analyses by the Puerto Rico Department of Labor suggest that about 70 per cent of the women working a short week, and 35 per cent of the men, consider themselves fully employed and do not want longer hours of work.

the gap should really be measured on an industry by industry basis. Table 3 indicates that, for selected industries which are important both in Puerto Rico and on the mainland, Puerto Rican wages rose from between 25 and 35 per cent of mainland levels in 1952 to between 50 and 70 per cent in 1962.

TABLE 3—AVERAGE HOURLY EARNINGS IN SELECTED INDUSTRIES: PUERTO RICO AS PER CENT OF U.S., 1952 AND 1962

Industry	1952	1962
Cigars	.30	.67
Broad woven fabrics	.38	.56
Knitting	.41	.70
Floor coverings	.26	.53
Men's and boys' furnishings	.32	.61
Women's and misses' outerwear	.26	.52
Women's and children's undergarments	.32	.70
Girls' and children's outerwear	.28	.59
Paperboard containers and boxes*	.36	.63
Drugs	.22**	.49
Leather footwear	.30	.52
Fabricated metal products	.31	.51
Machinery—nonelectrical	.39	.54
Household appliances	—	.56
Toys and sporting goods	.26	.51
Costume jewelry, buttons, and lotions	.33	.50

* The data for Puerto Rico are for the broader industrial group, paper and allied products; however, the bulk of the activity is to be found within the paperboard and box division.

** The ratio is for 1950.

Sources: The Puerto Rican data were derived from the annual *Census of Manufacturing Industries of Puerto Rico*, published by the Puerto Rico Department of Labor, Bureau of Labor Statistics. The wage data apply to the week ending nearest the first week of October for each year. The wage data for the United States were taken from the *Monthly Labor Review* and apply to the month of October for each year.

Even this comparison is not conclusive for appraising locational advantage. The Puerto Rican wage level in each industry should properly be compared with low-wage areas on the mainland which might be considered as alternative locations. One might also compare wages in Puerto Rican plants with those of mainland plants operated by the same company. One such study, which covered 50 companies in the spring of 1958, found that wages in the Puerto

Rican plant ranged from 35 per cent to 94 per cent of those in the mainland plant, with a median of 59 per cent [3]. Considering the continued improvement of Puerto Rico's relative position since 1958 shown by Table 3, a comparable survey today would probably show a median in the neighborhood of 70 per cent.

The large wage increases since 1950 have not been confined to manufacturing, but have been general throughout the economy. Manual workers in construction, public utilities, and the service industries have received increases of roughly the same percentage size as in manufacturing. There has been a serious lag, however, in agricultural earnings. In 1952 the average wage earner in agriculture earned about half as much as the average factory worker. By 1962 he earned less than one-third as much. The urban wage level has pulled away increasingly from the agricultural base.

It is hard to find an economic rationale for the rapid rise of the urban wage level. Some pressure on food supplies is suggested by the fact that consumer prices of domestically produced foodstuffs rose more than 50 per cent between 1947 and 1961. But 60 per cent of the food consumed on the island is still imported, and import prices have risen only slightly. Prices of nonfood items, and the over-all consumer price index, have risen at about the same rate as on the mainland. Thus there has been a rapid rise in real wage levels, and it is this which has to be explained.

Trade union organization in Puerto Rico is relatively weak. Pressure for higher wages has come mainly from the U.S. and Commonwealth governments, operating through legal minimum wages. Industries involved in external commerce are covered by special provisions of the Fair Labor Standards Act. There is also a Puerto Rico minimum wage law, passed originally in 1941 and revised and strengthened in 1956. This act can be applied to external commerce, but in practice the Commonwealth government has ceded jurisdiction in this area to industry committees appointed under the FLSA. The main impact of the Puerto Rican law is on intra-insular activities, where minima have been established for most of the major industries, including agriculture.

We are accustomed to regard minimum wage regulation in the mainland United States as rather unimportant. The reason is that the legal minimum is a flat rate, infrequently revised, and set well below the prevailing wage level of most industries. The control structure in Puerto Rico is quite different. Under both the federal and island legislation, minimum wages are set separately for each industry on the recommendation of tripartite industry committees. The minima are geared to the estimated wage-paying ability of each industry, and there is at any time a wide range between the highest and lowest industry rates. Most workers in each industry earn very close to the minimum rate; and as the minimum is raised, which happens every year or two, the industry wage level is forced up by a proportionate amount. There is convincing evidence that minimum wage regulation, rather than labor-supply conditions, is mainly responsible for the advance of real wages over the past 15 years.

TABLE 4—FREQUENCY DISTRIBUTION OF INDUSTRY WAGE MINIMA UNDER THE FLSA, 1949 AND 1963

Minimum Rates	1949	1963*
Under .25	37	0
.25–.299	20	1
.30–.349	17	1
.35–.399	16	0
.40–.449	35	0
.45–.499		2
.50–.599		2
.60–.699		2
.70–.799		27
.80–.899		20
.90–.999		19
1.00–1.149		38
1.15–1.249		36

* Data as of June 1963; a further automatic increase of 10 per cent in all rates was scheduled for November 1963.

Source: U.S. Department of Labor, Wage and Hour and Public Contracts Division.

The rate at which the legal minima have been raised, as well as the dispersion of industry minima at a particular time, is illustrated by Table 4. In 1949 the median minimum wage was about 30 cents an hour, and there were still many rates below 25 cents. By 1963 the median minimum wage was $1.00 an hour, and there were scarcely any rates below 70 cents. The impact of successive revisions stands out clearly from Puerto Rican wage statistics. When an industry's minimum is raised, average hourly earnings rise by about the same amount, though usually with some lag because the rates of upper occupational groups may not be revised immediately. After the increase, as before, the bulk of the labor force is found earning very close to the legal minimum.

The leaders of the Commonwealth government would doubtless have acted to raise the manufacturing wage level in any event. However one may view the classical model of capital accumulation in principle, the spectacle of very large profits and stagnating wages can scarcely be viewed with equanimity by a democratically elected government. Whether Commonwealth leaders, given completely free choice, would have moved so rapidly to reduce the island's locational advantage is uncertain, for they have been under strong pressure from the mainland. Each time Congress has revised the Fair Labor Standards Act, many mainland manufacturers and union leaders have urged that Puerto Rico be blanketed under the federal minimum to eliminate 'unfair' competition. Political and business leaders on the island have avoided this only by accepting substantial wage increases under the industry committee system.[7] Each industry committee contains union, industry, and public representatives from the mainland as well as from Puerto Rico. The Puerto Rico industry representatives, who alone have a strong incentive to resist wage increases, find themselves outnumbered; and the wage decision which emerges may well differ from that which would have been reached by a committee of island residents only.

We shall argue in a moment that rapid wage increases have operated to retard the expansion of factory employment in Puerto Rico. They have doubtless had advantages in other directions, and opinions will differ on where the balance of advantage lies. But even if one concludes that a more moderate rise of wages would have better served the interest of Puerto Rico, this is not necessarily a criticism of the economic judgment of Commonwealth officials. Domestic and external political pressures have operated to restrict their freedom of maneuver.

7 And even so, they have not always averted specific Congressional action. In the most recent FLSA revision, Congress provided that the mainland minimum of $1.00 was to be raised in two steps, to $1.15 in 1961 and to $1.25 in November 1963. In the case of Puerto Rico, all minimum rates were to be increased in two steps, simultaneously with the mainland increases and by the same relative amounts. Thus a 15 per cent increase was provided for the first step and a further 10 per cent increase for the second. Still higher minima, of course, could be set by industry committee action.

IV *Wages, Productivity and Employment*

The rapid rise of wages may have retarded the expansion of employment in two ways. It may have deterred some mainland companies from establishing branch plants in Pureto Rico, and it may have induced plants that were established to use more labor-saving methods of production. What evidence is there on the strength of these effects?

Puerto Rico has certain cost disadvantages which must be offset to make location there attractive. Transportation costs are often higher, especially where components are shipped from the mainland to Puerto Rico for processing or assembly and the finished product is re-exported to the mainland. Uncertainty of shipping is an additional cost, for the docks are well organized and dock strikes are not infrequent. Executives brought from the mainland to manage plants in Puerto Rico are usually paid a substantial premium over their mainland salaries to cover the cost of living in their accustomed fashion by buying imported U.S. goods, the cost of sending children to mainland schools and colleges, and vacation and other travel for themselves and their families. Companies seem also to expect a substantially higher profit margin on their Puerto Rico operations to offset additional risks and uncertainties.[8]

Labor efficiency appears to be an unfavorable consideration *ex ante,* although it is on the average a neutral factor *ex post.* Prominent in the thinking of companies which have decided against locating in Puerto Rico is an expectation that labor productivity will be sufficiently lower that, even with lower wage rates, there will be no saving in unit labor costs relative to the mainland. These expectations are in fact unduly pessimistic. The evidence suggests that well-managed plants designed to mainland standards can reach mainland productivity levels after a reasonable breaking-in period. For locational decisions, however, it is expectations which matter rather than facts; and productivity expectations have usually been unfavorable.

The main favorable factors are tax exemption, which is temporary

8 For evidence on this point see the study by Mrs. Griffith (3) based on interviews with 50 companies which have located in Puerto Rico and 50 companies which considered locating there but decided against it. It is possible, of course, that companies which require a high profit rate to locate in Puerto Rico initially may be willing to stay there for a lower rate. Despite large wage increase and eventual expiration of tax exemption, relatively few plants have been shut down. Of 95 E.D.A.-sponsored plants whose tax exemption had expired by the end of 1962, only 21 had been closed.

in nature, and a lower wage level. Many companies reason that the wage level should yield savings in labor cost sufficient to offset the cost disadvantages noted above, leaving them with the tax advantage as a net gain. Thus as the wage level in Puerto Rico approaches that of competing areas on the mainland, one may expect a rise in the proportion of companies deciding against a Puerto Rican location. Eventually one should reach an equilibrium leaving no net inducement for plant migration to Puerto Rico. But at this equilibrium, will Puerto Rican wages be 5 per cent below competitive areas on the mainland, or 10 per cent below, or 20 per cent below? This is hard to estimate, and the answer will differ from one industry to another.

There has been no absolute retardation in the movement of industry into Puerto Rico. On the contrary, the number of new E.D.A.-sponsored plants established in the island has risen from 283 during the four-year period 1952-55 to 388 during 1956-59 and 511 during 1960-63. It seems likely that inflow of plants would have been even larger had wage increases been less rapid; but it is hard to test this hypothesis.

We can speak with more confidence about the reactions of plants already established in Puerto Rico. They responded with productivity-raising improvements which were sufficient to offset most of the higher wage costs. But the offset was not complete. Average annual profits for all E.D.A.-sponsored manufacturing plants, calculated as a percentage of owners' equity, varied in the range of 35 to 40 per cent up to 1956. As the pace of wage increases accelerated in the mid-'fifties, the annual profit rate declined until by the early 'sixties it was in the range of 25-30 per cent.[9] In some labor-intensive industries, such as the important foundation-garment industry, pretax profits in Puerto Rico have fallen to about the mainland level, leaving only the tax advantage to the Puerto Rican producers.

How were productivity increases accomplished? The aggregate statistics for the manufacturing sector are revealing. The period of accelerated wage increase seems to have brought little change in capital-output ratios.[10] But over the years 1954-61 both capital

9 Calculations based on data from Economic Development Administration. *Annual Statistical Report of EDA Manufacturing Plants*, successive editions through 1962.

10 For E.D.A.-sponsored manufacturing plants of assets of less than $1 million, capital employed per dollar of sales receipts was $0.90 in 1954 and $0.87 in 1960. For plants with assets above $1 million, the corresponding figures are $1.27 in 1954 and $1.23 in 1960.

per worker and output per worker approximately doubled. There was a sharp reduction in the use of labor relative to *both* capital and output. Management found ways of dispensing with labor and of getting greater output from those who remained.

Introduction of labor-saving machinery in response to wage increases does not seem to have been of major importance. It is true that in some of the older native firms, wage pressure has forced modernization of the entire plant, with a consequent increase in the amount of capital employed. But in mainland branch plants, the capital equipment was usually already of recent vintage. With a few notable exceptions, mainland firms establishing branch plants in Puerto Rico did not adopt production techniques different from those employed in mainland plants. Where exceptions were made, they were generally in the direction of more labor-intensive methods of materials handling. Thus the possibility of factor substitution was limited, and seems inadequate to explain more than a small part of the increase in capital-labor ratios.

What mainly happened was that personnel and production management were much improved over the years. Field investigation of 85 recently established manufacturing plants in Puerto Rico, carried out in the mid-'fifties as part of the Manpower Resources Project, revealed remarkable instances of inefficiency. Among the managers of mainland branch plants whom we interviewed, almost half had never before occupied a management position, and some had no industrial experience of any sort. First-line production supervisors had been chosen largely from the Puerto Rican population, often on the ground of fluency in English, which is scarcely a sufficient qualification. Workers were often carelessly selected, training methods were inadequate, standards of expected output were low, waste of materials and spoiled work were excessive, labor turnover and absenteeism were high. Even at this time one encountered some well-managed establishments which were approaching mainland productivity levels. But in others the feeling seemed to be that, with wage rates so low, one could scarcely avoid showing a profit.

Efficiency would doubtless have risen over the years through normal learning. But the rising wage level was a powerful stimulus to learning. Each time a minimum wage increase was impending, most managements reviewed their personnel policies and production standards to see what might be done to offset the higher wage; and usually something could be done. Managers and supervisors were replaced, job layout was improved, work crews were trimmed down to minimum size, waste of materials and products was reduced through better training and supervision, standards of expected output were raised, costs of turnover and absenteeism were lowered. There is apparently considerable interdependence between how much management expects workers to produce, how much they were willing to produce, and the level of their earnings. Workers on incentive systems, who would have resisted a simple increase in output standards, as a 'speed-up', offen accepted such an increase cheerfully when it was offset by a proportionate rise in their minimum wage.

Thus labor requirements per unit of product were reduced, not so much through larger capital inputs as through larger (or higher-quality) *inputs of management effort*. Anyone familiar with industry realizes that this is possible in some measure. The Puerto Rican experience dramatizes the magnitude of the productivity gains which can be achieved in this way during the early stage of industrialization.

It is not clear how one should rationalize this process in terms of production theory. If one defines the production function as embodying *median current practice*, one would have to say that the production possibilities frontier moved outward as the wage level rose. If on the other hand one defines the production function in terms of *best available techniques* (say, in this case, the performance of a superior mainland plant in the same industry), one would have to say that most Puerto Rican plants started off well within their production frontier and moved toward it as a result of wage pressure. (Some plants, of course, failed to adapt rapidly enough and passed out of existence.) Alternatively, one could define management as a separate input; but the difficulty of quantifying this input would be a serious bar to statistical analysis.

It would be interesting to know, not just that wage increases had a negative effect on employment, but the approximate size of this effect. So an attempt was made to estimate the elasticity of demand for labor in Puerto Rican manufacturing.[11] The procedure involved a basic assumption that, within each of the subperiods for which the elasticity was estimated (1949-54 and 1954-8), the production

11 The method used was devised by my colleague, Peter Gregory, who also supervised the statistical calculations. Both the method and the results are described in greater detail in the forthcoming volume.

function of the Puerto Rican manufacturing sector was homogeneous of degree one. This abstracts from economies of scale as well as from technical progress. Following from this assumption is the proposition that, given constant relative factor prices, the increase in output during a period should have been accompanied by a similar increase in employment. Failure of employment to expand by the same amount as output could then be attributed to a change in the relative price of labor.

The procedure followed involved regression analysis using Census of Manufactures data on employment, production worker wage payments, and value added for the years 1949, 1954, and 1958. A simple linear regression equation was used, in which employment foregone (the difference between the rate of change in output and the rate of change in employment) was held to be a function of the rate of change in the wage. The regression was fitted by least squares. Separate calculations were made for two periods, 1949-54 and 1954-8. These periods were presumed to be long enough to permit adjustment of production operations to any change in the price of labor. Cross-section data were used, covering 37 industries for the earlier period and 50 industries for the latter. The finest available classification was used, so that most industries, particularly for the latter period, were defined at the 4-digit level. The value-added data for 1949-54 were deflated by the appropriate wholesale price indexes; those for 1954-8 were not deflated in view of the slight variation of price over this period.

Solution of the regression equations yielded an elasticity estimate of — 1.137 for the period 1949-54, and — 0.939 for 1954-8, neither of these being significantly different from unit elasticity by the *t*-test. So a change in the wage could be expected to be associated with an approximately equal proportionate change of employment in the reverse direction.[12] The regression equations can also be used to estimate the amount of employment foregone as a result of wage increases. This procedure yields an estimated loss of about 9,000 jobs between 1949 and 1954, and of 29,000 jobs between 1954 and 1958, in the manufacturing sector alone. This amounts to more than 5 per cent of the island labor force. Since the wage advance

12 This conclusion, of course, does not mean that the manufacturing wage bill in Puerto Rico remained constant from 1949-58. This would have happened only if the demand curve for manufacturing labor had itself remained constant. But in fact the demand curve has been shifting upward rapidly as a result of new investment.

was general, there was presumably a sacrifice of employment in other sectors as well.

These findings must be interpreted with caution. The procedure tends in some ways to overestimate, and in other ways to underestimate, the employment effect of wage changes; and one cannot be certain which bias predominates in the results.

On the side of underestimation, we have taken no account of the fact that actual and anticipated wage increase may have deterred plants from locating in Puerto Rico. Our estimate of employment in the terminal year of each period at the base-year wage was based on *actual output* of goods rather than what output might have been in the absence of a rise in wages. Locational effects are thus excluded. We have already given reasons for thinking that these effects may have been substantial.

On the other hand, two factors may have led us to overestimate the association of wage and employment changes. We assumed a homogeneous production function in order to estimate potential employment at the base-year wage level. If the actual function yields increasing returns to scale, then we will have overestimated the amount of employment that should have been associated with the output of year 1, and hence the employment foregone as a result of the rise in the wage. Moreover, the assumption of a stable production function within each time period ignores the likelihood that even without wage shocks management would have achieved economies in the use of labor through normal learning.

It must be remembered also that the elasticity estimates are averages for all manufacturing. Elasticities in different Puerto Rican industries can be expected to vary widely because of differences in product market conditions and production functions. That these elasticities do vary widely has been recognized implicitly by Congressional reluctance to apply an across-the-board general wage minimum to Puerto Rico, and by the actions of the industry committees which have tried to weigh the probable effects of varying wage increase in different industries.

V *Unlimited Labor, Wages, and Employment*

Unlimited supply of labor has been and is a reality in Puerto Rico. Employers in the modern sector have never had serious difficulty in recruiting labor, and it has not taken long to transform raw recruits into competent industrial workers. This labor has come from the sources which Lewis enumerated: agriculture, trade, domestic service, other service industries, and new entrants to the labor force.

Employment has not expanded, however, along the constant real wage line in Figure 1. The wage level has been raised repeatedly, and this has stimulated management responses which have restricted the rise of employment.

The actual course of events may be interpreted with the aid of Figure 2. The industrial wage level at time t_0 is OW, the schedule of marginal labor productivity is MPL, and employment is OE. Suppose that by time t_1 there has been new industrial investment which, by itself, would shift the productivity schedule proportionately upward to MPL_2 and, with no change in wages, would result in employment of OE_3. Meanwhile, however, government has raised the wage level to OW_1. Labor supply is unlimited, as before, but it is unlimited at a higher real wage level. (An interesting feature of the Puerto Rican case is that raising money wages does raise real

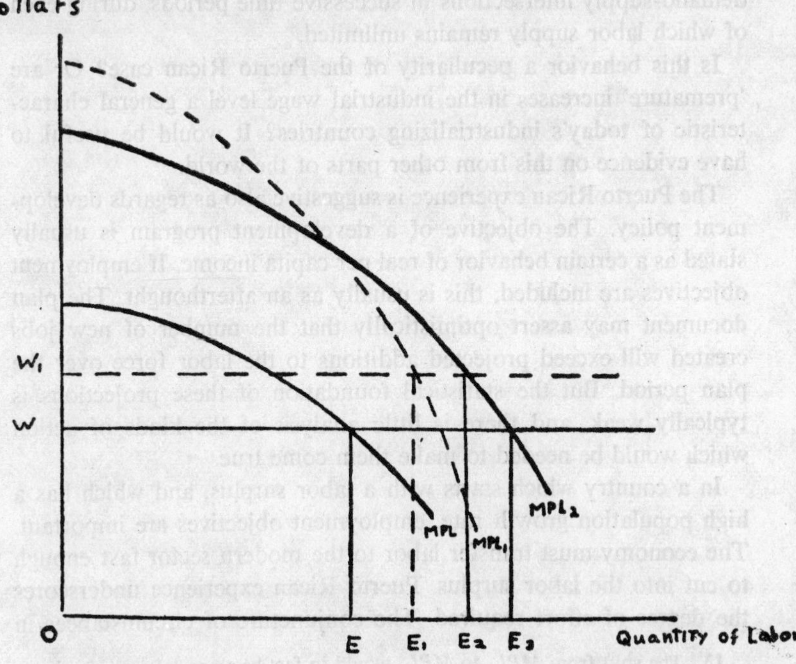

Figure 2

wages as well, since product prices are largely determined in the mainland market. This would not necessarily be true in a more closed economy.)

The wage increase stimulates management to make labor-saving innovations so that, with the investment of t_1, the labor productivity schedule is tilted to the position MPL_1.[13] The potential employment OE_3 is reduced on two counts. The wage increase alone would reduce it from OE_3 to OE_2; the labor-saving innovations cut it further to OE_1. Thus the substantial investment between t_0 and t_1 leads to only a slight increase in employment.

The upward shift of wages is repeated in the next time period, and similar management adjustments follow (Figure 3). Thus the wage-employment locus, instead of moving horizontally to the right along path I moves upward to the northeast along path II. If government wage policy is aggressive, and if management is very successful in saving labor, path II may be quite steep—large wage increases, small employment increases. Path II looks like a conventional upward-sloping labor-supply curve; but it is actually the locus of demand-supply intersections in successive time periods, during each of which labor supply remains unlimited.

Is this behavior a peculiarity of the Puerto Rican case? Or are 'premature' increases in the industrial wage level a general characteristic of today's industrializing countries? It would be useful to have evidence on this from other parts of the world.

The Puerto Rican experience is suggestive also as regards development policy. The objective of a development program is usually stated as a certain behavior of real per capita income. If employment objectives are included, this is usually as an afterthought. The plan document may assert optimistically that the number of new jobs created will exceed projected additions to the labor force over the plan period. But the statistical foundation of these projections is typically weak, and there is little analysis of the kinds of action which would be needed to make them come true.

In a country which starts with a labor surplus, and which has a high population growth rate, employment objectives are important. The economy must transfer labor to the modern sector fast enough to cut into the labor surplus. Puerto Rican experience underscores the degree of effort required. The conjuncture of circumstances in

13 The shift from MPL_2 to MPL_1 would in fact be a *very* labor-saving innovation in the Hicksian sense i.e. an innovation leading to reduced employment at the same wage level [*4*, Ch. 2] [*9*, Ch.3].

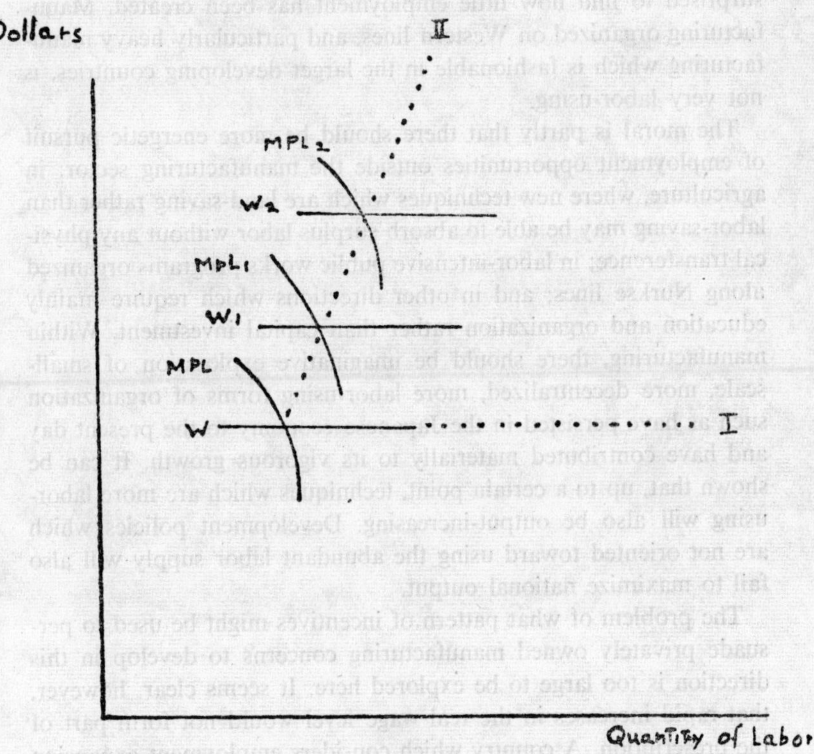

Figur e3

Puerto Rico since World War II has been unusually favorable, yet progress in reducing the labor surplus has been slow. In countries less favorably situated, such as India and Pakistan, the tide of surplus labor is rising and will continue to rise over the foreseeable future.

Development of modern factory-style manufacturing makes only a limited contribution to employment. The Puerto Rican industrial development program has been unusually vigorous and successful: but from 1952-62 the average annual increase of employment in E.D.A.-sponsored plants was about 5,000 a year. With present labor force participation rates, and in the absence of net emigration to the mainland, annual additions to the Puerto Rican labor force would be of the order of 40,000. One hears reports also from other countries which, after a decade or more of accelerated industrialization, are surprised to find how little employment has been created. Manufacturing organized on Western lines, and particularly heavy manufacturing which is fashionable in the larger developing countries, is not very labor-using.

The moral is partly that there should be more energetic pursuit of employment opportunities outside the manufacturing sector: in agriculture, where new techniques which are land-saving rather than labor-saving may be able to absorb surplus labor without any physical transference; in labor-intensive public works programs organized along Nurkse lines; and in other directions which require mainly education and organization rather than capital investment. Within manufacturing, there should be imaginative exploration of small-scale, more decentralized, more labor-using forms of organization such as have persisted in the Japanese economy to the present day and have contributed materially to its vigorous growth. It can be shown that, up to a certain point, techniques which are more labor-using will also be output-increasing. Development policies which are not oriented toward using the abundant labor supply will also fail to maximize national output.

The problem of what pattern of incentives might be used to persuade privately owned manufacturing concerns to develop in this direction is too large to be explored here. It seems clear, however, that rapid increases in the real wage level would not form part of the prescription. A country which considers employment expansion important should ponder the wisdom of raising the price of labor. Modern Western reasoning about wages, in which labor is taken as a scarce factor, may be quite misleading. Poor labor-surplus countries are still living in a classical world. Perhaps they should follow the classical route toward fuller employment.

REFERENCES

1 W. Baer, *The Puerto Rican Economy and United States Economic Fluctuations*. Barcelona 1962.

2 ———, 'Puerto Rico: An Evaluation of a Successful Development Program.' *Quart. Jour. Econ.*, Nov. 1959, *73*, pp. 645-71.

3 R. C. Griffith, *Factors Affecting Continental U. S. Manufacturing Investment in Puerto Rico*. Unpublished doctoral dissertation, Harvard Univ. 1961.

4 J. R. Hicks. *The Theory of Wages*. London 1932.

5 W. A. Lewis, 'Economic Development with Unlimited Supplies of Labour,' *Manchester School*, May 1954, *22*, pp. 139-91.

6 ———, 'Unlimited Labour: Further Notes,' *Manchester School*, Jan. 1958, *26*, pp. 1-32,

7 H. S. Perloff: *Puerto Rico's Economic Future: A Study in Planned Development*, Chicago 1950.

8 G. Ranis and J. C. Fei 'A Theory of Economic Development,' *Am. Econ. Rev.* Sept. 1961, *51*, pp. 533-65.

9 ———, *Development of the Labor-Surplus Economy: Theory and Policy*. Homewood 1964.

10 T. W. Schultz, *Transforming Traditional Agriculture*. New Haven 1964.

11 Puerto Rico Department of Labor, *Employment and Unemployment in Puerto Rico* (quarterly reports).

12 ———, *Median Weekly Earnings in Puerto Rico* (quarterly reports); and *Employment, Hours, and Earnings in Manufacturing Industries in Puerto Rico* (monthly reports).

13 Puerto Rico Economic Development Administration, *Annual Statistical Report of EDA Manufacturing Plants*.

14 Puerto Rico Planning Board, *Historical Statistics of Puerto Rico, 1959; Statistical Yearbook;* and *Economic Report to the Governor* (annual).

6

MIGRATION, UNEMPLOYMENT AND DEVELOPMENT: A TWO-SECTOR ANALYSIS

John R. Harris and Michael P. Todaro *

THROUGHOUT MANY less developed economies of the world, especially those of tropical Africa, a curious economic phenomenon is presently taking place. Despite the existence of positive marginal products in agriculture and significant levels of urban unemployment, rural-urban labor migration not only continues to exist, but indeed, appears to be accelerating. Conventional economic models with their singular dependence on the achievement of a full employment equilibrium through appropriate wage and price adjustments are hard put to provide rational behavioural explanations for these sizable and growing levels of urban unemployment in the absence of absolute labor redundancy in the economy as a whole. Moreover, this lack of an adequate analytical model to account for the unemployment phenomenon often leads to rather amorphous explanations such as the 'bright lights' of the city acting as a magnet to lure peasants into urban areas.

In this paper we shall diverge from the usual full employment, flexible wage-price models of economic analysis by formulating a two-sector model of rural-urban migration which, among other things, recognizes the existence of a politically determined minimum urban wage at levels substantially higher than agricultural earnings.[1]

We shall then consider the effect of this parametric urban wage on the rural individual's economic behavior when the assumption of

*The authors are assistant professors of economics, Massachusetts Institute of Technology and research fellow, Institute for Development Studies, University-College, Nairobi, respectively. They would like to thank the Rockefeller Foundation for making possible their research on economic problems of East Africa. Peter Diamond, Richard Eckaus, Joseph Stiglitz, two anonymous referees, and the managing editor made valuable comments on a previous draft. The authors, of course are responsible for remaining errors.

1 For some empirical evidence on the magnitude of these real earnings differentials in less developed economies, see Reynolds, Berg, Henderson, and Ghai.

no agricultural labor surplus is made, i.e., that the agricultural marginal product is always positive and inversely related to the size of the rural labor force.[2] The distinguishing feature of this model is that migration proceeds in response to urban-rural differences in *expected earnings* (defined below) with the urban employment rate acting as an equilibrating force on such migration.[3] We shall then use the overall model for the following purposes:

1) to demonstrate that given this politically determined high minimum wage, the continued existence of rural-urban migration in spite of substantial overt urban unemployment represents an economically rational choice on the part of the individual migrant;

2) to show that economists' standard policy prescription of generating urban employment opportunities through the use of 'shadow prices' implemented by means of wage subsidies or direct government hiring will *not* necessarily lead to a welfare improvement and may, in fact, exacerbate the problem of urban unemployment;

3) to evaluate the welfare implications of alternative policies associated with various back-to-the-land programs when it is recognized that the standard remedy suggested by economic theory—namely, full wage flexibility—is for all practical purposes politically infeasible. Special attention will be given here to the impact of migration cum unemployment on the welfare of the rural sector as a whole which gives rise to intersectoral compensation requirements; and, finally,

4) to argue that in the absence of wage flexibility, an optimal policy is, in fact, a 'policy package' including *both* partial wage subsidies (or direct government employment) and measures to restrict free migration.

2 We do not make the special assumption of an agricultural labor surplus for the following reasons: Most available empirical evidence to date tends to cast doubt on the labor surplus argument in the context of those economies of Southeast Asia and Latin America where such a surplus would be most likely to exist (see Kao, Anschel, and Eicher). Moreover, few if any economists would seriously argue that general labor surplus exists in tropical Africa, the area to which this paper is most directly related.

3 For a dynamic model of labor migration in which urban unemployment rates and expected incomes play a pivotal role in the migration process, see Todaro. However, unlike the present model which attempts to view the migration process in context of aggregate and intersectoral welfare considerations, Todaro's model was strictly concerned with the formulation of a positive theory of urban unemployment in developing nations. As such, it did not specifically consider the welfare of the rural sector, nor was it concerned with the broader issues of economic policy considered in the present paper.

I The Basic Model

The basic model which we shall employ can be described as a two-sector internal trade model with unemployment. The two sectors are the permanent urban and the rural. For analytical purposes we shall distinguish between sectors from the point of view of production and income. The urban sector specializes in the production of a manufactured good, part of which is exported to the rural sector in exchange for agricultural goods. The rural sector has a choice of either using all available labor to produce a single agricultural good, some of which is exported to the urban sector, *or* using only part of its labor to produce this good while *exporting* the remaining labor to the urban sector in return for wages paid in the form of the manufactured good. We are thus assuming that the typical migrant retains his ties to the rural sector and, therefore, the income that he earns as an urban worker will be considered, from the standpoint of sectoral welfare, as accruing to the rural sector.[4] However, this assumption is not at all necessary for our demonstration of the rationality of migration in the face of significant urban unemployment.

The crucial assumption to be made in our model is that rural-urban migration will continue so long as the *expected* urban real income at the margin exceeds real agricultural product—i.e., prospective rural migrants behave as maximizers of *expected* utility. For analytical purposes, we shall assume that the total urban labor force consists of a permanent urban proletariat without ties to the rural sector plus the available supply of rural migrants. From this combined pool or urban labor, we assume that a periodic *random job selection process* exists whenever the number of available jobs is exceeded by the number of job seekers.[5] Consequently, the expected

4 In tropical Africa especially, this notion that migrants retain their ties to the rural sector is quite common and manifested by the phenomenon of the extended family system and the flow of remittances to rural relatives of large proportions of urban earnings. However, the reverse flow, i.e., rural-urban monetary transfers is also quite common in cases where the migrant is temporarily unemployed and, therefore, must be supported by rural relatives. For an excellent discussion of this penomenon from a sociological point of view, see Gugler (pp. 475-8).

5 The qualitative conclusions of the model do not depend on the precise nature of the selection process. We have assumed random selection not merely for analytic convenience but also because it directly corresponds to an appropriate dynamic construct developed in Todaro's 1969 article. There it is shown that over time expected and actual earnings will converge to a positive number even though the rate of job creation is less than the rate of migration so that unemployment is increasing. It is interesting to note in this context that sociologist Gugler who has spent considerable time studying labor migration in Africa has recently concluded

urban wage will be defined as equal to the fixed minimum wage (expressed in terms of manufactured goods) times the proportion of the urban labor force actually employed (see equation (6)). Finally, we assume perfectly competitive behavior on the part of producers in both sectors with the further simplifying assumption that the price of the agricultural good (defined in terms of manufactured goods) is determined directly by the relative quantities of the two goods produced.

Consider now the following formulation of the model.

Agricultural Production Function:

(1) $$X_A = q(N_A, \bar{L}, \bar{K}_A), \qquad q' > 0, \; q'' < 0$$

where,

X_A is output of the agricultural good, N_A is the rural labor used to produce this output, $\bar{L}$ is the fixed availability of land, $\bar{K}_A$ is the fixed capital stock, q' is the derivative of q with respect of N_A, its only variable factor.

Manufacturing Production Function:

(2) $$X_M = f(N_M, \bar{K}_M), \qquad f' > 0, \; f'' < 0$$

where

X_M is the output of the manufactured good, N_M is the total labor (urban and rural migrant) required to produce this output. $\bar{K}_M$ is fixed capital stock, and f' is the derivative of f with respect to N_M, its only variable factor.

Price Determination:

(3) $$P = \rho\left(\frac{X_M}{X_A}\right), \qquad \rho' > 0$$

where

P, the price of the agricultural good in terms of the manufactured good, (i.e., the terms of trade) is a function of the relative outputs of

that rural-urban migration is essentially an economic phenomenon that can be portrayed as a 'game of lottery' in which rural migrants come to the city fully aware that their chances of finding a job are low. However, the great disparity between urban and rural wages makes the successful location of an urban salaried job so attractive that unskilled migrants are willing to take a chance (pp. 472-3). See also Hutton.

agricultural and manufactured good when the latter services as numeraire.[6]

Agricultural Real Wage Determination:

$$(4) \qquad W_A = P.q'$$

where

W_A, the agricultural real wage, is equal to the value of labor's marginal product in agriculture expressed in terms of the manufactured good.

Manufacturing Real Wage:

$$(5) \qquad W_M = f' \geqq \overline{W}_M.$$

The real wage in manufacturing, expressed in terms of manufactured goods, is equated with the marginal product of labor in manufacturing because of profit maximization on the part of perfectly competitive producers. However, this wage is constrained to be greater than or equal to the fixed minimum urban wage. In our analysis, we shall be dealing only with cases in which $f' = \overline{W}_M$ (i.e., there is never an excess demand for labor at the minimum wage).

Urban Expected Wage:

$$(6) \qquad W_u^e = \frac{\overline{W}_M N_M}{N_u}, \qquad \frac{N_M}{N_u} \leq 1,$$

Where the *expected* real wage in the urban sector, $W\epsilon_u$, is equal to the real minimum wage $\overline{W}_M$ adjusted for the proportion of the total urban labor force (permanent urban plus migrants, denoted as N_u) actually employed, N_M/N_u.[7] Only in the case of full employment in the urban sector ($N_M = Nu$) is the expected wage equal to the minimum wage (i.e., $W_u^\epsilon = \overline{W}_M$).

6 A sufficient, but not necessary, condition for this assumption is that all individuals in the economy have the same homothetic preference map. Again, the assumption is made for analytical convenience. The qualitative conclusions of our analysis will remain unaffected under several plausible assumptions about distribution of income and tastes.

7 This assumes a very particular form of wage expectation, namely that the expected wage is equal to the average urban wage. Although this is a convenient expression to work with, we could be more general and make the expected wage some function of the average urban wage. Indeed, the only restrictions on such a function that are necessary for our results are that, *ceteris paribus*, the expected wage varies directly with the minimum wage and inversely with the unemployment rate.

Labor Endowment:

(7) $$N_A + N_u = \overline{N}_R + \overline{N}_u = \overline{N}$$

There is a *labor constraint* which states that the sum of workers actually employed in the agricultural sector (N_A) plus the total urban labor force (N_u) must equal the sum of initial endowments of rural ($\overline{N}_R$) and permanent urban ($\overline{N}_u$) labor which in turn equals the total labor endowment ($\overline{N}$).

Equilibrium Condition:

(8) $$W_A = W_u^\epsilon$$

Equation (8), an equilibrium condition, is derived from the hypothesis that migration to the urban area is a positive function of the urban-rural *expected* wage differential. This can be written formally as

(9) $$\dot{N}_u = \psi\left(\frac{\overline{W}_M N_M}{N_u} - P.q'\right), \quad \psi' > 0, \quad \psi(0) = 0$$

where $\dot{N}_u$ is a time derivative. Clearly then, migration will cease only when the expected income differential is zero, the condition posited in (8).[8] It is important to note that this assumes that a migrant gives up only his marginal product.[9]

We thus have 8 equations in 8 unknowns X_A, X_M, N_A, N_M, W_A, W_u^ϵ, Nu and P. Given the production functions and fixed minimum wage $\overline{W}_M$, it is possible to solve for sectoral employment, the equilibrium unemployment rate and, consequently, the equilibrium expected wage, relative output levels and terms of trade. Let us analyze how such an unemployment equilibrium can come about.

8 $\psi(0)=0$ is purely arbitrary. If, instead, we assume $\psi(\alpha)=0$ where α can take on any value, migration will cease when the urban-rural expected wage differential is equal to α. None of the subsequent analysis is affected qualitatively by specifying $\alpha=0$. Equation (8) would merely be written as $W_A+\alpha=W_u^\epsilon$.

9 Other assumptions could be made. Much of the literature has stressed that in peasant economies producers receive their average product which is higher than their marginal product. Indeed, this is at the heart of the well-known Lewis and Fei-Ranis models. However, these models ignore the migration decision and seem to assume that migrants continue to receive their share of peasant production yet migrate only if jobs are actually available. In much of Africa it appears that migrants continue to receive income from land after migration and commonly hire labor to work on their farms in their absence. There is also a considerable group of landless individuals who work on farms for wages. Thus it would appear that our assumption is not unreasonable. The analysis could easily be modified to make earnings foregone equal to average product, however.

The essence of our argument is that in many developing nations the existence of an institutionally determined urban minimum wage at levels substantially higher than that which the free market would allow can, and usually does, lead to an equilibrium with considerable urban unemployment. In our model migration is a disequilibrium phenomenon. In equilibrium $\overline{W}_M N_M/N_u = P_q'$ and migration ceases. (See Appendix I for proof that this equilibrium is stable.) Now we know from equation (5) that in the competitive urban manufacturing sector, $\overline{W}_M = f'$. We also know from equation (7) that $\overline{N} - N_A = N_u$ and from equation (3) that $P = \rho(X_M/X_A)$. Therefore, we can rewrite our equilibrium condition (8) as

$$(8') \qquad \Phi = \rho(X_M/X_A)q' - \frac{f'N_M}{\overline{N} - N_A} = 0.$$

Since X_M and X_A are functions of N_M and N_A respectively Φ is an implicit function in N_A and N_M which, for any stated minimum wage, can be solved for the equilibrium combination of agricultural and manufacturing employment. From this solution the levels of urban unemployment and commodity outputs can also be determined. There will be a unique equilibrium associated with each possible value of the minimum wage, and the locus of these equilibria is plotted in Figure 1 as the line $\Phi = 0$ in N_A, N_M space.[10] The line $N_A + N_M = \overline{N}$ in Figure 1 is the locus of full employment points.

10 In Figure 1 we have assumed that $\frac{dN_A}{dN_M} = -\,[\Phi_{N_M}/\Phi_{N_A}] > 0$ although this need not necessarily hold true. Differentiating (8′) partially with respect to N_A we find that

$$\Phi_{N_A} = \frac{-\rho' f q'^2}{q^2} + \rho q'' - \frac{\rho q'}{\overline{N} - N_A}$$

which is unambiguously negative since $q'' < 0$ and $p' > 0$. Differentiating (8′) partially with respect to N_M we find that

$$\Phi_{N_M} = \frac{1}{\eta_{LW}} - \eta_P \frac{f'N_M}{X_M} + 1$$

which is less than, equal to, or greater than zero as

$$-\frac{1}{\eta_{LW}} + \eta_P \frac{f'N_M}{X_M} \gtreqless 1,$$

where

$$\eta_{LW} = -\frac{dN_M}{d\overline{W}_u} \cdot \frac{\overline{W}_u}{N_M}$$

is the wage elasticity of demand for labor and

$$\eta_P = \frac{dP}{d\left(\frac{X_M}{X_A}\right)} \cdot \frac{X_M/X_A}{P}$$

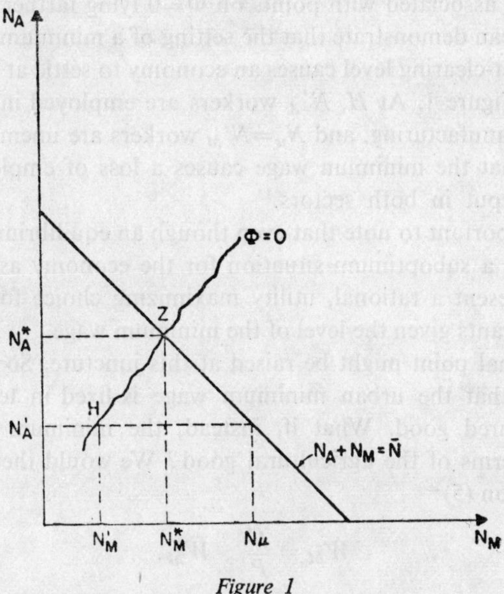

Figure 1

Point Z is the only equilibrium full-employment point in Figure 1 at which $N_M{}^*$ workers would be employed in manufacturing and $N_A{}^*$ in agriculture. Points on the locus $\Phi=0$ east of Z are infeasible and will not be considered further, while points to the west of Z are associated with minimum wages higher than the full-employment wage. There is a monotonic mapping such that higher minimum

is the elasticity of the terms of trade with respect to a change in relative outputs. It follows, therefore that the slope of the locus of equilibria, dN_A/dN_M depends on the respective employment and price elasticities.

A sufficient condition for Φ_{NM} to be negative (making dN_A/dN_M positive) is for the wage elasticity of employment to be less than one, a situation which recent empirical studies suggest is likely to exist (see Erickson, Harris and Todaro (1969), and Katz). However, even if η_{LW} exceeds unity, dN_A/dN_M can still be positive providing price elasticity is sufficiently high. The logic of these conditions is clear. If η_{LW} is less than one, a decline in the minimum wage will lower the urban wage bill even though employment and output increase. This causes the expected urban wage to decline thereby reducing the expected rural-urban earnings differential which gives rise to reverse migration and increased rural employment and output. If nLW exceeds unity, a fall in the minimum wage is accompanied by an increased urban wage bill and, hence, a higher expected urban wage. However, the expected rural-urban earnings differential can either increase or decrease in this case depending on the movement in terms of trade which raises the value of the marginal product in agriculture. For example, if η_{LW} were 1.5 and the wage share of manufacturing output $(f'N_M/X_M)$ were .50, then an agricultural price elasticity greater than 0.67 would be sufficient to make dN_A/dN_M positive.

wages are associated with points on $\Phi=0$ lying farther to the west. Thus we can demonstrate that the setting of a minimum wage above the market-clearing level causes an economy to settle at a point such as H in Figure 1. At H, N'_A workers are employed in agriculture, N'_M in manufacturing, and $N_u = N'_M$ workers are unemployed. It is evident that the minimum wage causes a loss of employment and hence output in both sectors.[11]

It is important to note that even though an equilibrium at point H represents a suboptimum situation for the economy as a whole, it does represent a rational, utility maximizing choice for individual rural migrants given the level of the minimum wage.

One final point might be raised at this juncture. So far we have assumed that the urban minimum wage is fixed in terms of the manufactured good. What if, instead, the minimum wage were fixed in terms of the agricultural good? We would then substitute for equation (5):

$$(5') \qquad W_M = \frac{f'}{P} \geqq \overline{W}_M.$$

Substituting (4), (5′), and (6) into (8) we get the equilibrium relationship

$$(11) \qquad Pq' = \frac{\left(\frac{f'}{P}\right).N_M}{N_u}.$$

We can then imagine an economy starting initially at the point on the production possibilities frontier at which X_M is that for which equation (5′) is satisfied and assume that

$$Pq' < \frac{\left(\frac{\overline{f'}}{P}\right).N_M}{N_u}$$

at that point. The equilibrium point will again be reached through a simultaneous raising of Pq' and lowering of W_u^e in response to migration. As relative agricultural output falls, P will rise. This in turn will cause output of the manufactured good to fall

11 If $dN_A/dN_M<0$, which we believe to be empirically unlikely, this statement would have to be modified. In such a case, increasing the minimum wage will decrease manufacturing employment but will increase agricultural employment and output. Unemployment will result from the imposition of a minimum wage but we can no longer assert that the level of unemployment will increase concomitantly with the level of the minimum wage.

as well, since producers will produce up to the point that $f' = \overline{\overline{W}}_M P$ which rises in terms of the manufactured good. Note that f' can be raised only through output restriction (since $f''<0$). Therefore in general, we would find that imposition of a minimum wage gives rise to an equilibrium characterized by unemployment and loss of potential output of both goods. A new locus $\Phi'=0$ will be defined in Figure 1 such that the point on Φ' corresponding to any given minimum wage will be west of the corresponding point on Φ.

Although our initial assumption is a bit easier to handle, the principal conclusion remains unaffected if we make the minimum wage fixed in terms of the agricultural good. Equilibrium is only achievable with unemployment. Actual minimum wage setting is usually done with reference to some general cost of living index, and food is the largest single item in the budget of most urban workers. (See Massell and Heyer, and the Nigeria report.) Hence, the second case may be somewhat more realistic. Note that in the first case the 'true' real wage was reduced somewhat by the rising agricultural price, while in the latter case it is increased by the falling relative price of the manufactured good.

III Implications For Development Policy

A. Planning in Terms of Shadow Prices

The standard solution to the problem of an institutionally determined wage that is higher than the equilibrium level is to employ labor in the public sector according to a shadow wage and/or to grant a payroll subsidy to private employers that equates private costs with this shadow wage.[12] Two main problems arise with this prescription: first, how can one determine the appropriate shadow wage? and, secondly, what are the implications of executing such a scheme when the institutional wage will continue to be paid to the employed? Our model can shed light on both of these issues.

12 Hagen (p. 498) states, 'a subsidy per unit of labor equal to the wage differential [between agriculture and industry] will increase real income further [than a tariff] and if combined with free trade will permit attaining an *optimum optimorum.*' Bardhan (p. 379) similarly adds. 'The best remedy for the misallocation caused by a wage differential is... an appropriate subsidy to the use of labor in the manufacturing industry.' It is important to recall that this argument is dependent on variable proportions production functions. If production coefficients are fixed, a wage subsidy will have no effect in the short run. The classic statement of this case is by Eckaus. Bardhan explores its implications for subsidy in a dynamic context. Both of these papers, however, posit surplus labor in agriculture, an assumption we do not wish to make in an African context.

In a static framework the appropriate shadow wage is the opportunity cost of labor hired by the industrial sector. Hence, if labor is hired to the point that its marginal product in industry is equated with the shadow wage which in turn is equated with the marginal product in agriculture, marginal productivity of labor will be equal in both sectors, a necessary condition for an optimal allocation of resources. Naturally, this assumes a positive marginal product in agriculture and sufficient factor mobility to ensure full employment of labor. The existence of urban unemployment, however, suggests that there may be a pool of labor that can be tapped without sacrificing output. Consequently, it might be suggested that even though agricultural labor is fully employed at peak seasons, the appropriate shadow wage for urban labor is likely to be one that is lower than the marginal product in agriculture. This would be correct if the two labor forces, urban and rural, were separate noncompeting groups. In linear programming terms, there are two labor constraints and each may well have a different associated shadow wage.

Now, the essence of our model is that the two sectors *are* intimately connected through labor migration. If one additional job is created in the industrial sector at the minimum wage, the expected wage will rise and rural-urban migration will be induced. In Appendix II it is shown that more than one agricultural worker will likely migrate in response to the creation of one additional industrial job. Hence, the opportunity cost of an industrial worker will exceed the marginal product of an agricultural worker. On the other hand, an increase in agricultural income will induce reverse migration with no diminution of industrial output. Thus, the opportunity cost of labor is lower to the agricultural than to the industrial sector!

The literature has been strangely silent for the most part about the full implications of using shadow-wage criteria. In a static context, Stolper has pointed out that financing subsidies or losses of public enterprises gives rise to fiscal problems, but unfortunately this issue has not yet been pursued in sufficient detail.[13] If the problem is considered at all, the analyst usually assumes that a system of non-distorting lump-sum taxes is available. Little, Lefeber, and Little and Mirrlees have pointed out that in a dynamic setting, the extra

13 Lefeber assumes that a wage subsidy can be financed by a profits tax, while other writers, e.g. Hagen, Bardhan, and Chakravarty never even consider the problem. Even Little and Mirrlees who present an excellent discussion of how to calculate a shadow wage never mention the fiscal problems of implementation.

consumption arising from payment of the institutional wage diverts resources from investment to consumption; thus some of the foregone future consumption should be considered in calculating the shadow wage. In our model, payment of the minimum wage to additional industrial workers will induce more rural-urban migration. Therefore, implementation of a shadow-wage employment criterion will have important effects on the level of agricultural output and on urban unemployment. The argument can be clarified with reference to Figure 2.

The initial equilibrium, given the minimum wage, is at point *D* with output of the manufactured good restricted to OX_M^*. If individuals did not migrate in response to expected wage differentials,

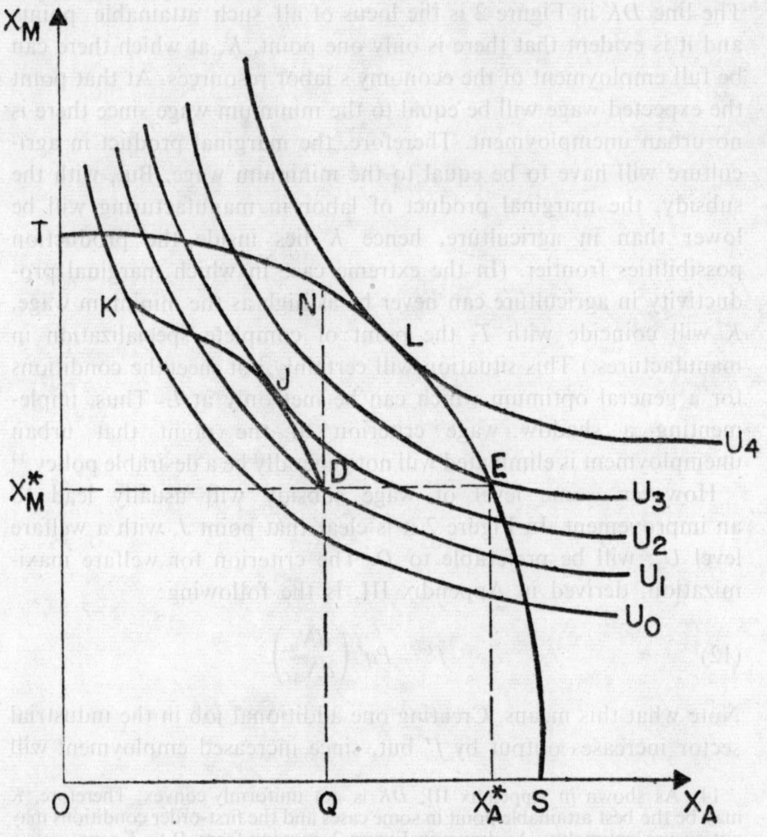

Figure 2

the economy could produce at point E, but migration reduces agricultural output to the level OQ. The theory of shadow pricing suggests that with an appropriate wage subsidy (or public-sector hiring rule) the economy could move to point L on the production possibilities frontier which, with the posited social indifference map, is the optimum position. Welfare would be increased from a level U, to a higher level U_4.

In the context of our model, such a point is unattainable. The effect of implementing a shadow wage will be to increase production of the manufactured good. But creation of an additional job at the minimum wage will induce some additional migration (see Appendix II) from the rural sector and therefore agricultural output will fall. Hence, movement from D can only be in a northwest direction. The line DK in Figure 2 is the locus of all such attainable points and it is evident that there is only one point, K, at which there can be full employment of the economy's labor resources. At that point the expected wage will be equal to the minimum wage since there is no urban unemployment. Therefore, the marginal product in agriculture will have to be equal to the minimum wage. But, with the subsidy, the marginal product of labor in manufacturing will be lower than in agriculture, hence K lies inside the production possibilities frontier. (In the extreme case in which marginal productivity in agriculture can never be as high as the minimum wage, K will coincide with T, the point of complete specialization in manufactures.) This situation will certainly not meet the conditions for a general optimum which can be met only at L. Thus, implementing a shadow wage criterion to the point that urban unemployment is eliminated will not generally be a desirable policy.[14]

However, some level of wage subsidy will usually lead to an improvement. In Figure 2 it is clear that point J, with a welfare level U_2, will be preferable to D. The criterion for welfare maximization, derived in Appendix III, is the following:

$$f' = Pq'\left(\frac{dN_u}{dN_M}\right) \tag{12}$$

Note what this means. Creating one additional job in the industrial sector increases output by f' but, since increased employment will

14 As shown in Appendix III, DK is not uniformly convex. Therefore, K may be the best attainable point in some cases and the first-order conditions may not ensure optimality. As drawn in Figure 2, moving from D to K represents a worsening of welfare, but this clearly is not a necessary conclusion.

raise the expected urban wage, migration will be induced in an amount dN_u/dN_M. The right-hand side of equation (12) states the amount of agricultural output sacrificed because of migration. Thus the shadow wage will be equal to this opportunity cost of an urban job and the amount of subsidy will be $\overline{W}_M - f'$. So long as $f' > Pq'(dN_u/dN_M)$, aggregate welfare can be increased by expanding industrial employment through subsidy or public sector hiring. Clearly the more responsive is migration to industrial employment, the higher is the social cost of industrialization and the smaller is the optimal amount of subsidy. In many African economies it is likely that dN_u/dN_M exceeds unity. If so, it will be optimal for the marginal product of labor in industry to be higher than in agriculture and urban unemployment will be a persistent phenomenon so long as minimum wages are set above a market-clearing level.

The discussion so far has ignored two other adverse effects of using a shadow wage. As mentioned earlier, several writers have noted that payment of a subsidized minimum wage to additional workers will increase total consumption, thereby reducing the level of resources available for investment. If foregone future consumption is positively valued, the opportunity cost of industrial labor will be higher than indicated in equation (12) and the shadow wage will be raised correspondingly. Furthermore, wage subsidies of public enterprise losses must be financed and if revenue cannot be raised through costless lump-sum taxes, the opportunity cost of raising taxes must be considered. Both of these effects will reduce the desirable amount of subsidized job creation in the industrial sector.

It is interesting to note that this model implies different opportunity costs of labor to the two sectors. While the creation of an additional job in the urban area reduces agricultural output through induced migration, additional employment can be generated in the agricultural sector without reducing manufacturing output. If this phenomenon is not taken into account, standard application of investment criteria is likely to be biased in favor of urban projects.

B. Migration Restriction

An alternative approach to the problem of urban unemployment is to physically control migration from the rural areas. Such controls have recently been introduced in Tanzania and have been used for some time in South Africa.[15] Other countries, such as Kenya, are giving serious consideration to instituting such a policy. Although we personally have grave reservations about the ethical issues involved in such a restriction of individual choice and the complexity and arbitrariness of administration, it seems desirable to investigate the economic implications of such a policy.

Looking at Figure 2 it is obvious that with the minimum wage such that industrial output is OX_M^*, prohibition of migration in excess of the labor required to produce that output will allow the economy to produce at point E. The movement from D to E arising from restriction of migration leads to an unambiguous aggregate welfare improvement providing appropriate lump-sum redistribution is effected. Since such compensation is notoriously difficult to carry out in practice, it will be useful to examine the welfare implications of such a move on each of the two sectors in the absence of compensation.

Recall that the two sectors were defined to be a permanent urban group and a rural sector that produces both agricultural goods and exports labor to the urban area in exchange for wages in the form of manufactured goods.[16] In Figure 3 the line $T'S'$ represents production possibilities for the agricultural sector when labor export is allowed. If its entire labor endowment is devoted to agricultural production, it can produce a quantity OS'. However, by exporting its labor, the agricultural sector can 'produce' the manufactured good (wages are paid in the form of this good). Hence this production possibilities frontier depends on market forces (wage levels and unemployment) as well as on purely technological factors. The amount of agricultural output foregone if a unit of labor is to be 'exported' is its marginal product; the amount

15 See Harris and Todaro (1969) for an analysis of the Tanzanian program.

16 In considering the welfare of the rural sector as a whole we are making the tacit assumption that there is redistribution of goods between individuals in this sector. This is a very strong assumption. Yet there is considerable evidence from tropical Africa that employed urban migrants repatriate substantial portions of their earnings to their kinsmen remaining in the rural areas and conversely that income both in cash and kind is received by unemployed migrants from kinsmen remaining on the farm. To the extent that the extended family system does redistribute goods between members, this assumption may be tenable as a first approximation. As Gugler (p. 480) has pointed out, is it appropriate to view the extended family as maximizing its income by allocating its members between agriculture and urban wage employment. Although there is some evidence that growing numbers of urban workers are settling permanently and gradually eliminating rural ties, it will be many years before such ties are completely severed.

of manufactured goods obtained by the exported labor unit depends on the wage, the amount of employment obtained by the exported unit, and its effect on employment of previously exported units.

In addition to these production possibilities, the rural sector also has the opportunity to trade some of its agricultural output with the permanent urban sector in exchange for manufactured goods.

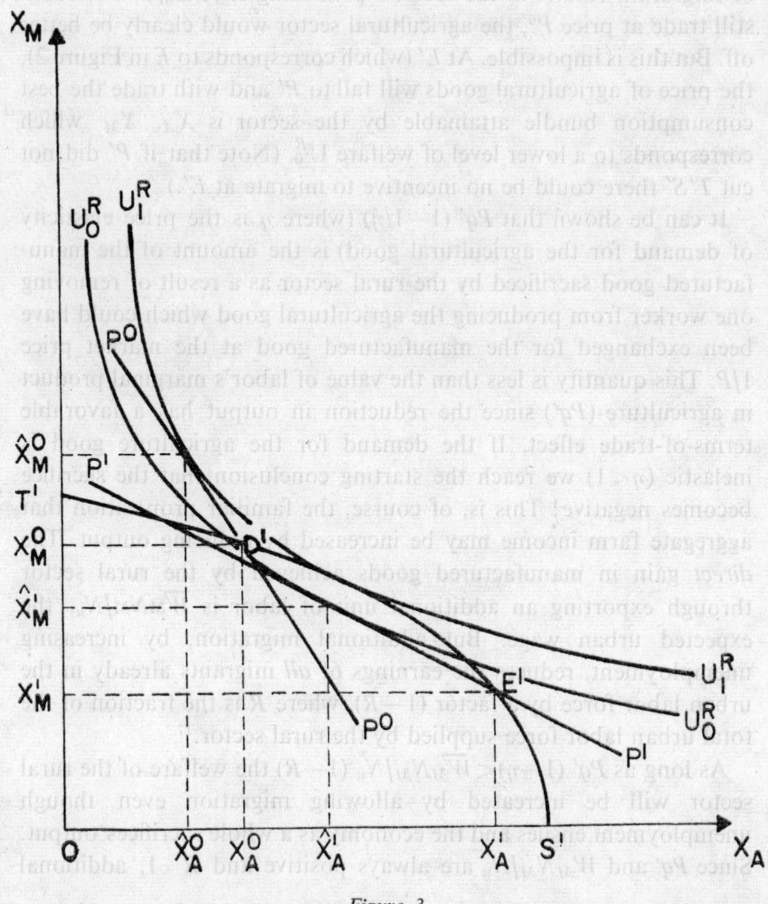

Figure 3

Corresponding to each point on the production possibilities frontier $T'S'$ there is a determinate price of the agricultural good. The manner in which alternative constellations of production and trade affect the sector's welfare can be illustrated by Figure 3.

D' corresponds to the initial unemployment equilibrium D (Figure 2). At that point the rural sector as a whole 'produces' $X_A{}^0$ and $X_M{}^0$ of the two goods. It also has the opportunity to trade at the price P^0. By trading some of its agricultural output to the permanent urban sector for additional manufactured goods, it consumes $X_A{}^0$, $X_M{}^0$ and achieves a welfare level of U^R_1. Restriction of migration results in the sector's producing X_A; X_M;. If it could still trade at price P^0, the agricultural sector would clearly be better off. But this is impossible. At E' (which corresponds to E in Figure 2), the price of agricultural goods will fall to P' and with trade the best consumption bundle attainable by the sector is X_A', X_M' which corresponds to a lower level of welfare U^R_0. (Note that if P' did not cut $T'S'$ there could be no incentive to migrate at E'.)

It can be shown that Pq' $(1—1/\eta)$ (where η is the price elasticity of demand for the agricultural good) is the amount of the manufactured good sacrificed by the rural sector as a result of removing one worker from producing the agricultural good which could have been exchanged for the manufactured good at the market price $1/P$. This quantity is less than the value of labor's marginal product in agriculture (Pq') since the reduction in output has a favorable terms-of-trade effect. If the demand for the agriculture good is inelastic ($\eta<1$) we reach the starting conclusion that the sacrifice becomes negative! This is, of course, the familiar proposition that aggregate farm income may be increased by reducing output. The *direct* gain in manufactured goods achieved by the rural sector through exporting an additional unit of labor is $\overline{W}_M N_M/N_u$, the expected urban wage. But additional migration, by increasing unemployment, reduces the earnings of *all* migrants already in the urban labor force by a factor $(1—R)$, where R is the fraction of the total urban labor force supplied by the rural sector.[17]

As long as Pq' $(1—\eta)<\overline{W}_M N_M/N_u$ $(1—R)$ the welfare of the rural sector will be increased by allowing migration even though unemployment ensues and the economy as a whole sacrifices output. Since Pq' and $W_M N_M/N_u$ are always positive and $R\leqslant 1$, additional

17 If urban unemployment was experienced only by migrants, this term would equal zero since the total amount of earnings through labor export would be constant. It can be positive only because the permanent urban labor force shares in unemployment, thereby reducing its share of the constant wage bill in the manufactured good industry. An interesting extension of the model would be to incorporate different employment probabilities for the permanent urban and migrant rural labor forces and then to check the sensitivity of results with our more simplified assumption of equal probabilities.

migration will always benefit the rural sector when $\eta < 1$. In general the lower is Pq', η, or R and the higher is $W_M N_M / N_u$, the more will the rural sector benefit from the opportunity to migrate.

From the foregoing, one can conclude that although migration restriction will improve aggregate welfare of the economy, given plausible values of n and R, substantial compensation to the rural sector will be required if it is not to be made worse off by removing the opportunity for free migration. The permanent urban labor force clearly will be made better off by becoming fully employed at the high minimum wage while also being able to buy food at a lower price. Each unit of labor exported by the rural sector will similarly earn more but this gain will be offset by reduced total labor exports and lower agricultural prices. Whether or not this will be true depends, of course, on the values of the specific parameters of the economy. If n is sufficiently high, the rural sector could be made better off by restricting migration in the absence of compensation, but this seems very unlikely.

C. A Combination of Policies

It has been shown that either a limited wage-subsidy or a migration-restriction policy will lead to a welfare improvement. Which of the two policies will lead to the better position cannot be determined without knowing all the relevant parameters for a particular economy. It is clear, however, that neither policy alone is capable of moving the economy to the optimum that could be achieved with competitive wage determination (point L in Figure 2).

At first sight it may seem strange that with a single market failure the wage level, a single policy instrument is unable to fully correct the situation.[18] The reason is that the wage performs two functions in this model. It determines *both* the level of employment in the industrial sector *and* the allocation of labor between rural and urban areas. While a subsidy changes the effective wage for determination of industrial employment, so long as the wage actually received by workers exceeds agricultural earnings there will be migration and urban unemployment. Restriction of migration prevents the minimum wage having its effect on unemployment but does nothing to increase the level of industrial employment. Therefore, if the optimum position is to be achieved, a combination of both instruments will have to be used. In order to reach point L

18 We wish to thank a referee of this *Review* for drawing this to our attention.

a wage subsidy must be instituted such that industrial employment will increase to the extent that with full employment the marginal product of labor will be equal in manufacturing and agriculture. The subsidy will be positive and equal to the difference between the minimum wage and marginal productivity. At the point $W_u^e = \overline{W}_M$ and $\overline{W}_M > Pq'$. Therefore, individuals would still find it in their interest to migrate and the point will not be attainable unless migration is restricted.

The agricultural sector has to be better off at L than at E since each additional unit of labor exported earns the full minimum wage, marginal productivity in agriculture is less than the minimum wage, and the price of the agricultural good rises. Whether the agricultural sector is better off at L than at D, however, depends again on the parametric values of the model.[19] It can be stated with certainty that the amount of compensation needed to make the rural sector *no worse off* than at D will be less at L than at E, and, furthermore it should be easier to finance since total income is greater.

Even so the fiscal requirements, of subsidy (or public enterprise losses) and compensation cannot be taken lightly.[20] A government may find it difficult to find nondistorting taxes capable of raising sufficient revenue. Perhaps a head-tax on all urban residents would be feasible although this too raises the question of how minimum wages are set (unions in tropical Africa, have in some cases, successfully fought to maintain the real after-tax wage). A tax on rural land is ruled out if there must be *net* compensation to the rural sector which, in the absence of pure profits in manufacturing, leaves an urban land tax as the remaining potential ideal tax.

All of the above suggests that altering the minimum wage may avoid the problems of taxation, administration, and interference with individual mobility attendant to the policy package just

19 As drawn in Figure 2, L must represent a higher welfare level than D for the rural sector since P rises and the sector produces more of both goods. In fact if L lies along TS north of the ray going through D there will be an unambiguous sectoral welfare improvement. However, if L lies south of the ray on TS, the rural sector could be worse off than at D since P falls.

20 This argument coincides with the statement by Stolper (p. 195), 'It should be noted, however, that even at best the application of shadow prices leads to the substitution of one problem, the budget, for another one, an imperfect market.'

We would not go as far as Stolper in rejecting out of hand any use of shadow pricing because of the fiscal implication. The general point is valid that one cannot disregard the consequences of implementation of shadow-price criteria if actual prices or wages continue to diverge from the shadow prices or wages.

discussed. Income and wages policies designed to narrow the rural-urban wage gap have been suggested by D. P. Ghai, and Tanzania has formally adopted such a policy along with migration restriction. In the final analysis, however, the basic issue at stake is really one of political feasibility and it is not at all clear that an income policy is any more feasible than the alternatives.

APPENDIX I

Proof of Stability of Unemployment Equilibrium

In order to prove that our urban unemployment equilibrium is stable, we can differentiate ψ (equation (9)) with respect to N_u remembering that $dN_u = -dN_A$ according to (7). We therefore obtain

$$\frac{d\dot{N}_u}{dN_u} = \psi'(.)\left[-\frac{\overline{W}_M N_M}{(N_u)^2} + P'' + \frac{\partial P}{\partial X_A}(q')^2\right]. \qquad (1.1)$$

Stability requires $d\dot{N}_u/dN_u < 0$ which is satisfied if

$$\frac{\partial P}{\partial X_A} < \frac{\frac{\overline{W}_M N_M}{(N_u)^2} - Pq''}{(q')^2}.$$

The right side of this inequality is unambiguously positive since $q'' < 0$. Hence our assumption that $\partial P/\partial X_A < 0$ will ensure stability and, indeed, is stronger than necessary. The adjustment mechanism may be made clear by the following phase diagram in which the function ψ is plotted. Its positive slope reflects the hypothesis that migration flows will increase with the magnitude of the urban-rural expected wage differential. In Figure 4, ψ is plotted under the assumption that $\psi(0)=0$, hence the horizontal intercept is at the origin (in general the intercept would be α). Furthermore, we have arbitrarily assumed that ψ is a linear function. The arrows show the direction of adjustment in accordance with (1.1). If $\overline{W}_M N_M/N_u - Pq' > 0$, then $\dot{N}_u > 0$ but we know that if $\dot{N}_u > 0$, the expected wage differential will decrease since $d\dot{N}_u/dN_u < 0$. Additional migration by increasing $\dot{N}_u$ without affecting $\dot{N}_M$ will reduce the expected urban real wage through increased unemployment. Concomitantly, the transfer of labor out of agriculture raises q' and reduced agricultural output also causes P to rise. Thus migration reduces the expected wage differential to zero and equilibrium is achieved when there is no further incentive for migration. See Todaro for a more detailed analysis of this process in a dynamic setting.

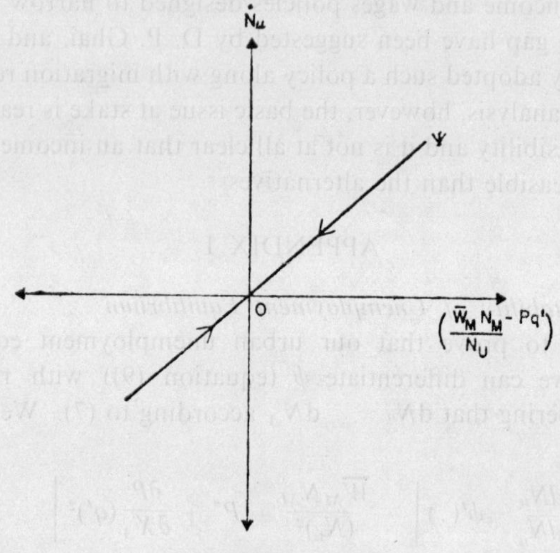

Figure 4

APPENDIX II

Differentiating the equilibrium condition (8) with respect to N_M, recalling that $dN_u = -dN_A$, we obtain the expression.

$$\frac{dN_u}{dN_M} = \frac{\dfrac{\overline{W}_M}{N_u} - q'p'\dfrac{f'}{X_A}}{\dfrac{\overline{W}_M N_M}{N_u{}^2} - \rho q'' + q'p'\dfrac{q' X_M}{X_A{}^2}} \qquad \text{(II.1)}$$

Defining the elasticity of demand for the agricultural good as

$$\eta_A = -\frac{\partial X_A}{\partial P} \cdot \frac{P}{X_A} = \frac{pX_M}{p'X_M}, \qquad \text{(II.2)}$$

(II 1) can be rewritten as

$$\frac{dN_u}{dN_M} = \frac{\dfrac{\overline{W}_M}{N_u} - \dfrac{pq'f'}{\eta_A X_M}}{\dfrac{\overline{W}_M N_M}{N_u{}^2} - pq'' + \dfrac{p(q')^2}{\eta_A X_A}} \qquad \text{(II.3)}$$

Differentiating the expression partially with respect to its various arguments it can be shown that dN_u/dN_M will vary directly with W_M, N_M, η_A and inversely with ρ, q', f', N_u, and q''. In general, the greater is the urban-rural wage differential and the less sensitive are prices and marginal products in agriculture, the greater will be the migration induced by creation of an additional job. If the minimum wage exceeds agricultural earnings, (II.3) will generally be positive and, with parameter values relevant for many African economies, will exceed unity.

When $dN_u/dN_M > 1$, creation of an additional job at the minimum wage will increase the absolute level of unemployment although the *rate* of urban unemployment will have to fall. This can be seen by converting (II.3) to an elasticity measure.

$$\frac{dN_U}{dN_M}\cdot\frac{N_M}{N_u} = \frac{\dfrac{\overline{W}_M N_M}{N_u^2} - \dfrac{N_M \rho q' f'}{N_u \eta_A X_M}}{\dfrac{\overline{W}_M N_M}{N_u^2} - \rho q'' + \dfrac{\rho (q')^2}{\eta_A X_A}} < 1 \qquad \text{(II.4)}$$

since $q'' < 0$.[21] To give an example of what this means, suppose that an economy initially has an urban unemployment rate of 25 percent. If in response to the creation of 100 additional industrial jobs, 125 additional individuals migrate to the urban area, the absolute number unemployed increases by 25 although the unemployment rate will drop, since the marginal unemployment rate is only 20 per cent.

APPENDIX III

If minimum wages are maintained and migration takes place in accordance with equation (8), aggregate welfare will be maximized if the following Lagrangean expression is maximized:

$$\Omega = U(X_A, X_M) + \lambda_1[q(\overline{N} - N_u) - X_A] + \lambda_2[f(N_M) - X_M]$$
$$+ \lambda_3 \left\{ \text{p} \left(\frac{f(N_M)}{q(\overline{N} - N_u)} \right) . q'(N - N_u) - \frac{\overline{W}_M N_M}{N_u} \right\} \qquad \text{(III.1)}$$

where U is the social welfare function and the succeeding terms are the constraints imposed by equations (1), (2), and (8) (recall that $N_A - \overline{N} - N_u$ from equation (7)).

Maximizing (III.1) we get the following first-order conditions:

$$\frac{\partial \Omega}{\partial X_A} = \frac{\partial U}{\partial X_A} - \lambda_1 = 0 \qquad \text{(III.2)}$$

21 We are grateful to Peter Diamond for deriving this expression.

$$\frac{\partial\Omega}{\partial X_M} = \frac{\partial U}{\partial X_M} - \lambda_2 = 0 \tag{III.3}$$

$$\frac{\partial\Omega}{\partial N_u} = -\lambda_1 q' + \lambda_3\left[p'\frac{fq'}{q^2} - pq'' + \frac{\overline{W}_M N_M}{N_u{}^2}\right] = 0 \tag{III.4}$$

$$\frac{\partial\Omega}{\partial N_M} = \lambda_2 f' + \lambda_3\left[p'\frac{f'q'}{q} - \frac{\overline{W}_M}{N_u}\right] = 0 \tag{III.5}$$

and the $\partial\Omega/\partial\lambda_i - 0$ ($i=1, 2, 3$) which ensures that the constraints hold.

Substituting (III.2) and (III.3) into (III.4) and (III.5) we get

$$\frac{\dfrac{\partial U}{\partial X_M} f'}{\dfrac{\partial U}{\partial X_A} q'} = \frac{\dfrac{\overline{W}_M}{N_u} - q'p'\dfrac{f'}{q}}{\dfrac{\overline{W}_M N_M}{N_u{}^2} - pq + q'p'\dfrac{fq'}{q^2}} \tag{III.6}$$

We know that in equilibrium $(\partial U/\partial X_M)/(\partial U/\partial X_A) - 1/P$ and it has been shown in Appendix II that the right-hand side of (III.6) is equal to dN_u/dN_M. Therefore (III.6) can be rewritten as

$$f' = Pq'\frac{dN_u}{dN_M}, \tag{III.7}$$

which is the condition used in the text to determine the optimal wage subsidy.

Condition (III.7) can also be written as

$$-P = \frac{-f'}{q'\dfrac{dN_u}{dN_M}} = \frac{dX_M}{dX_A}. \tag{III.8}$$

We know that $-P$ is equal to the marginal rate of substitution between the two commodities and dX_M/dX_A is the marginal rate of transformation. Hence (III.8) states the familiar condition for optimality: equate marginal rates of substitution and transformation. dX_M/dX_A is the slope of the line DK in Figure 2 and it clearly will be negative. However, its derivative with respect to N_M,

$$\frac{d\left(\dfrac{dX_M}{dX_A}\right)}{dN_M} = \frac{-q'\dfrac{dN_u}{dN_M}f'' - f'\left(\dfrac{dN_u}{dN_M}\right)^2 q'' + f'q'\dfrac{d^2N_u}{dN_M{}^2}}{\left(q'\dfrac{dN_u}{dN_M}\right)^2} \tag{III.9}$$

is of indeterminate sign since f'', $q''<0$ and $d^2N_u/dN_M{}^2$ will generally be negative as well. (III.9) must be positive if the effective production possibilities frontier (*DK*) is to be convex, a condition that is likely to hold but the possibility of concavity as full employment is approached must be considered. The slope of *DK* in Figure 2 seems plausible on *a priori* grounds.

REFERENCES

P. K. Bardhan, 'Factor Market Disequilibrium and the Theory of Protection,' *Oxford Econ. Pap.* (New Series), Oct. 1964, 16, pp. 375-88.

E. J. Berg, 'Wage Structure in Less Developed Countries,' in A. D. Smith, ed., *Wage Policy Issues in Economic Development*, London 1969.

A. Callaway, 'From Traditional Crafts to Modern Industries,' *ODU: University of Ife Journal of African Studies*, July 1965, 2.

S. Chakravarty, 'The Use of Shadow Prices in Programme Evaluation,' in Rosenstein-Rodan, ed., *Capital Formation and Economic Development*, London 1964.

Y. S. Cho, *Disguised Unemployment in Developing Areas, with Special Reference to South Korean Agriculture*, Berkeley, 1960.

R. S. Eckaus, 'The Factor-Proportions Problem in Underdeveloped Areas,' *Amer. Econ. Rev.*, Sept. 1955, 45, pp. 539-65.

J. Erickson, 'Wage Employment Relationships in Latin American Industry: A Pilot Study of Argentina, Brazil, and Mexico,' International Labour Office, 1969, typescript.

J. Fei and G. Ranis, *Development of the Labor Surplus Economy*, Illinois 1964.

D. P. Ghai, 'Incomes Policy in Kenya: Need, Criteria and Machinery,' *East Afr. Econ. Rev.*, June 1968, 4, pp. 19-35.

J. Gugler, 'The Impact of Labour Migration on Society and Economy in Sub-Saharan Africa. Empirical Findings and Theoretical Considerations," *African Social Research*, Dec. 1968, 6, pp. 463-86.

E. E. Hagen, 'An Economic Justification of Protectionism,' *Quart. J. Econ.*, Nov. 1958, 72, pp. 496-514.

J. R. Harris and M. P. Todaro, 'Urban Unemployment in East Africa: An Economic Analysis of Policy Alternatives,' *East Afr. Econ. Rev.*, Dec. 1968, 4, pp. 17-36.

——— and ———, 'Wages, Industrial Employment, and Labour Productivity: The Kenyan Experience,' *East Afr. Econ. Rev.* (New Series), June 1969, 1, 29-46.

J. P. Henderson, 'Wage Policy in Africa,' Paper prepared for delivery at the African Conference on Economics, Temple University, mimeo, April 1968.

C. R. Hutton, 'The Causes of Labour Migration,' in Gugler, ed., *Urbanization in Sub-Saharan Africa*, Kampala 1969.

C. H. C. Kao, K. R. Anschel, and C. K. Eicher, 'Disguised Unemployment in Agriculture: A Survey,' in C. K. Eicher and L. W. Witt, eds., *Agriculture in Economic Development*, New York 1964, pp. 129-44.

J. M. Katz, 'Verdoorn Effects; Returns to Scale, and the Elasticity of Factor Substitution,' *Oxford Econ. Pap.*, Nov. 1968, 20, 342-52.

L. Lefeber, 'Planning in a Surplus Labor Economy,' *Amer. Econ. Rev.*, June 1968, 58, pp. 343-73.

W. A. Lewis, 'Economic Development with Unlimited Supplies of Labour,' *Manchester Sch. Econ. Soc. Stud.*, May 1954, 22, pp. 139-91.

I. M. D. Little, 'The Real Cost of Labour, and the Choice Between Consumption and Investment,' in P. N. Rosenstein-Rodan, ed., *Pricing and Fiscal Policies: A Study in Method*, Cambridge 1964, pp. 77-91.

——— and J. A. Mirrlees, *Manual of Industrial Project Analysis*, Vol. II, 'Social Cost Benefit Analysis,' Paris 1969.

B. F. Massell and J. Heyer, 'Household Expenditure in Nairobi: A Statistical Analysis of Consumer Behaviour,' *Econ. Develop. Cult. Change*, Jan. 1969, 17, pp. 212-34.

L. G. Reynolds, 'Wages and Employment in a Labor-Surplus Economy,' *Amer. Econ. Rev.*, Mar. 1965, 55, pp. 19-39.

W. F. Stolper, *Planning Without Facts: Lesson's in Resource Allocation from Nigeria's Development*. Cambridge 1966.

M P. Todaro, 'A Model of Labor Migration and Urban Unemployment in Less Developed Countires,' *Amer. Econ. Rev.*, Mar. 1969, 59, pp. 138-48.

Nigeria, *Report of the Commission on the Review of Wages, Salary and Conditions of Service of the Junior Employees of the Governments of the Federation and in Private Establishment* 1963-64.

7

URBAN UNEMPLOYMENT AND ECONOMIC GROWTH IN AFRICA[1]

C. R. Frank Jr.

ONE OF THE characteristics of the less-developed economies of the world is a rapidly growing urban population and urban work force combined with a much slower increase in employment opportunities in the larger-scale urban establishments. The result has been either unemployment or under-employment in small-scale, often individual or family-run, establishments. This phenomenon has been noted in economies such as Puerto Rico and India with high population densities as well as in the relatively under-populated countries of Africa.[2] Those countries which are industrializing rapidly seem to suffer from this phenomenon just as much, if not more, than those which are not industrializing quickly.[3]

The growing mass of urban unemployed and under-employed is regarded by many as a great social evil and a prime source of human tragedy.[4] Others, including politicians in power, fear it as a source of political instability. The presence of large numbers of poverty-striken and jobless people in the cities puts a great deal of pressure on governments, national and local, to increase current expenditures rapidly to provide civil service jobs for the unemployed. At the same time governments are faced with demands on their capital budgets to spend more for development purposes. In addition, increasing urban population creates demands for urban services: housing,

1 This paper has benefited from comments by and conversations with numerous individuals including Jules Backman of New York University, Peter Clark of UCLA, Peter Kilby of Wesleyan, Donald Huddle, Stephen Hymer and Howard Pack of Yale University, Alan Strout of USAID and Brian Van Arkadie of Yale. Michael Duberstein and John Todd assisted capably as research assistants.

2 See Reynolds [24], Friedlander [12], Pearson [23], Calloway [6], and Doctor and Gallis [8]. References at the end of the article.

3 See Baer and Herve[1].

4 For example. Calloway [7], (p. 60) asserts that '.... no social and economic problem in Nigeria is so urgent as that of finding employment for the ever increasing number of school leavers. Nor is there any major policy issue of which the meanings and implications are so little understood'.

sewerage, lighting, roads, police, and fire protection and the like. A large mass of unemployed or under-employed do not generate the output or tax revenues which are needed to provide these services. For these and other reasons, the political consensus in most developing countries is that the pressures of urban unemployment and under-employment have to be relieved.

How best can this be accomplished? One might say the solution is through high rates of investment and rapid growth. The history of fast-growing countries and their continued inability to cope with the problem of unemployment indicate that something else besides rapid growth is required for a solution. Many writers suggest that growth must occur by investing in relatively labour-intensive activities rather than those which are capital-intensive. The argument runs that not only will this result in more rapid growth because of the low opportunity cost of labour relative to capital, but will increase the rate of growth of employment for any given level of investment. Even in cases, however, when the labour-intensive investment is less than optimal from the point of view of growth, it may be justified if a high enough priority is given to growth in employment and/or reduction in unemployment.

In this paper, we will attempt to show that for the typical African country[5] neither high rates of growth in the modern urban sector nor an attempt to resort to labour-intensive techniques in that sector is likely to have much effect on the magnitude of the urban unemployment problem. The answer, if one exists, to the problem of urban unemployment must be sought through examination of urban-rural income differentials and the distribution of public goods and services to urban and rural areas.

A *Composition of The Urban Labour Force*

The urban labour force constitutes only a small fraction of the total working force of most African countries. In Nigeria, for example, one of the most urbanized of the African countries south of the Sahara, the urban population (in cities having a population greater than 20,000) is only about 13 per cent of the total population. In Uganda, one of the least urbanized African countries, only about 2.5 per cent of the total population lives in cities and towns of 2,000 or more people, although many of those who work in the towns of

5 In referring to Africa in this paper, we generally mean Africa south of the Sahara exclusive of South Africa.

Uganda live outside the urban areas and commute by foot or bicycle.

The working force in the urban areas may be divided into two groups, those in the modern sector and those in the traditional sector. Since the line between the modern sector and the traditional sector is often hard to draw, this distinction is somewhat arbitrary. (We include government establishments in the modern sector.) Basically, the difference is one of scale of operations. Throughout urban Africa there are numerous very small-scale establishments often individually or family run. These include petty trading, individual craft activities (e.g. shoemaking, wood carving, furniture making) and very small-scale manufacturing and construction establishments (employing, say, less than ten people). Workers in the traditional sector typically use little capital, do not employ modern accounting and book-keeping methods, and receive little remuneration in the way of profits or wages. A great many of the employees in the traditional sector are unpaid apprentices or family labour. Many traditional sector workers are employed on a part-time or casual basis. Those employed part-time or seasonally often maintain very close connection with the rural areas, either spending a good part of each year in the countryside or returning to the rural areas periodically every few years.

Those employed in the modern or large-scale sector are better paid and more productive because of a higher capital to labour ratio. Many of the modern establishments are run and/or owned by Europeans. They employ modern methods of accounting and generally keep better records than the traditional establishments.

Of that part of the total work force living in the cities, only a fraction is engaged in the modern sector. In Nigeria, for example, workers in the modern sector account for about one-half of the urban work force or a little over 5 per cent of the total labour force. The rest of the urban labour force is either engaged in the traditional, low productivity sector or is completely unemployed.

B *Growth in The Urban Labour Force in Africa*

Few data are available on urban labour participation rates in Africa. Growth in the urban labour force must be inferred from urban population data. Table I gives the rates of growth for some major cities of Africa. These vary considerably from 1.7 per cent per annum (Addis-Ababa) to more than 15 per cent (Fort Lamy). While the data on which these figures are based are very inadequate,

TABLE I

SUB-SAHARAN AFRICA: URBAN POPULATION GROWTH

City	Year	Population ('000)	Year	Population ('000)	Annual growth (per cent)
Salisbury	1946	69	1961	300	10.3
Dar-es-Salaam	1948	69	1957	129	7.2
Brazzaville	1955	76	1961	134	9.9
Dakar	1945	132	1960	383	7.4
Accra	1948	136	1960	491	11.3
Nairobi	1948	119	1962	315	7.2
Abidjan	1955	127	1960	180	7.2
Monrovia	1956	41	1962	81	12.0
Fort Lamy	1955	29	1963	92	15.5
Cotonou	1945	26	1960	113	10.3
Mombasa	1948	85	1962	180	5.5
Bamako	1945	37	1960	127	8.6
Bulawayo	1946	53	1964	214	8.1
Lusaka	1950	26	1964	122	11.7
Yaounde	1955	38	1962	93	13.8
Douala	1954	118	1964	187	4.7
Addis-Ababa	1951	400	1964	505	1.7
Khartoum-Omdurman	1948	210	1960	315	3.4
Luanda	1950	150	1960	220	3.9
Leopoldville	1946	110	1961	420	9.3
Elisabethville	1950	103	1961	190	5.7
Kumasi	1955	75	1960	190	20.4
Lourenco-Marques	1950	94	1961	184	6.3

Source: United Nations, *Demographic Yearbook*, New York, various issues and William A. Hance, *The Geography of Modern Africa*, Columbia University Press, New York, 1964, p. 54.

the mean annual growth (weighted by initial size) of 6.8 per cent can be regarded as fairly typical. These differ considerably from the estimated growth of total population in the African countries which usually range between 2 and 3 per cent per annum. This means, of course, that the urban labour force is a growing percentage of the total labour force.

C *Growth in Demand for a Modern Urban Labour Force*

These very high rates of growth of the urban labour force have not been matched by correspondingly high rates of growth of the quantity of urban labour demanded by the modern larger scale establishments.

TABLE II

NON-AGRICULTURAL EMPLOYMENT INDICES IN SELECTED AFRICAN COUNTRIES (1958=100)

	Cameroons	Ghana	Kenya	Malawi	Nigeria
1955	102	82	107	88	n.a.
1956	104	91	105	95	95
1957	100	95	105	98	100
1958	100	100	100	100	100
1959	95	106	100	99	99
1960	91	111	102	96	106
1961	94	122	98	93	89
1962	72	128	97	87	113
1963	91	132	91	87	94
1964	92	n.a.	111	n.a.	n.a.
Rate of growth* (per cent)	—1.0	6.3	—0.5	—0.7	0.1

	Southern Rhodesia	Sierra Leone	Tanzania	Uganda	Zambia
1955	86	87	97	94	92
1956	92	87	104	93	100
1957	98	92	101	99	100
1958	100	100	100	100	100
1959	100	98	96	99	95
1960	101	101	98	99	93
1961	98	108	104	98	90
1962	95	112	101	93	88
1963	91	119	91	89	86
1964	90	125	95	89	91
Rate of growth* (per cent)	0.2	3.0	—0.4	—0.1	—0.9

Source: United Nations, *Statistical Yearbook, 1965*, New York, 1966, pp.109-10.

* Rates of growth calculated by fitting a logarithmic time trend.

Note: n.a. means not available.

Table II gives some representative rates of growth of total non-agricultural employment. Note that many of these rates of growth are negative. Furthermore, the growth in the Kenya non-agricultural labour force would be considerably more negative were it not for the extraordinary jump in employment between 1963 and 1964. This discontinuity was most likely the result of a mild export boom in

1964 and, more importantly, the signing of the so-called Tripartite Agreement by government, private employers, and the labour unions which called for employers to increase their employment by ten per cent and the unions to hold back on wage demands.

The low rates of growth in Table II cannot be attributed to a low growth in output. Some representative annual rates of increase of non-agricultural output between 1954 and 1964 are[6]

Kenya	6.5
Southern Rhodesia	6.7
Uganda	7.7

Non-agricultural output in Tanzania increased at a rate of 6.0 per cent between 1954 and 1958 and 9.1 per cent between 1960 and 1964.

The very high rate of growth of employment in Ghana is very atypical. The reason for it has, however, been a very high growth in government employment brought about by very rapid growth in government expenditures. Given the current limitations on Ghana's ability to finance further increases in government expenditure and their move away from government make-work projects, there should be little further growth in employment from this source.[7]

The low rates of growth of employment in Table II are, on the whole, considerably below the rates of growth of urban population in Table I. Thus, only a small portion of the annual increment in the urban labour force is being absorbed by the modern urban sector. The residual (those either unemployed or engaged in the traditional sector) are an increasing proportion of the urban work force. It is difficult to say how many of those in the residual are either under-employed or unemployed, but it is unlikely that the demand for the goods and services from the traditional urban sector has been growing at anywhere near the rate needed fully to absorb the growth of the residual labour force. In Nigeria, the large supply of workers to the traditional sector has kept the real wage-rate in the sector either constant or falling while real wages in the modern sector have risen considerably. (See Kilby[19].) The highly paid

6 These growth rates were calculated from data in United Nations, *Statistical Yearbook, 1965*, New York, 1966, pp. 27-31.

7 Between 1961 and 1964, private enterprise employment in Ghana fell from 138 thousand to 115 thousand while public sector employment increased from 212 thousand to 262 thousand, a net increase of 27 thousand. Employment in the services sector increased by 30 thousand, thus accounting for all of the increase in employment and then some. See Ghana, *Quarterly Digest of Statistics*, December 1962. p. 2 and *Ghana Economic Survey, 1964*, p. 105.

workers of the modern sector are becoming an increasingly smaller percentage of the urban work force while the wage differential seems to be widening.

D *Composition of Labour Demand*

There are several striking aspects of the composition of labour demand in Africa. First, the role played by government is very large. Government non-agricultural employment as a percentage of total non-agricultural employment for selected countries is given in Table III. It ranges from 37.6 to 52.1 per cent. Second, employment in trade, commerce, and miscellaneous services is the most important component of non-agricultural employment in most African countries, ranging from 45 to 65 per cent for those countries in Table IV. Finally, manufacturing and public utilities accounts for a relatively small portion of non-agricultural employment, roughly between 15 and 20 per cent (see Table IV). These characteristics of the composition of labour demand have very important implications for the growth in demand for labour.

TABLE III

DISTRIBUTION OF NON-AGRICULTURAL EMPLOYMENT BY TYPE OF EMPLOYER

	Year	Government (per cent)	Non-Government* (per cent)
Uganda	1964	52.1	47.9
Kenya	1964	41.4	58.6
Tanzania	1963	48.9	51.1
Nigeria	1962	37.6	62.4
Ghana	1961	45.6	54.4

Sources: *Uganda Statistical Abstract, 1965*, Entebbe, 1966, p. 93; *Kenya Statistical Abstract, 1965*, Nairobi, 1966, p. 122. *Tanzania Statistical Abstract 1964* Dar-es-Salaam, 1965, p. 142; *Nigeria Report on Earnings and Employment Enquiry, 1962*, Lagos, 1964, p. 12, and *Ghana Quarterly Digest of Statistics*, Accra, December, 1962, p. 2.

* Includes Government Corporations except for Uganda.

Government employment grows roughly at about the same rate as recurrent government expenditure less the rate of growth of the average wage or salary paid by government. Wages and salaries comprise a large proportion of this expenditure (typically 60 to 80 per cent) which tends to change very little through time for any

TABLE IV

DISTRIBUTION OF NON-AGRICULTURAL EMPLOYMENT BY SECTOR

	Manufacturing and public utilities	Commerce and services	Construction	Mining	Transport and communications
Uganda (1964)	20.2	56.2	15.0	3.0	5.6
Kenya (1965)	19.2	65.0	5.6	0.6	9.4
Tanzania (1963)	15.2	50.5	16.2	4.2	13.9
Nigeria (1962)	14.4	45.0	20.7	9.8	10.2
Ghana (1964)	13.9	47.6	19.3	8.6	10.2

Sources: Same as Table III except for Kenya and Ghana data which were obtained from International Labour Office, *Yearbook of Statistics, 1966*, Geneva, p. 268: and *Ghana Economic Survey, 1964*, Accra, 1965, p. 105.

given country. Government investment expenditure is a small fraction of the total government expenditure, and wages and salaries are a much smaller proportion than is the case with recurrent expenditure. In any case, much of the investment expenditure by African governments is in payments to private contractors and this does not affect government employment. Thus the growth in government employment opportunities is largely a function of the taxing and borrowing capabilities of African governments and their willingness to expand recurrent expenditures. It makes little sense to talk about greatly altering these relationships by the use of more labour-intensive techniques when government recurrent services are largely the services of labour anyway.

Value added in commerce, trade, and miscellaneous services, while including some profits and depreciation, is largely composed of wages and salaries (explicitly or implicitly). Thus, as is the case with government, employment tends to grow roughly the same as value added (in money terms) with an adjustment for increased average employee remuneration, i.e. employment tends to grow about the same as real value added. Furthermore, the commerce, trade, and miscellaneous services industries may be viewed basically as intermediate goods industries whose output tends to grow in fixed proportion to the general level of economic activity. To conclude, with regard to trade, commerce, and other service industries, there is little scope for increasing labour intensity and the growth of employment in this industry above that dictated by the overall growth of the economy.

The scope for increased employment growth through more labour intensity therefore lies in other urban-based industries such as mining, manufacturing, transport, construction, and public utilities which, however, generally account for less than 50 per cent of the total modern, urban labour force.

E *The Role of Labour Productivity*

The growth of employment in these other urban-based industries is considerably reduced by growth in labour productivity which occurs independently of the choice of technique with regard to output expansion. This growth in productivity occurs for several reasons:[8]

(1) Increasing quality of the labour force, particularly through on-the-job training and increased experience in a factory environment;
(2) Disembodied labour-saving technical change resulting from better management, organization, and work procedures;
(3) An increase in the share of the market for those firms which have achieved higher labour productivity because of better management or better labour quality;
(4) Economies of scale;
(5) Increasing capacity utilization resulting in increased productivity of maintenance and administration personnel.[9]

Of course, productivity may decrease through time if the labour force is deteriorating, or management control of operations becomes

8 Reasons (2), (3) and (4) cited here are similar to Leibenstein's notion of an increase in X-efficiency. See Leibenstein [20].

9 This cause of increased labour productivity is somewhat peculiar to the smaller size, less developed economies. In most African countries, there is usually only one railway company, for example. Maintenance of the right of way and administrative and clerical operations require some minimum of workers. The need for these kinds of workers does not expand nearly as rapidly as output expands. In most African countries, the railway accounts for a considerable portion of the labour force, and as the railways are used to fuller capacity, works per unit of output falls rapidly. There is also a tendency to build certain manufacturing plants substantially ahead of demand or to build a large enough size to handle demands during export booms (e.g. cement). As the average capacity utilization increases, maintenance and administrative personnel increase their productivity.

lax, but the main direction of change in Africa has been toward substantial increases in labour productivity.

The first three of these factors tend to operate independently of increases in output or value added. Thus, there is a tendency for some gain in productivity even though output is falling, stagnant, or growing slowly. Productivity increases resulting from economies of large-scale operation and/or increased capacity utilization come into play as output growth increases. Increases in output which begin to put a strain on the existing capital stock capacity may, however, cause the growth in productivity to fall off for very high rates of growth of output.

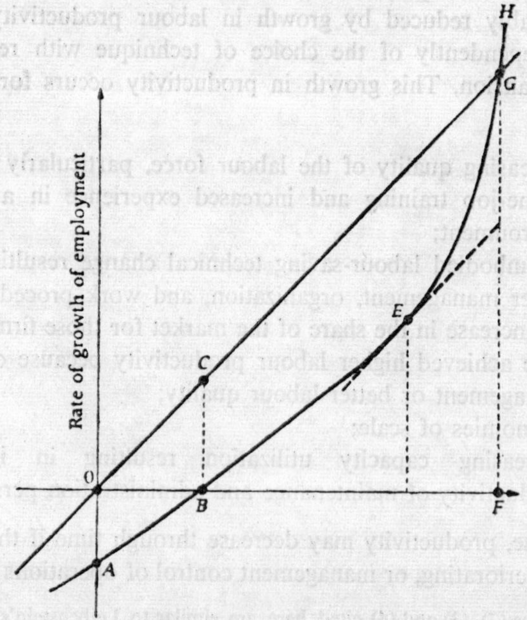

Figure 1

The curve ABEH in Fig. 1 shows the relationships between output growth, productivity growth, and growth in employment.[10] The vertical axis is the rate of growth of employment, and the horizontal axis is the rate of growth of output (value added). At zero rates

10 A derivation of the relationship between growth in employment and growth in output assuming that there are three factors, labour, skilled labour, and capital; and labour-augmenting and capital-augmenting technological change is contained in the appendix.

of growth of output the growth in employment is negative and equal to minus the distance of *OA*. The rate of growth of output must be greater than *OB* in order for there to be any positive increase in employment at all.

The growth in productivity is approximately given by the distance between the 45 degree line *OCG* which emanates from the origin. For example, when the rate of growth of employment is zero, the rate of growth of productivity is equal to *OA* (the rate of decrease of employment). When the rate of growth of output is *OB*, the growth in productivity is approximately given by *BC*. If the growth in output is *OF*, the growth of productivity equals zero. Whenever the slope of the curve *ABEH* is equal to unity (at the point *E* in Fig. 1), there is no change in the rate of growth of productivity. Below the point *E*, the rate of growth of productivity is increasing and above the point *E*, productivity growth decreases.

We place no great faith in the particular form of the curve *ABEH* shown in Fig. 1 other than the fact that (*a*) for most relevant rates of growth of output, it probably lies below the 45 degree line (on the average, at any relevant rate of growth of output there is a net increase in productivity) and (*b*) only for very high rates of growth of output would there be a tendency for productivity to decline, i.e. for a wide range in the growth of output, there is a tendency for the curve to have less than unitary slope.

In order to test the appropriateness of such a relationship among growth rates of output, employment, and productivity, we have analysed data from mining activities in three countries and for two railway systems in Africa.

a. Mining in Nigeria

In Nigeria, the bulk of employment in mining relates to tin and coal. The gains in labour productivity in both these industries has been remarkable. Between 1950 and 1957, despite an increase in tin output from 949 tons to 1096 tons per month or 15.6 per cent, employment *dropped* from 58.2 to 55.2 thousand or 4.6 per cent, implying an increase in productivity of 20.9 per cent or an average increase of 2.8 per cent per annum. Between 1950 and 1964, tin output hardly increased, but tin employment fell by 24.2 per cent, an increase of productivity of 36.8 per cent or 2.3 per cent per annum. Between 1950 and 1957 there was virtually no increase in labour productivity in coal, but between 1959 and 1964 coal output fell by 15.5 per cent, and employment fell by 60.5 per cent, an increase in productivity of 113 per cent or 11.4 per cent per annum.[11]

b. Mining in Ghana

In Ghana, most employment in the mining industry relates to gold. Between 1948 and 1964 output increased from 672,000 fine oz. to 865,000 fine oz. while employment dropped from 32.2 thousand to 20.6 thousand. Productivity increased by about 100 per cent over 16 years, an increase of about 4.4 per cent per annum.[12]

c. Mining in Zambia

Copper output (electrolytic and blister combined) in Zambia more than doubled (from 309 thousand to 635 thousand tons) between 1950 and 1963. Employment increased by only 4.5 per cent from 37.4 thousand to 39.1 thousand. The increase in productivity was 98 per cent or 5.0 per cent per annum over the 14-year period.[13]

d. The East African Railways

The East African Railways is the largest non-government employer in East Africa. Employment in 1949 was 47.1 thousand, but by 1963 this had dropped to 44.7 thousand. In the meantime, ton-miles carried increased from 1.2 million to 2.1 million or 75 per cent. The implied increase in ton-mile productivity was 60 per cent or 3.4 per cent per annum.[14]

e. Railways in Nigeria

Between 1948 and 1963, ton-miles carried by the Nigerian Railways increased from 554 thousand to 1,410 thousand or nearly threefold in 15 years. Employment meanwhile increased from 22,100 to 27,400, a gain of only 24 per cent. Productivity increased at about 5 per cent per annum over the 15 years. The gain in productivity has been particularly noticeable between 1952 and 1963; ton-miles per worker more than doubled, a gain of 7 per cent per annum.[15]

11 Data from Nigeria, *Quarterly Digest of Statistics*, various issues.
12 Data from Ghana, *Quarterly Digest of Statistics*, various issues.
13 Employment data from Northern Rhodesia, Chamber of Mines. *Year Book 1964*. Output data from Federation of Rhodesia and Nyasaland, *Monthly Digest of Statistics* and Zambia, *Monthly Digest of Statistics*, various issues.
14 Data are from East African *Economic and Statistical Review*, various issues.
15 Data from Nigeria, *op. cit.*, various issues.

We regressed annual percentage change in employment on annual percentage increase in output for each of the above industries. In the case of East African Railways, we added a third variable, the ratio of the increase in capital expenditure to employment.[16] The results are summarized in Table V. The constant term in each

TABLE V

EMPLOYMENT GROWTH—PRODUCTIVITY GROWTH REGRESSIONS

Industry	Regression	Data	Required growth in output to prevent employment from falling
Nigeria Coal	$Y = -7.1 + 1.704X_1$ ($R^2 = 0.28$)	1950-64 Output in tons	4.2%
Nigeria Tin	$Y = -1.5 + 0.875X_1$ ($R^2 = 0.90$)	1950-64 Output in tons	1.7
Ghana Gold	$Y = -3.8 + 0.720X_1$ ($R^2 = 0.46$)	1948-64 Output in fine oz.	5.3
Zambia Copper	$Y = -3.7 + 0.669X_1$ ($R^2 = 0.995$)	1950-63 Output in tons	5.5
East African Railways	$Y = -2.0 + 0.318X_1 + 1.432X_2$ ($R^2 = 0.48$)	1949-63 Output in ton-miles	6.7 6.7
Nigeria Railways	$Y = -1.2 + 0.216X_1$ ($R^2 = 0.70$)	1948-63 annual percentage changes in three-year moving averages of employment and output (ton-miles)	4.5

Note: Y is percentage change in employment; X_1 is percentage change in output and X_2 is ratio of increase in capital expenditures to employment.

of these equations is the rate at which employment *decreases* in these industries when output is stagnant. We converted these to percentage increases in output required to prevent a drop in employment by setting $Y = 0$ and solving for X_1. The results are presented in the last column of Table V.

Studies of various manufacturing industries as well indicate very large increases in productivity. For example, a study by Azarias

16 This variable was added as an explanatory variable since employment figures covered workers employed on capital projects.

Baryaruha of three firms in Uganda, Nyanza Textiles, Uganda Breweries, and British-American Tobacco Company, revealed average annual increases in physical labour productivity of 12.2, 6.6, and 3.4 per cent respectively over the 1960–64 period. Using employment figures from the annual enumeration of employees and Gross Domestic Product data, Baryaruha also revealed the following increases in labour productivity in Uganda over the period 1960–4:[17]

Cotton, Coffee, and Sugar Processing	6.9%
Manufacture of Food Products	2.7%
Miscellaneous Manufacturing	6.2%

In a study of the sugar industry in East Africa, the present author concluded that productivity in sugar processing in Kenya increased 52 per cent between 1958 and 1962 or an average of more than 10 per cent per annum.[18]

These studies also indicate that the increases in productivity could not be attributed to the adoption of more capital intensive techniques of production but rather to some of the factors mentioned above. For example, the increase in the productivity of the tobacco firm studied by Baryaruha occurred despite no new investment during the period and with a 10 per cent decline in production over the period. The productivity increases most likely were the result of more efficient operation and increases in worker skills. The increase in the productivity of sugar-processing in Kenya was basically the result of higher rates of utilization and efficiency of the existing processing equipment.

F *The Role of Wage Rates*

One possible way of stimulating a growth in employment opportunities is a reduction of wage rates or perhaps, more appropriately, a reduction in the growth of wage rates. In particular, wage-rate reductions can have a very significant influence on the growth of employment opportunities generated by government activity. For example, suppose government recurrent expenditures are expected to increase 5 per cent from one year to the next. If the average government wage also increases by 5 per cent, the increase in employment will be nil. If government wage increases are held to only 2 per cent and there is no change in the revenue

17 See Bharyaruha [2].
18 See Frank [11], p. 92.

and expenditure picture, the increase in employment will be about 2.9 per cent. Alternatively, the funds freed by holding the wage increase down to 2 per cent may be used, not for increased employment out of the recurrent budget, but for additional government investment activity which will have both direct and indirect stimulative effects on employment opportunities.

Several remarks are appropriate here, however, with regard to the use of wage restraint as an employment-stimulating device.

First, many industrial enterprises in Africa are foreign-owned, large-scale enterprises which use very capital intensive methods of production. Wage costs are small relative to value added and wage changes have very little effect on output decisions and the technology used.

Secondly, wage changes tend to have less effect on the labour-intensity of the already existing capacity than on the labour intensity of new investment. When new investment plans are made, the current wage structure can be taken into account by choosing the appropriate technology. Past investments may involve a given commitment to particular products and particular technologies, embodied, for example, in the type of equipment and plant layout used.

Thirdly, for those industries which are highly labour-intensive, such as trade and commerce, the effectiveness of wage restraint in stimulating employment depends on the price elasticity of demand for the services of these industries. If demand is inelastic, there will be little change in the employment opportunities.

Fourth, a reduction in wages at the lower scales may have an insignificant impact on employment opportunities if trained supervisors are relatively scarce. The hiring of additional unskilled workers even at very low wages may not be profitable if it is not possible to hire additional trained supervisors.

Fifth, a reduction in wages at the lower scales only may have an insignificant effect on government employment if there are large wage and salary differentials between skill levels. For example, in the *1959 Nigeria Report on Earnings and Employment Enquiry*, 11.7 per cent of those employed by the Federal and Regional governments together were classified as either professional, technical, administrative, executive, or managerial. The cash earnings of these senior employees comprised 41.5 per cent of the total wage and salary bill. At the other end of the scale, general unskilled labour accounted for 36.6 per cent of employment but received only 13.9 per cent of total earnings. A 10 per cent reduction in the lower wage scales could result in approximately a 10 per cent increase in unskilled employment at the same level of expenditure. A 10 per cent reduction of salaries of skilled personnel, which would adversely affect considerably fewer individuals could result in an increase in unskilled employment of approximately 30 per cent.

Finally, and most important, an advocacy of wage restraint as an employment-stimulating device must take into account the social and institutional factors which accompany the wage determination process in Africa. In the modern urban sector, the central government usually sets the pace in one way or another. Unlike in the developed western countries, in some areas such as in East Africa, British Central Africa, and Ghana, minimum wage legislation essentially determines the whole wage scale. Minimum wages are periodically adjusted upwards usually as the result of recommendations of minimum wages advisory boards which are appointed every few years. The increase in the minimum wage is very effective in raising the whole wage scale since the wages of most unskilled workers are at or near the current minimum wage. Recent increments in the minimum wage in many African countries have been very substantial. In Uganda, for example, minimum wages in the urban areas were adjusted in 1959, in 1962, and 1964. The minimum wage was set at Shs. 75.4, Shs. 120.0 and Shs. 152.0, respectively, implying more than a doubling of the money wage in five years.[19] The real minimum wage increased almost as much since there was little price inflation during those years.[20] In Ghana, minimum wage legislation was introduced in 1960. The result was a sharp shift upwards in wage rates.[21]

In those countries where minimum wage legislation is not the major factor in setting wage rates, the government wage scales have a substantial impact on wage scales throughout the modern sector of the economy. Such is the case in Nigeria today and Ghana before 1960.[22] There are two reasons why government scales set

19 See Uganda [27], pp. 9 and 18.

20 The index of retail prices in African markets in Kampala was 102 in June of 1959 and 102 in June of 1964. The cost-of-living index (based on expenditure patterns of middle-income civil servants) in Kampala was 138 in June of 1959 and 157 in June of 1964, an increase of about 14 per cent over five years.

21 See Birmingham, Neustadt, and Omaboe [4], p. 137.

22 See Kilby [19], pp. 13-20 and Birmingham *et al*, *op. cit.*

the pace for the rest of the modern sector. First, the preponderance of government as the largest single employer means that other employers set their scales at or near those of the government in order to hold their own labour force and to be in a competitive position to attract better quality workers at all levels. Secondly, the larger private employers, for political reasons, want to achieve and maintain a reputation as 'progressive employers'. In some instances, the private employers pay substantially above government rates for these reasons.[23]

The central government often raises its wage scales in large and discrete jumps. In Nigeria, for example, the traditional mechanism for raising government wage scales is the appointment of a commission of inquiry into wages and conditions of employment every few years. The commission's recommendations are usually adopted without substantial change, resulting in a discrete jump in wage scales which is changed only slightly until the next commission of inquiry is appointed. Government wage scales in Nigeria were adjusted upwards in 1954–5, 1959, and 1964 upon recommendations of the Gorsuch Commission in 1954, the Mbanefo and Morgan Commissions in 1959, and a second Morgan Commission in 1964. The minimum wage for general labour increased from 4*s.* 8*d.* in 1955 to 5*s.* 10*d.*, in 1959, to 7*s.* 8*d.* in 1964. The increase of 67 per cent in the money wage of general labour was accompanied by only small changes in the price level.[24]

The sharp increases in real wage rates brought about by changes in minimum wage legislation or changes in government wage scales, accompanied by increasing urban unemployment, indicate that the wage in the modern sector tends to be set institutionally and politically without great regard for achieving balance between the demand and supply of labour. An examination of available recent government documents which deal with the policy issue of wages confirms this fact. There are two main arguments used to justify

23 See Kilby [19], p. 20.

24 Changes in the Consumer Price Index for various Nigerian cities are as follows:

Lagos: 1953=100; 1964=112
Ibadan: 1953=100; 1964=127
Enugu: 1953=100; 1964=147
Kaduna: 1957=100; 1964=118
Port Harcourt: 1957=100; 1964=117.

Three indices are based on expenditure patterns of employees earning £350-400 per annum. See Nigeria, *Quarterly Digest of Statistics.*

the usual recommendation of a substantial increase in the wages paid to general unskilled labourers. The first is that a stable, modern, urban labour force requires that the lowest paid workers be able to maintain themselves and their families at a 'living wage' or what is necessary to provide a man and his family 'a minimum standard of health and decency'.[25] A good statement of this philosophy is contained in the Uganda Government's *Report of the Minimum Wages Advisory Board*, p. 5.

> The wages of unskilled workers in Uganda, in common with many other developing countries, are so low in many cases that they live in a state of permanent poverty and are generally 'underfed, underhoused and underclothed'. We feel, therefore, that until such time as they achieve a minimum wage which will enable them to live as decent human beings equipped, at least, with the basic necessities of life we cannot allow our consideration for any increase to be determined solely by the so-called 'economic laws', even though this may be contrary to the economist's usual ideas of how wage levels should be determined. It is of paramount importance to the country's future stability and prosperity that we achieve, as rapidly as possible, a wage structure based on the needs of the family unit. The realization of this objective should receive top priority and the full co-operation of both the Government and of the business community.

In practical terms, a minimum monthly wage of 240 shillings was deemed a living wage by the 1964 Uganda Minimum Wages Advisory Board which it felt ought to be achieved in a few years, implying a 58 per cent increase over and above their current recommendations.[26] Since the concept of a living wage is ephemeral, to say the least, once a wage of 240 shillings a month is achieved, this will no doubt be regarded as inadequate.

The second argument most often used relates to the very substantial differences in pay scales between the various labour categories. In Nigeria, for example, a young university graduate entering the civil service typically has a starting salary of £600 or £700 per annum with more or less guaranteed raises up to a maximum level of £1,400 or £1,500 a year. If he is lucky enough to be promoted to the so-called super-scales, he can earn close to £4,000 a year. A typical unskilled labourer will start at about £100 per annum and, unless he is able to qualify as an artisan by further training, cannot hope to rise much above £150 a year.

25 See Nigeria [22], pp. 11-12.
26 See Uganda [27], p. 15.

These large income disparities result in significant pressures and sentiment in favour of forcing a more equitable income distribution by raising the lower wage scales. The alternative policy of lowering the higher wage and salary scales has been attempted by Nkrumah and Nyerere with significant political repercussions. Few other African political leaders would probably attempt such a solution.

Granted that the African governments cannot set wage scales which are completely devoid of any considerations of demand and supply; nevertheless, within a very large range, they have the power and the apparent determination not to let 'economic forces' determine employee remuneration.

G Policy Measure to Stimulate Growth in Modern Sector Employment

In general, attempts to solve the urban unemployment problem by stimulating the growth in the demand for employment are likely to meet with difficulties. Efforts by government to increase its employment opportunities are limited by government budgetary considerations and the need to strike a balance between recurrent and investment expenditures. Attempts to impose a more labour-intensive regime in the private sector would have limited impact because of the relatively small proportion of the labour force employed in those industries with a significant scope for choice of technique.[27] In any case, a policy of more labour-intensive production in the modern private sector is difficult to implement. It requires either (*a*) direct government controls, (*b*) a system of taxes and subsidies to encourage the use of labour, or (*c*) a policy of wage restraint. The first two alternatives carry with them the danger that private investment may be discouraged and reduced in the process.

27 The author [11] conducted a study of the projected growth in the modern sector employment in Nigeria from 1963 to 1972. He used various assumptions, both optimistic and pessimistic, regarding the growth of government recurrent expenditure, growth of leading sectors, and the labour intensity of manufacturing investment. The annual growth in employment ranged from 24 per cent under the most pessimistic assumptions to 5.4 per cent under the most optimistic assumptions. The major conclusions derived from this study were the following:

(*a*) Assumptions concerning growth of government recurrent expenditure were the most important determinants of the growth of employment because of the importance of government in the total;

(*b*) The ratio of investment to total expenditure was an important determinant of the rate of growth of employment because of the indirect effect on the growth of construction, a relatively labour intensive industry; and

(*c*) A doubling of the labour intensity of investment in manufacturing had a very small impact on the growth rate of employment, resulting in an increase in the growth rate of from 0.4 to 0.6 percentage points.

The third alternative, wage restraint, involves some formidable social and political obstacles.

Perhaps the most discouraging argument against attempting to solve the urban unemployment problem by increasing employment opportunities is the tendency for supply and demand to interact[28] in such a way that an increase in employment is accompanied by an increase in unemployment. At any given wage rate and at any given point in time, the number of entrants into the urban labour force is not only a function of the prevailing wage rate, rural-urban real income differentials, etc., but probably also a function of the assessment of individuals of the subjective probability of getting a job. Prior to entering the urban labour force, a prospective entrant's assessment of this probability is likely to be very crude but nevertheless proportionately related to the ratio of the current stock of unemployed to the current number of persons gainfully employed.

Once a person has entered the labour force, any decisions to withdraw later from the labour force depends on whether he is gainfully employed or not. If he is not employed, his decision to withdraw, like his decision to enter, depends both on the wage rate and on his subjective assessment of the probability of getting a job which will change through time as the amount of his information increases through experience. Furthermore, the average length of time a labour force participant goes without a job is dependent on the ratio of those unemployed to those employed. The longer the labour force participant remains without a job, the more likely he is to leave the labour force both because his assessed probability of getting a job decreases the longer he remains unsuccessful in becoming employed and because his financial and intangible assets decrease. By intangible assets, we refer to his ability to live off relatives, friends, and tribesmen during his period of seeking work.

Once a person becomes employed, the likelihood of his leaving the labour force is reduced.

If the quantity of labour demanded increases autonomously, in the first instance, the ratio of unemployed to those employed in-

28 The relationship between quantity supplied of labour (labour force participation) and the numbers employed and unemployed has long been recognized with regard to the U.S. economy and recently has been the subject of intense empirical research. See Mooney [21] which contains a bibliography on studies of this nature. This kind of analysis has particular relevance for urban labour force participation rates in African countries because of the large stock of potential entrants into the urban labour force, i.e. those resulting in the rural areas.

creases as the number of employed increases. The fall in this ratio induces: (*a*) a greater flow of entrants into the labour force because of the increase in the subjective probability of obtaining a job and (*b*) reduces the flow of withdrawals from the labour force because of the increase in subjective probabilities, because of the reduction in the length of time a participant goes without a job, and because those who become gainfully employed are less likely to leave the labour force.

Thus, the quantity of labour demanded and quantity supplied to the labour force are not independent. An increase in quantity demanded brings forth an increase in the quantity supplied through a reduction in the flow out of the labour force and an increase in the number of new entrants. If the increase in the quantity supplied is greater than the increase in the quantity demanded, the net result will be an increase in the number unemployed.[29]

This analysis of interactions between supply and demand also indicates that the current rates of rural-urban migration may not be maintained for very long in the future. As the ratio of those not employed in the modern sector to those employed becomes very large, the subjective probability of obtaining a job will decrease. People are unlikely to continue to flock to the cities at current rates if there are so few jobs available. In the meantime, the stock of unemployed and under-employed is building up very rapidly and may be quite large before some sort of equilibrium is reached.[30]

29 In terms of a mathematical model, let w be the wage rate, Q_d be the quantity of labour demanded and Q_s be the quantity of labour supplied.

Then $$Q_d=f_d(w;a), \quad Q_s=f_s\left(w,\frac{Q_s-Q_d}{Q_d}\right)$$

where a is an automonous shift parameter. Equilibrium occurs when $Q_d=Q_s$ but the existence of equilibrium is not assured unless, among other things, there is some upper bound on Q_s, the total labour supply. For African countries, there is almost no effective upper bound on the numbers which can be supplied to the urban work force since it is such a small fraction of the total work force. A shift in demand (a change in a) results in the following change in quantity supplied if the wage rate is held constant: $\frac{\partial Q_s}{\partial a}$ etc.

where $e = (Q_s - Q_d)/Q_d$ is the unemployment ratio. The sign of df_s/de is negative for reasons discussed above. Thus the increase in demand at a given wage results in an even larger increase in supply if $\frac{Q_s}{Q_2}\frac{df_s}{de} > 1$.

With this kind of model, an increase in demand can actually lower the equilibrium wage even if the slopes of the demand and supply curve (*df_d/dw and df_s/dw*) are negative and positive, respectively.

30 For an analysis of the long-run unemployment equilibrium using a model similar to the one outlined here see Todaro [25].

Up to this point we have been concerned only with the possibility of increasing labour demand in the modern urban sector to alleviate urban unemployment. Other, perhaps more encouraging, alternatives exist. The first is a policy of encouraging the growth of the small-scale, mainly indigenous, urban entrepreneur. The second approach is to focus on policies which operate on the supply of labour rather than solely the demand for labour.

H *Encouraging the Small-Scale Producer*

Perhaps the most successful way of raising the labour intensity of investment is to give every encouragement, or probably more important, avoid every discouragement to the growth of the traditional small-scale sector. The employment effect of investment in the small-scale sector is much greater than in the modern sector. Estimates by Peter Kilby[31] and the National Manpower Board in Nigeria indicate that investment per worker in small-scale industry is about £100 to £200. In large-scale establishments, the average ratio is from £2,000 to £3,000 per worker.[32] With regard to encouragement of the small-scale sector, several points are worth making:

1 Aid to small-scale producers in the form of loan schemes or training schemes may not have much impact on increasing the labour absorptive capacity of small-scale establishments. The thrust of many schemes is to increase the efficiency of existing producers rather than to encourage expansion of total output and the entry of new firms. Increased efficiency often means less employment rather than more for a given level of output.

2 Investment in large-scale modern establishments sometimes competes directly with certain types of small-scale producers. The productivity of shoes and sandals and enamel hollow-

31 See Kilby [17], p. 5.

32 Analysis of the data in *Industrial Survey of Nigeria, 1963* (Lagos, Federal Office of Statistics 1966) indicates that paid-up capital alone (excluding debt-financed investment) amounts to about £1,700 per worker in manufacturing.

The National Developmant Plan, 1962-63 (Lagos, The Federal Ministry of Economic Development, 1962), p. 329, cites ten industrial undertakings in the western region having a total capital of £5.5 million and employing only 1,573 workers or an investment per worker of about £3,400. A forthcoming study by T. N. Yesufu reveals that the investment per worker in selected current and prospective development projects in Nigeria ranges from £1,700 to £34,000.

A survey conducted by the East African Manufacturers Association with 38 responses indicated a total paid up capital of £44 million and 19,626 workers. The range of variation in the capital labour ratio was £1,000 to £50,000.

ware in modern establishments may be examples where large-scale production has significantly replaced small-scale production and has led to a net decrease in employment in those industries. In other African countries, the establishment of large-scale government-owned wholesale and retail operations may have had a depressing effect on small-scale trading by private individuals. A few African governments have established large-scale, government trading corporations. If others should plan to do so in the future, the impact on small-scale trading should be considered.

3 Government regulation, licensing and controls may discriminate against the small-scale producers. While African countries, particularly those formerly controlled by the British, have had fairly liberal regimes, there have been many instances in other less developed countries where the unintended effect of government regulation and control has depressed small-scale production. Foreign exchange control, in particular, discriminates in favour of the large-scale, established producers. Exchange allocations are often based on past needs for imports and are difficult to obtain for small-scale, newer, and potentially growing establishments. The fixed costs involved in obtaining foreign exchange licenses, cutting through the red tape, bribery of officials, etc., can be absorbed more easily by the larger firms. Road transport licensing seems to have had an inhibiting effect on the growth of small-scale African run transport firms in East Africa.[33]

I *Reducing the Supply of Urban Workers*

Perhaps the most crucial variable which operates on both demand and supply is the rural-urban real income differential. Urban wage restraint must not be viewed so much as a stimulus to demand as a retardant operating on the supply of workers to the urban areas, especially if accompanied by policies which might raise rural real incomes.

It would be foolish to suppose that the real wage in the modern urban sector could be lowered by reducing money wages. If money wages are held constant or restrained, however, inevitably inflation would take its toll and real wages would deteriorate or rise only very slowly. As we pointed out above, the growth in money wages in

33 See Hawkine [14] Chapter VI.

Africa has come about mainly as the result of recommendations of commissions of inquiry into civil service wages and minimum wage legislation.

Rural real incomes might be raised in several ways. The pattern of development in many African countries has been one in which rural incomes have provided much of the surplus which has been used to finance expansion of social overhead facilities and modern sector development in the urban areas. The mechanism for providing this transfer has been agricultural marketing board policies (see Helleiner [15]), export taxes, and import duties on consumption goods. Direct income taxes on rural incomes and the channelling of savings through financial intermediaries has not been used to such a large extent. Two questions arise with regard to this policy. First, has the resulting reduction of peasant incomes been wise, given the rapid increase in real incomes of those employed in the modern sector? The transferring of the agricultural surplus probably has reduced peasant investment and contributed to the excessive draining off of workers to the city. Secondly, what has been the net impact on the rural sector of the investment financed through agricultural surpluses? Investment in urban construction, manufacturing, public utilities, and urban social overheads has often had little positive impact on the rural sector, especially when manufacturing of import substitutes involves higher prices to the rural consumers because of increased tariffs and monopoly protection. Investment in roads, rail, air travel, and port facilities has to some extent facilitated the movement of goods and services to and from and within the rural sector. All too often, however, a large proportion of the investment in roads is for widening, improving and paving the connections between main urban centres, and very little has been spent on agricultural and feeder roads. Most of the investment in air travel has been for improving the main international airports and purchasing aircraft for international service rather than for improving connections between rural centres.

More important, perhaps, than the bias of investment activity toward provision of services for the urban areas has been the bias of administrative and political effort towards satisfying the needs of urban areas. Improvement in the quality of rural life, say through increased activities of the departments and ministries concerned with rural community development, may not require so much increased investment in the rural areas as a redirection of thought, effort, and research towards that end and a political reform which gives rural interests a stronger voice in formulating government policy.

Finally, an approach based on limiting the growth of population might be possible.[34] Such a policy combined with attempts to reduce the urban-rural income differential could significantly reduce the population pressures on the cities. A report prepared for the Government of Kenya by several eminent experts on population control was fairly optimistic on the possibilities for population control in that African country. The government's response to the report was quite favourable. Perhaps some preliminary investigations of large-scale attempts at population control elsewhere in Africa are in order. Population control, however, is a very controversial subject and the deleterious effects of rapid population growth on development goals would have to be amply demonstrated before government acceptance could be obtained.

To sum up, the key to the solution of the unemployment, part-time and under-employment problem in the cities is a reduction of urban-rural real income differentials. This can be accomplished not only by urban real wage restraint and an increasing agricultural real incomes from cash crops, but by a redistribution of the benefits of social welfare schemes and public consumption goods toward the rural areas.

APPENDIX: THE RELATION BETWEEN GROWTH IN EMPLOYMENT AND GROWTH IN OUTPUT

In this appendix let us derive the relationship between growth in output and growth in employment using a general neo-classical type production function:

$$Y=f(Le^{\alpha t}, Ke^{\beta t}, S) \qquad (1)$$

where
L: Labour
K: Capital
S: Skilled Labour
Y: Output

34 Rapid rates of overall population growth tend to aggravate the urban unemployment problem for a number of reasons. First, the rapid growth of population means an increasing supply of potential entrants into the labour force. Secondly, while Africa is generally considered to be a land surplus area, there are certain regions of Africa where overpopulation is becoming an increasing problem. In other areas, a continued rapid growth in population will begin to result in pressures on the land in a few years. The increasing scarcity of land means that everything else being equal the rate of rural-urban migration will increase.

α: Rate of labour-augmenting technical change
β: Rate of capital-augmenting technical change
$L^* = Le^{\alpha t}$: 'effective' labour force
$K^* = Ke^{\beta t}$: 'effective' capital stock.

The equilibrium labour force at any time is determined by equating the marginal product of labour f_L with its price p_L:

$$f_L = p_L = f_{L^*} e^{\alpha t} \tag{2}$$

The change in (1) in (2) through time is determined by taking the total derivatives of both sides of these equations:

$$\dot{Y} = f_{L^*} \dot{L}^* + f_{K^*} \dot{K}^* + f_S \dot{S} \tag{1*}$$

$$\alpha f_L + f_{LL^*} \dot{L}^* + f_{LK^*} \dot{K}^* + f_{LS} \dot{S} = \dot{p}_L \tag{2*}$$

where the dot over a variable represents change per unit of time, f_x represents the first partial of f with respect to the variable x and f_{xy} represents the partial of f_x with respect to the variable y.

From (1*) and (2*) we may eliminate K^* and solve for L^*.

$$\dot{L}^* = \frac{[-f_{K^*}\dot{p}_L + (f_{LS}f_{K^*} - f_S f_{LK^*})\dot{S} + f_{LK^*}\dot{Y} + \alpha f_L f_{K^*}]}{(f_{LK^*}f_{L^*} - f_{LL^*}f_{K^*})} \tag{3}$$

Using the chain rule and product rule for differentiation we have the following relationships:

$$f_{L^*} = e^{-\alpha t} f_L; \qquad f_{K^*} = e^{-\beta t} f_K \tag{4}$$

$$f_{LL^*} = e^{-\alpha t} f_{LL}; \qquad f_{LK} = e^{-\beta t} f_{LK} \tag{5}$$

$$\dot{L}^* = e^{\alpha t}\dot{L} + \alpha L . e^{\alpha t} \tag{6}$$

Substitute (4), (5) and (6) into (3).

$$[-f_K \dot{p}_L + (f_{LS}f_K - f_S f_{LK})\dot{S} + f_{LK}\ \dot{Y} + \alpha f_L f_K] \tag{7}$$

where under the usual assumptions about production functions

$$D = (f_{KL} f_L - f_{LL} f_K) > 0 \tag{8}$$

We may rearrange (7) as follows:

$$\gamma_L = \alpha \frac{(f_L f_K - D.L)}{D.L} - \frac{f_K \dot{p}_L}{D.L} + \frac{(f_{LS} f_K - f_S f_{LK})}{D} \frac{S}{L} \gamma_S + \frac{f_{LK} Y}{D.L} \gamma_Y \tag{9}$$

where

$$\gamma_L = \frac{1}{L}\dot{L} \text{ rate of growth of labour (employment)}$$

$$\gamma_S = \frac{1}{S}\dot{S} \text{ rate of growth of skilled labour}$$

$$\gamma_Y = \frac{1}{Y}\dot{Y} \text{ rate of growth of output}$$

Equation (9) is represented in Fig. 1 assuming $\dot{p}_L$, r_S, and α are held constant at some fixed level. The effects of these variables will be to cause the intercept A in Fig. 1 to be negative if (*a*) wage rates rise ($\dot{p}_L > 0$); (*b*) if skilled labour grows (r_S positive) and skilled labour growth is on balance substitutable for growth in unskilled employment (($f_{LS} - f_S f_{LK}$) is negative); and/or (*c*) labour-augmenting technical change α is positive and $f_K f_L < D.L.$ The slope of the curve in Fig. 1 is the coefficient of r_Y in equation (9) and depends on the particular type of production function postulated.

BIBLIOGRAPHY

1 Baer, W., and Herve, M. E., 'Employment and industrialization in developing countries', *Quarterly Journal of Economics*, vol. 80, No. 1 (Feb. 1966), pp. 88-107.

2 Baryaruha, A., 'Productivity analysis and an attempt at employment projection', Kampala, East African Institute of Social Research, EDRP No. 76, July 1965.

3 Baumgartner, H. W., 'Potential mobility in agriculture: some reasons for the existence of a labor transfer problem', *Journal of Farm Economics*, Feb. 1965, vol. 47, pp. 74-82.

4 Birmingham, W., Neustadt, I., and Omaboe, E. N., *A Study of Contemporary Ghana*, vol. i, London, Allen and Unwin, 1966.

5 Calloway, A., 'Unemployment among African school leavers', *Journal of Modern African Studies*, vol. i, No. 3 (1963), pp. 351-71.

6 ——'School leavers and the developing economy in Nigeria', *Nigerian Institute of Social and Economic Research Conference Proceedings*, 1960, Ibadan.

7 Doctor, K. C., and Gallis, H., 'Modern sector employment in Asian countries: some empirical estimates', *International Labor Review*, vol. 89, No. 12 (Dec. 1964), p. 558.

8 Etherington, D. M., 'Projected changes in urban and rural population in Kenya and the implications for development policy', *The East African Economics Review*, vol. 1 (new series).

9 Fei, J. C. H., and Ranis, G., 'Innovation, employment and production in the development process', mimeographed.

10 Frank, C. R., Jr., *The Sugar Industry in East Africa*, Nairobi, East African Publishing House, 1965.

11 ——'Industrialization and Employment Generation in Nigeria', *Nigerian Journal of Economic and Social Studies*, Nov. 1967 (delayed).

12 Friedlander, S. L., *Labor Migration and Economic Growth*, Cambridge, Massachusetts, M.I.T. Press, 1965.

13 Galenson, W., 'Economic development and the sectoral expansion of employment', *International Labor Review*, vol. 88, No. 6.

14 Hawking, E. K., *Roads and Road Transport in an Underdeveloped Country, A Case Study of Uganda*, Colonial Research Studies, No. 32, H.M.S.O., London, 1962.

15 Helleiner, G., 'The fiscal role of marketing boards in Nigerian economic development', *Economic Journal*, Sept. 1964.

16 Johnston, B. F., 'Agriculture and economic development', *Food Research Institute Studies*, vol. vi, No. 3, 1966, Stanford University, Stanford, California.

17 Kilby, P., *The Development of Small Industry in Eastern Nigeria*, U.S. Agency for International Development, Lagos, Mar. 1962.

18 —— 'Organization and productivity in backward economies', *Quarterly Journal of Economics*, May 1962, vol. 76, pp. 303-10.

19 —— 'Industrial relations and wage determination in Nigeria', mimeographed.

20 Leibenstein, H., 'Allocative efficiency vs. X-efficiency', *American Economic Review*, June 1966, vol. 56, pp. 392-415.
21 Mooney, J. D., 'Urban poverty and labor force participation', *American Economic Review*, vol. 42, No. 1, Mar. 1967, pp. 104-19.
22 Nigeria Federal Republic, *Report of the Commission on the Review of Wages, Salary, and Conditions of Service of the Junior Employees of the Government of the Federation and in Private Establishments*, Lagos, 1964 (The Morgan Commission 1964 Report).
23 Pearson, D. S., 'Employment trends in a developing economy—the case of Southern Rhodesia', *The East African Economics Review*, vol. ii, No. 1, (June 1964), pp. 59-77.
24 Reynolds, L. G., 'Wages and employment in a labor surplus economy', *American Economic Review*, Mar. 1965, vol. 55, pp. 19-39.
25 Todaro, M., *The Urban Unemployment Problem in Less Developed Countries: An Analysis of Demand and Supply*, Chapter 3.
26 *United Nations*, *Statistical Yearbook* 1965, New York, 1966.
27 Uganda, *Report of the Minimum Wages Advisory Board*, Entebbe, 1964.

8

EMPLOYMENT AND WAGES IN DUAL AGRICULTURE

Robert Mabro

Introduction

THE PURPOSE of this paper is to analyse certain problems of employment and wage-determination in the agricultural sector of the labour-surplus economy.

In the elaborate theories of development propounded by Sir Arthur Lewis [18] and some of his followers [6], [7], [14], [15], agriculture is depicted by three simple assumptions. The institutional framework is uniform.[1] Labour is paid a subsistence wage whose level is determined by tradition or related in some ways to the average product. Disguised unemployment—a situation where the marginal product of labour is zero—prevails in the whole sector. In these models, the allocation of resources within agriculture is inefficient because of unfavourable endowments of land and capital. For many years this simplified picture has dominated the literature. As in other instances of the history of economics a set of convenient assumptions, legitimate perhaps in the framework of a given theory, has gained wide acceptance outside its original context and enjoyed over a long period the dubious legitimacy of a conventional view.

However, this acceptance was never universal. Criticisms were levelled at the concept of disguised unemployment soon after Nurkse and Lewis formulated the idea.[2] The reaction culminated with Schultz [27,], who purported to show that traditional agriculture, although poor, is efficient: the institutional framework is irrelevant to the issue of resource allocation; disguised unemployment is not a feature of agriculture in underdeveloped countries. Paglin [24] and Hansen [9], [11] among many other development economists

1 Often the institutional framework is not clearly specified, Lewis [18] alluded to an agricultural sector where the family holding is small. Fei and Ranis [6] considered first a peasant economy and in later chapters of their book analysed the behaviour of 'enlightened', presumably big, landlords. Neither Lewis nor Fei and Ranis examined the possibility of a dual structure in agriculture.

2 For a good summary of the debate see [5].

defended similar propositions. Schultz's views, though expressed in a form that few may accept without qualifications, represent a new and significant trend of thought, perhaps as influential today as Lewis' ideas fifteen years ago.

The empirical evidence accumulated in recent years for typical labour-surplus economies such as Egypt and India does not entirely support either Lewis' or Schultz's theories. The evidence will be reviewed in a later section; it will suffice here to note that it reveals a set of interesting features of agriculture in both countries.[3] (*a*) Agricultural wages are related to the marginal product of labour and seem to respond to the ordinary laws of supply and demand.[4] (*b*) The labour market is very active in certain regions especially during the seasonal peak. It attracts family workers from landed households and in some instances supplies small farmers with casual labour.[5] (*c*) Labour inputs per unit of land (and sometimes yields) tend to increase as the size of holdings decrease.[6] (*d*) Disguised unemployment may occur in some places[7] but is not a prevalent feature of agriculture in 'overpopulated' countries. (*e*) Under-employment—defined as a surplus stock of man-hours and measured by subtracting labour requirements from availabilities—seems to exist in many areas and to persist in some throughout the year.[8]

These findings suggest that the labour market is more perfect than Lewis and his followers led us to believe; that the assumption of a homogeneous agrarian system is not very helpful because modes of labour-utilization seem to differ according to type and size of farms; that the concept of disguised unemployment does not depict adequately the employment situation in agriculture. But they also point to the existence of surpluses and productivity differentials. Despite Schultz's contentions, poor agriculture is not efficient in all respects; the institutional framework may be relevant to the allocation of resources.

A question however arises: are the findings listed above consistent with each other? Is it possible to reconcile them all? The temptation is to retain some results in support of a preferred theory and to

3 The features are surprisingly similar for both countries.
4 See [9], [11].
5 See [8], [13], [19], [24], [31].
6 See [8], [13], [24], [31].
7 See [4].
8 See [12], [23].

dismiss the others. Paglin [24], for example, rejected the possibility of labour surpluses when he discovered that various groups of small farmers hire workers during the seasonal peaks. The validity of his argument depends on the assumption that *all* farms have recourse to outside labour, which is not the case. Hansen [9] took a similar line when he established that agricultural wages in Egypt behave according to the marginal productivity theory. But his reasoning implies that factor-markets are perfect, an assumption that may not be warranted everywhere. Some authors attempted to explain partial results excluding other aspects of the problem from consideration. The relationship between labour inputs, yields, and size of plots, for instance, received considerable attention. It was attributed alternatively to variations in soil fertility,[9] to the use of different techniques[10] or to differences in objectives.[11] Mazumdar [21], in a more elaborate explanation, argued that the supply price of family labour to their own farms is lower than that of hired workers,[12] but his interesting model is concerned with a case which does not exactly fit the evidence: it assumes that family workers do not enter outside employment and all farms hire wage-labour during the peak.

We shall attempt to analyse the conditions of agricultural employ-

9 The best statement of this hypothesis is that of Sen [29]: 'If two pieces of land are of the same size but holding A is more fertile than holding B, the former will provide a greater opportunity of earning income, so that family size may expand faster in the former case. This will lead to quicker subdivision of A than of B and soon a correlation may be established between smallness of the size of holdings and the fertility of soil. This argument is easy to see in the context of inter-regional variation, because it has been often observed that in fertile areas population expands faster both because of natural increase as well as migration. But the picture can be expected even within a given region particularly because of the ability of a family to withstand famines and other catastrophes is greater if the land it ownsis fertile than if it is not. Thus the correlation between size and fertility is not an odd result but one that can be expected on good economic grounds.' Sen, however, did not retain this hypothesis. See also Khusro [16].

10 However, according to Mazumdar [21, pp. 163-4], the Indian data suggest 'that the ratio of capital to labour input per acre does not vary much among farms of different sizes'.

11 Large farms aim at maximizing profits, small operators at maximizing output.

12 Mazumdar assumed that all workers have the same supply curve. But the supply price is a function of the number of days worked during the year. The agricultural year is divided into a busy and a slack season. In the busy season the labour force is fully employed and wages are equalized, but in the slack season wage labourers supply more days than family workers and their supply price is consequently higher. Sen [28] suggested also that a wage gap may exist. It may reflect either a distortion of the market or the higher social costs of hired labour as opposed to own labour or the higher efficiency of wage labour (higher wages attracting the best people and effecting productivity through better nutrition).

ment to show that the features disclosed by empirical research may be explained within a single framework. Differences of labour intensity on various farms may obtain despite factor mobility; physical underemployment is not necessarily eliminated by the operation of a competitive labour market. These features may be related to a well-defined tenure system. We do not aim at presenting a predictive theory but a 'model' which is both descriptive and analytical. The only claim is that it may encompass a wider range of phenomena than alternative explanations. The 'model' differs from both Lewis's and Schultz's in that it treats agriculture as a dual sector. There are two groups of farms which sell and purchase the services of labour and land because initial endowments are unequal. We are, however, in agreement with Lewis on the importance of unfavourable endowments, with Schultz on the rationality of peasants' behaviour, and with Sen and Mazumdar on the significance of wage-gaps in dual agriculture.

A. *Institutions and Behaviour*

(*a*) *The agrarian system*

We are concerned with an agrarian system defined by the rights of private property. Inequalities of land ownership are a usual feature of such a system. Farms vary in size along a spectrum from small holdings to large estates. It may be convenient to distinguish two types of farms according to the mode of operation, 'capitalist' (sometimes referred to as 'large') farms which rely on hired workers and 'family' (or 'small') farms mainly operated by the members of the household. The existence of a pool of landless workers[13] is typical of a system of private ownership. Some landless workers may be permanently attached to large estates;[14] others to small operators through family ties. Some, however, remain unattached and subsist by selling their services to farmers or by taking

13 The simultaneous existence of this pool of landless workers with that of labourers owning land has important implications often ignored in theoretical models. Neither Fei and Ranis [6] nor Lewis [18] concerned themselves with this problem. Berry and Soligo [2] studied wage labour as an *alternative* institution to peasant farming but did not explore the relationships that arise from their coexistence.

14 Attached workers are employed under various institutional arrangements. The nature and the strength of the bond vary from society to society. They may be paid either in cash or in kind or in some mixed form. In some areas, they may be required to supply a number of working days and receive in exchange the right to cultivate a small plot of land.

up non-agricultural jobs (construction, the services, transport, or trade) in rural areas.[15] This latter group is freely mobile, willing to enter casual day-to-day employment or to subscribe to longer-term commitments not only in the vicinity of their villages but sometimes in distant localities.[16]

The simultaneous existence in a given area of a large number of 'capitalist' farms and a sizeable group of landless workers creates the necessary conditions for a competitive market to develop. Competition is enhanced during the seasonal peak when labour requirements can be extremely high. Given these conditions we would expect wages to fluctuate seasonally on the labour market in response to the normal forces of supply and demand. Hansen's findings [9], [11] provide ample evidence for this phenomenon.

There is a market for the services of land which may be rented under various institutional arrangements: share-cropping or cash-tenancy. Cheung [3] has demonstrated convincingly that the choice of the suitable alternative ultimately depends on economic considerations, the risks attached to different crops, and the costs of drafting and implementing the tenancy contract. That alternative forms of contract are equivalent under certain conditions does not mean, however, that the land market is perfect. There are impediments that prevent potential tenants from optimizing the size of their holdings given their resources, their preferences for income and leisure, and the configuration of factor-prices. Imperfections in the land market arise for two main reasons. First, land is not mobile in the same sense as labour or capital are assumed to be. Hired labour moves *corps et biens* to the place of work; the services of land can be purchased but not transferred from one location to another. Family farms are not always able to rent either adjacent strips or pieces of land in the immediate neighbourhood and there is an economic limit to how many separate plots an individual farmer can operate at a time. Second, the willingness to let land depends to a certain extent on the credit-worthiness of potential tenants. Those who require more land are those who initially are less well endowed, landless workers, and owners of small plots; in other words, the least credit-worthy members of the rural community. Tenancy arrangements redistribute land from large owners to other farmers but they may fail to produce optimum adjustments. It is interesting

15 See Hansen [11, p. 300, Table 1].
16 See Ayrout [1, p. 55].

to note that in Egypt widespread inequalities of land 'holdings'[17] tend to persist[18] after tenancy arrangements are made notwithstanding the fact that some 47 per cent of the cultivated area is leased in various ways.

(b) Behaviour

We may infer from the ample evidence provided by empirical studies[19] on peasants' responsiveness to price incentives that farmers generally behave as 'rational' agents. The lack of response observed in certain cases is often due to the presence of risks which, at low levels of income, weigh heavily in the peasants' decisions. Those who argue that behaviour cannot be described in terms of economic 'rationality' tend to underestimate the importance of risks in poor agriculture. We shall assume that peasants maximize an objective given certain constraints and allowing for risks. Thus 'capitalist' or wage-labour farms tend to operate according to the postulate of profit-maximization. In the family sector individuals aim at maximizing their utility when they trade leisure for income (say corn) through work. Because of the dual structure of agriculture they may choose to work on the family holding or to enter wage-employment on large farms. Mobility is a corollary of rational behaviour when alternative opportunities are available. Landless peasants who find themselves unable to rent land can only supply their labour services for subsistence. They work for a positive wage which may not fall below the minimum necessary to compensate for the extra consumption that physical effort entails.

(c) Seasonality and the employment of labour

Agricultural production is seasonal in character. The demand for labour tends therefore to shift significantly from period to period

17 By 'holding' we mean here the plots, whether leased or owned, which are operated as a single unit.

18 The Agricultural Census of 1961 [30, part 1, section 1] shows the following distribution:

Size of 'holdings'	*Number of holdings*
less than 1 acre	423,951
1–2 acres	383,332
2–3 acres	285,607
3–4 acres	173,640
4–5 acres	99,318
5–10 acres	169,236
10–20 acres	55,420
20–50 acres	23,241
50–100 acres	6,271
100 and over	3,767

19 For an excellent survey see Krishna [17].

throughout the year. In certain instances, the market for casual labour ceases to function for lack of demand;[20] at other times competitive bidding may raise wages above the supply price of landless workers.[21] The production of a given crop entails a series of tasks linked in a time-sequence. Each has a specific technological characteristic. The demand for labour reaches a peak when the agricultural operation is labour intensive and/or must be performed within a short interval. Both the timing and the speed at which a given task should be performed may partly depend on occurrences which escape the farmer's control: maturity of plant, availability of water, weather, flood, pests. These simple features of agricultural production, often mentioned in the literature to emphasize the significance of seasonal underemployment, have other important implications for the present analysis.

The seasonal pattern of demand for labour affects the nature of the labour-contract that capitalist farmers tend to offer and the type of commitment landless workers would like to undertake at different times of the year. During the slack season, employers may require labour in limited amounts for very casual jobs. Their preference is for very short contracts: a day or two, a few hours here and there according to the nature and the importance of the task. Since labour is generally underemployed at that time, 'capitalist' farmers can easily enforce their preferences even if they do not correspond to the workers' desire for greater security. In Egypt, during the slack season, farms tend to employ labourers on a day-to-day basis for such tasks as sowing or watering the plants[22] and the system known as *tarhila* by which labour is recruited for four to eight weeks for the maintenance of canals and other irrigation works provides to some the security of a longer commitment outside the farm sector.[23] During the peak period farmers wish to secure the services of labour for the period necessary to the safe completion of the operation. Their preference is for an arrangement that commits labour or a subcontractor for the whole of the period. Saffa [26,

20 See [31, Report, D]. This survey records instances of Egyptian villages where no transactions have taken place on the labour market during certain weeks of the slack season, Also [9, p. 386].

21 Demand may exhaust the pool of wage labour, the supply curve of this group of workers thus becoming very inelastic. In Egypt, seasonal wage differentials are large. For men the average wage during the peak is 50 per cent higher than in the slack season, for women 100 per cent [11, p. 305, figure 1].

22 See Saffa [26, p. 411], 'Le journalier qui touche un salaire quotidien.... est charge d' accomplir un travel agricole tel que les semallies et l'arrosage.'

23 See Ayrout [1, p. 55], Saffa [26, p. 410],

p. 411] notes that for the wheat harvest and the gathering of cotton Egyptian farmers tend to employ *tâcherons* who are paid an agreed lump-sum each on completion of the task assigned. Others have recourse to a subcontractor (*kholi*) who guarantees a regular supply of labour for a fee or a commission.[24] Farmers succeed in enforcing their preferences at the price, perhaps, of higher labour costs or wages.

During the peak, the labour market, which operates in a manner that favours landless labourers, is less attractive to landed workers than it may, at first, appear. Family workers may wish to retain some control over the allocation of their services between their own farm and the outside employer while an important agricultural operation is being performed. Maximization of utility entails in some cases such a division of their time. If risks or costs are involved in the delaying of certain tasks the family worker would want to complete the job (say the harvest which represents the benefits of a year's effort) on his farm before he seeks other employment. In other circumstances he may value the convenience of being able to switch back to his own plot should an emergency arise after he has taken an outside job. The employer's preference for early and relatively long commitments from their workers during the peak restricts the choices of family labourers. Let us note, however, that the rigidities should not be attributed to the stipulations of a formal contract but to the relationship between the period of commitment sought by employers and the duration of the specific task performed at the time. A week-commitment seems short and flexible in the other labour markets. But it may represent a long and rigid undertaking for a family worker when the weather or other factors allow only ten or fifteen days for the safe completion of the operation in which all are engaged.

B. *Characteristics of Production and Employment in Agriculture*

(*a*) *Family farms*

Endowments of land are unequal on 'family' farms: households

24 See Saffa [26, p. 429] and Ayrout [1, p. 55], The *kholi Rom rais* commands a group of men who are attached to him by various bonds (relatives, clients, debtors). The worker receives a daily wage but is usually paid at the end of the week. The *kholi* can secure the workers' commitment by delaying payments in case of absenteeism. The workers often depends on the sub-contractor for

differ in size and plots in acreage. We shall characterize farms by the land to man ratio (hitherto referred to as '*n*') which may vary significantly from one end of the spectrum to another. To simplify the analysis the following assumptions are made: (*a*) Production: In the family sector peasants use the same techniques and cultivate a single crop—corn. Factors of production are homogeneous; the ratio of capital of labour is constant[25] and there are beyond a certain range diminishing returns to factors and constant returns to scale. (*b*) Households: The working members of a household are adult males of equal ability with identical preference maps for income (corn) and leisure. Neither corn nor leisure are inferior goods. If indifference curves were drawn they would be convex to the origin with a positively sloping income offer curve. The members of a given household supply equal amounts of work and acquire equal shares of the product.[26] Effort always implies some disutility.

Family workers can transform leisure into corn by working on their farms. Because of inequalities of endowments, workers from different households will operate at different points of their production functions and achieve different results.[27] (*a*) Both the marginal and average products of a given amount of labour inputs supplied by workers from different households vary directly with '*n*' (because the same quantity of labour is combined with larger tracts of land). (*b*) We may thus infer that, save in the absurd case where the income elasticity of goods is negative, the income of family workers increases with '*n*'. (*c*) The worker maximizes his utility on his own farm, given the production constraint determined by '*n*', by equating the marginal product of his labour (*MP*) with the marginal rate of substitution of leisure for goods (*MRS*). The equilibrium value of *MP* (= *MRS*) increases as '*n*' increases. (This proposition simply assumes that leisure is not a very inferior good.) (*d*) Implicit factor-prices are unequal for workers on different farms. The implicit wage-rate (*MP*), as noted earlier, increases and the implicit

works in construction or canal maintenance and for money advances during the slack season.

25 According to Mazumdar [21, pp. 163-4] the Indian data suggest 'that the ratio of capital to labour input per acre does not vary very much among farms of different sizes'.

26 The production function of a family farm has thus the same characteristics as the transformation curves (product/work) of a member of this farm.

27 For a similar description of features of family farms see [22]. Mellor, however, assumed that peasants' behaviour is characterized by 'low aspirations'. Our belief is that farmers in poor agriculture behave as any *home-oeconomicus*. They value leisure and income for both are 'goods'.

rental element decreases as '*n*' increases. The less well-endowed worker applies more labour inputs per acre than his more fortunate neighbour.[28] Other things being equal, yields will vary inversely with '*n*'. (*e*) Workers with a very unfavourable endowment may suffer from disguised unemployment. If average incomes are low, peasants may have to apply labour inputs up to the point where the marginal product is not significantly different from zero in order to secure their subsistence.[29] (*f*) Many workers could be physically underemployed in the sense that their actual supplies of labour fall short of some norm. Economists usually find this concept of underemployment wanting because of the arbitrariness involved in defining the 'full-employment' norm and the confusion between the notions of actual and intended supplies that may be implied. It is possible, however, to attach an economic meaning to this concept in the present context. Suppose that individual supplies are directly related to the amounts of land at the worker's command. Individuals although not involuntarily unemployed on the smallest farm (since all balance the marginal disutility of work, with its meagre marginal product) may be underemployed from the point of the economy as a whole if they are both able and willing to supply more work for a larger reward.

We have depicted the situation of family workers confined to their own farms. The higher the man-to-land ratio, the poorer is the worker, the smaller is the marginal product of his labour, and the greater is his marginal preference for goods in relation to leisure; the greater also is the likelihood of underemployment and disguised unemployment.

Family workers can improve their lot in two ways: by renting land or selling their labour services outside. We have argued that the imperfections of the land-market are significant. The poorer farmers are not able to maximize their utility through the optimum adjustment of their holdings of land. We must turn therefore to the labour market. Two situations may arise. First, family workers have no access to outside employment. There are places—villages with a concentration of small farms and no large estates in the neighbourhood—and times—slack seasons during which the labour market has ceased to function—when such a restriction may arise.

28 Which does not mean that the poorer worker supplies more units of labour to his farm.

29 There is no choice between goods and leisure at a level of income near subsistence.

In that case, the propositions established above would hold. Second, family workers have access to the labourmarket. This more general situation will be examined now.

(b) The labour market and family farms

We shall consider the agricultural sector at a time when a specific operation, say harvesting, is undertaken. Market wages ('*w*') are determined by the intersection of demand (larger farms) and supply (landless and certain groups of family workers). Capitalist farms operate at the point of their production functions which equates the marginal product of labour and the market wage. Family farms are able to hire or to supply labour.

At one end of the family farm spectrum[30] the marginal product of labour may exceed the market wage. Farmers belonging to this group will tend to hire outside workers in order to increase the welfare of their members. But perfect adjustments are not possible, save when labour time can be purchased in infinitely divisible amounts. The flexibility of adjustments mainly depends on two factors: the labour contract and the size of the employer's family. The greater rigidities are experienced when the contract is relatively long and the household small.[31] Their significance, however, should not be exaggerated. Family employers may attract some workers from poorer households who prefer shorter commitments than the ones offered by 'capitalist' farms. We may thus infer that the market equalizes the marginal product of labour with the wage-rate on a number of large family farms (those able to hire outside labour up to the optimum amount). Because of the rigidities mentioned above a number of odd farms operate at points of their production functions where $MP > w$.

At the lower end of the spectrum, the marginal product of labour is below the wage rate. Workers from these households may seek outside employment. The supply price of a landed labourer is a function of his marginal product (*MP*) on the family farm, the probability ('*p*') of finding a job, the disutility of having to supply a contractual amount of work (if it is in excess of the amount

30 Farms with a large endowment of land.

31 The services of a hired worker relieve all the members of the employer's family. We can thus assume that the services of an outside worker are equally distributed among all family workers. For any contract of duration '*t*' the larger the family, the greater are the opportunities to divide '*t*' among the family members.

supplied at home during a given agricultural operation or if it hinders a desired flexibility of the allocation of his time), and that of working under supervision. Other things being equal the supply price is an increasing function of *MP*, i.e. of the land-to-man ratio '*n*'. Given the wage-rate *w*, the market attracts workers from households at the lower end of the farm-scale up to a marginal household H^*.[32] On H^*, the worker is indifferent as between his own farm and the outside employer. The worker is indifferent (assuming that he is compensated by other members of the household for the rental element of his land) if

$$MP^* = wp\,(1-a); \quad o<a<1 \quad \text{and} \quad o<p<1, \qquad (1)$$

where '*p*' expresses the probability of finding a job and '*a*' the proportion of his expected wage which he sets against the disutility of outside employment.

If he is not compensated for the rental element, the condition becomes

$$AP^* = f(MP^*) = wp(1-a). \qquad (2)$$

The marginal product of the 'indifferent' worker on his own farm is always lower than the wage rate. The differential between MP^* and *w* is larger in (2) than it is in (1) because $AP > MP$.

During the peak, the probability '*p*' of finding a job is high but the disutility of outside employment may weigh significantly in the worker's decision.[33] On the contrary, '*p*' is low during the trough but the disutility is less significant. For one cause or another, the differential may persist in all seasons.

The labour market does not eliminate factor-price differentials on family farms. The *MP* of labour of family farms ranges between a lower limit MP^* ($<$ w) and a higher limit which may be equal to or greater than *w*. The range is probably wider during the slack

32 We assume that the household consists of more than one worker. When a member leaves the farm to take outside employment, his companions are left with more land each. They move up the '*n*'-scale and the equilibrium *MP* on his farm increases. (Note that the welfare of the man's companions does not increase if they compensate him exactly for the rental element.)

33 The supply price of a family worker may be different to family farmers with larger farms than to capitalist farmers: if the nature of the contract varies with the employer. During the peak, the disutility coefficient '*a*' may be smaller for employment on another family farm than on a capitalist farm but '*p*' also may be lower. The farm structure (capitalist/large family farm/small family farm) in an 'overpopulated' country such as Egypt is very broad at the base, narrower in the size range of 3–5 acres, and broader again above this size.

season when the market is not active (see previous section) than during the peak. That *MP* varies with '*n*' means that the rental rate, labour intensities, and yields are also related to the land-to-man ratio. Mazumdar [21] has shown that this conclusion will hold even if the differentials between the supply price of family workers to their own farm and the wage rate appear in only one of the two seasons (the slack). For labour inputs applied at different times of the year are complementary in agricultural production. We have argued, however, that differentials are characteristic of both seasons.

The labour market eliminates disguised unemployment in the case defined by equation (1). The worker whose marginal product is zero is induced to take an outside job because $wp\,(1-a)$ is always positive. Disguised unemployment may persist in the case defined by equation (2). The worker whose marginal product is zero will take an outside job if $wp\,(l-a)$ is equal or greater than his average product which is always positive.

Physical underemployment is consistent with the model. That it occurs during the trough does not require explanation. During the peak, family workers who are not occupied on their farms for the full duration of the agricultural operation may remain unemployed (*a*) if the free time at their disposal falls short of the minimum required by the labour contract; (*b*) if, having chosen because of risks and costs[34] to complete first the work on their own farms, they find themselves towards the end of the operation in a residual labour market where few jobs are offered.

C. *Results and Empirical Evidences*

We have treated the agricultural sector as a set of productive units with unequal endowments of labour and land. The agents are 'rational' and the markets competitive. For factor-equalization to obtain, one factor at least should be perfectly mobile. But there are imperfections. The labour market is affected by a single but rather minor restriction: the existence of contractual agreements. The land markets is more seriously hindered by geographical and institutional impediments. The time pattern of agricultural

34 Peasants' attitudes towards waiting are affected by uncertainty. They tend to gather cotton or harvest wheat as soon as the crop is ready if the risks of the weather turning are high. Waiting implies costs: watching the field at night (if he delays the harvest), losses arising from inadequate barns and stores (if he delays threshing), etc.

operations is subject to economic and technological constraints. These assumptions may not conform with traditional thinking on underdeveloped countries, usually influenced by Lewis' views on labour and Ricardo's on land. We suggested, however, that the most important are related to observed facts.

In our agriculture landed workers are mobile. They respond to the inducement of higher incomes by taking outside employment. Their supply price is among other things a function of land endowments. On the other hand, small farms may have recourse to outside help. The Egyptian survey on 'Employment Problems in Rural Areas'[35] undertaken with the help of the I.L.O. in 1964–5 and the Indian 'Studies in the Economics of Farm Management' provide ample evidence of this mobility. Paglin [24, p. 824] referring to India stated that 'available statistics show that the extent of outside work is quite considerable in many areas'. Data for both countries are presented in Tables 1 to 3. As expected, amounts of outside labour supplied or demanded by small farms are a function of farm and household size.

We have shown that total labour inputs per acre (and *ceteris paribus* yields) are a function of '*n*', the land-to-man ratio. If this ratio increases as the acreage of holdings decreases,[36] an inverse relationship between labour intensity and size would obtain. Such a relationship is well established empirically and has been discussed at length in the literature.[37] There is no need to expand this subject here.

In our analysis, the possibility of disguised unemployment is related to very special conditions. Empirical research, save for one significant instance, has failed to produce convincing evidence of disguised unemployment. Desai and Mazumdar [4, p. 49] having established that the marginal product of labour is not significantly different from zero for a sample of Indian farms, note, however, that (*a*) these farms use only family labour and (*b*) they are concentrated in villages where few wage-labour farms exist. For disguised unemployment to appear two conditions seem necessary: an unfavourable man-to-land ratio and a slack labour-market.

Most empirical studies on underemployment in agriculture apply a method known as the labour utilization approach which measures

35 For a summary of the results see [13].
36 For the evidence see [20, p. 168] and [8], [31].
37 The evidence for India is discussed in Mazumdar's and Paglin's important articles. See [21], [24]. For Egypt, see [31, Report C].

TABLE I

WORK SUPPLIED OUTSIDE OWN FARMS (EGYPT)

Size of farm (feddans)*	Size of household (no. of working members)	Work outside own farm** (% of hours worked annually)
0.5-under 2	3 and under	18
2.0-under 5	,,	4
5 and over	,,	3
0.5-under 2	more than 3	33
2.0-under 5	,,	14
5 and over	,,	5

* 1 feddan=1 acre approximately ** Adult males only

Sources: (31, statistical tables, table 10A, p. 29), (11, table 2, p. 301).

TABLE II

USE OF HIRED LABOUR ON SMALL FARMS (EGYPT)

Size of farm (feddans)	Holdings employing outside labour (%)
0.5-under 2	24*
2.0-under 5	36
5.0-under 10	53
10.0 and over	85

* Mainly temporary labourers

Source: (31 report C, p. 41).

the difference between the available amounts of labour units at a given place and time and actual (or required) inputs. They measure 'physical' underemployment and nothing else. The claim, often made in the past, that their results are evidence of disguised unemployment (a concept relating to the marginal product of labour inputs) has caused much confusion and unnecessary controversy. That disguised unemployment is unlikely to prevail when family farmers have access to a labour market has been established analytically and the empirical evidence referred to above

TABLE III

USE OF HIRED LABOUR ON SMALL FARMS (UTTAR PRADESH, INDIA)

Size of farms (acres)	Hired labour (% of total labour inputs)*
0-2.5	11
2.5-5.0	10
5.0-7.5	18
7.5-10.0	20
10.0-15.0	29

* Annual labour inputs are measured in days per acre.
Source: (24, table 4, p. 823).

provides some support. But we have argued that 'physical' underemployment is consistent with the existence of a labour market. The evidence suggests that agriculture holds a surplus of labour-time. It seems that availability exceed requirements throughout the year which led some authors such as Mohieldin [23] for Egypt and Mellor [22] for India to conclude that the 'surplus' is not simply a seasonal but a permanent feature of agriculture. Mohieldin also found that the excess stock of labour-time increases as the size of holdings decreases; that the size of the surplus varies significantly according to regions, categories of workers, and the nature of the agricultural operation. His quantitative estimates may exaggerate labour availabilities but the qualitative results seem well established. On the other hand, agricultural wages seem to behave in a way that indicates flexible response to supply and demand conditions.[38] We have focused our analysis on a relatively short time interval—the period during which a specific agricultural task is performed—to show that physical underemployment may exist when demand for labour is at its peak. The argument is (*a*) that structural factors (the pattern of land holdings) cause underemployment in the first place and (*b*) that the labour-market, given the complex preferences of various groups of employers and workers, may not succeed in achieving full employment.

Our analysis may be construed as an attempt to integrate a wider range of facts and relationships into a single theoretical framework.

38 See Hansen [9], [11], who produced very convincing evidence for Egypt.

It has limitations (we have excluded 'capital' from consideration and this factor may turn out to be important, especially on very large farms). It points to the need for more empirical research in the nature of agrarian institutions and the significance of market imperfections. One may raise further questions: is it legitimate to ignore differences between male labour and women and children? How rigid is the job distribution by sex and age in poor agriculture?[39]

Conclusion

That an inefficient allocation of resources characterizes the agricultural sector of a poor and overpopulated economy is the cornerstone of many theories of development. The concept of disguised unemployment used to provide an elegant and attractive explanation. Dissatisfaction with this concept culminated with the Schultz [27] argument that traditional agriculture is efficient in the use of resources. The interesting feature of the various studies and surveys mentioned earlier in this article is that they concur in their findings. They reveal similar patterns of allocation involving factor-price differentials and surpluses of labour-time: certain symptoms of inefficiency.

In our view, inefficiency should not be attributed—as in the disguised unemployment hypothesis—to irrational attitudes on the part of peasants, employers, and landowners in poor agriculture. The economic rationality of human agents may not be a function of development and wealth.

The pattern of resource allocation that seems to obtain in certain underdeveloped countries is attributed to the agrarian structure, widespread inequalities in the ownership of land, the absence of credit facilities to the tenants, and the arrangements that govern the employment of hired labour. This change of emphasis entails policy implications. For earlier writers, the concept of disguised unemployment was associated with idea of 'costless' transfers of labour from agriculture to industry. Our model points to the need of institutional reform *within* agriculture. Changes in the structure of land holdings and land ownership may result in a better use of resources. For incomes, yields, and employment are a function of the size of farms. On large estates, the labour force is more

39 See [11] and [23] for discussions of this problem.

fully employed but yields are usually low and a large share of agricultural income is transferred outside the rural sector to absentee landlords. On very small farms yields sometimes are significantly higher but the peasant's average income is low and family labour underemployed. A land reform ought to tackle the problem of size at both ends of the farm spectrum: the consolidation of small farms into larger production units (through co-operatives for example) may be as important as the breaking up of large estates. The likely effects of a successful land reform[40] are increased yields (and therefore total production), higher rural incomes, and a fuller utilization of family labour. Landless workers missed out by the redistribution measures may become temporarily worse off because of reduced employment opportunities on farms. A land reform, thus, may transform 'hidden' unemployment of family labour into open unemployment of landless workers.[41] If the land reform succeeds, however, in increasing the share of agricultural income retained by the rural population, employment opportunities will expand in the countryside in such activities as trade, construction, cottage industry, transport, and personal services Eventually, the landless workers displaced from large estates would be absorbed by the development of non-agricultural activities in rural areas.

To focus on institutions rather than behaviour may be more helpful for the purposes of economic policy. Theories that presuppose abnormal motives and attitudes on the part of peasants offer little scope for action in their favour. How does one go about changing these alleged attitudes? To claim against these theories that agriculture is efficient in underdeveloped countries may also lead to the same neglect of genuine needs for agrarian reforms. We have seen that such claims seem to contradict the empirical evidence.

40 A successful land reform entails complimentary measures the discussion of which is beyond the scope of this paper. For an excellent treatment see Warriner's classical work [32].

41 The theoretical implication is interesting for it suggests that institutional reform is a necessary condition for the success of the labour transfer mechanism postulated by Lewis and his followers.

REFERENCES

1 Ayrout, H., *The Egyptian Peasant*, Boston, 1968.

2 Berry, R. A., and Soligo, R., 'Rural-urban migration, Agricultural output and the supply price of labour in a labour surplus economy', *Oxford Economic Papers*, vol. 20, July 1968.

3 Cheung, S. N. S. *The Theory of Share Tenancy*, Chicago, 1969.

4 Desai, M., and Mazumdar, D., 'A test of the hypothesis of disguised unemployment', *Economica*, vol. 37, 1970.

5 Eicher, C. K., and Witt, L. W., *Agriculture in Economic Development*, New York, 1964.

6 Fei, J. C. H., and Ranis, G., *Development of the Labour Surplus Economy: Theory and Practice*, Homewood, Illinois, 1964.

7 Findlay, R. F., 'Capital theory and development planning', *The Review of Economic Studies*, vol. xxxix, Feb. 1962.

8 Government of India, Ministry of Food and Agriculture, *Studies in the Economics of Farm Management*, Delhi, 1957-62.

9 Hansen, B., 'Marginal productivity wage theory and subsistence wage theory in Egyptian agriculture', *Journal of Development Studies*, vol. 2, July 1966.

10 —— 'The distribution shares in Egyptian agriculture, 1897-1961', *International Economic Review*, vol. 9, June 1968.

11 —— 'Employment and wages in rural Egypt', *American Economic Review*, vol. 59, June 1969.

12 Hopper, W. D., 'Seasonal labour cycles in an eastern Uttar Pradesh village', *Eastern Anthropologist*, vol. 8, Nos. 3-4.

13 International Labour Organization, *Rural Employment Problems in the U.A.R.*, Geneva, 1969.

14 Jorgenson, D., 'The development of a dual economy', *Economic Journal*, vol. 71, June 1961.

15 —— 'Surplus agricultural labour and the development of a dual economy', *Oxford Economic Papers*, vol. 19, Nov. 1967.

16 Khusro, A. M., 'Returns to scale in Indian agriculture', *Indian Journal of Agricultural Economics*, vol. xix, July-Dec. 1964.

17 Krishna, R., 'Agricultural price policy and economic development' *in* Southwell, H. M., and Johnston, B. F. (eds.), *Agricultural Development and Economic Growth*, Ithaca, 1967, pp. 497-540.

18 Lewis, W. A., 'Economic development with unlimited supplies of labour' *Manchester School of Economic and Social Studies*, May 1954.

19 Mabro, R., 'Industrial growth, agricultural underemployment and the Lewis model. The Egyptian Case, 1937-1965', *Journal of Development Studies*, vol. 4, June 1967.

20 Mathur, A., 'The anatomy of disguised unemployment', *Oxford Economic Papers*, vol. 16, July 1964.

21 Mazumdar, D., 'Size of farms and productivity: A problem of Indian peasant agriculture', *Economica*, vol. 32, May 1965.

22 Mellor, J. W., 'The use and productivity of farm family labour in early stages of agricultural development', *Journal of Farm Economics*, vol. 45, Aug. 1963.

23 Mohieldin, A., 'Agricultural investment and employment in Egypt since 1935', PhD. thesis, London, 1966 (unpublished).

24 Paglin, M., 'Surplus agricultural labor and development: facts and figures', *American Economic Review*, vol. 55, Sept. 1965.
25 Pepelasis, A., and Yotopoulos, P. A., *Surplus Labour in Greek Agriculture* 1953-1960, Centre of Economic Research, Athens, 1962.
26 Saffa, S., 'Exploitation agricole et economique d'un domaine rural Egyptien', *Egypte Contemporaine*, vol. 50, 1949.
27 Schultz, T. W., *Transforming Traditional Agriculture*, New Haven, 1964.
28 Sen, A. K., 'Peasants and dualism with or without surplus labor', *Journal of Political Economy*, vol. 74, Oct. 1966.
29 —— 'Size of holdings and productivity', *Economic Weekly*, Annual Number, Feb. 1964.
30 United Arab Republic, *Agricultural Census of Egypt*, 1961, 5 vols. Cairo, 1968 (in Arabic).
31 United Arab Republic, Institute of National Planning, and International Labour Organisation, *Research Report on Employment Problems in Rural Areas, UAR*, 10 vols., Cairo, 1965-8.
32 Warriner, D., *Land Reform in Principle and Practice*. Oxford, 1969.

9

INDUSTRIAL SECTOR LABOR ABSORPTION*

Gustav Ranis

I

THE RECENT increased focus on the LDC unemployment problem takes many forms; like development itself, the issue is complex and many faceted. But perhaps no link in the chain of attempted understanding has been as uncertain and controversial as the question of the range of technology choice actually physically open to the contemporary LDC in its nonagricultural sector—even if it were of a mind to listen to relevant advice on the subject.

This paper is intended to throw some light on the particular question of LDC industrial sectors' ability to efficiently absorb unemployed or underemployed labor in the course of the development process. We know that in the past even where countries have been growing at 5 or 6 per cent annually in real terms—and overall growth has generally been quite satisfactory in the 1960s, as the Pearson Commission records—industrial sector growth rates of from 8 to 10 per cent annually have been accompanied by labor absorption rates of only 2-3 per cent. Moreover, the elasticity of industrial employment with respect to output has not only been low but also apparently falling over time.[1] Consequently, virtually everywhere in the LDC world some combined index of unemployment or underemployment seems to have been on the rise—and accompanied by an even more pronounced rise in the awareness of the inadequacy of per capita income as the main indicator of adequate performance.

When this somber historical record is combined with the fact that, even if 'zero population growth' policies were adopted everywhere tomorrow, the age structure of the present LDC population

* This paper was prepared with the support of the IBRD's Development Research Center and the Agency for International Development.

1 See Werner Baer and Michel E. A. Hervé, 'Employment and Industrialization in Developing Economies,' *Quarterly Journal of Economics*, 80, no. 1 (February 1966): pp. 88-107.

would yield a labor force explosion of major proportions (close to 3 per cent annually over the next decade or so), the dimensions of the problem become clear. If the developing world should be unable to absorb these inevitable projected additions to their labor force—never mind mopping up the substantial pool of underemployment already in existence in most places—the prospects are indeed grim.

The role of the industrial sector in this context—even when we define it broadly as including all nonagriculture except the 'spongy' services—of course tells only part of the story. Clearly, if an LDC is developing at all, it is likely to have to activate its preponderant agricultural sector in the process. Whether or not agricultural productivity increase in this context turns out to be labor using or labor displacing is extremely important to the size of the burden placed on nonagricultural sector absorption for any given rate of aggregate growth. But I shall concentrate here on the capacity of nonagriculture to efficiently absorb labor. Not only is there more misunderstanding on this—somehow most people seem to accept the realism of alternative scale, tenure, and input combinations in agriculture while holding religiously to fixed proportions in industry—but we also know, regardless of how the inquiries into the employment consequences of the Green Revolution come out, that, over time, people inevitably will be pushed out of agriculture, in the case of success, and pulled out, in the case of failure, and that the nonagricultural sector's ability to absorb them efficiently will play a crucial role in any total balanced development story.

In Section II, I try to place the generally poor record of industrial labor absorption in its proper historical and policy perspective. In Section III, I advance some preliminary notions of the differential nature of the innovation process over time in that context, and in Section IV, I attempt to demonstrate the empirical relevance of these notions, under conditions of a favorable policy environment, by reference to historical Japan and contemporary Korea and Taiwan.

II

It has by now become part of the conventional wisdom to criticize the so-called import substitution regime most LDCs followed during the fifties and sixties. This regime usually comprised a well-known syndrome of policies including exchange controls cum import licensing. budget deficits cum inflation, and low (sometimes negative) real rates of interest. The aim, generally speaking, was to redirect pre-independence traditional colonial flows to the creation of social and economic overheads and import-replacing, consumer-goods industries. The consequence was often a spurt in industrial output growth but of an inefficient—that is, capital and import intensive—character, accompanied by the discouragement of exports and of agricultural output, low rates of industrial employment, low rates of technological change, low domestic saving rates, and a relatively heavy dependence on foreign aid.

As LDC governments became increasingly aware of the economic costs of this set of policies, one could observe, during the sixties, a tendency, at least in some countries, to consider turning to an alternative set of policies. This set can be characterized, if again at the cost of oversimplification, as aiming at a reduction of some of the gross inefficiencies attending industrial development through the readjustment of a number of crucial, previously distorted, relative prices, including the exchange rate and the interest rate. By replacing quantitative controls in the foreign exchange market with tariffs and moving toward more realistic exchange rates, via either a de jure or de facto devaluation, and replacing severe credit rationing with higher interest rates, developmental access and participation could now be offered to medium- and small-scale industrial entrepreneurs for the first time. In the course of this second phase, industrial development is based less on natural and more on human resources; export substitution occurs, that is, new exports, especially of a non-traditional, labor-using variety, no longer discriminated against, begin to expand; domestic saving rates begin to move up into the 'take-off' range; agriculture is no longer fettered by unfavorable terms of trade and can begin to play its historical role in earnest, that is, generating surpluses which, when successfully channeled, provide simultaneous employment opportunities for the unskilled labor force being released; and indigenous technological change in both sectors can assume much greater importance.

While there exists as yet no marked trend toward such 'export substitution' policy packages in the less developed world generally, its adoption has indeed had remarkable results—for example, in Korea, Taiwan, and West Pakistan—in turning some situations of virtual overall stagnation in the fifties into high growth situations in the sixties.

Perhaps most important for us here is the fact that the new and better signals in this phase are likely to induce the adoption of different, more labor-using, or unemployment-reducing, technologies and output mixes. In this context, the vital role, for better or worse, of technological flows between rich and poor countries inevitably comes into play. The very coexistence of countries at very different levels of technology has to represent one of the most important influences on the performance of LDCs, past, present, and prospective. It is the precise nature of these technological flows, and the way in which they have been accommodated by LDCs, which has, in my view, had a decisive impact on overall performance during these past two decades of development. Alternatively put, it is also in this area in which the greatest potential for improved LDC performance in the seventies on both output and employment grounds can and must be located.

Under the influence of the record of the past, many have concluded that a conflict between these two objectives is inevitable. But before we accept such fundamentally dismal conclusions we have an obligation to carefully examine the validity of the proposition, especially in countries which seem to have performed well with respect to both output and employment growth in the past. Certainly such an examination is necessary before we can intelligently address the question of how the LDC world as a whole will be able to efficiently absorb the inevitable projected additions to their labor force, not to mention the existing backlog of the unemployed and underemployed.

As we look into the 1970s, three major schools of thought seem to be emerging with respect to the solution of the unemployment problem. One suggests we need more growth, that is, a higher growth rate, traditionally arrived at, with enough 'trickle down' to achieve full employment. This is clearly, at best, an expensive and unrealistic proposition, requiring huge volumes of foreign capital, for instance, if the rickety, import-substitution-dominated machinery of the sixties is to yield, without restructuring, substantially more employment. The second approach also assumes no major parameter shift in the behavioral relations of the system. It suggests, however, that after the traditional planning exercise has been consummated, a 'supplementary strategy' must be employed to mop up the remaining unemployed. This customarily means instituting labor-intensive public works programs. There is a real possibility here, especially where the rural infrastructure, for example, is inadequate, but evidence to date indicates that blueprinting and executing capacity may be a constraint as one goes from project to project. But most important, this approach fails to make the employment issue part of the primary strategy of development and relegates it to an afterthought, which—despite all 5-year-plan protestations to the contrary—was essentially the situation in the 1950s and 1960s.

The third approach attempts to change the nature of the growth pattern itself by making it more responsive to the factor endowment. This means that we don't try to 'dethrone the GNP,' except perhaps in political terms, but we try to place it on a 'sturdier throne.' In other words, once the open dualistic economy moves out of its administered-price, import-substitution hothouse and into a more market-oriented, export-substitution phase, it becomes possible for major efficient changes in output mix and technology—both in a labor-using direction—to take place. Such restructuring, as can be demonstrated in the cases of Taiwan and Korea, may permit the economy to have more of both, that is, more output *and* more employment, rather than having to make a choice between them. Moreover, such a move towards more market-oriented signals has absolutely nothing to do, as it is sometimes alleged, with a return to colonialism or handing the country over to unbridled free enterprise. The same desirability of letting the endowment 'be heard' in production decisions applies to the socialist countries; and, in fact, the market is increasingly being used as a tool of socialist planning, and in pursuit of socialist objectives, in Eastern Europe today.

Finally, we should note that income distribution, a third and increasingly important dimension of developmental performance, also stands to benefit. There are those who assume that any tendency at wage restraint at low levels, in keeping with the condition of labor surplus, must be bad for the 'little man.' In fact, quite the opposite is likely to be the case. Where the poverty problem is in considerable part an unemployment problem—due to the government's unwillingness or inability to redistribute fiscally—those who are hurt by wage restraint are the already employed or labor elite, not the usually disfranchised, unemployed, or underemployed. Not only total output, and hence per capita income, but also the wage bill is likely to rise once the economy moves to efficient labor-intensive technologies and output mixes. Figures on income distribution in a number of countries interestingly enough indicate that Taiwan is the best performer here as well, that is, sporting the most equal distribution of income in the sample. Even more instructive is the fact that Taiwan shows up as a much better performer on this count in 1964—when export substitution was in full swing—than in 1953—during its import-substitution phase. While economists who are conditioned to think always in terms of trade-offs will hate to admit it, labor surplus developing countries, well within their efficiency frontier, may be able—with the right policy changes—to enjoy more employment, more growth, and more income distribution at the same time.

With this realization, a lot more attention is now being paid to the importance of factor price distortions, over-valued exchange rates, inappropriate fiscal policies, 'premature' welfare legislation, and other institutional constraints which have obviously contributed to the low rate of labor utilization, especially in the LDCs' growing nonagricultural sectors. But much less attention has been paid to date to the actual technological choices available to the typical LDC—on the assumption its entrepreneurs and government officials could be brought to the point of facing a more reliable set of signals relative to the existing factor endowment and skill capacities. In other words, even if domestic fiscal, monetary, credit, and exchange-rate policies were ideal, would the choice of technology from the shelf available abroad and/or producible at home yield a substantially different kind of technology—or are there other, overwhelmingly severe, choice constraints forcing acceptance of technology currently available in the most advanced of the capital-exporting countries?

Many LDC officials, aid donors, and scholars still share the point of view that most technological change, especially in non-agriculture, must take place abroad and that the borrowing LDCs, in fact, have only a very narrow set of technological choices open to them. If only the coefficients attaching to the latest vintage machinery produced in the most advanced countries are relevant, all the talk about alternative factor proportions in response to alternative resource endowments becomes largely irrelevant or restricted to changes in output mixes via trade.

Such skepticism on the scope of technological choice is, of course, not unrelated to the still considerable dragging of the feet in abandoning the import-substitution policy package in much of the less developed world. In spite of the real world demonstration of what can, in fact, be accomplished, there remain formidable obstacles to the dismantling of the import-substitution regime. Direct controls imply absolute power—as well as supplementary incomes—for the civil service, which it is loath to surrender lightly. Moreover, the inevitably greater role for private enterprise under any liberalized regime runs up against associations with colonialism and fears of antisocial give aways. But one of the more powerful arguments on the side of conservative policy makers remains the supposed rigidity of the choices actually available. In large part it results from deducing the inevitability of fixed proportions from their historical prevalence during the import-substitution phase. I intend to investigate this issue by, first, attempting to elucidate the differential nature of the innovational process in each phase and then by demonstrating the potentially substantial scope for labor-using innovations by reference to the cases of historical Japan and contemporary Korea and Taiwan.

III

First and foremost, it should be remembered that, unlike in an advanced country where technological change is viewed as rather automatic and routinized or as capable of being generated through R & D expenditures according to some rules of cost/benefit analysis, in the contemporary developing societies technological change cannot either be taken for granted or afforded through basic R & D allocations. In this situation, we cannot avoid the question of what, given the existence of a shelf of technology from abroad, is the pattern by which the typical less developed economy, in fact, manages to innovate. This question in turn forces us to look at least at the following dimensions more carefully: (1) precise nature of that technology shelf, (2) the availability within the LDCs of required initial managerial and entrepreneurial capacity, and (3) the changing nature of that required managerial and entrepreneurial capacity in the course of transition to modern growth.

The technology shelf developed in the mature industrial economies abroad may be described by a set of unit activities following a smooth envelope curve as in figure 1. A particular technology can be described by an L-shaped contour producing one unit of output with a given pair of capital and labor coefficients. The technology shelf is composed of the complete set of such activities or technologies which have been demonstrated to be feasible somewhere in the advanced countries at some historical point in time, including the present. Since there exists a number of technology-exporting countries—for example, the United States, Germany, the United Kingdom, and Japan—with continuous technological transfers among themselves as well as with the LDCs, it is not unreasonable to postulate the existence of a single technological shelf for the lending world as a whole. For example, unit technology

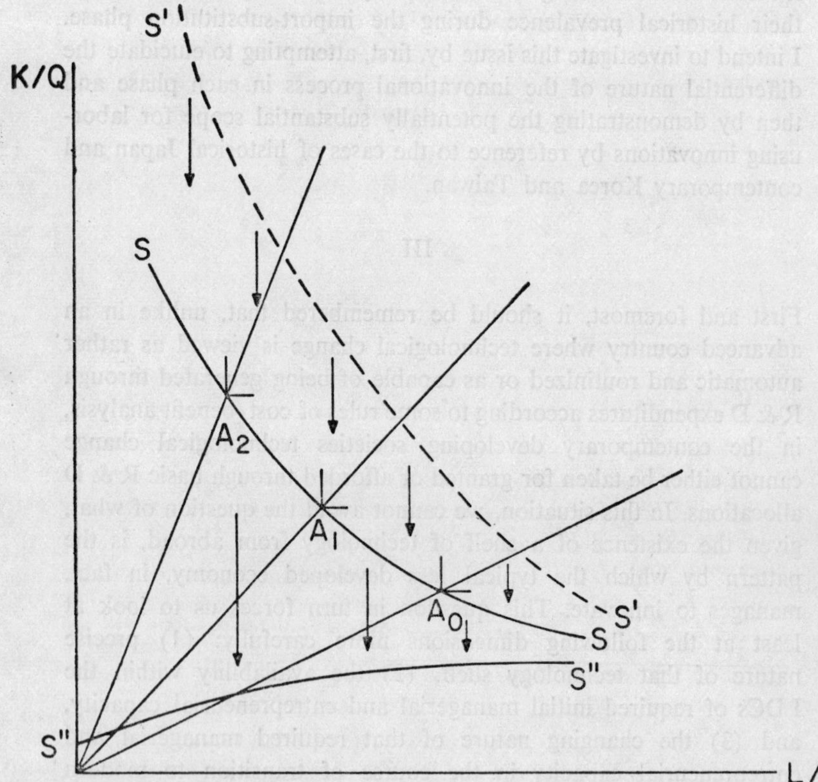

Figure 1

A_0 may have been generated in Germany in 1920, A_1 in the United States in 1920, and A_2 in the United States in 1950. In other words, as we move to the left along the shelf we run into more 'modern' technology, that is, technology of more recent vintage and of higher capital intensity. As capital per head increases this means that the typical worker has learned to cooperate with more units of capital of increasing technical complexity. This capital-deepening process, in other words, is more complicated than the textbook version of 'homogeneous' labor being equipped with more units of 'homogeneous' capital.

At any point in time the typical LDC is, then, theoretically free to borrow a particular unit activity from anywhere along this shelf. What technology is chosen and what happens as an immediate and ultimate consequence of that choice, that is, what secondary processes and reactions are set off, is, of course, all part and parcel of the innovation process taken as a whole. The quality of that process, each step of the way, in turn depends on both the economic environment, that is, the nature of the relative price signals, and on the entrepreneurial, managerial, and skilled labor capacity of the borrower.

The role of innovation must therefore be seen as intimately related to the stage in which the developing economy finds itself. In other words, the role of technological change in output and employment generation must be viewed as sensitive to the same discernible phases of growth as the economy moves in transition from open agrariansim to Kuznets' modern economic growth. In the first post-independence or import-substitution phase previously mentioned, an effort is made to increase the supply of domestic entrepreneurship and the economy's learning capacity, partly through the importation of people via aid but mainly through the system of protection established by government policies. In fact, the most reasonable explanation for the import-substitution syndrome is that it is a response to a real (or imagined) shortage of entrepreneurship and that it permits time, through informal learning by doing or more formal educational processes, for this entrepreneurial capacity to develop.[2]

2 Some few countries, like Malaysia, with command over a very strong and reliable natural resources base, may be able to avoid such a phase altogether. Moreover, there clearly exist better and worse (i.e., less and more costly) import-substitution packages to choose from (e.g., compare Brazil and Ghana), but I cannot expand on this very interesting subject in the context of the present

In terms of figure 1, this means that, although the technological shelf may look as indicated by curve *SS*, the *actual* choices available to the developing country during the import-substitution phase are more aptly described by $S'S'$. In other words, due to the inadequate state of entrepreneurial capacity during the early post-independence period of physical controls, the efficiency of generating output per unit of capital in the borrowing country is likely to be substantially below that in the lending country. This is likely to be more true the more capital intensive the import, that is, the further removed from the cultural inheritance and experience of the borrower. Such technological imports are often accompanied by imported engineers, even managers and supervisors—adding up to what is called a 'turn-key project.' The most advanced and sophisticated technology can, of course, be made to 'work,' in the physical sense, even in the most backward developing economy. But a shiny new plant embedded in a society many decades distant is bound to be substantially less efficient. This is true for a thousand direct reasons, such as the absence of even minimal skilled labor supplies, domestic subcontracting, and repair and maintenance possibilities, as well as for many more subtle sociological reasons which enter into the total milieu in which the plant is required to operate. The more sophisticated and removed from the rest of the economy the technological transplant, in other words, the greater the relative inefficiency, as indicated by the shape of the $S'S'$ curve.

If and when the economy then moves away from the import-substitution phase and enters into the second phase of liberalization and export substitution, a second important, if unintentional, type of innovation is likely to appear, namely, a reduction in the extent of the inefficiency of the original transplanted technology. Call it *X* efficiency if you like, but the cost of the pure transplantation is likely to be reduced, quite unintentionally, that is, largely as a result of factors external to the profit-maximizing behavior of the productive unit itself. This increase in productive efficiency over time will increase in quantitative significance as the import-substitution hothouse temperature is gradually turned down and a more competitive economy emerges. In figure 1, the effects of

paper (see, however, my 'Relative Prices in Planning for Economic Development,' in *International Comparisons of Prices and Output*, ed. D. J. Daly [Columbia University Press, 1972], pp. 287-302).

gradual enhancement of efficiency may be represented by the arrows tending, over time, to move $S'S'$ back toward the original SS position.[3]

Another more conscious and quantitatively more important type of innovation begins to gather importance during this same second phase of transition. This phenomenon may be called innovational assimilation—innovating 'on top of' imported technology in the direction of using relatively more of the abundant unskilled labor supply. As the economy shifts from a natural-resource-based growth pattern in the import-substitution phase to a human-resource-based system in the export-substitution phase, there is an increasing sensitivity to the continuously changing factor endowment, first in terms of the efficient utilization of the domestic unskilled-labor force, and later in terms of the incorporation of growing domestic skills and ingenuity. In other words, the appropriate type of technology finally in place must be one in which not only the initial choice from the shelf but also the adaptations and adjustments consciously made thereafter, in response to changing domestic resource and capability constraints, play an important role.

The more liberalized the economy, in terms of the government's performing a catalytic role through the market by indirect means rather than trying to impose resources allocation by direct controls, the better the chances that the millions of dispersed decision makers can be induced, by the sheer force of profit maximization, to make the 'right' decision. As the gap between shadow and market prices narrows—coupled with the expectation of continued labor surpluses for years to come—we would expect transplantation choices to become more flexible, that is, labor intensive. However, since shelf choices are likely to continue to be severely constrained—partly by a lack of illumination of substantial portions of it, partly by such institutional inhibitions as prestige, aid tying, and so forth—we can realistically expect relatively less benefits from liberalization to accrue in the transplantation process. On the other hand, we can expect much more from the assimilation type of innovational

3 A more sophisticated analysis, differentiating between the labor- and capital-saving nature of this move, depending on the region in which the economy is operating, is possible but will not be introduced here (see also G. Ranis and J. C. H. Fei, 'LDC Innovation Analysis and the Technology Gap,' in *The Gap between the Rich and the Poor Nations*, ed. Gustav Ranis, Macmillan Co., 1972, New York, pp. 312-35).

behavior which now tends, for the same reasons, to be more slanted in a labor-using direction. In the typical labor surplus type of economy—or one likely to become one over the next decade (as is probably the case in much of Africa)—all this means a much greater possibility for the efficient accommodation of pure labor services.[4] Whether this will lead to a sectoral output shift in favor of labor-intensive export commodities or a mix change predominantly addressed to the domestic market, of course, depends on, *ceteris paribus,* income elasticities of demand, the government's fiscal prowess, and the type (e.g., size) of the economy. Moreover, no strong generalization as to the relative importance of shifts in output mix versus changes in technology for given mixes is likely to be valid. It should be clear, however, that the important issue is that the search for innovation can now be considered a conscious activity of the individual entrepreneur and—given the combination of more realistic relative price signals after liberalization plus greater entrepreneurial capacity—that it is likely to be mainly directed toward various forms of indigenous capital stretching on top of the imported technology. Such capital stretching can be represented by a reduction in the capital coefficient per unit of output. The effective post-assimilation set of unit technologies, that is, *after* domestic assimilation, may thus be represented by curve $S''S''$ in figure 1, with the strength of the indigenous labor-using innovative effort indicated by the amount of the 'downward' shift in the capital coefficient.

It should be noted here that a negatively sloped technology shelf, for example, SS, representing pure technological transplantation, permits, as we move to the left, higher labor productivity levels, but only at increasing capital cost. In a country characterized by capital scarcity this may mean increased technical unemployment (à la Eckaus) and hence a lower value of per capita income for the economy—in spite of the higher level of labor productivity achieved. Domestic capital stretching, however, can materially affect that situation by enabling more workers to be employed per unit of the capital stock. If the post-assimilation unit technology set, $S''S''$, for example, is upward sloping from left to right, higher labor

4 It is important to emphasize the word 'efficient' since I am not concerned here with the, possibly also legitimate, objective of employment creation as a separate social goal to be weighed against output growth.

productivity levels become consistent with lower capital/output ratios.[5]

In summary, once the overall policy setting has turned more favorable and permitted the economy to enter the second phase of transition, it is this indigenous capital-stretching capacity which I consider to be of the greatest importance—especially for the contemporary developing economy facing the formidable labor force explosion predicted for the seventies and eighties. It is in this specific area also where the skepticism of planners, engineers, and aid officials generally is most pronounced—especially with respect to the full range of technological choice really available when all the dust has settled. Historical examples from the Japanese case, as well as contemporary evidence from Korea and Taiwan, permit us to demonstrate the existence and potential importance of such capital-stretching innovations for the labor surplus developing country.

IV

As has been pointed out by many observers, including Allen and Lockwood,[6] the most significant feature of the Japanese economy in the early Meiji period—which followed hard on two centuries of self-imposed, nearly complete isolation—was her ability to choose relatively freely from among the items on a technological shelf perfected in the West. The reopening of foreign trade and the resumption of other related contacts, especially the flow of technical personnel in both directions, led immediately to the stimulation of technological change by direct borrowing. But while the Japanese have often been characterized as possessing a consummate ability to copy and imitate, it is noteworthy that, in fact, very soon the majority of domestic innovation activity 'consisted of the adaptation of foreign techniques to domestic conditions.'[7]

5 The historical evidence within individual now developed Western countries over time seems to indicate an approximation to constancy in the capital/output ratio, i.e., approximating a horizontal position for $S' S'$, the 'final' locus of unit technologies achieved there.

6 George C. Allen, *Japanese Industrialization: Its Recent Development and Present Conditions* (New York: Institute of Pacific Relations, 1940); W. W. Lockwood, *Economic Development of Japan, 1868-1928* (Princeton, N.J.: Princeton University Press, 1954).

7 M. Miyamoto, Y. Sakudo, and Y. Yasuba, 'Economic Development in Pre-industrial Japan: 1859-1894,' *Journal of Economic History* 25, no. 4

The reasons for this relatively early move to a responsiveness of the industrial sector's technology to domestic endowment conditions are complicated and cannot be dealt with here. Suffice it to say that post-Restoration Japan did not engage in very extensive or prolonged import-substitution policies—partly because extra-territoriality deprived her of the ability to establish strong protective import barriers and partly because the government quite early thought it more efficient to work through the market, that is, by using taxes and subsidies rather than through extensive controls and government ownership. These government plants in directly productive areas which were established during the immediate post-Restoration period were viewed mainly as pilot projects and sold off to private interests by 1890. Thus, Japan moved relatively quickly into the export-substitution phase.

In assessing the importance of capital-stretching innovations, it is useful to recognize distinctions between innovations relating to the machine proper, innovations relating to the production process as a whole (emphasizing the importance of activities within the plant but peripheral to the machine), and innovations with respect to the production process as a whole (emphasizing plant size and organization at various stages of that process).

With respect to machine-related, capital-stretching innovations, the simplest and quantitatively probably most important example was the running of machinery imported from the United Kingdom and the United States at rates and speeds substantially in excess of those used abroad. For example, once the kerosene lamp made night work possible, spinning could be done on two, sometimes three, shifts daily, with but two or three rest days a month. This meant that the average work week per machine was two to three times that encountered in the country of origin, and, since physical depreciation is much less important than economic obsolescence, using a machine twice as intensively does not wear it out twice as fast. This heavy use of machinery typical of the nineteenth-century Japanese industrial sector meant that the normal gap between the physical and economic life of a machine was substantially narrowed and capital was considerably 'stretched.'

(December 1965): p. 557. The same authors also report (p. 563) that similar capital or land-stretching innovations took place during the same period in the agricultural sector, mainly via new cultivation methods on the intensive margin (see also my 'Factor Proportions in Japanese Economic Development,' *American Economic Review* 46 [September 1957]: pp. 594-607).

Moreover, there was a related speedup of the very same spinning machines. By running the machines at faster speeds and/or by substituting cheaper raw materials (in this case, raw cotton, which necessitated a greater number of women to handle the resultant increase in the number of broken threads), industry achieved an additional major saving in capital.

> Certain differences in the industries of the two countries are important and must be noted. The raw material is essentially different. Though the Japanese do use some American raw cotton, the bulk of their cotton is from India and is of shorter staple, more likely to breakage...and requiring more labor to put it through the machinery. The yarn spun has much more of the coarser counts that require more labor....By adding more labor it is run somewhat faster than American practice....All of these factors are in some way related to the cheap labor policy. They are there because the labor is cheap.[8]

Japanese spindles were equipped with a seven-eighth inch instead of a one inch front roll to accommodate the shorter staple cotton when operated at higher speeds.

For these reasons, differences in the yarn count and differences in the speed of the machine as well as differences in the number of shifts, we find that there was a very marked substitution between capital and labor in the cotton-spinning industry. For example, Orchard reports that a competent Japanese spinner working on a 20-yarn count operated from 300 to 400 spindles, while an American spinner on the same yarn count tended from 1,020 to 2,688 spindles, that is, two and a half to seven times as many.[9] As the U.S. Tariff Commission reported: 'In order to distribute the fixed overhead charges in the way of high interest and depreciation costs, and to earn the large amounts needed to pay a normal rate of dividend, every effort has been made to obtain the largest possible output from the expensive equipment and plant. Machinery is therefore run at high speed, and almost since their inception the Japanese spinning mills have been operated night and day, employing two 12-hour shifts (22 actual working hours) for an average of 27 days a month.'[10]

8 John E. Orchard, *Japan's Economic Position*, McGraw-Hill Book Co., 1930, p. 367.

9 Ibid., p. 367.

10 U.S., Tariff Commission, *The Japanese Cotton Industry and Trade*, (Washington, D.C.: Government Printing Office, 1921), p. 99.

Here again, given a standard count of yarn, the average Japanese spinner is seen as tending 240 spindles, while the American counterpart on the same machine tends about 1,000 spindles. As late as 1932, weekly man-hours per 1,000 homogeneous spindles of the same quality ranged from 328.8 in Japan to 164.8 in the United Kingdom and 143.1 in the United States.

A somewhat similar story can be told with respect to cotton weaving. Once again: 'The high cost of mill construction is considerably reduced if you consider the hours during which the mill is being put to effective use. So far in Japan the wheels have turned round during 20 out of 24 hours, while in Europe only eight hours are being worked. Effective working time in England is less than 38 hours per week, as two hours out of those are devoted to cleaning; this is done in Japan after working hours.'[12] Again, the U.S. Tariff Commission reports that 'in weaving staple cotton sheetings, the ordinary Japanese weaver seldom operates more than two plain looms, while the American weaver, with perhaps some assistance in supplying fresh bobbins, normally tends from eight to ten plain looms.'[13]

Perhaps the most convincing evidence that these adjustments along the machines proper constituted a rational response to very marked differences in factor endowments was that in weaving, in contrast to spinning, the latest automatic equipment from abroad was not, in fact, invariably imported. Quite frequently, non-automatic looms were taken from the shelf instead, permitting more stretching than would have been possible in the case of initially more capital-intensive technologies. Unlike some of the contemporary less developed countries, Japan clearly did not wish to 'transplant' ahead of its entrepreneurial and skilled labor capacities.[14] As the Tariff Commission put it:

> The price of the automatic loom is more than twice that of the plain loom, which, with the additional expense involved in the importation from the United States or Great Britain, made the

11 *The World Textile Industry: Economic and Social Problems* (Geneva: International Labour Office, 1937), 1:209.

12 Arnold S. Pearse, *Japan and China*, Cotton Industry Report, International Federation of Master Cotton Spinners' and Manufacturers' Association (Manchester, 1929), p. 86.

13 U.S. Tariff Commission, p. 100.

14 The U.S. Tariff Commission reported that a shipment of automatic looms, imported shortly after the turn of the century, had been found so difficult to operate that, after removing the batteries and warp-stop motions, they were nstead run as plain looms, two looms to a weaver (p. 116).

> total outlay too high in a country where the interest charges on money were relatively much higher than the cost of labor Japanese mill managers have, therefore, hitherto preferred to employ more workers and to forego the more labor-saving but more expensive machinery, in contrast to the situation in the United States where the high-priced labor is economized rather than the machinery.[15]

Taking cotton spinning and plain loom weaving on similar products together, they concluded, in summary, that

> the average Japanese spinner or weaver tends about one-fourth the number of spindles or looms usually assigned to one person in an American mill. A comparison of the total number of persons employed in the two countries to operate individual plants of similar size, and, viewed more broadly, a comparison of the total number of persons employed in the whole American industry, per 1,000 spindles, with the number that would be required on the similar balanced basis under the Japanese conditions, confirms the general relation observed, that the Japanese mills require between three and one-half and four times as many operatives as the American.[16]

In the case of silk production, which, with cotton, made up more than 70 per cent of total industrial output until the turn of the century, we have similar evidence of the ability to innovate in a capital-stretching direction on the machine proper. In raw silk, for example, the Japanese employed more than twice as many women as did the reeling basins in Italy. In other areas, well into the twentieth century, Japanese railways employed 19 workers per mile of track compared with seven in the United States.[17] In the production of printed goods, the following account may be instructive:

> Recently, a Japanese manufacturer of plain linoleum decided to undertake the production of printed goods. He despatched a representative to the United States to purchase the necessary equipment. The representative was familiar with the modern linoleum printing machine, printing several colors at one time and turning out as much as 15,000 square yards in 9 hours, but he considered it too expensive a piece of equipment, especially

15 Ibid. A related interesting example of technical flexibility far beyond what most engineers are willing to admit to is provided by the Toyoda automatic loom, one of the few indigenous Japanese inventions in this area. Subsequently manufactured by Platt's and Oldham's under a Japanese patent, it was advertised to require 20 workers per loom in England; 50 workers had always been used in Japan.

16 Ibid., p. 113.

17 Orchard, p. 375.

since his labor was being paid only about 50 cents a day, and so he sought out, in an American plant, an old hand block printing outfit. It was not for sale. Its parts were lying about in a storeroom of the factory. Some of them were 40 years old, and the whole outfit had been discarded 15 years before. But the Japanese representative purchased it and had it shipped to Japan. In the immediate outlay of capital he saved money, for he purchased the old equipment at the price of a printing machine or even below the prices of a new hand outfit, but he installed in his plant equipment that could only have been disposed of as junk in the United States. He started in Japan a new industry in a stage of technical development that had become obsolete years before in the older industrial countries.[18]

Many of the extra workers in Japanese plants were not engaged on the machine proper but in what might be called machine-peripheral or handling activities. In place of mechanical conveyor belts, human conveyor belts were devised. Packaging was more often done by hand. As Orchard again reports, 'At one of the largest copper smelters in Japan, clay for the lining of the furnaces is carried down from a nearby hillside on the backs of women. At the plant of the Tokyo Gas Company, coke is put into bags by hand and then carried by coolies, some of them women, to the barges in the adjacent canal. Coal, even in the larger Tokyo plants, is unloaded by hand and carried in baskets to the power houses.'[19] The ability to substitute labor for capital in such activities peripheral to the machine proper apparently existed, and the quantitative incidence was substantial. Very often such activities were machine paced in the Hirschman sense, that is, while they might have looked wasteful to the untrained Western eye, they were, in fact, paced by well-spaced machinery as part of the same production line which contained large numbers of unskilled laborers.[20]

A third type of capital-stretching innovation of which much use was made in historical Japan is what might be called the plant-saving variety. This is often characterized by the coexistence of different historical stages of production in the same industry. Raw silk production and cotton weaving represent outstanding examples.

18 Ibid., p. 246.

19 Ibid., p. 255.

20 This is very similar to contemporary methods of construction with the use of reinforced concrete in India and Pakistan. Here a cement mixer is linked to the final pouring of the concrete by a long chain of workers passing the cement from hand to hand; the cement is put in place just before it is ready to cool and harden.

In the former industry, silkworm rearing and cocoon production were handled mainly by farmers' wives in small homemade sheds, extensions of the rural households. In cotton weaving, most of the yarn was 'put out' to farm households, with individual, looms dispersed in farm houses and worksheds. But even in the more modern factory-style spinning industry, preparatory and finishing processes were carried out largely at the cottage level.

This rather remarkable survival of domestic industry on a subcontracting basis must be explained largely in terms of the exploitation of complementarities between many small labor-intensive operating units and the large industrial-management unit. The traditional merchant middleman, as a representative of the subcontracting unit, served as both supplier and market for the goods to be worked up domestically. A specialization of functions as between workshops, even as between the members of a given family developed. One-roof economies could be achieved in this fashion that is, by using cheap labor in cooperation with old-fashioned machinery at the workshop level, while economies of scale could be achieved in the financing, purchasing, and merchandising stages.[21] The continued relative importance of this household type of enterprise is quite remarkable; cottage-style industry contributed more than two-thirds of industrial output in 1878, almost 60 per cent in 1895, and retained substantial importance well into the twentieth century. Not only lacquerware, pottery, porcelain, sake, fruit and fish canning but also such new consumer goods coming to the fore over time as bicycles, electric lamps, and rubber exhibited the same characteristics.

Purchase or construction of plants amounts to more than 50 per cent of total investment in plant and equipment in most countries. The ability to utilize households for putting-out operations, and thus reduce expenditures on a plant, undoubtedly amounted to a major kind of capital-stretching innovation. By scattering familiar but improving machinery over large numbers of scattered miniplants, large amounts of unskilled labor could be deployed in both direct production and in satisfying the resulting increased demand for transportation and handling activities. In this fashion, Japanese entrepreneurs were able to, first, incorporate pure

21 'Sometimes even a single part is not completed in one shop or home but is shaped in one and painted or plated in another' (H. G. Aubrey, 'Small Industry in Economic Development,' *Social Research* 18, no. 3 [September 1951]: pp. 269-312).

labor services and, later, domestic ingenuity and skills into the industrial production processes, largely for export.

An examination of the capital/labor ratio in the non-agricultural sector in Japan during the period discussed indicates the effectiveness of capital-stretching innovations at the aggregative level; while the average annual rate of capital deepening was 4.3 per cent between 1906 and 1917, the earlier period, between 1892 and 1900, was characterized by capital deepening at a rate of 2.8 per cent annually, declining to 1.7 per cent between 1900 and 1906.

This seems to at least suggest that Japanese entrepreneurs were getting better and better, through a learning-by-doing process, at innovating in a relatively labor-using direction, before the unlimited supply of labor condition came to an end as the reserve army of the unemployed and underemployed was substantially mopped up after World War I.

In contemporary Korea, devaluation in 1964 and a major interest rate reform in 1965 laid the basis for substantial changes in technology as well as output mix. Examples of capital-stretching adaptations of imported technology abound in textiles, electronics, and plywood production. In the manufacture of silk, for example, one woman operates two looms in contrast to contemporary Japan where one woman operates 6.8 looms. In reaction to the now rising wages in Japan, Korea is taking over the lower quality yarn spectrum where more workers can be employed to make up for the inferior quality of the raw material. In cotton weaving, one worker operates three looms in Korea, four looms in Japan; in spinning, the contrast is between 600 and 900 spindles. Moreover, Korean machinery is run for three eight-hour shifts daily as contrasted with only two such shifts in Japan. Peripheral to the machines proper, the contemporary Japanese use a conveyor belt system, for example, between the carding, gilling, and combing operations, which is replaced by human hands in Korea.

In the production of plywood, what appears at first as production processes very similar to those carried on in the United States, that is, fixed proportions, in fact, turn out to be quite flexible—interestingly enough mainly because of the greater machine speed combined with much more labor-intensive repair methods used. In the United States, defective pieces of lumber are cut out automatically by machine and discarded. In Japan, defective pieces of lumber are cut out by hand and the section is discarded. In Korea, defective sections are cut out by hand, the scraps saved, and the defect plugged manually. Here, once again, a lower quality raw material can be upgraded through the application of cheap labor. Consequently, overall, there are twice as many workers per unit of capital equipment in Korea—123 workers are engaged per equivalent capital production line as contrasted to 72 in Japan. Moreover, a Korean line is worked 22 hours a day compared to 20 in Japan. At the same time, in the production of Korean plywood, between 10 and 15 per cent more workers are engaged in inspection, repair, and maintenance of both materials in process and the machinery in place.

In Korean electronics, machine-related, labor-using innovations and adaptations are most prominent. In transistor assembly operations, for instance, the given wage rates are 1/10 of those of equivalent operators in the United States (for the same firm), the machinery is run at physical full capacity, that is, six days, three shifts a day, which is 20 per cent above the U.S. equivalent. Moreover, certain special operations such as feeding and packaging are usually done by hand on the assembly line, instead of automatically. In spite of the greater use of labor, productivity per worker seems to be higher due partly to the faster learning process (it was repeatedly stated that it takes at least two weeks less to train Korean women in assembly line work than Americans) but mainly to the greater discipline and attentiveness on the assembly line throughout. For example, in one firm the difference in speed of assembly on identical equipment yields a 30 per cent differential in output (from 68 units per machine hour to 85), and in a die-mounting process it rises to more than 100 per cent (from 113 units per hour to 240). These greater speeds of operation, either due to faster machine or operator pacing, are once again accompanied by putting additional women into more intensive testing, inspection, and repair efforts than in Japan or the United States. Defective pieces are not thrown away but are repaired by hand. Similarly, with machinery itself working at physical full capacity, considerably more manpower is allocated to the maintenance and repair of the in-place capital equipment.

With respect to other organizational and plant-related technological choices, the most important phenomenon is clearly sub-contracting, both domestic and international. Domestically, sub-contracting to local equipment and parts manufacturers is being increasingly practiced, especially in the electronics industry; sometimes, as the experience of several companies indicates, it takes two to three years before the domestic sub-contracting supplier, via a learning-by-doing process, becomes a lower cost producer than the main plant or import alternatives. While such capital-saving innovations, mainly via the reduction of plant and large-scale urban overhead requirements, are not yet as widespread in Korea as in historical Japan (and contemporary Taiwan), they are markedly on the increase in a number of other industries as well. Internationally, of course, accepting a sub-contract for the labor intensive phase of a multistage and, elsewhere, technologically demanding production process is a potentially very efficient way of harnessing virtually pure labor services to the development process. Bonded export processing schemes—consisting of tariff-free zones into which, often under subsidiary or sub-contracting arrangements with Japanese or American firms, raw materials are imported and then re-exported, after value in the form of cheap labor has been added—can be most helpful. This scheme now yields close to 20 per cent of a Korean export volume which itself has been rising at an almost incredible 30-40 per cent annual rate over the past three years.

But it is to the larger question of the productive absorption of labor through changes in the output mix and trade that we must turn in this connection. In 1962, land-based foodstuffs and raw materials made up 75 per cent of total exports, while labor-based light manufacturing industries as a whole, including plywood, raw silk, cotton textile, wigs, and footwear amounted to 15 per cent. By 1968, the situation had been completely reversed, with 77 per cent of the exports in manufacturing and only 14.5 per cent in foodstuffs, livestock, and raw materials. It should, moreover, be noted that small-scale manufacturing exports, that is, in units of less than ten workers (undoubtedly the most labor-intensive part of the spectrum), grew from 18.6 per cent of the total in 1963 to 31.4 per cent in 1968.

As a consequence of all this, manufacturing employment doubled between 1963 and 1969, with light industry, in particular, increasing its employment at a rate even in excess of value added (see table 1).[22] At least until Korea began to reverse its liberalization trend, after 1968,[23] the capital/labor ratio for manufacturing as a whole actually

22 I would like to acknowledge the assistance of Sung-Hwan Jo of Sogang University, Seoul, in connection with the plant interviews.

23 This reversal is part of a larger story which cannot be dealt with in the context of this paper.

TABLE I

KOREA

Year	Employed Industrial Labor Force (in 1,000s)	Annual Growth Rate (%)
1952	..	..
1953	..	..
1954	..	..
1955	989	
1956	2,223	
1957	2,716	
1958	2,444	
1959	2,729	10.3 (1955–1963)
1960	3,062	
1961	2,139	
1962	3,136	
1963	3,360	
1964	3,809	
1965	4,199	6.5 (1963–1967)
1966	4,312	
1967	4,680	

TABLE II

CAPITAL INTENSITY BY ESTABLISHMENT SIZE: KOREAN MINING AND MANUFACTURING, 1968

Estimated Size	Fixed Assets	No. of Workers	Capital/ Labor Ratio
5–9	23,722	82,183	.289
10–19	28,601	79,141	.361
20–49	38,367	100,586	.381
50–99	28,695	73,467	.391
100–199	28,406	76,485	.371
200–499	68,512	120,875	.567
500 +	188,421	258,446	.729

Source: Economic Planning Bureau, Korean Development Bank, *Report on Mining and Manufacturing Census, 1968;* and Paul Kuznets, 'Labour Absorption in Korea since 1963' (paper presented to the Conference on Manpower Problems in East and Southeast Asia, Singapore, May 22-28, 1971), table 8.

declined after 1964 (see fig. 2). There is also evidence, for example in table 2, that a good deal of disparity by scale exists here, as in many other, less 'well-behaved' countries.[24] This is due to the well-known discrepancies in residual factor price distortions affecting large and small firms, with real wages lower and capital costs higher for the smaller units.

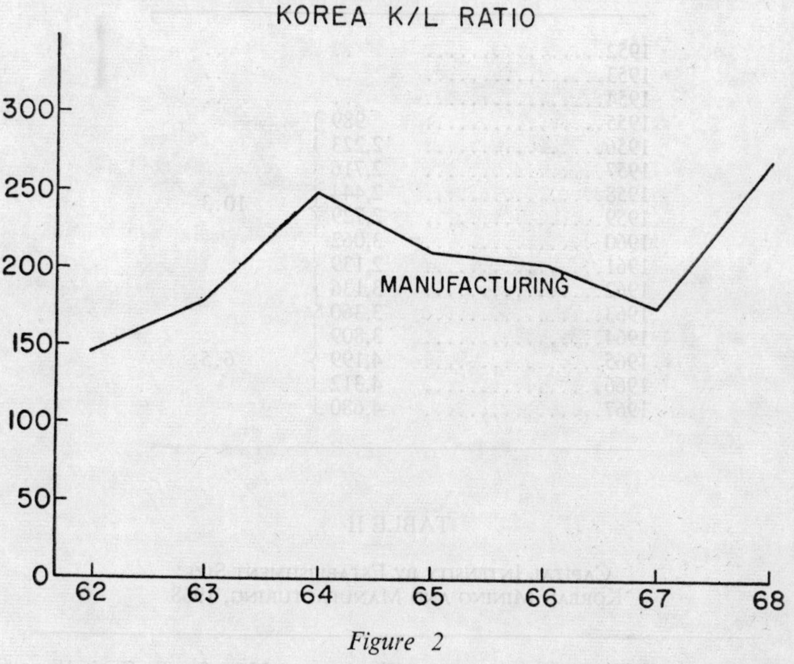

Figure 2

Relevant microeconomic data are harder to come by, as firm interviews proved unsuccessful in eliciting reliable data at the firm level. The leading Korean timber company, however, did show a decline in its capital/labor ratio from 35.8 in 1965–6 to 27.8 in 1968–9.

In Taiwan, too, once the liberalization policies of early sixties had substantially reduced some of the major distortions in relative prices which comprise the import substitution syndrome, marked labor-using innovations took place in the textiles, electronics, and

24 From Paul Kuznets, 'Labour Absorption in Korea since 1963' (paper presented to the Conference on Manpower Problems in East and Southeast Asia, Singapore, May 22-28, 1971).

food-processing industries. Large-scale mushroom and asparagus production as forms of agricultural by-employment (similar to silk in early Japan),[25] combined with related processing and canning activities, provided major markets for surplus unskilled labor, especially female. With time, and facilitated by the establishment of the Kachsiung Export Processing Zone, export substitution via a dramatic expansion of labor-intensive manufacturing took place.

At the microlevel, on the basis of 20 firm interviews conducted, I found that most of the capital stretching in evidence clearly took place in fabricating, as opposed to continuous processes.[26] One large plastics factory produced both intermediate and finished products. Its board chairman reported that in the intermediate continuous process (of producing resin) the capital/labor ratio of his plant was about the same as that of other plants of the parent company in the United States, while in the fabricating process the capital/labor ratio was about one-half of that of the American plants.

The use of labor is most intensive in the electronics assembly industry. While parts are mainly assembled with the aid of machines in the United States, this work is performed by women workers in Taiwan. According to the general manager of one major electronics firm, the amount of labor used in assembling one television set in the Taiwan plant is 50 per cent greater than that in a plant of the parent company in the United States. In fact, most of the electronics firms interviewed were making efforts in one way or another to introduce labor-intensive methods. While the capital/labor ratios in this industry have been generally rising through time the largest electronics factory in Taiwan has experienced an increase of capital by nine times and an increase of employment by 16 times between 1965 and 1969. Throughout the electronics industry, capital/labor ratios have apparently fallen during the sixties. Many of the managers interviewed pointed out that the wage bill was lower in spite of the substantially larger relative volume of employment.

One tentative conclusion which may be derived from these plant visits is that the closer the production process is to the raw material processing stage, that is, backward linkages, the smaller the chances for efficient labor/capital substitution statically or capital-stretching

25 In fact, such non-farm earnings comprised 72 per cent of agricultural incomes in 1962.

26 I would like to acknowledge the assistance of N. R. Chen of Cornell University in connection with the plant interviews.

innovations dynamically; the closer the process to the finished product stage, the greater are these possibilities.

In 1952, rice and sugar constituted 78 per cent of Taiwan's export earnings. By 1969, this had shrunk to 4.8 per cent. During the same period, non-traditional agricultural products, including fresh and canned fruits and vegetables, rose from 0 to 10 per cent of the total; and, most impressively, manufactured goods, including wood and plywood products, rose from 5 per cent to 69 per cent of the total. The full dimensions of this structural change are recognized when it is noted again that total export earnings were rising very rapidly, at rates in excess of 20 per cent annually, especially during the 1960s.

At the macrolevel, consequent to all this, industrial employment grew at rates of 3.0 per cent annually between 1952 and 1959 (see table 3), but accelerated to 8.1 per cent annually for the decade of the sixties, once the transition to export promotion had been completed. If non-agriculture is divided into Kuznets' M and S sectors, it can be seen that the rate of labor absorption rose from 4.6 per cent annually in 1950-60 to 7.5 per cent in 1960-9 in the M sector, and from 3.2 per cent to 6.5 per cent for the same periods in the S sector.[27] Equally significant is the fact that once interest rates and other reforms had been completed—in addition to the exchange and land reforms which took place earlier—this trend seems to have accelerated—for the 1964–5 period the relevant rates are 8.7 per cent for the M sector and 7.2 per cent for the S sector.

In conclusion, the above, largely episodal approach, is consistent with, though it admittedly does not conclusively prove, my main point, that the typical developing country, especially one which is open and not too large in size, can expect—with appropriate policy changes taking place—to transit from import substitution, with pure technological transplantation the order of the day, to export substitution, with labor-using innovations taking on major significance. Once shortages in domestic entrepreneurial capacity and other economic overheads have been repaired, if and when the hothouse temperature is gradually reduced, labor-using types of technological change, both of the unintentional and of the intentional variety, assume increasing importance. In this phase, the famous

27 These data are from Harry Oshima, 'Experience of Labour Absorption in Postwar Taiwan' (paper presented to the Conference on Manpower Problems in East and Southeast Asia, Singapore, May 22-28, 1971).

conflict between output and employment objectives in industrial development may be subject to fundamental challenge. Both the historical experience of Japan and that of Korea and Taiwan in recent years illustrate that the current widespread skepticism concerning the supposed tyranny of the rigid technical coefficients may be seriously in error. This error derives in the main from an underestimate of the potential inventiveness of indigenous entrepreneurs, once they are given access, at a price, to the required inputs. And this is no trivial matter. For if our skepticism here is unwarranted, this would be among the most powerful arguments for accelerating the current rather slow and uneven trend toward liberalization and the erosion of the substantial shadow price—market price differentials in factor and commodity markets.

TABLE III

TAIWAN

Year	Employed Industrial Labor Force (in 1,000s)	Annual Growth Rate (%)
1952	1,198	3.0 (1952–1959)
1953	1,223	
1954	1,261	
1955	1,291	
1956	1,304	
1957	1,366	
1958	1,418	
1959	1,481	
1960	1,536	6.4 (1960–1969)
1961	1,598	
1962	1,689	
1963	1,781	
1964	1,843	
1965	1,938	
1966	2,034	
1967	2,239	
1968	2,480	
1969	2,679	

10

SOME QUESTIONS CONCERNING GROWTH, TRANSFORMATION AND PLANNING OF AGRICULTURE IN THE DEVELOPING COUNTRIES[1]

K. N. Raj

I The Questions

RECENT LITERATURE on agriculture in the developing countries has tended to draw a sharp distinction between those that have been able to accelerate the rate of growth in this sector to phenomenally high levels over a short period of time and those that have failed to do so. This difference in performance has been attributed to the successful transformation of traditional agriculture in the former through changes in technology. The inference has also been drawn that the same or similar changes in technology in other developing countries would lead to comparable breakthroughs in agriculture and to high rates of growth within relatively short periods.

It is necessary to examine closely the factual basis of this hypothesis and its analytical and policy implications. For if the facts and the hypothesis are correct, one would be justified in assuming that the institutional framework of agrarian economies is not a serious obstacle to growth and that what is needed above all is concentration on specific questions relating to the mechanics of the technological change required in each and the supply of the necessary inputs. Moreover, if growth rates of the order usually mentioned in this context can be achieved in agriculture, many other problems that developing countries face, such as inflation, foreign exchange shortage and idle manpower, would be much easier to solve than has appeared.

Two countries that are generally cited as having achieved phenomenally high rates of growth in agriculture in the post-war period

1 This paper was written originally for the *Journal of Development Planning*, no. 1, then a new publication of the Centre for Development Planning, Projections and policies of the Department of Economic and Social Affairs of the United Nations Secretariat.

are Mexico and Taiwan. The Mexican experience has been highlighted particularly in Professor Schultz's analysis of how to transform traditional agriculture and of the possibility of doing so in a short period:

> Agricultural production in Mexico has been increasing at the unusually high rate of 7.1 per cent per year. The lesson to be learned from what Mexico has accomplished is especially germane to many low income countries seeking to develop a modern economy. Mexico entered upon this growth very recently. The foundations for growth were not laid by an earlier gradual development spread over many decades.[2]

At the other end of the spectrum, as an example of a country in which agriculture has failed to grow rapidly, India has often come in for considerable attention.

It would therefore be of interest to examine in some depth the growth rates achieved in agriculture in Mexico, Taiwan and India, the factors which have contributed to their respective growth performances, and the lessons that could legitimately be drawn.

II The Experience of Mexico

It is clear enough from the available data that, while agricultural production in Mexico was stagnant in the period between the two world wars,[3] it has been increasing rapidly since the early 1940s. What is open to doubt is the accuracy of the growth rates mentioned in this context and some of the inferences drawn from the Mexican experience in the latter period covering approximately two decades.

In the first place, an examination of the data shows that the high rate of growth in Mexican agriculture during this period is attributable to a large extent to a phenomenally high rate recorded in the earlier half of this period; in the second half there was a perceptible and fairly sharp decline. Thus the rate of increase of agricultural

2 Theodore W. Schultz, *Transforming Traditional Agriculture* (1964) p. 19.

3 Given below are the index numbers of the volume of agricultural production in Mexico (with 1929 as the base year):

1925-8:	114.1
1931-4:	105.2
1935-8:	111.5
1941-4:	152.2

Source: Nathan L. Whetten, *Rural Mexico* (1948) p. 255. The index numbers are those constructed by the Secretariat of National Economy of the Government of Mexico.

output as a whole was 6.5 per cent per annum between 1939 and 1949, but it dropped to 3.7 per cent per annum in the following decade.[4] Similarly data for crop output alone for the period 1948-63 show that while it grew at a compound rate of 8.5 per cent per annum between 1948 and 1955, the rate of growth declined to 4.1 per cent between 1955 and 1963.[5]

Most of the assessments made of the Mexican performance relate to the period as a whole and do not make any attempt to distinguish between factors that might have contributed to the very high rates of growth in the earlier phase and those underlying the deceleration and lower rates later. A typical example is the following summing-up by three agricultural scientists who were closely associated from the early 1940s with the development of the plant varieties and agronomical practices adopted in Mexico and were in fact the pioneers of the movement:

> Then was 1943; now is 1963. The place is Mexico, both then and now; but it is not the same Mexico now as it was then, for there has been a revolution between then and now.... The population increased 70 per cent between then and now, but the production of the three basic foods increased 300 per cent.... Even more noteworthy, however, is the way in which it was accomplished, for it was done not so much by using more acres as by helping each acre produce more...... Agricultural revolution is no mere figure of speech, for Mexico is indeed on the road to tremendous progress. The 1941 agriculture was traditional; now it is progressive. And it will continue to progress because it is continually becoming more scientific.[6]

Other appraisals of Mexican agriculture made in the middle of this period have, however, some light to throw on the factors responsible for the high rates of growth recorded in the first half. Given below are extracts from a report by a group of experts sponsored by the World Bank and the Government of Mexico in 1952:[7]

4 W. W. Wicks, 'The Agricultural Development of Mexico, 1940-60,' unpublished doctoral thesis submitted to the Food Research Institute of Stanford University in October 1965 (available in microfilm). Extensive use has been made in this paper of the statistical material contained in this volume, which is an important and extremely valuable contribution to the available literature both on Mexico and on problems of agricultural development in general.

5 U.S. Department of Agriculture (Economic Research Service), *Changes in Agriculture in 26 Developing Nations, 1948 to 1963*, Table 4.

6 E. C. Stakman, Richard Bradfield and Paul C. Mangelsdorf, *Compaign against Hunger* (Harvard University Press, 1967) pp. 1-9.

7 *The Economic Development of Mexico*, Report of the Combined Mexican Working Party, published for the International Bank for Reconstruction and Development (1953) chap. ii (italics mine).

The average annual rate of increase of agricultural production, which amounted to 4.7 per cent in the period 1940 to 1949, increased slowly from 4.4 per cent in 1940-4 to 5.0 per cent in 1945-9; according to preliminary estimates, the increase in production in 1950 amounted to 16.1 per cent.... *The rise in the use of arable land, extension of cultivated area and improvement of old and new lands by irrigation. Greater use of new and improved lands made it possible to grow more valuable crops and to increase yields. Better farming methods contributed little to higher yields.* (p. 27)

From 1939 to 1950, the average increase in harvested area was 3.1 per cent per annum. As in the case of agricultural production, the area harvested expanded slowly up to 1949, the increase averaging 1.9 per cent annually in 1940-4 and 2.3 per cent in 1945-9; also as with production, preliminary and somewhat tentative estimates for 1950 show a greater than usual increase, 13.4 per cent over the previous year. (p. 27)

The increase in yields accounted for 23 per cent of the rise in agricultural production in the twelve years from 1919 to 1950 .... *The increase in yields between 1939-50 were due primarily to the extension of cultivation to superior new lands and to improvements of old lands placed under irrigation. On the other hand, no significant rise in yields occurred in the older unimproved agricultural regions.....The higher yields obtained on the new lands were due to the virgin soil, to relatively greater use of irrigation, and in some cases, to more favourable climatic conditions than in the older regions....the increase in yields is attributed only in limited degree to the use of improved seed and of fertiliser, or to other improvements in agricultural methods...*.On the basis of an estimate....that the use of hybrid seed increases yields by about 25 per cent per hectare, it can be determined that *less than 2 per cent out of an overall increase of 58 per cent in corn production between 1939 and 1950 was attributable to the use of hybrid seed distributed*....(pp. 28-29)

Between 1939 and 1950, important changes occurred in the distribution of crops over the total cultivated area which produced a relative increase in the area devoted to crops with higher yields and unit values. Thus, corn declined from 71 per cent of the harvested area in 1939, to 66 per cent in 1945-9, and 65 per cent in 1950. On the other hand, the harvested area for cotton rose from 3.8 per cent of the total in 1939 to 5.1 per cent in 1945-9 and 8.5 per cent in 1950. Similarly the harvested area for oilseeds increased from 1.4 per cent of the total in 1939, to 2.9 per cent in 1945-9, and 3.3 per cent in 1950....*These changes in the crop pattern were responsible for 60 per cent of the rise in agri-*

cultural production in 1940-4 and therefore had more effect on output than the increase in harvested area or than the higher yields per hectare; in 1945-9, such changes accounted for 32 per cent ....(p. 31)

It is clear from this that whatever growth took place in Mexican agricultural output as a result of applying new 'modern' inputs was recorded in the second rather than in the first half of the period of two decades normally considered in this context.

A closer examination of the data[8] also reveals striking regional differences in agricultural performance, the growth rate in the older and more densely populated regions of the country being much lower than in the northern part (more specifically in the North and Pacific North regions) which, though more sparsely populated, received the bulk of the investment in irrigation after 1939.[9]

It will be seen from Table I that in the Central region—which has about one-half of the country's population—the rate of growth of agricultural production was only two and a half per cent per annum between 1949 and 1959.

The North and Pacific North regions were not only sparsely populated but arid and dry, for which reason they were largely unaffected by the ceilings on the size of agricultural holdings imposed by earlier land reforms:

> Holders having more than 1,000 hectares, although accounting for only 0.3 per cent of the holders, had 61.9 per cent of the land (in all Mexico); those having more than 40,000 hectares had one-fourth of all the land censused in 1940. Large holdings, however, persist mostly in the semiarid region where the land is not suitable for cultivation and can be used only for grazing or for a very extensive type of agriculture....two-thirds of all holdings having more than 1,000 hectares are found in the north and north Pacific regions, where it is too dry for farming without irrigation.[10]

These large holdings were consequently the greatest beneficiaries of the subsequent investment in irrigation in these regions.[11]

8 Hicks, 'The Agricultural Development of Mexico, 1940-60'.

9 Irrigation accounted for 12-16 per cent of the total public investment per annum in Mexico between 1939 and 1950; public investment itself formed nearly two-fifths of gross domestic investment during this period. Consequently the area under irrigation increased from 0.24 million hectares in 1939 to 1.19 million hectares by 1950: *The Economic Development of Mexico*, Tables 15 and 20. The share of irrigation in public investment continued to be high after 1950—not to mention private investment, which also picked up.

10 Whetten, *Rural Mexico*.

11 Between 1939 and 1959 the total irrigated area in Mexico increased from 1.7 million to 4.3 million hectares; of the increase of 2.6 million, the share of the North and Pacific North regions was 1.6 million.

TABLE I

RATE OF GROWTH OF AGRICULTURAL OUTPUT PER ANNUM IN MEXICO

	1939-49	1949-59	1939-59
Mexico	6.5	3.7	5.1
North	8.9	4.9	6.9
Pacific North	11.9	7.9	9.9
Central	7.7	2.5	3.6

Within the North and Pacific North regions the agricultural growth that took place was concentrated mainly in seven states: Baja California, Coahuila, Chihuahua, Durango, Sinaloa, Sonora and Tamaulipas. These states accounted in 1940 for only about three-fifths of the total population of these regions, and for less than a sixth of the total population of the country. They claimed, however, 50 per cent of the area irrigated after 1939, and accounted in 1957 for nearly 70 per cent of the total area in the irrigation districts of Mexico. By 1957 nearly the whole of the cotton production (to be exact 95 per cent) and about two-thirds of the wheat production of the country were also grown in these seven states. The extent to which agricultural performance in Mexico in the period 1939-59 was a reflection of the increase in production recorded in these states will be evident from Table II. It will be seen that the seven

TABLE II

INCREASES IN AREA, PRODUCTION AND VALUE OF OUTPUT OF COTTON AND WHEAT IN MEXICO, 1939-59

	Cotton			*Wheat*		
	1939-49	1949-59	1939-59	1939-49	1949-59	1939-59
Mexico						
Area harvested ('000 hectares)[a]	337	212	549	—18	400	382
Production ('000 metric tons)	352	558	910	95	747	842
Value of output (million pesos)	739	1,934	2,673	175	862	1,037
Seven States						
Area harvested ('000 hectares)	246	276	522	25	256	280
Production ('000 metric tons)	332	527	859	59	472	531
Value of output (million pesos)	700	1,824	2,524	106	522	628

Source: Hicks, 'The Agricultural Development of Mexico, 1940-60'.

[a] The total area harvested (under all crops) rose in Mexico from 6.7 million hectares in 1939 to 8.6 million hectares in 1949 and to 12 million hectares by 1959, recording an increase of 80 per cent in the course of the two decades.

states accounted for 85 per cent of the increase in the total value of output of cotton and wheat in the two decades.

It is also important to note that, in these states, while the production of cotton increased by 544 per cent (from 158,000 to 1,017,000 metric tons) between 1939 and 1959 and wheat by 207 per cent (from 257,000 to 788,000 metric tons), the area under these crops also increased during this period by no less than 272 per cent (from 192,000 to 714,000 hectares) and 101 per cent (from 271,000 to 551,000 hectares) respectively. A large part of the increase in production is therefore attributable merely to the extension of the area under cultivation (not to mention the fact that most of this additional area was also newly irrigated).

Within these seven states themselves the growth was concentrated to a significant degree in two, namely Sinaloa and Sonora, since the largest percentage increases in harvested area took place within their territory. Between 1949 and 1959 in particular the harvested area expanded at the compound rate of nearly 68 per cent per annum in Sinaloa and 10½ per cent per annum in Sonora.[12] By 1961 Sonora was producing nearly one-half of Mexico's total output of wheat; naturally the higher productivity here had a significant impact on the average for all Mexico: 'it was the increase in the wheat area in Sonora, where yields were high and increasing rapidly, that was largely responsible for the increase in the average yield in Mexico'.[13]

As for the increase in cotton production in the northern region, it was to a large extent due to the ceilings on cotton acreage imposed in the United States which made it attractive to grow cotton in the areas south of the border in Mexico. Not only, therefore, did the cotton produced have a ready market, but considerable financial assistance became available from private merchants for extension of the area under cotton in Mexico.[14]

12 In 1940, Sinaloa and Sonora together had a population of less than 900,000 out of a total population of nearly 20 million in Mexico: Whetten, *Rural Mexico*, Appendix, Table 2.

13 Hicks, 'The Agricultural Development of Mexico, 1940-60'. According to Hicks, since this was a state in which yields were already high, the extension of harvested area accounted for more than twice as much of the increase in production as did the increase in yield.

14 Loans given by private merchants to agriculture increased by over 1,400 million pesos between 1949 and 1959, and loans given by all sources of credit (including the government) by over 6,400 million. About three-fourths of the former and two-thirds of the latter were concentrated in the northern region. Private merchants included international cotton merchants like Anderson & Clayton: Hicks, ibid.

These facts place in a broader perspective the performance of Mexican agriculture in the period following the Second World War. It is fairly clear that it was largely a kind of 'enclave' development made possible by heavy investments in irrigation opening up new areas for cultivation as well as by certain special circumstances such as that of location—more particularly the proximity to the United States which favoured this region.

> The analysis of cotton and wheat yields in the seven states on a state-by-state basis suggests that the expansion of irrigation into new areas of northern Mexico where techniques, machinery, fertilisers, insecticides, and credit from the United States were adopted may have accounted for the bulk of the increase in production.[15]

It is reasonable to suppose that the large size of holdings in this region (comparable to that on the other side of the border in the United States) as well as similar soil and climatic conditions facilitated such transfer.

That what has been accomplished in Mexico is not very dissimilar to the kind of development that has taken place in limited regions under favourable circumstances in many other countries in the course of the last century, and that transformation of traditional agriculture as such was not even attempted in Mexico, is borne out also by others closely associated with the experiment:

> It would be most unfair to suggest that the irrigated Yaqui Valley in northwest Mexico is representative of the total of Mexico's agriculture. It is, however, representative of a type of agriculture in Mexico and also of a type of agriculture which may be found in many other countries in Latin America and I expect also in other parts of the world; a type of agriculture which is the direct result of an attempt to increase the size of the technological sector relative to the traditional sector. Where the attempt has not been to accomplish a rapid transformation of the traditional into the technological but in contrast has been to guide 'new growth' into the technological.[16]

Past experience also suggests that, however high the resulting rates of growth in agriculture might be over certain periods, such development does not necessarily lead to transformation of agriculture but often only to the emergence of dualism within this sector. That the

15 Ibid.

16 Donald K. Freebairn, 'Relative Production Efficiency between Tenure Classes in the Yaqui Valley, Sonora, Mexico', *Journal of Farm Economics* (Dec. 1963). Mr. Freebairn was attached to the Rockefeller Foundation and associated with the co-operative agricultural research programme of the Mexican Secretariat of Agriculture.

Mexican experience during this period has nevertheless been cited as a demonstration of the possibility of transforming traditional agriculture is a remarkable example of the kind of casual empiricism that is abundantly in evidence in the literature on development problems.

III The Experience of Taiwan

The rate of growth of agricultural production in Taiwan is somewhat lower than that claimed for Mexico. For the period 1948-63 the estimated rate of growth of crop output is only $4\frac{1}{2}$ per cent per annum (compared to nearly $6\frac{1}{4}$ per cent per annum for Mexico).[17] The inclusion of forestry, fishery and livestock output would no doubt raise the rate, and figures of $5\frac{1}{2}$ per cent per annum and more have sometimes been mentioned for certain periods (such as for 1953-64). Nevertheless, most assessments covering the entire period since the early 1950s place the rate of growth of agricultural output at only about $4\frac{1}{2}$ per cent per annum.[18]

This growth rate in agriculture supported a phenomenally high rate of growth of the economy of Taiwan during this period. The gross national product (at constant 1964 prices) increased at a rate of over $7\frac{1}{2}$ per cent per annum from the early 1950s, as a result of which the per capita income in the country went up by more than 75 per cent by 1964 despite rapid growth of population in the intervening period.[19] In fact, at the beginning of this period the level of income per head of the population was no higher in Taiwan than in most of the underdeveloped countries (i.e. the equivalent of less than or around $U.S. 100 per annum); but by the middle of the 1960s its per capita income had doubled and was nearly $U.S. 200 per annum. The performance in the agricultural sector during this period contributed materially, therefore, to carrying the economy of Taiwan to a more advanced stage of development.

Taiwan's is also clearly a more genuine case of transformation of traditional agriculture than Mexico's: Even before the Second World War over 70 per cent of the farms were less than 3 hectares in size and the average size of farms in Taiwan was only a little over 2

17 *Changes in Agriculture in 26 Developing Nations*, Table 4.

18 U.S. Department of Agriculture, *Taiwan's Agricultural Development: Its Relevance for Developing Countries Today*, Foreign Agricultural Economic Report No. 39 (Apr. 1968) p. vii.

19 Neil H. Jacoby, *An Evaluation of U.S. Economic Aid to Free China, 1951-1965* (Agency for International Development, Department of State) chap. viii.

hectares; by 1960, more than 85 per cent of the farms were less than 3 hectares in size and the average size of farms had declined to 1 hectare.[20] The high growth rates recorded have been mainly in farms within this size range based mainly on family labour.

The growth performance of Taiwan during this period is, however, rooted in large part in the trends established in an earlier period of its history. An appreciation of these earlier trends and of the factors contributing to them is essential for an assessment of the post-war experience and its implications for other countries.

Fig.1 shows on semi-logarithmic scale the movements of an index of agricultural output for Taiwan covering the period 1901-60.[21] In these six decades taken as a whole the growth rate was a little over 3.1 per cent per annum. It will be seen that though the post-war period recorded much higher rates of growth—in fact over 8½ per cent per annum if we take the fifteen years starting from 1945—they represented to a large extent a process of catching up with the earlier trend line.[22]

The relatively high rate of growth of agricultural output in Taiwan in the pre-war period was the result of policies actively followed by Japan as a colonial power. Japan was short of food and other agricultural products and needed to develop Taiwan as an additional source of supply. A large part of the agricultural growth recorded during this period was due to extension of the cultivated land area—this area having more than doubled between 1901 and 1940 (from 376,000 hectares to 860,000 hectares)[23]—but a significant part is also attributable to changes in technology. Higher-yielding plant varieties and techniques of intensive cultivation such as multiple cropping of land and use of chemical fertilisers—all of them familiar

20 *Taiwan's Agricultural Development*, p. vii. See also S.C. Hsieh and T. H. Lee *Agricultural Development and its Contributions to Economic Growth in Taiwan* (Apr. 1966) Appendix, Table 12.

21 Yhi-min Ho, *Agricultural Development of Taiwan, 1903-60* (1966) chap. 3, Fig. 4. The first five years of the century represented, however, a period of recovery from the first Sino-Japanese war and recorded exceptionally high rates of growth; if these years are excluded, the growth rate for the period 1906-39 would work out to only about 2.6 per cent per annum.

22 '... 1939 was the peak year of agricultural production in Taiwan before the war. Not until 1952 did Taiwan break this previous record in its agricultural production. If 1952 is regarded as the year ending the post-war reconstruction period, the growth rate for the post-war period then became 3.22 per cent, which is slightly lower than the pre-war rate of 3.32 per cent (of 1906-39) ... Because the year of 1939 was far off the linear trend, it seems to be more appropriate to take the long-term growth rate of 2.57 per cent as the representative growth rate for the pre-war period': ibid., p. 33.

23 Ibid., p. 48.

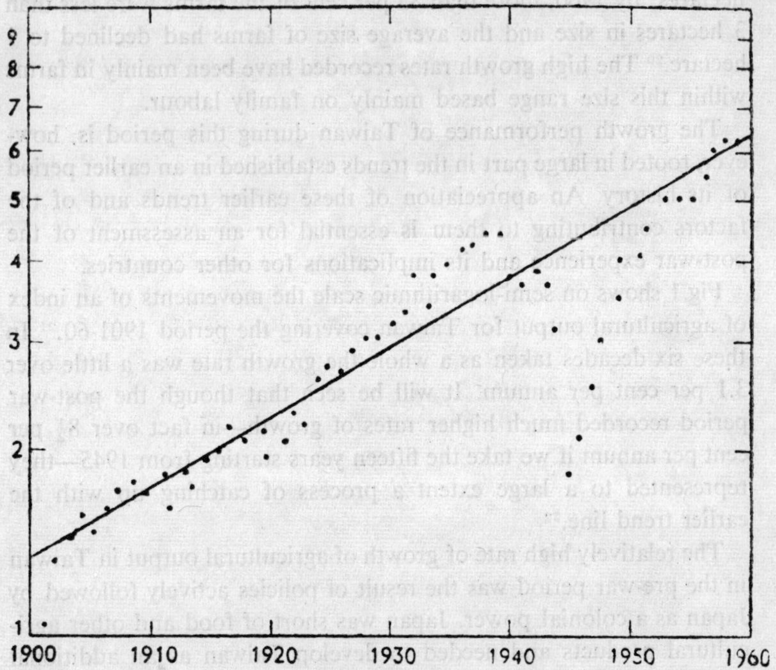

FIG. 1 Index of agricultural output in Taiwan, 1901–60, shown in semi-logarithmic scale

to Japan—were introduced into the country during this period. But no changes were made in the land tenure system, which remained highly oppressive.

The performance of Taiwan's agriculture before the Second World War, it is therefore evident, was due in the main to extension of the cultivated area and technological improvements. Both, however, were dependent on a large-scale expansion of the area under irrigation. From around 30 per cent of the cultivated area at the turn of the century, the share of irrigated land in the total area under cultivation was raised under Japanese rule to nearly 62 per cent by 1940.[24]

The Japanese also used somewhat unconventional methods for getting the new crop varieties and methods of cultivation adopted in Taiwan as will be evident from the following extract:

It was tacitly assumed, and even frequently expressed by experts at the Taipei agricultural station research bureau, that police

24 Ibid., Table 16, p. 49.

power had to be employed to force new farming techniques on to rural communities resisting change. One observer evaluated the police force's role in these terms: 'In each district throughout the island the chief of police exercised the power to protect and change traditional behaviour as well as introduce new customs and ideas; he also was dedicated to stimulating industry and increasing the wealth of his area and laying the groundwork for a new communication system. There are many benefits to be derived in this way for developing an area'.[25] Since the police penetrated to every village household through the *ho-ko* (*pao-chia*) system, it was relatively easy for them to insist on the adoption of new sugar cane or rice seeds and supervise their use.

Through the use of the police force for this purpose is more forgivable than other uses often made of it by imperial powers in their colonies, it is important to bear in mind that, in the absence of a land tenure system providing the necessary incentives for the transformation of agriculture, methods of this kind were needed to produce the results that were shown in Taiwan.

Once a breakthrough was achieved, the further development of agriculture in Taiwan was much easier. After the Second World War there was little scope for further extension of the cultivated area, but it was possible to increase the area under irrigation, extend multiple cropping, introduce new and even better plant varieties, and increase the intensity of input of nutrients. It should, however, be observed that (*a*) the quantity of commercial fertiliser consumed in Taiwan in 1960 was only 20 per cent higher than in 1940;[26] (*b*) the growth of agricultural output in the period since the war has been to a large extent due to high rates of growth recorded in the forestry, fishery and livestock subsectors as well as in food products like vegetables and fruits—which in turn were made possible by the rapid growth in demand on account of the doubling of per capita income during this period;[27] and (*c*) the rate of growth of output of rice, which was the dominant item in production and

25 Ramon H. Myers and Adrienne Ching, 'Agricultural Development in Taiwan under Japanese Colonial Rule', *Journal of Asian Studies*, XXIII, 4 (Aug. 1964). The quotation is from a publication in Taiwan of 1959.

26 1938: 472,000 metric tons
1939: 489,000 metric tons
1950: 555,000 metric tons
1958: 682,000 metric tons
1959: 679,000 metric tons
1960: 665,000 metric tons

Yhi-Min Ho, chap. 5, Table 21.

27 The growth of output in vegetables and fruits, particularly during the recent years, has been to a larger extent attributable to export demand as well as a general diversification of demand in the economy due to rising income.

consumption earlier, has been much lower than that of these other agricultural products—in fact only about 3 per cent per annum.[28]

It should also be recalled that in the period following the Second World War the land reforms that were carried out in Taiwan altered significantly the institutional framework of agriculture. Not only were many of the larger holdings broken up, but a much higher proportion of holdings came to be owner-cultivated and without large rents having to be paid as before by cultivating tenants.

> Before 1949, 39 per cent of the total farm families in Taiwan were tenant farmers. They were reduced to only 17 per cent of the total in 1957. Changes in the number of owner farmers were also accompanied by a change in the acreage of owner-cultivated land. Of a total area of 680,000 hectares of private cultivated land, the proportion cultivated by owner farmers was increased from 61 per cent to 85 per cent.[29]

In sum, the rapid growth of agricultural output in Taiwan in the post-war period was not simply due to technological changes introduced during this period; the foundations for technological progress has been laid earlier over a period of four decades. Indeed the more immediate contributory factors were the recovery to the pre-war trend line, the rapid growth in demand for agricultural products other than cereals generated by growth in income, and the increased incentive given to farmers by land reform for more intensive application of inputs.

IV Experience In India

In comparison with the performance of agriculture in Mexico and Taiwan, the growth recorded in India since the early 1950s is clearly less impressive, being only around 3 per cent per annum

28 The agricultural sector as a whole grew at an average rate of 5.9 per cent per annum in the period 1953-64, but the rate of growth of output of forest products during this period was 7.5 per cent per annum, of fisheries 9.9 per cent per annum, and livestock 7.3 per cent per annum, so that the rate of growth of agricultural products excluding these was only 4.6 per cent per annum. Within this group, output of rice increased at an average rate of just 3.1 per cent per annum. See *Taiwan Statistical Data Book* (Ministry of Economic Affairs, 1967) p. 24.

29 Hsieh and Lee *Agricultural Development and its Contributions to Economic Growth in Taiwan*, p. 83. Before the war over two-thirds of the land under rice was under tenancy. 'The numerous tenants competed among each other for rental of land. Tenancy contracts were short, usually only for one year. They were oral contracts. . . . Rental rates were high. Tenants paid 50 per cent or more of their main crops to landlords for use of land': *Taiwan's Agricultural Development*, pp. 44-5.

compound rate for the sector as a whole. For crop output also the rate of growth has been no higher. It is probable that in the national income statistics there has been some underestimation of growth in some of the subsectors, in particular of livestock products, but it is unlikely that this would make a great deal of difference to the overall growth rate in the agricultural sector.

What the growth rate for India as a whole conceals, however, are important inter-regional differences in agricultural performance. While the rate has been lower than the national average in some regions—so much lower that, in seven of the fourteen major states in the country, growth of population has outpaced the growth of foodgrain production—it has been much higher in some others. This will be evident from Table III.

The rates of growth recorded in some of these states were comparable to, and even exceeded, the rates achieved in Mexico and Taiwan. Though agricultural output in Mexico grew at the rate of a little over 5 per cent per annum in the period 1939–59, the rate recorded in the second half of this period was (as observed earlier) only about 3.7 per cent per annum. Even this is likely to be

TABLE III

RATES OF AGRICULTURAL GROWTH IN INDIA (COMPOUND), 1952-3 TO 1964-5

	All crop output	Foodgrain output	Population
Punjab	4.56	4.17	2.16
Gujarat	4.55	2.06	2.61
Madras	4.17	3.66	1.25
Mysore	3.54	3.31	2.08
Bihar	2.97	3.05	2.12
Maharashtra	2.93	2.20	2.32
Rajasthan	2.74	2.42	2.68
Andhra Pradesh	2.71	3.21	1.63
Madhya Pradesh	2.49	2.32	2.51
Orissa	2.48	2.39	2.16
Kerala	2.27	3.68	2.33
West Bengal	1.94	1.14	2.92
Uttar Pradesh	1.66	0.85	1.84
Assam	1.17	0.76	3.15
All India	**3.01**	**2.50**	**2.19**

Source: Ministry of Food and Agriculture (Government of India,) *Growth Rates in Agriculture 1949–50 to 1964–65*. The rate of growth of crop output is a little higher, at 3.19 per cent per annum, for the period 1949-50 to 1964–5.

an overestimate, as the data for Mexico do not fully allow for the progressive increase in the coverage of the government estimates of agricultural production (more particularly of corn).[30] In Taiwan too the rate of growth of agricultural output—excluding forestry, fishery and livestock products—was no more than 4.6 per cent per annum between 1953 and 1964; and (as already pointed out) the rate of growth of output of rice, the main foodgrain grown in Taiwan, was only 3.1 per cent per annum during this period. Table IV shows the growth rates for different crops in the three shares of India in which rates comparable to those recorded in Mexico and Taiwan were achieved in the period 1952–3 to 1964–5.

TABLE IV

RATE OF GROWTH OF OUTPUT OF DIFFERENT CROPS IN THE PUNJAB, GUJARAT AND MADRAS STATES IN INDIA, 1952-3 TO 1964-5

Crop	*Punjab*	*Gujarat*	*Madras*
Wheat	5.38	3.12	—
Rice	8.68	5.59	4.98
Maize	3.83	—	—
Jowar	0.98	1.06	4.20
All foodgrain crops	3.66	2.06	4.17
Cotton	7.06	5.42	4.56
Sugarcane	6.72	10.56	7.68
Tobacco	—	6.51	0.70
Groundnuts	—	9.01	4.55
All non-foodgrain crops	7.04	6.62	4.17
All crops	4.56	4.55	4.47

30 There is also some additional circumstantial evidence for suspecting the accuracy of the official Mexican estimates of the rates of growth in agriculture which have been used uncritically by Professor Schultz and others. For instance, though per capita income in Mexico was no more than $150 in 1939, the share of agriculture in the total national product was only 22 per cent—which is exceptional for economies in this range of income. Moreover, in spite of the per capita income in Mexico doubling itself in the following two decades, the share of agriculture was still 20 per cent in 1960, i.e. only a little lower than in 1939. If the underestimation of agricultural production earlier is allowed for, it is not improbable that the share of agriculture was higher to begin with and that it fell more sharply during this period: Hicks, 'The Agricultural Development of Mexico, 1940-60'.

It should perhaps be added that, by allowing for the increase in the area coverage of the official estimates of agricultural production in India, foodgrain production in 1949-50, which was originally estimated to be 48 million tons, has been subsequently placed at over 60 million tons; the estimates of rates of growth of agricultural production in India are based on the index numbers of agricultural production revised to take into account the extensions in coverage. While these revised index numbers for India are still defective in some respects and have occasionally come in for critical comment, the Mexican data on agricultural output have been generally accepted uncritically.

The increases in output recorded in these states can be broken down according to certain proximate and identifiable sources of growth, namely, extension of area under crops, changes in the crop pattern (in the direction of more highly valued crops) and increases in crop yield per unit of land. The results of such an exercise[31] based on the data available for individual states and covering the period 1951–4 to 1958–61, are given in Table V.

TABLE V

RELATIVE CONTRIBUTIONS OF DIFFERENT ELEMENTS TO THE GROWTH OF CROP OUTPUT IN THE PUNJAB, GUJARAT AND MADRAS STATES

	Percentage increase attributed to				
State	Area increase	Change in crop pattern	Increase in crop yield	'Interaction'[a]	Total
Punjab	69.93	22.38	7.98	0.29	100.00
Gujarat	22.16	68.21	21.29	11.66	100.00
Madras	19.70	25.00	52.70	2.60	100.00

[a] 'The interesting term in our scheme is essentially in the nature of a balancing entry': Minhas and Vaidyanathan, op. cit.

While extension of area under crops was the major source of growth in the Punjab, and changes in the crop pattern in Gujarat, the more important source of growth in Madras is increase in crop yield per acre. One needs to consider what it is that made these the main sources of growth—which would indicate also why these states were able to achieve rates of growth comparable to those recorded in Mexico and Taiwan.

The Punjab's is a particularly interesting case. For a number of historical reasons the north-western region of India—including (and in fact more particularly) that part of the Punjab which is now in the territory of Pakistan—received the bulk of the public investment undertaken during the British period, and a high proportion of this went into irrigation. Thus, in the period 1898–1914, when gross public investment annually was itself in the range of 3¾ to 5½ per cent of the national income (and net public investment about

31 B. S. Minhas and A. Vaidyanathan, 'Growth of Crop Output in India, 1951-54 to 1958-61: An Analysis by Component Elements', *Journal of the Indian Society of Agricultural Statistics* (Dec. 1966). Data for different crops within each state are not fully corrected for errors due to extensions in the coverage of official agricultural statistics; this has to be borne in mind in interpreting the results of this analysis, more particularly in the case of states like Rajasthan where such extensions are known to have been very large.

$2\frac{1}{2}$ to 4 per cent), and irrigation accounted for about one-eighth of this investment, no less than 50 per cent of the gross investment in irrigation was in the Punjab.[32] As a result there was an increase of as much as 150 per cent in the stock of irrigation assets in this region during the period and a more than proportionate increase in the area irrigated. While the Punjab accounted for only 4.5 million acres out of 13.5 million acres under irrigation in British India in 1899–1900, its share went up to 7.0 million acres out of 17.0 million acres by 1913–14, which in turn led to the production of wheat in the Punjab increasing by about 60 per cent during this period and of raw cotton by no less than four and a half times.

The partition of the Punjab resulted in the greater part of the irrigated area of the region falling into the territory of Pakistan, and this fact, together with the need to rehabilitate the refugees who migrated into India, made it necessary to make heavy investments in irrigation in the eastern part of the Punjab in the years immediately following 1947. Most of it was on the Bhakra Nangal Project—the largest multi-purpose project in India's First Five-Year plan.[33] This project not only helped to increase the area under irrigation in the region but—as in Mexico at about the same time—brought into cultivation some relatively arid and dry areas, thereby increasing the total cropped area itself. The net area irrigated in the Punjab State (of the Indian Union) increased from 38 per cent of the net sown area in 1950–1 to 43 per cent in 1962–3; alongside, the gross cropped area in the state increased by nearly one-third during this period.[34]

The northern part of the state, and even some areas in the centre, already had canal irrigation from earlier investments in irrigation (as in the West Punjab in Pakistan) and the areas where irrigation was newly provided were therefore mainly in the extreme south and south-west. It will be seen from Fig. 2—which depicts the

32 See M. K. Thavaraj, 'Public Investment in India, 1898-1914: Some Features,' *Indian Economic Review*, II, 4 (Aug 1955): also his paper on 'Capital Formation in the Public Sector in India: A Historical Study, 1898-1938', in *Papers in National Income and Allied Topics*, (Indian Conference on Research in National Income), ed. V. K. R. V. Rao, S. R. Sen, M. V. Divatia and Uma Datta. The data presented in this paragraph are taken from these two papers.

33 For more information on this project, see K. N. Raj, *Some Economic Aspects of the Bhakra Nangal Project: An Analysis in Terms of Selected Investment Criteria* (Asia Publishing House, 1960).

34 The extension of the area under cultivation in the Punjab as a result in irrigation during this period was of course proportionately much less than of Mexico.

annual growth rates, district-wise, between 1952–3 and 1959–60—that these areas in the south recorded rates of growth of over 10 per cent per annum during this decade and that even in some of the other areas benefited by the project crop output grew at a rate of between 5 and 10 per cent per annum.[35]

The total population of the Punjab in 1961 was over 20 million (of which the population in the seven districts in which crop output increased fastest was nearly 3½ million); the total area under cultivation was around 8 million hectares (of which these seven districts accounted for nearly one-half). Considered in terms of the size of the population and cultivated area, the Punjab, it will be seen, is therefore about two-thirds as large as Mexico, while in the areas within the state in which the growth rate has been highest both the population and the area under cultivation are clearly larger than in the corresponding regions of Mexico. Though the average size of holdings is larger in the Punjab than in most other parts of India, it is very much smaller than in the northern regions of Mexico; the degree of concentration in the ownership and operation of land holdings also appears to be much lower in the Punjab.[36] If the achievement of high growth rates in relatively small-sized holdings based on family labour is the criterion, the performance of agriculture in the Punjab since the Second World War is therefore perhaps more worthy of attention than that in Mexico during this period.

The state of Madras, and more particularly some of the directs within it, has similarly many features in common with Taiwan. The area under crops as well as the population are no doubt much higher (about ten and three times as high respectively as in Taiwan),

35 It would appear from some unpublished data made available to the author that the picture is broadly the same even for the peirod 1952-3 to 1964-5. Bhatinda, Patiala and Hissar recorded increases in crop output of approximately 10 per cent or more per annum, while in Karnal, Mahendragarh, Ludhiana and Jullundur crop output grew at the rate of between 5 and 10 per cent per annum.

36 The average size of an agricultural holding in the territory of the Punjab State (as in 1953-4) was only 11.0 acres, which was slightly larger than the all-India average of 7.5 acres. See *Report on Land Holdings (4), Rural Sector—States* (The National Sample Survey, No. 66) Tables 2–5. Taking into account all the assets (including land but excluding some financial assets) held by households in the rural sector, it has been estimated that the top 10 per cent of the households in the Punjab State accounted for only 47 per cent of the assets held by all households in the state (compared to 56.5 per cent in Madras and 60 per cent in Andhra Pradesh, both in South India). See 'Distribution of Value of Total Assets among Households Resident in the Rural Sector of India', *Reserve Bank of India Bulletin* (Oct. 1966). Transfers of land through leasing also do not significantly alter the size distribution of holdings in the Punjab.

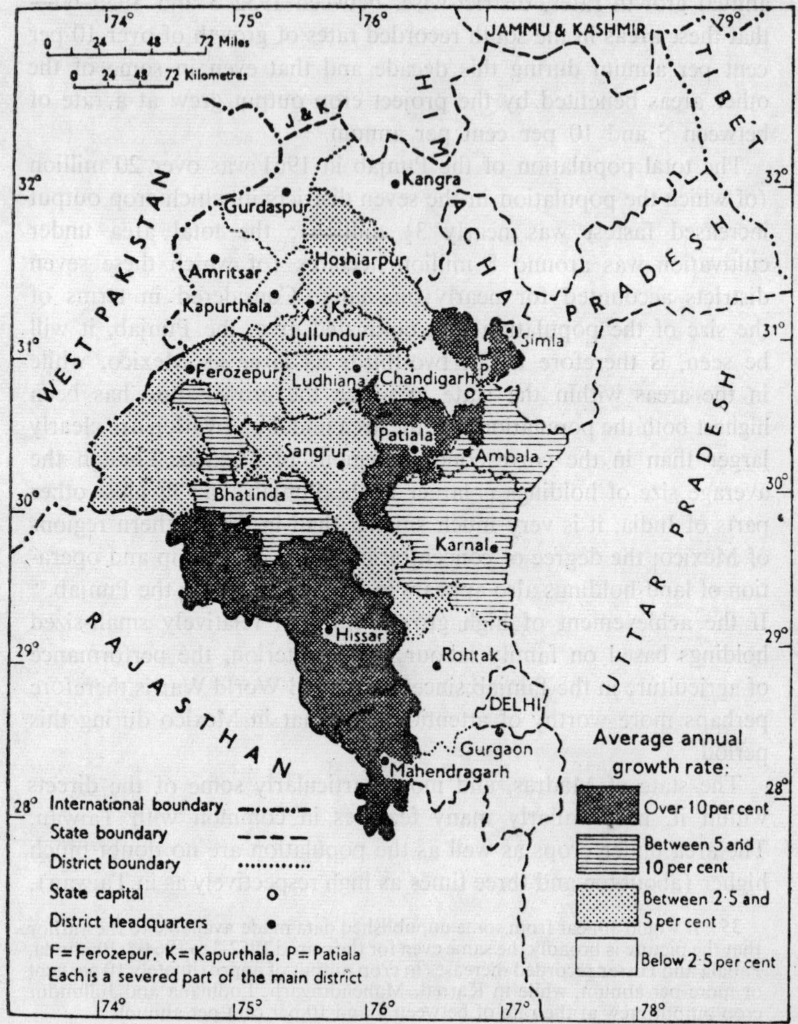

FIG. 2 Growth rates in agriculture in the Punjab between 1952–5 and 1959–62

but in both cases a high proportion of the cultivated area has been under irrigation for a fairly long period as a result of earlier investments. (The irrigated area in Madras has increased in recent years, from about 35 to 41 per cent of the net sown area.) In fact in the Thanjavur district of the state, where the area under crops is nearly four-fifths as high as in Taiwan and the population about one-fourth in size, nearly 80 per cent of the cropped area is irrigated. As in Taiwan, the main foodgrain grown in Madras is rice: and the Thanjavur district, often described as 'the rice-bowl' of South India, grows about one-fourth of the total production of rice in the state. With the high percentage of land under irrigation, the state of Madras (and more particularly the districts like Thanjavur) has also come in for special attention in recent years through programmes for intensive agricultural development formulated as part of the Five-Year Plans.

However, the highest rates of growth of crop production in Madras in the period since the late 1940s have been recorded (as in the Punjab) in the districts in which the irrigated area *increased* most. As will be evident from Table VI, this is because the gross area sown has registered the largest increases in districts where the percentage increase in irrigated areas has been highest. These were also generally districts in which productivity per acre was relatively lower than elsewhere in the state, and so the effect of extension of irrigation was to raise productivity by a larger percentage than in other districts where productivity was higher to begin with. It will be seen that in districts which already had extensive areas under irrigation and the further increases in irrigated and gross sown areas were relatively much smaller, not only was growth of crop output dependent to a larger extent on increases in crop yield per acre, but the rate of growth of output recorded was itself much lower (exactly as in the areas of Mexico and Taiwan that had been under irrigation earlier). In Thanjavur district, where the area under irrigation and productivity per acre were highest to begin with, the recorded growth rate of crop output was no more than 3.3 per cent (which is of the same order as of rice output in Taiwan in the same period).

Gujarat presents a special case of a state in which the irrigated area is relatively small (less than 10 per cent of the net sown area) but where the climatic and soil conditions favour the cultivation of non-foodgrain crops with relatively high productivity per acre. These crops accounted for 48.3 per cent of the total cropped area in Gujarat even in the early 1950s (compared to 24.5 per cent for all India). In response to rapid growth in demand (particularly

TABLE VI

GROWTH OF CROP OUTPUT[a] IN TEN SELECTED DISTRICTS OF MADRAS STATE (SOUTH INDIA), 1949-50 TO 1962-3

	Growth rate per annum (compound)	Percentage of gross area sown 1949-51	Output per acre 1949-51 (in rupees)	Percentage of gross area irrigated 1949-51	Percentage increase in gross irrigated area 1949-51 to 1960-2	Percentage increase in gross area sown 1949-51 to 1960-2	Percentage increase in output per acre 1949-51 to 1960-2	Percentage contribution of increases in crop yield to growth of output 1949-51 to 1962-3[b]
Group I:								
Chingleput	8.8	40.6	95.8	56.3				
Ramanathapuram	7.4	34.4	93.3	42.2				
North Arcot	5.9	44.3	129.1	34.0				
Coimbatore	5.4	46.3	103.1	25.4				
Average	**6.9**	**42.0**	**105.3**	**35.5**	**63.2**	**34.6**	**60.4**	**46.7**
Group II:								
Salem	5.0	41.0	91.7	19.0				
Tirunelveli	4.7	45.1	121.0	37.9				
Madurai	4.5	44.6	129.2	40.7				
Average	**4.7**	**43.2**	**113.9**	**31.0**	**25.1**	**20.6**	**33.7**	**52.8**
Group III:								
Thanjavur	3.0	69.5	185.9	80.0				
South Arcot	3.0	58.1	140.7	37.7				
Tiruchirappalli	2.8	50.9	126.5	33.7				
Average	**3.0**	**58.3**	**151.0**	**50.4**	**21.4**	**9.9**	**29.9**	**62.7**

Source of data: R. Thamarajakshi, 'Growth of Agriculture in Madras State, 1949-50 to 1962-63', *Agricultural Situation in India* (Ministry of Food and Agriculture, Dec. 1967); also her paper on *Agricultural Growth in Madras State, 1949-50 to 1962-63*, occasional paper No. 1 (Agricultural Economics Research Centre, University of Delhi).

a The study covers fifteen crops accounting on average for 90 per cent of the total area under crops in the selected districts.

b The method used for isolating the contribution of increases in crop yield to the growth of production is the same as in the paper by Minhas and Vaidyanathan referred to earlier.

for raw cotton and groundnuts) their share went up to 53.9 per cent by 1964–5, the area under raw cotton and groundnuts alone accounting for over 37 per cent of the total cropped area in the state and for 70 per cent of the area under non-foodgrains. With the introduction of improved varieties, additional inputs of fertiliser, and probably some diversion of better quality land, the productivity per acre also went up during this period by no less than 25 per cent in the case of groundnuts. The high growth rate recorded in Gujarat was therefore essentially due to the special circumstances governing the demand for and the production of raw cotton and groundnuts.

V *Conclusions*

The implications of these empirical findings are important. A feature common to Mexico, Taiwan, the Punjab and Madras, as will have been evident, is that they only had considerable irrigation facilities as a result of past investments, but that there was an extension in the irrigated area during the period in which high rates of growth were recorded. Such extension led to an increase in the gross area under crops during the period and was responsible to a significant degree for the increases in output. When irrigation was extended to areas with good soil but where productivity of land was relatively low earlier, owing to inadequate supplies of water, such extension led not only to an increase in the cropped area but to higher productivity all round.

No doubt new and higher-yielding plant varieties evolved by scientific research made a contribution too—more particularly in Mexico and Taiwan—but many of these new varieties yielded more only with substantial complementary inputs of chemical fertilisers and other plant nutrients, and they in turn required assured supplies of water at specified intervals. Without such supplies there was danger not only of the complementary inputs becoming infructuous but, in some cases, of the yield being lower than by the use of the older varieties without applying these inputs.

The percentage area of the land that can be provided with assured supplies of water therefore imposes a limit to the rates of growth that can be realised by technological change. In a country like India that has had a long tradition of irrigation, and where past investments have already exploited a large part of the more easily available water resources, not only is the scope for further extension more limited than in some other countries but it is likely to be much more costly. There might of course be particular regions in which subsoil water could be tapped at relatively low cost by use of modern technology, but one must be careful not to generalise from the performance of regions in which conditions for such exploitation of water resources are favourable. Moreover, since the areas with such assured supplies usually already have higher productivity than elsewhere, the rates of growth that can be achieved are generally lower than one might be tempted to assume as feasible from the recorded rates of growth in regions in which irrigation has been newly provided.

An important factor in the feasible rate of growth of output by absorption of an altogether new technology based on 'modern' inputs is the degree of risk attached to its adoption. This may in part reflect purely subjective considerations, such as the unwillingness of farmers to experiment with new methods, but not infrequently such conservatism on their part is itself founded on experience. Agriculture is generally exposed to many uncertainties, and the capacity of farmers to bear risks is so limited that one must expect the rate of assimilation of new techniques to be relatively slow unless it is proven beyond doubt that the risks involved are negligible or adequately covered by higher returns. A closer examination of the conditions that need to be satisfied for the realization of higher crop yields shows very often that there are many objective and clearly identifiable considerations responsible for the absorption of the new technologies in agriculture (particularly those involving chemical fertilisers) being slower than one might expect from the high rates of return they seem to offer from tests made in experimental stations (and even in the field under favourable conditions).

Consider also the steps that have to be taken in most regions of India (including those in which some kind of irrigation is available) for the adoption of new plant varieties. They include not only provision of adequate supplies of seed and fertiliser, but a number of other related measures with a significantly different orientation from steps taken earlier:

> The dreadful famines of the late nineteenth century, and the brush with famine conditions at several intervals of the twentieth century, led to a dominant concern with a need to produce crop varieties that were disease, insect and drought resistant.... Research was not the only aspect of twentieth-century agricul-

> tural development dominated by the need for stability. Irrigation projects were designed and built to distribute water over as many acres as possible to assure a harvest in years of drought. State plant protection services were established to act when the threat of insect attacks reached a level that presaged severe crop loss....
> ...The difference between the present varietal work and that of the past is more than just the pursuit of higher yields. The new varieties that are beginning to emerge are a significant break with traditional agriculture for they are being selected for response to inputs that are not part of conventional Indian farming. Most notable among these, of course, is fertiliser....In addition to fertiliser, these varieties will require pampering with a range of other non-traditional inputs. Plant protection measures must be stepped up. As plant stands thicken with high fertility conditions, insect population and the opportunity for the spread of disease will increase. To capture the high yield potential bred into the plant by the geneticists will require constant control of pests, plant parasites, and noxious weeds....
> The interaction between irrigation water and the uptake of fertiliser is a favourite example of the package concept of agricultural growth where the total benefits from the application of both are greater than the sum of the benefits of each taken singly. Higher yielding varieties able to make use of high dosages of fertilisers will demand levels of water application that go far beyond those available from irrigation systems designed for drought protection....The social and political problems of re-designing existing irrigation systems for intensive production will be very large....[37]

The re-designing of irrigation systems to suit the requirements of the new varieties has indeed very far-reaching implications. Thus it has been indicated that the full requirements of the new varieties of wheat would need a twenty-four-hour delivery of a cusec of water to be spread over no more than 60 acres, compared to the present practice in North Indian canal and tube-well systems of spreading it over 200 and 400 acres.[38] If adequate supplies of water are available for meeting the higher requirements of both the new varieties and of the areas previously supplied, only the cost of securing additional supplies (such as of further investment in tube-wells) need be taken into account. But adequate supplies of water cannot be taken for granted and, if more intensive irrigation is possible only at the cost of lower area coverage, many other

37 W. David Hopper, 'The Mainsprings of Agricultural Growth', Rajendra Prasad Memorial Lecture delivered at the 18th Annual Conference of the Indian Society of Agricultural Statistics, Jan 1965.

38 Ibid.

considerations become relevant. It certainly cannot be assumed that high rates of growth promoted by intensive irrigation are necessarily to be preferred even if the result is to have, along with high growth rates, fluctuations in output of vastly greater magnitude.[39]

There are also specific problems relating to each crop which often come in the way of quick absorption of a new technology. For instance, the new varieties of rice—essentially hybrids based on the Indian and Japanese types—require the fulfilment of certain important conditions. There are significant differences in the factors governing the supply of water in India and Japan, the seasonal variations in rainfall in rice-growing areas being generally much less sharp in Japan (and even in Taiwan) than in most parts of India. Since the yield of plants is affected not only by drought but by excessive supplies of water at the germination, seedling and later stages of growth, the need for drainage and other techniques of controlling water supply is vastly greater in India. The varieties hitherto grown in India were 'tough, vigorous plants, chosen to withstand and produce under all but the worst the monsoon could do'; the introduction of the new varieties poses a wholly new kind of problem which might require both considerable investment and time to resolve (except perhaps in certain regions). There are also other problems involved in introducing the Japanese type in the

39 Note in this connection the following findings and observations based on a study of the fluctuations in foodgrain output in India from 1901 to 1966:

> '... there is a marked difference in the situation obtaining in 1951-52 to 1965-66 and that obtaining in the two earlier periods. The growth between 1900-01 to 1923-1924 was very slow and it occurred mainly due to extension of area. Droughts were quite frequent and severe and had relatively greater impact on marginal land. Between 1924-25 and 1950-51, there was a general stagnancy in production, droughts were relatively less frequent and less severe and the extension of irrigation in certain areas of the country was also having a somewhat stabilizing effect. There was hardly any increase in the use of inputs like fertilisers and the risk from this factor was absent. In the period 1951-52 to 1965-66, there was not only an unprecedented increase in the rate of the growth but there was also a sharp increase in both acreage and use of inputs like fertilisers. There was, no doubt, an appreciable increase in irrigation also, but it was neither sufficient in volume nor utilised with sufficient care and economy so as to compensate for the destabilising effect of the first two factors. So, when a widespread and severe drought struck the country in 1965, there was a sharp decline of as much as 17 million tons in foodgrain production, an order of decline which the country had not seen for over 40 years.

S. R. Sen, 'Growth and Instability in Indian Agriculture', Address to the 20th Annual Conference of the Indian Society of Agricultural Statistics, Jan. 1967.

tropics, due both to its greater vulnerability to disease[40] and to consumer preferences in India.[41]

Apart from the technical problems associated with the adoption of new technology, there are usually institutional impediments resulting from the pattern of ownership of land and the factors governing transfers of land and capital (including finance) for production purposes. In the absence of economies of scale, the optimum size of the farming units may be small (particularly in countries with relatively abundant supply of labour), but the risks associated with leasing out land tend to restrict the scale of such transfer from those with large holdings to those with little or no land, and consequently the size distribution of 'operational holdings' is often not markedly different from that of 'ownership holdings'.[42] Moreover, the ability to borrow tends to be very closely linked with holdings of land and other assets, with the result that those who have small holdings are unable to secure credit for applying inputs (other than labour) on the necessary scale. Thus, given the additional risks associated with the new technology, it is sometimes only the larger holdings that are in a position to adopt them, and this too only to the extent that the returns at the margin appear to them adequate to cover the risks of hiring more labour and the other costs that have to be incurred. The smaller holders usually have an advantage in so far as the new technology requires intensive application of labour (as in the case of rice); but inadequate credit, as also the risks attached to the new technology, set limits to the application of other inputs. The tendency of the bigger holders of land is generally neither to lease out land to small-holders nor to hire labour on a large scale, but to adopt labour-saving techniques

40 'Japanese rice has a resistant quality against rice stem-borers. Both the number of egg-mass and larvae that actually bore into the plant is small and the damage is little. However, with the other [Japanese] type in foreign countries, the number that actually bore into the plant is larger and increases with the more abundant use of nitrogenous fertiliser.' Cf. Takekazu Ogura (ed.), *Agricutural Development in Modern Japan* (1963) Appendix to Part III, pp. 611-12.

41 The quality of the rice produced by the new varieties is different, and in some cases thought to be inferior by consumers to the quality produced by existing varieties in India. This would naturally affect the price expectations of producers-particularly when large increases in yield are expected to be realised from the new varieties and discourage their adoption beyond a point. This tendency is already evident in certain regions in India, more so because of the zonal system which restricts the free movement of foodgrains between different states.

42 An analysis of these and related phenomena is attempted in my forthcoming book on *Capital Accumulation and Growth in Agrarian Economies*.

as far as possible and utilise available land and other inputs only to the extent consistent with these techniques. The result is that, even when there are no economies of scale, the availability of modern technology very often leads only to dualism in the agricultural sector (as in Mexico) rather than to the transformation of traditional agriculture.

Given all these constraints, the rate of growth of agricultural output would also tend to be much lower than one might expect on the basis of norms established from experiments conducted under favourable conditions. Strategies of development based on the expectation that phenomenally high rates of growth can be realised in agriculture might therefore prove to be a serious mistake in many countries, even if there are examples of such a strategy having succeeded in some. Certainly the high rates of growth recorded in regions like northern Mexico, Taiwan, Madras and the Punjab are unlikely to be realised in large areas of the underdeveloped world in which the natural conditions for transforming the technology of agriculture are much less favourable.

There is as much danger in overestimating the potentialities of growth in agriculture and basing other policies on the assumptions of phenomenally high rates of growth in this sector as in not recognising the importance of agriculture to economic growth. From one extreme the pendulum has recently swung to the other, and some correction of perspectives is perhaps now called for. Unfortunately, the policies and diplomacy of foreign aid encourage both donors and recipients of such aid to play up particular achievements without an objective assessment of all the relevant factors.

Clearly, if the areas in which the technology can be rapidly transformed are limited by inadequate supplies of water, the case for making the most efficient use of resources in the regions in which such transformation is possible (as well as elsewhere) becomes even stronger than otherwise. This is where the need to make institutional changes in agriculture comes in. It is generally the case that the regions which are most fertile have a relatively higher percentage of land under tenancy; but the terms on which tenants operate often discourage the kind of investment and intensive input of labour that agriculture in these regions calls for. Further, as indicated, in many of the developing countries today transfers of land through leasing do not alter significantly the size distribution of land holdings to the extent required to promote the full utilisation of the available labour in these economies. If the rates of growth are still higher than elsewhere, it only shows the dominant influence of the favourable technical conditions in these regions, not that the most efficient use is being made of the available resources. This aspect of the problem has been getting increasingly neglected in recent years in the belief that technological changes in agriculture can by themselves yield high rates of growth and that, since institutional reforms call for strong political action that might meet with resistance, it is wiser to concentrate on the former. Most developing countries do not in fact have such a choice, and have to advance on both fronts to realise the rates of growth in agriculture they require for rapid economic development.

11

ECONOMIC THEORY AND AGRARIAN REFORM[1]

V. M. Dandekar

COUNTRIES with retarded economic growth are in general characterized by a large proportion of their population depending for its subsistence on agriculture. Therefore among the actions intended to release the forces which may initiate or accelerate the process of economic growth, agrarian reform usually receives a high priority. In most non-communist countries, where an agrarian reform has been initiated, it has usually taken the form of a movement aimed at creating individual peasant holdings. This has happened in countries with such widely different historical and cultural backgrounds as Japan, India, Iraq, Egypt, Cuba, and Bolivia. Everywhere, without question, the principle seems to have been accepted that in conditions of agricultural overpopulation, individual peasant holdings is the best economic policy. However, the economic rationale of this policy is generally understood only inadequately and in fact there often exist lurking doubts whether it is all economic policy. Recently, Georgescu-Roegen[2] has provided such a rationale. In fact, he comes to the conclusion that, 'the proposition that capitalism and controlled socialism provide the best systems for developing an underdeveloped economy is patently false, at least for an overpopulated economy' and further that 'the intuition that led the Agrarians to their double negation—not Capitalism, not Socialism—proves to have been surprisingly correct'. The purpose of this paper is to examine this conclusion in the light of the theoretical schemata put forward by Georgescu-Roegen and by taking his argument a step beyond where, it seems, he has left it somewhat incomplete.

1 The paper was originally submitted to the International Seminar on Paths to Economic Growth held in Jan. 1961 under the auspices of the Congress for Cultural Freedom and the Gokhale Institute of Politics and Economics, at Poona, India.

2 N. Georgescu-Roegen, 'Economic Theory and Agrarian Economics', *Oxford Economic Papers*, xii (1960), pp. 1-40.

The analysis is confined to the situation of overpopulation which is recognized as a certain critical relation between the total population or total labour force and the total of available land-capital resources. It is this relation which ultimately governs the marginal productivity of labour under conditions of full employment. Georgescu-Roegen defines overpopulation to be the situation in which, under conditions of full employment, the marginal productivity of labour falls short of the minimum subsistence of the worker. In the more extreme situation, the marginal productivity of labour may even reach zero before the conditions of full employment are realized. Georgescu-Roegen distinguishes this by calling it a condition of 'strictly' overpopulation. Most underdeveloped countries do show such signs of overpopulation in a more or less extreme form. The process of economic growth consists in accumulating more and more land-capital resources so that the marginal productivity may progressively rise—first above the zero and then above the minimum subsistence. It is then that the condition of overpopulation ceases to exist.

From the standpoint of agrarian reform, it should be recognized further that, in the countries concerned, the agricultural sector is usually much more acutely over-populated than is the economy as a whole. This is because the non-agricultural sector in these economies is usually organized on the capitalist principles and hence does not permit workers in unless they can contribute to the production more than the wages they receive in return. Consequently, the entire residual population is thrown on the agriculture which by its nature and tradition employs or accommodates whatever population is thrown on it without reference to the marginal productivity of labour. Conceived as a part of the problem of economic growth, the agrarian problem consists in holding on to this population until an increasing part of it is withdrawn to the non-agricultural sector and in the meanwhile in employing it usefully so as to maximize the total output of the agricultural sector.

That capitalism cannot offer a solution to this problem is easily demonstrated. Because capitalism, understood as an economic system regulated by profit maximization, cannot offer employment to labour beyond the point where its marginal productivity equals the wages paid to it. Under conditions of over-population, this means that the capitalist system cannot employ labour beyond the point where its productivity equals its minimum subsistence. A part of the labour force thereforce remains unemployed. Apart from its social consequences, this is obviously not even an economic solution for, though it maximizes the profit-rent of the capitalist-entrepreneur, it fails to maximize the total output of the agricultural sector. Maximization of the total output requires that the entire labour force or at least the same up to the point of zero marginal productivity is employed. Capitalism does not provide an institutional structure to make this possible.

In this context, we should refer to the theoretical construction put forward by Leibenstein[3] with the purport of explaining how, even under the incentives of profit maximization, landlords may employ labour beyond the point where its marginal productivity equals the wages paid to it. In his theoretical construction, Leibenstein postulates that the productivity of labour depends not only on the kind of technology used and the amount of land-capital resources available per employed worker but also on the level of wages paid because it affects the amount of work effort a worker might put forth. Therefore, on this construction, there is not one curve of average or marginal productivity but several such curves appropriate to the different wage levels. Given a wage level and the corresponding marginal productivity curve, there is an optimum number of workers whom the landlords as a group would hire if they were to maximize their group income and this optimum is determined, as usual, at the point where the wage is equal to the marginal productivity of the employed workers. But the wage level is not given and the landlords as a group have the choice of so fixing it as to maximize their group income. As for the supply of labour, under conditions of over-population, the whole of it is supposed to be available at the minimum subsistence level. Under the usual construction where the labour productivity is not supposed to depend upon the level of wages paid, there is no incentive for the landlords to raise the wages above the minimum subsistence level. But now under the Leibenstein construction, the landlords might want to offer wages above the minimum because that might raise the labour productivity and more than compensate the landlords so that their total income might in fact rise. In general, under this construction, the group income of the landlords is maximized at a wage level somewhere above the acceptable minimum. The

3 Harvey Leibenstein, *Economic Backwardness and Economic Growth*, John Wiley & Sons, pp. 58-76.

landlords will therefore choose to offer this wage. They will of course employ only the optimum amount of labour appropriate to that wage level and the marginal productivity of the employed workers will equal the proposed wage. Nothing unorthodox has so far happened except that the proposed wage level is above the acceptable minimum and simultaneously a number of workers remain unemployed.

But now it seems that in the face of a large number of unemployed workers, the landlords find it difficult to maintain the proposed wage level even though it is in their interest to do so. The competition among the unemployed and the employed workers depresses the wages. To counter this, the landlords must offer to employ the entire labour force. This they cannot do at the proposed wage level. It seems that finally they reach a compromise solution and offer a wage somewhere below the proposed one but nevertheless somewhere above the acceptable minimum and what is more important, at this compromise wage, they offer to employ the entire labour force and not only the optimum appropriate to that wage level. In other words, they employ labour beyond the point where the marginal productivity equals the wage. Thus two things happen: In the first instance, the landlords offer a wage higher than the acceptable minimum; this they do because it raises the labour productivity and on the whole they make larger income than they would do if they employed the labour at the minimum subsistence. Secondly, at the proposed wage level, they offer to employ the entire labour; on this they lose because the marginal productivity of the employed labour falls below the wage level but, nevertheless, they do it because it enables them to maintain the wages at the proposed level and on balance they still make more income than they would otherwise do.

The crucial part of the solution is that the landlords find it profitable to pay a wage higher than the minimum subsistence and in addition to employ the entire labour force at this wage. Of course, this is not inevitable; it might happen that the landlords do not find it profitable to do so and therefore they may allow the wages to be depressed to the minimum subsistence level. If and when this happens, this is important; the landlords have no interest in employing the entire labour force or in fact any labour beyond the point where the marginal productivity equals the minimum subsistence. Leibenstein does not specify the conditions under which the landlords may find it profitable to maintain the wage rate above the minimum subsistence and in particular it is not clear whether this would be true under conditions of over-population as defined by Georgescu-Roegen wherein the marginal productivity of labour falls below its minimum subsistence or even to zero. In the Leibenstein construction, this would mean that there is no wage level equal to or above the minimum subsistence, where under full employment, the marginal productivity of labour would not be less than its minimum subsistence. Leibenstein is aware of this possibility but does not examine its consequences. But it appears that under these conditions Leibenstein's special solution would not hold good and that the landlords would offer no more than the minimum acceptable wage and employ labour only to the extent where its marginal productivity equals the wage. The rest of the labour would then remain unemployed.

It is, of course, possible to presume that under conditions of over-population, the landlords are not quite unfettered in their pursuit to maximize their incomes and that they work under some kind of institutional obligations to employ the entire labour force somehow. But then these are not quite the capitalistic institutions. We may, therefore, say that in general the capitalist system does not provide a solution to the basic agrarian problem. We should, therefore, look for some other institutional structure and it seems that it will have to be basically non-capitalistic.

In point of fact the traditional agriculture in over-populated countries has developed its own characteristic institutions which among other things, achieve precisely the same purpose, namely, to maximize the total output by maximizing the employment beyond the point where its marginal productivity falls below the minimum subsistence, or even to zero. For instance, as Georgescu-Roegen points out, feudalism provided such an institution. For here, the entrepreneur-landlord was compensated not by profit-rent, but by means of a tithe or a share of the total produce. Therefore, for a given ratio of the share, in order to maximize the tithe, the total produce had also to be maximized. Feudalism thus did provide the needed structure. But feudalism is no longer serviceable, if for no other reason, for the reason that having come in close contact with capitalistic institutions, it ceases to be sufficiently feudal. The capitalist economy in the non-agricultural sector offers new opportunities to the landlords and they are anxious to free themselves from the obligations of a traditional society. This leads to absentee landlordism, rack-renting, and all those evils which ruin agriculture. Therefore, feudalism has to be replaced.

And replaced it is, almost with a vengeance. Its place is taken by the new agrarian doctrine of individual peasant holdings and the new doctrine seems to work, at any rate up to a point. In explanation, Georgescu-Roegen points out that the principle of individual peasant holdings meets the requirements of the situation because it is essentially the old feudal formula under a new and a better form. From the standpoint of economic theory it is still feudal because the employment of the family labour is not governed by considerations of marginal productivity but by considerations of maximizing the total output. The family labour presumably works to the full limit of zero marginal productivity and it works because it is rewarded by the entire product of its labour, no share going to the erstwhile landlord—an echo of Leibenstein's postulate that productivity is influenced by the reward.

But, as we shall see, the principle works only up to a point and in particular does not create certain important conditions for rapid economic growth. In the first instance, the principle does not remain confined to the creation of individual peasant holdings. It soon takes the form of a wider doctrine of self-employment, namely, that under conditions of over-population, self-employment provides the most favourable conditions for maximizing the total output under conditions of over-population, self-employment provides the most favourable conditions for maximizing the total output. [The principle is easily extended to industry, and small-scale and cottage industry is recommended on grounds that it promotes self-employment.] Labour-intensive techniques are thus often equated to self-employment techniques. This leads to serious consequences in agriculture. An immediate consequence is the elimination of the large peasant holdings because such holdings, even though effectively peasant proprietorship do involve a considerable amount of wage employment. Proposals for ceiling on family holdings are not always put forward explicitly on these grounds; more often they are based on general egalitarianism and more particularly on the need to satisfy the land hunger of the landless families. Also, the ceiling limits are not always placed sufficiently low to eliminate or at any rate minimize wage employment. Nevertheless, it is obvious that it would be more rational to base such proposal on the principle of maximization of self-employment. Such a principle may also provide a more rational and meaningful basis for a fixing of the ceiling.

What concerns us here is that whatever may be the basis of the principle of ceiling on peasant holdings, it can have very serious consequences on the agricultural sector. For, whatever its justification, a ceiling on land holding is a ceiling on how far a peasant may go as long as he remains a peasant. As a result, it is feared that the ability and enterprise which cannot be contained within the ceiling limits, would sooner or later leave the agricultural sector. Thus the agricultural sector would become progressively depressed and politically weak. These fears are all genuine. Nevertheless, it should be understood that they are the consequences of the initial proposition that in an over-populated economy, the agricultural sector must be organized on some principle other than the capitalist enterprise. We should remind ourselves of the initial fact: Because, the non-agricultural sector is usually organized on the capitalist principle, the residual burden of the population is thrown on agriculture. Therefore, if a capitalist sub-sector were permitted within the agricultural sector, its immediate consequence would be to accentuate the conditions of over-population in the remaining part of the agricultural sector. Therefore these fears regarding ceiling on holdings will have to be countered by means other than permitting or promoting capitalist enterprise within the agricultural sector.

If the advocacy of a ceiling on holdings were based primarily on maximizing self-employment, the reform would still remain within some limits. However, as more often is the case, when the advocacy of the ceiling has a pronounced egalitarian base, the process does not stop at elimination of large holdings. The reform is then aimed at not only the creation of family holdings which can be cultivated by the family labour, but of equal family holdings or more strictly of equal holdings after making due allowance for the size of the family. The streak of egalitarianism is usually strong among the agrarian reformers and it would have in fact gone longer than it has, were it not for some serious physical problems of equalization of agricultural holdings. These are not always realized and equalization of holdings or reducing of existing inequalities in them is sometimes attempted within the existing physical layout. For instance, the Cuban agrarian reform provides for bringing the small land holdings up to a certain minimum by appropriately redistributing the land expropriated above the ceiling. The small holdings are of course too numerous and the expropriated land, even if adequate to meet the requirement, is seldom located conveniently for adding to the small holdings. Therefore the objective of bringing up the small holdings up to a certain minimum would require not only the expropriation of the land above the ceiling, but also of the land in the small holdings and its completely new allocation—in other words a complete redrawing of the physical layout of the individual holdings. Egalitarianism has therefore to push forward more slowly than it would otherwise. When the physical layout of the holdings has to be redrawn anyhow because of considerations of agricultural technology, as in Iraq, the reform does provide for the creation of more or less equal family holdings.

It is, of course, true that even complete equalization of the family holdings can be justified on economic principles by following to its logical extreme the previous argument for maximizing the total product. However, this is not always done and equal holdings are advocated, somewhat apologetically, on egalitarian grounds because some other considerations equally relevant to the problem of maximizing the total output appear running contrary to the objective of equal family holdings.

One such consideration is the size of the production unit. For various technological considerations, it seems that even in agriculture, in order to realize maximum output from given amounts of resources, the production unit has to be of an optimum size. Under conditions of over-population, the principle of a holding for every peasant family and for that matter an equal holding obviously does not lead to an optimum size of the production unit. In fact, it might be argued that it puts the entire agriculture in production units below the optimum. Georgescu-Roegen recognizes this defect of the principle of a holding for every peasant family and remarks that 'it led to a sub-optimum size of the production unit' and further that 'this prevented the crystallization of the existing capital in the most efficient form compatible with the prevailing factor ratio and the available techniques'. But he does not consider how the defect may be remedied. Instead he leaves this important point with the remark: 'The facts just mentioned do not justify the prejudice of Stalinist governments in favour of large and highly mechanized farms of the North American type.

This prejudice errs in the opposite direction: it leads to a size far greater than the optimum compatible with over-population, and hence it uses labour inefficiently.' This may be so. But the fact remains that something has to be done to the individual peasant holdings in order to secure an optimum production unit and the result may not be individual peasant holdings at all.

This question of the size of the production unit is often raised in the literature on the subject, but is not always understood in the same sense as it is being raised here. It will be useful, therefore, to make the distinction clear. In the context of the principle of individual peasant holdings, the question of the size of the optimum unit is usually discussed from the standpoint of the peasant proprietor and the optimum holding is supposed to give him minimum or a desired or an optimum family income. To the extent that it is also considered as an efficient production unit, its efficiency is judged as that of a capitalist enterprise—the peasant proprietor is supposed to behave like a capitalist-entrepreneur and offer employment on the principle of marginal productivity. For instance, it is on some such understanding of the problem of the size of production unit that the ceiling on holding is sometimes disputed. It is obvious however that if the optimum size of the production unit is to be determined on such principles, it will not satisfy the initial requirement, namely, that in order to maximize output, the maximum amount of labour resources must be utilized. Therefore, the only result of such determination of the optimum holdings is to show that under conditions of over-population, not all the peasant families can have optimum holdings and that their creation would only lead to the creation of a large agricultural proletariat. The point is therefore given up as a hopeless idea for it appears to run against the egalitarian principle. The peasant proprietorship and equal family holdings therefore continue to be advocated with greater egalitarian zeal and with a lurking fear that the reform in these directions might affect the total output adversely.

Therefore it should be understood that the question of the optimum size of the holding is not being raised here from the standpoint of an individual peasant proprietor. The elementary principle that in order to maximize the total output, all the available resources must be utilized and in the particular context of the over-populated countries, that all their labour resources or at least a maximum amount of them, must be utilized has to be firmly held on to.

Therefore, given the quantity of land in agriculture and the number of people it must absorb and support, the size of the individual holding is automatically determined and one can hardly improve upon the principle of equal family holdings. Therefore, if the question of the optimum unit of production is to be raised, it must be clearly understood that the optimum must be determined under conditions that the optimum unit, whatever its size, must carry its proportionate burden of the population. In other words, while discussing the question of the optimum size of the production unit, one should not be discussing whether an individual should have a smaller or a bigger holding, for there is no choice in that respect; rather, one should be discussing whether the equal peasant holdings should be operated, as production units, individually or whether there is an advantage in operating them jointly and, if so, how large such joint units should be.

To be sure, the question is sometimes understood in this light. For instance, this was how the Mexican agrarian reform approached the problem in its initial stages. Also, more recently, both the Iraqi and the Cuban agrarian reforms provide for the creation of the more or less equal individual holdings and their almost immediate merger into some form of co-operative production units. However, more often, co-operation like egalitarianism is regarded as valuable *per se* and is advocated without a full realization of its economic basis and implications. When these become fully apparent, the advocates of co-operation often fight shy of their initial advocacy.

The reasons for not realizing fully the implications of co-operativizing the individual holdings is that the economic basis for the advocacy of individual peasant holdings is not firmly understood so that one does not realize fully what is lost in the process of co-operativization. As Georgescu-Roegen points out, the main advantage of the individual peasant holdings, in conditions of over-population, is that they afford conditions under which labour may be employed without reference to its marginal productivity. Once the individual holdings are put in the form of a co-operative production unit, this advantage is lost because usually the conditions of employment in a co-operative farm are governed by considerations of marginal productivity. As a result, even the family workers of the members of a co-operative cannot be employed beyond the point where the marginal productivity equals the minimum subsistence wage. In terms of the usual formulation the co-operative organization brings to surface the unemployment which otherwise appears in the disguised form of self-employment. This formulation is correct as far as it goes but it misses the important point that, in addition, the co-operative organization also in fact reduces the employment if its decisions in this matter are allowed to be governed by the considerations of marginal productivity. This is in fact what usually happens because the manager of a co-operative farm, by training and background is more often a capitalist-entrepreneur than a feudal-landlord. Also he is called upon to function in an economy where the growing non-agricultural sector is worked on capitalist principles and consequently his own management is judged by the same criteria of efficiency. It is for this reason, mainly, that the co-operative organization of the individual holdings, in the sense it is usually understood and advocated, defeats its own purpose. There is, of course, no other method of achieving the optimum size of the production unit, except by pooling the individual holdings in some form of co-operative joint production units. But for them to fulfil the original purpose, namely to achieve maximum output through a maximum utilization of labour, the co-operative farm has to be basically feudal and not capitalist.

In its feudal form, the co-operative organization should resemble a household rather than a business enterprise. The members of a co-operative organization are, in fact, often exhorted to act and behave like the members of a family. But usually, such exhortation is more romantic than realistic. Because, logically, the primary responsibility of the manager or the managing committee of a co-operative organization conceived as a household, would be to feed its members and to occupy them usefully, and it is rarely that individual households are willing to yield themselves to a common discipline which may be necessary for the purpose. In any case, it takes more than an occasional exhortation for them to agree to such a submission.

Of all the responsibilities which may be put on the manager or the managing committee of a co-operative production unit, the most serious is that of usefully employing all its labour resources. Overpopulation, strictly speaking, means that under conditions of full employment, the marginal productivity of labour is zero. This means that labour cannot be employed beyond the point of zero productivity without being detrimental to the total output. Obviously therefore all the labour cannot be utilized in current production. Therefore, a part of it must be utilized on capital works, that is on works which directly lead to capital creation. It is this possibility which enables the joint production units to create additional employment and to utilize the unemployed labour resources disguised as self-employed in family farms. The superiority of the joint production units lies in this that they alone, as distinct from individual family holdings, can undertake certain categories of capital works. The optimum size of the production unit must therefore be decided, not by the exclusive considerations and techniques of current production, but also, and perhaps mainly, by the requirements of discovering, planning, and executing capital works. Thus conceived, it will be noted that few individual holdings, including even those above any proposed ceiling, can be regarded to be of the optimum size. In fact, thus considered, the optimum production units will be sizeable agricultural regions. This is not what is usually conceived by way of co-operative organization of individual holdings.

With the accumulation of capital in the agricultural sector and with the withdrawal of a part of the agricultural population into the growing non-agricultural sector, the ratio of land-capital to labour in the agricultural sector improves and causes an upward shift in the marginal productivity curve. A stage is then reached when even under conditions of full employment, the marginal productivity of labour in the agricultural sector is no longer zero—it is positive but still less than the subsistence wage. In terms of the definitions given by Georgescu-Roegen, the condition of overpopulation still persists but not quite strictly. Under this condition, the management has a difficult choice to make between capital works and current production. However, what is more important in the present context is that under these conditions, in order to maximize the total output, the labour must be used to its fullest capacity. As Georgescu-Roegen points out, at this stage of development, the working class can have no leisure at all. The co-operative organization of the individual holdings, as it is usually understood, does not create conditions compelling everyone to work to his full capacity. For that purpose, something more than the co-operative spirit is required.

It seems, therefore, that the individual peasant holdings or even these same organized in what are loosely called co-operatives do not provide a solution to the agrarian problem under conditions of overpopulation. The solution has to be found in an organization of the agrarian sector in large units of land and population, feudal in theory, modern in technology and oriented to a socialistic purpose. Because the basic production units would be large, it is inevitable that the relation between man and land in them should be much looser than the one implied in individual peasant holdings. There is another reason why this relationship should be rather loose and certainly short of proprietary rights in land. The starting-point of this discussion, it will be remembered, was the problem of how to seek an institutional structure which would hold and employ the residual population until an increasingly larger portion of it was withdrawn into the non-agricultural sector. Therefore the holding operation must be such as would facilitate the timely release of a part of the labour force when needed. In particular, while settling the whole population in agriculture, care must be taken to see that the settlement is not done in a manner which may obstruct this eventual withdrawal of a large part of the population or which may cause dislocation in agriculture when such withdrawal takes place. Individual proprietary interests in land in general create such difficulties. Therefore it will be advisable to avoid creating such rights in land. In many countries such rights in land already exist, and possibly they have to be taken cognizance of. Nevertheless, two broad principles may be enunciated: Firstly, no individual rights should be created in lands where they do not already exist or where they have been destroyed for one reason or another, such as by expropriation or by the application of a ceiling. Secondly, granting of individual rights in land to persons who do not already have any should be avoided; in other words, permanent or long-term settlement of landless persons in agriculture should be avoided. On the other hand, those who are not yet settled on land, should receive the highest priority and preparation for being withdrawn from the agricultural sector into the non-agricultural sector.

These are some of the considerations of internal organization of the agricultural sector which indicate that individual peasant holdings do not provide the requisite structure. There are also other compelling reasons which point in the same direction. One such consideration concerns the relation between the agricultural and the non-agricultural sectors. In the process of economic growth, when the non-agricultural sector continually grows, one of the crucial functions of the agricultural sector is to produce enough food and to release it for the use of the non-agricultural sector at reasonable price. There is no need to spell this problem more fully. The conflict is well known and is known to become spiny under conditions of overpopulation and peasant proprietorship. When food is in short supply, its equitable distribution becomes crucial. In other words, if the process of growth is not to be hindered on this account, the non-agricultural sector must be able to secure its due share of the food production. Whatever the form of the institutional structure we may desire to have for the agricultural sector, it must provide for a feudal overlord who will collect the tithe and hand it over to the non-agricultural sector.

To repeat, all these considerations lead to the same conclusion, that the individual peasant holdings, though feudal in form and therefore answering the purpose up to a point and found culturally satisfying, do not meet several other requirements of economic growth. Further, this principle when it is associated with romantic egalitarianism with its doctrine of self-employment, puts a ceiling on individual achievement and enterprise, depresses the agricultural sector and makes it politically weak. The argument leads inevitably to a structure composed of large production units managed not on capitalist principles, but for collective good. It will be seen that such a structure also offers a large network of institutions, where the enterprise and ability of individuals may find the fullest scope and where it may be amply rewarded, though rather differently. In the light of this it is difficult to accept Georgescu-Roegen's recommendation of the agrarian doctrine of individual peasant holdings and cottage industry involving the double negation—not Capitalism, not Socialism.

12

MONETARISTS, STRUCTURALISTS, AND IMPORT-SUBSTITUTING INDUSTRIALIZATION: A CRITICAL APPRAISAL

David Felix

THE MONETARIST-STRUCTURALIST debate is more than the Latin American version of the international dispute concerning the efficacy of monetary controls in stabilizing the price level. It also involves a deep disagreement over the ability of the price mechanism to bring about a socially acceptable rate of growth and distribution of income in the Latin American context. Finally, the temperature of the polemics tends to be heated by mutual accusations of political bias to a higher degree than is characteristic of professional debates elsewhere. The interweaving of these three issues accounts for some of the murkiness of the monetarist-structuralist debate. This paper deals, however, with only the first two issues.

The practical focus of the debate has been whether the package of policies—credit constraints, devaluation, the elimination of exchange and price controls, and related measures—invoked in a number of Latin American countries in recent years to halt inflation would succeed, and, if so, whether success would be at the expense of economic growth. These programs have generally been undertaken under the aegis of the International Monetary Fund. In fact the IMF has insisted, as a condition for granting stand-by credits, on setting exact limits to the rate of credit expansion, unification of the exchange rate, and complementary measures.[1] It is evident that the IMF's ability to impose terms has depended in good part on the willingness of U.S. governmental lending

1 For tactical reasons, the specific terms of the agreements are not publicized, so that it is not possible, except on the basis of 'inside knowledge.' to know the precise range of commitments nor the degree of flexibility permitted in carrying out the commitments. It is clear, however, that as the going got more sticky, the authorities tended to push credit expansion beyond agreed-upon limits and to fudge on other commitments, and that the IMF was often forced to accede, albeit reluctantly.

agencies, with their more ample resources, to make the granting of credits contingent on an IMF agreement being reached. Such collaboration was the rule during the Eisenhower administration, but under Kennedy's Alliance for Progress the two suppliers of credit have tended at times to part company, and as a result the IMF's leverage has been weakened.

It is by now evident that the stabilization programs have been largely unsuccessful, particularly in the larger Latin American countries. In Argentina, after a period of exchange rate stability between May, 1959 and March, 1962 and of near price stability between January, 1960 and March, 1961 (there was an 8 percent rise in the cost of living in this period), the dam broke, and by 1962 accelerating inflation and exchange depreciation were again underway. A similar, if as yet less dramatic, denouement also occurred in 1962 for the Chilean stabilization program.[2] In neither country, moreover, was there a sustained rise in the growth rate during the stabilization period. Uruguay is at this writing still maintaining its exchange rate, but without the price stability and export expansion needed for long-run support. Peru, with moderate inflation and a stable exchange rate anchored in expanding exports, is apparently the one important victory in the array of partial or total defeats.

Events seem, then, to have given the debating cup to the structuralists. But was this because the stabilization programs miscalculated political limits, or because they were economically misconceived? Would the Argentine and Chilean programs have succeeded if the authorities could have held on a bit longer or turned the screws a bit tighter? It is the contention of this paper that the basic fault lay elsewhere, that the programs were simply not reallocating resources in the *directions* needed to create viable growing economies. This seems to have been due to excessive confidence in the efficacy of the price mechanism and to a failure to take account of the adverse effect of the import-substituting pattern of industrialization followed by Argentina and Chile on the structure of consumer demand and on the capacity to import.

2 The Chilean effort has had two phases. The first stabilization plan (the so-called Klein-Saks program, after the Washington consulting firm which drew up the plan and advised the Chilean government) was instituted in late 1955 and was patently running down by 1958. A second effort followed in December, 1958 under a new presidential regime. The Argentine program was begun in January 1959.

The first defect has been a central part of the structuralist critique, but the second has not.[3] This paper is, thus, also a partial critique of standard structuralism. It is, however, structuralist in spirit, and its policy suggestions share the greater catholicity in the choice of policy instruments which is characteristic of this school of thought.

The IMF Stabilization programs and Their Rationale

Two features of the IMF-sponsored stabilization programs should be emphasized at the outset. The first is that credit tightening was only one of a composite set of measures designed to achieve exchange and price stability and to stimulate the rate of growth. The second is that the programs were premised on the explicit awareness that supply rigidities were retarding the growth rate. These rigidities were, however, considered in large part the consequence rather than the cause of inflation. That is, they could in effect be classified into two types: 'distortions,' engendered by price expectations built up during the long inflation, and supply inelasticities which were the result of 'distortions' in the structure of relative prices due to controls.

The first type refers to inflated business inventories, luxury construction, and similar manifestations alleged to be associated with inflationary expectations. In fact, it is not at all easy to sort out behavior due to inflationary expectations from that related to more enduring socioeconomic determinants. Inventorying in poorly integrated economies relying heavily on long distance imports is bound to take a larger share of investment than in advanced economies.[4] Babylonian excesses have been more conspicuous in Caracas, where there was until recently virtually no inflation and easy importation of more mobile forms of conspicuous consumption,

3 *Inflation and Growth*, the valuable five-volume mimeographed study prepared by the Economic Commission for Latin America for the Rio Conference on Inflation and Growth, in particular the sections on the Argentine economy (Vol. IV) and the Chilean economy (Vol. V).

4 A. S. Shaalan finds that in 1953-59 underdeveloped countries put twice as large a percentage of their gross investment in inventories (exclusive of agricultural surpluses) than did advanced countries. In addition, he finds an *inverse* correlation in his sample group of underdeveloped countries between the average rate of inflation and the percentage of inventory accumulation in gross domestic investment. He does, however, find a positive correlation for some Latin American countries, including Chile, between rises in the rate of inflation and increases in the inventory percentage of gross investment. ('The Impact of Inflation on the Composition of Private Domestic Investment,' *International Monetary Fund, Staff Papers*, Vol. IX (July, 1962), pp. 243-63.)

than in the residential and commercial construction in and about Santiago or Buenos Aires, where neither condition has prevailed. It is not clear how much the stabilization programs hoped to alter such behavior, although attacks on luxury housing, of course, made good public relations material for the programs.[5]

The second type of 'distortion' referred primarily to overvalued exchange rates, underpriced public services, and underpriced agricultural prices. That is, an inadequate capacity to import, power and transport bottlenecks, and a poor growth rate of agricultural output were explicitly recognized, just as in structuralist analysis, to be key points of strangulation. The 'over- and under-pricing' viewpoint, however, assumed that there was an attainable set of equilibrium prices which would remove these bottlenecks.

In reality, it was much less a matter of removing price controls, despite some loose usage, than of trying to change the relative position of controlled prices. This was obvious for public utility and transport rates. But the same also was true of the exchange rate. For while the full goal of the programs was the establishment of a single stable rate in place of multiple rates, to be held by orthodox pegging operations, in actuality it was only the form rather than the substance of exchange control which changed. After the initial devaluation and formal unification of the rate there was less stress on quantitative import controls. But the shifting of goods between a permitted and a prohibited list of imports in order to protect industry and to meet foreign exchange pressures was one of the important tools of foreign exchange policy. In place of a formal structure of multiple rates, import deposits and other temporary surcharges and direct controls on invisible transfers were also varied in a discriminatory manner to achieve the same two objectives. In Argentina, in addition, export taxes were selec-

---

The latter relationship for Chile is supported by a recent analysis of the asset structure of a sample of large Chilean firms, which also indicates that inventories rose more when the rate of inflation rose. *See* Instituto de Economia, Universidad de Chile, *Formación de Capital en Las Empresas Industriales* (Santiago, 1961), p. 124, Table III.

5 Construction fell drastically during the Klein-Saks period in Chile, generating high rates of unemployment among construction workers. The drop however, was due in good part to cutbacks in public works and the general slowdown of economic activity. There was a similar decline in construction during the first year of the Argentine stabilization program, which seems also to have been due in large part to similar causes. In the second Chilean effort, construction rose at the outset from the extremely depressed 1958 level as a result, in part, of a more active public works program.

tively reduced on occasion to encourage exporting, although reduction was limited by the importance of these taxes in the federal budget.[6] Only when these methods failed, and exchange reserves plus the availability of new stabilization credits were patently inadequate, was the exchange rate allowed to fall once more. Severe and unexpected declines in international prices for the major exports did complicate the effort of the Klein-Saks program of Chile to attain an 'equilibrium' exchange rate. Copper prices fell from an average of $0.44 per lb. in 1955 to a low of $0.247 in 1958. But no such declines disturbed the other two efforts. During the second Chilean effort, begun at the end of 1958, copper prices rose moderately, the average for the three subsequent years being slightly below $0.30 with little annual variation.[7] Moreover, annual export volume of the foreign-owned mining sector in 1959-61 averaged 10 percent higher than in 1955-58. Similarly, Argentine export prices and terms of trade were moderately higher during 1959-62 than in the previous three years.

Apart from special difficulties in the Klein-Saks effort to stave off falling copper prices, the common problem for these stabilization attempts was to limit the general rise of domestic prices in the private sector while bringing about a relative rise of agricultural prices, as well as of controlled prices, sufficient to remove the critical bottlenecks in supply.[8]

The first part of this problem was met primarily by efforts to restrict the expansion of credit to the private sector and monetary

6 They were the third most important source of tax revenue. Compare Bank of London and South America, *Quarterly Review*, January, 1961, pp. 116-22.

7 London price for electrolytic copper. *See* Banco Central de Chile, *Boletin Mensual*, April, 1962.

8 The stress put by protagonists on the favourable effects which the removal of domestic price controls in the private sector would have on the structure of relative prices is difficult to fathom. In the first place, such controls as were applied were weakly enforced. At most they had a short-run delaying effect, which in shortage economies subject to severe speculative flurries is probably justifiable.

Secondly, they did not alter the direction of movement of relative prices which excess demand conditions suggested would take place. In Chile, for example, agricultural prices rose 1.32 times more than industrial prices during the pre-stabilization period 1940-55. During the subsequent six years of progressive decontrol, it was industrial prices which, interestingly enough, rose the more rapidly. (See ECLA, *op. cit.*, Vol. V, p.57; and for the more recent period the components of the wholesale price index in Banco Central de Chile, *Boletin Mensual*, April, 1962). In Argentina also, except for the short period in the late 1940's when a strong effort was made to hold agricultural prices, they rose in 1949-59 almost 1.5 times more than industrial prices, with the relationship reversing direction in 1960 and 1961. (See ECLA, *op. cit.*, Vol. IV, pp. 44,53.)

wages. In Chile, during the Klein-Saks period the rise in money wages was held down by utilizing the already existing pattern of legislated annual wage adjustments, but restricting the increases to a fraction of the previous year's rise in the cost of living. This policy, however, ran into increasing opposition, so that the fraction was back to unity in 1958. The subsequent Chilean stabilization effort also began with a fractional adjustment in 1959, with the fraction forced upward in subsequent years by labor unrest and political pressures. In Argentina the principal device used seems to have been a tougher policy toward unions on the part of the government. However, this, too, ran into increasingly heavy sledding.[9]

The second part of the problem would, it was hoped, be solved by an elastic response of the private sector to more profitable opportunities to export and to increase agricultural production, to be supplemented by a greater inflow of private foreign investment which more stable prices and exchange rates would hopefully induce. The transportation and energy bottlenecks would, it was recognized, take more time to resolve, since they required heavy investments by the public sector. While these could be met in part by long-term loans from the IBRD and other foreign sources, the noninflationary financing of such investments would also require a substantial current account surplus in the public sector through cutbacks in current expenditures and increases in tax revenues, as well as higher rates for public services.[10] Thus fiscal reform and a cutback of current budgetary expenditures were key elements in the stabilization programs. However, to bridge the interval required to achieve such reforms and to promote the expansion of the private sector,

---

Thirdly, after formal decontrol the governments continued to use informal pressures to restrain price increases. In Chile, for example, the government decreed decontrol but threatened to restore controls unless industrialists held the line on prices. To check retail price increases, consumer committees were organized to publicize establishments guilty of raising prices. Probably these methods were about as effective as the previous price controls in restraining price increases.

9 According to an informed observer, while labor relations in Argentina had shown 'remarkable stability' in the 'face of a substantial reduction in real wages in 1959 and 1960,' there were significant signs by the end of 1960 of 'a more militant attitude of trade unions indicating that the working classes are not prepared to accept any further reductions in their standard of living.' (Bank of London and South America, *Quarterly Review*, January, 1961, p. 113.)

10 A relatively quick response was achieved in Argentina in removing the heavy drain on foreign exchange from petroleum imports. The state petroleum agency was authorized to open up oil reserves to foreign firms, who were guaranteed remunerative prices for all their ouput and liberal profit transfer rights. Domestic oil production rose rapidly as a result, so that Argentina by 1961 was

short-term credits were obtained from the IMF, various U.S. and European governmental agencies, and foreign banks. These were to meet budget deficits in a non-inflationary manner as well as to amplify imports and sustain capital formation during the critical adjustment period.[11]

Tactics differed on how rapidly to attempt the relative price changes and the retrenchment of governmental current expenditure. The Klein-Saks program took the most gradual approach, perhaps as much because of governmental foot-dragging as from the original intent of the program advisors. The second Chilean effort tried to make many of the adjustments more speedily; the exchange rate adjustment in 1959 was particularly abrupt. The Argentine effort was the most abrupt of all, setting off a spiral of prices and wages in 1959 during which wholesale prices rose 145 percent and real wages fell by about 25 percent.[12] The last two efforts, however, were each followed by about three years of exchange rate stability and a shorter period of near price stability, while the Klein-Saks effort, bedeviled by falling copper prices, never achieved even this brief triumph. Nevertheless, since all three efforts ultimately failed, the most evident lesson to be drawn seems to be that differences in timing were probably unimportant in explaining the ultimate failure of the efforts.

Reasons for the Failure of the Stabilization Programs

Why did the programs fail? It is quite arbitrary to single out any one of the propagating factors, to use ECLA's terminology, as responsible. The collapse of exchange rate stability in all three cases did set off a more rapid price rise. But in each program the exchange rate came to be held up by drawing on foreign credits and exchange reserves long after rising prices had already wiped

largely self-sufficient in crude petroleum. However, the longer-run gain in foreign exchange savings from the reduced outlay on the import of petroleum products is being partly offset by the substantial profit transfers which the foreign contracts entail. In point of fact, many of the contracts were made in 1958 before the formal initiation of the stabilization effort, but they were clearly consistent with the economic philosophy motivating the stabilization program.

11 They are the main reasons why the Chilean balance of payments deficit on current accounts, which was negligible during the early 1950's rose to 72 percent of gross capital formation during the Klein-Saks period (1956-58) and to 22 percent in 1959-60. *See* UN, *Yearbook of National Accounts Statistics*, 1961, section on Chilean accounts.

12 ECLA, *op. cit.*, Vol. IV, p. 41; Vol. III, p. 126.

out the initial cost-price gap created by devaluation.[13] The rise in domestic prices, in turn, can be attributed alternatively to wage pressures or to budget deficits which forced an expansion of the money supply and thus permitted the upward adjustment of wages and prices. But, since wages had substantially lagged behind prices during the earlier phase of the stabilization efforts, it seems uncharitable to blame the workers for resisting further cuts in real wages. Similarly, rising prices and the disappointingly low rate of growth of output and employment undoubtedly made it more difficult to cut back public employment or to resist raising badly lagging public salaries. Hence one of the key elements in the failure to create a current account surplus was the inability to slow markedly the increase of current expenditure. In particular, initial gains in public transport and utilities tended to be lost through rising operating costs.

The failure significantly to increase tax revenues can be less easily dismissed in this manner. A large tax bite would not have generated widespread destitution among the Argentine or Chilean higher income classes, particularly during a period when their relative and absolute position had significantly if temporarily, improved. However, given the slow longer-run growth of income in the private sector, resistance to increased taxation was understandably sharpened. Moreover, the substantial increase in taxes needed for stabilization would probably have led initially to a further curtailing

13 The exchange picture is currently most critical for Argentina. Despite a number of earlier debt renegotiation agreements, the short-term external debt obligations (five years or less maturity) of the central bank and government were reported in Fall, 1962 as follows.

1962	$ 277,200,000
1963	$ 384,500,000
1964	$ 459,700,000
1965	$ 318,500,000
1966	$ 246,500,000
Total	$ 1,686,400,000 (U.S. dollars)

In addition the external debt of the private sector, chiefly short-term, was reported as £283,700,000, while the long-term external debt (maturity of over five years) was reported as £751,600,000. (Bank of London and South America, *Quarterly Review*, October, 1962, p. 216.) This is even more serious in the light of the fall of central bank gold and foreign exchange reserves from a high of £705 million in the first quarter of 1961 to £215 million in the third quarter of 1962, and average annual exports in recent years of $1,000,000,000. Moreover, profit transfers from the foreign petroleum contracts and the increased inflow of private direct investment in 1958-61 are now generating an additional service demand for foreign exchange.

of private construction, reduced employment in some of the more sumptuary domestic industries, and an increase in the relative importance of the public sector which would run counter to the economic philosophy of the managers of the stabilization program.[14] Hence, despite the commitment of the programs to budget balancing (apart from foreign loans for capital expenditures), there was a general dragging of feet on tax questions.

How does one break through this circle? Leaving the tax question to one side for the moment, the most promising entry is via the slow growth achieved during the stabilization efforts. Actually, growth declined markedly from the pre-stabilization rates only during the Klein-Saks period, and even in this case the decline had already set in during the preceding quinquennium. In the second Chilean effort, the growth rate in 1959-61 was about equal to that of the Klein-Saks period, while in Argentina output and employment fell absolutely in 1959, recovered in 1960-61, with the average over the three years only slightly below the sluggish rates prevailing in the preceding decade. What this meant, however, was that in none of these cases did the economy respond to the apparent opportunities opened up by the wage lag, devaluation, and foreign credits, either with increased exports or with a sustained rise in domestic output.[15]

The General Structuralist Explanation

The failure of the programs to overcome the sluggishness of the postwar Argentine and Chilean economies strengthens the view that the major rigidities are deeper-rooted than had been assumed by the monetarists, and were causes rather than results of inflation. Of these, two are singled out by the structuralists as, in effect,

14 This was particularly the case in Argentina, where *smithianismus* had gotten a new lease on life as a reaction to the Perón era. In Chile, however, there has been a marked shift in emphasis to public investment since 1960. This seems to have been due partly to the disappointingly slow growth of the private sector, but it was also impelled by reconstruction needs resulting from the earthquake of May, 1960. The change of heart, however, has not yet affected tax policy.

15 The moderate increase in exports in the foreign-owned mining sector in Chile during the second stabilization effort had relatively little to do with the stabilization programs. The firms of this sector are not required to return their foreign exchange receipts to the central bank or government except as needed for local outlays on labor and materials or to pay taxes. Local nontax outlays have averaged less than 30 percent of sales in the postwar period, so that devaluation can only have a modest effect on production costs of these firms. Moreover, as taxes, which since 1955 have been levied on profits, take up a large percentage of sales receipts, the modest gains from lowered production costs as a result of devaluation are partly offset by increased tax payments.

primordial: the slow growth of agricultural output and the limping capacity to import. The first is attributed primarily to institutional defects in agriculture, the second to unfavorable trends in world primary products markets.[16] The consequences of these two rigidities on output and inflation can be rather summarily treated, since their analysis is by now a familiar feature of economic development literature in Latin America and elsewhere.[17]

Briefly, in a closed economy, with money wages and industrial prices rigid downward, prices will rise if the growth of per capita income times the income elasticity of demand for food exceeds the rate of growth of food production per capita. Since the income elasticity of demand for food in poor countries is likely to be quite high—on the order of 0.5-0.6—a slow rate of growth of food production per capita (in Chile the rate has been negative over the past 25 years) limits the noninflationary increase in aggregate output per capita to perhaps twice the rate of growth of food output per capita. There is, moreover, a redistributive effect if the noninflationary limit set by the food supply is exceeded, since food outlays take up a larger share of working-class than of upper-class budgets. Thus money wages are likely to react to rising food prices, generating a wage-price spiral. In other words, excess demand inflation in the agricultural sector becomes cost inflation for the rest of the economy.

Opening the model to bring in the capacity to import makes it more realistic, since underdeveloped economies depend on imports for some of their consumer goods including food, much of their industrial materials and fuels, and most of their capital goods. With the income elasticity of demand for imports greater than unity, cost pressures are felt via import shortages and rising import prices when the capacity to import grows less rapidly than domestic output. These shortages and rising prices, however, also provide opportunities for import-substituting industries to develop, although this development will be associated with a rising price level.

The model now becomes more complex and can take off in

16 However, in the case of Argentina, whose exports are predominantly agricultural, the inadequate capacity to import in the 1950's has been related to agricultural supply rigidities as well as to the unfavourable trend in world agricultural prices. See ECLA, *op. cit.*, Vol. IV, pp. 10-21.

17 The food-price relationship is explored in considerable detail in Geoffrey Maynard, *Economic Development and the Price Level* (London; Macmillan & Co., 1962). See in particular Chapter III. The other is part of the well-known Prebisch thesis. Both are elaborated upon in ECLA, *Inflation and Growth*.

various directions, depending on the relative growth of food output and the capacity to import, the nature of the labor market and wage pressures, the rate of growth of productivity in industry, etc. For example, if we separate the industrial enterprise sector from the household sector, it will be noted that the redistribution effect of substituting domestic production for consumer imports works against the higher income households in whose budgets such consumables take up a larger share than in working-class budgets. The extent to which this is compensated for by profits received as owners of industrial enterprise depends on wage and productivity trends in the industrial sector and on the dividend policy of corporate enterprises. For example, in Argentina and Chile real wages in corporate industry prior to the stabilization efforts seem to have risen at least as fast as man-hour productivity,[18] although workers in smaller enterprises and in services fared much worse. Profits of the Chilean corporate sector tended downward in the 1950's, and firms resorted to progressively higher profit retention to finance inventory and fixed capital formation.[19] The fact that household savings turned negative in Chile during the 1940-55 inflation may, therefore, be due at least in part to the redistribution effect of import-substituting industrialization, rather than to the supposed depressing effect of inflation as such on the propensity of households to save.

Thus, whereas in the closed model there is a strong presumption that the share of wages will fall and the aggregate savings rate will rise as a result of inflation, in the open model there is no firm basis for such a presumption. In point of fact, the wage share was quite stable in Chile during the 1940-55 inflation, tending downward only during the subsequent stabilization period.[20] In Argentina there was a remarkably large rise in the wage share during the late 1940's, the share subsequently sagging somewhat and then falling rapidly in 1959 to the early postwar level. In both countries the savings rate declined in the 1950's.

Industrial growth, however, may still proceed fairly rapidly despite unaccommodating wage movements, as long as there is a large

18 For Argentina, see ECLA, *op.cit.*, Vol. III, p. 130, graph 2. The short period fluctuations in the relationship have been quite substantial, so that it is possible to claim an up or down trend, depending on the choice of dates for measuring the trend.

19 Instituto de Economia, *op. cit.*, *pp.* 110-11, 166-69.

20 The reference is to the Klein-Saks period. I have not seen any income shares data for the more recent period.

margin of consumer imports to be compressed and foreign exchange to be diverted to import-substituting industries at subsidized rates. Thus inflation and exchange discrimination in favor of industry may for a time raise the growth rate of the economy beyond what would occur from a policy of monetary constraints designed to keep the rate of growth from upsetting price and exchange rate stability. But as consumer imports contract toward an incompressible minimum, the ability to divert foreign exchange to the industrial sector falls correspondingly, although such diversions to new industries may still occur at the expense of the older ones. And since inflation is unable progressively to depress the wage share, industrial capital formation and economic growth decline. This is the stage which Argentina and Chile had reached by the 1950's, according to structuralist analysis, and since the two primordial rigidities have continued to prevail during the stabilization periods, the rate of growth has remained low.

The structuralist model is, in fact, more richly embellished with sociopolitical propositions than the above skeletal statement. Other constraints are also recognized as coming into play during the inflationary spiral; for example chronic infrastructure bottlenecks due to lagging transport and energy prices and cuts in public investment in order to restrain mounting budget deficits. Such constraints are judged, however, to be largely derivatives of the two basic rigidities. That is, the apparently greater confusion and contretemps in Argentine and Chilean policy than in the policies of some other Latin American countries is related to two essentially sociological observations. One is the plausible proposition that growth with a lagging capacity to import puts more severe pressure for rapid adjustment not only on the economic structure but also in the administrative and policy-making machinery. The second, rather paradoxical, proposition is that the more industrialized and technologically advanced Latin American economies with their correspondingly greater urbanization adjust less easily to economic shocks than do the less developed countries. Thus the greater success of the recent stabilization effort in Peru is attributed in large part to a comparatively favorable capacity to import, which in turn put less pressure on the economy to industrialize.[21]

21 ECLA, *op. cit.*, Vol. III, pp. xiv-xv. The assumption that Peru's favorable capacity to import in recent years has been due more to exogenous factors than to astute monetary and exchange rate policies is by no means implausible. In the foreign-owned mineral industries—most notably in copper—and the partially

Import-Substituting Industrialization and Structural Rigidities

Has the sluggishness of agricultural supply and of the capacity to import been, in fact, grounded in institutional or exogenous forces? In the case of Chilean agriculture, the evidence that this is so appears convincing enough. That is, neither the trend in relative prices, nor agricultural taxation, nor the evidence on agricultural profits suggest a situation which should have depressed a reasonably responsive, technologically alert agricultural sector.[22] Argentine evidence is not as clear cut. Government price fixing, which depressed relative agricultural prices by 25 percent in 1946-49, undoubtedly damaged agricultural output. However, the sluggish supply response to the rise of about 50 percent in relative prices during the subsequent 13 years plausibly suggest institutional deficiencies.[23]

The capacity to import presents, however, a more complex picture. Granted that world excess capacity in minerals, coupled with import restrictions by a number of leading industrial powers, have held down earnings from Chile's mineral exports. Granted that a somewhat similar situation has prevailed for Argentina's agricultural exports.[24] Granted also that in the circumstances a lavish resort to devaluation or to greater concessions to foreign mineral investors might be only a beg from my neighbor policy which would evoke mutually damaging responses from other depressed primary exporters. What remains to be explained is why Argentina and Chile, with their sizeable industrial sectors, have been unable to become significant industrial exporters both prior to and during stabilization efforts. This calls for closer analysis of the import-substituting industrialization pattern. But since what follows is not based on re-

foreign-owned fishing industry, investments to expand capacity were under way some years before the stabilization effort in 1959. They came to completion fortuitously when the stabilization effort was under way.

22 Supplementing the data referred to in the ECLA *Inflation and Growth* study is a recent calculation of Chilean agricultural production over the longer run which indicates that the average annual increase in 1921-40 was 1.9 percent or only slightly in excess of the rate of population growth. In the period of 1941-57, the annual increase fell to 1.7 percent, while the population growth rate rose to over 2 percent per annum. See Tom E. Davis, 'The Growth of Output Employment, Capital Stock and Real Wages in Basic Sectors of the Chilean Economy', in *Hearings before the Sub-Committee on Inter-American Relationships, Joint Economic Committee*, 87th Cong., 2nd sess. (Washington D.C.: Government Printing Office, 1962), p. 104, Table 1.

23 Compare ECLA, *op. cit.*, Vol. IV, pp. 11, 17-22.

24 In actuality, the slow growth of agricultural output and relatively favorable home prices have also depressed the volume of Argentine exports in the postwar period.

search in depth, careful economic analyses of Latin American industries being still rather sparse, the discussion will perforce be in rather general terms. To the extent that it is valid, however, the analysis may fit other industrializing economies of Latin America—Brazil, for example—as well as Argentina and Chile.

In form the import-substituting pattern recapitulates the conventional pattern of capitalist industrialization. That is, the initial industries are generally consumer goods or building materials producers with a relatively simple technology and a low capital requirement per worker and per unit of output. They are then followed by consumer goods industries requiring a more sophisticated technology and larger capital outlay, shading subsequently into industries producing relatively complex consumer durables, steel, engineering, and chemical products.

The patterns diverge, however, in two important respects. The first is that, in contrast to European, North American, or even Japanese industrialization, Latin American countries have lacked an extensive structure of handicraft industries from which to draw skilled labor and entrepreneurial talent. The development of such a structure was inhibited by the highly stratified two-class society which characterized most Latin American countries prior to World War I, in particular by the absence of a middle class of farmers and merchants to provide an extensive market for such industries. Argentina, it should be noted parenthetically, is a partial exception, since much of its population was of recent European, albeit of largely poor peasant origin. The industrialization efforts, therefore, have been forced to draw on a particularly inexperienced stock of human inputs. To a varying degree, deficiencies in entrepreneurship and capital accumulation have been compensated for by foreign firms which have established branches and subsidiaries, in good part to avoid a threatened loss of the local market due to import restrictions, and by government-financed industries when capital outlays have been too large to interest private investors. But at the same time the highly protected monopolistic market environment which has been created to induce private investment lessens pressure on industrial firms to increase productive efficiency. To this must be added the notorious lag of Latin American education in developing trade and technical schools to augment the supply of industrial and scientific skills. The consequence has been that even with modern plants and low wages, domestic industries tend to have considerably higher unit costs than foreign equivalents.[25]

The second major difference is that widening of the industrial spectrum has taken place more rapidly than had been characteristic of the conventional pattern of capitalist industrialization. The pace has been more rapid the more sluggish the capacity to import, for then the saving of foreign exchange by encouraging import-replacing industries became high policy. This has also tended to give the industrialization pattern a bias toward producing middle class products, such as consumer durables, since it is the less essential imports which have been restricted most severely. But even when efforts are made to check this bias, policy still tends to favor the allocation of foreign exchange and tax concessions to establish new industries which would save foreign exchange, as against the modernization and expansion of existing industries.

Two significant consequences have followed from this precocious widening of the industrial spectrum. Firstly, it has meant a rapid movement toward the production of technologically sophisticated products in which complex economy of scale factors are especially critical determinants of production costs, even though the domestic market has often been inadequate to exploit such economies. These scale economies relate not merely to the size of individual plants, but also to the size of the intricate complex of feeder firms. Thus, whereas in advanced economies with larger domestic markets supplemented by exports, the market size and level of organizational competence permit complex flow production within and between plants, the smaller markets and lower organizational competence in Latin America has meant batch production, lags in supply, larger inventories, and other cost elevating deficiencies. Secondly, output curves have tended to be kinked, rising rapidly when exports are being replaced, but flattening out when further growth of demand has been grounded in the growth of domestic income. Profits have also followed this kinked pattern. Thus industries have moved rapidly from high profit and growth to precocious 'maturity,' at which point they fall back to monopolistic quiescence with lower profit rates, a reduced level of investment, and aging plant and equipment.

25 For a detailed appraisal of the factors involved in one important industry, see ECLA, *Labor Productivity of the Cotton Textile Industry in Five Latin American Countries* (New York, 1951).

The inability of even the more industrialized Latin American countries to develop export markets follows from the general pattern described. The initial cost disadvantage stemming from the lack of skills and deficient organization could, taken by itself, be overcome in time, particularly in industries of lesser technological sophistication with relatively low capital-output ratios. Precisely because the initial skill differential vis-à-vis older foreign competitors is great, the learning curve in Latin American countries is likely to slope more steeply, despite the absence of internal competitive pressures. This, plus a slower growth of real wages relative to foreign competitors, plus devaluation, might bring down costs in such industries to a profitable exporting level. Of course, even this possibility could well be thwarted by the effect on wages of relatively rising food prices. For the relevant wage relationship is real wages in terms of industrial product, and the latter would rise more rapidly than real wages as such when the industrial terms of trade are worsening.

But even if these terms of trade do not completely thwart the narrowing of the cost gap, the added effect of the relative aging of the capital stock in industries with export potential may well do so. For one of the convincing generalizations emerging from contemporary analysis of productivity is that its growth is positively correlated with the growth of capacity because this results in a stock of plant and equipment which is more *au courant* with the latest technological developments in the industry. This is due not merely to a more rapid addition of capacity, but also to a more rapid rate of replacement. The combined effect of an inadequate growth of food production and of the import-substitution pattern followed in Latin America may, therefore, create a continual state of dynamic cost disadvantage.

The argument can be developed more formally. Whether or not an import-substituting industry reaches exporting efficiency depends on the interplay of at least four sets of forces: (1) the effect on the industry's productivity of the growth of other industries; (2) the effect on its productivity of its own growth in output; (3) the growth in productivity of competitors abroad, (4) wage and exchange rates trends.

The first set of forces, the external economy-diseconomy problem, may for our purposes be disposed of quickly. If the establishment of new industries always lowers unit costs in existing industries, then the rapid widening of the industrial spectrum would be broadly justifiable, and the case against continuing import-substituting industrialization much the weaker. But, clearly, industries also compete for scarce resources. Indeed, deepening shortages of foreign exchange (imports) and public services have, as already indicated, been a major cause of the slackening of industrial growth in recent years in Argentina and Chile. Between specific subclusters of industries, complementary relations in production may perhaps outweigh the competitive ones,[26] but this would still mean that the choice of industries to encourage can critically affect a country's ability to become an industrial exporter.

The other sets of forces are combined in Diagram 1 which, after a necessary if tedious explication of its components, will be used to illustrate how the interplay of these sets of forces can render import-substituting industries incapable of exporting.[27]

The T (textiles?), A (automotive?) and E (electronic?) industries are selected to represent industries in different portions of the industrial gamut created by import-substitution. They broadly represent an ordering in terms of increasing technical sophistication and probably, also, in terms of recency of establishment, although the last is incidental to the argument. The ordering is assumed capable of being extended to other industries, so that we may imagine an array of curves filling the space around those actually depicted. The *Pf*-line represents the annual rates of increase in labor productivity in the equivalent exporting foreign industries. For our purposes this is simply exogenous information. The line slants to the right because the evidence suggests that in recent years the productivity increases have been higher the more technically sophisticated the industry.[28]

The *Px*-line is the export-efficiency line. Starting from current levels of output, let us provisionally take both the exchange rate and the differences between domestic and foreign wages and between

26 The *pôles de croissance* theory of François Perroux is built on this notion of complementary clusters. 'Note sur la notion de pôle de croissance,' *Economie Appliquée*, January-June, 1955, pp. 309-20.

On the other hand, the view attributed to Nurkse (perhaps wrongly) that complementarity in demand insures that the external effects between industries are positive, is analytically incorrect. See Marcus Fleming, 'External Economies and the Doctrine of Balanced Growth,' *Economic Journal*, June, 1955, pp. 241-56.

27 This is a revised version of a diagram in the original draft of this paper presented at the Rio conference. I am grateful to the Quantitative Seminar of the London School of Economics for useful criticisms which caused me to reconstruct the diagram. Far from the revised version being the responsibility of the seminar, however, its members would probably resent such an implication.

28 For a bit of evidence on this, *see* UN, *World Economic Survey*, 1961, Tables 2-13.

other factor prices also as given. Let us fix the time interval at the end of which the industrial sector is to become capable of exporting. There will then be a point on each industry curve representing the rate of increase in its output and productivity necessary to allow it to export. The *Px*-line connects such points. As drawn, no industry is initially capable of exporting—approximately the current situation in Latin America.

The curves are derived by combining four functional relations between industry output and productivity. A fifth is incorporated in the *Px*-line.

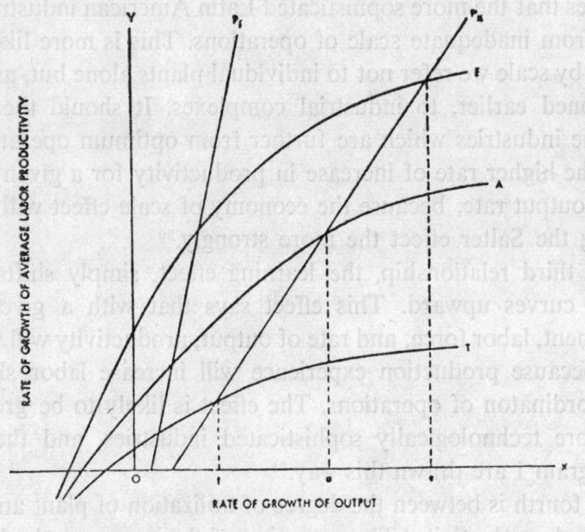

Diagram 1

The first relation we call the Salter effect.[29] New technology is incorporated in any industry mainly through gross investment in currently most advanced equipment. Since plant and equipment is durable, each industry, soon after its founding, comes to consist of layers of plant and equipment of different vintages, the older the vintage the less efficient the equipment. Consequently, the faster the growth of output, the younger will be the age structure of the industry's plant and equipment and the larger the growth of average

29 After W. E. G. Salter, who first made important use of a major fact about capital structures which had been ignored by capital theory. *See* his *Productivity and Technical Change* (Cambridge: Cambridge University Press, 1960).

productivity of its capital and labor. Higher rates of growth of output will hasten both the expansion of capacity and the obsolescence rate for old equipment. The relationship between growth of output and productivity is curvilinear, approximately as in Diagram 1, rather than linear, for reasons which should be apparent to the reader.

The curves array themselves approximately as indicated in the diagram because of a second relationship, the economy of scale effect. It is generally accepted that Latin American industries suffer in varying degrees from inadequate scale of output. The productivity effect of this is depicted in rather oversimplified form by Diagram 2, where current rates of output are taken as given. The diagram assumes that the more sophisticated Latin American industries suffer most from inadequate scale of operations. This is more likely to be true if by scale we refer not to individual plants alone but, as already mentioned earlier, to industrial complexes. It should then follow that the industries which are further from optimum operations will have the higher rate of increase in productivity for a given increase in the output rate, because the economy of scale effect will be reinforcing the Salter effect the more strongly.[30]

The third relationship, the learning effect, simply shifts the industry curves upward. This effect says that with a given plant, equipment, labor force, and rate of output, productivity will rise over time because production experience will increase labor skills and the coordinaton of operations. The effect is likely to be greater for the more technologically sophisticated industries, and the curves in Diagram 1 are drawn this way.[31]

The fourth is between the degree of utilization of plant and equipment and productivity. The extension of the curves to the left-hand quadrant of Diagram 1 indicates that productivity increases as output falls below the full capacity level.

30 For a perfect ordering, it is necessary for the downward sloping section of all long-run industry cost curves to have approximately the same slope. This is unlikely to be the case, although how far off the mark such an assumption is cannot be assessed directly, since we have limited information on the shape of such curves. It can, however, be assessed indirectly by testing our model's prediction that, for example, the industries in Argentina or Chile with the highest increases in productivity per given increase in output also have the greatest shortfall in productivity levels relative to foreign competitors. This prediction depends on the legitimacy of arraying the industry curves as in Diagram 1 and the array is derived from the economy-of-scale ordering in Diagram 2.

31 This is also an oversimplification. The learning-by-repetition influence on the efficiency of a given plant, equipment, and labor force should peter out in time. Correcting for this should, however, strengthen rather than weaken the main conclusions derived from Diagram 1.

Finally, industrial efficiency may be enhanced for technological borrowers, such as Latin American countries, if they can lower unit costs by adapting imported technology to their lower wages and higher capital costs. The consequence of effectively substituting labor for capital is to increase total productivity, but to lower labor productivity. Such substitution would therefore lessen the increase in output per head and the corresponding rate of increase in output required to attain export efficiency. The *Px*-line and the industry curves may thus be expressed in terms of labor productivity, as in Diagram 1.[32] The more sophisticated, however, the

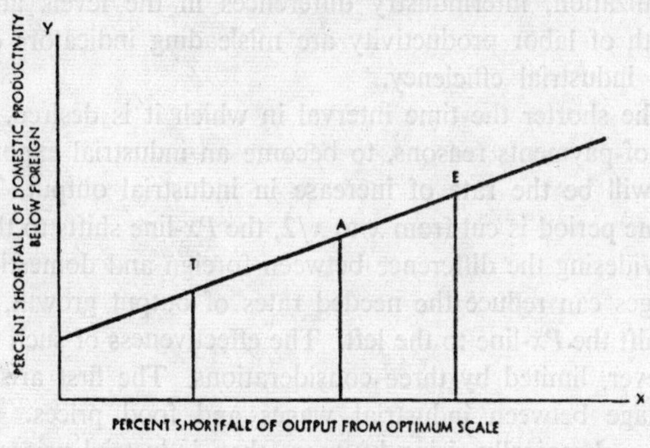

Diagram 2

imported technology, the less the ability of Latin American countries, with their limited engineering and managerial cadres, effectively to make such adaptations. Empirically, this should show up for each country in smaller differences between the capital-labor ratios at home and abroad per given plant, the more sophisticated the industry. That is, the capital-labor ratio for T-type industries should be lower than in foreign equivalents by a greater percentage than for A- and E-type industries, a hypothesis which I believe is broadly valid, and should at any rate be testable.[33] The *Px*-line, therefore, slants further to the right than the *Pf*-line, because it is

32 The Salter, economy of scale, and learning effects presumably influence total productivity, that is, both capital and labor efficiency, proportionately. Hence, the resulting curves should be the same whether expressed in labor or total productivity.

33 Alternatively, a possible definition of that sexy but imprecise concept, technological sophistication, could be concocted in terms of ratios between capital-labor ratios at home and abroad. This, however, might be giving too many hostages to stochasticism.

given an added tilt by the declining ability to substitute labor for capital as we move from the less to the more sophisticated sections of the industrial spectrum.

We may now, at long last, manipulate Diagram 1 to indicate a number of conclusions concerning import-substituting industrialization.

1. Despite higher rates of increase in output per head, the more sophisticated industries will require greater sustained rates of increase in output to reach export efficiency than the T-type industries; $O_e > O_a > O_t$. Under the import-substituting pattern of industrialization, interindustry differences in the levels and rates of growth of labor productivity are misleading indicators of comparative industrial efficiency.

2. The shorter the time interval in which it is desired, say for balance-of-payments reasons, to become an industrial exporter, the greater will be the rate of increase in industrial output. That is, if the time period is cut from x to $x/2$, the *Px*-line shifts to the right.

3. Widesing the difference between foreign and domestic industrial wages can reduce the needed rates of output growth, that is, it can shift the *Px*-line to the left. The effectiveness of such a policy is, however, limited by three considerations. The first arises from the linkage between industrial wages and food prices. If food prices are chronically rising by more than industrial prices, as has been the case in Argentina and Chile, the fall in wage costs per unit of industrial product may be much smaller than the widening of differences between domestic and foreign real wages. The second is that if industrial wage costs are reduced by a sufficient cut in wages, consumer demand would shift from T-type consumables to sophisticated A- and E-type consumer goods. The implication of this for the failure of the Argentine and Chilean stabilization programs is discussed in the following section. The third is that if it is necessary to depress industrial output and employment in order to force down real wages, productivity falls. That is, we move into the left-hand quadrant of Diagram 1. Although the *Px*-line may have been moved to the left by the fall in wages, the output and productivity gap which has to be bridged in order to reach export efficiency can remain as wide as ever.

4. Devaluation as a means of promoting industrial exporting is also subject to at least two constraints germane to the model. The first is that if the redistributive effect of devaluation is toward greater

income inequality, the shift in consumer demand will be toward A- and E-type goods. This point is elaborated below. Secondly, the ability of devaluation to shift the *Px*-line leftward is limited by the degree to which higher price of imports feeds back on industrial costs. The degree appears to be substantial, because the import-substituting pattern relies heavily on Professor Hirschman's strategy of establishing industries and letting the backward linkages come along later. Hence, the industrial sector develops with a heavy dependence on imported materials, fuels, and parts.[34]

5. The extension of import-substituting to capital goods establishes new industries which are likely to be in the A- and E-range of the industrial spectrum. Whether the *Px*-line shifts to the right or left depends on whether the higher price of such goods to industrial users is offset by more ready availability and, hence, lower inventory costs. There is no *a priori* reason for assuming that the extension will improve the prospects for industrial exporting. It depends on which industries are established and what their economy of scale shortfall might be.

6. Economy of scale deficiencies are obviously less of a problem the larger the domestic market. Hence the industry curve array should be narrower for Argentina than for Chile, and somewhat narrower for Brazil than for Argentina.

The general presumption is that economies which have pushed import-substituting industrialization in the context of stagnating agriculture to the extent to which Argentina and Chile have, tend to box themselves in. As industrial growth slows down when imports become less compressible, the industrial sector, for reasons suggested by the above analysis, is unable to revive its momentum by exporting. Clearly the analysis needs to be tested more carefully against the facts than I have been able to do. The model, however, provides us not only with a plausible set of reasons for the incontrovertible fact that neither Argentina nor Chile (nor Brazil) has been able to become an industrial exporter, but also, I believe, with a useful agenda for empirical research on this problem.

34 This has been brought out in a number of recent ECLA studies of the growing 'rigidity' of imports in the more industrialized Latin American countries.

Due to the monopolistic character of Latin American industry increases in costs are also passed along rapidly, and even anticipated. Wage demands may then set off a wage-price spiral which can wipe out in short order the gain from devaluation. This is clearly a serious problem for economic policy. The points made under 4, however, concern not the speed of adjustment of money incomes but whether devaluation can shift resources so as to facilitate industrial exporting.

Import-Substituting Industrialization and the Failure of the Stabilization Programs

The analysis also helps explain why, despite the fall in real wages, devaluation, and foreign credits, the IMF stabilization programs failed to promote a breakthrough to industrial exporting. Basically it was because the programs worked against the reallocation of resources needed for such a breakthrough. There appear to be three major reasons for this.

The first is that the reduction of real wages and the wage share tended to divert investment in the industrial sector excessively and indiscriminately to consumer and capital goods industries in the A- and E-portions of the industrial gamut. This resulted partly from the fact that the less-sophisticated consumer goods industries at the T-end of the gamut are generally industries whose demand depends more heavily on wage income.[35] The resulting stagnation of T-industry demand was further accentuated by sharp changes in relative prices for manufactures consumed by the nonwage households whose real income position had improved. Recall that import-substituting industrialization and the restrictions of sumptuary imports when the capacity to import is tight tend to raise drastically the prices of goods which are more important in the budgets of nonwage than wage households. The most glaring examples in Argentina and Chile in the 1950's were, of course, automobiles, which because of import restrictions sold for five to six times their price in the United States or Europe. But price disparities of a significant, if less spectacular, degree existed for most consumer durables, even when domestic production or assembly was the main source of supply. Some of the greater supply of foreign exchange made possible by stabilization credits was used to increase imports of consumer durables and luxury goods. A much larger share was used to import equipment and supplies for new durable consumer goods industries and to enlarge the output of existing ones. The particularly high income elasticity of demand for such goods among nonwage households combined with the fall in their relative prices to divert a major share of the increased nonwage income to industries produc-

35 However, since they are also industries with lower capital-labor ratios, they should reap the greater cost benefits from lower wages. Offsetting this is the fact that they tend to be less dependent on imported inputs and thus benefit less from a greater availability of foreign exchange. The argument in the text is, therfore, essentially an empirical judgement that the cost advantages which might have accrued to the T-industries from the stabilization programs were not enough to offset the disadvantages stemming from the shifts in consumer demand.

ing these products. In turn, this stimulated the demand of domestic suppliers to these industries and encouraged their expansion. Parenthetically, the falling wage share may also help to explain why, contrary to the expectations of the program, the removal of price controls was followed by a fall in relative agricultural prices.[36]

Secondly, most of the augmented inflow of foreign manufacturing investment during the stabilization periods[37] also went into A- and E-type industries. This was due not only to the increased demand for such products from the income distribution changes described above; it was also related to the special characteristics of such investment in Latin America. This investment tends to be limited-risk investment designed to obtain or keep a foothold in the local market when direct exporting is blocked by import restrictions, hence is made despite the fact that local costs of production are often substantially higher.[38] It is limited-risk investment because, to the maximum degree commensurate with local regulations, foreign manufacturing firms seek to rely on imported parts and other imports, and to finance operations from local borrowing and retained profits. The gains to the parent firms tend to come from the sale of goods and services to their Latin American subsidiaries as much as from the profits of these subsidiaries. Thus, despite the fact that profit rates of U.S. branches and subsidiaries in Latin America declined progressively in the 1950's[39] and from 1951 on have averaged much less than the profit rate after taxes earned in U.S. manufacturing, the annual inflow of such investment rose until 1958. The flow of such investment tends, therefore, to be heavily influenced by the prospective availability of foreign exchange for importing and, to a lesser extent, for the transfer of profits. But it reacts only slowly to changes in the rate of profit earned by branches and subsidiaries.[40] The greater availability of foreign exchange during the earlier phases of the stabilization effort attracted, there-

36 See footnote 9. The greater impact of devaluation on industrial costs was probably the other main factor.

37 The inflow, however, was negligible in Chile during the Klein-Saks period.

38 For a more detailed discussion of this characteristic, see *United States. Business and Labour in Latin America*, prepared at the request of the Subcommittee on American Republic Affairs, Committee on Foreign Relations, U.S. Senate, 86th Cong. (Washington, D.C.: Government Printing Office, 1960), Chapters I-III.

39 *Ibid.*, p. 12, Table 9.

40 In contrast to investment in extractive industries for export. *Ibid.*, pp. 13-15, Charts 1-3.

fore, an increased volume of manufacturing investment which went into the partial domestic production of sophisticated products. The most notorious example was, of course, the Argentine automotive industry. Between December, 1958 and November, 1961, Argentine authorities approved automotive investment plans submitted by foreign firms to the amount of $97 million (U.S.). This resulted, by 1961, in the establishment of 22 automotive firms, wholly or partly foreign-owned, in a country with an estimated market potential for motor vehicles in the half-decade ahead of at the most 150 to 200 thousand units per annum. In 1961 alone, the industry imported $153 million in parts, supplies, and equipment, or about 16 percent of that year's imports, in order to produce 136,000 units.[41] An additional volume of imports, impossible to qualify without an input-output table, was consumed by the steel industry and domestic-parts manufacturers in order to fill orders for the automotive industry. While there were no such spectacular examples in Chile, an accumulation of small-scale partial production of sophisticated consumer goods, including automotive assembly, took place, to which foreign investors contributed.[42]

The third reason is that the policy of tighter credit diverted private finance to A- and E-type firms. When credit is tight, the activities of firms with higher rates of profits are usually less affected, since they are better able to finance internally through retained earnings and also have superior credit ratings. This seems to have been true in both Argentina and Chile.[43] Moreover, since credit was tightened primarily by imposing global limits on bank lending to the private sector, a nonbank lending market emerged in each country with extremely high interest rates, in which the more profitable operations could obtain marginal funds but which was

41 Bank of London and South America, *Quarterly Review*, July, 1962, pp., 124-30.

42 There was a particulary heavy concentration of such new industries in the northernmost province of Tarpacá. In order to offset the decline of the nitrate industry, ports in this province were given free importing privileges. It became highly profitable, therefore, to locate industrial activity in these ports, even though the market (the central provinces) was located 1300 miles to the south.

43 For Argentina, see Bank of London and South America, *Quarterly Report*, July, 1962, p. 148. For Chile, some rather indirect evidence is indicated in Instituto de Economía, *Formación de Capital.* The latter shows that while domestic loans financed a decreasing percentage of gross capital formation for the sample of corporations studied, the firms with the most rapid growth of real assets had both the highest rate of retained profits and received a higher rate of loans as a percentage of profits. In addition, see some general remarks in ECLA, *op. cit.*, Vol. III, pp. 86-103.

too costly for less profitable firms.[44] It is difficult to assess the quantitative importance of these diversions although their direction seems clear enough. During the earlier phases of the stabilization programs, when budget deficits were largely met by foreign credits, the squeeze on the private sector as a whole does not seem to have been very severe. But, as the net inflow of foreign credits fell off, a larger portion of government budgets had to be financed by central bank borrowing. To keep within the credit limits agreed upon with the IMF, loans to the private sector were restricted more severely, chiefly by raising marginal reserve ratios of the commercial banks. The effect was felt most acutely, evidently, by less profitable firms. In Argentina, in particular, this led to a serious credit crisis in June, 1962, during which the central bank had to undertake the emergency rediscounting of industrial paper to enable firms to meet wages and other current commitments.[45]

In sum, the effect of the IMF stabilization policies on the industrial sector was mainly to shift an excessive proportion of resources to A- and E-type industries. The cul-de-sac into which the industrial sector had worked itself prior to the stabilization efforts was made a bit roomier, but no breakthrough to exporting occurred because the stabilization policies, rather than directing resources to industries with export potential, continued the pattern of precocious widening of the industrial spectrum. Even the apparent gain in labor and productivity for the industrial sector as a whole was partly illusion (see Table I). For, while tighter credit probably did force an increase in efficiency, part of the apparent gain in productivity seems to have been merely due to a shift in output toward industries with higher capital/labor ratios made possible by greater capital imports.[46]

44 Interest rates in the nonbank credit markets in Chile during the Klein-Saks period and in Argentina during the recent stabilization period ranged to well over 40 percent per annum. For Argentina, see Bank of London and South America, *Quarterly Review*, January, 1962, pp. 25-26. The most important single use of the high interest credit in Argentina was to finance motor car sales.

45 Earlier in the same year, the Minister of Economy had appealed to the automotive industry to obtain foreign funds for retail financing in order to relieve pressure on the local credit market. (Bank of London and South America, *Fortnightly Review*, March 24, 1962, p. 233.)

46 Two-digit industry classes are too gross to be very illuminating about output and productivity trends. Moreover, it is not clear how well the data gatherers make allowance for new products in these classes. (The small rise in output of the Argentine vehicle and nonelectric machinery class does not seem to conform with the information on automotive expansion.) For what they are worth, the sectoral data in Table 2 are offered.

TABLE I

	Argentina 1952=100		Chile 1953=100	
	Manufacturing Production	Manufacturing Employment	Manufacturing Production	Manufacturing Employment
1957.. ..	..	..	103.7	95.7
1958.. ..	123.7	95.7	106.9	91.8
1959.. ..	107.4	91.6	122.1	93.4
1960.. ..	109.5	84.2	119.3	96.9
1961.. ..	120.1	81.6	127.5	102.6

Sources: Argentina: Dirección Nacional de Estadística y Censos, *Boletin Mensual de Estadistica*, January, 1961; March, 1962. Chile: Banco Central de Chile, *Boletin Mensual*, April, 1962.

The need for drastic measures to slow inflation and stimulate growth in Argentina and Chile has been obvious beyond question. One cannot but conclude, however, that the IMF-type programs were based on a misappraisal of where some of the leading difficulties lay, as well as on an erroneous normative perspective. The contention that under quite restrictive assumptions a free market economy will necessarily be improved merely by making it 60 percent does not support the corollary that the performance of a half-free economy will necessarily be improved merely by making it 60 percent free. Yet it is this sort of reasoning, buttressed by an uncritical faith in the benefits of private foreign investment, rather than detailed analysis of the structure of the Argentine and Chilean economies, which seems to have guided much of the stabilization programs.

Policy Implications

If the analysis of this paper is broadly correct, Argentina and Chile have reached another major impasse in their frustrating climb to self-sustaining growth, similar to that of the 1930's. Then, the decline and stagnation of their primary export markets made clear that the economic growth of Argentina and Chile could no longer be supported primarily by a handful of primary exports for which substantial Ricardian rents provided by nature offset the technological backwardness of the economy. The impasse, temporarily

TABLE II

Argentina					1952=100							
	Vehicles and Nonelectrical Machinery		Electrical Products and Machinery		Rubber Products		Food and Drink		Textiles		Leather	
	O	P	O	P	O	P	O	P	O	P	O	P
1958	99	102	128	109	123	103	133	121	102	122	90	101
1959	80	97	123	115	119	105	114	115	81	117	70	98
1960	103	111	136	116	144	114	110	123	85	116	66	107
1961	109	123	122	105	199	140	115	131	90	122	73	110

Chile					1953=100									
	Metal Products other Than Machinery		Electrical Products		Chemicals		Rubber Products		Food Products		Textiles		Leather	
	O	P	O	P	O	P	O	P	O	P	O	P	O	P
1957	118	108	111	101	112	101	93	89	103	106	93	106	103	104
1958	124	112	104	118	122	109	99	106	99	102	93	112	103	110
1959	149	132	106	131	121	106	134	140	107	110	107	127	103	122
1960	155	130	112	134	126	109	147	139	111	93	95	121	90	91
1961	195	149	115	139	134	114	161	150	114	84	103	122	102	123

O=Output.
P=Labor productivity (Man-hour output in Argentina; per worker output in Chile).
Source: See footnote 41.

overcome by import-substituting industrialization, has now reappeared in a new guise. Import-substituting industrialization has also proved inadequate to elevate the economy to growth-sustaining efficiency. Continued agricultural backwardness, inadequate investment in public overhead capital, and precocious widening of the industrial spectrum have combined with a fall in the external terms of trade to bring Argentina and Chile to their present impasse. How is this to be overcome?

Firstly, the preceding analysis underlines—if such emphasis is still needed—the necessity to accelerate agricultural development by agricultural reforms and related measures and to augment substantially public investment in education, transport, and power. The attempt to outflank technological backwardness by import-substituting industrialization without such ancillary measures has failed. Nevertheless, the attempt has given Argentina and Chile a substantial heritage of industrial skills and experience which should now be utilized to supplement their primary exports. Indeed, the viability of their economies required this, for the growth of their traditional exports is hardly likely alone to support their import needs, even under optimistic projections of world primary market trends. In brief, they must also turn to industrial exporting. But the existing demand structure as well as ingrained industrial habits stand in the way of a simple market solution to the problem of restructuring their industrial sector. What are required, therefore, are more direct and drastic measures, conceived in the spirit of Mrs. Robinson's dictum that the 'task is not merely to study the coefficients but to change them.' More specifically, the following lines of policy are suggested :

1. Taxation should be used to alter the structure of consumer demand. It is not sufficient to raise taxes in order to finance more public investment. The tax incidence must also fall much more heavily than is now the case on consumer durables and other sumptuary items of consumption, whether imported or domestically produced, with the object of curtailing new investment in such products. This requires some combination of heavy indirect taxes on A- and E-type consumables and augmented and progressive taxation of *personal* income.

2. A larger share of industrial investment must be directed to T-type industries with good export potential. This implies cost and market studies to identify such industries and input-output studies

to estimate the direct and indirect demand for foreign exchange of alternative industrial investments. Given such information, exchange and capital issues controls, tax concessions, and public funds will probably have to be used to help proportion industrial investment so as to maximize net foreign exchange availability and to direct entrepreneurial perspectives outward rather than toward the domestic market. Since the required scope and rigor of such measures would vary inversely with the buoyancy of traditional exports, the authorities should link these measures to medium-term projections of traditional exports. Similarly, government outlays on power, transport, manpower training, and industrial research should be channelled to facilitate the industrial exporting effort.

3. Foreign manufacturing investment must also be screened with the same criterion in mind. The authorities must not be seduced by the appearance of direct exchange saving, or by the fact that such investments may not compete with existing industries, into overlooking possible indirect defects of such investments in augmenting the demand for foreign exchange and stimulating low priority complementary investment.

4. Foreign technical assistance should be sought to assist in modernizing promising T-industries.

5. Vigorous efforts should be made to get the United States and Europe to open their markets to T-exports from Latin America.

In short, the emphasis, particularly while the exchange crisis resulting from stagnating markets for primary exports lasts, must be on export promoting industrialization. The focus, however, should be on raising promising industries to long run exporting efficiency, not on indiscriminately subsidizing industrial exports.

Let me finally anticipate three lines of criticism.

The first is that world demand for T-industry products has generally risen less rapidly than for A- and E-industry products. While this is not necessarily the case for all items, it is broadly true for the general class of less sophisticated industrial products. Yet it is also true that world demand for such products has expanded more rapidly in recent years than for primary products. Moreover, in more advanced industrial economies the rapid rise of A- and E-industries has been pulling up real wages and labor costs in T-industries, so that imports have been progressively supplementing and even replacing domestic production of many T-type items. Coupled with this is the growing middle-class taste in these countries for exotics, which also favors the demand for technologically less-sophisticated industrial imports. To hasten the gradual process in the advanced countries of substituting imports for domestic output of T-products undoubtedly requires further liberalizing of the import restrictions against T-imports.[47] What is disturbing is that while the industrially more advanced Latin American countries are pressing hard for the removal of import restrictions against primary products, they have shown little interest in measures which would promote industrial exports to hard-currency markets.[48]

The second objection is that the Argentine and Chilean governments have been singularly inept in administering controls. This is, however, a *tu quoque* argument, for neither has the private sector been notably efficient. More importantly, the objection tends to confuse the essential issue. As indicated in the preceding discussion, a strong measure of discriminatory controls in Argentina and Chile is unavoidable. The quest, for example, for an equilibrium exchange rate proved to be chimerical. Exchange controls took on different guises in the stabilization periods, but have shared the major weakness of earlier efforts; namely, they attempted to check immediate symptoms without central guidance on allocation priorities from a general development program. It would be far the wiser course to recognize the inevitability of discriminatory controls and to concentrate more fruitfully on relating them to a coherent development strategy, of which the promotion of industrial exports should surely be a major component.

A third objection is that the stricture against excessive A- and E-type investment overlooks that the feedback on industrial skills and managerial experience is greater from such industries than from T-industries. There is some merit to this criticism, although one

47 The Alliance for Progress could well devote some of its efforts to promoting such liberalization and to encouraging the industrial export potential of the relatively industrialized countries of Latin America. The benefit to their balance of payments and to their industrial confidence might lessen the danger of the Alliance becoming little more than a supplier of stabilization credits to demoralized economies. Such funds could be used to better mutual advantage even if partly spent in the United States to ease the transfer of resources out of industries adversely affected by the liberalization of entry to Latin American industrial exports.

48 The Latin American Free Trade Association is not an exception to this statement, since at present it is largely an effort to extend import-substituting industrialization in A- and E-type goods to the entire region. This is not necessarily a criticism, although it is clear that the limited amount of intraregionall trade, the timidity of the Montevideo Treaty, and the difficulties of compensating the less developed members of the LAFTA for the burden of diverting their

should not overlook the favorable feedback on cost and quality control and marketing skills which would derive from exporting T-products. The basic problem is to determine the point at which the educational gain from establishing A- and E-industries is being purchased at too great a cost in short-run resource misallocation. If we use the growth rate as a rough guide, it seems reasonably evident from the critical plight of the Argentine and Chilean economies in the past decade that they have gone beyond the point, and need now to find more economic ways of picking up industrial skills and experience.

Growth economics is not able, of course, to indicate any single right path to maximizing the long-run growth rate, although it can indicate some of the necessary conditions for mounting each path successfully. There is, for example, the path formalized by the turnpike theorem and illustrated, perhaps, by the Soviet Union. That path would indeed call for an intensification of A- and E-investment in capital goods, heavy outlays on education and technical training, compression of real wages and consumption whenever necessary to offset bottlenecks and misallocations in the capital goods sector, and other hard, painful measures. It is possible that by taking this dangerous, long, and tortuous detour the turnpike to rapid economic growth can be reached. I doubt that Latin Americans, who are notoriously wild drivers, are capable of managing the difficult detour. But even if they are tempted, they should at least realize that the Russian people did not make it over the detour to the turnpike in Zils and Moskvitches or outfitted with household durables. If one prefers a less distant payoff in such goods, then one had bettter choose an easier, if perhaps ultimately slower, road to travel. But even on this road it is possible to break down from the weight of excess baggage, or to tip over from a badly unbalanced load.

imports of A- and E-goods to higher-priced Brazilian, Argentine, or Chilean production makes it likely that expansion of intraregional trade in industrial products will be slow. It does not provide, therefore, a sufficiently persuasive argument for foregoing the effort to develop hard-currency industrial exports. The LAFTA consultation machinery, on the other hand, could be used to coordinate plans for developing T-type exports, so as to avoid needlessly competitive efforts.

13

IMPORT SUBSTITUTION AS AN INDUSTRIALIZATION STRATEGY

John H. Power

Introduction

AN INDUSTRIALIZATION STRATEGY biased toward import substitution is, I think, almost an inevitable phenomenon in less developed countries. Often it emerges in an apparently natural way—perhaps even inadvertently—following the imposition of import controls in response to a *balance of payments problem*. What is initially viewed as a curb on the consumption of less essential imports soon becomes rationalized as a protective device to encourage production of their substitutes. Since the market is already there for the taking, a sufficient degree of protection will promise quick easy gains in industrial output, primarily in finished consumption goods even though materials and parts, as well as capital equipment, must be imported.

Moreover a dual theoretical rationale for an import substitution orientation in development strategy easily emerges to justify its continuance.[1] World demand for primary commodities is held to be growing too slowly for their export to play a leading role in economic growth. The export of manufactures in competition with developed countries appears unpromising both because of the disadvantages of technological backwardness and small scale and because of protection in the wealthy countries where the principal markets are. This leaves production for the home market, balanced in relation to home market demand, as the seemingly most promising avenue of growth.

The first aspect of the rationale for an import substitution bias is a defensive one, implying, in effect, that this is the only way out of a difficulty. The other has a more positive character, however,

1 The description of this rationale that follows is obviously based on well-known theories of R. Nurkse and W. A. Lewis. It by no means does justice, however, to the sophistication and depth of their views. Popular versions of famous theories, which serve as the rationale for political decisions, are often unfortunately only caricatures of the originals.

suggesting the possibility of an emerging self-sustaining growth mechanism. Behind import controls the domestic manufacturer can obtain high prices for goods even of inferior quality, thereby 'earning' high profits that can be saved and reinvested. This means turning the terms of trade against agriculture (and other non-protected sectors) to create the saving for industrial growth. Eventually, it is hoped, agriculture too will benefit as industrial progress reduces costs and prices, and as industrial expansion offers higher productivity employment to rural labor.

This line of thinking has a natural appeal in newly developing countries. It promises less dependence on traditional exports—hence, less fear that 'export lag' or declining terms of trade (or both) will inhibit development. The problem of competition with the more advanced technology in developed countries is avoided by curbing imports and not encouraging new exports. The balance of payments problem —the need to import growing quantities of capital goods—is solved instead by saving foreign exchange through import substitution. The difficult problems associated with increasing agricultural productivity can be pushed into the background, since it is the twist of the terms of trade that initially wrests saving from agriculture. And, via this shift in income distribution to the 'capitalist sector' and the latter's response, a cycle of profit-saving-reinvestment-increased productivity-higher profit-etc. can supposedly emerge to render growth self-sustaining.

While this is, no doubt, an over-simplified view of the origins of an import substitution strategy as well as of its rationale, it is suggestive, I think, of the experience of a number of developing countries that have had some success in the first stage of implementation of such a strategy—the take-over of an existing market for consumption goods from the foreign supplier. Common also to their experience, however, seems to be the greater difficulty of meeting the challenges that lie beyond the first stage—namely, extending production backward to intermediate goods, capital goods and raw materials, and breaking into the world market with exports of manufactures. Yet these are crucial to ultimate success in that, without one or both, the pace of industrial growth must falter and the emergence of a self-sustaining growth mechanism is frustrated. For expanding consumption goods production only, unless this results in growing exports or import replacement, is incompatible with growth of saving.

The conclusion is, then, that beyond the first stage in an import substitution strategy—the expansion, behind protection, of finished consumption goods production to the limits of the domestic markets—lies the necessity of developing production of intermediate goods, capital goods, and raw materials; or expanding exports; or both. It is a simple matter to formulate and implement a policy of protection for the first stage. Often this happens almost inadvertently, as was suggested above. But the crude policies of protection that may serve adequately in the first stage, and the economic structure that they encourage, are likely, in my opinion, to become barriers to growth in subsequent stages.[2] Why this is so, and what might be done to prevent it or correct it, is the subject of this paper.

Section 1 comprises a discussion of the emergence of barriers to growth under three headings: economic inefficiency (misallocation of resources); technical inefficiency (failure to minimize costs); and the saving gap (failure to achieve an adequate rise in domestic saving). While the distinctions may not always seem clear-cut, this scheme of presentation does serve to emphasize that a naive import substitution strategy can impede growth via an adverse influence on the marginal saving rate, as well as on the social product; and that its influence on the latter over time depends as much on inducements to efficiency and innovation as on resource allocation.

There follows in Section II a brief summary of the policy implications of the critique of such an import substitution strategy.

I Economic Inefficiency

An import substitution bias means a balance of payments policy that favors import control or restriction (often via exchange control) over export encouragement. This, in turn, implies a lower value for foreign exchange than that appropriate to a policy of equal encouragement to exports and import substitution. If market prices were given and could be taken to represent unit costs and utilities at the margin, the resulting resource allocation would require a

2 Because of a rising import bill of materials, parts and equipment to sustain production in the protected industries, and because of a resistance on the part of unprotected sectors and income groups (e.g. agriculture and labor) to any deterioration of their terms of trade, barriers to growth taking the form of balance of payments difficulties and inflation may arise long before the first stage is completed.

greater value of resources to save an additional unit of foreign exchange through import substitution than to earn an additional unit of foreign exchange through export expansion.

Since this kind of welfare loss is generally well understood, the persistence of this direction of bias in balance of payments policies suggests either that considerations other than economic efficiency are held to be more important, or that the assumptions underlying this kind of welfare judgment are considered to be invalid. About all an economist can do with regard to the former is to point to the cost and, since this emerges anyway in a discussion of economic efficiency, I will focus on the latter.

Before turning to the validity of the assumptions on which welfare judgments against interference with free market results are based, however, we should note another kind of misallocation that appears to be both very likely and very substantial in the context of an import substitution strategy. That is the bias against production of intermediate goods, capital goods and raw materials. The reason is, of course, that these are inputs in the industries which develop in the first stage and, as such, are usually more liberally imported than are finished consumption goods that compete with the emerging domestic industries. This means not only a bias against vertical balance in import substitution—i.e., backward linkage is discouraged—but also an inflated and irrationally differentiated structure of protection at the finishing stages of production.

This is so because the total rate of protection depends not only on the particular rate of protection that applies to the product of that industry, but also on the particular rates that apply at the preceding stage in the production process. The former acts as a subsidy while the latter act as taxes on value added in a particular industry. It may be useful to put these relationships more formally at this point.[3]

Let Y_i represent the output of any industry and $\sum_j a_{ji} Y_i$ its intermediate inputs, both valued at given world prices—i.e., the prices that would prevail with free trade. Then

$$V_i = Y_i - \Sigma a_{ji} Y \quad (1)$$

3 The formal exposition is patterned closely after that of Harry G. Johnson in his 'Tariffs and Economic Development,' *Journal of Development Studies* (October 1965), p. 20.

is value added at free trade prices, and

$$V_i(1 + T_i) = Y_i(1 + t_i) - \Sigma a_{ji}(1 + t_j)\ Y \tag{2}$$

is actual value added under the system of protection. The t's represent the proportions by which the system of protection permits the actual domestic prices of the outputs of various industries to exceed their free trade prices, while T_i is the total rate of protection of the ith industry—the proportion by which its value added can exceed what would be its free trade value. This can be written also as

$$V_i(1 + T_i) = Y_i + t_i Y_i - \Sigma a_{ji} Y_i - \Sigma a_{ji} t\ Y_i$$

and by substituting (1) in the right-hand side

$$V_i(1 + T_i) = V_i + t_i Y_i - \Sigma a_{ji}\, t_j Y_i$$

We can solve this for the total rate of protection

$$T_i = \frac{V_i + t_i Y_i - \Sigma a_{ji}\, t_j Y_i}{V_i} - 1$$

or

$$T^i = \frac{t_i - \Sigma a_{ji}\, t}{V_i / Y_i} \tag{3}$$

From (3) we can see that the total rate of protection of an industry will be greater the greater is its own particular rate of protection, the smaller are the particular rates of protection of its supplying industries, and the smaller is the proportion of its value added to the total value of its output. Now consider the distorted pattern of protection that can result from a policy of restricting most severely the import of consumption goods, while permitting inputs into these industries to be more liberally imported.

First, as was noted above, exports are penalized by the lower value of foreign exchange that is consistent with the bias toward import restriction. But the extent of the bias can be much greater than the particular degrees of protection would suggest. Suppose, for example, that the protective device employed were a 50 per cent duty on consumption goods while intermediate inputs could be imported at free trade prices. Then if value added in manufacturing (at free trade prices) were 25 per cent of total (free trade) value, equation (3) tells us that the total degree of protection would be

200 per cent! If the protection is effective, the economy is paying marginal resources adding value in import-substituting industries 200 per cent more, for each unit of foreign exchange saved, than it is paying marginal resources earning a unit of foreign exchange in export industries. This could mean either higher rewards per unit of resources, or more resources—i.e., less efficiency, or both.[4]

A similar magnification of the distortion in degrees of protection excurs, of course, between industries producing consumption goods and those producing materials, parts and equipment when the latter are more liberally imported. Thus, the bias against backward-linkage import substitution is more pronounced than a simple comparison of particular rates of protection would suggest. Moreover, the resulting relative lack of domestic sources of supply for these inputs, together with the fact that the total degree of protection is inversely related to the (proportional) value added contribution of the industry, means that such a system of protection particularly encourages heavy users of foreign exchange. Finally, we should note that in protecting the balance of payments via import restriction, it is a very common practice to restrict most severely the least essential imports. This tends to bias import substitution, albeit perhaps inadvertently, in favor of less essential industries.

The conclusion is that an import substitution bias in development strategy, when accompanied—as is, I think, typical—by relatively liberal import policies with respect to 'essential' imports (both in the form of inputs for domestic industries and special categories of consumption goods), can create a rather extreme distortion of incentives away from the pattern that would result from free markets. Moreover, the direction of distortion appears to be unfortunate in that it particularly discourages export expansion and backward-linkage import substitution, one or both of which is crucial to sustained industrial growth, as noted above; while it gives the greatest encouragement to industries most heavily requiring foreign exchange to produce less essential products.

Despite this, protection is often defended as a means of correcting 'market failures,' and once we abandon the assumption that free market prices are necessarily the best welfare indicators we are obliged to consider several more or less respectable arguments for this view.

Johnson has argued that the only economic justification for tariffs

4 This assumes no terms of trade effect.

is the terms of trade effect of trading more or less.[5] For an open economy that can affect via trade the prices of the goods it buys and sells, full Paretoan optimality requires equality between the ratio of domestic prices of exports and imports and the *marginal* terms of trade, rather than the international price ratios. This means restricting trade until

$$\frac{p_h}{q_h} = \frac{p_w}{q_w} \cdot \frac{1 + \frac{1}{\eta}}{1 - \frac{1}{e}} \qquad (4)$$

where p represents the price of imports and q the price of exports, the subscripts h and w indicating home and world prices, while η and e are the world elasticities of supply of imports and demand for exports, respectively.[6] This could be accomplished by establishing a dual exchange rate system, the price of foreign exchange for imports exceeding that for exports in the proportion

$$C = \frac{1 + \frac{1}{\eta}}{1 - \frac{1}{e}}$$

(the 'correction' for terms of trade effects). The more common method of favoring import substitution over exports, however, is by tariffs or exchange control. In this case imports should be restricted (and the price of foreign exchange reduced) until the condition described by equation (4) is met.

How does this description of optimality relate to the picture of misallocation which preceded it? First, the general degree of protection would have to be equal to $(C-1)$ and it should apply uniformly at all stages of the production process. If all industries were effectively so protected the total rate of protection for each industry would be equal to its particular rate—i.e., the uniform general rate $(C-1)$. This can be seen by setting $t_i = t_j = t$ in equation(3)

$$T_i = \frac{t - \Sigma_j a_{ji}\, t}{V_i / Y_i} \qquad 3(a)$$

5 Johnson, *op. cit.*, p. 8.

6 S. Alexander, 'Devaluation versus Import Restriction as an Instrument for Improving the Trade Balance,' *IMF Staff Papers* (April 1951), p. 379.

and since

$$V_i / Y_i = \frac{Y_i - \Sigma_j a_{ji} Y}{Y_i}$$

$$T_i = \frac{t(1 - \Sigma_j a_{ji})}{1 - \Sigma_j a_{ji}} = t.$$

As Johnson has pointed out, however, for a trading country the export industries' rates of protection (in the absence of export taxes) must effectively be zero.[7] If any of these exportables are inputs in other domestic industries, total rates of protection will differ among industries in accordance with their use of these inputs and their (proportional) value added contributions. This does not mean, however, that resources will be misallocated in this case, since the resulting pattern of protection is just what is needed to bring domestic rates of transformation between exports and imports in line with the international *marginal* terms of trade.

Put this way there seems to be a perfectly respectable argument for protection when the marginal terms of trade are below the average. The appropriate rate of protection is $(C-1)$ and to avoid inter-industry distortions in the pattern of protection the simple rule is a uniform rate for all industries.

There are, however, two serious weaknesses in the argument. First is the assumption of a single elasticity of demand for all exports[8]—presumably a weighted average. For most developing countries, however, the primary reason for a value of C in excess of unity is the relatively low elasticity of demand for one or a few primary exports which weigh heavily in the total. Basing a system of protection on the weighted average elasticity would mean a strong bias against all of the other (actual and potential) export industries.

7 Johnson, *op cit*., p. 22. This assumes that the export industries are competitive. If they are not they can act as discriminating monopolists behind protection. But if they (all) exploit their monopoly power in the world market there is no need for the government to do so via a policy of protection. Since, however, the most important cases of high value for C are likely to be associated with primary commodity exports, the assumption that the home prices of exports are equal to the world prices (or below them by the amount of export taxes where these play a role in the adjustment to the condition described by equation (4)) is probably a reasonable one.

8 A single elasticity of supply for all imports is also assumed, but this is normally more defensible.

This strongly suggests that the few exports with low elasticity of demand be removed from the jurisdiction of general trade policies and treated as special cases requiring taxes, supply restrictions, or something of the sort. If this is done, however, the second weakness, alluded to above, of the terms of trade argument for protection becomes more apparent. For the argument assumes no retaliation—an assumption that might be valid in the case of modest across-the-board protection, but which can be held with less assurance in the case of a much stronger price influence concentrated on one or a few commodities. It is, in other words, precisely where the potential terms of trade gains from trade restriction are greatest that the threat of retaliation is most likely.

A situation where a country can avoid serious misallocation of resources only by means that hurt others and invite retaliation calls for some kind of international agreement to resolve the inherent conflict. So what appears to remain as valid of the terms of trade argument for protection is that it should apply selectively to a relatively few commodities, and that this should lead to an international agreement on prices. Short of achieving this kind of international cooperation it is probably in the interest of the developing countries to apply supply restriction schemes for these commodities because of the paramount importance of freeing all other exports from the penalty of an undervaluation of foreign exchange.

What of the other common arguments for protection: infant industry, external economies, and factor price disequilibrium? Johnson has argued that since these do not involve a failure of international price ratios (or marginal terms of trade) to represent true opportunity costs in international trade, any policy designed to implement these arguments that simultaneously disturbs the relation between domestic and international price ratios will thereby create, as well as correct, distortion.[9] The appropriate measures to bring true social costs and values into line in each of these cases would involve a system of taxes and subsidies, not a system of trade restriction. His argument is correct on the assumption that the government can in fact implement a fiscal policy that itself involves less distortion than, say, taxing imports. If, on the other hand, the fiscal measures available are quite limited for institutional reasons,

9 Johnson, *op.cit.*, pp. 8-9. It is assumed here that the relation has already been corrected for terms of trade effects.

the argument is weakened. Nevertheless, the advantages of fiscal remedies are so pronounced in each of these cases that the argument for trade restriction is, in my opinion, very dubious. Let me consider each of these cases, in turn.

The infant industry argument has two roots. One is the relation of efficiency to scale and the other is the relation of efficiency to time. Increasing returns to scale and a time-consuming learning process then serve as valid bases of the case for protection of infant industries.

The logic of the argument calls for specific protection of certain industries, however, rather than general protection of the sort described above (in the introduction) as an import substitution strategy. The reason is two-fold. First, industries differ with respect to their scale-efficiency and time-efficiency relationships. Long-run comparative advantage depends in part, then, on their relative differences in the response of efficiency to scale and time. Second, the extent and pace of response is itself likely to be a function of the concentration of resources. That is, even if all industries had the same response functions it would normally pay to concentrate on fewer industries, at least up to a certain point in their development, rather than to disperse resources across a broad front.

This is obvious for the scale-efficiency relationship, but it may be true for the time-efficiency relationship, as well. That is, a concentration rather than a dispersion of investment, technical and organizational skills, and education and training may mean a more rapid average rate of progress in efficiency for the whole economy. Scitovsky emphasizes in this connection the relationship between the pace of growth of an industry and its rate of innovations, concluding that the rapid pace made possible for some industries (as opposed to the pedestrian rate for all in a balanced growth context) means concentrated growth would permit and encourage a more rapid overall rate of increase of productivity.[10]

So the logic of the infant industry argument calls for concentrated industrial growth rather than growth balanced in relation to domestic demand, implying greater emphasis on exports and less on import substitution. But protection against imports penalizes exports via the lower value of foreign exchange. An optimal set of policies would include, therefore, subsidies to exports from the

10 T. Scitovsky, 'Growth—Balanced or Unbalanced?,' *Papers on Value and Growth* (Stanford University Press, 1964), pp. 107-109.

selected industries equal to their rates of protection, both set (somehow) equal to the (discounted) future relative advantage of these industries.

There remains another problem, however. We do not have in this case a uniform degree of protection across the economy, with the result that industries using as inputs the outputs of the protected industries would be penalized, the degree of penalty depending not only on the amount used of the various protected goods, but also on each industry's (proportional) value added contribution. In order to avoid misallocation from this source, these differential penalties would have to be offset by matching subsidies. At this point Johnson's argument for avoiding all of this 'patching up' by subsidizing directly the 'infant industries' in the first place appears very sound.[11]

The presence of external economies is another reason sometimes given to defend protection. Broadly viewed external economies comprise all elements of interdependence among industries, both direct and through the market. It will be convenient for what follows to distinguish within these simply between interdependence in production and interdependence in consumption.

An emphasis on interdependence in consumption leads to 'horizontally balanced' growth in line with market demand. While this yields external economies via complementarities in consumption, it means that external diseconomies prevail in interdependence in production via competition for scarce resources. In contrast, an emphasis on interdependence in production leads to 'vertically balanced' growth in line with backward and forward linkages in production. This, of course, yields external economies on the supply side, but ignores complementarities in consumption, thus requiring an ability to sell in the world market to solve the demand problem.

There seems to be no obvious reason for giving greater emphasis in general to one kind of interdependence over another—i.e., for generally favoring horizontal balance and import substitution over vertical balance and export expansion because of the existence of external economies. On other grounds a preference could be established. For example, if the terms of trade were the only criterion, horizontal balance should be preferred. Or, if saving and growth

11 Johnson also rightly stresses the loss in consumer surplus from distorting the relationship of domestic to international prices. *Op. cit.*, p. 10.

were the only criterion, vertical balance should be preferred.[12] But if the world market is available to fill the gaps in demand and supply the external economies argument does not necessarily favor either domestic supply balance or domestic demand balance.

The essence of the external economies argument for protection, however, is the inability of private decisions based on market criteria to take account of the results of interdependence.[13] While this may be a nearly universal phenomenon in the context of a dynamic growth process, there will be certain areas where the total gains from interrelated decisions can be judged to be particularly large in relation to what the market promises atomistic decisions. These then should be treated in a manner similar to that suggested above for infant industries. And the same argument for subsidy rather than protection applies. In the absence of any reason for altering the relation between domestic and international prices, the only defense for protection in these cases would be that import duties were the least inefficient method of taxation available to the government.

I turn finally to the factor price disequilibrium argument for protection of manufacturing. Put in its simplest form it is that wage rates in manufacturing[14] exceed the opportunity cost of labor from other sectors and this puts domestic manufactures at an unwarranted disadvantage with imports. Protection of domestic manufactures is then the suggested remedy.

Lary has argued correctly that, since the factor price disequilibrium applies to manufacture for export as well as for import substitution, the former should be equally encouraged. He has advocated a dual exchange rate—a higher price of foreign exchange for both exporting and importing manufactures and a lower price for trading agricultural products.[15] This is a step in the right direction in that it corrects an unwarranted bias against exports. But there remains a bias against the use of labor in the factor mix and a bias against the use of domestic manufactures as inputs. These can be eliminated along with the others, however, by a simple subsidy on the employment of labor where its market price is above its

12 See below.

13 T. Scitovsky, 'Two Concepts of External Economies,' *Papers on Value and Growth, op. cit.*, pp. 69-83.

14 This need not be restricted to the manufacturing sector.

15 H. Lary, 'Economic Development and the Capacity to Import—National Policies,' in *Lectures on Economic Development* (Istanbul University, 1958).

opportunity cost. Again it seems that restriction of imports is an inept and costly way to correct a market failure.

The conclusion that emerges from this analysis of the economic efficiency of favoring import substitution via protection is somewhat depressing. First, the system as it develops in the first stage is likely to misallocate resources by means of a strong bias against exports, against backward linkage import substitution, in favor of less essential industries, and in favor of heavy users of foreign exchange. Nor can any of the arguments for correction of market failures bolster very much the case for this kind of protection. Even the terms of trade argument appears dubious when a concern with low world demand elasticities for a few exports dictates an under-valuation of foreign exchange that heavily penalizes all other exports (actual and potential).

This is a qualitative judgment, of course, and the really important question is its quantitative significance. Some striking evidence bearing on this has been presented recently by Soligo and Stern for Pakistan.[16] Using the Tims-Stern input-output model for 1963-64, they have calculated implicit rates of protection for forty-eight manufacturing industries. Their 'implicit' rates correspond to my 'total' rates, but with an important difference. In my notation theirs is

$$U_i = \frac{t_i - \sum_j a_{ji}\, t_j}{V_i / Y_i + (t_i - \sum_j a_{ji}\, t_j)} \qquad (5)$$

which can be compared with equation (3) above.

Put more simply the difference is this:

$$T_i = \frac{W_i - V_i}{V_i}$$

and

$$U_i = \frac{W_i - V_i}{W_i}$$

where W_i is $V_i(1 + T_i)$, actual value added under this system of protection (see equation (2) above). If follows that their implicit rate of protection.

16 R. Soligo and J. Stern, 'Tariff Protection, Import Substitution and Investment Efficiency,' *Pakistan Development Review* (Summer 1965), pp. 249-270.

$$U_i = T_i \ . \ \frac{V_i}{W_i} = \frac{T_i}{T_i + 1}$$

The Soligo-Stern measure of the rate of protection has one very decisive advantage in that it can apply to cases where V_i is negative, which my T cannot. And this turns out to be of considerable importance in assessing the Pakistan data.

A negative V_i means that for an industry, the value of output at world prices is less than the value of intermediate inputs at world prices. Abandoning production and importing the finished product would save both foreign exchange and domestic resources.

This was found to be true for twenty-three industries in Pakistan, including food processing, beverages, cigarettes, textiles and wearing apparel, petroleum and coal products, furniture, cycles, and motor vehicles. Since V was negative for each of these industries, U was greater than unity. Among the twenty-five with values for U less than unity (implying no absolute waste of resources from the activity), the values varied widely from −0.27 for grain milling to 0.92 for matches (suggesting relative waste of resources). The pattern of differential protection corresponds to what one would expect from an import substitution bias.

In general (i) consumer goods are much more heavily protected than either intermediate or investment and related goods, (ii) within the consumer goods industries, non-essentials, such as beverages and cigarettes, are much more heavily protected than essential industries such as grain and rice milling, salt and tea, (iii) textiles are the most heavily protected group of industries, although the protection is approximately the same for all components of the group and (iv) the least protected industries are those producing heavy machinery, both electrical and non-electrical, and transport equipment other than motor vehicles and cycles. Fertilizer is also among the least protected group.[17]

A similar study of protection is in process for the Philippine economy and some preliminary results are presented in the accompanying table for 55 manufacturing industries, accounting for more than 80 per cent of gross value added in manufacturing. While the estimates should be taken as tentative and subject to revision, they indicate broadly, I think, the range of degrees of protection accorded manufacturing by the system of tariffs and indirect taxes.

17 Soligo and Stern, *op. cit.*, p. 259.

TABLE I

TOTAL RATES OF PROTECTION FOR SELECTED PHILIPPINE MANUFACTURING INDUSTRIES[a]

(*Preliminary Estimates*)

ISIC Code		*U*	*T*
2441	Embroideries (not exported *U* = .60)	—.29	—.22
*2031	Pineapple canning	—.24	—.20
*3811	Ship repairing	—.19	—.16
2331	Cordage, wine and net	—.15	—.13
*2514	Plywood	—.15	—.13
3121	Coconut oil and copra cake	—.13	—.12
2511 & 2513	Lumber	—.08	—.07
2131	Brewery and malt products	—.04	—.04
2093	Desiccated coconut	—.02	—.02
2024	Milk processing	.04	.04
3621	Agricultural tractors	.11	.12
*3114	Fertilizers	.13	.15
3641	Food products machinery	.13	.15
3211	Petroleum refining	.17	.20
3831	Motor trucks and buses	.18	.22
3113	Compressed, liquefied or solidified gases	.22	.29
*3192	Medical and pharmaceutical preparations	.25	.33
2072	Sugar central and refinery products	.27	.36
*3411	Basic iron and steel products	.31	.45
3731	Batteries	.35	.53
2095	Coffee	.41	.69
3194	Soap and other cleaning compounds	.42	.71
3321	Glass containers	.43	.76
3832	Motor vehicles engines, parts and bodies	.48	.91
3021	Tires and tubes	.48	.94
2721	Paper stationery	.50	.98
2433	Women's & children's garments	.54	1.19
2723	Cartons, cardboards, boxes	.58	1.40
2712	Paper and board mill products	.59	1.45
3993	Fabricated plastic products	.63	1.67
3673	Household sewing machines	.65	1.84
2431	Men's and boys' garments	.66	1.94
3531	Fabricated structural iron and steel	.66	1.97
2411	Shoes, except rubber	.67	2.04
3391	Structural concrete products	.67	2.05

TABLE I—*Contd.*

ISIC Code		U	T
3733	Electric wires and wiring devices	.69	2.21
3322	Flat glass	.70	2.36
*2053	Wheat mill products	.72	2.51
*3341	Cement	.72	2.63
3532	Architectural metal work	.73	2.72
2320	Knitting mill products	.73	2.77
3722	Radios, phonographs & TV	.79	3.79
2141	Soft drinks	.87	6.62
3011	Rubber shoes, slippers and boots	.91	10.07
2097	Starch and its by-products	.93	13.77
2096	Prepared animal feeds	.95	21.03
2611	Wood & rattan furniture, not upholstered	1.02	
3542	Metal closures and crowns	1.10	
3131	Paints and varnishes	1.14	
2081 & 2082	Candy, cocoa and chocolate products	1.19	
2211	Cigarettes	1.21	
**2314	Cotton textile mill products	1.32	
2094	Vegetable lard and margarine	1.34	
3193	Perfumes, cosmetics and other toilet preparations	1.44	
3831	Autos	2.03	

[a] See Appendix for notes on the method of estimation.

* These industries are exempted from taxes on imported machinery and equipment. The exemption will decline each year until it disappears in 1969. The effect of this, which has not been taken into account in the above estimations, would be to raise only slightly the rates of protection for these industries, since duties on machinery and equipment are generally very low.

** The cotton textile industry has special tax exemption under R. A. 4086. The exemption will decline each year until it disappears in 1971. Without this exemption U would be 1.04.

The estimates, however, are based on value added in domestic prices and the system of duties and indirect taxes, with value added in world prices deduced by discounting outputs and inputs by their particular rates of protection.

Thus

$$U_i = \frac{W_i - V}{W_i} = 1 - \frac{\dfrac{1}{1+t_i} - \sum_j \dfrac{a_{ji}}{1+t_j}}{W_i / X_i}$$

and

$$T_i = \frac{U_i}{1 - U_i}$$

This means that they measure the total rates of protection accorded to these industries.

Any inferences from this data about efficiency of resource allocation, however, involve an assumption about the extent to which the protection accorded is actually used. Casual empiricism suggests to the writer, for example, that the soft drink industries do not take full advantage of the protection available to them. This may be true of many other industries, as well. In general, absence of a significant volume of imports would suggest the possibility that a portion of the accorded protection is redundant. Moreover, there are many ways, both legal and illegal, to get around the nominal set of duties and taxes. Finally, however, the data in the table do not take into account the tax and duty exemptions accorded certain industries under the Basic Industries Law, the effect of which would be to raise slightly their total degrees of protection.

These qualifications should warn the reader to be cautious about drawing conclusions about relative efficiency in the use of resources from these preliminary estimates. Nevertheless, to see what they suggest about the pattern of bias, we can classify the industries in five groups, as follows:

I. EXPORTS

Coconut Oil
Embroideries
Pineapple Canning
Cordage
Plywood
Lumber
Brewery and
Malt
Desiccated Coconut
Sugar

II. CAPITAL GOODS

Ship repair
Agricultural tractors
Food machinery
Trucks and buses

III. INPUTS INTO CONSTRUCTION

Plywood
Lumber
Flat glass
Cement

Structural iron and steel	Architectural metal
Structural concrete products	Paints and varnishes
Electric wires, etc.	

IV. INTERMEDIATE GOODS

Fertilizers	Glass containers
Petroleum refining	Tires and tubes
Compressed gases	Cartons, Cardboards
Basic iron and steel	Electric wires, etc.
Batteries	Prepared animal feeds
Motor vehicles, parts and bodies	Metal crowns

V. IMPORT-SUBSTITUTE CONSUMPTION GOODS

All other (24 industries)

The significance of the classification is obvious except, perhaps in the case of group III. Capital formation involves the acquisition of equipment and structures (neglecting inventories as not relevant here). Protection of equipment producing industries is favorable to allocation of resources to investment goods industries, while protection accorded to inputs into construction is unfavorable. Therefore, high rates in group II and low rates in group III would indicate a bias in favor of expansion of the investment goods industries, and vice versa.

The median industry is 'Cartons, cardboards, boxes,' which is in group IV—intermediate goods. Eight others in that group have rates below the median, while only three have rates above. In contrast, eighteen of the twenty-four industries in group V—import-substitute consumption goods—have rates above the median. All nine export industries have rates below the median and eight of them have negative rates. The exception is sugar which is protected by the U.S. quota and restrictions on imports.

All four capital goods industries have rates below the median, while seven of nine construction input industries have rates above the median. Consequently there is a dual bias against the investment goods industries.

Unweighted averages of rates for each group show the same pattern of bias:

Group	*Average Rate*
Exports	— .14
Capital goods	.06
Inputs into construction	.56
Intermediate goods	.49
Import-substitute consumption goods	.83

Thus the bias appears to follow the pattern we should expect from a naive import substitution strategy. Consumption goods industries are strongly favored over intermediate goods and capital goods industries. Moreover, the bias is strongly in favour of luxury goods industries like autos, pèrfumes and cosmetics, cigarettes, candy and chocolate products, and radio and TV sets. On the other hand, not all of the highest rate industries are luxury industries. In any case, we can conclude that the system of protection is biased towards industries that are less essential on growth criteria, and probably also on consumption criteria, and that the overall extent of distortion in resource allocation is probably very great.

The present system of protection has been in effect, of course, only since decontrol. Most commentators refer to the period of exchange control during the 1950's as the period of import restriction leading to industrialization. Decontrol is assumed to have involved a liberalization of import restriction. This is, no doubt, correct, although many duties have been raised since decontrol. The implication is, then, that protection was overall greater in the 1950's, so that the bias against exports was even more pronounced. Moreover it is the heavily import dependent industries that suffered most from decontrol and, by implication, were more strongly favored under exchange controls. These tend to be the high rate industries because of the relatively low value added (in world prices) at the finishing stages of production. Thus, it is possible that the system of protection was more distorted (in the same pattern), as well as more protective overall.

If this pattern of protection was in existence during the period of rapid advance in manufacturing in the 1950's, we should expect to see some of its influence on trends in international trade and industry. No attempt will be made here to set forth a statistical picture of the industrialization and trade of that period. A casual observation of the readily available data suggests, however, that the growth of manufacturing was mainly concentrated in consumption goods industries and that capital goods and materials for consumption goods industries rose sharply in importance in the import bill, at the expense of manufactured consumption goods. Exports of manufactures failed to develop to any significant extent, despite rapid increases in production. Finally, the pace of industrial growth retarded markedly in the second half of the period. This is seen in Table II which gives the year-to-year percentage changes in the industrial production index of the Central Bank. (There is good reason to believe that this index has increasingly understated the gains in industrial production, so that the retardation may have been less striking than Table II indicates.)

TABLE II[18]

PERCENTAGE CHANGES IN INDUSTRIAL PRODUCTION

Year	*% Change from Previous Year*
1950	20.7
1951	17.3
1952	5.3
1953	13.0
1954	12.4
1955	12.6
1956	15.7
1957	8.0
1958	7.7
1959	8.3
1960	3.2
1961	6.6
1962	5.7
1963	6.4
1964	8.3
1965	2.0

It appears, then, that the major trends in manufacturing and trade roughly correspond to what one would expect from an import restriction bias in industrialization strategy, and are consistent with the pattern of incentives implied by the structure of protection that developed.

18 Central Bank of the Philippines, *Statistical Bulletin* (March 1966), p. 247.

Technical Inefficiency

A relatively high total rate of protection for an industry may, of course, imply high factor incomes or relative inefficiency, or both. I have no evidence to present on this point, but it seems to me that for several reasons we might expect relative inefficiency to be widespread among those industries with the highest total rates of protection. First, a system of protection of the kind under discussion will inevitably include under its umbrella all kinds of comparatively disadvantageous industries. Second, for others (including 'infant industries'), the protection against foreign competition permits monopolistic or oligopolistic market positions that take the edge off the drive for efficiency and technical progress. Third, the dispersion of resources in horizontally-balanced industrial growth sacrifices potential gains from economies of scale and the stimulus to innovations and learning from faster concentrated growth.

It is possible, on the other hand, that some of these highly protected industries have a real comparative advantage and are reasonably efficient, so that the protection permits high factor incomes. The factor-price disequilibrium case fits here. The protection may permit the industry to pay the required excess above labor's opportunity cost that the market dictates. We have seen above, however, that this is no more than a third-best sort of argument for protection.

Finally, however, the high degree of protection may mean high profits, and high profits suggest the possibility of a saving-reinvestment growth mechanism. This brings us, then, to the effects on saving of an import-substitution bias in development strategy.

The Saving Gap[19]

I have argued above (page 309) that to carry an import substitution strategy successfully beyond the first stage requires either breaking into the export market or extending production backward to materials, intermediate goods, and equipment. Continuing expansion of finished consumption goods for the domestic market, while

19 The following discussion owes much to analyses of the Pakistan and Indian experiences. See A. R. Khan, 'Import Substitution, Consumption Liberalization and Export Expansion,' and my 'Industrialization in Pakistan: A Case of Frustrated Take-Off?,' both in *Pakistan Development Review* (Summer 1963). For India, an unpublished paper by V. V. Desai of the University of Bombay, entitled 'Import Substitution, Growth of Consumer Goods Industries and Economic Development' was particularly useful.

perfectly compatible with a non-accumulation economy (wherein the growth of income occurs exogenously), can permit growth in capital accumulation (other than accumulation of stocks) only so long as it reduces consumption goods imports.[20] When the first stage is completed, of course, this is no longer possible. But even during the first stage there is a very real possibility that a bias toward the production of consumption goods balanced in relation to domestic demand will tend to erode the constraints on consumption that are needed to permit accelerating growth.

To see how this might be so, consider first the identity

$$C_d + I_d + E_d = C_m + C_d + S \qquad (7)$$

where C_d, I_d, and E_d are value added in domestic production for consumption, investment, and exports. S is domestic saving and C_m is the imported component of consumption. The left-hand side represents the national product and the right-hand side, the disposal of national income.

A rise in any component of the left-hand side implies an equal rise in saving (and investment—domestic or foreign) if consumption does not rise. Thus a case of pure import substitution (the rise in C_d being matched precisely by a fall in C_m) increases saving exactly as does a rise in the production of capital goods or exports when consumption is constant. The analysis can be extended to the more general case in which consumption rises by some proportion of the rise in national product, and the conclusion is the same. The change in saving associated with a rise in output depends on the change in consumption regardless of the kind of goods the output increase embodies.

The key question is, then, how the marginal consumption rate might be affected by alternative patterns of investment leading to different mixes of output increase. This is usually analyzed in terms of the associated sectoral income increases and saving propensities, but I propose to look at it briefly from the other side—to consider how the supply mix itself can affect consumption and saving.

Consider the following simple model of a closed economy.

$$\Delta Y = kI \qquad \text{(i)}$$
$$\Delta S = s\Delta Y \qquad \text{(ii)}$$

20 Of course rising capital imports could permit growing capital accumulation without any rise in domestic saving. I am assuming here, however, that some rise in domestic saving is essential.

$$\Delta I = kaI \qquad \text{(iii)}$$
$$\Delta S = \Delta I \qquad \text{(iv)}$$

Y is national product, I is investment, S is saving, s is the marginal propensity to save, k is the incremental output-capital ratio (identical for all sectors of the economy), and a is the proportion of investment allocated to the investment goods sector.

Given ΔY (the growth target) and the investment coefficient, k, these four equations determine I, ΔS, ΔI and either s or a if the other is given. If both are given the system is overdetermined. That is, consistency is required between the marginal saving rate and the proportion of investment allocated to the investment goods sector. This leaves open the question of how consistency is achieved, however. If saving propensities govern, a must adjust to s—the allocation of investment must respond to the pattern of final demand. Alternatively, however, marginal saving could be constrained by the output mix of consumption and investment goods as determined by the investment allocation—i.e., by a. It is this latter possibility that I want to explore in the context of an import substitution strategy.

To do this we must introduce international trade into the model. This can be done most simply by assuming that any increase in exports or substitution of domestic production for imports going into consumption will result automatically in investment via import of equipment with the foreign exchange earned or saved. Allocation of investment to sectors producing for export or import substitution will then raise the rate of capital accumulation exactly as will investment in the capital goods sector, and a can refer to the proportion of investment going to these sectors taken together.

Marginal saving depends, then, on a—the allocation of investment to capital goods production, to production of exports, and to import substitution. But the import substitution strategy described above is strongly biased via the system of protection against both exports and the production of capital goods. And within the category of import substitution it is biased against investment in the production of materials and parts. A high a must depend mainly then on (1) the rapid expansion of capacity to add value at the finishing stages of consumption goods production, and (2) the use of this capacity to reduce the import bill rather than to supply an expanding home consumption.

At first these conditions may easily be met as import restriction serves not only as a balance of payments control, but also as a principal constraint on consumption. As domestic capacity expands rapidly in response to high rates of protection, however, two things happen. First, a kind of automatic decontrol of consumption takes place as the proportion of consumption constrained by import controls declines. This is partly due to the increase availability of goods and disappearance of scarcity premiums, and partly due to the shift in income distribution from government (customs duties) and profits of importers to income recipients in the new industries.

At the same time the expansion of consumption goods industries creates a rapidly growing demand for imports of materials, parts, and equipment. These two developments shift the focus of control over consumption to taxes and imports of inputs for the new industries. If control over the latter is tightened there arises the phenomenon of excess capacity due to scarcity of imported supplies. While this should be attributed to the misallocation of investment resulting from biases in the system of protection—too much capacity installed to produce consumption goods and too little to produce materials, parts, and equipment, the pressures are inevitably on the side of permitting the necessary imports. For the availability of excess capacity always promises a cheap way to get an increase in production. Since the increased production will be consumption goods, however, this also precludes the imposition of new taxes to offset the steady erosion of control over consumption. The result is what Khan has called 'consumption liberalization.'[21]

Consumption liberalization occurs, in a static context, when the rise in domestic output of consumption goods is not fully matched by a decline in imports—i.e., in equation (7) (above), when the rise in C_d exceeds the fall in C_m with a corresponding diminished effect on saving. In a dynamic context we must expect consumption to grow with growing output and the question of whether an increase in production serves to replace imports or liberalize consumption is a more complex one.

Khan's solution[22] was to calculate a 'normal' increase in consumption of a good based on population growth, per capita income increase, the planned marginal saving rate, and an expenditure elasticity of demand. Any increase in supply from production plus imports that was not exported or absorbed by normal consumption

21 Khan, *op. cit.*, p. 209. 22 *Ibid.*, pp. 208-212.

was defined as consumption liberalization. He then attempted to measure this over the period of 1951/52 to 1959/60 for four of Pakistan's important import substitution industries: cotton cloth, sugar, cigarettes, and paper. In each case he found that a very high proportion of the output increase resulted in consumption liberalization—from almost 50 per cent in cotton cloth to over 100 per cent in paper.

Desai, in a similar study for India, found that consumption per capita of nine categories of 'less-essential' consumption goods increased in the period of protection-induced import substitution (1950's and 1960's) almost twice as much as would have been estimated from an income elasticity derived from a pre-protection base period (1948/49-1953/54).[23]

These results are at least consistent with the hypothesis that a part of the explanation for the low saving rates in India and Pakistan during this period (despite rapid industrialization) was the bias toward consumption goods production for the home market.[24] On the other hand, because of shifts in income distribution and in the proportions of rural and urban populations, because of the existence of controls and other abnormal influences affecting consumption, and finally because of the general complexity of the relation between the consumption of particular goods and aggregate consumption, one cannot be sure how important this was.[25]

Nevertheless, on theoretical grounds a strong case can be made against an import substitution bias in development strategy because of its likely effect on saving. First, the various aspects of economic and technical inefficiency discussed above mean lower incomes, and especially lower profits, with obvious implications for saving. Second, the bias toward producing goods that can be consumed and against goods that cannot (e.g., capital goods and some exports) is likely to make political control of consumption more

23 Desai, *op. cit.* The nine categories are automobiles, electric fans, radios, air-conditioners and refrigerators, motor cycles and scooters, rayons, sewing machines, bicycles and pharmaceuticals.

24 A case could be made for liberalizing the consumption of certain goods (via price or other inducements) to take advantage of economies of scale or other advantages of concentration. This 'consumption distortion' has merit particularly if the favored goods are essential mass consumption goods. To avoid a general consumption rise, however, taxes would have to be raised elsewhere.

25 The use of cross-section expenditure elasticities of demand to estimate 'normal' consumption may also be open to criticism. In the case at hand, however, the change in per capita income was so slight that their influence on the results was negligible.

difficult.[26] Finally, at some points there is an absolute necessity to move into exports or to the earlier stages of production, or both; and the longer it is postponed and the more biased against it is the system of protection, the more likely is the economy to find itself in the kind of trap that leads to consumption liberalization.

II

The conclusion I reach from this critique of an industrialization strategy biased toward import substitution is that it does not promise an easy path around the difficulties facing less developed countries. This is not a happy conclusion for the difficulties are very great and the alternatives to an import substitution strategy are not very promising either.

In any case, for what they are worth the policy implications, as they pertain to a single country, have more or less emerged in the course of the critique itself. They are, in general, to avoid the kind of excessive and distorted protection that biases growth toward a horizontal balance of consumption goods production for the domestic market, penalizing both exports and backward-linkage import substitution. The costs of such a policy go beyond simple resource misallocation to adverse effects on technical efficiency, innovations and saving. More emphasis on vertical balance would seem to be essential to success in industrial growth beyond the first stage of import substitution.

This does not mean that policies should be biased against import substitution. What is needed rather are rational choices, both between import substitution and export expansion and among various potential import substitution industries. Especially important in helping the economy (public or private) to make rational choices in this area is to find some means of correcting the undervaluation of foreign exchange. Despite its obvious advantages, however, this is the kind of advice that will be widely ignored. Let me suggest two reasons why this is so, only one to which I have any kind of an answer.

First is the terms of trade disadvantage from devaluation when

26 This has now become officially recognized in Pakistan. See the Preface to the Pakistan Third Five-Year Plan (Karachi, Government of Pakistan, March 1965), p. viii.

world demand elasticities are significantly below infinity for important categories of exports. Insofar as these are primary commodities a particular country will normally count only a few in this category and can easily isolate them from the effects of the devaluation if international price agreements are beyond reach. If, however, new manufactured exports also face relatively low demand elasticities because of 'reactive protectionism' in established manufacturing countries, there is a case for maintaining 'overvalued' currencies even though this further penalizes such exports. How real is this case is difficult to estimate. Pakistan has discovered that a *de facto* partial devaluation by means of an export bonus scheme has elicited a very strong response from non-traditional exports. Whether what is true for one would be true for all less developed countries it is not possible for me to judge, however.

In some Latin American countries, apparently, another inhibition against devaluation is an automatic anticipation of an ensuing inflation that hastens it and renders the devaluation almost immediately ineffective.[27] So far as I can judge, economics is not able to teach us how to deal very effectively with social-psychological behavior of this sort. It might be of interest in passing to note, however, that the export bonus scheme was not generally recognized in Pakistan as a form of devaluation until economists began explaining it in these terms.

Beyond the difficulties of implementing exchange rate policy, however, lie more fundamental issues around which doubts will certainly arise. For what the above critique may appear to do is to reverse the classic argument of Nurkse in his lectures on 'Patterns of Trade and Development.'[28] There it was the difficulties faced by both traditional and new exports that dictated the option for balanced growth in relation to domestic demand. If the latter has all of the disadvantages catalogued above, however, the last escape route from economic stagnation would seem to have been closed off.

It is only fair to remind ourselves that Nurkse's view of an import substitution strategy bore little resemblance to that pictured above. He emphasized especially the prime importance of rising agricultural productivity in balanced growth and considered the

27 John B. Sheahan, 'Imports, Investment, and Growth: Colombian Experience Since 1950,' (mimeographed).

28 Ragnar Nurkse, *Equilibrium and Growth in the World Economy*, Haberler and Stern [eds.], (Harvard, 1961), pp. 282-324.

inherent difficulties in carrying through an agricultural revolution to be the reason that 'industrialization for domestic markets appears as a much more formidable task.'[29]

In addition he argued that: 'When industrialization for the home market has taken root, it becomes easier to increase exports of manufactured goods to the more advanced economies.'[30] It follows, I think, that he would have opposed measures that unnecessarily penalize such exports. Nevertheless, he was not sanguine about their prospects and I confess that I somewhat share his view.

The reason is that the distorted pattern of protection, described above, that tends to magnify greatly the total rate of protection for industries adding the final values to products is not a phenomenon peculiar to less developed countries. It is rather the rule for most countries.[31] Thus there is a strong general bias in the world against trade in finished manufactures—the end of the production line at which less developed countries typically start.

But Nurkse suggested another escape route—one which has by now achieved a popularity in principle far beyond its realization in practice. He wrote: 'Manufacturing for home markets in the less developed countries must include also production in these countries for export to *each other's markets*.'[32] This is clearly one way of resolving the Nurkse dilemma. What would appear to each individual country as new exports would represent a more rational pattern of import substitution for the group of countries. More stress on vertical balance within each country would be combined with some horizontal balance for the group.

Whether this is a first-best or second-best solution to the trade problems of developing countries is a question that I won't attempt to answer here. Let me simply register my opinion that the less developed countries trade (proportionally) more with the developed countries and (proportionally) less with each other than is optimal from their standpoint. I hope to elaborate this point at some future date.

29 *Ibid.*, p. 315.
30 *Ibid.*, p. 320.
31 Harry G. Johnson, 'The Theory of Tariff Structure, with Special Reference to World Trade and Development,' *Etudes et Travaux de l'Institut universitaire de hautes Etudes internationales de Geneve*, Vol. IV (1965), pp. 17-18.
32 Nurkse, *op. cit.*, p. 318 (Italics are Nurkse's).

APPENDIX

ESTIMATION OF THE TOTAL RATE OF PROTECTION

1. The total rate of protection is defined as the proportion by which actual value added could exceed free trade value added when the partial rates of protection of both outputs and inputs are evaluated at the margin of competition with foreign supply. Foreign supply is assumed to be infinitely elastic and its price is the landed cost of imports.

2. Let W represent actual value added under protection and V, the value added that would be allowed by world prices under free trade. Then $W - V$ is the amount by which the system of protection permits greater value added.

3. $W - V$ could be put as a proportion to either V or W.

$$\text{Let } T = \frac{W - V}{V} \text{ and } U = \frac{W - V}{W}$$

$$\text{Then } T = \frac{U}{1 - U} \text{ and } U = \frac{T}{T + 1}$$

4. If we start with world prices we could find T_i in the following way:

$$T_i = \frac{W_i}{V_i} - 1$$

$$= \frac{Y_i(1 + t_i) - \sum_j a_{ji} Y_i(1 + t_j)}{V_i} - 1$$

$$= \frac{Y_i + t_i Y_i - \sum_j a_{ji} Y_i - \sum_j a_{ji} Y_i t_j}{V_i} - 1$$

$$= \frac{V_i + t_i Y_i - \sum_j a_j \; Y_i t_j}{V_i} - 1$$

$$= \frac{t_i - \sum_i a_{ji} \; Y_i t_j}{V_i / Y_i}$$

where a_{ji} represents the input coefficients as they would be measured if world prices prevailed. The t's represent partial rates of protection applying to the outputs of particular industries. Y_i is output at world prices.

5. But the data we usually have is for the input coefficients as measured with actual prices. Since these are

$$\frac{I_j(1+t_j)}{Y_i(1+t_i)} \quad \text{while}$$

$$a_{ji} = \frac{I_j}{Y_i} \text{ (where } I_j \text{ is an intermediate input valued at world prices)}$$

the measured input coefficients

$$c_{ji} = a_{ji}\,\frac{1+t_j}{1+t_i}$$

6. T can also be derived from actual prices and measured coefficients

$$T_i = \frac{W_i - V_i}{V_i} = \frac{W_i}{V_i} - 1 = \frac{W_i/X_i}{V_i/X_i} - 1$$

$$= \frac{W_i/X_i}{\dfrac{1}{1+t_i} - \sum_j \dfrac{c_{ji}}{1+tt}} - 1$$

Where $X_i = Y_i(1+t_i)$.

7. The T measure has some advantages—e.g., if all goods are protected at rate t, $t = T$ for all. It has one important disadvantage, however. If V is negative T cannot be measured. For this reason we need another measure of the total rate of protection.

$$U_i = \frac{W_i - V_i}{W_i} = 1 - \frac{V_i}{W_i} = 1 - \frac{V_i/X_i}{W_i/X_i}$$

$$= 1 - \frac{\dfrac{1}{1+t_i} - \sum_j - \dfrac{c_{ji}}{1+t_j}}{W_i/X_i}$$

8. The t's are partial rates of protection on the outputs of particular industries. They include tariffs plus other indirect taxes on foreign goods. For goods that are imported an indirect tax is an offset while one on its domestic suppliers is ignored, since both are assumed to be absorbed, unless matched by a tax on the foreign supply.

Hence $t_i = t'_i + f'_i - d_i$ while

$t_j = t'_j + f_j$

where t' refers to the tariff rate and d and f are indirect tax rates on goods of domestic and foreign origin, respectively.

9. If a good is exported we assume that $t_i = 0$ and that $t_j = d_j$ since taxes on foreign products are irrelevant while domestic taxes are passed on to the buyer.

10. Moreover, if a good is neither exported nor imported (in any substantial volume), t_i could range from 0 to $(t'_i + f_i - d_i)$ and t_j from d_j to $(t'_j + f_j)$.

11. The standard assumption is that domestic price = world price $(1 + t)$ for any good. If domestic price is greater than this, the presumption is that either a scarcity premium has arisen from import restriction, or some element of t has been left out or mis-estimated.

    If domestic price is less than this, either domestic competition has prevented the industry from taking full advantage of protection from foreign competition or it is efficient enough even with monopoly pricing not to need it (assuming t has not been mis-estimated).

12. It has been assumed above that foreign and domestic goods are of the same quality. Often, however the latter is priced at a discount for quality—or imagined quality—reasons. In this case the value derived for the world price is a hypothetical one that would be appropriate to like quality world goods if they existed; and what is protected is inferior quality rather than high price. But what if the discount for the domestic product is not justified by quality differences?

    What if, for example, the foreigner is able to sell in some volume only because a certain class of people place snob value on foreign goods? It could be argued that the industry is being 'protected' from a bias against domestic products, but the welfare implications are quite different in this case.

13. Values for U greater than unity imply negative value added in world prices. While this may reflect inaccurate estimates of the relevant variables, there are other possibilities that could explain such a result:

    (1) Higher transport costs for the parts shipped separately than for the finished product (though more often the reverse would probably be true).

    (2) Monopoly power of the foreign supplier of parts, especially where the investment is foreign and the activity is simply assembing (Why shouldn't a part of the gain from protection be taken in

the form of higher prices and profits for the home branch of the firm?)

(3) Failure to use wastes, scrap, etc. to the same extent as in advanced countries.

(4) Higher incidence of theft, breakage, etc.

(5) Higher relative costs of non-traded inputs.

While it is unlikely that any one of these by itself could render value added negative, a combination of them might easily do so.

14

THE POLITICAL ECONOMY OF IMPORT-SUBSTITUTING INDUSTRIALIZATION IN LATIN AMERICA

A. O. Hirschman

There is now a new school of thought on Latin America which casts the whole matter into a biblical mold and amounts to transposing the doctrine of original sin onto the social terrain. Here is a summary of this thesis: Latin America, with its evil destiny, was forced into the world capitalist system by the European powers right after Columbus and the Conquest. A great many calamities derive from this historical fact, yet they are small if compared to what happens during the next stage when the Continent is fully inserted into the international order organized by the 'truly' capitalist nations, with Great Britain at the helm. That stage is reached in the nineteenth century after Independence. Subsequently, with export-led growth really taking hold, the evils become even greater and more numerous. But this is not the end of Latin America's 'purgatory in life.' Another phase of expiation and, in a way, of even greater degradation was yet to come. It duly arrived with 'inwardlooking' development and 'dependent' industrialization whose adverse repercussions and insuperable limitations have been described ad infinitum.

Such reasoning makes one wonder whether the first and foremost trouble with Latin America was not perhaps the departure of Columbus from the port of Palos. . . its basic weakness [consists in] the complete failure to understand the contradictory character of every social process.

—Aníbal Pinto Santa Cruz

Disenchantment with Industrialization in Latin America

Not long ago, industrialization ranked high among the policy prescriptions which were expected to lead Latin America and other underdeveloped areas out of their state of economic, social, and political backwardness. In the last few years, however, considerable disenchantment with this particular solution of the development problem has set in. The present paper will survey some characteristics of 'import-substituting industrialization' (ISI) in an attempt to appraise its evolution and the principal difficulties it has encountered. Some purely economic aspects of the problem will be discussed, but particular attention has been directed to interrelations with social and political life. The ease with which such interrelations could be suggested—mostly in the form of tentative and untested hypotheses—indicates serious neglect by social scientists of a fertile terrain.

To set the stage for our inquiry it is useful to illustrate, through quotes from Latin America's most prominent economists, the change in attitude toward industrialization as a cure of the area's ills. In his well-known 'manifesto' of 1949 Raúl Prebisch said:

> Formerly, before the great depression, development in the Latin-American countries was stimulated from abroad by the constant increase of exports. There is no reason to suppose, at least at present, that this will again occur to the same extent, except under very exceptional circumstances. These countries no longer have an alternative between vigorous growth along those lines and internal expansion through industrialization. Industrialization has become the most important means of expansion.[1]

Thirteen years later, Prebisch wrote another basic paper on Latin America, in a sense his farewell message to his Latin American friends upon assuming his new post as Secretary-General of the United Nations Conference on Trade and Development. Here industrialization is presented in a rather different light:

> An industrial structure virtually isolated from the outside world thus grew up in our countries.... The criterion by which the choice was determined was based not on considerations of economic expediency, but on immediate feasibility, whatever the cost of production...tariffs have been carried to such a pitch that they are undoubtedly—on an average—the highest in the world. It is not uncommon to find tariff duties of over 500 per cent.
>
> As is well known, the proliferation of industries of every kind in a closed market has deprived the Latin American countries of the advantages of specialization and economies of scale, and

1 *The Economic Development of Latin America and Its Principal Problems* (New York: United Nations, 1950), p. 6. See chap. 13 for a more detailed account of the Prebisch and ECLA doctrines.

owing to the protection afforded by excessive tariff duties and restrictions, a healthy form of internal competition has failed to develop, to the detriment of efficient production.[2]

If we take a look at the writings of Celso Furtado, the shift in the climate of opinion stands out even more starkly. In 1960, after a decade or more of rapid industrial advance, Furtado celebrated the resulting 'transfer of decision centers' from abroad to Brazil in almost lyrical terms:

> By now the Brazilian economy could count on its own dynamic element: industrial investments supported by the internal market. Growth quickly became two-dimensional. Each new impulse forward would mean an increasing structural diversification, higher productivity levels, a larger mass of resources for investment, a quicker expansion of the internal market, and the possibility of such impulses being permanently surpassed.[3]

Only six years later, after Brazil had suffered a series of political and economic setbacks, a disillusioned Furtado wrote:

> In Latin America...there is a general consciousness of living through a period of decline.... The phase of 'easy' development, through increasing exports of primary products *or through import substitution* has everywhere been exhausted.[4]

Considering these two pairs of quotes one could easily conclude that we have here an instance of the acceleration of history. The phase of export-propelled growth (*crecimiento hacia afuera*) in Latin America lasted roughly from the middle of the nineteenth century until the Great Depression; and it took another twenty years, from 1929 to the Prebisch manifesto of 1949, before the end of export-propelled growth became official Latin American doctrine. Then came the next phase of Latin American growth, *crecimiento hacia adentro* or growth via the domestic market. It gathered strength during the Depression and World War II, flour-

2 *Towards a Dynamic Development Policy for Latin America* (New York: United Nations, 1963), p. 71.

3 Celso Furtado, 'The Brazilian Economy in the Middle of the Twentieth Century,' mimeographed (Israel: Industrial Conference on Science in the Advancement of New States, 1960), p. 5. See also chap. 13, p. 303.

4 'U.S. Hegemony and the Future of Latin America,' *The World Today* 22 (September 1966), p. 375 (my italics). Detailed critiques of the ISI process in Latin America can be found in two influential articles: Maria de Conceicão Tavares, 'The Growth and Decline of Import Substitution in Brazil,' and Santiago Macario, 'Protectionism and Industrialization in Latin America,' both in *Economic Bulletin for Latin America* 9 (March 1964), pp. 1-61 and 62-102.

ished briefly in both theory and practice during the fifties and was pronounced either dead or a dud in the sixties. It looks, therefore, as though the acceleration of technical progress in the developed countries were matched in the underdeveloped ones by an increasingly rapid accumulation of failures in growth experiences!

As will be seen, there may be considerable exaggeration in the announced failure of import-substituting industrialization just as, in spite of the supposed demise of export-propelled growth, Venezuela, Ecuador, Peru, and Central America achieved notable economic gains in the two postwar decades through rapidly growing exports of petroleum, bananas, fishmeal, and cotton, respectively. While *fracasomania,* or the insistence on having experienced yet another failure, certainly has its share in the severity of the recent judgments on industrialization, the widespread criticism of ISI—in Pakistan and India very similar problems are being discussed—indicates that there is real substance to the concern that is being expressed. But the rapidity of the reversal in the climate of opinion makes one rather suspect that ISI had, from its very onset, both positive and negative aspects, with the latter simply coming into view a few years after the former. Our inquiry will therefore start out with a brief survey of the principal characteristics which set off ISI from other types of industrialization.

Four Impulses of Import-Substituting Industrialization (ISI)

Wars and depressions have historically no doubt been most important in bringing industries to countries of the 'periphery' which up to then had firmly remained in the nonindustrial category. The crucial role of the two world wars and of the Great Depression in undermining acceptance of traditional ideas about the international division of labor between advanced and backward countries is well known.[5] But industrialization has not only been the response to sudden deprivation of imports; it has taken place

5 Apparently even earlier crises had positive effects on industrial growth in Latin America. The following quote is instructive: 'There is no ill wind that does not blow some good . . . the crisis the country is going through is tremendous—and yet this is a perfect wind for national industry. Many of our industries have had a more or less vigorous protection through customs duties. But all of this would not have been enough had it not been for the crisis of 1875 which gave the impulse to industry and for that of 1890 which strengthened and diffused it.' Quoted from *El Nacional* in Adolfo Dorfman, *Desarrollo industrial en la Argentina* (Rosario, 1941), p. 11 (my translation).

in many erstwhile nonindustrial countries as a result of the gradual expansion of an economy that grows along the export-propelled path. As incomes and markets expand in such a country and some thresholds at which domestic production becomes profitable are crossed, industries come into being without the need of external shocks or governmental intervention—a process I have described as 'import-swallowing'[6] and which has been perhaps more aptly termed industrialization through 'final demand linkage,' as distinct from the continuation of the process via backward and forward linkage effects.[7] Gradual import substitution in response to the growth of domestic markets accounts for the widespread establishment of industries which have substantial locational advantages because of the weightiness of the product (cement, beer) and of those, such as textiles, whose market is large even at low per capita incomes.

Over the past two decades import-substituting industrialization has, of course, no longer been exclusively a matter of natural market forces reacting to either gradual growth of income or to cataclysmic events, such as wars and depressions. It has been undertaken in many countries as a matter of deliberate development policy, carried out no longer just by means of protective duties, but through a wide array of credit and fiscal policy devices, through pressures on foreign importing firms to set up manufacturing operations as well as through direct action: the establishment of state-owned industries or, increasingly, of development corporations or banks which are then entrusted with the promotion of specific ventures.

It is useful to keep in mind these distinct origins of ISI—wars, balance of payments difficulties, growth of the domestic market (as a result of export growth) and official development policy—in focusing on the distinctive characteristics of the process.

Clearly, there is not just one ISI process. An industrialization that takes place in the midst and as a result of export growth has a wholly different *Gestalt* from one that feeds on foreign exchange deprivation. For example, in the latter situation it seems much

[6] Albert O. Hirschman, *The Strategy of Economic Development* (New Haven: Yale University Press, 1958), chap. 7.

[7] See Melville H. Watkins, 'A Staple Theory of Economic Growth,' *Canadian Journal of Economics and Political Science* 29 (May 1963), pp. 141-58; and Richard E. Caves, 'Vent-for-Surplus Models of Trade and Growth' in *Trade, Growth and the Balance of Payments*, Essays in honor of Gottfried Haberler (Chicago: Rand-McNally, 1965), pp. 95-115.

more likely that inflationary developments will accompany the industrialization process than in the former. Or, to proceed to one of the alleged—and often criticized—characteristics of the industrialization process itself, namely its tendency to concentrate on nonessential, luxury-type goods. This tendency to give importance to what is unimportant will be present only when the primary impulse to industrialization arises out of unexpected balance of payments difficulties which are fought routinely by the imposition of quantitative import controls. The controls will aim at permitting continued supply of the more essential goods traditionally imported at the cost of shutting out nonessentials and will thus cause domestic production of the latter to become especially profitable.

It is easy, however, to make too much of this situation. Of the four motive forces behind ISI—balance of payments difficulties, wars, gradual growth of income, and deliberate development policy—only the first leads to a bias in favor of nonessential industries. The last, deliberate development policy, is likely to produce exactly the opposite bias; and the remaining two causes are neutral with respect to the luxury character of the industry. Wars cause interruption of, or hazards for, all international commodity flows, essential or nonessential, and therefore provide a general unbiased stimulus to domestic production of previously imported goods. The same is true for the stimulus emanating from the gradual growth of markets. It seems likely, therefore, that the role of nonessential goods within the total ISI process has been exaggerated by the 'new' critics who, in stressing this role, sound almost like the old-line Latin American laissez faire advocates who were forever inveighing against the introduction of 'exotic' industries into the countries.

Characteristics of the Initial Phase of ISI

Industrialization by Tightly Separated Stages

No matter what its original impulse, ISI starts predominantly with the manufacture of finished consumer goods that were previously imported and then moves on, more or less rapidly and successfully, to the 'higher stages' of manufacture, that is, to intermediate goods and machinery, through backward linkage effects. The process can and does start here and there with capital or even intermediate goods insofar as such goods are imported prior to any industrialization because they are needed in connection with agricultural or transportation activities. Machetes, coffee hulling machines, trucks and fertilizers are examples. In the textile industry, the crushing superiority of machine spinning over hand spinning, combined with a lesser advantage of machinery in weaving, has made sometimes for the installation of spinning mills ahead of weaving mills, especially in countries where a strong handweaving tradition had not been previously destroyed by textile imports from the industrial leaders.

But the bulk of new industries are in the consumer goods sector and as they are undertaken in accordance with known processes, on the basis of imported inputs and machines, industrialization via import substitution becomes a *highly sequential*, or *tightly staged*, affair. Herein lies perhaps its principal difference from industrialization in the advanced countries. This aspect is so familiar and seemingly inevitable that it has not received quite the attention it deserves. It is the basic reason for which the ISI process is far smoother, less disruptive, but also far less learning intensive than had been the case for industrialization in Europe, North America, and Japan.

This is not the place for renewing the discussion over the advantages or drawbacks of an early or late start in industrialization. Suffice it to point out, however, that those who have stressed the advantages of a late start have often had in mind the ability of newcomers to jump with both feet into a newly emerging dynamic industrial sector (as Germany did with chemicals) instead of remaining bogged down in sectors that had long passed their prime (as England in textiles and railways construction). But the 'late latecomers' with whom we are concerned here are not apt to jump in this fashion. Industrialization is here at first wholly a matter of imitation and importation of tried and tested processes. Consider by way of contrast the following description of the establishment of new industries in advanced countries:

> Young industries are often strangers to the established economic system. They require new kinds or qualities of materials and hence make their own; they must overcome technical problems in the use of their products and cannot wait for potential users to overcome them; they must persuade customers to abandon other commodities and find

specialized merchants to undertake the task. These young industries must design their specialized equipment and often manufacture it.[8]

Not much of this travail occurs when a new industry is introduced intio the 'late late' starting countries. It is in this connection that one must be on guard against studies purporting to show that the history of industrialization is substantially the same in all countries, working its way from light consumer goods industries, to heavy and capital goods industries, and eventually to consumer durables. The apparently similar pattern of the earlicr and 'late late' industrializers in this respect conceals an essential qualitative difference. Even when the earlier industrializers were predominantly in the light consumer goods stage (from the point of view of labor force or value added), they were already producing their own capital goods, if only by artisan methods. As Marx wrote: 'There were mules and steam-engines before there were any laborers whose exclusive occupation it was to make mules and steam-engines; just as men wore clothes before there were tailors.'[9] But the 'late late' industrializers will import, rather than make, their clothes until such time as they are able to set up a tailor in business all by himself. This situation forecloses, of course, for a considerable time any fundamental adaptation of technology to the characteristic of the importing countries, such as the relative abundance of labor in relation to capital. Whether and to what extent such an adaptation is desirable is an idle question under these circumstances; given the sequential pattern of industrialization there is remarkably little choice. ISI thus brings in complex technology, but without the sustained technological experimentation and concomitant training in innovation which are characteristic of the pioneer industrial countries.

'Late' vs. *'Late Late' Industrialization*

The 'late late' industrialization sketched so far may be contrasted not only with that of the presently advanced industrial countries in general, but particularly with that of the so-called latecomers among

8 George Stigler, 'The Division of Labor is Limited by the Extent of Market,' *Journal of Political Economy* 59 (June 1951), p. 190.

9 *Kapital*, 1 (Vienna-Berlin, 1932), p. 399. This passage and the previous one by Stigler were brought to my attention by Nathan Rosenberg's article 'Capital Goods, Technology and Economic Growth,' *Oxford Economic Papers*, 15 (November 1963), pp. 223-24.

them. The 'late' industrialization of countries like Germany, Italy and Russia has been depicted by Gerschenkron through the following propositions:

1. The more backward a country's economy, the more likely was its industrialization to start discontinuously as a sudden great spurt proceeding at a relatively high rate of growth of manufacturing output.
2. The more backward a country's economy, the more pronounced was the stress in its industrialization on bigness of both plant and enterprise.
3. The more backward a country's economy, the greater was the stress upon producers' goods as against consumers' goods.
4. The more backward a country's economy, the heavier was the pressure upon the levels of consumption of the population.
5. The more backward a country's economy, the greater was the part played by special institutional factors designed to increase the supply of capital to the nascent industries and, in addition, to provide them with less decentralized and better informed entrepreneurial guidance; the more backward the country, the more pronounced was the coerciveness and comprehensiveness of those factors.
6. The more backward a country, the less likely was its agriculture to play any active role by offering to the growing industries the advantages of an expanding industrial market based in turn on the rising productivity of agricultural labor.[10]

Of these six characteristics only the last one applies unconditionally to the 'late late' industrializers. Special institutions designed to supply capital and entrepreneurial guidance (point 5), became important in most of Latin America after the ISI process had already been underway as a result of private, decentralized initiative for a considerable time. As to the remaining four points, almost the opposite could be said to hold for our 'late' latecomers. Their industrialization started with relatively small plants administering 'last touches' to a host of imported inputs, concentrated on consumer rather than producer goods, and often was specifically designed to improve the levels of consumption of populations who were suddenly cut off, as a result of war or balance of payments crises,

10 Alexander Gerschenkron, *Economic Backwardness in Historical Perspective* (Cambridge, Mass.: Harvard University Press, 1962), pp. 343-44.

from imported consumer goods to which they had become accustomed. Even though the rates at which new plants were built and at which their output expanded were often respectable, the process thus lacked some of the essential characteristics of Gerschenkron's 'great spurt.'

As a result, 'late late' industrialization shows little of the inspiring, if convulsive élan that was characteristic of the 'late' industrializers such as Germany, Russia and Japan. This is perhaps the basic reason for the feelings of disappointment experienced by Latin American observers who had looked to industrialization for a thorough transformation and modernization of their societies.

Naturally, the difference between the two types of industrialization must not be overdrawn. At least one experience in Latin America, that of Brazil during the fifties, came fairly close to the picture drawn by Gerschenkron: sustained and rapid progress of steel, chemical and capital goods industries during this decade was here combined with a 'special institutional factor designed to increase supply of capital,' namely inflation, and even with the flowering of a 'developmentalist' (*desenvolvimentista*) ideology.[11] But what looked like the hopeful beginning of a 'Brazilian economic miracle' was thrown into disarray by the political crises and related economic and social setbacks of the sixties. The gloom that pervades the Latin American mood at present stems precisely from the convergence of frustrations over the unexciting character of 'late late' industrialization in most Latin American countries with the despair felt over the stumblings of the one country whose advance had assumed the more inspiring characteristics of the 'great spurt.'

The Sources of Entrepreneurship

A number of important characteristics of 'late late' industrialization remain to be surveyed. What has been said so far permits, first of all, some discussion of the sources of entrepreneurship. As industry is started primarily to substitute imports, those engaged in the foreign trade sector are likely to play a substantial role in the process. This is the reason for the industrial prominence of

11 While not included in the six points cited above, support by a vigorous movement of ideas has been stressed elsewhere by Gerschenkron as a characteristic of 'late' industrialization. See, for example, his *Economic Backwardness*, pp. 22-26. For a survey of developmentalist-nationalist ideas in Brazil during the fifties, see Frank Bonilla, 'A National Ideology for Development: Brazil', in K. H. Silvert, ed., *Expectant Peoples: Nationalism and Development* (New York: Random House, 1963), pp. 232-64.

(a) the former importers of Lebanese, Jewish, Italian, German, etc., origin, and (b) of the large foreign firms intent on maintaining their market and therefore turning from exporters into manufacturers. Once again, however, it is useful to distinguish between an industrialization which is brought underway under conditions of expanding income from exports and one that is ignited by deprivation of previously available imports (due to war or balance of payments troubles). Only in the latter situation are local importers and foreign exporting firms likely to be the main promoters of industrial enterprise. When foreign exchange income is expanding, one may rather expect industrial opportunities to be exploited by indigenous entrepreneurship. Under such conditions, the importing interests are apt to be well satisfied with their lot and activity; industrial development will run clearly counter to their short-run interests, especially when it requires the imposition of even a moderate level of protection. Some evidence in support of our distinction may be cited: in both Brazil and Colombia, coffee booms in the late nineteenth and early twentieth centuries gave rise to periods of industrial expansion led by domestic entrepreneurs who were in no way tied to the importing interests.[12] The latter, on the other hand, were prominent in these and other Latin American countries during the high pressure drives toward import substitution which marked the world wars and the Great Depression.

The importance of foreigners, of minorities or, generaly speaking, of non-elite-status groups in the total industrialization process has on occasion been held responsible for the fact that industrial interests do not wield in Latin America the political influence and social prestige which have been theirs in the older industrial countries. Insofar as the phenomenon is real, it can also be explained by the kind of industries most characteristic of the first phases of import-substituting industrialization: opinions of the owners of soft drink bottling plants or of cosmetic or pharmaceutical industries are unlikely to command as much attention as those of steel and machinery manufacturers. In addition, the industrialists of the leading industrial countries always gained considerable influence by virtue of being exporters; as such they achieved prestige abroad, acquired contacts and gathered information—all accomplishments

12 Warren Dean, 'The Planter as Entrepreneur: The Case of São Paulo,' *The Hispanic American Historical Review* 46 (May 1966), pp. 138-52; Luis Ospina Vásquez, *Industria y protección en Colombia (1810-1930)* (Medellín: E. S. F., 1955), chap. 8.

that were highly prized by their governments.[13] This source of influence is quite unavailable to the import-substituting industrialists who are usually aiming only at supplying the domestic market.[14]

The Exuberant Phase of ISI and Its Political Consequences

A final characteristic of the early phases of import-substituting industrialization is the growth pattern of the newly established industries. It has been suggested that

> output curves in newly established import-substituting industries have tended to be kinked, rising rapidly when exports are being replaced, but flattening out when further growth of demand has been grounded in the growth of domestic income. Profits have also followed this kinked pattern. Thus industries have moved rapidly from high profit and growth to precocious maturity, at which point they fall back to monopolistic quiescence with lower profit rates, a reduced level of investment, and aging plant and equipment.[15]

The extent to which the kinked pattern of output growth is really a fact rather than an inference from the nature of import substitution remains to be established. After all, newly established industries have to overcome initial production and organization problems, they encounter some sales resistance due to preference for the imported product so that the early portion of their sales data may still approximate the logistic curve which has given a good fit for the time shape of the expansion of many industries in the advanced countries.[16]

13 In Germany, for example, social prestige was granted to industrial entrepreneurs only to the extent that they were active in 'fields which made a direct contribution to Germany's economic strength [such as] coal, steel, chemicals, industrial engineering' or that they exploited 'the all-important export markets' (William N. Parker, 'Entrepreneurial Opportunities and Response in the German Economy,' *Explorations in Entrepreneurial History* 7 [October 1954], p. 32).

14 The proposition that the comparative *lack* of political power of the industrialists can be explained by the *lack* of industrial exports becomes perhaps more convincing when one states its positive counterpart: namely that the continuing political influence of the land-owning interests throughout the period of industrialization in Latin America is explained by the continuing almost total dependence of the capacity to import on exports of primary products. This point is made for Brazil in Francisco C. Weffort, 'Estado y masas en el Brasil,' *Revista Latinoamericana de Sociologia* 1 (March 1965), pp. 53-71.

15 David Felix, 'Monetarists, Structuralists and Import-Substituting Industrialization,' in W. Baer and I. Kerstenetzky, eds., *Inflation and Growth in Latin America* (Homewood, Illinois: Irwin, 1964), p. 384. (See p. 276 above.)

16 Simon S. Kuznets, *Secular Movements in Production and Prices* (Boston: Houghton Mifflin, 1930), Arthur F. Burns, *Production Trends in the United States since 1870* (New York: National Bureau of Economic Research, 1934).

Nevertheless, it is probably legitimate to speak of a particularly 'easy' phase of import substitution when the manufacturing process is entirely based on imported materials and machinery while importation of the article is firmly and effectively shut out by controls. Under such conditions, the early experience of the new manufacturers is likely to be most gratifying. It is this phase of import substitution that gives rise to the often noted exuberance and boom atmosphere during which demand is easily overestimated. In any event, low duties or preferential exchange rates for machinery imports make for lavish orders. As a result, the new industry is likely to find itself saddled with excess capacity as soon as it reaches the kink.[17]

It is tempting to speculate about the psychological-political consequences of this pattern of industrialization. Progressive Latin Americans had long hoped that industry would introduce new, much-needed disciplines into the behavior of their governments. The very nature of industrial operations—their precision, the need for exact timing, punctuality, reliability, predictability and all-around rationality—was expected to infuse these same qualities into policy making and perhaps even into the political process itself. This sort of inference was based on the nature—or supposed nature—of industrial operations at the plant level. It disregarded, however, the larger financial and economic aspects of the process which had, of course, a much more direct and determining impact on politics. Thus the ease with which new industries were installed in spite of dire warnings and often in the midst of war and depression, the rapid growth they experienced and the handsome profits they realized during the first phases made import-substituting industry appear as a new incarnation of some primary product that would suddenly

17 Even if expansion plans of competing firms are known all around and there is no excessive optimism, demand tends to be overestimated for two special reasons: with protection the price of the domestically produced product is going to be higer than that of the imported one; and market studies based on import statistics often overestimate the domestic market for the new domestic industry also because the statistics usually include a fair volume of specialty products which the domestic industry is unable to supply. In the case of intermediate products, however, demand may be *under*estimated for an important reason: by looking primarily at the volume of imports of such products as an indication of the room for substitution, the analyst would overlook opportunities that arise as import substitution is undertaken with respect to products which use the intermediate good as an input. See Samuel A. Morley and Gordon W. Smith, 'On the Measurement of Import Substitution,' *American Economic Review* 60 (September 1970), pp. 728-35.

erupt with an old-fashioned world market boom. Little wonder, then, that the hoped for achievement of rationality in economic policy making and in the political process in general failed to occur. On the contrary, the 'exuberant' phase of import substitution was accompanied by flamboyant public policies which badly overestimated the tolerance of the economy for a variety of ventures, be they income redistribution by fiat, the building of a new capital, or other extravaganzas. Here we can do no more than touch upon these matters; but it may be conjectured that in their very different ways, Perón, Kubitschek, Rojas Pinilla, and Pérez Jiménez could all be considered victims of the delusions of economic invulnerability fostered by the surprising early successes and rapid penetration of industry into a supposedly hostile environment.

The Alleged Exhaustion of Import Substitution

Then, suddenly, the honeymoon was over and the recriminations began. Import-substituting industrialization was officially added, as we have seen, to the long list of certified *fracasos* in Latin American policy making. We shall now attempt to sort out and evaluate some of the elements in this reversal of opinion.

Four principal accusations have been leveled against the industrialization process as it has appeared in Latin America:

1. Import-substituting industrialization is apt to get 'stuck' after its first successes, due to the 'exhaustion of easy import substitution opportunities'; it leaves the economy with a few relatively high-cost industrial establishments, and with a far more vulnerable balance of payments since imports consist now of semi-finished materials, spare parts and machinery indispensably required for maintaining and increasing production and employment.
2. Import-substituting industry is affected by seemingly congenital inability to move into export markets.
3. The new industries are making an inadequate contribution to the solution of the unemployment problem.
4. The new industries often tend to be established as branch plants and subsidiaries of foreign firms and hereby foster a new type of 'dependency' for Latin America.

In the following we shall concentrate on the first two critiques; the other two cannot be adequately discussed within the limits of the present essay.

A Naive and a Seminaive Exhaustion Model

The argument on ISI getting stuck is put forward in several forms. Most frequently and crudely, the assertion is made that the process faces 'exhaustion' after a certain period during which the 'easy' import substitution opportunities are taken up. Exhaustion evokes the image of a natural resource available in strictly limited quantities which is being depleted; and we must ask now to what extent the image is sensible. One model which could underly the exhaustion concept is an exceedingly simple one: at any one point of time, a country imports commodities $A, B, C, \ldots$; the annual import volumes of these commodities are M_A, M_B, $M_C \ldots$. Next, one assumes the existence of economies of scale such that the minimum economic sizes of plants which are to produce these various goods can be unequivocally defined. If the annual capacities of such plants are designated by P_A, P_B, $P_C, \ldots$ then import substitution opportunities are limited to those products (say, $A, C, E, \ldots$) for which imports (the M's) exceed the minimum economic sizes (the P's).

This would be a truly naive model rationalizing the exhaustion concept, and it is perhaps too much of a caricature of what the critics of import substitution have in mind. The more sophisticated among them, at least, do realize that the first steps of ISI open up new opportunities for the establishment of domestic manufactures through both income and backward linkage effects. In the first place, the domestic production of A, C, and E creates new incomes which may enlarge the market for a number of additional final demand goods to the point where their domestic production becomes, in turn, feasible. Secondly, domestic production of A, C, and E, which is *ex hypothesi* set up on the basis of imported inputs, opens up new opportunities for the establishment of domestic manufacturing facilities turning out these inputs.

The income effect is likely to result in a convergent series of new investment opportunities. Thus it postpones exhaustion in relation to the naive model, but does not overcome it. When backward linkage effects are taken into account, however, the exhaustion concept tends to evaporate unless it is bolstered by some additional assumptions.

Again a rather naive, let us call it 'seminaive,' exhaustion model could be built up as follows. Industry A requires imported inputs $a_1, a_2, a_3, \ldots a_i, \ldots$; industry C inputs $c_1, c_2, c_3, \ldots c_i, \ldots$ and so on. It seems plausible that imports of any individual input, such as

$M_{a1}, M_{a2}, M_{a3}, \ldots M_{ai}, \ldots$ should be smaller than M_A had been before domestic production of A started. On the other hand, it could be surmised (and frequently is unquestioningly assumed) that minimum economic plant size increases as one ascends to 'higher' stages of production. If this is so, then we have $P_{ai} < P_A$ while $M_{ai} > M_A$. Under these circumstances the chances that imports will exceed the minimum economic sizes for any large number of imported inputs for A, C, and E decrease rapidly as one ascends via backward linkage toward the higher stages of production.

Criticism of the Seminaive Model: The Importance of Policy

I believe that something like this seminaive model is indeed in the minds of those who speak of exhaustion. For this reason it is useful to spell it out, for as soon as that is done, it is easy to perceive where such an exhaustion model goes wrong and what are, therefore, the requirements of an industrialization process that would 'beat' exhaustion.[18]

Two modifications of the model serve to make it look both more realistic and less exhaustion-prone. In the first place, some of the inputs needed for the initial import-substitution industries are likely to be identically the same (steel, paper, glass are needed as intermediate inputs in a wide variety of final demand products). As a result of this product convergence of industrial processes the a_i's are not always distinct from the c_i's and e_i's so that imports of a number of intermediate goods may well be larger than the previous imports of final demand goods.[19]

Secondly, it is of course not necessarily true that minimum economic plant size increases regularly as one ascends toward the higher stages of production. I am not aware of any systematic study relating

18 One way of staving off the exhaustion predicted by the naive or seminaive model would be to enlarge total market size, either for *all* products through the amalgamation of several national markets, or for *some* products particularly important for industrial progress, through appropriate income redistribution within a given national market. Accordingly the formation of common markets and a redistribution of income which would result in larger domestic markets for mass-produced articles have held an important place in the discussions that arose after the 'exuberant' phase of ISI was over. There can be no doubt that the creation of a larger market through either or both of these moves would contribute much to dynamic industrial growth. But we wish to argue here that they are not the only available instruments or, in other words, that market size is not as rigid and definite a barrier as the exhaustion thesis claims.

19 Moreover, because of this product convergence the opportunities for import substitution are much greater, in the case of intermediate goods, than appears from a look at the import statistics.

to this point. But it is well known, for example, that automobile assembly plants deal with a number of suppliers and subcontractors for many needed components, just as a single steel plant will draw for its supply of coal on several mines. Large capacity plants do characterize the technology of a few important intermediate and basic products; but at every stage—particularly in the machinery and equipment industries which, in a sense, represent the 'highest' stage of production—small and medium-sized establishments are also to be found.[20]

If we put these two considerations together, one particularly favourable possibility appears: minimum economic size could providentially be, and in fact often is, large in those industries for whose products (steel, glass, paper) the convergence phenomenon is important. But even apart from such a happy coincidence, the preceding considerations make the exhaustion concept lose the physical and predictable definiteness it had assumed with the previous models. It appears instead that the difficulties that may well dog the backward linkage process are to a considerable extent a matter of economic environments and policies, instead of being determined exclusively by objective quantities such as market and minimum economic plant sizes.

We have a few more words to say on the latter topics before we turn to the economic and sociopolitical reasons for which the backward linkage process may or may not get stuck. It must be recognized that one implication of the above considerations is to stress even more the importance of market size. In the seminaive exhaustion model, market size sets definite limits to the number of industries which a given country can set up. With increasing market size, an additional number of industries, all of larger size than could be accommodated previously, become possible. But if one gives up the idea that minimum economic size and stage of production are closely correlated, the advantages of market size can become larger rather than smaller, for a larger market permits the installation not only of an industry requiring that market, but, in its wake, of a host of other plants supplying that industry; the required market

20 For striking evidence on the smallness of the typical machine tool firm in the United States and on low concentration ratios in the industry, see Murray Brown and Nathan Rosenberg, 'Prologue to a Study of Patent and Other Factors in the Machine Tool Industry,' *The Patent, Trademark and Copyright Journal of Research and Education* 4 (Spring 1960), pp. 42-6. One reason for this situation is that capital/labor ratios are typically low in the machinery industry.

size of these plants may be much smaller, but they could not be established without the prior establishment of the industry requiring the larger market and which might therefore be called the 'bottleneck industry.'

These considerations make us understand better the tremendous importance of market size (so well illustrated by the exceptional achievements in Latin America of Mexico and Brazil) if the backward linkage process is to be vigorous. But they also lead to some interesting policy conclusions: with the seminaive model, the industrialization process is bound to stop at a given point. It can be likened to the ascent of a mountain which gets steeper all the time; the country is the mountain climber and the larger it (or rather its market) is, the higher up the mountain it gets. If this were really so, there would not be much point in pushing it up a bit higher through special incentives or promotion of public enterprise, and any infant industry protection should be uniform. But if we abandon the seminaive model, the mountain alters its shape; at one point its slope does become forbiddingly steep, but then it flattens to turn up again only much later. Under those conditions it becomes exceedingly important to climb the forbidding portion (the bottleneck industry) of the mountain as then the traveling can be continued with ease for some time. In other words, the existence of the bottleneck industries is a powerful argument for special protection, or direct promotion, and even better, for efforts to export the portion of the industry's output that cannot be accommodated by the domestic market. In any event, public policy is very much back in the saddle with this view of the industrialization process.

A further remark along similar lines. The phenomenon of product convergence can also be utilized to help a country negotiate the steeper slopes of its bottleneck industries. When an intermediate product industry faces inadequate domestic demand and cannot therefore be established on an economic scale, it is possible to canvas possibilities for setting up industries which might generate additional demands for the bottleneck industry's output. While this may be difficult in practice, the argument leads to a counsel of caution in policies directed against so-called 'non-essential' industries: the demands for intermediate products emanating from these industries can be very precious in permitting *essential* intermediate product industries to be established.

Economic, Political and Technological Determinants of Backward Linkage

While the preceding considerations ended up by stressing the importance of policy, they were still focused on the *mechanism* of industrialization through backward linkages. We must now address ourselves directly to the political economy of the process.

The importance of market size and of an adequate supply of foreign exchange in setting some limits to the process is undoubted; nevertheless, the industrialization processes of countries which are not too dissimilar with respect to these constraints still display considerable variation so that curiosity is aroused about the role of other factors, such as the behavior of private industrialists and of public authorities.

As is well known by now, the setting up of an industry based on imported inputs has two contradictory effects: it becomes possible, and in some to be defined ways attractive, to set up industries producing inputs for the initial industry; but at the same time, the very establishment of that industry sets up resistances against backward linkage investments. Several reasons for such resistances had already been noted in my *Strategy of Economic Development:*

> The industrialist who has worked hitherto with imported materials will often be hostile to the establishment of domestic industries producing these materials. First, he fears, often with good reason, that the domestic product will not be of as good and uniform quality as the imported one. Secondly, he feels that he might become dependent on a single domestic supplier when he could previously shop around the world. Third, he is concerned about domestic competition becoming more active once the basic ingredients are produced within the country. Finally, his location may be wrong once the source of supply of the materials he uses is thoroughly altered. For all these reasons, the interests of the converting, finishing, and mixing industries are often opposed to the establishment of domestic sources of supply for the products that they convert, finish, or mix.[21]

Another powerful factor making for resistance has since received much attention: high tariff protection for the initial industry combined with low or zero tariffs or preferential exchange rate treat-

21 Hirschman, *Strategy*, p. 118. I am quoting myself here because the critics of ISI have sometimes taken me to task for having overrated the power and automaticity of the backward linkage process.

ment for the industry's inputs.[22] The greater the difference between the level of protection accorded to the import-substituting industry and that applying to its imported input, the more will the profit margin of the industry depend on preventing domestic production of the inputs. For it is a fair assumption that the backward linkage industries would, once established, be eligible for a level of protection similar to that benefiting the initial import-substituting industry, and it is at least doubtful whether the initial industry can obtain a compensatory tariff increase for its own output or, in general, whether the resulting increase in costs can be passed on to the consumers without loss in sales volume.

For those various reasons, the newly established industries may not act at all as the entering wedge of a broad industrialization drive. The high customs duties on their outputs, combined with low (or negative) duties on their inputs, could almost be seen as a plot on the part of the existing powerholders to corrupt or buy off the new industrialists, to reduce them to a sinecured, inefficient, and unenterprising group that can in no way threaten the existing social structure. Indeed, like the workers' aristocracy in Lenin's theory of imperialism, these pampered industrialists might go over to the enemy—that is, make common cause with agrarian and trading interests which had long been opposed to the introduction of 'exotic' industries.

The possibility that the industrialists who first appear in non-industrial countries may not be all that much in favor of dynamic industrial development leads to an interesting sociopolitical puzzle. Sociologists and political scientists have frequently deplored the weakness of the middle class and particularly of the industrialists in Latin America, its lack of self-assertion and its failure to influence public affairs. Earlier we have tried to account for this phenomenon by some characteristics of 'late late' industrialization. But at this point, one begins to wonder whether it would really be a good thing if the new industrialists were much more self-assertive and

22 See, for example, Santiago Macario. 'Protection and Industrialization.' and R. Soligo and J. J. Stern. 'Tariff Protection, Import Substitution and Investment Efficiency,' *Pakistan Development Review* 5 (Summer 1965), pp. 249-70. A general critique of import substitution on the grounds that the concentration on, and strong protection of, consumers' goods it usually implies make for misallocation of resources, for obstacles to further industrial growth, and for a bias in favor of consumption is in John H. Power, 'Import Substitution as an Industrialization Strategy,' *Philippine Economic Journal* 5 (Second Semester 1966), pp. 167-204.

powerful than they are—perhaps they would then really be able to choke off further industrialization, something which generally they have not been able to do! Considering what we called the tightly staged character of 'late late' industrialization it may in fact be preferable for the governments of the 'late late' industrializing countries to be run by *técnicos*, by groups of planner-technicians, rather than by the new industrialists themselves. It has been in fact due to the regulations issued by the *técnicos* of the Kubitschek administration that backward linkage was enforced rapidly in the Brazilian automotive industry in the late fifties. In Mexico, on the other hand, assembly plants had existed for decades without any progress being made toward the local manufacture of motors and parts until measures similar to those in Brazil were adopted in the sixties. Thus the resistance of the initial industrialists to backward linkage combine with other already noted characteristics of 'late late' industrialization to enhance the potential contribution of public policy to the process.[23]

But we dare not rely on such policies emerging simply because they are needed and because we issue a call for them. Could the resistance to backward linkage be overcome otherwise than by state action? While the resistances of the new industrialists are perfectly rational, one cannot but feel that they are based on a myopic, excessively short-run view of the development process. In this manner, we can supply a concrete justification for the view of a Brazilian sociologist according to which the traditional Western, Puritan-ethic-imbued, rational, profit-maximizing businessman is not really the type that is most needed in the situation of Latin America; what is required, he feels, are entrepreneurs who can identify themselves with the general developmental aspirations of their society, be it even at the expense of some rationality in their everyday business operations.[24]

But, once again, one cannot rest content with issuing a call for the *desenvolvimentista* entrepreneur; it would be more useful to be able to explain his appearance or nonappearance by a series of economic and social factors. This will be our next task. While it is

23 That a policy of forcing backward linkage investments has problems and pitfalls of its own is shown in Leland L. Johnson, 'Problems of Import Substitution: The Chilean Automobile Industry,' *Economic Development and Cultural Change* 15 (January 1967), pp. 202-16.

24 Fernando H. Cardoso. 'The Industrial Elite' in S. M. Lipset and A. Solari, eds., *Elites in Latin America* (New York: Oxford University Press, 1967), pp. 96-9.

true that backward linkage meets with certain resistances and obstacles, we have yet to inquire about the existence of other forces working in the opposite direction, that is, in the direction of making backward linkage work. This appraisal of the comparative strength of forces and counterforces is probably the key to understanding why industrialization has been more vigorous and continuous in some developing countries than in others—long before they ran up against any barriers of market size.

As is the case for the start of 'late late' industrialization, so will the continuation of the process through backward linkage be strongly influenced by the industrializing country's balance of payments. The opposition of the initial industrialists to backward linkage investments is likely to be considerably reduced if they occasionally experience curtailments, due to foreign exchange shortages, in the flow of imported inputs; on the other hand, the backward linkage investments require availability of foreign exchange for the importation of machinery. Consequently it is likely that some alternation of foreign exchange stringency and abundance would be optimal from the point of view of generating both the motivation and the resources required for the process. I have previously made this point[25] and considerable attention has been paid to the foreign exchange constraint.[26] Hence, it will be more useful to focus here on other forces affecting the process. There surely exist many situations in which some backward linkage investments are neither impossible in the light of foreign exchange availabilities, nor wholly compelled because of previous searing experience with foreign exchange shortages. We are interested here in the conditions that make for vigorous continuation of industrialization in these situations.

In line with our previous arguments, we posit a certain level of resistance of the new industrialists to the manufacturing of currently imported inputs. The resistance, while rational on the part of the initial industrialists, is undesirable from the point of view of the economy in the sense that profitable production of some inputs is assumed to be possible provided some average or normal level of protection is extended to them. In other words, there is room for, but resistance against, further industrialization along reasonably

25 *Strategy*, pp. 173-76.

26 See, for example, Carlos F. Díaz-Alejandro; 'On the Import Intensity of Import Substitution,' *Kyklos* 18 (1965), pp. 495-511.

efficient lines of comparative advantage.[27] We now inquire what conditions other than balance of payments developments could make this resistance weaken or disappear.

The principal point to be made here is very simple: the resistance is almost wholly premised on the supposition that manufacturing in the higher stages of production is going to be undertaken by entrepreneurs other than the already established initial industrialists (or other than members of his immediate family). For if he himself undertakes it, most of the listed objections to the expansion of manufacturing via backward linkage fall to the ground. Thus, the fear of unreliability and poor quality of the domestic article should abate and the fear of domination by a monopoly supplier will disappear entirely. True, domestically produced inputs may have to be purchased at a higher price than was paid for the previously imported product which was perhaps obtained duty free or bought at some preferential exchange rate. But even if the increase in input costs that comes with domestic manufacture cannot be passed on, vertical integration would take the sting out of it; for the decrease of profits in one operation of an integrated industrial concern does not seriously matter if that decrease is compensated by the emergence of profits in another, newly established operation. To realize such profits the industrialist who contemplates the manufacture of hitherto imported inputs will usually have to obtain for those inputs some 'normal' level of protection. It must be assumed, therefore, that he does not consider existing customs

27 In somewhat more rigorous terms: the established, protected industries are earning excess profits which they would lose if industries supplying inputs to them were to be established with a 'normal' level of tariff protection. The excess profits of the first ISI industrialists thus have an interesting contradictory character: they set up resistances against further industrialization, but at the same time they represent an obvious and attractive source of possible finance for that very process. Protection of the backward linkage industries achieves quite simply the needed transfer: as is now familiar, this protection lowers the level of effective protection of the industries catering to final demand. The numerous studies which have lately been devoted to the topic of effective protection have paid little attention to this important mechanism, presumably because they were rooted in the desire to denounce the evils and inefficiencies of ISI. That some of these evils are possibly self-liquidating as ISI proceeds, that an industry protected by infant industry tariffs can 'grow up' not only because those tariffs are reduced but because supplier industries with their own tariff protection spring up, was specifically suggested by W. M. Corden in his fundamental article, 'The Structure of a Tariff System and the Effective Protective Rate,' *Journal of Political Economy* 74 (June 1966), p. 229. But this implication of the theory of effective protection seems to have been forgotten by the many researchers who have followed in Corden's footsteps.

duties and exchange rate preferences as unchanging parameters immune to his will and influence; the opposite assumption is sometimes made in the literature on import substitution (with pessimi stic consequences for the prospects of ISI), but it is manifestly unrealistic for most investment decisions.

If the disposition of the initial industrialists themselves to move farther back into the industrial structure is an important element in overcoming obstacles to the backward linkage process, a brief inquiry into the factors making for a disposition of this sort is in order.

The economist can contribute a general reason for which backward linkage investments are likely to be carried on by the new industrialists themselves: the mere fact that they have been earning profits and are therefore presumably looking for new investment opportunities. Once the new industries have reached the point at which imports have been wholly substituted so that horizontal expansion is no longer profitable, vertical expansion into the 'higher stages' of production may well offer the best available and, in any event, the most obvious outlet for investment funds that have accumulated as a result of the profitable operation of the existing industries. The availability of profits from the first phase of import substitution thus provides a generalized incentive for the successful import-substituting industrialist to plunge once again, naturally after appropriate modification of the tariff and exchange rate policies affecting the products whose manufacture is to be undertaken. The likelihood that the new industrialist will look in this particular direction, is increased by two interrelated factors: one, by the special difficulty of moving into export markets, to be commented on in the next section; and secondly by what we called the sequential or 'tightly staged' character of 'late late' industrialization. The industrialist manufacturing a final demand good during earlier cycles of industrialization was likely to call into life domestic producers of inputs and of the required machinery; therefore, once he was no longer able to expand his domestic sales volume, he found the higher stages already occupied by others and was therefore impelled to look elsewhere, including to exports, for further expansion. The situation is very different when production is undertaken wholly on the basis of imported inputs.

The availability of profits and resulting search for new profitable investment opportunities act, as has been said, as a general counterweight to the hostility toward backward linkage investments on the part of new industrialists. Whether or not this counterweight will outweigh the hostility is difficult to say. Under the worst of circumstances the combination of the two forces may result in a dog-in-the-manger situation: the new industrialists are able to prevent others from entering the backward linkage arena, but are not sufficiently motivated to enter it themselves.

To carry the analysis a bit further and to account for the different degrees of strength which the backward linkage dynamic has displayed in different countries, it is tempting to make a brief foray into the realm of sociology. The eagerness of an industrialist to move into related fields of activity instead of being satisfied with his existing operation based on imported inputs, may, for example, be reinforced if he has the feeling that his sons are locked into his own class and career. If an industrialist's sons are able and eager to enter the professions or the government, there is no need for father to think about finding new industries for the sons to expand into and to manage (preferably one for each son so they won't fight). But if industrialists look down on government and the professions, or if the latter look down upon the former, or, as happens frequently, if dislike and disdain are mutual, or simply, if the social distance between the industrialists and other groups is considerable, then the advantage of providing jobs for the family may fully compensate for the inconveniences, headaches, and even for minor monetary sacrifices that may be entailed by backward linkage investments. It appears once again, although from a rather different angle, that it is perhaps not a bad thing for the initial entrepreneurs to belong to a group of immigrants or of some other outsiders, with no immediate prospects of joining the established upper class or of moving into politics or the professions.

Social distance is bred by geographical distance. For this reason, one might expect that an industrialization process which, at least in its beginnings, is strongly identified with one or several centers other than the national capital stands a better chance to spill over vigorously from one industry to another than one which has its base in the capital city itself. The importance of having a somewhat isolated, inbred and self-consciously proud industrial center during the early stages of industrialization is demonstrated by the roles played by São Paulo, Monterrey, and Medellin. No similar pioneering center outside the capital city arose in Chile and Argentina, and it is perhaps not a coincidence that these two countries have provided the critics of the ISI process with far better examples of its alleged irrationality and propensity to exhaustion than Brazil, Mexico, and Colombia.

A final subject of speculation is the differential impact of technology on the comparative strength of the linkage process in different industries. When a backward linkage effect points to an industry which is technologically quite distinct from the one requiring the input, the input-utilizing industrialist is less likely to be attracted to the input-producing industry than if the latter is closely related to processes and techniques with which the industrialist is already familiar. For example, the backward (and forward) linkage dynamic may show more spontaneous vigor in the 'inbred' metalworking and chemical industries than in, say, the textile industry whose inputs come in large part from technological strangers such as, precisely, the chemical industry. Thus the backward linkage dynamic may be held back at some point simply by 'technological strangeness.' This point is of particular importance for the machinery industry since machinery is usually a technological stranger to the industry in which it is utilized. An inquiry into the technological determinants of the differential propensity of different industries toward linkage investments could be of considerable value. To identify and then to remove this sort of bottleneck should be a principal task of public agencies concerned with industrial development.

The purpose of the preceding observations was to convince the reader that there is far more to the vigor or weakness which 'late late' industrialization displays in various countries than minimum economic size of plants, market size and even foreign exchange availabilities. We have left the naive and seminaive exhaustion models far behind and have instead generated a highly complex 'field' of forces and counterforces. If the reader feels a bit confused, we have achieved our purpose: for essentially we wished to show that the process is not nearly so straightforward and constrained as it has recently been made to look, and that it depends far more on public and private acts of volition than has sometimes been granted as well as on numerous economic, sociological and technological factors which remain to be investigated.

The Inability to Export Manufactures: 'Structural' Causes and Remedies

It is hardly necessary to stress how desirable it would be for our 'late late' industrializing countries to become exporters of the outputs of their new industries:

1. Through exports they would overcome whatever obstacles of market size limit their growth or prevent their establishment.
2. Through exports they would loosen the balance-of-payments constraint which may otherwise prevent capacity operation of existing industries as well as establishment of new industries.
3. Finally, by competing in world markets, industries would be forced to attain and maintain high standards of efficiency and product quality and would thereby acquire defenses against oligopolistic collusion and decay to which they often succumb in highly protected, small local markets.

Unfortunately, the intensity with which one would wish for exports of manufacturers from the 'late late' industrializers is matched by the solidity of the arguments which appear to foreclose any real prospects of success in this direction.

Once again, the arguments are familiar: the new industries have been set up exclusively to substitute imports, without any export horizon on the part of either the industrialists themselves or the government; the foreign branch plants and subsidiaries, which have taken an important part of the process, often are under specific instructions not to compete abroad with the products of the parent company; even more decisive than these obstacles deriving from attitudes and institutions, is the fact that the new industries, set up behind tariff walls, usually suffer from high production costs in countries that are, moreover, permanently subject to strong inflationary pressures—hence there is no real possibility of these industries competing successfully in international markets even if they were disposed to do so.

These are weighty arguments and they seem to meet the test of a satisfactory explanation in that they put one's mind to rest. But do they? After all, there are many industries which started out producing for the home market and eventually spilled over into foreign markets. Prior, successful acceptance of a manufactured commodity in the home market has even been considered to be a prerequisite for successful exporting.[28] Secondly, foreign firms have been known to be quite adaptable in their manufacturing and export policies. Just as they have been coaxed by national policies to produce or procure domestically a larger proportion of their inputs, so they could be induced to engage on export drives. Finally, even the most impressive explanation of the inability to export—the cost disadvantage of new industries set up under tariff protection—loses some of its persuasiveness when one remembers that protection of industries in Germany and the United States has not prevented considerable success of those protected industries in world markets. Industrialization of the nineteenth century latecomers was in fact frequently accompanied by both tariff protection and a vigorous export drive which threatened the previous dominant position of the old established industrial countries in a number of important markets. Again, the behaviour of the 'late late' industrializers could not be more different and it now begins to appear that we may be in need of some further, perhaps more fundamental explanations of the inability to export that afflicts them. While such a 'structuralist' strategy of problem solving may show the problem to be even more deeply rooted than had been thought it can also uncover new, hitherto unsuspected ways of attacking it.[29]

One additional explanation of the difficulty of exporting has already been given in the preceding section. It was asserted that in view of the sequential character of industrialization, 'late late' industrialists looking for new profitable business opportunities will frequently have the option between investing in backward linkage industries and expanding into export markets, whereas late industrialists had primarily the latter course open to them since the backward linkage industries were already in existence. Little wonder, then, that the 'late late' industrialists decide to stay cozily at home much longer than the 'late' industrialists who were under a far greater compulsion to make the plunge into foreign markets if they were going to expand. It would therefore be unrealistic to

28 S. B. Linder, *An Essay on Trade and Transformation* (New York: Wiley, 1961), p. 87 ff.

29 A general plea for 'structuralist' analysis of Latin American economic problems along with a good bibliography is to be found in Osvaldo Sunkel, 'El trasfondo estructural de los problemas del desarrollo latino-americano,' *Trimestre Economico* 34 (January-March 1967), pp. 11-58. For an interpretation of structuralism as a strategy for problem solving, see my *Journeys Toward Progress* (New York: Twentieth Century Fund, 1963), pp. 210-16 and 231-35.

expect an industry to become an exporter before it has truly taken root in the country through a variety of the more obvious backward linkage investments. And the expeditious undertaking of these investments is therefore desirable not only per se, but also as a necessary way station to the opening of the export phase.

Another structural reason for the inability to export derives from the circumstances under which resources have been channeled into the industrial sector in many Latin American countries. Industrial investments became attractive not only because of customs protection, but additionally because of the combination of internal inflation, overvaluation of the currency, and exchange controls. In effect, maintaining an overvalued exchange rate meant that the exporters of traditional primary products would receive a smaller real income than with an equilibrium or undervalued exchange rate. At the same time, the overvalued exchange rate permitted the acquisition at favorable prices (in domestic currency) of those imports that were let in by the control authorities. And since machinery and essential industrial materials enjoyed preferential status, the overvalued exchange rate acted in effect as a mechanism to transfer income from the traditional export sector to the new industries.[30]

At the same time, however, the overvalued exchange rate acted as a bar to exports from these industries. This probably was not a serious drawback and certainly was not felt as such during the earlier stages of import-substituting industrialization when exports on the part of the nascent industries were not a real prospect. But as a vigorous industrial establishment grew up in various countries one may well ask the question why a different institutional arrangement was not chosen. For example, why not tax the export sector, subsidize the new industries and do away with the overvalued exchange rate so that industrial exports are encouraged? To ask this question is to answer it: in most Latin American countries such a course would have been politically impossible. The power of the groups tied to the primary export sector would hardly have permitted so direct an assault, as is attested by the strong, per-

30 Alexandre Kafka, 'The Theoretical Interpretation of Latin American Economic Development,' in H. S. Ellis, ed., *Economic Development in Latin America* (New York, St. Martin's Press, 1961), p. 21; and Celso Furtado, 'Industralization and Inflation,' *International Economic Papers* 12 (1967), pp. 101-19.

manent and occasionally successful pressures that were exerted against the indirect squeeze of the sector which Latin American monetary authorities had more or less inadvertently stumbled on. The great advantage of the inflation-cum-overvaluation arrangement was in fact not only that it resulted in an indirect rather than direct squeeze of politically and socially powerful groups, but that this mechanism was an unintended and, for a long time, an unnoticed by-product of a course of action which had the perfectly respectable objective of 'defending the national currency against depreciation.'[31]

Viewed in this way, the inability to export manufactures appears as the price which had to be paid for building up an industrial sector under adverse sociopolitical conditions. Should we then perhaps be simply gratified that industrialization was contrived at all, and be happy to pay the price? Not necessarily. As industrialization proceeded, the desirability of the overvaluation device became increasingly questionable from the point of view of industry itself. For overvaluation not only impeded exports, but interfered, in ways already analyzed, with the vigorous exploitation of the backward linkage dynamic. Moreover, in several countries, industries became sufficiently vigorous and integrated so that the help stemming from the procurement of a few imported inputs at bargain prices (via the overvalued exchange rate) was bound to be more than offset, for an increasing number of firms, by the loss of potential profits that could have been realized through the exports at a nonovervalued rate of exchange. It could thus be suggested that, at a certain point, overvaluation of the currency turned from a stimulus to industrial progress into a drag on it.

It appears that the much advertised noncompetitiveness of Latin American industry may be rooted more in the failure to modify institutions than in any inability to bring down real costs. The question then arises why the industrial interests have not vigorously pressed for institutional arrangements—export subsidies, preferential exchange rates, or more radically, an exchange rate that is undervalued rather than overvalued—that would make exporting

31 The policy originated, ironically enough, in an attempt to *defend* the export interests, e.g., in the case of Brazil to maintain the cruzeiro price of coffee in the face of falling world market prices during the Great Depression. This policy led to an increase in the money supply, and thereby caused domestic inflationary pressures which would eventually result in the inflation-cum-overvaluation arrangement. Cf. Furtado. *Industrialization and Inflation*, p. 103.

profitable. Are there some grounds on which industrialists could be basically *reluctant* to commit substantial resources to an export drive?

This question leads to a third structural reason for—or speculation about—the difficulties of exporting. It has to do, once again, with the distribution of power in Latin American societies. To stage an export drive, an industrialist must frequently make special investments in research, design and packaging: he must assemble a specialized sales force, delegate considerable authority, launch an entirely different advertising campaign; in short, he incurs special risks and new overhead costs which will be recoverable only over a comparatively long period of successful exporting. Therefore, an industrialist will consider exporting only when he can be sure either that the basic institutions and policies which vitally affect his foreign operations are highly stable or, as a minimum, that his interests will be given the most serious attention when these institutions and policies are altered.

In effect we have just spelled out a 'prerequisite' for a determined and successful export drive for manufactures; to undertake such a drive with all its risks and special costs, the industrialist class must feel reasonably sure that it can control certain crucial fiscal and monetary policies of its government. Differently put: only a cohesive, vocal, and highly influential national bourgeoisie is likely to carry industrialization beyond relatively safe import substitution to the risky export-oriented stage. It will be noted that this assertion—the industrialists do not export because they are not influential—completes the second half of a vicious circle whose first half asserted that the ISI industrialists are lacking in influence because they are not 'conquering foreign markets' (see p. 351 above). Obviously we should not take inordinate pride in having fashioned a new vicious circle or in having identified a new prerequisite to the economic progress of the developing countries. Rather, we shall consider in a moment ways of breaking out of the circle and of doing without the prerequisite or of finding, à la Gerschenkron, a substitute for it. But we must nevertheless pause at this point in our reasoning and take notice that conditions for a strong export drive by the private sector are highly unfavorable in Latin America: in no country of that continent do the industrialists feel securely in control of vital economic policies affecting them. Policy makers positively cultivate unpredictability and distance from interest groups; at the same time, they are highly manipulative. Changes in fiscal, monetary, and foreign exchange policies are therefore frequent while communication about these changes with the affected interest groups is infrequent. These are the sociopolitical traits that account, perhaps more fundamentally than the cost-price structure of the new industries, for their poor export performance.

Having uncovered ever more cogent reasons for the inability to export, have we encountered by the same token a 'fundamental' remedy? One way of staking such a claim would be to expect that, as a result of our analysis, Latin America will change the nature of its politics and that its powerholders will henceforth become less manipulative and more communicative. Unfortunately analysis is not likely to act as so powerful a solvent. But is it really necessary to wait until a trusting and intimate relationship between the industrialists and the policy makers emerges or is it conceivable that countries which find it difficult to establish such a relationship could travel an alternative road?

A radical reaction to the problem would be for the state itself to take over the foreign merchandising function. The spectacle of the state rendering difficult or impossible the performance of an important function by the private sector and then taking over that function because the private sector is ostensibly falling down on the job, is by no means uncommon. If this course of action has not been taken so far for the export of manufactures, one reason is that the importance of this function is only beginning to be appreciated. Also, state enterprise is hardly likely to be at its best in selling a wide variety of manufactures in foreign markets; for by its nature, this task requires levels of initiative, flexibility, risk-taking and decentralized decision making which it has been difficult for state enterprise to attain.

A less radical and more promising solution would be for the state simply to take an active role in promoting exports by private enterprise. As already mentioned in connection with exports from foreign-owned branch plants and subsidiaries, the state could very well tie the granting of tax and other incentives to the attainment of export targets in a manner analogous to that with which backward linkage has been enforced in the Brazilian automobile industry. From the point of view of the industrialists, such a policy would have the advantage that one sector of the bureaucracy would become committed to the export drive and could then be relied on to do battle with those sectors whose policies interfere with the success of the drive.

Quite a different solution consists in leaving alone, at first, the obstacles to exporting that derive from the actions of one's own government and in concentrating instead on those that are caused by other governments. This is in fact what is being attempted at present through the United Nations Conference on Trade and Development and its campaign for preferences for the manufactures of developing countries in the markets of developed countries. Perhaps this request can be viewed more sympathetically than it has been if it is considered as a compensation to the exporters of the newly industrializing countries for some of the extra burdens they must bear because of the policies and frequent policy changes of their own governments. In this reasoning, one may also discern a hope that such preferences would be temporary: once exports in volume would have been achieved, the first half of the vicious circle we have identified—industrialists are not influential because they do not export, and they do not export because they are not influential—would have been shattered. There would then be hope that government policies would become more finely attuned to the needs of the exporting industrialists who might therefore dispense in due course with the special privileges obtained from other governments.

The need for common markets among developing countries can also be better appreciated from this perspective. The common markets would not only provide preferential treatment for the industrialists of the participating countries; for these mutual arrangements to be durable, monetary and foreign exchange policies would have to become more uniform and stable than they have been; and such a development would be even more important than the customs preferences themselves in promoting exports from the common market countries, not only to each other, but also to third countries. It is, however, precisely the prospect of less freedom of movement in monetary and foreign exchange policies which makes national governments so skittish about entering effective common market commitments.

Finally our problem could be alleviated by developments in the structure of international trade in manufactures. According to some observers, countries of recent industrialization should be acquiring a comparative advantage in certain types of highly standardized industrial products.[32] To sell such goods abroad may not be possible, in a number of lines, without special international market and firm connections, but it does not require either expensive advertisement campaigns or any special adaptation to foreign tastes and conditions. As a result, the overhead cost of exporting would be cut and the risks deriving from the instability or unpredictability of official economic policies would be correspondingly reduced.

In the preceding pages an attempt has been made to describe the varieties and characteristic features of import-substituting industrialization, and to derive from them sociopolitical consequences which in turn affect the process. Among the characteristics of ISI the possibility of proceeding sequentially, in tightly separated stages, because of the availability of imported inputs and machinery, plays, as was shown, a particularly commanding and complex role, direct and indirect, positive and negative.

Thus, the sequential or staged character of the process is responsible not only for the ease with which it can be brought underway, but also for the lack of training in technological innovation and for the resistances to both backward linkage investments and to exporting that are being encountered. The most important consequence of sequentiality, however, is the fact that it has become possible for industrialization to penetrate into Latin America and elsewhere among the 'late' latecomers without requiring the fundamental social and political changes which it wrought among the pioneer industrial countries and also among the earlier group of latecomers. The repercussions of this situation on the industrialization process itself are ambivalent: on the one hand, the lack of political power of the new industrialists means, as we have just seen, that exporting meets with political and institutional, rather than purely economic, obstacles; on the other hand, this very lack of power neutralizes in various ways some of the possible adverse effects of sequentiality, for example, the resistance of the new industrialists to backward linkage.

In addition, the fact that import-substituting industrialization can be accommodated relatively easily in the existing social and political environment is probably responsible for the widespread disappointment with the process. Industrialization was expected to change

32 Raymond Vernon. 'International Investment and International Trade in the Product Cycle,' *Quarterly Journal of Economics* 80 (May 1966), pp. 202-07.

the social order and all it did was to supply manufactures! Hence one is only too ready to read evidence of total failure into any trouble it encounters.

This paper has by no means denied the various difficulties which the ISI process is apt to experience; in fact, they have on occasion been shown to be more deepseated than had been thought. At the same time, our exploration of the characteristics of the process has made it possible to discern avenues toward continued industrial growth that remain open to the 'late' latecomers.

15

A STAPLE THEORY OF ECONOMIC GROWTH

Melville H. Watkins

THE STAPLE APPROACH to the study of economic history is primarily a Canadian innovation; indeed, it is Canada's most distinctive contribution to political economy. It is undeveloped in any explicit form in most countries where the export sector of the economy is or was dominant.[1] The specific terminology—staple or staples approach, or theory, or thesis—is Canadian, and the persistence with which the theory has been applied by Canadian social scientists and historians is unique.

The leading innovator was the late Harold Innis in his brilliant pioneering historical studies, notably of the cod fisheries and the fur trade;[2] others tilled the same vineyard[3] but it is his work that has stamped the 'school'. His concern was with the general impact on the economy and society of staple production. His method was to cast the net widely. The staple approach became a unifying theme of diffuse application rather than an analytic tool fashioned for specific uses. There was little attempt to limit its application by the use of an explicit framework.[4] Methodologically, Innis'

1 The American economic historian, Guy S. Callender, however, devoted considerable attention to the importance of international and interregional trade in staples in the United States, an aspect of American growth which has been much neglected but has recently been revived by Douglass C. North. See Callender, *Selections from the Economic History of the United States, 1765-1860* (Boston, 1909), and North, *The Economic Growth of the United States, 1790-1860* (Englewood Cliffs, NJ, 1961).

2 See his *The Fur Trade in Canada: An Introduction to Canadian Economic History* (Toronto, 1930; 2nd ed., 1956); *The Cod Fisheries: The History of an International Economy* (Toronto, 1940; 2nd ed., 1954). For a collection of his writings in the Canadian field, see *Essays in Canadian Economic History* (Toronto, 1957). For a complete bibliography of his writings, see Jane Ward, The Canadian Journal of Economics and Political Science, (CJEPS), XIX, May, 1953, pp. 236-44.

3 W. A. Mackintosh is sometimes given credit as a co-founder of the staple theory; see his 'Economic Factors in Canadian History' *Canadian Historical Review*, IV. March, 1923, pp. 12-25, and 'Some Aspects of a Pioneer Economy,' CJEPS, II, Nov., 1936, pp. 457-63.

4 This point has often been noted; see, for example, Richand E. Caves and Richard H. Holton. *The Canadian Economy: Prospect and Retrospect* (Cambridge Mass. 1959), p. 30; and W. T. Easterbrook, 'Problems in the Relationship of

staple approach was more technological history writ large than a theory of economic growth in the conventional sense.[5]

Once solidly entrenched in Canadian studies, the staple approach has now fallen on more uncertain days as its relevance has come to be questioned by Canadian economic historians.[6] The strongest attack has come from Kenneth Buckley who maintains that it is 'practical and efficacious' as a theory of economic growth to 1820, but that thereafter 'other sources of national economic growth and change' are impossible to ignore; he concludes that Canadian economic historians should 'replace the notion of an opportunity structure determined by geography and natural resources with a general concept of economic opportunity without specifying determinants.'[7] Vernon C. Fowke's emphasis on agriculture serving the domestic market as an impetus to investment and hence to economic growth in central Canada prior to Confederation involves a devaluation of the role of staple exports.[8] W. T. Easterbrook has argued, after extensive review of the literature, that the staple theory no longer constitutes—and apparently ought not to—an adequate unifying theme for the study of Canadian development.[9] On the other hand, Hugh G. J. Aitken has remained satisfied with the approach. His own recent writings have been focused on the new resource industries of the twentieth century;[10] in commenting on Buckley's paper he suggested that the staple approach was relevant at least to 1914,[11] and he has subsequently maintained that 'it is still true that the pace of development in Canada is determined

---

Communication and Economic History,' *Journal of Economic History*, XX, Dec. 1960, p. 563.

5 Kenneth Buckley makes this point strongly; see his 'The Role of Staple Industries in Canada's Economic Development', *Journal of Economic History*, XVIII, Dec., 1958, p. 442.

6 For its use in communication study—where, following the later Innis, the media become the resource or staple—see Marshall McLuhan. 'Effects of the Improvements of Communication Media.' *Journal of Economic History*, XX, Dec., 1960, pp. 566-75, and *The Gutenberg Galaxy* (Toronto, 1962), particularly pp. 164-6.

7 'The Role of Staple Industries,' pp. 444, 445.

8 Fowke, *The National Policy and the Wheat Economy* (Toronto, 1957), chap. 2.

9 Easterbook, 'Trends in Canadian Economic Thought,' *South Atlantic Quarterly*, LVIII, Winter, 1959, pp. 91-107; and 'Recent Contributions to Economic History: Canada,' *Journal of Economic History*, XIX, March, 1959, pp. 76-102.

10 Aitken, 'The Changing Structure of the Canadian Economy' in Aitken et al., *The American Economic Impact on Canada* (Durham, N. C., 1959) and *American Capital and Canadian Resources* (Cambridge, Mass, 1961).

11 'Discussion', *Journal of Economic History*, XVIII, Dec. 1958, p. 451.

fundamentally by the exports that enable Canada to pay its way in the world.'[12]

The sample is small, but so too is the number of practising Canadian economic historians. There would appear to be declining confidence in the relevance of the staple approach, especially if consideration is given to what has been said as well as what has been written. But, curiously, the decline has been paralleled by rising interest among non-Canadians who may or may not refer to Innis and Canada. The leading advocate of the staple approach today is Douglass C. North, whose work may well have set the stage for a reconsideration of the causes of American economic growth from the American Revolution to the Civil War.[13] Two American economists, Richard E. Caves and Richard H. Holton, have critically re-examined the staple approach from the viewpoint of modern economic theory as a prelude to forecasting the state of the Canadian economy in 1970, and have given it a surprisingly clean bill of health.[14] R. E. Baldwin has provided a brilliant theoretical article on the impact of staple production on an economy. and both North and Caves and Holton have acknowledged their indebtedness to him.[15] Mention must also be made for the analytical approach used by Jonathan V. Levin in his study of the role of primary product exports in Peru and Burma,[16] of the implications for the staple approach of the application of modern income and growth theory to the classic problem of the transfer mechanism for capital imports in the Canadian balance of payments, particularly in the great boom before the First World War,[17] and of the

12 *American Capital and Canadian Resources*, p. 74.

13 North, 'Location Theory and Regional Economic Growth,' *Journal of Political Economy*, LXII, June, 1955, pp. 243-58; 'International Capital Flows and the Development of the American West,' *Journal of Economic History*, XVI, Dec., 1956, pp. 493-505; 'A Note on Professor Rostow's "Take-off" into Self-sustained Growth,' *Manchester School of Economic and Social Studies*, XXVI, Jan. 1958, pp. 68-75; 'Agriculture and Regional Economic Growth,' *Journal of Farm Economics*, XLI, Dec., 1959, pp. 943-51; *The Economic Growth of the United States, 1790-1860*.

14 Caves and Holton, *The Canadian Economy*, Part I.

15 Baldwin, 'Patterns of Development in Newly Settled Regions,' *Manchester School of Economic and Social Studies*, XXIV, May, 1956, pp. 161-79.

16 Levin *The Export Economies: Their Pattern of Development in Historical Perspective* (Cambridge, Mass, 1960).

17 G. M. Meier, 'Economic Development and the Transfer Mechanism: Canada, 1895-1913,' *The Canadian Jour. of Eco. and Pol. Science*, XIX, Feb., 1953, pp. 1-19: J. C. Ingram, 'Growth and Canada's Balance of Payments,' *American Economic Review*, XLVII, March, 1957, pp. 93-104; John A. Stovel. *Canada in the World Economy* (Cambridge, Mass, 1959).

distinction made by Harvey S. Perloff and Lowdon Wingo, Jr., between 'good' and 'bad' resource exports in the context of American regional growth.[18]

The simultaneous waning of the reputation of the staple approach among Canadians and its rise elsewhere has created a gap in the literature which this paper will attempt to bridge. It will argue that the staple theory can fruitfully be limited to distinct type of economic growth; restate a staple theory so constrained in more rigorous form, primarily by drawing on the literature cited in the paragraph above; contrast this staple theory with other models of economic development; and finally, consider again the relevance of a staple approach to the Canadian case.

I

The linking of economic history and the theory of economic growth is a prerequisite to further advance in both fields. One obvious link lies in the development of theories appropriate to particular types of economic growth. The staple theory is presented here not as a general theory of economic growth, nor even a general theory about the growth of export-oriented economies, but rather as applicable to the atypical case of the new country.

The phenomenon of the new country, of the 'empty' land or region over-run by the white man in the past four centuries, is, of course, well known. The leading examples are the United States and the British dominions. These countries had two distinctive characteristics as they began their economic growth: a favourable man/land ratio and an absence of inhibiting traditions.[19] From these initial features flow some highly probable consequences for the growth process, at least in the early phase: staple exports are the leading sector, setting the pace for economic growth and leaving their peculiar imprint on economy and society; the importation of scarce factors of production is essential; and growth, if it is to be sustained, requires an ability to shift resources that may be hindered

18 Perloff and Wingo, 'Natural Resource Endowment and Regional Economic Growth' in Joseph J. Spengler, ed., *Natural Resources and Economic Growth* (Washington, 1961), pp. 191-212, this article draws on Harvey S. Perloff. Edgar S. Dunn Jr., Eric E. Lampard, and Richard F. Muth, *Regions, Resources and Economic Growth* (Baltimore, 1960).

19 Both features are recognized by W. W. Rostow in *The United States in the World Arena* (New York, 1960), p. 6; the first is also cited by Bert F. Hoselitz, 'Patterns of Economic Growth,' *The Canadian Journal of Economics and Political Science*, XXI, Nov., 1955, pp. 416-31.

by excessive reliance on exports in general, and, in particular, on a small number of staple exports. These conditions and consequences are not customarily identified with underdeveloped countries, and hence are not the typical building blocks of a theory of economic growth. Rather, the theory derived from them is limited, but consciously so in order to cast light on a special type of economic growth. Because of the key role of staple exports it can be called a staple theory of economic growth.

II

The fundamental assumption of the staple theory is that staple exports are the leading sector of the economy and set the pace for economic growth. The limited—at first possibly non-existent—domestic market, and the factor proportions—an abundance of land relative to labour and capital—create a comparative advantage in resource-intensive exports, or staples. Economic development will be a process of diversification around an export base. The central concept of a staple theory, therefore, is the spread effects of the export sector, that is, the impact of export activity on domestic economy and society. To construct a staple theory, then, it is necessary to classify these spread effects and indicate their determinants.

Let us begin with the determinants. Assume to be given the resource base of the new country and the rest-of-the-world environment—the international demand for and supply of goods and factors, the international transportation and communication networks, the international power structure. The sole remaining determinant can then be isolated, namely, the character of the particular staple or staples being exported.

A focus on the character of the staple distinguished Innis' work. C. R. Fay expressed the point most succinctly: '. . . the emphasis is on the commodity itself: its significance for policy; the tying in of one activity with another; the way in which a basic commodity sets the general pace, creates new activities and is itself strengthened or perhaps dethroned, by its own creation.'[20] The essence of the technique has been thrown into sharp relief by Baldwin. Using

20 Fay, 'The Toronto School of Economic History,' *Economic History*, III, Jan. 1934, pp. 168-71. See also Easterbrook, 'Problems in the Relationship of Communication and Economic History,' p. 563.

the method of ideal types, he contrasts the implications of reliance on a plantation crop and a family farm crop respectively for the economic development of an area exporting primary products. The important determinant is the technology of the industry, that is, the production function, which defines the degree of factor substitutability and the nature of returns to scale. With the production function specified and the necessary *ceteris paribus* assumptions—including the demand for goods and the supply of factors—a number of things follow: demand for factors; demand for intermediate inputs; possibility of further processing; and the distribution of income.

These determine the range of investment opportunities in domestic markets, or the extent of diversification around the export base. If the demand for the export staple increases, the quantity supplied by the new country will increase. This export expansion means a rise in income in the export sector. The spending of this income generates investment opportunities in other sectors, both at home and abroad. By classifying these income flows, we can state the staple theory in the form of a disaggregated multiplier-accelerator mechanism. In Hirschman's terms, the inducement to domestic investment resulting from the increased activity of the export sector can be broken down into three linkage effects: backward linkage, forward linkage, and what we shall call final demand linkage.[21] The staple theory then becomes a theory of capital formation; the suggestion has been made but not yet elaborated that it is such.

Backward linkage is a measure of the inducement to invest in the home-production of inputs, including capital goods, for the expanding export sector. The export good's production function and the relative prices of inputs will determine the types and quantities of inputs required. Diversification will be the greatest where the input requirements involve resources and technologies which permit of home-production. The emphasis usually placed in studies of economic development on barriers to entry into machinery production suggests a high import content for capital-intensive staples, and hence a small backward linkage effect. Caves and Holton, however, emphasize the importance of capital-intensive agriculture in supplying linkage to domestic agricultural machinery production. Theory and history suggest that the most important example of backward linkage is the building of transport systems for collection

21 Albert O. Hirschman, *The Strategy of Economic Development* (New Haven, 1958), chap. 6.

of the staple, for that can have further and powerful spread effects.

Forward linkage is a measure of the inducement to invest in industries using the output of the export industry as an input. The most obvious, and typically most important, example is the increasing value added in the export sector; the economic possibilities of further processing and the nature of foreign tariffs will be the prime determinants.

Final demand linkage is a measure of the inducement to invest in domestic industries producing consumer goods for factors in the export sector. Its prime determinant is the size of the domestic market, which is in turn dependent on the level of income—aggregate and average—and its distribution.

The size of the aggregate income will vary directly with the absolute size of the export sector. But a portion of the income may be received by what Levin has called 'foreign factors'—factors which remit their income abroad—rather than 'domestic factors.' To the extent that income received by foreign factors is not taxed away domestically, final demand linkage will be lessened. The servicing of capital imports is a case in point. Primary producers are notoriously susceptible to indebtedness, and the burden will be greater the more capital-intensive the staple. Leakage can also result from wages paid to migratory labour and from immigrants' remittances.

The average level of income, that is, the *per capita* income of the domestic factors, depends on the productivity of 'land' or the resource content of the staple export, for other factors are importable. The distribution of income, on present assumptions, is determined by the nature of the production function of the staple, in Baldwin's models being relatively unequal for the plantation crop and relatively equal for the family farm crop.

The impact of these two market dimensions on final demand linkage can be seen by classifying consumer spending in two ways. Firstly, consumer spending may be either on home-produced goods or on imports, and the higher the marginal propensity to import the lower the final demand linkage. Secondly, it may be either on subsistence goods and luxuries, or on a broad range of goods and services; the latter are more likely to lend themselves to those economies of mass production which lie at the heart of on-going industrialization, while luxury spending—other than for labour-intensive services—is likely, given the tendency to ape the tastes of more advanced countries, to be directed towards imported goods, that is, to create in Levin's terminology 'luxury importers.'

Final demand linkage will tend to be higher, the higher the average level of income and the more equal its distribution. At a higher level of income, consumers are likely to be able to buy a range of goods and services which lend themselves to domestic production by advanced industrial techniques. Where the distribution is relatively unequal, the demand will be for subsistence goods at the lower end of the income scales and for luxuries at the upper end. The more equal the distribution the less the likelihood of opulent luxury importers and the greater the likelihood of a broadly based market for mass-produced goods.

The discussion of the linkages so far has assumed that investment is induced solely by demand factors. But on the supply side the expansion of the export sector creates opportunities for domestic investment which may or may not be exploited. Consideration must be given to the relationship between staple production and the supply of entrepreneurship and complementary inputs, including technology.

The key factor is entrepreneurship, the ability to perceive and exploit market opportunities. Entrepreneurial functions can be fulfilled by foreigners, and to the extent that this makes available technical and marketing skills the result can be advantageous to the new country. But the literature on economic development, and particularly on the dual economy, raises many doubts as to the adequacy of foreign entrepreneurship. It may flow freely into the export and import trades, but fail to exploit domestic opportunities. Exports may be regarded as safer, in part because they earn directly the foreign exchange necessary to reimburse foreign factors, but largely because export markets are better organized and better known than domestic markets. Foreign domination of entreprenuership may militate against its general diffusion.

An adequate supply of domestic entrepreneurship, both private and governmental, is crucial. Its existence depends on the institutions and values of society, about which the economist generalizes at his peril. But the character of the staple is clearly relevant. Consider, for example, Baldwin's polar cases. In the plantation case, the dominant group with its rentier mentality on the one hand, and the mass of slaves who are prevented from bettering themselves on the other, can produce a set of institutions as inimical to entrepreneurial activity as is to be found in any tradition-ridden society. Business pursuits may be castigated as "money grubbing'; education—which, as North has emphasized, is very important—is likely to be confined to the élite and to slight the development of technical and business skills; political activity tends to be devoted to the defence of the *status quo*. On the other hand, in the family-farm case, as in wheat areas, the more equal distribution of income can result in attitudes towards social mobility, business activities, education, and the role of government which are more favourable to diversified domestic growth. These are gross differences; the more subtle ones could be worked out for specific staples.

Even where domestic entrepreneurship is forthcoming, its effectiveness rests on the availability of labour and capital, both foreign and domestic. The 'push' from the old countries has in the past created a highly elastic supply of labour, although not, as the slave trade attests, without some resort to the use of force. But the individual receiving country has to create conditions sufficiently favourable to the inflow of labour to compete with other receiving countries. The original staple may create a social structure which is unattractive to the immigrant with skill suitable for the development of domestic economic activity. Where the staple is land-intensive, as is fur, the staple producers may find it in their own self-interest to discourage immigration and settlement. The transport technologies associated with particular staples provide varying passenger fares and hence differential stimuli to immigration. The availability of labour domestically will depend on the competing attractions of staple production and the quality of the labour force that has resulted from the exploitation of the particular staple. The staple activity may attract excess labour through non-pecuniary advantages: the romantic life of the fur trader and the aristocratic life of the planter are frequently alleged to have had detrimental consequences for other sectors of the economy. The quality of the labour force is significantly related to education.

Foreign capital, both in substance and in preference for foreign trade over domestic industry, is difficult to distinguish from foreign entrepreneurship, which we have already discussed. The availability of capital domestically will depend on the extent of domestic saving and the biases of the savers in placing their funds. The amount of saving will be determined by the production function for the staple. For example, Baldwin argues that savings will be higher with the skewed income distribution of the plantation crop than with the equal distribution of the family-farm crop. This would be the conventional view, although the opposite would be true if it were assumed that saving was encouraged by greater investment opportunities at home or discouraged by a greater concern with consumption for status in a more hierarchical society. But the amount of saving may not matter greatly. For domestic savers, like foreign capitalists, may be biased against domestic activities; they may prefer to expand the export industry further or to invest in the import trade. They may also prefer to invest abroad, for in as open economy capital can flow out as well as in. It is only when there are abundant opportunities in domestic markets waiting to be exploited that the amount of domestic saving will significantly determine the rate of investment.

The technology applied in domestic sectors is likely, to the extent that it is up to date, to be substantially borrowed from abroad. The newness of the country will minimize the difficulties of adapting borrowed technology and create a potential minimum growth rate not significantly lower than that achieved by advanced economies. The inflow of foreign technology will be facilitated by the inflow of foreign entrepreneurship and capital. To the extent that innovation is necessary and possible in the export sector, confidence may be gained by domestic entrepreneurs which will facilitate creative responses in domestic sectors. As domestic entrepreneurship emerges, innovations should become more appropriate to domestic factor proportions and the requirements of the domestic market.

A historically relevant theory must allow not only for the differing character of particular staples but also for the impact of the resource base of the new country and the international environment. For any particular new country the initial conditions can vary, and these conditions can change over time, both autonomously and as a result of the actions of the new country consequent on its success in exploiting its particular staple or staples.

Although these points are important, it is difficult to say much in general about them. For any given inducement to invest offered by the market, an appropriate resource base is necessary; the best of all possible staples will do little to encourage development if the resource base is sufficiently bad, and the impact of a particular staple can vary widely depending on the resource base of the particular country.[22] The resource base itself can change through discovery, and success in staple production, at least for some staples may expedite the process.[23]

So too the international environment can vary in its suitability for the development of new countries. Staple producers begin as colonial outposts of old countries and differences among the latter, in their markets for staples, their supplies of factors for export, their institutions and values, and their colonial policies, will affect growth prospects. Change can take place in any of these dimensions: in foreign demand and foreign supply, which can destroy old staples and create new ones; in transport facilities, which can cheapen internationally traded goods; in the 'push' of factors from the old countries and the 'pull' from other new countries; in colonial policy and in the frequency of wars which can either encourage or discourage growth. And the new country, to the extent that it is successful, may gain power to mould the environment to suit its needs. It can develop a transport system adequate for both domestic and export requirements; it can pursue a commercial policy by which it can cause further processing of its exports and promote import-competing industry without unduly interfering with the optimal allocation of its resources.

What is the likely growth path of a staple economy? Growth is initiated by an increase in demand for a staple export. If the spread effects are potent, as the export sector grows so too will the domestic sectors. The result will be increasing demand for factors. Domestic slack, if it exists at all, will be quickly absorbed, and the continuation of growth will depend on the ability to import scarce factors. If the supply of foreign factors is elastic, the customary tendency for the expansion of one sector—in this case exports—to affect domestic sectors adversely by driving up factor prices is mitigated. This explains the very strong booms that are a feature of growth in staple economies.[24]

22 North's book is weakened by his failure adequately to appreciate the importance of the resource base. He applied Baldwin's polar cases to the American South and West in the period prior to the Civil War, but has very probably exaggerated their efficacy in explaining rates and types of development by understating differences in the general resource base which favoured the West.

23 Note the Canadian mineral discoveries consequent on railway building and hence linked ultimately to the development of the western wheat economy.

24 On external diseconomies generated by an expanding sector when factor supplies are inelastic, see Marcus Fleming, 'External Economies and the Doctrine of Balanced Growth', *Economic Journal*, LXV, June, 1955, pp. 241-56. On the character of export-led booms in Canada, see the literature cited in n. 17.

But what of the nature of growth in the long run? In a staple economy, as in any other, sustained growth requires an ability to shift resources at the dictates of the market—what C. P. Kindleberger calls 'a capacity to transform.' Particular export lines can create prosperity, but typically only for a short time. Over the longer pull they cease to be profitable either because of diminishing returns on the supply side, or adverse shifts in demand consequent on competition from cheaper sources of supply or from synthetics, or because of the income-inelasticity of foreign demand, or simply because of changes of taste. This tendency can be slowed up by attempts to improve marketing and by seeking out cost-reducing innovations. The possibility of the latter depends on the character of the staple; for example, because of the physical properties of the plants, cotton production was historically much more resistant to mechanization than wheat-growing. But the law of diminishing returns cannot be checked indefinitely. Sustained growth, then, requires resource flexibility and innovation sufficient to permit shifts into new export lines or into production for the domestic market.

The probability of long-run success for the staple economy is significantly increased by its two distinctive initial features: a favourable man/land ratio and an absence of inhibiting traditions. The first implies a relatively high standard of living which facilitates expanding domestic markets and substantial factor mobility. The fact that new countries do not start their development with population pressing against scarce resources gives them an enormous advantage over the typical underdeveloped country. Specifically, they have neither a large subsistence agricultural sector severely limiting markets for domestic industry, nor a pool of cheap labour permitting industrialization to proceed with only limited impact on the incomes of much of the population. Subsequent population growth, in part by immigration, means that the size of population is closely related to economic opportunity at a relatively high standard of living. The second feature, the lack of traditions, means that institutions and values must be formed anew, and although there will be a substantial carry-over from the old world, the process will be selective and those transferred are likely to take a form more favourable to economic growth.

These are substantial advantages, and go far to explain the extraordinary success of some new countries. But even for the staple economy, historians have insisted that the process of growth is not without pitfalls. It is frequently alleged, at least implicitly, that the achievement of a high level of national income masks deficiencies in the structural balance of the economy. W. W. Rostow charges that the high levels of welfare achieved in new countries by exploiting land and natural resources will delay their reaching the 'take-off' stage.[25] If the concept of take-off is interpreted as meaning simply the growth and diversification of the manufacturing sector, this argument runs counter to the staple theory. Rostow's claim, however, is no more than an untested hypothesis. He has not outlined the specific mechanism by which primary exports delay industrialization. It is not clear that he is saying anything more than that if a country has a comparative advantage in primary exports it will perforce have a comparative disadvantage in manufactures. This static view communicates nothing about the process of growth in a world where factor supply can be highly elastic and the composition of imports can shift radically over time. The first peril, then, is illusory.[26]

A more real difficulty is that the staple exporters—specifically, those exercising political control—will develop an inhibiting 'export mentality,' resulting in an overconcentration of resources in the export sector and a reluctance to promote domestic development. Our previous comments on the social and political structure associated with particular staples are relevant here, but the literature on economic development in general is replete with other hypotheses and examples. Easterbrook, developing a theme of Innis', has commented that bureaucratic institutions concerned with 'playing it safe' tend to emerge in the face of the initial uncertainties of a marginal status, and then to persist.[27] In the Cuban case, H. C. Wallich emphasizes the importance of the 'sugar mentality' which 'gives sugar an economic and political dominance even greater than its true weight in the economy.'[28] H. W. Singer has pointed out that, when export earnings are high, the country is able to finance development but lacks the incentive to do so; when the earnings are

25 Rostow, *The Stages of Economic Growth* (Cambridge, 1960), p. 36.

26 North, after appeal to the American case, reaches a similar conclusion.

27 See his 'The Climate of Enterprise,' *American Economic Review*, XXXIX, May, 1949, pp. 322-35; 'Uncertainty and Economic Change,' *Journal of Economic History*, XIV, Autumn, 1954, pp. 346-60; 'Long Period Comparative Study: Some Historical Cases,' *Journal of Economic History*, XVII, Dec., 1957, pp. 571-95.

28 Wallich, *Monetary Problems of an Export Economy* (Cambridge, Mass., 1960), p. 12.

low, the incentive exists but the means are lacking.[29] In Canada, there is evidence of a boom-and-bust psychology; excessive optimism causes booms to proceed beyond their proper limits,[30] while depressions are met by resort to tariffs which are 'second best' in the short run and probably inappropriate in the long run and which persist once introduced.[31] One is led to conclude that staple economies are often believed to be much more at the mercy of destiny than they actually are. As Levin has demonstrated in his study of Burma, planning can alter income flows, thereby strengthening linkages and increasing domestic investment.

The serious pitfall is that the economy may get caught in a 'staple trap.' Sustained growth requires the capacity to shift attention to new foreign or domestic markets. The former requires a favourable combination of external demand and available resources. The latter requires a population base and level of *per capita* income that permit taking advantage of the economies of scale in modern industrialism. Both require institutions and values consistent with transformation and *that* requires the good fortune of having avoided specialization in the wrong kind of staple, such as Baldwin's plantation crop. If the staple is unfavourable or if stagnation persists for any extended period because of a weak resource base, the staple economy can take on the character of the traditional underdeveloped country in both respects stressed by Rostow. Firstly, institutions and values can emerge which are inimical to sustained growth, and the process of remoulding will be difficult. Secondly, a population problem can be encountered as the population initially established through immigration continues to expand through natural increase. Persistent unemployment and underemployment will become characteristic of the economy. Immigration may be replaced by emigration, as resort is had to the Irish solution. In the absence of alternative opportunities, factors will tend to accumulate excessively in the export sector or in subsistence agriculture. In the former case, growth may become 'immiserized' as the terms of trade turn against the

29 Singer, 'The Distribution of Gains between Investing and Borrowing Countries,' *American Economic Review*, XL, May, 1950, p. 482.

30 The classic example is the building of two additional transcontinental railways during the wheat boom, 1896-1913. The general phenomenon is noted by A. F. W. Plumptre, 'The Nature of Economic Development in the British Dominions," CJEPS, III, Nov., 1937, pp. 489-507.

31 The high correlation between depressions and tariff increases is noted by John H. Young, *Canadian Commercial Policy*, A study done for the Royal Commission on Canada's Economic Prospects (Ottawa, 1957).

country.[32] In the latter, the economy will face a problem common to most underdeveloped countries: development will depend on the interdependent growth of agriculture and industry. In any event, the initial opportunities for easy growth will no longer exist.

If the pitfalls are avoided—if the staple or staples generate strong linkage effects which are adequately exploited—then eventually the economy will grow and diversify to the point where the appellation 'staple economy' will no longer suffice. Population growth will come to result more from natural increase than from immigration. *Per capita* income will rise beyond the level consistent with any customary definition of underdevelopment. With the gaining of entrepreneurial confidence and the expanding opportunities of domestic markets, domestic entrepreneurs will persistently usurp markets from foreign suppliers.[33] A well-developed secondary manufacturing sector serving domestic markets and possibly even foreign markets will emerge. Staple exports and imports of manufactured goods may fall as a percent of national income. If 'land' remains relatively abundant, this may not happen; that should not be taken as proof of backwardness, however, for it may be no more than the momentary outcome of the operation of the law of comparative advantage.

III

We have taken pains throughout to emphasize the special character of the staple theory. Consideration of the range of relationships possible between foreign trade and economic development will underline the point. In a recent synthesis of the literature, Kindleberger has put forth three models relating foreign trade and economic development; these cover cases where foreign trade is, respectively, a leading, a lagging and a balancing sector of the economy.[34] In the model in which it leads, autonomous foreign demand, typically accompanied by technological change in the developing country, sets the pace, and economic development is a

32 For a formal presentation of the theory of immiserizing growth, see J. Bhagwati, 'Immiserizing Growth: A Geometric Note,' *Review of Economic Studies*, XXV, June, 1958, pp. 201-5, and 'International Trade and Economic Expansion,' *American Economic Review*, XLVIII, Dec., 1958, pp. 941-53.

33 This mechanism has recently been emphasized by Hirschman, *The Strategy of Economic Development*, p. 120 ff.

34 C. P. Kindleberger, *Economic Development* (New York, Toronto, London, 1958), chap. 14.

process of diversification around an export base. The staple economy is clearly a special case of this model.

In the model in which foreign trade lags, domestic investment leads, tending to create pressure on the balance of payments which is met by import-substitution. A large number of underdeveloped countries believe that this is the relevant model. The restrictive nature of the commercial policy of developed countries, combined with the tendency for import demand to expand more rapidly than income in the early stages of development—chiefly because of the need to import capital goods and possibly also industrial raw materials and food—lend credence to this belief. The contrast between the leading and lagging models is that between development based on trade expansion and development based on trade-contraction.

The model in which foreign trade is the balancing sector covers the case of trade-expansion which is not demand-led, but rather based on autonomous supply pushes in the export sector. It applies to the case where domestic investment leads, creating balance of payments difficulties which are met by pushing exports rather than by limiting imports. A trade pattern based on exporting manufactures, in order to import food and take the strain off domestic agriculture, has been espoused by both W. Arthur Lewis and the late Ragnar Nurkse, and is a particular version of the balancing case.[35]

Kindleberger's classification applies to countries already in the process of development. The limitations of the staple theory emerge most clearly when we consider the case where export production is superimposed on a pre-existing subsistence economy. For the staple economy, the export sector can be an engine of growth; for the subsistence economy, the consensus appears to be that the export sector will have either limited or adverse effects on the economy. The linkage effects are likely to be slight, regardless of the character of the export good, because of the internal structure of the underdeveloped country, including the existence of non-competing groups in the domestic and foreign sectors.[36] Even where groups are competing, if there is disguised unemployment in the subsistence sector, increases in productivity in the export industry will not

35 Lewis, *The Theory of Economic Growth* (Homewood, Ill., 1955); Nurkse, *Patterns of Trade and Development*, Wicksell Lectures, 1959 (Stockholm, 1959).

36 H. Myint, 'The Gains from International Trade and the Backward Countries,' *Review of Economic Studies*, XXII, 1954-55, pp. 129-42.

bring increases in real wages; these depend on raising productivity in the subsistence sector and to this exports make little or no contribution.[37] The country might have been better off if it had never exported in the first place. Growth may have become immiserized, as was previously noted. Domestic factors may have been drawn into export production when they could have been more productively applied to domestic manufacture.[38] Investments made complementary to the export sector may generate pecuniary external economies which excessively encourage primary export production.[39] Imports which flood in as a result of exporting may destroy existing handicraft production, and if the export sector does not absorb the labour which is displaced, the gains from trade may be negative.[40] If exports and domestic investment compete for available saving, then a rise in the export volume can directly reduce the rate of growth of income.[41]

IV

The closeness of the link between the staple approach and Canadian historical research makes it unlikely that the application of a more explicit theory will add much to our understanding of Canadian economic development. Nevertheless, a few comments are in order, both to clear up some specific ambiguities and to resolve the issue of the relevance of the staple theory to Canada's economic development, past and present.

1. The cod fisheries and the fur trade were clearly the leading sectors of the early period. Neither staple required much permanent settlement, although as the fur trade came to rely less on the Indian and penetrated further west and as the cod fisheries shifted from the green cure to the dry cure—an example of forward linkage—the impetus to settlement increased. In New France the distribution of income consequent on the fur trade may have been such as to lower

37 W. Arthur Lewis, 'Economic Development with Unlimited Supplies of Labour,' *Manchester School*, XXII, May, 1954, pp. 139-41.

38 Singer, 'The Distribution of Gains.'

39 Lewis, *The Theory of Economic Growth*, p. 348.

40 G. Haberler provides a geometric demonstration of a case where free trade is harmful given rigid factor prices. 'Some Problems in the Pure Theory of International Trade,' *Economic Journal*, LX, June, 1950, pp. 223-40. The argument is extended in Steffan Burenstam Linder, *An Essay on Trade and Transformation* (New York, Stockholm, 1961), chap. 2.

41 R. J. Ball, 'Capital Imports and Economic Development: Paradoxy or Orthodoxy,' *Kyklos*, XV, 1962, fasc. 3, pp. 610-23.

final demand linkage—although it would hardly bear comparison with that resulting from a plantation crop—and the aristocracy may have been as much feudal as *bourgeois* in its attitudes, although the drive of men such as Jean Talon should not be forgotten. But neither character of the staple nor the Frenchness of the colony explain the slow growth relative to the American colonies. Rather, what is fundamental was poor location compared with New England for supplying the West Indies market. This limited the diversity of exports and thus retarded the development of commercial agriculture, lumbering, and above all the carrying trade and shipbuilding which were then the keys to development. A small population base, established more for reasons of imperial design than of economics *per se,* grew rapidly by natural increase. In the face of limited economic opportunities, labour accumulated in subsistence agriculture and New France came to approximate a dual economy, with a compact agricultural community of *habitants* and the moving frontier of the fur traders, which had only limited contacts one with another.[42] By the time of the Conquest the colony had clearly taken on some of the coloration of an 'old' society and was partly ensnared in the staple trap.

In the Atlantic colonies, New England's success in developing an aggressive commercial economy around the fisheries shows that the character of cod as a staple can hardly explain the slow growth of Nova Scotia and Newfoundland. Rather, proximity to the markets of the West Indies and southern mainland colonies and, to a lesser extent, good agricultural land and the possibility of a winter fishery, were the prerequisites that were lacking. The effects of a poor location and a weak resource base—the latter being particularly applicable to Newfoundland—were intensified by the frequency of imperial conflict and the commercial and military aggressiveness of New England. The result militated against either England or France taking the effort that was necessary to create an environment favourable to further development. The area was not so much trapped as buffeted about and ignored.

Absence of economic opportunity because of geographic factors was the crucial constraint on both continental and maritime developments. Innis' method has obscured this point and has led to exaggerated emphasis on the character of the staples, particularly

42 Dietrich Gerhard, 'The Frontier in Comparative View,' *Comparative Studies in History and Society*, I, March, 1959, pp. 205-29.

of fur. But if the nature of the staples is insufficient to explain the absence of rapid growth, lack of diversified development imprints more clearly the character of those staples around which some success is found and increases the probability that their peculiar biases will persist in institutions and values. Thus, with fur came the life of the *habitant* and the vision of a centralized transcontinental economy; with cod, parochialism and a commitment to the sea.

2. Fowke has argued that commercial agriculture in Upper Canada rose above the subsistence level prior to the 1840's in the absence of substantial external demand. Although allowance must be made for 'shanty demand' linked to timber exports, the point is conceded, and with it the implication that some growth is possible without exports as the leading sector. But the quality of the growth that took place was unimpressive. The census of 1851 shows industrial development to be confined to flourmills and sawmills, both of which were on an export basis, and to the small-scale production of the simpler types of manufacture for the local market.[43] The population and income levels that had been attained were not sufficient to sustain a large or technologically sophisticated manufacturing sector. Buckley rightly insists that the economy became more complex after 1820 and that the range of economic opportunity widened, but this does not mean that staple exports ceased to be of critical importance.

3. One of Buckley's criticisms of the staple approach is its tendency 'to ignore any section once the staple which created or supported it is no longer expanding,' and he cites as an example the slighting of Quebec's economic development since the decline of the fur trade.[44] His point has some validity, at least so far as Quebec is concerned, but the neglect is not inherent in a properly stated staple theory of economic growth. As the new country (or region) ages, whether it be successful or unsuccessful, it takes on the character of an old country and becomes amenable to analysis as such. In Quebec in the nineteenth century, it is clear that the expansion of timber and ships as staple exports, the entrepreneurial drive and accumulated capital of the English commercial class carried over from the fur trade, and emigration which relieved the

43 J. Firestone, 'Development of Canada's Economy, 1850-1890' in *Trends in the American Economy in the Nineteenth Century* (Princeton, 1960), pp. 217-52.

44 'The Role of Staple Industries,' p. 447.

pressure of population on scarce resources combined to lessen the probability that the region would become too deeply enmeshed in the staple trap. Nevertheless, it is the interrelationship between agriculture and industry in the context of a rapidly growing population that should be made the focus of study, as one would expect to be done for any presently underdeveloped country. Statistics on the relative rates of growth of Ontario and Quebec indicate, incidentally, that if one gives credence to the alleged anti-commercial attitudes of the French Canadian, then given the less favourable man/land ratio Quebec inherited from New France, what needs to be explained is the remarkable success of Quebec.

4. The period of Canadian economic history on which most controversy has focused recently has been the 'Great Depression' of 1873-96. So long as it could be properly regarded as a great depression, it was amenable to the staple approach. Its bad reputation was based on the slow growth of population and persistent emigration, and this could be linked to the failure of the western wheat economy to expand in a sustained fashion in the face of a trend decline in the world price of wheat. The absence of rapid extensive growth made it possible for the period to be passed over quickly in the history books, and to be remembered more for the attempts that were made to promote development than for the actual growth achieved. Recent research, however, particularly the statistical work of Firestone, McDougall, Hartland, and Bertram,[45] makes it impossible to continue to regard these years as a great depression; they witnessed, in fact, an impressive increase in real *per capita* income, comparable to that in the United States, considerable industrial expansion, and substantial capital inflow.

The growth in real income can be attributed partly to the export sector. Exports did fall as a percentage of national income. Nevertheless, the real value of exports grew absolutely; there were important shifts in the composition of exports which generated new investment, from wood products to agriculture, and within the latter, from grain to animal products, with cattle and cheese emerg-

45 O. J. Firestone, *Canada's Economic Development, 1867-1953* (London 1958), and 'Development of Canada's Economy, 1850-1900'; Duncan M. McDougall, 'Immigration into Canada, 1851-1920,' CJEPS, XXVII, May, 1961, pp. 162-75; Penelope Hartland, 'Canadian Balance of Payments since 1868' in *Trends in the American Economy in the Nineteenth Century*, pp. 717-55; Gordon W. Bertram, 'Historical Statistics on Growth and Structure of Manufacturing in Canada, 1870-1957,' Canadian Political Science Association Conference on Statistics, June 10-11, 1962.

ing as the new staples, probably exports became more highly manufactured—the growth of cheese factories is striking—and more capital-intensive, railway building provided an important stimulus to growth and its *primum causum* was the expectation of large exports of western grain.

Exports, then, continued to play their conventional role as a leading sector. They can hardly be given full credit, however, for the increase in real income of this period. Factor increments shifted from export markets to domestic markets with a success inconsistent with a markedly backward economy. Yet the extent to which the adaptation was made to a declining stimulus from the export sector should not be exaggerated. The decade rates of growth of manufacturing after 1870 are not comparable to those of the first decade of the twentieth century when exports were expanding rapidly, and at the end of the century Canadian industry was still backward relative to that of such countries as Britain, the United States, and Germany. There was substantial net emigration in every decade from 1861 to 1901. The Canadian economy was not growing fast enough to generate employment opportunities for increments to the labour force by natural increase; while this may be no cause for concern from an international perspective, contemporary political debate and newspaper comment leaves no doubt that Canadians regarded this steady outflow of population as evidence of an unsatisfactory performance by the economy.

5. A restatement of the staple theory might be expected to cast new light on the hoary issue of the long-run impact of the Canadian tariff. A conventional argument has been that the tariff permanently increases population because export industries are less labour-intensive than import-competing industries.[46] Young would appear to have effectively disposed of this line of reasoning,[47] but there may be some validity to the population-sustaining argument for a tariff if one looks at its effect in a boom period, such as 1896 to 1913. It is clear that, by reducing the marginal propensity to import, the tariff increases employment in import-competing industries. At the same time, the fact that factors are in highly elastic supply limits the extent to which costs rise for the export industries,

46 W. A. Mackintosh, *The Economic Background of Dominion-Provincial Relations, A Study Prepared for the Royal Commission on Dominion-Provincial Relations* (Ottawa, 1939), p. 84 ff.; and Clarence L. Barber, 'Canadian Tariff Policy,' *The CJEPS*, XXI, Nov., 1955, pp. 513-30.

47 Young: *Canadian Commercial Policy*, p. 89 ff.

while the sheer strength of the boom, which is being further increased by investment in import-competing industries, keeps imports high in spite of the tariff, thus tending to eliminate foreign repercussion. The tariff would appear to increase employment opportunities, and thereby the population-sustaining capacity of the economy. If, as is probable, the infant industry argument is not valid, however, then the real income has been lowered. We return to the customary view that the Canadian tariff has increased population while lowering real income. But there is an important qualification, as a result of which population may not be increased in the long-run. The tariff will tend to strengthen a boom which is already excessive and thus to increase the problems of readjustment that have to be faced eventually. To the extent that these problems are not otherwise solved, emigration to the United States with its higher wages is likely to be greater than it would have been in the absence of the tariff.

6. The period 1896 to 1913 was undeniably an example of a classic staple boom. But the industrial development which was achieved in its wake so increased the complexity of the Canadian economy as to make it impossible to continue to use staple industries as the unifying theme of economic growth, or so the implicit reasoning seems to run in the best of the textbooks.[48] The notion of a discontinuity in Canadian economic development in the early twentieth century, though superficially attractive, is difficult to maintain, as Caves and Holton have demonstrated. The manufacturing sector appears to have been filling in slowly over a long period of time, without passing through any critical stage of economic maturity. Patterns of short-run change consistent with the staple theory are to be found in all three periods of rapid growth in this century, 1900-1913, 1920-1929, and 1946-1956: the rate of investment closely reflects the demand for exports, current and prospective; production for domestic markets expands around the export-base, replacing imports; excessive optimism leads to over-expansion in the export sector and complicates the subsequent problems of readjustment; and the quantity of saving adjusts itself to investment demand, in part by inducing capital imports.

Is the staple theory, then, relevant to Canada today, or has it

48 W. T. Easterbrook and H. G. J. Aitken, *Canadian Economic History* (Toronto, 1956).

been long irrelevant? Does the evidence adduced by Caves and Holton on the common character of growth patterns in the twentieth century, which could be extended to include the boom of the 1950's, reflect historical necessity or historical accident? Is Canada unable to grow at a satisfactory rate unless exports lead, or able to do so but relieved of the necessity until now by good luck? There is no doubt that luck is a neglected factor in Canadian economic history. Nevertheless, the fundamental fact is the pervasive interdependence with the North Atlantic community, and particularly with the United States. Canada is a small and open economy, a marginal area responding to the exogenous impact of the international economy. The basic determinants of Canadian growth are the volume and character of her staple exports and the ability to borrow, adapt, and marginally supplement foreign technology. These guarantee for Canada a minimum rate of growth that cannot diverge too widely from that achieved elsewhere, particularly in United States. They create no assurance, however, of a rate of growth sufficient to maintain full employment, even if the expansion of the labour force be limited to natural increase. The probability that borrowed technology and staple exports will provide a sufficient impetus to the economy has diminished as staples have become more capital-intensive.

That expanding exports and satisfactory economic growth have been correlated in the past is clear. How this is interpreted depends on a judgment as to the freedom of action that Canada possesses. The emphasis increasingly placed by economists on the link between the inefficiency of Canadian secondary manufacturing industry and the Canadian tariff[49] suggests that the major difficulty is an inhibiting export mentality, the elimination of which lies within Canadian control. From this point of view, economic institutions and political values, an inefficient structure of industry combined with an unwillingness to do anything about it have in the past prevented Canada from growing at a satisfactory rate in the absence of a strong lead from primary exports, but this need not be true for the indefinite future.

49 See H. E. English, 'The Role of International Trade in Canadian Economic Development since the 1920's,' unpublished Ph.D. thesis, University of California, 1957; S. Stykolt and H. C. Eastman, 'A Model for the Study of Protected Oligopolies,' *Economic Journal*, LXX, June, 1960, pp. 336-47; Roger Dehem, 'The Economics of Stunted Growth,' *CJEPS*, XXVIII, Nov., 1962, pp. 502-10.

16

COMPARATIVE ADVANTAGE AND DEVELOPMENT POLICY

*Hollis B. Chenery**

IN THE GREAT REVIVAL of interest in economic development that has marked the past decade, attention has centered on two main questions: first, what determines the over-all rate of economic advance?; second, what is the optimal allocation of given resources to promote growth? Analysis of the growth rate has relied mainly on the Keynesian tools and has produced a multiplicity of aggregate growth models. The second question, however, reopens more ancient economic issues, and their analysis must start from the classical and neoclassical solutions. Only very recently have the two types of discussion tended to come together in the more comprehensive framework of general equilibrium analysis.

In the field of resource allocation, controversy centers around the implications of the classical principle of comparative advantage, according to which growth is promoted by specialization. The defenders of this principle draw their inspiration from David Ricardo, J. S. Mill and Alfred Marshall, while the lines of attack stem from Friedrich List, J. A. Schumpeter, A. A. Young and J. H. Williams. The chief criticism is that comparative advantage is essentially a static concept which ignores a variety of dynamic elements.

This issue is of great practical importance to the governments of underdeveloped countries, most of which take an active part in allocating investment funds and other scarce resources. The main purpose of the discussion has therefore been to discover workable principles for the formulation of development policy. The classical approach derives these principles from international trade theory, while its critics base their analysis on modern growth theory.

* I am indebted to Moses Abramovitz, Bela Balassa, and Lawrence Krause for helpful comments. Research for this article was undertaken at the Cowles Foundation for Research in Economics under Task NR 047-006, Office of Naval Research. [This is the third in a series of survey articles for which the Rockefeller Foundation has provided support.]

Elements of a dynamic, general-equilibrium theory are needed to resolve the differences between the two approaches. The more general analysis is of very limited value, however, unless its empirical implications can be ascertained.

The present paper discusses the analysis of resource allocation in less developed economies from three points of view. Section I tries to ascertain the extent to which the allocation principles derived from trade theory and from growth theory can be reconciled with each other without losing their operational significance. Section II compares various approaches to the measurement of optimal resource allocation in terms of their logical consistency and their applicability to different conditions. Section III examines some of the practical procedures followed in setting investment policy in underdeveloped countries in the light of the earlier discussion. Finally, some of the theoretical issues are re-examined to indicate their practical importance.

I *Conflict Between Trade Theory and Growth Theory*

The main contradictions between comparative advantage and other principles of resource allocation derive from their different orientation and assumptions. The classical analysis focuses on long-run tendencies and equilibrium conditions, while modern theories of growth are concerned with the interaction among producing and consuming units in a dynamic system. Since both approaches are familiar, I shall only try to identify the differences in assumptions and emphasis that lead to different policy conclusions.

A. *The Implications of Comparative Advantage for Resource Allocation*

The modern version of the comparative cost doctrine [20] is essentially a simplified form of static general equilibrium theory.[1] The optimum pattern of production and trade for a country is determined from a comparison of the opportunity cost of producing a given commodity with the price at which the commodity can be imported or exported. In equilibrium, no commodity is

1 An excellent discussion and synthesis of the several versions of trad- theory is given by Caves [7]. The terms 'comparative advantage' and 'comparative cost' are used interchangeably in most discussions.

produced which could be imported at lower cost, and exports are expanded until marginal revenue equals marginal cost. Under the assumptions of full employment and perfect competition, the opportunity cost of a commodity, which is the value of the factors used to produce it in their best alternative employment, is equal to its market value. Market prices of factors and commodities can therefore be used to determine comparative advantage under competitive conditions. Long-term changes are not ignored but they are assumed to be reflected in current market prices.

The Heckscher-Ohlin version of the comparative cost doctrine has been widely recommended as a basis for development policy because it provides a measure of comparative advantage that does not depend on the existence of perfect competition and initial equilibrium. This version states that a country will benefit from trade by producing commodities that use more of its relatively abundant factors of production. It will export these commodities and import commodities using more of its relatively scarce factors unless its pattern of domestic demand happens to be biased toward commodities using domestic factors. The critical assumptions in this analysis are that factors of production are comparable among countries and that production functions are the same. These assumptions are not required by classical trade theory.

The applicability of the comparative cost doctrine to present-day conditions in underdeveloped countries has been re-examined by Viner and its validity has been reaffirmed with some modifications. Viner criticizes the Heckscher-Ohlin version because its assumption of comparable factors does not allow for observable differences in their quality [63, p. 16]. In this recent answer to critics of the comparative cost approach [64], however, Viner admits the necessity of interpreting comparative advantage in a dynamic setting in which the efficiency of production may change over time, external economies may exist, and the market prices of commodities and factors may differ from their opportunity cost. As Nurkse points out [64, p. 76], these modifications rob the original doctrine of much of its practical value. It is now necessary to have an explicit analysis of the growth process itself before it is possible to determine, even theoretically, where comparative advantage lies; market prices and current opportunity costs are no longer sufficient.

B. *Implications of Growth Theory for Resource Allocation*

Modern growth theory is concerned with the interactions over time among producers, consumers, and investors in interrelated sectors of the economy. In the writings of such economists as Rosenstein-Rodan [43], Lewis [29], Nurkse [36], Myrdal [34], Rostow [44], Dobb [12], and Hirschman [23], there is much more emphasis on the sequence of expansion of production and factor use by sector than on the conditions of general equilibrium. Growth theory either ignores comparative advantage and the possiblities of trade completely, or it considers mainly the dynamic aspects, such as the stimulus that an increase in exports provides to the development of related sectors or the function of imports as a carrier of new products and advanced technology. With this different point of view, growth theorists often suggest investment criteria that are quite contradictory to those derived from considerations of comparative advantage.

The conflicts between these two approaches to resources allocation may be traced either to differences in assumptions or to the inclusion of factors in one theory that are omitted from the other. Growth theory contains at least four basic assumptions about underdeveloped economies that differ strongly from those underlying the comparative cost doctrine: (1) factor prices do not necessarily reflect opportunity costs with any accuracy; (2) the quantity and quality of factors of production may change substantially over time, in part as a result of the production process itself; (3) economies of scale relative to the size of existing markets are important in a number of sectors of production; (4) complementarity among commodities is dominant in both producer and consumer demand.

Some of the implications of these factors are developed by Rosenstein-Rodan [43] and Nurkse [36] as arguments for 'balanced growth,' by which is meant simultaneous expansion of a number of sectors of production.[2] Assuming an elastic supply of either capital or labor, these authors show that investment will be more profitable in related sector, because of horizontal and vertical interdependence, than in the same sectors considered separately. Market forces will not necessarily lead to optimal investment decisions

2 The term 'balanced growth' has been given a variety of meanings, but the idea of simultaneous expansion on several fronts is common to all of them.

because present prices do not reflect the cost and demand conditions that will exist in the future. This effect of investment in one sector on the profitability of investment in another sector, via increased demand or reduced costs, has been called by Scitovsky [47] a 'dynamic external economy.' The imputation of these economies to the originating sectors may seriously affect the estimate of comparative advantage.

If we assume fixed investment resources instead of an elastic supply, the same set of factors provide an argument for concentrated or unbalanced growth [48] [50]. In order to achieve economies of scale in one sector, it may be necessary to devote a large fraction of the available investment funds to that sector and to supply increased requirements in other sectors from imports (or to curtail them temporarily). The optimal pattern of investment will then be one which concentrates first on one sector and then on another, with balance being approached only in the long run. Streeten [53] has developed further dynamic arguments for unbalanced growth from the fact that technological progress may be more rapid if increases in production are concentrated in a few sectors, while Hirschman [23] argues for imbalance to economize on entreprenurial ability.

The historical significance of the balanced growth argument has been examined by Gerschenkron [18], Rostow [44], and Ohlin [38], in the context of nineteenth-century industrial development in Europe. They show that vertical interdependence has been important in stimulating the growth of related industrial sectors, although the nature and origin of these complexes differ from country to country. In one case they may be related to exports, in another to expansion for the domestic market. The importance of interdependence among producers emerges fairly clearly from these historical studies.

The net effect of the discussion of dynamic interdependence and balanced vs. unbalanced growth is to destroy the presumption that perfect competition, even if it could be achieved, would lead to the optimum allocation of resources over time. Since the doctrine of comparative advantage in its conventional form is a corollary of general equilibrium theory, the theoretical qualification that apply to the latter also apply to the former. If, then, the doctrine of comparative advantage is to be useful for development policy, the essential elements of the growth analysis must be combined with it.

C. *Dynamic Modifications of Comparative Advantage*

Classical trade theory does not exclude changes in the supply of factors and other data over time, but it does insist that under perfect competition the effects of such changes will be reflected in the market mechanism. If, on the other hand, we take comparative advantage as a principle of planning rather than as a result of market forces, we can include any foreseeable exogenous changes in technology, tastes, or other data without going beyond the framework of comparative statics.

Some of the modifications suggested by growth theory are dynamic in a more essential way, in that a particular change depends not only on the passage of time but on other variables in the system. For example, the rate of increase in the productivity of labor in an industry may depend on an increasing level of production in that industry. Some of these dynamic elements can also be analyzed by methods of comparative statics if our purpose is only to choose among alternative courses of action.

The four assumptions of growth theory discussed above (Section B) lead to the following requirements for the analytical framework to be used in determining comparative advantage in a growing economy:[3] (1) recognition of the possibility of structural disequilibrium in factor markets; (2) the inclusion of indirect (market and nonmarket) effects of expanding a given type of production; (3) simultaneous determination of levels of consumption, imports, and production in interrelated sectors over time when decreasing costs result from the expansion of output; and (4) allowance for variation in the demand for exports and other data over time.

These changes destroy the simplicity of the classical system, in which allocation decisions can be based on a partial analysis because adjustments in the rest of the economy are reflected in equilibrium market prices. In the dynamic analysis, it may not be possible to state that a country has a comparative advantage in producing steel without specifying also the levels of production of iron ore, coal and metal-working over time. In short, we are forced to compare alternative patterns of growth rather than separate sectors, and we cannot expect to find simple generalizations of the

3 Some of these criticisms of static analysis were made years ago by Williams [66], and a number of the elements were, of course, recognized by the classical economists themselves. I am not concerned with explicit criticism of the classical analysis, but with the possibility of reconciling it with growth theory.

Heckscher-Ohlin type concerning the characteristics of individual lines of production.

Since there is no well-developed body of theory concerning the formal properties of the system just outlined,[4] I shall only try to indicate in a general way the modifications that some of these elements of growth theory will produce in the analysis of comparative advantage.

Factor Costs. It is generally agreed that costs of labor and capital in underdeveloped countries do not reflect their opportunity costs with any accuracy because of market imperfections, but there is wide disagreement as to the extent of the typical discrepancies. Some types of labor may be overvalued while particular skills are undervalued. Factor costs may also change markedly over time as a result of economic development, so that an advantage based on cheap labor may prove quite limited in duration. As Lewis [29] and Hagen [21] show, the effects on comparative advantage of correcting for disequilibrium factor prices are often very substantial. (The effects of disequilibrium in factor markets are discussed further in Part II.)

Export Markets. Two of the main arguments against the trade pattern produced by market forces concern (1) the fluctuating nature and (2) the low income and price elasticities of the demand for primary products. The existence of cyclical fluctuation is well established, but the income and price elasticities vary considerably among primary commodities. Their net effect on the terms of trade of primary producers over time is a matter of dispute [64]. These characteristics are often used as an argument for reducing specialization in underdeveloped countries and for expanding industry for local consumption rather than expanding primary exports [41] [51].

These factors can be admitted without seriously modifying the principle of comparative advantage. The market value of the stream of export earnings should be reduced to reflect the drawbacks to the economy resulting from its variable characteristics, and this social value should be used in comparing investment in primary exports to other alternatives. When export demand has a low elasticity, marginal revenue should be used in place of average revenue. Since it is quite likely that the market evaluation of the

4 In his survey of modern trade theory, Caves [7] shows that attempts to introduce dynamic elements have been concerned mainly with particular aspects and have led not to new principles, but rather to extensions of static results.

attractiveness of an investment in exports will differ from this social evaluation, some form of government intervention may be warranted. It is wrong, however, to conclude from this analysis that continued specialization in primary exports may not be the best policy, because even the corrected return on exports may be greater than that on alternative investments. The supply of foreign investment may also be greater for export production.

Productivity Change. The possibility of rising efficiency as labor and management acquire increasing experience in actual production has long been recognized [66] and forms the basis for the infant industry argument. This argument has been generalized to include the effects of increasing production in any industry on the supply of skilled labor and management available to other industries. Since manufacturing is thought to have more important training effects than primary production [33] [41], the fact that improvements in factor supply are not reflected in the market mechanism may introduce a bias against manufacturing. The empirical basis for this argument has been questioned by several economists [46] [63], who assert that there is often as much scope for technological improvement in agriculture as in industry. Without trying to settle the empirical question that has been raised, it may be concluded that productivity change is an important factor and therefore that comparative advantage should be measured over time. It cannot be said, however, that allowance for this factor will always favor manufacturing.

Dynamic External Economies. As indicated above, dynamic external economies are received by an industry from cost reductions or demand increases in other sectors. Cost reductions may result from economies of scale, productivity increases, or new technology. The customary analysis of comparative advantage on a sector-by-sector basis would require that the cost reduction from simultaneously developing interrelated sectors be allocated separately to each. However, if a group of investments will only be profitable when they are undertaken together, comparative advantage can only be determined for alternative combinations of investments. As shown in [11], not only do market prices fail to produce the best investment allocation in this situation, but any structure of equilibrium prices may also be an inadequate guide in the presence of economies of scale.

There is considerable evidence that external economies are more important in the industrial sectors than in primary production because of internal economies of scale, training effects, and high demand elasticities. Their omission from the market mechanism is therefore likely to bias resource allocation against manufacturing. The quantitative significance of this factor is very hard to determine, however, since it involves simultaneous changes in a number of sectors.

Uncertainty and Flexibility. The limited ability of policy-makers to foresee changes in demand and supply conditions puts a premium on flexibility in the choice of a development strategy. This factor not only argues against specialization in one or two export commodities but it also favors the development of a diversified economic structure which will enable the economy to shift to new types of exports or import substitutes when changing trade conditions may require them. Kindleberger [26] sees this factor as the main explanation for his finding that the terms of trade have favored developed countries although they have not favored countries exporting manufactured goods in general.[5] The argument is similar to that of Stigler [52] concerning the optimum choice of techniques in a manufacturing plant. The optimum design for a changing market is likely to differ from the optimum under static conditions because in the former case the proper criterion is lowest-cost production for varying operating levels and with changes in product design. Similarly optimum development policy should result in a pattern of resource allocation that allows for unforeseen changes in supply and demand conditions even at the cost of some loss of short-term efficiency.

II *The Measurement of Optimum Resource Allocation*

The development of an adequate theory is only the first step in formulating economic policy. In order to reach practical conclusions, it is also necessary to specify the environment in which the policy-maker functions. Relevant aspects of a particular society include its general objectives, the policy instruments to be considered, and the information available. The theory must then be combined with these elements in such a way as to yield guides to action or 'decision rules' for particular situations.

Although the growing science of operations research is concerned

5 This argument is also discussed by Caves [7, pp. 264-6].

with the development of decision rules for business and military operations, less progress has been made in developing an operational approach to long-run economic policy. Tinbergen [55] and Frisch [15] have outlined a general framework for policy analysis, but it has had relatively little impact on the discussion of the development of underdeveloped countries. In this field the failure to specify adequately the decision-making environment and to distinguish between decision rules and the corollaries of pure theory has led to great confusion.

Since the information needed for over-all economic analysis is available to a very limited extent in underdeveloped countries, there has been a considerable effort to derive decision rules or 'investment criteria' that can be based on partial analysis. I shall group the various suggestions into three categories: (1) factor-intensity criteria; (2) productivity criteria; (3) programming criteria based on accounting prices. Although these various approaches often lead to contradictory results, each has some merit as a form of decision rule if properly qualified. In general, the theoretically more valid formulations require more information and must be replaced by cruder approximations when adequate data are not available. Since a major part of the literature in the development field has been devoted to the discussion of investment criteria, it is important to identify the sources of conflict among them and to specify the circumstances under which each may be approximately correct.

In economic theory, capital and labor are assumed to be separately allocated in single units to different uses. In national planning, however, it is more convenient to consider the decision to install a given productive process or plant, representing the allocation of a group of inputs in specified quantities, as the basic choice. Investment criteria are customarily formulated for 'projects' of this sort, since they form the basis for the decisions of planning authorities. This procedure recognizes that very small productive units are uneconomical, and it permits a consideration of different scales of output. The choice of techniques can be considered as a choice among projects producing the same output from different input combinations. In this way the allocation procedure can be divided into two steps: the choice of the best technique for a given type of product, and the decision whether to produce the commodity at all. The principle of comparative advantage is more directly relevant to the second type of choice, but the two cannot be separated entirely.

A. *Factor-Intensity Criteria*

The simplest approach to any allocation problem is to concentrate on the scarcest resource. Since this is often capital in underdeveloped countries, it seems reasonable to choose the technique that uses the least capital to produce a given output. The same logic is applied to the choice of sectors of production: an underdeveloped country is advised to produce and export commodities that use relatively less capital per unit of output and to import items requiring more capital. Statements of this type occur in many economic writings of the past fifteen years. Buchanan [5] was among the first to state this criterion for investment in underdeveloped countries and to base policy recommendations upon it.

The 'minimum capital-output ratio' criterion is only valid under the following restrictive conditions:[6] (1) Either capital is the only scarce factor in the system, or other inputs are so abundant relative to capital that the latter is the dominant element in determining cost differences. (2) Either the same output is produced by each investment alternative, or the market values used to compare the different products coincide with their social values. (3) Production takes place under constant costs.

The use of the capital-output ratio theoretically requires a measurement of the total capital used in producing a given commodity, including the capital used in producing all materials and services purchased. Alternatively, the indirect use of capital can be allowed for by deducting the cost of purchased inputs from the value of output and expressing the criterion as the ratio of capital to value added. This procedure requires the further assumption that market prices correctly reflect the use of capital in the rest of the economy.

A closely related allocation criterion is the capital intensity: the ratio of capital to labor. This test is derived directly from the Heckscher-Ohlin version of the comparative cost doctrine. If the same production functions exist in all countries and if capital is scarce relative to labor in the underdeveloped countries, com-

6 A rigorous analysis of the validity of marginal and average factor-output ratios as indicators of optimum allocation in a two-factor system is given by Bator [4].

parative advantage in the latter can be identified by low capital-labor ratios. This approach does not assume that labor has zero opportunity cost, as does use of the capital-output ratio, but only that the ratio of labor cost to capital cost is lower than in the country's trading partners. To allow for differences in the quality of labor among countries, it is sometimes suggested that the assessment of relative labor cost should be made for labor units of equal efficiency—e.g., the labor required in each country to perform a given type of operation with the same capital goods and organization.

A principal criticism of the use of both these ratios is that they ignore the existence of other factors of production, such as natural resources. If either labor or natural resources has a significant opportunity cost, the capital-output measure must be replaced by the more general marginal productivity of capital criterion, which is discussed in the next section.

To judge comparative advantage by the capital-labor ratio is to assume either that this ratio will be the same for the same industry in all countries, or that capital is equally substitutable for labor in producing all the commodities traded. Deviations from these assumptions, along with the omission of other inputs and variations in efficiency by sector, make the capital-labor criterion a very crude approximation indeed to a proper estimate of comparative advantage.

B. *Marginal Productivity Criteria*[7]

A more comprehensive allocation criterion is the social marginal product of a given unit of resources in a given use. Where the factor-intensity criteria are at best only correlated with the increase in national income produced by a project, the productivity criteria try to measure the increase. The marginal productivity test is in turn less general than the over-all programming approach, because it is based on a partial equilibrium analysis that is only valid for relatively small changes in the economic structure.

The several forms of marginal productivity criterion that have been proposed differ in the assumptions made about the social welfare function and in the extent to which allowance is made for the indirect effects of a given allocation. All versions are alike in

7 Surveys of these and other investment criteria are given by Castellino [6] Vaidyanathan [62], and the United Nations [61].

assuming that the government controls, directly or indirectly, a certain fraction of the investible resources of the country and wishes to allocate them in such a way as to maximize future welfare.

Since the productivity criteria are usually applied to investment projects rather than to single units of capital, they are 'marginal' only in the sense that a project normally constitutes a small fraction of the total capital invested in a given year. For very large projects a breakdown into smaller units would be more appropriate.

The Static SMP Criterion. As proposed by Kahn [25], the social marginal product (SMP) is a general equilibrium concept which is conventionally defined as the net contribution of a marginal unit (project) to the national product.[8] The related decision rule is to rank investment projects by their SMP and to go down the list until the funds to be allocated are exhausted. Alternatively, any project having an SMP above a given level can be approved.

Kahn uses the SMP criterion to show the fallacies in the factor-intensity measures that had been advocated by Buchanan [5], Polak [40], and other writers. He points out that: 'The existence of a particular natural resource, specialized skills, particular climatic conditions, or the importance of a particular product or service may make the SMP of capital higher in a line which is more capital intensive than in another which is less so' [25, p. 40]. He also argues that even when there is substantial rural unemployment, a considerable amount of capital and other inputs are required to transport, train, and house the workers who are to be employed elsewhere. Kahn's arguments against the simple capital-intensity criteria appear to have been generally accepted, although he admits that a lower capital-output ratio may be a useful guide when other information is lacking.

Some modifications in the SMP criterion were suggested by the present author [8] to allow for artificial elements in the price system (tariffs, subsidies, etc.) and to provide for the evaluation of labor and foreign exchange at opportunity cost rather than at market value. Further allowances for the difference between market price and social value can be made by estimating the benefits to be provided to other sectors in the form of external economies, and

8 To be more accurate, cost and output streams should be discounted to the present, but I shall not be concerned with differences in the time pattern of output of different projects.

by including overhead costs in the estimate of the cost of labor. All of these elements are included in Eckstein's synthesis and extension of the productivity approach [14].[9]

The SMP criterion is entirely consistent with the general programming approach discussed below, which derives opportunity costs from an explicit analysis of total factor use. In the absence of such an overall analysis, the corrections suggested for the calculation of the productivity of investment are likely to be quite approximate. There is no logical conflict between the results of the SMP analysis and the dictates of comparative advantage because each is a corollary of a general equilibrium solution over a given time period.

The Marginal Reinvestment Criterion. A sharp criticism of the SMP criterion was made by Galenson and Leibenstein [17], who challenge some of its basic premises. They would substitute a different social welfare function in which the aim is to maximize per capita income at some time in the distant future rather than to maximize a discounted stream of income over time. They also assume severe restrictions on the policy instruments available to the government, and in particular deny its ability to affect the rate of saving by fiscal measures. Under these assumptions, it is necessary to take account of the division of income resulting from a project between profits and wages, since savings from the former are higher.

To maximize the total output at some distant future time, Galenson and Leibenstein easily show that the most 'productive' project is not necessarily the one which maximizes national income in the near future but the one which leads to the highest savings. Since it is assumed that neither voluntary saving nor taxes can be extracted from wages, the most productive project will be the one with the highest profit rate per unit of capital invested.[10] The assumption that profits are saved and reinvested leads to the 'marginal reinvestment quotient' as a decision-rule to be applied in place of the SMP.

Galenson and Leibenstein push their argument one step further

9 Eckstein points out that the assumption of capital rationing implies a social judgment as to both the amount of investment in the current period and the discount to be applied to future outputs, since the market rate of interest is rejected for both purposes.

10 I omit the possibility of an effect on population growth, which leads Galenson and Leibenstein to state the criterion on a per capita basis.

and identify the most profitable project as the one with the highest capital-labor ratio. This result leads them to the paradoxical conclusion that the factor-intensity rule should be reversed: countries should prefer the most capital-intensive rather than the least capital-intensive techniques in order to promote savings and future growth. This conclusion involves an implicit assumption about the nature of production functions: that increasing the capital intensity will necessarily raise the average return to capital in each sector of production. This is obviously not true in general and is not necessarily true of existing productive techniques. The savings effect of a given project should therefore be measured directly and not assumed to vary in proportion to the capital-labor ratio.

Galenson and Leibenstein have been widely criticized for their extreme assumptions [4] [14] [24] [35], in particular for the use of a social welfare function in which the starvation of half the population in the near future would appear to be a matter of indifference and for the assumption that limitations on fiscal policy make a lower income preferable to a much higher one if the former has a higher savings component. Their analysis has nevertheless been useful in emphasizing that other effects of an investment beside its immediate contribution to the national product should be included in the productivity criterion.[11]

The Marginal Growth Contribution. Eckstein [14] has successfully reconciled the conflict between the Kahn-Chenery SMP approach and the Galenson-Leibenstein reinvestment approach, and in so doing he has provided a considerable generalization of each. First, he assumes that the social objective is to maximize the present value of the future consumption stream. With a zero discount rate, this objective approximates the long-term income objective of Galenson and Leibenstein, while with a high discount of future consumption it leads to the maximization of income in the short term. Second, Eckstein assumes that there is a different savings (reinvestment) coefficient associated with each project, but he allows for any savings rate out of wages and profits. From these assumptions, he derives a measure of the 'marginal growth contribution' of a given project that consists of two parts: (1) an *efficiency term*, consisting of the present value of the consumption stream; and

11 In [28], Leibenstein restates in more restrained form his arguments for including labor training, savings, population growth, and other indirect effects in a comprehensive productivity measure.

(2) a *growth term*, consisting of the additional consumption to be achieved by reinvesting savings.

The relative importance of the two terms depends largely on the rate of discount that is applied to future consumption. Even with a low rate of discount, the significance of the second term depends on how much variation there is in the fraction of income saved among different projects. If the savings ratio is not related to the form of income generated, then, as Bator [4] shows, there is no conflict between maximizing income in the short run and in the longer run. Eckstein's formula provides for all possible intermediate assumptions between the two extreme views of the determinants of savings.[12]

In principle, one might include other indirect dynamic effects, such as the value of the labor training provided, in the measurement of the total productivity of a given project. There is a danger of double counting if partial-equilibrium analysis is extended too far, however, and most indirect effects can be more readily evaluated in the more general programming framework considered below.

C. *Programming Criteria and Accounting Prices*

The allocation rules discussed up to now are based on the existing economic structure and are strictly applicable only for relatively small changes in it. Although it may in many instances be necessary to rely primarily on these marginal criteria for lack of data on the rest of the economy, it is important to have some way of testing larger changes and of evaluating the errors that are introduced by the marginal procedure. Furthermore, without a more comprehensive analysis it is impossible to reconcile fully the conflicting policy implications of comparative advantage and growth theory.

The difficulties of partial analysis increase with the number of modifications that have to be applied to market prices in order to arrive at social value. Both the factor-intensity ratios and the partial productivity measures assume that there is one principal restriction on the system, the scarcity of capital. They do not allow for the fact that in allocating capital according to any one of these rules some other restriction on the system, such as the supply of foreign exchange, of skilled labor, or of a particular commodity, may be exceeded.

12 Sen [49] independently formulated a more general investment criterion that is very similar to Eckstein's, in which the SMP and reinvestment criteria are shown to be limiting cases.

The programming approach to resource allocation begins with the problem of balancing supply and demand for different commodities and factors of production. Until quite recently, practical programming methods have been more concerned with ensuring the consistency of a given allocation of resources with certain targets than with testing the efficiency with which resources are used. Historically speaking, the programming approach is thus the operational counterpart of the theory of balanced growth, from which much of its conceptual framework is derived.

One of the earliest attempts at formulating a comprehensive development program for an underdeveloped area was Mandelbaum's illustrative model for Southeastern Europe, undertaken during the war [31]. He starts, as many subsequent programs have done, from an estimate of the increase in national income required to absorb a prospective increment in the labor force. The allocation of capital and labor is made initially from demand estimates and by analogy to the structure of more advanced countries. The principle of comparative advantage is only introduced intuitively in modifying the initial projection. The main test of resource allocation is the balance of demand and supply for each sector and factor of production.

The development of mathematical programming methods makes it possible to carry out this type of analysis in a much more precise way. In several countries, consistent development programs have been formulated by using input-output analysis, as in the studies of the Economic Commission for Latin America [58] [59] [60]. It is only with the development of linear programming, however, that it is possible to reconcile the consistency criteria and the productivity criteria in a systematic way.

A link between the test of consistency (feasibility) in resource allocation and the test of productivity (efficiency) is provided by a consideration of the price implications of a given allocation. Assume that a set of production levels has been worked out so as to be consistent with the available supplies of labor, capital and natural resources, given the structure of consumer demand and the country's trading possibilities. These sector production and trade levels constitute a 'feasible program.' Any such program implies a unique set of commodity and factor prices if the economy is in equilibrium. If production activities are assumed to operate at constant costs, linear programming provides a method of calculating the 'shadow prices' corresponding to the equilibrium conditions, in which the price of each commodity is equal to its cost of production.[13] Prices are determined by the solution to the following set of simultaneous equations, one for each production activity included in the program:

$$a_{1j}P_1+a_{2j}P_2+\ldots+a_{nj}P_n=0 \qquad (j=1\ldots n) \tag{1}$$

where a_{ij} is the input or output of commodity or factor i by activity j, and P_i is the shadow price of commodity or factor i. The input coefficients may be measured at existing prices or in other convenient units. In an open economy, activities of importing and exporting are also included in the system, and the price solution contains the equilibrium price of foreign exchange. An example of this calculation is given in Table 1, which will be explained shortly.

The use of shadow or 'accounting' prices in evaluating investment projects has been suggested by Tinbergen [54] [56], Frisch [15] [16], and Chenery [9] [10]. Although Tinbergen does not use a linear programming framework, his accounting prices for factors have the same meaning as shadow prices: the opportunity cost implied by a given resource allocation.[14] He suggests computing the costs associated with a project by using accounting prices; any project that shows a positive net return over cost (including capital cost) should be approved. This test is equivalent to the SMP criterion, as shown below.

The general linear programming problem is to maximize the value of a linear objective function subject to linear constraints. In development programs, the principal constraints are that the demands for commodities and factors should not exceed their supplies; the function to be maximized is usually taken as the national income. Alternatively, the objective may be the achievement of a given increase in output at minimum cost in investment (including foreign investment). Other social objectives, such as a minimum employment level or a specified degree of regional balance, can be included as additional restrictions on the program. The

13 The assumptions of linear programming and methods of finding solutions to programming models have been discussed in a number of recent publications, such as [13].

14 Tinbergen [56, p. 39] defines accounting prices as those 'that would prevail if (i) the investment pattern under discussion were actually carried out, and (ii) equilibrium existed on the markets just mentioned' [i.e., labor, capital, foreign exchange markets]. The relation between accounting and shadow prices is discussed in Chenery [10] and Qayum [42].

TABLE 1

EVALUATION OF PRODUCTION AND IMPORT ACTIVITIES BY ACCOUNTING PRICES[a]

Commodities and Factors	Production Activities				Import Activities			Accounting Prices				Restrictions
	X_1	X_2	X_3	X_4	M_1	M_2	M_3	Trial a	Trial b	Trial c	Trial d	
	(1)	(2)	(3)	(4)	(5)	(6)	(7)	(8)	(9)	(10)	(11)	(12)
1. Metal Products	**1.00** (3.41)				**1.00** (3.41)			2.55	3.42	3.41	2.26	1000
2. Iron and Steel	**− .22** (− .89)	**1.00** (4.03)				**1.00** (4.03)		3.60	4.82	4.03	3.50	1000
3. Iron Ore		**− .08** (− .25)	**1.00** (3.12)				**1.00** (3.12)	3.30	4.42	3.12	2.19	0
4. Foreign Exchange				**1.00** (4.01)	**− .85** (−3.41)	**−1.20** (−4.81)	**−1.10** (−4.41)	3.00	4.02	4.01	2.92	0
5. Other Inputs	**− .20** (− .62)	**− .25** (− .78)	**− .70** (−2.17)	**− .10** (− .31)				3.00	3.20	3.10	2.20	—
6. Labor	**− .70** (−1.05)	**− .20** (− .30)	**− .30** (− .45)	**−1.00** (−1.50)				1.50	1.50	1.50	.50	—

TABLE 1 (Contd.)

Commodities and Factors	Production Activities				Import Activities			Accounting Prices[a]				Restrictions
	X_1	X_2	X_3	X_4	M_1	M_2	M_3	Trial a	Trial b	Trial c	Trial d	
	(1)	(2)	(3)	(4)	(5)	(6)	(7)	(8)	(9)	(10)	(11)	(12)
7. Capital	**− .70** (− .70)	**−2.70** (−2.70)	**− .50** (− .50)	**−2.20** (−2.20)				1.00	1.00	1.00	1.00	—
Social Profitability[b]												
Trial a	− .59	− .41	+ .25	−1.00	0	0	0					
Trial b	− .03	+ .37	+1.23	0	0	0	0					
Trial c	+ .15	0	0	0	0	− .78	−1.29					
Trial d	0	− .03	0	0	− .32	0	−1.32					
Production and Import Levels												
Trial a	0	0	0	2050	1000	1000	0					
Trial b	0	1000	80	850	1000	0	0					
Trial c	1000	1220	98	0	0	0	0					
Trial d	1000	0	0	1464	0	1220	0					

[a] Based on Chenery [11], Table 1. Prices satisfy equation (1) except for P_4 in trial 1. Figures in parentheses are $(a_{ij} Pi)$ for trial c.

[b] Calculated from equation (4).

instrument variables can also be constrained to fall within specified limits, as in the models of Frisch.[15]

To illustrate the meaning and use of shadow prices in evaluating investment projects, I shall take up a very simplified programming model that is worked out in more detail elsewhere [11]. The truncated system given in Table 1 covers only a small part of the economy, but it will serve to illustrate the way in which interdependence influences investment decisions and the effect of having more than one scarce factor.

The model contains four production activities (X_1,X_2,X_3,X_4) and three import activities (M_1,M_2,M_3). Each activity is represented in Table 1 by a column of coefficients, a_{ij}, showing the amount of input $(-)$ or output $(+)$ of commodity i when the activity is operated at unit level. (These coefficients are the boldface figures in columns 1 to 7.) The net output is taken as unity in all cases. The production activity X_1, for example, represents the production of one unit of metal products from .22 units of iron and steel, .20 units of 'other inputs,' .70 units of labor, and .70 units of capital. The import activity M_1 provides an alternative way of supplying a unit of metal products by an expenditure (input) of .85 units of foreign exchange. A similar choice is provided between X_2 and M_2 (iron and steel) and between X_3 and M_3 (iron ore). The fourth production activity shows the resources used in the marginal export sector to provide a unit of foreign exchange.

In a complete programming model, the amounts of all commodities required for final use at a given level of income would be entered as restrictions on the solution. Similarly, the amounts of available capital and labor of different types would be specified. In this limited illustration, the problem is to supply requirements of 1000 each for metal products and iron and steel at minimum cost. Iron ore and foreign exchange are therefore taken to be intermediate goods having not net outside demand. 'Other inputs,' labor and

15 Frisch is one of the strongest advocates of the use of linear programming for development planning, as indicated in the preface to a recent methodological study: 'In the beginning of 1959, during my work as a United Nations expert in Cairo, I was confronted with the problem of working out a methodology for *optimal investment programming* in a rapidly expanding underdeveloped country. I have always believed—and my Cairo experiences have confirmed it—that such a method must be formulated in terms which ultimately make the problem amenable to linear programming. Otherwise one is practically certain to be taken by surprise afterwards in unexpected balance of payments difficulties and other troubles' [16, p. 1].

capital are supplied from outside the model at prices reflecting their opportunity costs in the rest of the economy. The main difference in principle between this submodel and a complete programming system is that the prices of only the first four commodities are determined in the model in the present case, while in general all prices are so determined.

The four restrictions in the model consist of equations stating that the supply of each of the first four inputs must be equal to the specified demand:[16]

$$
(2)\qquad
\begin{aligned}
X_1 + M_1 &= 1000 \\
-.22X_1 + X_2 + M_2 &= 1000 \\
-.08X_2 + X_3 + M_3 &= 0 \\
X_4 - .85M_1 - 1.20M_2 - 1.10M_3 &= 0
\end{aligned}
$$

The objective is to minimize the amount of capital required to supply the given final demands, with the use of labor and 'other inputs' valued at their opportunity costs in terms of capital. This is the same as supplying each commodity at minimum unit cost, since the amount of each to be supplied is fixed.

A feasible solution to the model contains either a production or an import activity for each of the three commodities plus the export activity for foreign exchange. The corresponding activity levels can be determined from equations (2) and are shown at the bottom of Table 1. The amounts of the outside factors (Fi)—labor, capital, and 'other inputs'—required by each solution can then be determined from the following equations:

$$
(3)\qquad
\begin{aligned}
&\text{Other inputs: } & F_5 &= .20X_1 + .25X_2 + .70X_3 + .10X_4 \\
&\text{Labor: } & F_6 &= .70X_1 + .20X_2 + .30X_3 + 1.00X_4 \\
&\text{Capital: } & F_7 &= .70X_1 + 2.70X_2 + .50X_3 + 2.20X_4
\end{aligned}
$$

The programming model thus contains two types of equations: price equations of the type of (1), and equations for the supply and demand of commodities and outside factors, (2) and (3). As outlined in [10], the general procedure for solving a programming model of this type involves three steps: (a) finding a feasible program or set of activity levels that satisfies the supply-demand restrictions; (b) calculating the shadow prices associated with the given program; (c) using these prices to determine whether any

16 I omit the possibility of overfulfilling demands, since there are no joint products in the present case.

improvement in the initial program is possible. This procedure is repeated as long as any further improvements can be made.

The programming criterion used to compare projects or activities is the social profitability of each as measured from the shadow prices. Any profitable activity should be included in the program. It is the recalculation of prices that distinguishes this procedure from the partial programming approach suggested by Tinbergen. In either case, however, the test of social profitability of activity j can be expressed as:

$$\Pi_j = \sum_i a_{ij} P_i \qquad (4)$$

By definition, the activities that were used in determining the shadow prices will have a profitability of zero. The optimum solution is identified by the condition that all other activities have zero or negative profitability.

Some idea of the type of adjustment that results from moving from partial toward general equilibrium analysis may be given by determining solutions to the model in Table 1 under four different procedures: (a) the use of market prices; (b) correcting for the overvaluation of foreign exchange; (c) finding the optimum solution for the submodel alone; (d) finding the optimum solution for the submodel with changes in the opportunity costs of labor and other inputs determined from a general programming model. The accounting prices corresponding to each assumption are shown in columns 8 to 11 of Table 1. The calculation of social profitability of each activity, given the accounting prices, is illustrated in the table for trial c by giving cost and revenue figures in parentheses in columns 1 to 7.

Trial a. Assume that market prices are based on the cost of importing and are determined by setting profits on the import activities equal to zero, with a given foreign exchange cost of 3.00. The exchange rate is assumed to be overvalued, so that the price of foreign exchange is less than the cost of securing it through expanded exports. At these market prices, only activity X_3 (iron ore) is profitable, but there is no domestic demand for iron ore unless steel is also produced (the export price is lower than that of imports because of transport costs). The use of market prices therefore leads to imports of steel and metal products, since the opportunity cost of expanding exports is not taken into account.

The corresponding activity levels are shown at the bottom of the table.

Trial b. Assume now that we correct for the existing structural disequilibrium by setting the price of foreign exchange equal to its opportunity cost of 4.02 as determined from the export activity X_4. Allowance is also made for a rise in the accounting price of 'other inputs,' some of which are imported. A new set of accounting prices for commodities 1–3 is determined from the cost of imports. Substituting these prices into equation (4) shows that X_2 and X_3 are both profitable ($\pi_2 = .37$, $\pi_3 = 1.23$). Investment should therefore take place in steel, iron ore, and exports on this test.

Trial c. To find the optimum solution to the submodel by linear programming, we can start from trial *b* and recalculate the shadow prices from the activities that are included: X_2 X_3 X_4 M_1. The four shadow prices P_1 to P_4 are determined by applying equation (1), taking the prices of the outside inputs (P_5, P_6, P_7) as given. The elimination of excess profits from the prices of iron ore and steel lowers the cost of producing metal products, providing an example of pecuniary external economies. Instead of a loss, activity X_1 now shows a profit of .15 and should be substituted for the import activity M_1. With the original prices for labor and capital, the optimum solution to the submodel is therefore to produce all three commodities and import nothing, since all import activities are unprofitable.

Trial d. If a similar analysis is carried out for the economy as a whole, it is likely that the initial estimate of the opportunity cost of labor (equal to its market price) will be revised. Assume that the shadow price of labor (equal to its marginal product in the rest of the economy) is only a third of its market price, or .5 units of capital. This lower labor cost will reduce the costs of production in different activities in proportion to their use of labor. Since exports are cheapened more than steel production by this calculation, it now becomes socially profitable to import steel and produce metal products. The optimality of this solution is shown by the prices in trial *d*, in which there is a loss of $-.03$ on X_3. The optimum quantity solution is shown at the bottom of the table. Valuing other inputs and labor at their accounting prices, it has a capital cost of 5760, compared to 8200, 7470, and 7290 in trials *a*, *b*, and *c*.

The programming approach of trials *c* and *d* adds two elements to the analysis of accounting prices. The first is the inclusion of repercussions on input prices from investment in supplying sectors. This is one of the main types of dynamic external economies which are omitted from partial analysis. It is much more significant when there are economies of scale. The second element is the revision of the initial estimate of the opportunity costs of labor, capital, and foreign exchange. This revision is determined by the relation between supply and demand for these factors and thus takes into account the requirements of feasibility.[17]

The profitability criterion (usually called the 'simplex' criterion) *that is used in linear programming is logically equivalent to the SMP test if the same prices are used in both.* The two can be put in a comparable form as follows:

(4a) Social profit on activity j: $$\Pi_j = \sum_i a_{ij}P_i - k_j$$

(5) SMP of investment in activity j: $$(\text{SMP})_j = \frac{\sum_i a_{ij}P_i}{k_j} = \frac{\Pi}{k_j} + 1$$

where $-kj$ is used for the capital input coefficient instead of a_7j. An activity having a positive social profit in equation (4a) will have an SMP of greater than 1.0 in (5), and the same projects would be accepted by either test. *If the prices used are not the equilibrium prices, however, the project rankings by the two formulae will not necessarily be the same.*

Although the example given here contained only one technique of production for each commodity, linear programming methods readily encompass alternative techniques. In a trial application of linear programming to Indian planning, Sandee [45] includes three alternative ways of increasing agricultural output—increased use of fertilizer, irrigation, and extension services—which are substitutes over a limited range. The four alternative techniques for producing textiles cited by Galenson and Leibenstein [17] could also be more properly evaluated in a programming model in which the cost variation associated with their different requirements for materials, maintenance, and skilled labor could be included. However, *it is only necessary to include alternative techniques in a pro-*

17 An example in which these successive adjustments are calculated in detail is given in [10]. Frisch has outlined a computational procedure for handling large numbers of investment projects without going beyond the capacity of simple calculating equipment [16].

gramming model when the choice between them depends on the outcome of the solution. Probably in most cases the range of shadow prices can be foreseen accurately enough to determine in advance which technique is more efficient for a given country. The initial assumption can always be verified after the analysis has been completed by using the resulting prices.

Linear programming can be extended to include many of the indirect effects of investment that are suggested by growth theory. The production of trained labor, the effect on savings, or other indirect benefits can be considered as joint outputs whose value can be specified in the objective function. Similarly, indirect costs of production, such as the provision of housing to urban workers, can be included as additional inputs. The shadow prices computed from such an expanded system will therefore reflect nonmarket as well as market interdependence to the extent that it can be specified in quantitative form.

In formal terms, it is also quite easy to extend the programming model in time and to compute future prices for commodities and factors. The measurement of social profitability could then be made against a pattern of changing future prices. Given the degree of uncertainty attached to all future economic magnitudes, however, this is not likely to be a very useful procedure beyond the customary five-year planning period except in the most general terms. It would, however, be desirable to estimate the change in the equilibrium prices of foreign exchange and labor over a longer period of time, since these are the most important variables in choosing among investment projects.

D. *Investment Criteria and Comparative Advantage*

The linear programming approach provides a convenient link to the principle of comparative advantage because the optimal pattern of trade is determined simultaneously with the optimum allocation of investment. The model is considerably more general than that of market equilibrium because it allows for different social objectives and takes account of costs and benefits other than those entering the market. The limitations to the programming model are of two sorts: the form of the restrictions that are specified, and the omission of relationships that cannot be expressed in quantitative form.

The introduction of inelastic demands or increasing costs does not create any more theoretical difficulty in a programming model than in the corresponding general equilibrium system, although the computational aspects of such models have not been widely explored. The accounting prices perform the same function as guides to proper allocation, but the test of social profitability must be applied in marginal rather than average terms. In development programs, this modification is particularly important in the case of exports, where the price elasticity of demand is often rather low.[18] As Nurkse [37] points out, marginal comparative advantage for the underdeveloped countries may for this reason be quite different from that inferred from the average costs and prices of primary exports.

The existence of increasing returns creates the same problem for the programming model as it does for equilibrium theory. Marginal-cost pricing is not sufficient to determine whether an investment should be undertaken, and the total cost of alternative solutions must also be considered. Although practical methods of solving programming models containing decreasing costs are now being developed, they do not give allocation criteria that rely only on accounting prices. It is approximately correct to say that beyond a certain output level country A has a comparative advantage in the production of steel, but the precise determination of the break-even point depends on the level of output in other sectors also.[19]

The most serious theoretical qualification to the principle of comparative advantage comes from the type of nonquantitative interdependence among sectors that is assumed by Hirschman [23]. If, as he supposes, one growth sequence is more effective than another because it economizes on decision-making ability or provides a greater incentive to political action, a set of criteria having little or nothing to do with comparative advantage is implied. The empirical significance of these psychological and sociological factors remains to be established, but they lead to a conflict that cannot be resolved in economic terms.

When the practical limitations on information and analysis are recognized, the possibilities of conflict between comparative advantage and growth theory are greatly increased, and Wiles [65]

18 A programming model including this feature is given in Chenery [9].

19 The nature of solutions to this type of problem is considered in [11], from which the data in Table 1 were taken. In this situation of decreasing average cost, the programming model may provide a greater improvement over the solution using partial criteria.

suggests that marginal efficiency calculations may be less important. An aversion to risk-taking may be a valid reason for limiting the extent of specialization in the export of primary products beyond the amount that would be optimum in the light of more accurate information. An inability to measure the extent of economies of scale, labor training, and other sources of external economies also makes possible a continuing disagreement as to their magnitude.

III *Comparative Advantage and Balance in Development Programs*

The inconsistent procedures that governments employ in formulating development policies are probably the most important source of conflict between the dictates of comparative advantage and of growth theory. Official pronouncements on development policy usually allege that both types of criteria have been (or should be) utilized in drawing up the program that is put forward, but the procedure followed in reconciling conflicts between the two is rarely made explicit. Since the analytical basis of most development programs is quite limited, it is important to look into the procedure that is actually used in order to discover sources of bias.

Development programs must simultaneously confront two sets of problems. In the short run, progress is hampered by structural disequilibrium in factor markets and in the demand and supply of particular commodities. This disequilibrium is reflected in the balance-of-payments difficulties that beset most low-income countries as they try to accelerate the process of development. In the long run, the choice among sectors becomes increasingly important because the pattern of growth in each period will depend on the choices made previously. Development programs that are influenced mainly by the existing structural disequilibrium therefore tend to stress the need for greater balance between domestic demand and supply, while those that take a longer view tend to pay more attention to comparative advantage.

Although the procedures actually followed cannot be ascertained with any accuracy by an outside observer, these two aspects can be identified from characteristic elements in the analysis. The balanced growth approach is generally associated with target-setting in key sectors, stress on the avoidance of bottlenecks, and attempts to equate the supply and demand of labor, capital, and the more important commodities. The extreme cases of this type of procedure are found in the communist countries. Less extreme examples, in which some attention is paid to comparative advantage, are the procedures of the Indian Planning Commission and the U.N. Economic Commission for Latin America.

Characteristic elements of the comparative advantage approach are attempts to measure the relative efficiency of different types of production, the weighing of balance-of-payments improvements against other benefits to the economy (by means of accounting prices or otherwise), and usually a greater emphasis on partial analysis than on over-all projections. Examples that will be cited are Puerto Rico, the Philippines, and Israel.

A. *Procedures Emphasizing Domestic Balance*

The planning procedures developed in the USSR and applied with some modification in other communist countries represent in extreme form the use of balance as a criterion for resource allocation and the virtually complete omission of any test of comparative advantage. As revealed in recent studies by Montias [32] and Balassa [1], the main tool of Soviet-type planning is a very detailed system of material balances specified in quantitative terms. Policy objectives are translated into production targets in which priority is given to heavy industry and other sectors that are expected to contribute to further growth ('leading links'). Prices are used mainly as rationing devices and have no necessary connection with production costs. The cumbersome calculations involved in arriving at balance of supply and demand for a large number of commodities limit the alternatives that can be tried out, so the main effort is to find a feasible program [32].

The question of comparative advantage scarcely arises in the USSR because of its size and diversified resources, although similar problems arise in connection with the choice of production techniques. When the Soviet planning system was transplanted to the satellite countries, however, it ran into difficulties because of its inability to determine the advantages to be secured from trade. According to Balassa [1, p. 264], the idea of comparative advantage did not exist in Hungarian development policy (at least until very recently) although trade has a high ratio to GNP. Exports are determined by import 'needs' and the institutional structure is such as to encourage exporters to meet targets for exports without regard to production costs. Since prices do not reflect resource use, it is impossible to determine where comparative advantage lies and to what extent the trade pattern deviates from the optimum.

Despite their violation of most short-term welfare considerations, the success of Soviet planning methods in producing a rapid rise in the national product makes them attractive to many underdeveloped countries. In India, for example, Mahalanobis' 'plan-frame' for the second five-year plan [30] draws heavily on Soviet methodology. He starts from the assumption that the rate of investment is determined by the level of domestic production of capital goods: 'As the capacity to manufacture both heavy and light machinery and other capital goods increases, the capacity to invest (by using home-produced capital goods) would also increase steadily, and India would become more and more independent of the import of foreign machinery and capital goods' [30, p. 18]. His analysis implies that export possibilities are so limited that they can be ignored, so that the composition of demand is limited by the composition of domestic output. In order to raise the level of investment, Mahalanobis concludes that investment in industries producing capital goods should be increased from less than 10 per cent to 30-35 per cent of total investment in the second five-year plan.

As Komiya [27] has shown, Mahalanobis' approach to development ignores price and demand considerations completely. The targets for the four sectors in his model appear to be based mainly on the goal of creating heavy industry, which is assumed to be the key to future growth. Criteria of efficiency and comparative advantage are entirely omitted from his analysis.

Although there are traces of the Mahalanobis approach in the second and third five-year plans formulated by the Indian Planning Commission, the final results are much less extreme. One basic problem is that exports are expected to rise only half as fast as national income between the first and third plan periods, while demand for the goods initially imported tends to rise much more rapidly. The inelastic demand for traditional Indian exports means that a considerable proportion of investment must be devoted to commodities that are presently imported. Within this category, the principles of comparative advantage should apply. In actuality, the emphasis has shifted somewhat from heavy industry in the second plan to agriculture in the third. In the latter document [19], increasing self-sufficiency in basic industrial commodities—steel, petroleum, machinery, etc.—is listed as a high-priority objective, but so is the maximum development of agriculture. Whether the resulting targets are consistent with comparative advantage is not considered in the published analysis.[20]

The balance-of-payments difficulties of many Latin American countries have also been a major factor in shaping the programming procedure developed by the Economic Commission for Latin America [57]. This approach has been applied in considerable detail in studics of Colombia [58], Argentina [59], and Peru [60]. One basic conclusion of these studies is that the growth of exports will be much slower than the growth of demand for goods that are currently imported. Investment therefore has to be heavily oriented toward import substitution, and the equality of supply and demand must be tested on a commodity basis to avoid balance-of-payments difficulties. In the three cases mentioned, this balancing process is carried out by means of an input-output analysis in which imported goods are distinguished from domestic products in each category.

In principle, comparative advantage can be used in the ECLA procedure as a basis for the choice of import substitutes, but this has apparently been done only to a limited degree. Since the main emphasis is on balance, there is a danger that the initial assumptions as to levels of exports will not be re-examined after the extent of import substitution required by a given program has been determined. The result may be a considerably lower productivity of investment in import substitutes than in exports if the two are not systematically compared. The drawbacks to this procedure are more serious in small countries like Colombia and Peru than in a large country like India, in which imports supply a smaller fraction of the total demand for commodities.

B. *Procedures Emphasizing Comparative Advantage*

Among countries having development programs, procedures that stress comparative advantage are less common than those emphasizing balance. Practically all policy statements list among their priority criteria factors presumably leading to comparative advantage, but there is little evidence as to how they are applied in drawing up programs.

20 On the basis of a simplified linear-programming model, Sandee [45, p. 25] finds that 'up to 1970 more effective ways to employ capital for development exist than highly capital intensive steel-making,' suggesting that an analysis of comparative advantage would indicate more reliance on imports. The nonmarket benefits of production are omitted from his analysis, however.

The development procedures of the government of Puerto Rico come as close to being a pure application of comparative advantage as Soviet procedures are of principles of balanced growth. Unlike many low-income countries, Puerto Rico has an elastic demand for its exports to the U.S. market and can attract U.S. capital for profitable investments. The government's policy has been to give tax remission for ten years and to provide overhead facilities, labor training, and other inducements to industries that will benefit the island's economy. In deciding which industries to promote, the Economic Development Authority has studied the long-term comparative advantage of a large number of alternative projects, since comparative advantage will lead to both satisfactory profits and maximum income. Low-cost labor (even with allowance for differences in productivity) has been the main element in comparative advantage, since most industrial materials must be imported. Allowance is also made for external economies in industries that will supply inputs to other sectors.[21]

Under this policy, the growth of per capita income has been as rapid (nearly 5 per cent annually) and the development of industry as marked (from 19 per cent to 25 per cent of GNP) over the years 1948-1958 as in any country following a deliberate policy of balanced growth. The planning procedure depends very largely on the particular relation of Puerto Rico to the United States and its small size. These factors make it unnecessary to worry about the elasticity of demand for exports or the dangers of dependence on foreign sources for essential imports, which so preoccupy the Indian and Latin American planners. With reliable export and import markets, domestic balance is not a problem.

Since the assumptions of the classical model are not approached so closely in most underdeveloped countries as in Puerto Rico, the calculation of comparative advantage usually departs farther from the market evaluation. In a more typical case the Philippine National Economic Council has outlined a procedure for applying the SMP formula under Philippine conditions [39]. This analysis starts from the market evaluation of the profitability of an investment and adds corrections for the project's effect on the balance of payments, its use of domestic materials, and its use of domestic

21 The Puerto Rican experience is discussed by Baer [2]; the evaluation procedures are described in mimeographed reports of the Economic Development Authority.

labor, each with a suitable weight. This procedure may be justified by comparison to the linear programming criterion of social profit. In principle the proper correction to private profit is obtained by giving each a value equal to the difference between its shadow price and its market price.[22] In the Philippines, this would mean a bonus for labor and a penalty for foreign exchange use (or a bonus for foreign exchange saving). Higgins [22, pp. 654-62] shows that the weights assigned in the Philippines tend to exaggerate these effects. The use of the same weight for all domestic materials may lead to serious error, since not all are overvalued by market prices.

The government of Israel has developed one of the most systematic procedures for measuring comparative advantage as a basis for allocating investment funds and foreign exchange. In effect, the Ministry of Finance evaluates projects on the basis of accounting prices for foreign exchange and capital, taking into account the indirect use of foreign exchange in sectors supplying inputs such as power or industrial materials. The calculation is summed up as the cost in domestic resources of a dollar earned or saved, and it is applied equally to exports and to import substitutes. The calculation of domestic value added is also made by exporters as a basis for export subsidies [3, p. 23]. In allocating the governments development budget, priority is given to projects whose domestic cost of earning or saving foreign exchange is less than the current estimate of its accounting price. This procedure can also be rationalized by means of the linear programming criterion of social profitability. Instead of measuring the value derived per unit of investment with accounting prices for foreign exchange and labor, as in the SMP formula, the cost per unit of foreign exchange acquired is computed using an accounting price for capital. When the same shadow prices are used, all three measures give the same result.

Although it is dangerous to generalize from the limited evidence on development policies that is available, there appears to be some

22 The social profit, Πj, may be expressed as:

$$\Pi = \bar{\Pi} j + \sum aij \Delta P_i, \tag{4b}$$

where $\bar{\Pi} j$ is private profit per unit of output calculated at market prices and ΔP_i is the difference between the market price and shadow price of commodity i. The elements ΔP_i may be regarded as weights attached to each input or output coefficient.

relation between the type of procedure adopted and the characteristics of the economy in a number of the cases examined. *Small countries are forced to pay more attention to comparative advantage because they cannot hope to produce the whole range of manufactures and primary products,* while large countries may be tempted to follow more autarchic policies.[23] The importance given to balanced growth also depends to a large extent on the country's recent experience with its export markets and the state of its foreign *exchange reserves and borrowing capacity.* Puerto Rico and Israel can both count on substantial capital inflows which make it unnecessary for them to approach balanced trade in the near future, while India has much less leeway.

IV *Conclusions*

This paper has considered development policy from the standpoint of economic theory, as a problem in operations research, and as it is actually carried on by governments. Much of the confusion in the field stems from a failure to distinguish these different levels of analysis. Theorists are prone to suggest decision rules that omit some of the relevant institutional limits, while economists who have been working in particular areas often arrive at conclusions that do not fit other cases. As in other fields of economics, most of the disagreement can be traced to implicit differences in assumptions.

There are a number of contradictions between the implications of trade theory and growth theory. To make the two theories consistent, it is necessary to discard the assumption of equilibrium in factor markets, to allow for changes in the quantity and quality of factors of production over time, and to take account of internal and external economies of scale. Although under these assumptions market forces do not necessarily lead to efficient resource allocation, a pattern of production and trade can be determined that maximizes income over time. The commodities to be produced and traded cannot be determined by a simple ranking procedure along the lines of classical comparative advantage because of the interdependence among sectors. At best, it may be possible to say, for example, that a country has a comparative advantage in steel production for a specified set of production levels in supplying and

23 Japan is one exception to this generalization, partly due to its dependence on imported raw materials.

using sectors. In advanced countries, this qualification may be unimportant, but in the less developed ones it crucial in a number of industries.

Much of the attack on the use of comparative advantage is based on its omission of various nonmarket elements. It is assumed that the inclusion of the latter favors the development of industry, and special benefits are often attributed to capital goods and heavy industry. The intangible benefits stemming from trade in the form of new products, improved technology, and technical assistance tend to be overlooked in this discussion. Although I support the critics who wish to include more of growth theory in determining the desirability of specialization, I doubt that this extension will favor balanced growth to the extent that they suppose.

The other main theoretical attack on comparative advantage is aimed at its supposed support for continued specialization in primary exports. Granting the low elasticity of demand for many primary products, it is wrong to conclude that comparative advantage is thereby superseded by principles of balanced growth. The increasing shortage of foreign exchange makes it even more important to economize on its use and to seek efficient ways for increasing its supply. The comparison of domestic to foreign sources of supply that is implied by comparative advantage is no less relevant to this situation than to the case in which investment is more evenly divided between exports and import substitutes.

The aspects of growth theory which do not seem to be reconcilable with the notion of comparative advantage are the sociological and political effects of choosing one production pattern instead of another. While the concept of opportunity cost can be extended to include a number of nonmarket phenomena, such as labor training and overhead facilities, it can hardly be stretched to cover differences in fertility rates or political attitudes. So far as I can see, in the present state of knowledge of social phenomena, considerations such as these may be used to modify the results of economic analysis but cannot be directly incorporated into it.

At the level of operations research, the search for simple decision rules for investment in low-income countries seems to have been useful mainly in exposing the fallacies in some of the common rules of thumb. One can specify conditions under which ratios such as the capital intensity or the effect on the balance of payments would be a valid indicator of the desirability of an investment, but the apparent gain in simplicity is offset by the danger of applying the test in inappropriate circumstances. A more fruitful approach to partial equilibrium analysis is provided by the use of accounting prices to compute the social profitability of a given use of resources. This method allows simultaneously for several overvalued or undervalued inputs, and it can include whatever elements of general equilibrium analysis are available.

Since market forces cannot be relied on to balance supply and demand under conditions of initial disequilibrium and accelerated growth, a principal concern of development policy is to ensure the consistency of production levels with commodity demands and factor supplies. The technique of linear programming is designed to combine the test of consistency with the test of the social profitability of a given resource use. Although it cannot be applied very extensively in underdeveloped countries as yet, the programming methodology serves as a guide to improved practical measures.

To most economists, a survey of the procedures actually followed in designing development policy would probably suggest that balance is overemphasized and that the potential gains from trade are often neglected. This emphasis may be partly justified by the greater uncertainties attached to trade and by an aversion to risk that is greater than seems warranted to the outside observer. Better understanding of the working of the underdeveloped economies and better information for planning is needed to redress the balance and enable countries to secure the potential gains from trade without conflict with measures for domestic development.

REFERENCES

1 B. A. Balassa, *The Hungarian Experience in Economic Planning*, New Haven 1959.
2 W. Baer, 'Puerto Rico: an Evaluation of a Successful Development Program,' *Quart. Jour. Econ.*, Nov. 1959, **73**, pp. 645-71.
3 Bank of Israel, *Annual Report*, **1959**, Jerusalem 1960.
4 F. M. Bator, 'On Capital Productivity, Input Allocation, and Growth,' *Quart. Jour. Econ.*, Feb. 1957, **71**, pp. 86-106.
5 N. S. Buchanan, *International Investment and Domestic Welfare*, New York 1945.
6 O. Castellino, 'La Scelta degli Investimenti nei Programmi di Sviluppo Economico,' *L'Industria*, 1959, No. 1, pp. 60-76.
7 R. E. Caves, *Trade and Economic Structure*, Cambridge 1960.

8 H. B. Chenery, 'The Application of Investment Criteria,' *Quart. Jour. Econ.*, Feb. 1953, **67**, pp. 76-96.
9 ———, 'The Role of Industrialization in Development Programs,' *Am. Econ. Rev., Proc.*, May 1955, **45**, pp. 40-57.
10 ———, 'Development Policies and Programmes'; *Econ. Bull. for Latin America*, Mar. 1958, **3**, pp. 51-77.
11 ———, 'The Interdependence of Investment Decisions,' in Abramovitz et al., *The Allocation of Economic Resources*. Stanford 1959.
12 M. Dobb, *An Essay on Economic Growth and Planning*, London 1960.
13 R. Dorfman, P. A. Samuelson, and R. M. Solow, *Linear Programming and Economic Analysis*. New York 1958.
14 O. Eckstein, 'Investment Criteria for Economic Development and the Theory of Intertemporal Welfare Economics,' *Quart. Jour. Econ.*, Feb. 1957, **71**, pp. 56-85.
15 R. Frisch, *A Method of Working out a Macroeconomic Plan Frame with Particular Reference to the Evaluation of Development Projects, Foreign Trade and Employment*. Oslo 1958 (mimeo.).
16 ———, *A Powerful Method of Approximation in Optimum Investment Computations of the Normal Type*. Oslo 1959 (mimeo.).
17 W. Galenson and H. Leibenstein, 'Investment Criteria, Productivity, and Economic Development,' *Quart. Jour. Econ.*, Aug. 1955, **69**, pp. 343-70.
18 A. Gerschenkron, 'Economic Backwardness in Historical Perspective,' in B. Hoselitz, ed., *The Progress of Underdeveloped Areas*, Chicago 1952.
19 Government of India Planning Commission, *The Third Five Year Plan*, New Delhi 1960.
20 G. Haberler, 'Some Problems in the Pure Theory of International Trade,' *Econ. Jour.*, June 1950, **60**, pp. 223-40.
21 E. Hagen, 'An Economic Justification of Protectionism,' *Quart. Jour. Econ.*, Nov. 1958, **72**, pp. 496-514.
22 B. Higgins, *Economic Development*. New York 1958.
23 A. O. Hirschman, *The Strategy of Economic Development*, New Haven 1958.
24 ———, 'Investment Criteria and Capital Intensity Once Again,' *Quart. Jour. Econ.*, Aug. 1958, **72**, pp. 469-71.
25 A. E. Kahn, 'Investment Criteria in Development Programs,' *Quart. Jour. Econ.*, Feb. 1951, **65**, pp. 38-61.
26 C. P. Kindleberger, *The Terms of Trade: A European Case Study*, New York 1956.
27 R. Komiya, 'A Note on Professor Mahalonobis' Model of Indian Economic Planning,' *Rev. Econ. Stat.*, Feb. 1959, **41**, pp. 29-35.
28 H. Leibenstein, 'Why Do We Disagree on Investment Policies for Development?' *Indian Econ. Jour.*, Apr. 1958, **5**, pp. 369-86.
29 W. A. Lewis, 'Economic Development with Unlimited Supplies of Labor,' *Manchester School*, May 1954.
30 P. C. Mahalanobis, 'The Approach of Operational Research to Planning in India,' *Sankhya*, Dec. 1955, **16**, pp. 3-131.
31 K. Mandelbaum, *The Industrialization of Backward Areas*, Oxford 1945.
32 J. M. Montias, 'Planning with Material Balances in Soviet-type Economies,' *Am. Econ. Rev.*, Dec. 1959, **49**, pp. 963-85.

33 H. Myint, 'The Classical Theory of International Trade and the Underdeveloped Countries.' *Econ. Jour.*, June 1958, **68**, pp. 317-37.
34 G. Myrdal, *Economic Theory and Under-developed Regions*, London 1957.
35 H. Neisser, 'Investment Criteria, Productivity and Economic Development,' *Quart. Jour. Econ.*, Nov. 1956, **70**, pp. 644-47.
36 R. Nurkse, *Problems of Capital Formation in Underdeveloped Countries*, Oxford 1953.
37 ———, *Patterns of Trade and Development*, Stockholm 1959.
38 P. G. Ohlin, 'Balanced Economic Growth in History,' *Am. Econ. Rev., Proc.*, May 1959, **49**, pp. 338-53.
39 The Philippines National Economic Council, *The Five-Year Economic and Social Development Program for Fiscal Years* **1957-1961**, Manila 1957.
40 J. J. Polak, 'Balance of Payments Problems of Countries Reconstructing with the Help of Foreign Loans,' *Quart. Jour. Econ.*, Feb. 1943, **57**, 208-40.
41 R. Prebisch, 'Commercial Policy in the Underdeveloped Countries,' *Am. Econ. Rev., Proc.*, May 1959, **49**, pp. 251-73.
42 A. Qayum, *Theory and Policy of Accounting Prices*, Amsterdam 1959.
43 P. Rosenstein-Rodan, 'Problems of Industrialization of Eastern and South-Eastern Europe,' *Econ. Jour.*, June-Sept. 1943, **53**, pp. 205-16.
44 W. W. Rostow, 'The Take-Off into Self-Sustained Growth,' *Econ. Jour.*, Mar. 1956, **66**, pp. 25-48.
45 J. Sandee, *A Long-Term Planning Model for India*, United Nations pub., New York 1959.
46 T. W. Schultz, 'Latin American Economic Policy Lessons,' *Am. Econ. Rev., Proc.*, May 1956, **46**, pp. 425-32.
47 T. Scitovsky, 'Two Concepts of External Economies,' *Jour. Pol. Econ.*, April 1954, **62**, pp. 143-51.
48 ———, 'Growth—Balanced or Unbalanced,' in M. Abramovitz et al., *The Allocation of Economic Resources*, Stanford 1959.
49 A. K. Sen, 'Some Notes on the Choice of Capital Intensity in Development Planning,' *Quart. Jour. Econ.*, Nov. 1957, **71**, pp. 561-84.
50 J. Sheahan, 'International Specialization and the Concept of Balanced Growth,' *Quart. Jour. Econ.*, May 1958, **72**, pp. 183-97.
51 H. W. Singer, 'The Distribution of Gains Between Investing and Borrowing Countries,' *Amer. Econ. Rev., Proc.*, May 1950, **40**, pp. 473-85.
52 G. Stigler, 'Production and Distribution in the Short Run,' reprinted in Am. Econ. Assoc., *Readings in the Theory of Income Distribution*, Philadelphia 1946.
53 P. Streeten, 'Unbalanced Growth,' *Oxford Econ. Papers*, June 1959, **11**, pp. 167-91.
54 J. Tinbergen, 'The Relevance of Theoretical Criteria in the Selection of Investment Plans,' in M. Millikan, ed., *Investment Criteria and Economic Growth*, Cambridge 1955.
55 ———, *Economic Policy: Principles and Design*, Amsterdam 1956.
56 ———, *The Design of Development*, Baltimore 1958.
57 United Nations, Department of Economic and Social Affairs, *Analyses and Projections of Economic Development*, New York 1955.
58 ———, *Analyses and Projections of Economic Development*, **III**, *The Economic Development of Columbia*, Geneva 1957.

59 ———, *Analyses and Projections of Economic Development*, **V**, *The Economic Development of Argentina*. Mexico City 1960.
60 ———, *Analyses and Projections of Economic Development*, **VI**, *The Industrial Development of Peru*. Mexico City 1959.
61 United Nations, *Manual of Economic Development Projects*, New York 1959.
62 A Vaidyanathan, 'A Survey of the Literature on Investment Criteria and Development of Underdeveloped Countries,' *Ind. Econ. Jour.*, Oct. 1956, **4**, pp. 122-44.
63 J. Viner, *International Trade and Economic Development*, Oxford 1953.
64 ———, 'Stability and Progress: The Poorer Countries' Problem,' in D. Hague, ed., *Stability and Progress in the World Economy*, London 1958 (with comment by R. Nurkse).
65 P. Wiles, 'Growth versus Choice,' *Econ. Jour.*, June 1956, **66**, pp. 244-55.
66 J. H. Williams, 'The Theory of International Trade Reconsidered,' *Econ. Jour.*, June 1929, **39**, pp. 195-209. Reprinted in Am. Econ. Assoc., *Readings in the Theory of International Trade*, Philadelphia 1949.

17

ECONOMIC GROWTH AND INTERNATIONAL TRADE IN PURE THEORY*

Jaroslav Vanek

I Introduction

MANY OF MY FELLOW international economists may have experienced the same difficulties as I have in teaching graduate courses in our field. Considering the importance that economic science is giving lately to the problem of economic growth, one feels that a substantial part of the graduate offering in international trade ought to contain a synthesis between the theory of economic growth on the one hand and the pure theory of trade on the other. But very often one does not get very much beyond contributions such as those of J. Bhagwati, H. G. Johnson, or T. N. Rybczynski,[1] wherein exogenously given changes in factor endowments or technology are translated into changing production possibilities and changing patterns of trade.

The explanation why generally one finds it very difficult to go beyond these writings is that the literature integrating the theory of growth with that of international trade is quite difficult. For example, the paper by P. K. Bardhan and that of H. Oniki and H. Uzawa (cited below) are, judging from my experience, too difficult for an average graduate student in international economics.[2]

I would like to submit that this difficulty is by no means a

*In preparing this paper I benefited from discussions with Mr. Alan Deardorff of the Cornell Department of Economics and Professor Trent Bertrand of Johns Hopkins University.

1 Jagdish Bhagwati, 'International Trade and Economic Expansion', *American Economic Review*, XLVIII, No. 4 (Dec. 1958), pp. 941-53. Harry G. Johnson, *International Trade and Economic Growth* (Cambridge: Harvard University Press, 1958). T. N. Rybczynski, 'Factor Endowment and Relative Commodity Prices,' *Economica*, n.s. XXII, No. 4 (Nov. 1955), pp. 336-41.

2 Bardhan, P.K., 'Equilibrium Growth in the International Economy,' this *Journal*, LXXIX, No. 3 (Aug. 1965), pp. 455-64. H. Oniki and H. Uzawa, 'Patterns of Trade and Investment in a Dynamic Model of International Trade', *Review of Economic Studies*, XXXII (1), No. 89 (Jan. 1965), pp. 16-38.

necessary one, and the first purpose of this paper is to substantiate this claim by offering a considerably simpler, yet rigorous, growth theory for an open economy. But this is not the only purpose. In the course of presenting the simplified theory I am able either to derive new results or to establish results previously obtained through new methods. In the following section I derive the rate of growth and study the existence and stability of growth equilibrium for a small country. In Section III, I derive the effects of changes in the terms of trade on the equilibrium growth solution. In Section IV the rate of growth, existence, and stability of equilibrium is studied in the context of a large country facing a less than infinitely elastic foreign offer curve. In Section V, I extend the theory of growth with technological progress to situations involving international trade, and, finally, in Section VI, I derive some conclusions regarding golden rule solutions for an open economy.

II The Rate of Growth, Existence and Stability of Equilibrium for a Small Open Economy

The economy whose growth behavior under international trade we want to examine is very simple. The defining characteristics that will remain with us for all five sections of this paper are as follows. The economy produces in each period from capital and labor two products, a consumer good x and a capital good y. The production functions are neoclassical, subject to constant returns to scale and diminishing returns to a single factor everywhere, and do not involve any interindustry flows. A constant share of national product s_0 is saved every year and invested in capital goods that can be either procured domestically or imported in exchange for the other nationally produced commodity. The rate of growth of the labor force is exogenously given; call it n. In addition to those assumptions, which will remain with us throughout this paper, we assume for the purposes of the present section an infinitely elastic foreign offer curve. In other words, the international and internal prices are perfectly invariant in the course of the process of growth.

Consider now Figure Ia, defined by two coordinate axes reflecting labor supply L and the capital availability K of the economy. More specifically, consider the factor endowments given by points L_0 and K_2. Corresponding to these endowments, to the fixed international terms of trade, and to the given production functions, the efficient allocation of resources is to be found at point *a* on the contract curve in the box diagram.

On observing that the marginal rates of substitution at *a*, indicated by the common tangency passing through *a*, are equal to the slope of the line $Z_2 0_y^2$, it is immediately apparent that the segment $0_x Z_2$, measures national product in terms of capital wage units. The ratio of that segment to the segment $0_x K_2$ thus measures, except for a constant factor of proportionality, the output-capital ratio Z/K. Of course, the factor of proportionality must be there to convert the nondimensional ratio of the two segments to the output-capital ratio expressed in terms of income at world market prices per physical unit of capital.

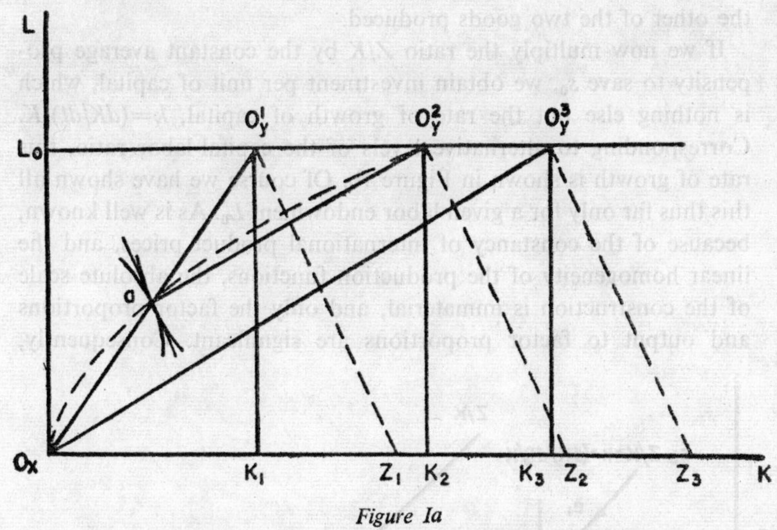

Figure Ia

We now observe that, if the capital endowment of the economy changes with that of labor remaining invariant, the dimensions of the box will change. However, the significant price ratios within a certain range will not change. As we know from the proof of the factor price equalization theorem, as long as international prices remain the same and as long as the economy does not specialize, changes in factor endowments in the economy will not affect factor prices. And consequently we can now expand the capital availability from K_2 to K_3, leaving labor supply unchanged at L_0, and this will make the national income increase to $0_x Z_3$. It is immediately apparent from the construction that the output-capital ratio Z/K must have declined, as the result of an expansion in supply of capital. Similarly, a contraction of the stock of capital to K_1 would increase the Z/K ratio.

Thus, at least for the range of no specialization corresponding to levels of capital supply K_1 through K_3, we have established that the output-capital ratio will be declining. This is shown in Figure Ib. When we expand the supply of capital beyond K_3, or contract it below K_1, the relationship between the capital endowment and the output-capital ratio still will be of the same declining nature. However, the rate of decline will be somewhat more pronounced because of the effect of changing relative factor prices and diminishing returns that must occur once the economy specializes in one or the other of the two goods produced.

If we now multiply the ratio Z/K by the constant average propensity to save s_0, we obtain investment per unit of capital, which is nothing else but the rate of growth of capital, $k=(dK/dt)/K$. Corresponding to alternative levels of the capital-labor ratio, this rate of growth is shown in Figure Ib. Of course we have shown all this thus far only for a given labor endowment L_0. As is well known, because of the constancy of international product prices, and the linear homogeneity of the production functions, the absolute scale of the construction is immaterial, and only the factor proportions and output to factor proportions are significant. Consequently,

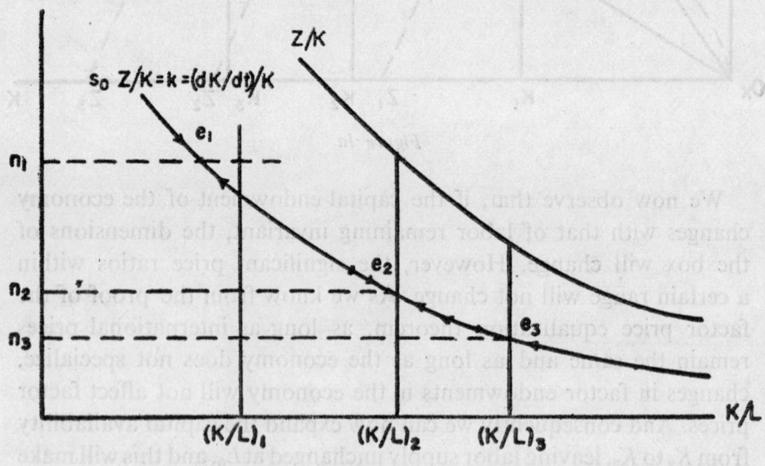

Figure Ib

Figure Ib has a general validity whatever the absolute levels of factor endowments.

For a prescribed rate of growth of the labor force n the equilibrium capital-labor ratio, that is, the capital-labor ratio belonging to the corresponding steady state, will now be found at the intersection of the contour k with a horizontal line drawn at the level n. For example, for a prescribed rate of growth of population n_2 we find the equilibrium e_2 in Figure Ib. It is apparent that for the rate of growth n_2 the economy will indefinitely keep producing both products x and y in the proportions indicated in Figure Ia by the resource allocation at point a. Of course it is not important that the output levels of product y, that is, of the capital goods, exactly match the capital requirements of the economy. Whatever the net excess or deficit of capital goods, the economy can barter it in the world markets at the prescribed market prices.

On the other hand, if the labor force experiences a considerably higher rate of growth, such as the one indicated by n_1 in Figure Ib, the steady state of the economy will be found at equilibrium point e_1 corresponding to a full specialization by the economy in the consumer goods. The economy must now acquire all of its capital goods year after year from the world market by bartering them for exports of consumer goods. On the other side of the spectrum, for a very low rate of growth of the labor force, such as n_3 or lower, the economy indefinitely specializes in the production of the investment goods. It is also apparent that, with rates of growth of population falling short of n_3, wages and the relative income share of labor must be higher than that found at points e_3 or e_2. Of course, the results regarding specialization depend critically on the relative factor intensities and would be reversed if x were capital-intensive and y labor-intensive.

Because the locus k is single-valued with respect to the vertical axis in Figure Ib, there can be only one equilibrium steady state for each prescribed level of rate of growth of the labor force. Moreover, the negative slope of the locus guarantees stability of all the equilibria, such as e_1, e_2, or e_3. As is indicated by the arrows in the vicinity of these equilibrium points, if the economy is temporarily away from equilibrium (for a prescribed rate of growth of the labor force), it will gradually return to equilibrium. This becomes immediately apparent if we realize that, for example, for points to the left of e_2, the rate of growth of capital exceeds the rate of growth of labor. Under such conditions, of course, the capital-labor ratio must be increasing, that is, the point must be moving along the k contour in the direction of e_2. And the process will not be arrested until e_2 is reached.

Noting, moreover, that everywhere, even for extremely high levels or extremely low levels of the capital-labor ratio, the contour k in Figure Ib must be negatively sloped, we also establish the global stability and uniqueness of the equilibrium point.

We have thus come to what we have set out to do in this section. We have found for a small open economy its steady state growth solution and established the uniqueness and local as well as global stability of such an equilibrium state. Obviously the comparative simplicity of the solution of this two-sector growth model resides in the fact that the economy need not supply all of its capital goods. The Uzawa closed-economy model, although it also contains only two sectors, is a good deal more complicated, because the economy has another constraint to operate under, namely, to secure exactly the amount of capital goods it needs for all investments.

III The Terms of Trade and the Growth Solution for a Small Open Economy

The effects of a change in the terms of trade on the growth equilibrium of a small economy need not detain us very long. Given what we have done already, the answers can be obtained very easily. In Figure II we show an instantaneous production possibility locus of our small economy as of a given period. Suppose that the economy is in a steady state at P_0 facing international terms of trade given by the slope P_0. Without loss of generality we have drawn our diagram in such a way as to make the economy exactly self-sufficient.[3] The equilibrium corresponding to P_0, analogous to Figure Ib, is found in Figure III at e_0, for the exogenously prescribed rate of growth of the labor force n_0.

Suppose now that the terms of trade line becomes steeper and assumes the position C_1P_1. In other words, the consumer good has now become more expensive in international markets. As is indicated in Figure II, more of x and less of y will now be produced, and at the new terms of trade there will be a need to trade from P_1 to C_1.

3 Of course, any other position involving exports or imports of the consumer good x in the (initial) steady state would be conceivable.

The point C_1 is characterized by the fact that the same proportion of national product as at P_0 is allocated to the consumer good; the savings propensity s_0 is some 40 or 45 percent.

Now what does this instantaneous change in the terms of trade do to the rate of growth of capital? It must be obvious that over short periods of time, with capital stock remaining by and large unchanged, the increase in demand for capital goods and investment from that indicated by P_0 to that indicated by C_1 must have raised instantaneously the rate of growth of capital. Such an increase is shown in Figure III from e_0 to e_0'. But, as we have noted in the preceding section, the k line drawn against the capital-labor ratio must always be downward sloping. Consequently the improvement in the price of x, that is, the improvement in the terms of trade of

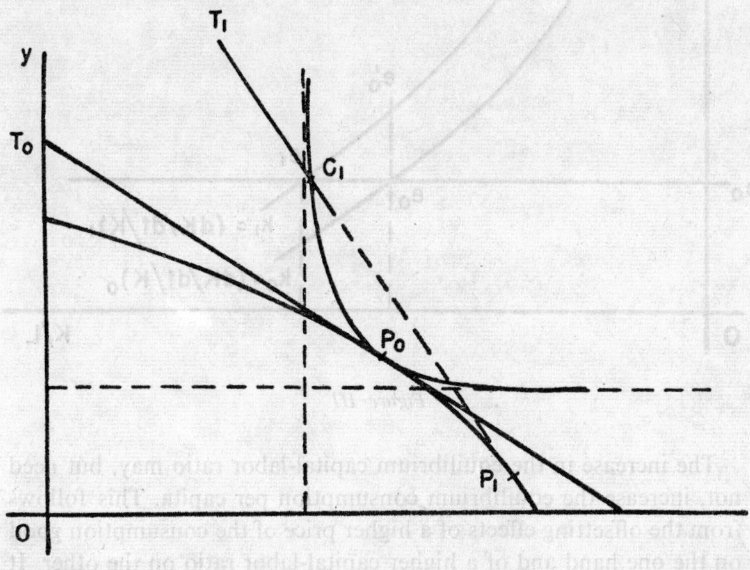

Figure II

our small country, must eventually lead to a new equilibrium point for the prescribed rate of growth of population n_0, found at point e_1. Unambiguously at that point the equilibrium capital-labor ratio is higher than the initial ratio corresponding to e_0. Now, observing that the price consumption line in Figure II must always show an increase in demand for capital if the price of capital goods declines in international markets, we find that the result that we have just obtained for points P_0 and P_1 becomes perfectly general. Specifically, an increase in the price of the consumer good in international markets must always lead to an increase in the equilibrium capital-labor ratio of the small trading economy. It follows from the nature of the proof that the result does not depend on relative factor intensities.

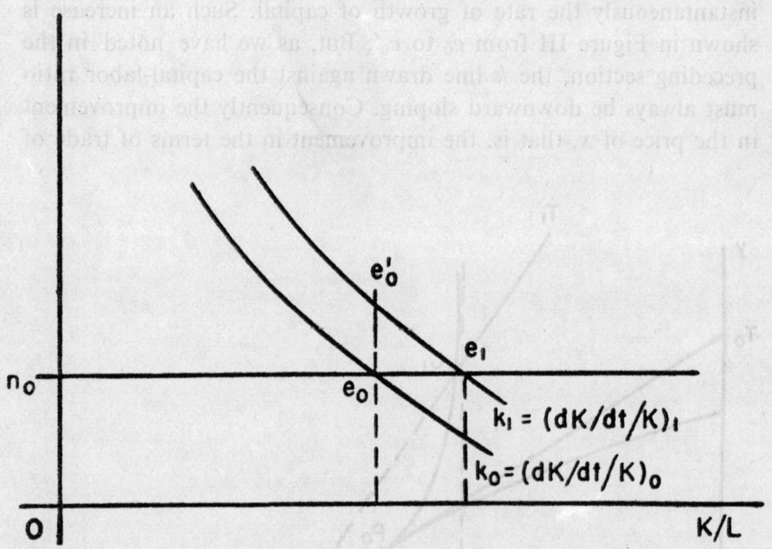

Figure III

The increase in the equilibrium capital-labor ratio may, but need not, increase the equilibrium consumption per capita. This follows from the offsetting effects of a higher price of the consumption good on the one hand and of a higher capital-labor ratio on the other. It also follows that an improvement in terms of trade, or introduction of trade starting from autarky, need not imply an improved living standard for a country in the long run. In fact, it is now possible to show without difficulty that steady state consumption per head will be maximized for extreme (zero and infinite) values of the terms of trade, and a minimum consumption per head will correspond to some intermediate terms of trade ratio, generally different from the autarky ratio.

IV The Rate of Growth, Existence and Stability of Equilibrium in a Large Open Economy

Once the assumption of an infinitely elastic foreign offer is abandoned, matters become more complicated because of the increased technical difficulty not only of analysis, but also of conception. What do we mean by a less than infinitely elastic foreign offer curve in the case of an economy that is indefinitely growing? Obviously, if we assume a foreign offer curve of finite elasticity, which is fixed and does not expand with time, we have only to wait until our economy grows large enough and becomes entirely dependent on its own resources, and cannot trade any significant amounts with the rest of the world. In that case we are back in the traditional Uzawa closed-economy model, and except for the transitional period during which the economy is expanding to assume its large size, Uzawa's results and conclusions obtain. On the other hand, if we postulate that the foreign offer curve expands over time at a rate exceeding the rate of growth of the labor force in the economy considered, then again it is only a matter of time for the foreign offer curve to become, from the point of view of the growing country, infinitely elastic; and in that case we are back in what we have done in Section II.

Thus we have two extreme solutions characteristic of two more general situations. One involves a rate of expansion of the foreign offer curve falling short of the rate of growth of population and labor force in the country considered, and the other, a rate of expansion of the foreign curve that is higher. In the very long run we do not have to worry about either of the two because they will eventually degenerate into cases known to us already. The first will turn into the Uzawa closed model, while the second will become the case of a small country studied in the previous sections of this paper.

Thus the only remaining case that we must be concerned with is the one where the rate of expansion of the foreign offer curve that is less than infinitely elastic equals the rate of growth of the labor force in the country considered.

Recall from the small country case studied in Section II that in a steady state where the economy expands at the rate n, vectors such as P_1C_1 in Figure II must expand also at the rate n per annum. If it so happened in our discussion of Section II that the expanding trade vector was exactly matched by an expanding foreign offer curve of finite elasticity, which for the prescribed terms of trade corresponds to the required volume of exports and imports, then the steady state solution of Section II would in effect have become a steady state solution of a large country facing a less than infinitely elastic foreign offer curve, expanding at the rate n.

And thus we can conclude that a steady state solution exists for the large country case provided that the rate of expansion n is also the rate of expansion of the foreign offer curve.

A question that remains to be answered is whether such an equilibrium is stable, or under what conditions it will be stable. Because the likelihood that the foreign offer curve would expand at the rate n is one out of infinity, we will not devote much space to the question. However, the reader will find it easy to verify, using the analytical apparatus of this paper, that, as in the Uzawa closed-economy model, the sufficient condition of stability now is the relative capital intensity of the consumption good, and the necessary (but not sufficient) condition of instability is the relative labor intensity of the consumption good.

V The Open Economy Growth Models and Technological Progress

Obviously, all the models that we have discussed up to this point are highly unrealistic in the sense that in a steady state the income per man remains unchanged. In fact all such models could just as well be called theories of secular stagnation, rather than theories of economic growth. To obtain actual growth we must bring into the picture technological progress, and that is the purpose of this section. Of course matters can become quite complicated, and consequently we will have to restrict ourselves to some simple assumptions. I will discuss rigorously only the case where Hicks-neutral technological progress takes place, and proceeds at the same rate A in both industries. Afterwards I will make some general and less rigorous remarks about other more general situations. I will proceed fairly rapidly, relying on a previous article of mine dealing with technological progress in a closed economy.[4] Through-

4 Jaroslav Vanek, 'A Theory of Growth With Technological Change,' *American Economic Review*, LVII, No. 1 (March 1967) pp. 73-89.

out I will be dealing with the case of a small country facing fixed international prices.

Let us place ourselves in the initial period, and postulate that the world market prices are fixed at p_x and p_y, respectively. We want to construct for the base period a relation between the value of national product per unit of labor on the one hand and the capital-labor ratio on the other. Let us call the function relating the former to the latter variable f. The task is a comparatively simple one if we turn to Figure Ia. Let us make the additional assumption that L_0 as it appears in that diagram is exactly equal to 1. We know already that if the capital endowment of the country falls short of K_1 in Figure Ia, then only the consumer good can be produced. For such values of capital stock the function f, the value of the national product per laborer, can be obtained by multiplying the fixed price p_x by the amounts of output read from the isoquants of the production function of x in Figure Ia. This portion of the function f is plotted for the range of capital-labor ratios between 0 and $(K/L)_1$ in Figure IV as the broken contour stretching from the origin 0 to b.

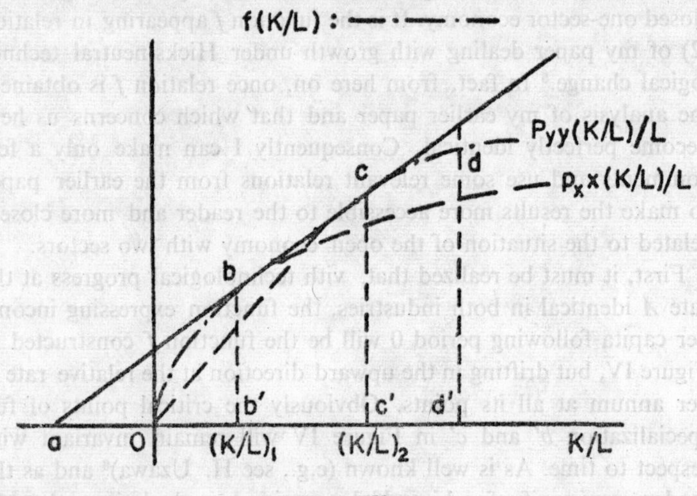

Figure IV

On the other hand, if in Figure Ia the capital endowment of the country exceeds the level K_3, the country will specialize in the capital good y; and thus the value of national product per laborer can now be easily constructed by multiplying by the fixed price p^x

the amounts of physical output x read from Figure Ia for points to the right of $0_y{}^3$.

Finally, for the stretch of relative capital endowments between K_1 and K_3 the value of gross national product per laborer can be obtained from the conventional box diagram by reading the levels of output at such points as a in Figure Ia, and multiplying these outputs by the corresponding fixed market prices. The reader will easily verify that this stretch of the function f in Figure IV must be a straight line. An intuitive proof can be obtained if we realize that for movements of the capital endowment to the right of K_1 in Figure Ia the point, such as Z_1, moves to the right at the same rate as does K_1. More specifically, for every inch of movement of K_1, Z_1 also moves by one inch; of course this holds only up to the point K_3, beyond which the relationship becomes nonlinear.

Thus we have obtained for the base period the entire function f for the whole range of capital-labor ratios between 0 and infinity. Except that it is expressed in terms of value at constant world market prices, it is the same as the all-important function f encountered in the analysis of growth with technological change for a closed one-sector economy. It is the function f appearing in relation (2) of my paper dealing with growth under Hicks-neutral technological change.[5] In fact, from here on, once relation f is obtained, the analysis of my earlier paper and that which concerns us here become perfectly identical. Consequently I can make only a few comments and use some relevant relations from the earlier paper to make the results more accessible to the reader and more closely related to the situation of the open economy with two sectors.

First, it must be realized that, with technological progress at the rate A identical in both industries, the function expressing income per capita following period 0 will be the function f constructed in Figure IV, but drifting in the upward direction at the relative rate A per annum at all its points. Obviously the critical points of full specialization b' and c' in Figure IV will remain invariant with respect to time. As is well known (e.g., see H. Uzawa)[6] and as the reader may verify for himself by a simple calculation, the all-important competitive income share of capital ϕ, depending on K/L only, can now be obtained for any point of f by a simple construc-

5 *Op. cit.*

6 Uzawa, 'On a Two-Sector Model of Economic Growth,' *Review of Economic Studies*, XXIX (1), No. 78 (Oct. 1961), pp. 40-47.

tion. For example, at b, ϕ is equal to the ratio Ob' divided by ab'. Of course a point such as a always must be the foot of a tangency to the broken line f. The generalized asymptotic rate of growth of capital k^*, given in relation (10) of my earlier paper, is now illustrated by the solid line marked k^* in Figure V. The formula defining k^*, also shown in the diagram, is

$$k^* = n + A/(1 - \phi). \tag{1}$$

The actual rate of growth of capital k, on the other hand, can be derived from the divergence of the actual rate from the asymptotic rate and from initial conditions. The key formula here is relation (15) of my earlier paper, given below in relation (2), where $(dk/dt)/k$ is the rate of acceleration of capital:

$$(dk/dt)/k = A\,\frac{k^* - k}{k^* - n}. \tag{2}$$

A typical path of the actual rate of growth of capital is shown by the curved broken line in Figure V, corresponding to the initial condition k_0. As is required by relation (2), k passes through an extreme level (maximum or minimum) when it crosses the asymptote k^*. Also, it will be noted that whenever k is above k^* it must be declining, and whenever it is below it must be increasing. It is that property that I have in my earlier paper referred to as asymptotic. The reader will also find it easy to verify that for the stretch of incomplete specialization, that is between endowments $(K/L)_1$ and $(K/L)_3$, the generalized asymptote must be linear. This is also indicated in Figure V.

Because k^* can never fall short of n, and given the nature of convergence of k to k^*, shown in relation (2), it is obvious that k can never remain indefinitely at or below n. Consequently, the capital-labor ratio with positive technological progress (that is, $A > 0$) must always be increasing in the long run. But this indicates that on the assumptions made it is only a matter of time for the economy to reach a state of complete specialization in the capital-intensive product, that is, in the case actually envisaged in Figure Ia and throughout most of this paper, in the capital good y. To remain in the nonspecialization range, it would be necessary either for the terms of trade to keep gradually changing in favor of the labor-intensive product or for the technological progress to be biased in favor of the labor-intensive good.

The latter alternative would, as can easily be verified by considering Figure IV, make the contour marked $p_x x\ (K/L)/L$ drift upwards at a faster rate than the rate corresponding to the movement of the contour marked $p_y y(K/L)/L$. This, loosely speaking, would keep shifting the linear stretch, such as *bc*, to the right and upwards together with the increasing capital-labor ratio. It is also apparent from Figure V that if the actual rate of growth of capital remains in the vicinity of the asymptotic rate without specialization for a substantial period of time, then it must be accelerating.

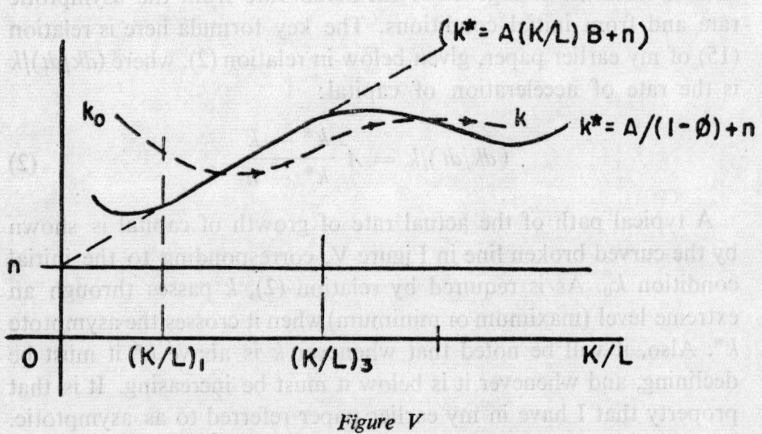

Figure V

VI. The Golden Rule Solutions

The function $f\,(K/L)$ of the preceding section (as derived in Figure IV) makes it possible to study the golden rule for a growing small open economy.[7] Its slope, $f'\ (K/L)$, is the marginal productivity of capital, measured at world market prices, p_x and p_y. As is well known, for a golden rule solution—that is, a steady state in which consumption per capita is maximum—s_0 must be so selected as to make $f'\ (K/N) = n(=k)$.

But it is immediately apparent from the linearity of f within the nonspecialization range that f' must be a constant for that range, call it f_0'. And thus, the small economy's golden rule never will necessitate production of both goods, x and y. Exceptionally, with $n = f_0'$, the economy may produce both goods, but it might just as

7 Of course, we now abandon the assumption of technological progress.

well have specialized then in either product without loss in per capita consumption.

It may also be interesting to note the effects of changes in product prices on the golden rule. For example, an increase in p_x in Figure IV will shift the linear nonspecialization range of f to the right and lower f_0'. If initially the country followed the golden rule and specialized in the (capital-intensive) product y, the increase in the other good's price may now call for a switch in specialization and a considerable change in the saving rate if the golden rule is to be retained.

18

EXTERNAL ECONOMIES, ECONOMIC DEVELOPMENT, AND THE THEORY OF PROTECTION[1]

Pranab Bardhan

I

THE CONCEPT of external economies has had a chequered career. It provided Marshall a means for 'saving' his long-run competitive model. In the twenties it came to be dismissed as more or less an 'empty economic box'. In the last two decades it became the *idée maitresse* of economists of development. While the importance of external economies in the early stages of industrialization in underdeveloped countries is now widely accepted, there are grounds to believe that this is not adequately reflected in the literature of international trade theory. The notorious historical lag with which trade theory is said to develop may have been operative here as well.

Not that trade theory has not dealt with the concept of external economies at all. It appeared in the (muddled) Graham protection controversy (although Graham himself declared the question of economies being external or internal as 'immaterial to the theory') in R. C. O. Matthews's demonstration of the stability of incomplete specialization of a country with decreasing costs industries, in the brief but definitive treatment of Haberler in his celebrated 1950 paper, and in certain scattered remarks of Meade in his *Trade and Welfare*. But most of these writers were doubtful about the reality and significance of external economies and treated the matter as a possible, but not very important, aberration. Thus Viner, after conceding a 'conceivable' case for protection on the basis of external economies, concludes that this is 'little more than a theoretical curiosity.'[2] Haberler, after establishing a case for protection on

1 I am indebted to Professor J.E.Meade for helpful comments on an earlier draft.

2 See Viner, 'Studies in the Theory of International Trade', pp.480-1. More

grounds of a divergence between private marginal costs and social opportunity costs (brought about by external economies), hastens to assure us: 'Most economists who have given serious thought to these problems have reached the conclusion that roughly, and as a rule, the ratios of private money costs do reflect the true social real cost ratios.'[3]

We need not detain ourselves here to establish the pervasive importance of external economies in the context of economic development in underdeveloped countries. The stress on external economies, as Rosenstein-Rodan argues,[4] is a major mark of the difference between traditional static equilibrium theory and the theory of economic development. Our purpose in this paper is to reformulate the existing theory in this field and to integrate into trade theory some aspects of the concept of external economies which are supposed to be important in the development process.

Since external economies have been classified in diverse ways by different writers,[5] it is better to be clear at the outset as to which classification we choose to follow. In this paper we shall analyse first in terms of 'horizontal' and then of 'vertical' external economies. Three points should be noted here. First, we have chosen this particular taxonomic device only to focus on certain key aspects of the types of external economies that we discuss. Secondly, although our classification has verbal similarity to that of Fleming, it is necessary to point out that his 'horizontal' variety is mainly concerned with those external economies which the development of one

---

recently, Viner referred to the 'increasingly fashionable' idea of external economies as providing an argument for protection, but he thought that it might 'call for major qualifications if it is presented as having much practical significance'; see his 'Stability and progress: the poorer countries' problem' in D. Hague (ed) 'Stability and Progress in the World Economy', 1958, pp.56-58 (page 40, last para).

3 Haberler, 'Some problems in the pure theory of international trade', *Economic Journal*, June 1950, pp. 237-8.

4 See his 'Notes on the theory of the big push' in H. S. Ellis (ed.), *Economic Development in Latin America*, 1961.

5 In the twenties we heard of economies 'external to the firm but internal to the industry', economies external to both firm and industry, &c., Viner ('Cost curves and supply curves' in Boulding and Stigler (eds.), *Readings in Price Theory*) introduced the perspicacious distinction between 'technological' and 'pecuniary' external economies; Meade distinguishes between 'atmosphere-creating' external economies and those due to the existence of 'unpaid factors' (*Economic Journal*, 1952); Scitovsky (*Journal of Political Economy*, 1954) talks about static and dynamic external economies, Fleming (*Economic Journal*, 1955) about horizontal and vertical external economies, and Bator (*Quarterly Journal of Economics*, 1958) about three types—ownership externalities, technical externalities, and public good externalities.

consumer-goods industry transmits to another via increased purchasing power and consumer spending,[6] whereas ours is with the distinct problem of interdependence of *production functions* at the same stage of production.[7] Thirdly, we shall deal with only those externalities that are particularly important in the early stages of economic development, and have very little time to observe how apple blossoms provide honey to bees (free of cost) and bees pollinate apples (free of cost), etc.

II

The type of horizontal external economies that are relevant in the context of economic development differs from the traditional static external economies on the essential point that the former are mostly irreversible,[8] i.e. they appear with an expansion of output but do not disappear with subsequent contraction. It can also be seen that this formed much of the basis of the age-old infant-industry case for protection which was applied in many countries in the early stages of their development. We shall shortly examine some aspects of this case in some details and also note that its validity extends beyond the rationale provided by irreversible external economies, contrary to what is sometimes thought. It is also important to realize, in view of the tenor of usual discussion on this point, that here is not just another exception to the doctrine of free trade;[9]

6 We decide to ignore this problem partly because the extension of the concept of external economies to include the effects of increases in consumer income seems not very desirable and partly because in countries with planned economic development the problem of demand deficiency due to low purchasing power may be less important than other complementarities of investment.

7 Vertical external economies, in our paper, are those which are transmitted from one stage of production to another. One possible objection to the use of the term 'vertical' is that this brings in the quaint Austrian notion of 'higher' and 'lower' order of goods while input-output interdependence may very well be circular. But the term may still be of some use in view of Chenery and Watanabe's observation that more than 90 per cent of all input-output flows can usually be arranged in a triangular pattern; see their 'International comparisons of the structure of production', *Econometrica*, Oct. 1958.

8 Bastable, Edgeworth, and others had noted this asymmetry between increasing and diminishing returns to scale, but later writers were often prone to relegate such disturbing phenomena to 'dynamic theory' and then forget all about them. The irreversibility argument was also put forward by K. S. Anderson against Graham's case for protection; see his 'Tariff protection and increasing returns' in *Explorations in Economics*, Notes and Essays Contributed in Honor of F.W. Thussig. (Page 42, last para.)

9 It is doubtful, despite Viner, if the infant-industry case formed an integral part of the classical theory. There is no doubt, however, that in subsequent

what is involved is the problem of a structural change in the pattern of specialization which may be all too important in the early stages of economic development in the underdeveloped countries. Here is a crucial conflict between what are called marginal and total conditions of welfare optimum. In formal terms, a protection-induced movement along the transformation curve towards more production of importables may bring an irreversible shift outwards of the curve itself, and this outer curve may conceivably lie totally outside the existing Baldwin-envelope curve (which is actually the open-economy availability frontier). In this case even no trade can be (potentially) better than some trade.

But what are the factors that actually operate behind such a shift? One of the most important of these, of course, the fact of external economies connected with on-the-job training of labor in a non-slave growing economy.[10] This is particularly important in underdeveloped countries, since laborers require long training to acquire industrial aptitudes after the change-over from rural life, and since labor turnover is often very high. External economies are also important in the well-known case of basic research and where a firm develops a process that cannot be patented or kept secret. (Even in case of applied research the relationship between research spending and private returns is often erratic.) Non-profit public institutions of research may, however, be a better (though partial) solution than protection. It might seem that the problem of underinvestment in research is less important for firms in underdeveloped countries, since they can depend on technology developed abroad (i.e. taking advantage of *international* external economies). But techniques can hardly be borrowed without much adaptation to the particular pattern of available resources, factor prices, market possibilities, &c., and the effort of acclimatization may take a difficult and longish learning period when protection may be necessary. Domestic external economies arise here since once the

literature it has often been relegated to an obscure corner of 'exceptional' cases. (Page 42, last para.)

10 External economies may, however, be substantially reduced, if, as Gary Becker ('Investment in human capital', *Journal of Political Economy*, Oct. 1962) contends, laborers themselves agree to pay for their own training by accepting a wage less than their marginal productivity for the period of apprenticeship (this is not unlikely particularly in underdeveloped countries where the labor market is often a buyers' market due to overt and disguised unemployment all around), or if the training happens to be highly specific to the firm providing it. Pension plans with incomplete vesting privileges, long-term contracts, &c., may also be some of the ways out.

technical knowledge about the best methods of producing a commodity in the particular economic and social environment of the country (this may not be the best or 'latest' method of producing it abroad) is learnt, it becomes common knowledge to other producers in the same country, although, it should be granted, all imitation, whether international or domestic, requires some effort of adaptation. There is another type of learning, what Arrow[11] calls 'learning by doing', which makes unit costs in many manufacturing processes a decreasing function of the cumulative volume of output (even when static scale economies are ruled out). This productivity effect of knowledge and experience accumulating over time has been much emphasized in recent literature and the traditional infant-industry argument can easily be reformulated in these terms.[12] Some of the effects of learning by the growing firm may also be freely available to late-comers in the field (in the form of external economies), but much of the 'know-how' may well be specific to the learning firm.

In all the different cases where no infant can learn without simultaneously teaching others (without pay), the infant-industry argument coincides with the (irreversible) external economies argument. But in cases where the potential external economies are successfully internalized, as in the cases of completely specific labor training, fully patented research, learning of specific know-how, etc. it has often been argued[13] that protection is not really necessary for the growing firm. Losses made on early operations should be counted by the entrepreneurs as part of their capital costs, and firms should be started only if the expected ultimate returns discounted at the current rate of interest are sufficient to give an economic yield (a situation where the entrepreneurs will start the firm anyway). But this argument is hardly relevant to developing economies. In its logical extreme it goes against all planning for economic development: an investment project should be started only if it is profitable in the long run, and if it is so, private business will see to that! The point is that in most cases society (through its

11 'The economic implications of learning by doing', *Review of Economic Studies*, June 1962.

12 For a more intensive analysis of the implications of different types of learning processes in the context of trade theory, see my 'Technical change as a learning process, economic development and trade theory', forthcoming.

13 See, for example, Kemp, 'The Mill-Bastable infant-industry dogma', *Journal of Political Economy*, 1960. See, however, Fellner, 'Individual investment projects in growing economies' in Millikan (ed.), *Investment Criteria and Economic Growth*.

development planners) may discount the future at a significantly lower rate than the market. Not only is the 'pure' time preference smaller for society as a whole than for individual entrepreneurs, the risk premium which is included in the gross interest rates used by them for discounting the future may be far less for the planners. In underdeveloped countries, where private enterprise is more at home in trading and speculative activities where the entrepreneurial horizon is very short, the State, if it is not itself in a position to do the pioneering job (as in Japan in late nineteenth century), may have to coax and cajole private business to invest in an industry that will be socially profitable in the long run. In this sense, the infant-industry argument for protection stretches beyond the (irreversible) external economies case.[14]

It might be interesting to note briefly some of the implications that the introduction of irreversible external economies may have for some of the accepted theorems in the literature on protection theory. Let us take, for example, the question of effects of tariffs on the terms of trade. As soon as we recognize that because of external economies protection might bring about an irreversible shift in the existing transformation curve for the economy, we can utilize here some of the results obtained in the literature of economic expansion and terms of trade[15] (with the difference that economic expansion is now endogenous and not given from outside the system as in the Hicks-Johnson-Corden-Bhagwati models). We shall not go into details here, but it may be interesting to note two 'perverse' cases. The customary analysis of the effects of a tariff on the terms of trade concludes,[16] under certain assumptions, that the terms of trade of the protecting country will improve or deteriorate according as the country's price-elasticity of demand for imports is greater or less than the marginal propensity to consume importables of whoever spends the tariff revenue. But if an infant-industry tariff induces

14 Kemp argues that the infant-industry case should also pass what he calls the 'Bastable test' that the ultimate saving in costs should compensate the community for the high costs (in terms of sacrifices on the part of the consumers or taxpayers) of the protected learning period. Needless to say, much again here will depend on the rate at which society discounts the future, and for a developing economy the 'Bastable test' should not be very stringent after all. (page 44, last para.)

15 For an excellent survey of the literature see Bhagwati and Johnson 'Notes on some controversies in the theory of international trade', *Economic Journal* 1960: see also my 'Technical progress and terms of trade,' *Arthaniti* (*Journal of Economics*, Calcutta University) July 1961.

16 See, for example, Metzler, 'Tariffs, the terms of trade and the distribution of national income', *Journal of Political Economy* Feb. 1949. (page 44, last para.)

an irreversible shift in production conditions in the importables industry, the consequential change in the output and consumption of importables might easily produce a negative excess demand for importables even when the marginal propensity to consume importables of whoever spends the tariff revenue happens to be *greater* than the country's price-elasticity of demand for imports: terms of trade will *improve*. Secondly, it is recognized in the literature of economic expansion and terms of trade that a sufficiently labor-saving improvement in the capital-intensive importables industry of a country may lead to an adverse movement in the terms of trade.[17] If an infant-industry tariff induces such a type of expansion, it may ultimately turn the terms of trade *against* the country even when its elasticity of demand for imports is *greater* than the marginal propensity to consume importables of whoever spends the tariff revenue.

When we bring in irreversible external economies the Marshall-Lerner theorem on the symmetry of import and export taxes may also go overboard. The essential point of this theorem is that the 'real' effects of the two taxes are similar since the import tax by making import-substitution more profitable *pulls* resources out from the exportables industry, while an export tax by making the latter industry less profitable *pushes* some of its resources towards the importables industry. But when we take account of learning and improvements induced by protection, with an import tax the import-competing industry may expand (with an endogenous improvement in the use of factors) not necessarily at the expense (ultimately, at least) of the exportables industry; whereas with an export tax production in the exportables industry will contract and resources will be driven to the importables industry. So there is an asymmetry in even the 'real' effects of the two taxes.[18]

III

Now we pass on to the case of 'vertical' external economies[19] where the expansion of one industry affects the profitability of other

17 See Findlay and Grubert, 'Factor-intensities, technological progress and the terms of trade', *Oxford Economic Papers*, 1959.

18 This and the preceding paragraph draw upon a part of my paper on 'Technical change as a learning process, economic development and trade theory', forthcoming.

19 These vertical external economies have not been as yet adequately integrated in international trade theory, at least to the extent in which they are supposed to

industries, higher up or lower down in the production structure. Historically, there is evidence enough[20] to believe that the vertical transmission of external economies has been very important in stimulating the growth of inter-related industries. Nor have these externalities been ignored in Marshallian value theory. But by the end of the twenties, the idea gained ground that no extra-market treatment is here called for since such economies will be reflected in market prices (hence Viner's term 'pecuniary' economies) of inputs and will be a part of the market's co-ordinating mechanism. But in a realistic environment of imperfect knowledge and insufficient communication of information, current prices are a poor signal of future profitability (especially in the context of economic change grafted on a small initial base) and what Koopmans[21] calls 'secondary uncertainty' hovers menacingly around all investment decisions in early stages of economic development (in the absence of speculators bearing the brunt of faulty communications in the purely academic world of perfect futures markets). Hence the need for centralized intervention in the decision-making process.[22]

Vertical externalities can be operative in a number of ways. We shall consider the cases where expansion (induced by protection) in one industry leads to the expansion (or establishment) of an industry using otherwise unused resources or of an industry which can now reap economies, internal or external.

---

be important in the theory of economic development. The problem has been touched upon, but not elaborated, in the context of trade theory in Viner, 'Stability and progress: the poorer countries' problem', loc. cit.; Chenery, 'Comparative advantage and development policy', *American Economic Review*, 1961; and Bhagwati, 'The theory of comparative advantage in the context of underdevelopment and growth,' *Pakistan Development Review*, Autumn 1962. An attempt to measure the significance of such investment complementarities in terms of a hybrid programming model of an open economy has been made by Chenery, 'The interdependence of investment decisions', in *The Allocation of Economic Resources*, Essays in Honor of B. F. Haley. (page 44, last para.)

20 See for example G. Ohlin 'Balanced economic growth in History', *American Economic Review*, May 1959. (page 46, last para).

21 See Koopmans, 'Three Essays in the State of Economic Science,' p. 154. While it is not absent in developed countries, this uncertainty and the caution or pessimism of entrepreneurs in the face of it are certainly greater in underdeveloped countries. For an analysis of different kinds of uncertainty arising from producer interdependence in a market where information is limited, see Malmgren, 'Information, expectations and the theory of the firm', *Quarterly Journal of Economics*, 1961 pp. 405-7. (page 46, last para.)

22 One other possible way out would have been the vertical integration of firms so that the said external effects are internalized. But there are limits to its feasibility (in view of organizational and financial difficulties particularly in underdeveloped countries) or to its desirability (in view of its probable distortion of the competitive allocation pattern) (page 46).

Take the case[23] [of a country where investment in extracting its reserves of iron ore is unprofitable because there is no domestic steel industry to use it and because it cannot compete with foreign iron ore in selling to the foreign steel industry due to high transport costs. On the other hand, domestic steel production is unprofitable because iron ore is not extracted domestically and because production with the help of foreign iron ore cannot compete with imports of foreign steel.[24] In such a case a temporary (infant-industry) protection to steel industry is in order. Steel industry will be economic in the long run when domestic iron ore is available. This is a case where the sheltered production of one industry leads to the establishment of another industry using hitherto unexploited resources.

Then there may be the case where the expansion of one industry under protection may induce expansion in a supplementary industry where the latter may have its costs reduced because of the productivity effects of learning and other horizontal external economies, and this in turn might increase the profitability of the protected industry and enable it ultimately to stand on its own feet.

In the third, and empirically perhaps the most important, case the protected expansion of an industry may give its input-providing industry a sufficient jolt to go over the 'hump' and reap internal economies of scale, enhancing by turn the profitability of the protected industry using cheapened inputs.[25] Of course, in this case

23 Chenery ('Interdependence of investment decisions', loc. cit., pp. 96-7) cites a similar case to show that external economies can occur even without economies of scale elsewhere in the economy (page 46, last para.)

24 It may be useful to go beyond verbal arguments to bring out the restrictive nature of the case. Suppose C_x is the cost price of a unit of steel in the domestic economy, C_y is the cost per unit of domestic iron ore, t_y is the cost of transporting a unit of iron ore either way between the countries, k is the number of units of iron ore required in producing a unit of steel and P_x is the total costs (other than those of iron ore) of producing a unit of steel; priced variables refer to the foreign country. Our assumptions above imply that $P_x+k(C'_y+t_y)>$price (c.i.f.) per unit of imported steel in the home country $>P_x+k.C_y$; and that $C'_y<C_y+t_y$. It can be seen from these two conditions that for this case for protection to be plausible the cost of domestic iron ore (C_y) must be in a particular range, or, $C'_y+t_x>C_y>C'_y-t_y$. The range is larger, the larger are the transport costs of iron ore. For a roughly similar exercise, see J. N. Wolfe, 'Transport costs and comparative advantage', *Journal of Political Economy*, 1959. As a matter of fact, transport costs may be a significant fraction of total costs of basic commodities such as steel, cement, chemicals, and in all 'weight-losing' process industries.

25 It is easy to see that in cases where both the exportables and the importables industries draw upon the same input-providing industries, an export subsidy may serve the same purpose as an import tax (contrary again to the implications of the Marshall-Lerner symmetry theorem).

In a case where protection of the importable industry enables the indigenous capital-goods industry to realize productivity effects of learning or economies

competition is likely to break down in the input-providing industry, but it may still share its economies with its buyers if the monopolist cannot or does not (there is plenty of reason why) practice perfect price discrimination (Pigou's first degree discrimination). In measuring the gains from protection in this case, one should match the allocative losses of market imperfections with the gains from external economies. Whether protection will bring any *net* benefit or not will depend on the increase in the rate of growth under protection (because of irreversible external economies), the static costs of protection (in terms of greater burden on domestic consumers and the allocative losses from monopolistic output restriction) and the *social* rate of time preference with which the future income is to be discounted.

We may, in passing, illustrate, with the help of a simple diagram, how protection may be *harmful* in this case. In Fig. 1 *AM* is the current transformation curve[26] for *A* (exportables) and *M* (importables), *PC* is the given free-trade price ratio, *P* and *C* are the

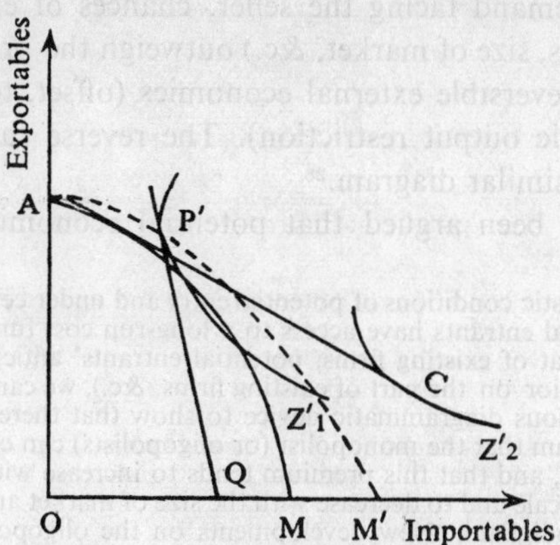

Figure 1

of scale, the cheapening of capital goods will lower the rental price of capital as a factor of production (at a given rate of interest) and the resultant factor-substitution may increase the marginal productivity of labor throughout the economy. Protection may thus raise the real wage of labor even if it happens to be the relatively *abundant* factor.

26 It is to be recognized, however, that the 'catch-all' transformation curve of trade geometry is a clumsy tool in an analysis of vertical externalities, since it normally presumes vertically integrated production processes, and in a sense assumes away our problem. We use it only for the purpose of a simple, if crude, illustration. (Page 48, last para.)

Vanek in a recent paper (*Quarterly Journal of Economics*, Feb. 1963) has tried to draw the transformation curve when inter-industrial flows are permitted. But his construction seems to raise more problems than it answers. (Page 48, last para.)

production and consumption points respectively under free trade. With protection giving rise to irreversible vertical external economies within the M-industry (complex)—as between its different (unintegrated) stages—the transformation curve shifts in the next period. AM' is, however, *not* the next period's transformation curve as such but the next period's transformation curve as evaluated (and telescoped) in the current period. In other words, AM' represents the optimal output combinations of the next period all discounted by the social rate of time preference, making the two curves comparable. If the price ratio under (prohibitive) protection and with monopoly *now* operating in an earlier stage of M-production and projected into the price charged in the final stage (Lerner's case of 'transitive' monopoly) is indicated by $P'Q$, production and consumption point P' is on an indifference curve Z'_1 lower than the free-trade indifference curve Z'_2. Evidently what happens is that the consumption costs of protection in terms of higher prices (the height of the price charged[27] depending on the rate of tariff, the elasticity of demand facing the seller, chances of entry, extent of scale economies, size of market, &c.) outweigh the production gains in terms of irreversible external economies (offset, to some extent, by monopolistic output restriction). The reverse case can also be shown with a similar diagram.[28]

It has often been argued that potential economies (internal or

27 Under realistic conditions of potential entry and under certain assumptions (e.g. that potential entrants have access to a long-run cost function identical in all respects to that of existing firms, potential entrants' anticipation of utmost belligerent behavior on the part of existing firms, &c.), we can use Modigliani's simple but ingenious diagrammatic device to show that there is a well-defined maximum premium that the monopolist (or oligopolists) can command over the competitive price, and that this premium tends to increase with the importance of economies of scale and to decrease with the size of market and the elasticity of demand. See Modigliani, 'New developments on the oligopoly front', *Journal of Political Economy*, 1958, pp. 216-20.

28 Although there is no decisive empirical presumption regarding likely magnitudes, more than casual empiricism often suggests that the static losses from misallocation (due to tariffs, monopolistic distortions, &c.) in underdeveloped countries are not likely to be substantial. See, for example, Harberger, 'Using the resources at hand more effectively', *American Economic Review*, May 1959. What about 'dynamic' losses from misallocation? Many free traders have eloquently referred to the 'dynamic benefits' (see Haberler's Cairo Lecture on *International Trade and Economic Development*) of free trade in its 'trust-busting' role; but, as Harberger testifies, correction of market imperfections is not likely to boost the rate of growth very much in underdeveloped countries (see also Higgins's comment on Harberger's paper, *American Economic Review*, May 1959). On the contrary, one need not have to be a Schumpeterian to point to the frequently observed 'dynamic' role of monopolies (even when tariffs happen to be the ignominious 'mother' of such trusts).

external) may be largely offset by rising factor costs (diseconomies) in a general equilibrium situation.[29] It is pointed out, quoting Marcus Fleming,[30] that industries are not only occasionally complementary, they are also, in most cases, competing for factors of production. The case for protection is to that extent qualified. Two general points can be noted here. First, this argument starts from a static model with full employment of the constant amount of resources. But even apart from structurally unemployed labor and unexploited natural resources (as in our transport-costs case) in many under-developed countries, in the dynamic context of development we have to take account of endogenous productivity changes (induced as in our analysis, by protection itself) and of exogenously growing labor force and a positive net investment. Secondly, if our purpose is to examine the doctrine of comparative advantage as a principle of planning, the question is one of alternative uses of investible resources, and, to quote Chenery: 'there is no *a priori* assumption that a coordinated programme which realises external economies will utilise more of any factor than the alternative investments that would take place without coordination. In fact, it is quite possible that coordination will use less of both capital and labor to obtain the same result as uncoordinated investment.'[31]

If we are after a principle of planning that will simultaneously determine the optimal pattern of trade as well as the optimal pattern of allocation of investible resources, comparative advantage, as is traditionally interpreted, will be a poor guide, particularly in view of vertical external economies.[32] In such a setting it may not be possible to ascertain a country's comparative advantage in a particular commodity without at the same time knowing the production conditions prevailing over time in the industries 'higher' and 'lower' in the vertical production structure, or with respect to the whole complex of interrelated activities. In this connexion it may

29 See Caves, *Trade and Economic Structure*, p. 168; Viner, 'Stability and progress, &c.', loc. cit., p. 57.

30 Fleming, op. cit.; Fleming himself, however, relaxes his argument in case of vertical external economies.

31 Chenery, 'Interdependence of investment decisions', loc. cit., p. 112.

32 Viner (op. cit.) continues paying his homage to the 'Lord Justice Comparative Cost' (Robertson's term) even in the context of economic development, since, as he tells us, he and the classicists have always intended the doctrine to be a long-run one 'including all the dynamic factors that could be foreseen or provided for in advance'. But as Nurkse in his comments on Viner's paper ('Stability and progress', loc. cit.) aptly points out, comparative advantage as a principle of planning is rather an empty formula; it does not give us any very useful tools with which to foresee or provide for the dynamic factors to which Viner refers.

be interesting to note that in contemporary regional analysis also it is being increasingly realized that the industry-by-industry comparative cost approach misses the heart of inter-industry relationships, and it has to be supplemented by techniques like industrial complex analysis using an inter-activity matrix (i.e. an inter-industry matrix with alternative processes and with added data which permit adjustments for certain non-linearities and scale economies).[33]

IV

The question may arise as to how we are to choose between different complexes of activities and why, as Haberler and others ask, the external-economies argument should apply only to industries devoted to import-substitution. As a matter of fact, Douglas North[34] and others have referred to the historically important vertical external-economy relationships between the 'export base' (of staples like American cotton and wheat, Scandinavian timber, Canadian wheat, &c.) and industries subsidiary to exports. On the other hand, we know that the primary export sector of many underdeveloped countries, despite considerable expansion in the nineteenth century, did not serve as a propulsive sector. Partly it may be due to the fact that the export 'enclaves' *economically* belonged to the metropolitan country,[35] partly due to market imperfections and institutional rigidities,[36] but to a significant extent it may be due, as Hirschman[37] seems to suggest, to the small 'linkage' effects of primary production in underdeveloped countries, especially since only a very small fraction of it receives elaborate processing, which usually takes place abroad.[38]

Hirschman's linkage effects should not, however, be identified (as it is sometimes done) with vertical external economies. The linear

33 See Isard, *Methods of Regional Analysis*, 1960, ch. 9.

34 Location theory and regional economic growth', *Journal of Political Economy*, 1955.

35 See Singer, 'The distribution of gains between investing and borrowing countries', *American Economic Review*, May 1950.

36 See Myint, 'The gains from international trade and the backward countries', *Review of Economic Studies*, 1954-5; also, Baldwin and Meier, *Economic Development*.

37 *The Strategy of Economic Development*, pp. 109-10.

38 Rostow (*The Stages of Economic Growth*, p. 56) recognizes the potential role of primary products as leading sectors, provided they involve the application of modern processing techniques.

homogeneity and additivity assumptions of input-output analysis in terms of which the structural linkages are estimated do not allow for economies, internal or external. We have seen that vertical external economies arise mainly because of internal economies of scale, irreversible horizontal external economies, productivity effects of learning, &c., in input-providing industries. Data on economies of scale are very scanty particularly with respect to underdeveloped countries. We may, however, accept Chenery's weighty evidence[39] regarding economies of scale in machinery, transport equipment, metals, and some other intermediate goods used in manufacturing operations.[40] As for productivity effects of learning, there is some evidence as to their importance in some basic producer goods industries.[41] Once economies of scale, &c.—the *root* of vertical external economies—can be traced in the input-providing industries, the structural linkages may give us only a very rough idea as to the *extent* of their transmission into the rest of the economy. It can be seen from a recent estimate[42] of structural linkages in the Indian economy that the forward linkage effects of many of the input-providing industries (iron and steel, &c., where economies of scale, &c., are generally believed to be important) are particularly high, indicating the likely importance of vertical external economies induced by an expansion of the industries that use those inputs. (The data also indicate a highly skewed deliveries distribution for those inputs, i.e. their deliveries are absorbed relatively highly by only a few sectors of the economy.) On the other hand, primary production has, as is commonly expected, very weak *backward* linkages, so that they cannot enjoy much of vertical external economies even when their sources potentially exist in input-

39 'Patterns of industrial growth', *American Economic Review*, Sept. 1960; see also J. Haldi, *Economies of Scale in Economic Development*, Memorandum No. E-7, Stanford Project for Quantitative Research in Economic Development for similar evidence.

40 *A Study of the Iron and Steel Industry in Latin America* (ECLA), 1954, testifies to the quantitative importance of economies of scale in steel production.

41 Hirsch notes ('Firm progress ratios', *Econometrica*, 1956) a number of empirical studies which have produced 'progress coefficients' for various types of machines and machine tools varying from 16.5 to 24.8 per cent in magnitude.

42 See K. R. Bharadwaj, 'Structural linkages in the Indian economy', *The Economic Weekly* (Bombay), Aug. 18, 1962. In contrast to the table for structural linkages in the economies of Italy, Japan, and the U.S.A. which Hirschman (op. cit., pp. 106-7) borrows from Chenery and Watanabe (op. cit.). Bharadwaj goes further and also estimates for the Indian economy the Rasmussen indexes of 'power of dispersion' and 'sensitivity of dispersion' (see Rasmussen, *Intersectoral Relations*, ch. viii) which are akin it, but, as Hirschman himself admits, are more refined than his 'backward' and 'forward' linkages respectively.

providing industries. One should, however, be careful not to put too much faith in the meaningfulness of these linkage coefficients.[43]

On all counts, however, the prospects of a machinery-steel-iron complex are bright indeed (unless the country concerned is very small, in which case the problem of the size of market can be solved by inter-regional integration, &c.). Economies of scale are substantial in the iron and steel industry,[44] and its forward linkage effect is also large. What is more, although circumstances differ widely for different underdeveloped countries, this is probably one of the few cases where the conflict between considerations of initial factor endowments and those of making the most of (vertical) external economies is likely to be the least sharp. The underdeveloped countries possess 57.3 per cent of the probable total of iron-ore resources of the world, while their crude steel production is only about 4.6 per cent of the world total.[45] Even their marked deficiency in coking coal can now be overcome with newer processes such as the Krupp-Renn sponge iron and Tysland-Hole process. It is in the light of these considerations that some, though not all, aspects of current protectionism in many underdeveloped countries with respect to this vital industrial complex can be rationalized, and also some of the past failures of the colonial governments in those countries be exposed. As regards the latter, it can be said that many of those governments had sinned not as much by 'exploiting' the colonial economy as by tenaciously following a policy of *laissez-faire* too long.

43 In her remarkable paper Bharadwaj also questions the operational usefulness of these structural relationships in determining investment priorities in economic planning, since the input-output matrix from which they are drawn are 'still pictures abstracted from time patterns of inputs and outputs', since there is the possibility that lower productivity might counteract lower inter-sectoral purchases to give a high backward linkage and so on.

It should also be noted that Hirschman introduces his linkage effects in a somewhat different context from ours. His framework of analysis in which entrepreneurial decision-making ability is the scarcest of resources and where linkage effects are important because of their capacity to generate, through excess demand and pressures, a compulsive sequence of development, is totally different from models like ours which concentrate on the supply side of the picture. Hirschman's purely 'demand' approach to economic development has been criticized by Myint, 'The demand approach to economic development', *Review of Economic Studies*, 1959-60.

44 The productivity effects of learning may also be considerable. The Indian iron and steel industry has been protected, in one form or another, since the twenties, and, it is held, the continuous fall observed in 'works costs' in major lines of production in the inter-war period is explainable, to a large extent, by a process of learning that ensued. I am indebted to A. K. Bagchi of Cambridge for drawing my attention to this example.

45 *World Iron Ore Resources and their Utilisation* (UNO), 1950, quoted in N.J.G. Pounds, *The Geography of Iron and Steel*, 1959, p. 168.

Even in a country like India, which in some respects (natural resources, entrepreneurship, cheap labor, potential size of market, &c.) had been more favorably placed than many other underdeveloped countries for creating such an industrial complex, the absence of any proper fiscal policy in the nineteenth and early twentieth century is commonly regarded to be one of the major factors responsible for stagnation.[46]

While all this is obviously important and will readily find loud supporters in underdeveloped countries, there are some considerations which protectionists would do well to remember. If the factors giving rise to vertical external economies are not adequately reflected in the market because of imperfect foresight and information on the part of private entrepreneurs, it has often been questioned whether the planners are so many supermen to be always endowed with necessarily better foresight.[47] The answer is not, however, difficult. Let us quote Scitovsky:[48]

> Uncoordinated investment plans are likely to be made up at different points of time; and the mere difference in timing causes them (or at least some of them) to be based on less information than would be available if the same investment decisions were coordinated and taken simultaneously. The better information, therefore, of the planners—that is, of the people, who coordinate simultaneous investment decisions—depends not on their better foresight or superior intelligence but solely on the simultaneity of inter-related decisions.

But when vertical complementarity thus demands that several things be done simultaneously, *not* successively, protection by tinkering with the price mechanism at one point (relying on a process of successive adaptation) may not be enough; it is to be supplemented by subsidies and other expansionary policies with respect to the whole hierarchy of stages that make up the particular industrial complex, or it may not work at all.

But if Koopmans's 'secondary uncertainty' is sought to be overcome by a policy of pushing on a wide front (or 'depth', one should say) without the government's participation in production

46 For one suggestive historical example, see G. Rosen, 'A case of aborted growth: India, 1860-1900', *The Economic Weekly* (Bombay), 11 Aug. 1962.

47 See, for example, Stockfisch, 'External economies, investment and foresight', *Journal of Political Economy*, 1955.

48 'A reply', *Journal of Political Economy*, 1955.

itself, another type of uncertainty may loom large. Whenever there is a necessity of simultaneous decision-making on the part of private entrepreneurs in the presence of reciprocal interdependence in production, game-theoretic uncertainty cannot be ruled out.[49] A complex game of strategies is easily conceivable here, and any convergent equilibrium solution might be unattainable through government tax-subsidy policy. A more direct government participation might be needed.[50]

This leads us to a more general point. Protectionists often argue out—occassionally successfully—a case for government intervention and planning, but a case for planning is not necessarily a case for the negative method of protection. In countries committed to overall economic development planning, as many underdeveloped countries today are, the exigencies of planning might necessitate more direct controls in the foreign trade sector.[51] A protectionist policy relying on (modified) market forces may be quite out of place. Once the market mechanism is shown to be fundamentally deficient, there may not be any half-way house to direct planning.

49 For a game-theoretic treatment of the 'non-separable' external economies between firms at the same stage of production, see O. A. Davis and A. Whinston, 'Externalities, welfare and the theory of games', *Journal of Political Economy*, June 1962.

50 One interesting (albeit partial) way out may be the method of 'put options' utilized by the U.S. Government to effect desired investment in the aluminium and nickel industries during the Korean war. For explanation of this point, see Haldi, op. cit., pp. 151-2.

51 For an emphasis on this conflict between a policy of protection and of development planning, 'more important and more immediate in the setting of the present-day underdeveloped countries than the traditional conflict between protection and free trade', see H. Myint's paper on 'Protection and economic development', contributed to the Brissago Conference of the IEA. I am indebted to Dr. Myint for letting me see a copy of this paper.

19

TRADE POLICIES IN DEVELOPING COUNTRIES

*Bela Balassa**

THE PURPOSE OF THIS paper is to examine some of the implications of the author's findings concerning the effects of trade policies followed by developing countries on their export performance and economic growth. In the discussion, use will be made of the results of several studies carried out in recent years: an investigation of the growth strategies of six semi-industrial countries, two of which, Argentina and Chile, are customarily included in the developing country category;[1] a comparative study of the structure of protection in Brazil, Chile, Mexico, Western Malaysia, Pakistan, the Philippines, and Norway;[2] and a study of industrial policies in Taiwan and Korea.[3] Following a brief summary of the findings, guidelines will be suggested for trade policies by developing countries.

I

Instruments of trade policy employed by developing countries include import tariffs and surcharges, export taxes and subsidies, multiple exchange rates, as well as quotas and licenses. By affecting the relative prices of inputs and outputs, these measures influence the allocation of resources, including new investment, and provide

* This paper was written as part of a consultant arrangement with the World Bank.

1 Bela Balassa, 'Growth Strategies in Semi-Industrial Countries', *Quarterly Journal of Economics*, February 1970, pp. 24-47.

2 Bela Balassa and Associates, *The Structure of Protection in Developing Countries*, Baltimore, Md., The Johns Hopkins University Press, 1971. For a discussion of some of the methodological issues and a summary of the estimates of effective rates of protection, see 'Effective Protection in Developing Countries' in *Trade, Balance of Payments and Growth: Papers in International Economics in Honor of Charles P. Kindleberger* (J. Bhagwati, R. Jones, R. A. Mundell, and V. Vanek, eds.), Amsterdam, North Holland Publishing Co., 1971—In the present paper, results pertaining to Norway will not be considered. Furthermore, in the case of Argentina, Brazil, and Chile, the paper will consider the situation existing prior to the changes in policies introduced in the late sixties. These policy changes will be briefly referred to at a later point in the paper.

3 Bela Balassa, 'Industrial Policies in Taiwan and Korea,' *Weltwirtschaftliches Archiv*, Band 105, Heft 1, 1971. To be reprinted in a volume in honor of Raul Prebisch.

incentives—or disincentives—to import-substituting and export activities.

Discrimination among economic activities introduced by the use of trade measures exists to varying degrees in the nine countries studied.[4] Argentina, Brazil, Chile, Pakistan, and—to a lesser extent —the Philippines provide considerable incentives to manufacturing industries at the expense of primary activities. The extent of discrimination in favor of manufacturing and against primary production is relatively small in Mexico; it is even less in Korea and Taiwan; and, on the average, virtually nil in Western Malaysia (for short, Malaya).

Discrimination in favor of manufacturing entails the protection of domestic manufacturing industries against imports whereas primary exports are penalized by tariffs on their inputs and by the lower exchange rate associated with protection. The protection of manufactured goods and discrimination against primary exports usually go hand-in-hand, the principal exception being Malaya, which levies a tax on its major primary exports, rubber and tin, but does not protect manufactures.

In Argentina, Brazil, Chile and the Philippines, there is also a substantial bias in favor of import substitution and against exports in protected manufacturing industries. Firms producing for home markets can get the domestic price raised by high import protection while, in the absence of export subsidies, they could obtain only the world market price in exporting. By contrast, the bias against exports in manufacturing industries is relatively small in Mexico and Malaya where levels of protection are low and it is practically nonexistent in Pakistan, Taiwan, and Korea. In Pakistan, manufacturing industries receive high protection irrespective of whether they produce for domestic or foreign markets; in Taiwan and Korea the extent of import protection is rather low and, on the average, it is matched by subsidies to manufactured exports.

II

The trade policies followed during the postwar period have affected export performance and economic growth in the countries

4 The results cited in the paper have been taken from the four studies cited above and do not include recent changes in the policies that will be noted below. Some of the estimates on exports and growth have been reproduced in Tables 1 and 2.

under consideration. The unfavorable treatment of primary exports has contributed to the decline in the shares of Argentina, Brazil, Chile, and Pakistan and, to a lesser extent, the Philippines in the world market for their major export commodities and has retarded the development of new exports. Malaya, too, has experienced a decline in the market shares of its major primary exports, but it has expanded its minor exports which receive more favorable treatment. Finally, Mexico and to an even greater extent Taiwan and Korea have been successful in raising the world market share of their major primary exports and in introducing new export products. In the latter two countries, these developments have taken place during the sixties following a shift in economic policies from import substitution to export promotion.

The expansion of primary exports in individual countries has further been affected by world demand conditions in the markets for their major export commodities. The main beneficiaries of favorable world market trends have been Chile (copper) and the Philippines (oilseeds) while the slow growth of world demand and unfavorable price changes for rubber and tin have depressed export earnings in Malaya.

The trade policies followed, together with changes in world market conditions, largely explain intercountry differences in the rate of growth of primary exports. Table 1 shows Korea and Taiwan in the lead, followed by Chile, the Philippines, Mexico, Argentina, Malaya, Brazil and Pakistan. Comparisons of growth rates are less meaningful for manufactured exports because several of the countries under consideration started from a very small base. Instead, we use the share of manufactured exports in manufacturing output and in total exports as indicators of success in exporting manufactures.

In countries with a substantial bias against the exports of manufactured goods, these commodities continue to account for less than 3 percent of manufactured output and account for at most 10 percent of total exports. Among countries with a lesser bias, Mexico's manufactured exports have reached 5 percent of manufacturing output and 25 percent of total exports. In Malaya 10 percent of manufactured output is exported although, given the relatively low share of manufacturing and the high share of exports in GNP, manufactured goods provide no more than one-tenth of total exports.

In Taiwan and Korea, manufactured exports have been stimulated to a considerable extent by the adoption of export-oriented policies around 1960. As a result, exports of manufactures have increased to a considerable extent in the two countries, both as a proportion of total exports and of manufacturing output. By 1969, these proportions reached 67 and 37 percent in Taiwan and 76 and 18 percent in Korea.

Following the introduction of the Export Bonus Scheme in 1959, manufactured exports have also assumed importance in Pakistan, with jute and cotton textiles being the principal items. But, owing to policies penalizing primary exports, foreign sales of raw jute and cotton have declined in an amount exceeding the rise in textile exports. Moreover, high subsidies to manufactured exports, together with the high protection of import substitutes, have imposed a substantial cost on the national economy.

Owing to their favorable performance in both primary and manufactured exports, Korea and Taiwan are far ahead of the other countries studied in terms of the expansion of total exports (Table 1). Exports have increased more than the average also in Mexico where the growth of tourism and border trade (not included in the export figures) have further contributed to increases in foreign exchange earnings. For reasons noted earlier, exports have risen relatively rapidly also in Chile and the Philippines while increases have been small in Argentina, Brazil, and Pakistan.

III

The expansion of exports contributes to economic growth directly by raising national income and indirectly by providing foreign exchange for the import needs of the domestic economy. An export-oriented policy also permits specialization according to comparative advantage—both between primary and manufactured activities and within the manufacturing sector. In particular, exports of manufactured goods enable firms to lower costs by employing large-scale production methods, reducing product variety, and participating in the international division of the production process through the manufacturing of parts and components for assembly abroad. Moreover, familiarity with foreign markets provides incentives for technological change and produce improvement.

Import substitution, too, can be a source of economic growth in

TABLE 1

EXPORTS IN SELECTED DEVELOPING COUNTRIES

	Argentina	Brazil	Chile	Mexico	Korea	Malaya	Pakistan	Philippines	Taiwan
Average annual rate of growth of exports									
Primary goods									
1950-60	0.1	−0.9	5.3	4.0	−3.5	1.9	−7.5	5.4	−1.2
1960-69	3.6	4.2	8.4	5.5	21.0	0.6	2.5	6.0	16.4
1950-69	1.7	0.6	6.8	4.7	16.7	1.1	−2.9	5.7	8.3
Manufactures									
1950-60	−7.6	15.6	11.1	12.2	0.2	29.0	35.0	4.7	30.5
1960-69	17.3	19.1	10.7	19.9	69.0	12.7	14.5	25.0	34.0
1950-69	3.5	16.3	10.9	15.8	35.6	19.0	24.0	13.3	32.5
All commodities									
1950-60	−0.5	−0.6	5.6	5.0	−2.8	2.0	−2.3	5.4	3.6
1960-69	4.6	5.1	8.5	7.2	38.9	1.2	6.3	6.8	24.0
1950-69	1.9	1.1	7.0	6.0	18.2	1.7	0.4	6.0	14.9
Manufactured exports as a percentage of									
output—1969	2	1	3	5	18	10	8	3	36
total exports—1969	10	9	6	25	76	10	51	10	67

Note: For Taiwan and Korea the base year is 1953 instead of 1950. For Brazil, Chile, Malaya, Pakistan, and the Philippines, the terminal year is 1968 instead of 1969.

Source: National and international trade statistics.

particular cases. A number of developing countries attained rapid rates of growth of manufacturing output and, to a lesser extent, national income, in the early stage of import substitution, which entails replacing the imports of nondurable consumer goods and their inputs by domestic production. Industries producing such commodities are the prime candidates for import substitution in developing countries since they employ chiefly unskilled and semi-skilled labor, do not require the application of sophisticated technology, and need few inputs from ancillary industries. Nor does the limited size of national markets constitute an important handicap for the development of these industries since the efficient scale of operations is relatively low and costs are not substantially higher in smaller plants.

But, in the absence of exports, the expansion of industries producing nondurable consumer goods and their inputs necessarily slows down after imports have been replaced since domestic production cannot continue to grow faster than home demand. Moreover, in the small domestic markets of developing countries, increasing difficulties are encountered in import substitution in other intermediate products, capital goods, and durable consumer goods. These commodities have higher technological and skill requirements, require the availability of materials, parts, and components from other industries, and need large-scale production for efficient operations with costs being substantially higher at lower output levels. Last but not least, in the event of continuing protection, there will be few inducements for technological improvements.

These considerations help to explain intercountry differences in rates of economic growth (Table 2). In Taiwan and Korea, the growth of GDP has accelerated to a considerable extent following the adoption of export-oriented policies. In expanding the exports of nondurable consumer goods, the two countries have utilized their educated manpower while the capital requirements of these industries are relatively low. The leading role of exports in the growth process is indicated by the high incremental ratio of exports to GDP; in 1960–69, this ratio was 39 percent in Taiwan and 29 percent in Korea.[5]

Exports have also importantly contributed to Mexico's economic

5 The incremental exports-GDP ratio (the ratio of the absolute increase in the value of exports to that of GDP) was calculated in constant prices from data given in national and international sources.

growth and the relatively low protection of manufacturing industries has limited the cost of import substitution. In turn, the low degree of discrimination among economic activities has made it possible for Malaya to attain a rate of growth of national income substantially above that for exports.

The remaining countries of the group are characterized by import substitution behind high protective barriers. In these countries, the relationship between import substitution and economic growth has been influenced by their market size and the level of their economic development. Thus, the expansion of manufacturing output has slowed down to a considerable extent in the Philippines after the mid-fifties by which time the 'easy' stage of import substitution had been largely completed. Despite rapid increases in exports due to favorable market conditions, there has been a decline in the rate of growth of GDP as well.

Argentina and Chile had replaced practically all nondurable consumer goods and their inputs before the period under consideration, and their small domestic markets have made the expansion of industries producing other intermediate products, capital goods, and durable consumer goods both difficult and costly. These countries have built up an industrial structure which entails the use of small-scale and often outdated production methods, inadequate specialization, and the manufacturing of products of low quality.[6] Discrimination against agriculture, associated with the high protection of manufacturing activities, has further hindered their economic growth and helps to explain why they have experienced the lowest growth rates among the nine countries studied.

Brazil, too, had completed the first stage of import substitution prior to the period under consideration. Its large domestic market, however, provided possibilities for the continued expansion of manufacturing during the fifties, mostly in intermediate products, capital goods, and durable consumer goods. But, as the possibilities for import substitution have been increasingly exhausted, industrial expansion has slowed down in this country also.

Pakistan had practically no industry prior to independence and it was able to achieve rapid rates of economic growth by substituting domestic production for the imports of nondurable consumer goods and their inputs. Subsequently, the adoption of the Export

6 For a detailed discussion, see Bela Balassa, 'Growth Strategies in Semi-Industrial Countries,' *op. cit.*, pp. 45-6.

TABLE 2

ECONOMIC GROWTH IN SELECTED DEVELOPING COUNTRIES

	Argentina	Brazil	Chile	Mexico	Korea	Malaya	Pakistan	Philippines	Taiwan
Average annual rate of growth of value added									
Agriculture									
1950-60	2.3	4.7	1.2	5.4	2.3	3.2	1.4	5.1	3.9
1960-69	2.0	4.2	2.5	4.0	4.6	3.9	3.7	4.6	5.0
1950-69	2.1	4.5	1.8	4.5	3.6	3.6	2.5	4.9	4.5
Manufacturing									
1950-60	4.7	8.8	3.3	8.0	13.6	5.1	7.8	10.2	10.1
1960-69	4.6	5.9	5.9	2.0	16.0	11.7	8.6	4.5	16.1
1950-69	4.6	7.5	4.5	8.4	15.0	8.0	8.2	7.8	13.5
GDP									
1950-60	3.4	5.8	3.7	5.8	5.0	4.1	2.5	6.8	6.9
1960-69	3.4	4.3	4.5	7.1	9.2	5.7	5.6	5.1	9.9
1950-69	3.4	5.1	4.0	6.4	7.4	4.8	4.0	6.1	8.6

TABLE 2 (Contd.)

	Argentina	Brazil	Chile	Mexico	Korea	Malaya	Pakistan	Philippines	Taiwan
Per capita GDP									
1950-60	1.4	2.8	1.2	2.8	3.0	1.1	0.4	3.5	3.1
1960-69	1.8	1.3	2.3	3.6	6.4	2.5	2.9	1.6	6.6
1950-69	1.6	2.1	1.7	3.2	4.9	1.7	1.6	2.7	5.1
Population									
1950-60	2.0	3.0	2.3	2.9	2.0	2.9	2.1	3.2	3.6
1960-69	1.5	3.0	2.2	3.4	2.6	3.1	2.6	3.4	3.0
1950-69	1.8	3.0	2.2	3.1	2.3	3.0	2.3	3.3	3.3

Note: For Taiwan and Korea the base year is 1953 instead of 1950. For Brazil and Malaya, the terminal year is 1968, for the Philippines, 1967.

Source: National and international statistics.

Bonus scheme has contributed to its relatively rapid industrial expansion. Continuing discrimination against agriculture has however adversely affected the growth of the Pakistani economy. If national income is measured at world market prices rather than at the domestic prices distorted by protection, increases in per capita terms appear to have been small.[7]

IV

The experience of the countries under consideration suggests the conclusion that while the protection of the manufacturing sector may permit rapid growth at an early stage of import substitution, it will eventually have adverse consequences for economic growth. Discrimination among industries does not permit specialization according to comparative advantage; the high protection of domestic industry induces the establishment of high-cost import-substituting activities; and the bias against exports retards the development of manufactured exports. Finally, in the absence of foreign competition, there will be little incentive for technical progress in small protected domestic markets.

The increasing difficulties experienced by countries at higher stages of import substitution have recently led some governments to reconsider their economic policies. In Argentina, the extent of discrimination against primary production and exports has been reduced and the protection of manufacturing industries has been moderated through a simultaneous devaluation and a lowering of tariffs. Manufactured goods also receive export subsidies in Argentina and such subsidies have assumed an important role in Brazil. Furthermore, in Chile, an effort has been made to lessen the degree of over-valuation of the currency while subsidies have been used to promote the exports of manufactured goods.

Efforts made to reform the structure of protection, however, have gone only part of the way and further progress is made difficult by resistance on the part of vested interests. Businessmen are opposed to changes in the status quo which ensures comfortable profits, and they demand continuing protection from foreign competition, whether this comes from the industrial countries or from developing nations as in the case of LAFTA. Additional problems

7 For such an adjustment, see Bela Balassa, *The Structure of Protection in Developing Countries*, Ch. 2.

are that transition to a more open economy would entail dislocation in particular industries and regions.

It appears, then, that once an industrial structure geared to import substitution has been established, change becomes increasingly difficult. This observation points to the need for making appropriate policy choices at the time when a country embarks on an industrialization program. In the following, guidelines will be suggested for trade policies by developing countries.[8] Apart from their application to countries at an early stage of industrialization, the guidelines can provide a basis for improvements in the policies of countries presently engaged in import substitution.

V

International trade theory tells us that small countries which do not affect the prices of their exports and imports will maximize welfare by specializing in accordance with price relations on the world market. Developing countries can generally take their import prices as given and they will not affect the prices of most of their manufactured exports either. This will not be the case, however, for traditional primary exports whenever increases in the country's exports lead to a fall in prices. For these exports, then, the relevant decision rule will involve equating marginal costs to marginal revenue from exports rather than to price. This can be accomplished by converting foreign exchange earnings from such exports at a less favorable exchange rate or—what amounts to the same—imposing an export tax on them. Export tax rates on individual commodities should be set by allowing for the elasticity of world demand, the country's share in world exports, and the possible reactions on the part of foreign competitors.[9]

The application of these measures would take account of market limitations for traditional primary exports, without unduly dis-

8 In formulating the guidelines, the author has drawn on the results of the studies referred to above, his experience in advising developing countries on trade policies, and the pertinent economic literature. Limitations of space have not permitted, however, the detailed consideration of particular issues.

9 An extreme case is that of coffee where producing countries would be advised to set the export tax (differential exchange rate) at a level calculated to ensure that domestic supply be equal to quota allocations under the International Coffee Agreement. In this way, profits due to the price-raising effects of quotas in international markets accrue to the government and, rather than providing incentives to surplus production, the proceeds of an export tax can be transferred to other activities where higher returns are obtained.

couraging their production as has often been the case in the past. A further question is whether manufacturing industries should be favored over nontraditional primary production, and if so, to what extent and by the use of what measures. In this connection, note should first be taken of arguments for infant industry protection, designed to compensate for assumed differences between social and private profitability. On the firm level, such differences may arise if the lack of credit facilities, the overestimation of risks, or simply the desire to exclude the possibility of bankruptcy provide disincentives for investment, although eventual cost reductions through the learning process or through increases in the scale of operations would make the investment socially desirable. Other instances are when some of the benefits of the pioneering firm's activities are enjoyed by others who utilize the know-how generated by the firm or hire away skilled labor and technicians it has trained.

It has often been said that infant industry arguments justify using production subsidies rather than tariffs since the latter limit the size of the domestic market by raising the price of the commodity in question. But while tariffs contribute to government revenue, subsidies represent a claim on this revenue. Budgetary reasons, then, may explain why developing countries use tariffs in preference to production subsidies. In fact, tariffs often account for a large part of government revenue in these countries, and their replacement by other forms of taxation may encounter practical difficulties.

The arguments for subsidies in preference to tariffs gain in force in cases when a particular distortion or cost disability needs to be corrected. This will be so if the cost of industrial labor to manufacturing enterprises exceeds its social cost in the form of the output foregone in primary activities from which labor is drawn. In some overpopulated countries, such a situation may exist on family-type farms where the contribution of the marginal worker is said to be less than his consumption. There is further the possibility that unemployment will persist at the existing wage rate which cannot be reduced lest it decline below a socially acceptable minimum. Mining industries, for example, utilize relatively little labor and countries relying on mineral exports may not be able to fully employ their labor force without providing special incentives for labor use.

In the cases described, the appropriate measure would be subsidizing the use of labor rather than imposing tariffs. Tariffs encourage the use of labor as well as capital in protected industries and they favor using labor in such industries in preference to other sectors of the national economy. Moreover, tariffs may provide incentives for the development of industries that would not be profitable under free trade even if wages were nil. In such instances, there is a trade-off between employment and growth since resources are channelled into industries with relatively high costs. Some of these industries may also have limited possibilities for improving productivity as is said to be the situation in the Indian cottage industry that receives considerable inducements. Finally, while employment-creating measures tend to improve the distribution of income, they may adversely affect savings and hence the prospects for future growth. The choice between employment and growth, then, becomes a choice between present and future employment.

Subsidizing labor use may take the form of taxing output and rebating the tax on the basis of the number of employees. This method would encourage the expansion of labor-intensive industries which use a developing country's abundant resource, labor, and would also provide incentives for employing labor-intensive production methods. However, there is no reason to restrict the application of this method to manufacturing industries, but it should be extended to all sectors other than family farming.

Particular cost disabilities, or handicaps of manufacturing industries owing to inadequate overhead facilities, can also best be corrected by specific action rather than by protection. But again, the provision of such facilities should not be restricted to manufacturing. Thus, roads and electricity are needed for agricultural activities, just as an increase in the educational level of the labor force would contribute to the development of industry as well as to the modernization of agriculture.

VI

The question remains whether, apart from temporary protection on infant industry grounds and the correction of particular cost disabilities, manufacturing should receive preferential treatment. In support of this proposition, it has been adduced that productivity tends to rise more rapidly in manufacturing than in primary production and that the expansion of manufacturing industries provides indirect benefits by inducing investments in other branches of industry and improving the quality of the labor force.

The first claim holds true if we compare manufacturing with agricultural activities that employ traditional techniques, although modern advances in agriculture offer possibilities for improvements in productivity. Furthermore, linkages among industries often favor the establishment of related branches of manufacturing, but one should not condone on this basis the establishment of inefficient industries which supply inputs to other industries at a high cost. There is finally some merit to the argument that manufacturing contributes to improvements in the quality of the labor force to a greater extent than does even modern agriculture.

From the point of view of long-term policy making, further consideration should be given to possible future changes in the supply and demand of primary products. In some developing countries either the supply of primary commodities or foreign demand for them would eventually prove to be a limiting factor for the country's economic growth. In such a situation, the preferential treatment of manufacturing industry, where supply and demand limitations are negligible, would be warranted not only vis-à-vis traditional primary commodities, but also in comparison to the primary sector as a whole.

These considerations indicate the difficulties encountered in appraising the claims made for the superiority of manufacturing over primary production. The difficulties are compounded if we attempt to quantify these alleged advantages. Nevertheless, one may argue that manufacturing offers *some* advantages over primary production in the form of labor training and in encouraging the expansion of related industry that do not enter into the profit calculations of the firm but benefit the national economy. Moreover, manufacturing will improve the growth potential of the economy whenever supply or demand limitations would eventually impinge on primary activities.

There is some presumption, then, in favor of promoting manufacturing industry in developing countries. The word 'promote' is used advisedly as it includes protection of production for domestic markets (import substitution) as well as assistance to firms exporting manufactured goods. Since, for reasons mentioned earlier, bias against manufactured exports entails an economic loss, equal incentives need to be provided to production for domestic and for foreign markets. This can be accomplished by granting a subsidy to the exports of manufactured goods at a rate equal to the tariff applied to the same commodity, or by using differential exchange rates for the manufacturing sector. Given the cost and uncertainties of entering foreign markets, it might even be desirable to provide additional incentives to exports of manufactured goods on a temporary basis.

Further questions are what are 'reasonable' rates of tariffs and export subsidies and whether all manufactured goods should receive equal treatment. Assuming that particular measures are used to correct special cost disabilities and that the employment objectives are served by a direct or indirect subsidy to the use of labor, as a first approximation one may suggest providing effective protection at equal rates to all manufacturing activities that have passed the infant industry stage.[10] In this way, one would apply the 'market principle' in the sense that firms will be established that are profitable under such conditions and existing firms would have to improve their operations, change their product composition or disappear altogether. At the same time, nonessential imports could be restricted by levying excise taxes that bear also on domestic production.

The choice of a 'reasonable' rate of tariffs and subsidies for mature industries in the developing countries will depend on the particular circumstances of the situation and on the range of other policy measures available to a particular country. It may be suggested, however, that since most developing countries have small domestic markets, they should aim at eventually reducing the net effective protection of manufacturing to levels observed in countries such as Denmark and Norway, i.e., to approximately 10 percent.

Exceptions to the proposed equality of effective rates may be made if there is evidence that profitability on the firm level greatly understates (or overstates) the contribution of a particular industry to the national economy. But such exceptions should apply to entire industries rather than to individual firms and only in cases that are well-documented so as to avoid a 'slippage' in protection. In other

10 In 'Decision Rules for Effective Protection in Developing Countries' (mimeo, November 1970), Trent Bertrand provides elegant proof of the proposition that maximizing welfare subject to the constraint that a certain amount of value added is geenrated in the manufacturing sector involves equalizing effective rates of protection within this sector. In a more general model, the desired amount of value added in the manufacturing sector and the rate of effective protection of this sector would be jointly determined.

words, the burden of proof should be on those who request favorable treatment.

Standard rates of protection should be applied also in the case of infant industries and one should avoid 'tailor-made' tariffs. While it is difficult to judge how much protection would be justified on infant industry ground, it does not appear likely that, exceptional cases aside, a rate of effective protection more than double that for mature industries would be warranted.[11] This additional protection of infant industries should be set on a declining scale so that its eventual disappearance provides incentives for improvements.

VII

The described scheme may be implemented by using a basic exchange rate for nontraditional primary products, export taxes on traditional primary exports, and a combination of tariffs and subsidies on manufactured goods. The same result could be achieved by applying differential exchange rates to the three groups of commodities, with further adjustments made for differences in the elasticity of demand among traditional primary exports. The choice between the two alternatives, or a combination thereof, would have to be made on the basis of considerations of political and administrative feasibility, with further account taken of the implications of the choice of exchange rates for invisibles and for capital movements.[12]

Compared to the policies of industrial protection followed by developing countries engaged in import substitution, the application of these guidelines would entail providing more favorable treatment to nontraditional primary commodities, reducing the protection of manufactured products, and equalizing the incentives for manufactured goods sold in domestic and in export markets. Also, as

11 According to an OECD study, economies of scale and external economies can hardly justify effective protection of infant industries exceeding 20 percent even if direct subsidies to labor use are not provided. This figure declines to 10 percent if labor use is subsidized. Cf. Ian Little, Tibor Scitovsky, and Maurice Scott, *Industry and Trade in Some Developing Countries*, London, Oxford University Press, pp. 158-59.

12 In some cases, however, neither of these alternatives might be feasible because of constraints in policy making. In Chile, for example, the government is said to have obligated itself not to levy special taxes on copper, the major export commodity. Accordingly, the basic exchange rate would have to be applied to copper while tariff-subsidy schemes would need to be used both for nontraditional primary products and for manufactured goods.

a general rule, equal incentives would be provided to all branches of manufacturing other than infant industries, and additional protection to infant industries on a temporary basis.

For countries that have already embarked on industrialization, behind high protective barriers, the application of the guidelines would entail a revamping of the structure of protection. Needless to say, this could not be undertaken instantaneously but would require a transitional period, the length of which would depend on the particular circumstances of the country in question. There would also be differences in the mode of application of these guidelines, again depending on political and institutional factors. Finally, the relative emphasis on direct measures and on the tariff-subsidy scheme may differ among countries at different levels of industrialization.

20

THE TWO GAP APPROACH TO AID AND DEVELOPMENT: COMMENT

Henry J. Bruton

THE CENTRAL IDEA of the 'gap analysis' of Hollis Chenery and his various collaborators is that development tends to create situations which, at various points in time, are characterized by a plentiful supply of all but one or a few of the factors 'required' for continued development.[1] For these few, a gap between the quantity supplied and that required slows growth or halts it completely. When growth is thus limited by a bottleneck, there is underutilization of other factors. Foreign aid can then serve as a means of breaking the bottleneck, thereby permitting fuller utilization of all resources and a continuation of development.

Chenery *et al.*, concentrate most of their attention on a saving-investment gap and an import-export gap. A target rate of growth is postulated and a capital-output ratio is accepted as a datum. Hence a specific saving rate is derived as necessary to achieve the targeted growth rate. Similarly, a fixed relationship between imports and growth of output is postulated from which one may derive the level and rate of growth of imports required. A saving gap appears when the domestic saving rate is below the level necessary to permit the investment required to achieve the target, while imports are adequate. Aid covers the saving gap, and permits the achievement of the target. A trade gap appears however if with adequate savings, the flow of imports is below the required level. Here aid breaks the import bottleneck and permits the target to be reached. In this latter case, the key assumption is that the country is unable to transform its potential savings into exports. Furthermore in a typical developing country, one expects a specific time sequence of the bottlenecks.

In the exchange between John Fei and Gustav Ranis [8] on the one hand and Chenery and Alan Strout [7] on the other, primary

1 The principal paper is [6], but there are a number of others equally useful. See especially [1], [5].

attention was given to the meaning and empirical validity of the parameter values necessary to produce the time sequence of gaps specified by Chenery. The present note seeks to pose a prior question, namely the significance of the parameter values necessary to produce a distinction between the gaps at all. Essentially the point here is that aid is gap producing, not gap covering, and that accepting it as the latter can in fact impede, rather than facilitate, development. To demonstrate this, two issues are considered: (1) the existence of two distinct gaps during a given short interval of time, and (2) the origins of the separate gaps. These issues will be taken up in turn.

I The Existence of Two Gaps

Chenery's major argument as to the existence of two gaps is familiar. Emphasis is given to a 'structural' argument, i.e., in any given time period a developing economy can neither increase its exports nor decrease its imports without imposing underutilization on the economy. Export earnings for the bulk of products are largely determined by foreign demand conditions, and 'a rapid increase in exports typically requires the development of new export products which is limited by productive capacity as well as organizational and institutional factors' [6, pp. 689-90]. Imports are required by the nature and limited flexibility of the productive system and of the composition of consumer demand. With such rigidity assumed, if the trade gap is larger than the saving gap, saving potential is 'wasted' as resources released from consumer goods production can be used neither to produce capital goods nor exports. To change this structure requires extra resources (aid) and time.

1. The simplest assumption is that all (and only) capital goods are imported, that all exports are consumer goods, and that there are no changes in inventories of consumer goods or foreign exchange reserves. With this assumption, to try to save is to reduce consumption and actually to save is to do that and to export. Consider Figure 1. Let *dd* be the domestic demand curve for a typical export (consumer good) and *Cf* the foreign demand curve, i.e., foreign demand is perfectly elastic. The total demand curve (the curve relevant to the producers) is *daf*. The supply curve is *ss* and the quantity supplied at equilibrium price *OC* is *Cb* of which *Ca* is

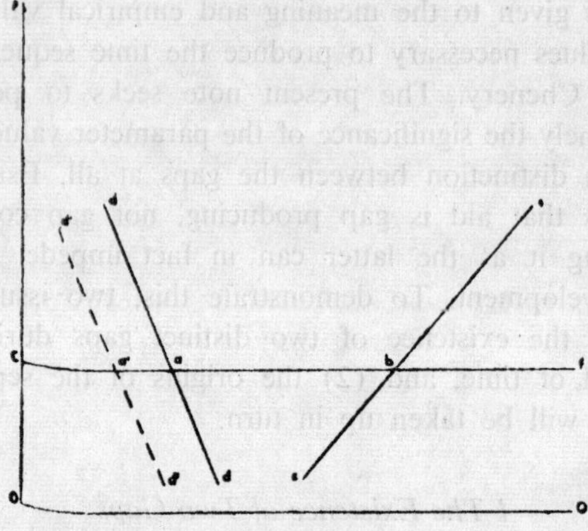

Figure 1

consumed domestically and *ab* is exported. The export of *ab* represents saving, the corresponding imports are capital, and the limitation on the rate of capital accumulation (and hence on growth in the Chenery model) is the saving rate. If the saving rate is increased, the domestic demand curve shifts leftward to $d'd'$, domestic consumption is reduced and exports and capital formation are increased by the same amount. Evidently there can be no trade gap distinct from the saving gap with these assumptions.

Suppose, however, that the foreign demand curve were vertical, as in Figure 2. The curve *tt* is obtained by summing horizontally *dd* and *ff*. In this event an increase in the saving rate, shown by the shift of *dd* to $d'd'$, has no effect on exports. The product price may tend to fall from OP_1, but this cannot help because the foreign demand curve is completely inelastic, and indeed the fall in price must induce an increase in the quantity demanded domestically until the new equilibrium is reached at price P_2, or unemployment will result. Evidently a similar result follows if *ff* has an elasticity greater than zero but less than unity over the relevant range. If the elasticity of *ff* exceeds unity and is less than infinite, and prices fall as domestic demand falls, the rate of capital formation will rise with an increase in the saving rate, but become increasingly expensive, i.e., a given increase in the rate of capital formation requires more saving (more resources devoted to export production) than at price P_1. At some point the curve will become inelastic and the rate of capital formation will have reached its maximum. If the target rate of growth requires a higher growth rate of capital than this maximum, then a trade gap emerges which cannot be closed by increasing the saving rate.

This explanation of a two gap situation depends on assumptions about the elasticity of the foreign demand curve. There may be

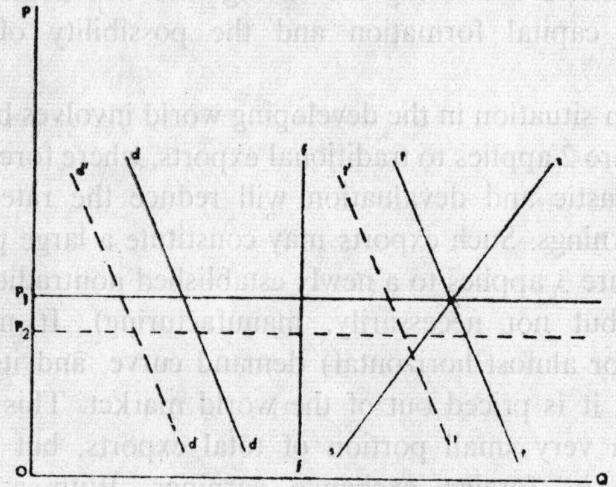

Figure 2

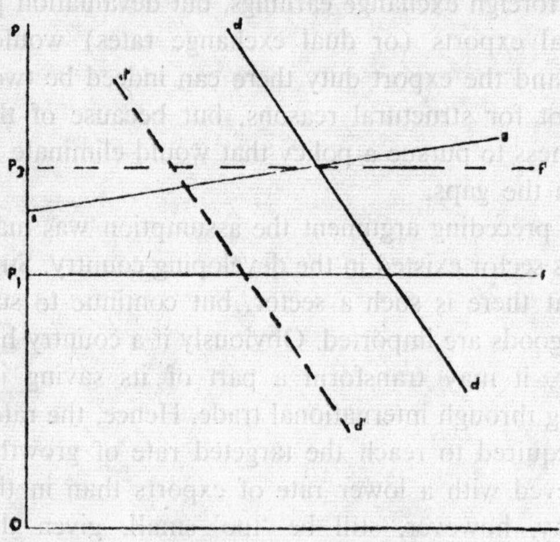

Figure 3

a problem on the supply side in a heavily protected domestic market. In Figure 3 the foreign demand curve is again horizontal at price OP_1. At this price, however, domestic suppliers are unwilling to export at all and survive only because they are protected from foreign competition. An increase in the saving rate will move the domestic demand curve to $d'd'$, but no increase in exports will be forthcoming. Devaluation will help in this case. In terms of the domestic currency, devaluation will result in the foreign demand curve rising, and a sufficient devaluation would then push P_1f to (say) P_2f', where increasing the saving rate will necessarily raise the rate of capital formation and the possibility of two gaps disappears.

A common situation in the developing world involves both Figures 2 and 3. Figure 2 applies to traditional exports, where foreign demand is quite inelastic and devaluation will reduce the rate of foreign exchange earnings. Such exports may constitute a large part of total exports. Figure 3 applies to a newly established nontraditional sector (probably, but not necessarily, manufacturing). It may face a horizontal (or almost horizontal) demand curve, and its costs may be such that it is priced out of the world market. This sector now constitutes a very small portion of total exports, but devaluation would raise its foreign exchange earnings. With a very large traditional sector and a small new sector, simple devaluation may not increase foreign exchange earnings, but devaluation plus a duty on traditional exports (or dual exchange rates) would. Without devaluation and the export duty there can indeed be two gaps, but they exist not for structural reasons, but because of the inability or unwillingness to pursue a policy that would eliminate the distinction between the gaps.

2. In the preceding argument the assumption was made that no capital goods sector existed in the developing country. Suppose now, however, that there is such a sector, but continue to suppose that only capital goods are imported. Obviously if a country has a capital goods sector, it may transform a part of its saving into capital without going through international trade. Hence, the rate of capital formation required to reach the targeted rate of growth of output can be achieved with a lower rate of exports than in the previous case. It may, however, still be 'too' small, given the level of exports, and the foreign exchange bottleneck appears as a consequence of the demand situation described above.

Consider now a more subtle point. A capital goods sector is one in which machines, equipment, plant, and other forms of physical capital are produced, and as such it is reasonably well defined. So defined, its capacity to produce can clearly be quite small. Recent literature, however, has emphasized the importance to development of education, technical research, health, and a variety of factors other than physical capital. These sources of growth are not free, but use up investible resources, i.e., the use of resources to improve education, health, etc. is a form of capital formation. The 'capital goods sector' must then include all activities which have the effect of increasing the productive capacity of the economy. With this broad definition of 'capital goods sector,' the notion of the fixity of size of the sector becomes virtually untenable. For one would then have to say that there is no use of investible resources that will raise the productive capacity of the economy.

Suppose foreign demand were such that there really was no way to increase foreign exchange earnings. Investible resources used to increase the capacity of the export sector will, in this case, have a social marginal product (*SMP*) of zero (or a capital-output ratio infinitely high). Resources used in other—domestic—capacity-increasing activities (improving or extending education, technical research, economic policy research) will have (in virtually all cases) a positive *SMP* (or a finite capital-output ratio). Evidently, then, investible resources should be applied to these latter activities. If when available investible resources are applied in this way, the target rate of growth of *GNP* is not reached, the problem is that the saving rate is too low. i.e., there is again not two gaps, only one.

3. The assumption was made in both 1 and 2 that only capital goods were imported. Consider now the consequence of a given structure of production that requires imports of raw materials and spare parts to keep the existing capacity fully utilized.[2] For example, automobile assembly plants may exist with no domestic source of steel, and to operate the assembly plants at any given level of capacity requires imports of steel at some specific rate. If steel imports are not available at this rate, the level of utilization of automobile assembly capacity must fall. To curtail imports for this purpose (maintenance imports) in order to step up capital goods imports means that the economy is penalized in the form of under-utilization of existing plant and equipment. This situation then imposes a lower limit below which maintenance imports cannot be reduced without sacrificing the level of output as well as the rate of growth of output.

Even here, however, with a given structure of production, to

2 One may also introduce consumer good imports but the consequence of reduced imports of these products on the argument is self-evident.

assume that import requirements are independent of available policy measures is to give in much too easily. It is easy to find examples where domestic policies are such that a high rate of consumption of import intensive services occurs. This applies especially to the pricing of many public services, e.g., passenger transportation and electric power. The pricing of these (import intensive) services is such that their consumption is encouraged, where with more realistic pricing either greater savings or a shift in consumption would occur, either of which would contribute to resolving the trade gap. A less obvious point may be of greater relevance. If domestic demand for consumer products falls as policies to increase the saving rate are implemented, the appearance of excess capacity (at going prices) may, as noted, bring about reduced prices which might help a bit. The possibility that declines in domestic demand will lead entrepreneurs to make a greater effort to export is important in the present context. This greater effort takes the form of more intensive market efforts, attempts to maintain announced schedules, possibly financing arrangements, and the like. If domestic demand is strong, then producers have less incentive to search out export markets.[3]

II The Origins of the Two Gaps

Although it is possible to devise a set of circumstances where saving cannot be transformed into capacity-creating activities, the possibilities are neither numerous nor empirically convincing. Indeed the arguments surely suggest quite strongly that, although the cost of growth may rise, the distinction between the two gaps as an empirical phenomenon is a rarity, and its explanation, where it does exist, as a structural phenomenon, i.e., a phenomenon not lending itself to short-term policy measures, is most unlikely. Emphasis may be placed on the fact that this conclusion does *not* depend on assumptions as to the empirical magnitudes of the several relevant elasticities. Neither does it depend on neoclassical assumptions as to flexibility and adaptability of all inputs. Such assumptions would of course eliminate the problem completely.

3 Evidence on this point is, of course, not beyond question. Perhaps the most useful has to do with evidence that in periods of downturns or recessions, in some of the developing countries exports rise even though export prices do not fall or fall only moderately. This seems especially true for some of the Latin American countries. See [11] *passim*.

Suppose, however, that a structure does exist where it is meaningful to speak of two gaps; there is still a prior question: namely, where did this structure come from? If it emerged as a necessary and endemic consequence of the nature of the development process, that is one thing. If it emerged as a consequence of specific policy measures, that is, of course, another matter. Consider now the origins of a two gap situation.

Professor Chenery explains the origin of a two gap economy in terms of the effect of aid—supported exchange rates on investment allocation relative to that allocation called for after aid has been reduced or discontinued entirely. Chenery writes [6, p.726].

> 'If investment and other allocation decisions are based on the exchange rate that is appropriate for a substantial flow of aid, they are not likely to induce sufficient import substitution or increased exports to make possible a future reduction in the capital flow. Planning should be based on the higher equilibrium exchange rate that would be appropriate to a declining flow of aid in order for the necessary changes in the productive structure to be brought about in time.'

After aid is reduced, the inflexibility and unadaptability of the system prohibits adjustments that would have to be made if the two gaps were not to appear. There are several reasons why this argument may be questioned.

The first point is purely empirical. Chenery cites Greece, Israel, Taiwan, and the Philippines as instances of successful uses of aid. There is no evidence, however, that in these countries investment allocation was based on the higher equilibrium exchange rate that is presumed to be appropriate after aid is reduced. In the absence of such evidence one may think that the success of these countries is due to factors other than the one isolated by Chenery.

More important than the empirical evidence, however, is the argument that the same exchange rate can be appropriate for a situation where aid is flowing in and for the situation after aid has been reduced. The central point seems *not* to be the exchange rate, but rather the composition of investment, especially the division between the consumer goods sector and the capital goods sector, and the rate of growth of productivity.

In the first part of this paper it was shown that, with a very narrow interpretation of capital and defining physical capital as the chief or sole source of growth, the size of the capital goods sector was strategic in the existence of a two gap situation. If the domestic capital goods sector were large enough, then the required savings could be, by definition, transformed into the physical capital necessary to produce to targeted rate of growth of output. Thus if the capital goods sector expands enough during the aid-receiving period, then in subsequent periods the two gap problem will not emerge.

Why doesn't the capital goods sector expand in the 'balanced' way necessary to keep the foreign exchange gap from appearing? There are many possible reasons, but one is surely dominant and leads to a widely applicable conclusion. A developing country, seeking to industrialize, almost always proceeds by way of curtailing imports. In choosing the manufacturing sectors to protect, it is understandable that policymakers select sectors which are least disadvantaged in terms of costs or are least 'essential' in some sense.[4] In a great variety of countries consumer durables fall in these categories and have become the major types of activities to replace imports. Rarely can one find a case where capital goods fall in the protected categories, as the difference between imported price and domestic costs is usually much larger than it is for consumer goods and of course no one classifies capital goods as luxuries. So the economy has new consumer goods industries. It has used aid to import capital to build industries and possibly to import raw materials and spare parts to support them. The country has new activities the products of which it cannot export and which cannot be used to produce capital goods. As this process continues, the country acquires more activities of this sort. As the amount of investment rises, more imports of capital goods and more maintenance imports are demanded, and the kind of situation shown in Figures 2 and 3 emerges.

Suppose aid were maintained in sufficient quantities to support the investment for a number of years, and then reduced. Evidently, the investment rate would have to fall. Now does the gap problem emerge because of the exchange rate question referred to by Chenery? It is difficult to believe so. There is indeed a signal problem, but it is not a question of the exchange rate signal. It is rather the absence of a signal. Investing in the least disadvantaged sector creates activities whose relevance for a general equilibrium solution

4 For a very lucid, thoroughly documented discussion of this point as it applies to Latin America, see Santiago Macario [9].

is purely coincidental and one must fall back on a projection of the 'structure' of the economy to ascertain the correct allocation of investment, i.e., the allocation that will prevent the growth process from grinding to a halt when aid is tapered off.

Suppose the activities which are initially least disadvantaged are all consumer goods industries. Then as aid falls and the bottleneck previously described emerges, this is a signal that investment should have occurred in the capital goods sector in order for the growth to continue. To produce capital goods domestically is by assumption, and in fact, more costly than producing consumer goods. If this were not the case, capital goods would have been produced initially domestically rather than consumer goods. As the country reaches the point where additional substitution of domestic production for imported consumer goods is not possible, it must begin to build capital goods. Then the cost of growth begins to rise. In this event, one would be saying not that the country had hit a foreign exchange barrier, but rather that the country was too poor to support its own development. This, however, is precisely the saving problem.[5] The only difference between this stage and the previous one is the size of the development bill, and the notion that the developing country can pay the lower price, but not the higher one. Obviously, this is a saving problem, not a trade gap problem.

If one argued that the country could not build capital goods because it did not have the labor skills, organization skills, and technical knowledge to do the job, this fact (assuming it to be a fact) is itself evidence of the wrong allocation of investment at some point in the past. Thus when Chenery writes that the 'existing economic structure at any moment of time also limits the feasible growth of export earnings' [6, p. 689] and that 'a rapid increase in exports typically requires the development of new export products, which is limited by productive capacity as well as organizational and institutional factors' [6, pp. 689-90] and that these difficulties can be removed only over time, he is saying that investment allocation in the past has now proved to be wrong. It was wrong in the sense that it produced a 'structure' that cannot now be fully exploited.

5 The usual view of the development process in the USSR illustrates this point. The Soviet Union depended little, if at all, on imports, and did not hit a trade barrier. In the simplest terms, the explanation is that the Soviet leaders were willing and able to force a level of saving on the economy that did permit the construction of a large and costly capital goods sector. More directly, the great capacity of the Soviet government to force saving solved the trade gap problem. On the general argument see Winston [10].

Where the difficulties are now skills and technology, the conclusion is that earlier investments should have been in activities that developed these aspects of the economy.

What emerges from these arguments is quite orthodox, and very much in line with what Chenery has taught us in his several papers on investment allocation criteria [3] [4]. The point here is to emphasize that the special difficulties attributed by Chenery to exchange rates with aid and after the end of aid are not really the heart of the issue. The problem is simply the old one of achieving the optimal saving rate and an investment composition that follows the social marginal productivity criterion. This criterion, broadly defined,[6] is of course difficult to apply in any circumstance, but that is not the point. In this case one must project the structure and allocate the investment to seek to prevent gaps in this structure from emerging. The allocation criterion must be gap prevention rather than least disadvantaged or some other cost based argument.

There is a final point of great relevance. Suppose a trade gap appears due either to distortions emphasized here or to Chenery's structural arguments. Aid can then provide the resources to correct or change this set of circumstances. Aid can also do something else. It can provide the resources with which an economy can continue to function acceptably *without* bringing about the elimination of the distortions or changing the structure. By relieving the pressure on the system, aid may also reduce not only the incentive to make painful changes, it may hide the location of the right allocations. The point here is, not that international aid should be reduced, but rather that its effective use places great demands on the policy-makers as to the understanding of the development process. Policies built around the assumption that a trade gap is a necessary condition of development may impede that understanding.

III Conclusion

This paper has argued three things: (1) the distinction between the two gaps is due to particular policies that themselves are growth impeding, and not to some inherent characteristic of the develop-

6 'Broadly defined' means inclusive of the 'side' or 'indirect' effects, e.g., effect on saving rates, on labor training, population growth, now commonly included in allocation analysis. See [2, Chapter 15].

ment process; (2) that foreign aid based on the assumption that there are two gaps may tend to perpetuate these growth impeding policies; and (3) that the traditional investment allocation issues remain strategic in development policymaking.

REFERENCES

1 Adelman, I. and Chenery, H. 'Foreign Aid and Economic Development: The Case of Greece,' *Rev. Econ. Stat.*, Feb. 1966, **48**, pp. 1-19.

2 Bruton, H. *Principles of Development Economics*, Englewood Cliffs. 1965.

3 Chenery, H. 'The Application of Investment Criteria,' *Quart. Jour. Econ.*, Feb. 1953, **67**, pp. 76-96.

4 ———, 'Comparative Advantage and Development Policy,' *Am. Econ. Rev.*, Mar. 1961. **51**, pp. 18-51.

5 ———, and M. Bruno, 'Development Alternatives in an Open Economy: The Case of Israel,' *Econ. Jour.*, Mar. 1962, **72**, pp. 79-103.

6 ———, and A. Strout, 'Foreign Assistance and Economic Development,' *Amer. Econ. Rev.*, Sept. 1966, **56**, pp. 679-732.

7 ———, 'Reply,' *Amer. Econ. Rev.*, Sept. 1968, **58**.

8 Fei, J. C. H. and Ranis, G. 'Foreign Assistance and Economic Development Revisited,' *Am. Econ. Rev.*, Sept. 1968, **58**.

9 Macario, S. 'Protectionism and Industrialization in Latin America,' *Econ. Bull. for Latin America*, Mar. 1964, **9**, pp. 61-102.

10 Winston, G. C. 'Consumer Goods or Capital Goods—Supply Consistency in Development Planning,' *Pakistan Develop. Rev.*, Autumn 1967, **7**, pp. 348-378.

11 Economic Commission for Latin America, *The Process of Industrial Development in Latin America* (Mimeo), Santiago, 1965.

21

THE EFFECTIVE EXCHANGE RATE EMPLOYMENT AND GROWTH IN A FOREIGN EXCHANGE-CONSTRAINED ECONOMY*

Richard R. Nelson

I Introduction

THE 'DECADE OF DEVELOPMENT' bodes turning into a decade of despair. In place of the optimism regarding the prospects of the less developed countries that marked the speeches of the early 1960s, a sense of helplessness is evolving on the part of economists and policy makers concerned with development. The despair is rooted, first, in growing awareness that forecasts and promises of large flows of assistance from the rich to the poor countries will not be fulfilled, and, second, in a developing belief that without massive assistance the less developed countries can do little on their own about lagging growth and rising unemployment.

Colombia's present economic problems or, more saliently, the way these problems and possible remedies are perceived, reveal the syndrome.[1] Growth rates have lagged behind plans. A major urban unemployment problem is developing. Yet Vanek and others have argued that higher investment required for faster growth is blocked by the balance-of-payments constraint (Vanek 1967). Similarly, attempts to increase employment through such measures as public works are seen to be impossible because of foreign exchange shortage (Currie 1967). The same syndrome of problems and pessimistic analysis exists in Brazil, India, and many others countries. To lend concreteness to the discussion, in the following analysis I occasionally shall refer to Colombia; however, the problem and the analysis are quite general.

While it is true that countries like Colombia will have much

*The study from which this paper evolved was financed partly through a contract with the Agency for International Development and partly by the RAND Corporation. The author is indebted to Robert Aliber, Paul Johnson, John Koehler, Donald Keesing, Stephen Resnick, Paul Schultz, Robert Slighton and the referee for useful comments and suggestions.

1 For a detailed discussion and analysis, see Nelson (1967) and Slighton (1968).

greater difficulty coping with their problems when foreign assistance is scarce than when it is plentiful, it is the contention of this paper that at least part of the felt futility resides in the persistence in looking at the constraints and policy options in terms of a model better suited to reveal the payoffs from more assistance, than to explore what can be done without more assistance. The blinders of the 'two-gap' model draw attention away from the central question of how an economy can learn to cope with an environment where imports must be financed largely through exports. In particular, it represses a powerful instrument of policy—the effective exchange rate.

Section II will examine the basic factors and assumptions behind the impotency of domestic policy alone to increase employment and investment implied by the two-gap model. Section III will present a model incorporating factor-substitution possibilities and factor prices. Section IV reconsiders the policy options and in particular considers the effective exchange rate as an instrument of policy.

II The Basic Two-Gap Model and the Implied Policy Dilemma

Considering fine structure as well as basics, the variety of 'gap' models is great and growing.[2] But underneath the apparent diversity, all the gap models have a roughly equivalent two-gap core, which can be developed in the following indirect but illuminating way.

Assume that an economy has available to it four basic activities: domestic production of investment goods, imports of investment goods, domestic production of consumer goods, and imports of consumer goods. A unit level of an activity can be chosen as 'a dollar's worth'. All activities require imports. The two production activities also require domestic inputs. The activity matrix is below.

		I_P	I_M	C_P	C_M
Output	I	1	1	0	0
	C	0	0	1	1
Input	M	a_1	1	a_c	1
	V	b_1	0	b_c	0

2 Among the most important articles are Chenery and Bruno (1962), Chenery and Strout (1966), McKinnon (1964), and Vanek (1967).

The column headings are the four activities; the subscripts P and M stand for production and imports, respectively. The first two rows are output of investment goods and consumer goods, I and C. The last two rows are use of imports M and domestic capacity V (for value added). It is assumed, and this is important, that production of investment goods is more important and less domestic input-intensive than production of consumer goods.[3]

Assume a given capacity. The constraints on the activities then are:

$$M^* \geq a_I I_P + a_C C_P + I_M + C_M$$

$$V^* \geq b_I I_P + b_C C_P$$

For our purposes we thus are ignoring any specialization of domestic production capacity between investment and consumer goods.

These constraints limit the choice set for consumption and investment available to the economy to the frontier *abd* in figure 1.

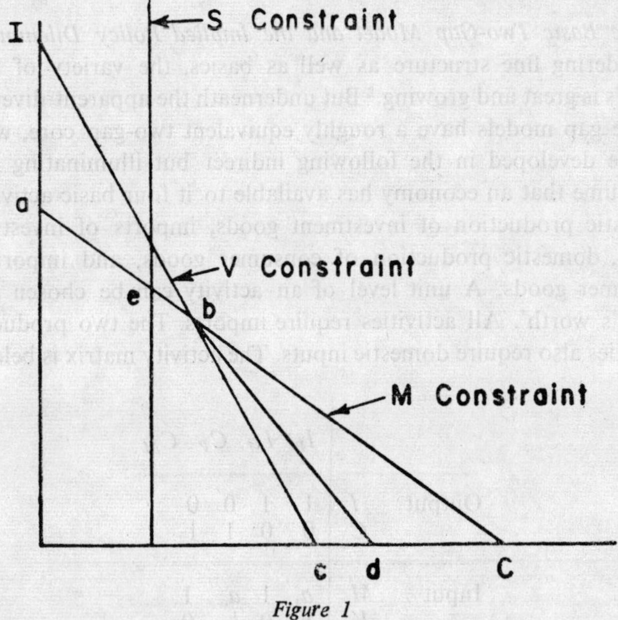

Figure 1

3 That is, $a_I > a_C$ and $b_C > b_I$. This certainly is so for Colombia and appears to be so for other less developed countries. For a discussion of some possible reasons, see Nelson (1967). It probably is not so for more developed countries. See Cooper (1968).

If we ignored the two direct import activities, the frontier would be *abc*. But because import capacity not used up for intermediate goods can be directly converted, one to one, for consumer and capital goods, to the right of *b* the frontier is *bd* , not *bc*.

If the economy is operating in the *bd* range, both domestic capacity and import capacity will be fully employed, imports will be employed in production of consumer goods and investment goods, and, in addition, some consumer and investment goods will be directly imported.[4] Along *ab*, import capacity will be fully utilized, but there will be unutilized domestic capacity. The asymmetry between imports and domestic production capacity is fundamental to the two-gap model. Domestic inputs must be complemented by imports to produce final product. In contrast, imports can provide final product directly (as well as complement domestic inputs).

To approach the two-gap formulation, we must introduce another constraint—a savings or minimal consumption constraint. With this constraint incorporated, the economy is limited to areas to the right of the savings constraint, as well as below the two input constraints—that is, to the frontier *ebd*. Next, it is necessary to transform the *IC* choice set into a growth-consumption choice set. In the standard two-gap model, it is implicitly assumed that capital is a binding constraint on domestic output. Then *I* can be associated with an increase in domestic capacity ΔV.[5]

Finally, it is necessary to transform the increment to capacity into a percentage rate of growth, and to eliminate the *V* constraint.[6] This we can do by having the horizontal axis refer to C/V and the vertical axis to the growth rate, $\Delta V/V$, which is proportional to $I/$V. This is done in figure 2. The former *V* constraint now becomes a constant in the problen and over time (so long as b_1 and b_2 do not change). The two constraints in figure 2 that can be manipulated are the 'savings' constraint and the foreign exchange constraint. We now have a 'canonical' two-gap formulation.

A central concern of the two-gap analysis is estimating the effects of shifting one or the other of these constraints. Regarding the savings constraint, notice that the effect on the growth rate of

4 If *V* is measured in dollars, then the slope of the *bd* facet can be shown to be -1. The slope of *ab* facet is $-a_C/a_I$.

5 Specifically $\Delta V = BI$. Obviously depreciation is being ignored.

6 By this I mean, of course, to eliminate it as a variable in the formulation of the problem. The domestic resource constraint on production always will exist (although it may not always be binding).

shifting the savings constraint to the left (reducing minimal C/V) is significantly greater when the savings constraint is to the right of *b* than when (as depicted above) it is to the left of *b*; Vanek's pessimistic conclusions regarding Colombia's ability to increase her own growth rate imply that the current position is to the left of *b*. And if this model does reflect reality, not only would it take a lot of reduced consumption to gain only a little added growth,

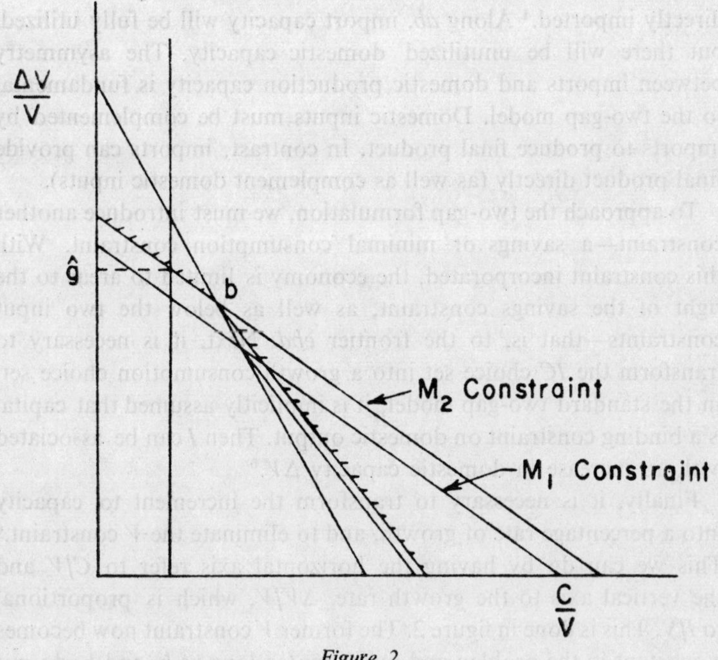

Figure 2

but there would also be rising unemployment. Although all of the imports released by cutting back consumption would be used for investment activity, the greater import intensity (lesser domestic input intensity) of investment means that the domestic resources so released would not be fully reemployed in investment. Thus employment and growth objectives are in conflict.

The relative returns to 'more foreign assistance' (holding consumption constant) also vary depending on whether the economy is operating to the left or right of *b*. In figure 2, notice how much more the frontier is shifted upward to the left, as compared with to the right of b, as a result of an increase in import capacity from M_1 to M_2.

In the model, as posed above, an increase in savings, like an increase in import capacity, will always permit an increase in the growth rate.[7] Thus it is misleading to say that one or the other of these constraints is *not* binding at any time. Nevertheless there clearly are sharp differences in the returns to more savings and returns to more imports, in terms of an enhanced growth rate, depending on whether the economy is to the left or right of b. In a loose sense, one can say that, to the right of b more savings are needed; to the left of b more import capacity is needed. This is the spirit of the two-gap distinction.

The foreign exchange gap, which Vanek (and others) attempt to estimate, can be defined as the increase in import capacity needed to achieve a given growth target, given the savings constraint. If, in figure 2, the growth target is $\hat{g}$, the foreign exchange gap is M_2-M_1, given the existing savings rate.[8] (As a bonus, the unemployment rate would be reduced as well). Of course the gap would be smaller if the savings constraint could be pushed to the left. But, given that the constraint already is to the left of b, it takes much increased savings to gain only a slight reduction in the gap.

The two-gap model, together with evidence (or assertions) that the economy is to the left of b, is ingeniously well designed to provide a case for more foreign aid. But it is diabolically well designed to engender a sense of helplessness in policy-makers regarding what they can do without additional aid. When more aid is not likely, it is imperative to develop another way of looking at the problem that illuminates additional options.

The two-gap model assumes fixed proportions. For consideration of short-run options this assumption probably is quite realistic, although overly strong even for the short run. When the focus is on the long run, the assumption of no substitution possibilities

7 In some of the earlier formulations, imports used in the production of consumer goods were ignored. Thus a_c was assumed to be zero—hence the curve of the import constraint to the left of b is flat. In this case, reduced consumption does not permit any increase in investment, once consumer goods imports have been eliminated (that is, to the left of b).

8 Specifically, the foreign exchange gap in dollars as a fraction of V is $(a_I/B)(G)$, where B is the value added to capital ratio, a_I is the import intensity of investment and G is the vertical distance between the M_2 and M_1 constraints. This can be shown as follows. The required increase in the growth rate, given the savings constraint, is G. This will require an increase in I of $(G/B)(V)$. The import requirements are $(a_I/B)(GV)$.

clearly is absurd. For at least the last twenty years, the basic thrust of Colombia's industrial development has been import substitution, and policy has deliberately and effectively stimulated this process. Several of the two-gap models do augment the basic core with a time tread in the coefficients.

Yet when focusing on the long run, and factor substitution is admitted—indeed is a major objective of policy—the question of incentives, costs, and factor prices, repressed in the conventional formulation, begs for attention. Colombia's problems are not new to her; Colombia has been suffering from a shortage of imports, and a growing unemployment problem since the coffee crisis of the mid-1950s, and with extreme severity for at least the last six years. In such a chronic situation the cost of imports relative to domestic factor prices ought to matter. Is it possible that Colombia has compounded her problems, and failed to consider an important path toward alleviating them, by having too low an effective exchange rate?

III A Neoclassical Input, Output, and Price Model

It seems apparent that any model designed to explore the possibility of substituting domestic inputs for imports (and for exploring the possibility of increasing import capacity through exports) must incorporate explicitly the following characteristics of the Colombian situation. Imports are largely intermediate goods in consumer- or producer-goods industries, and direct purchases of capital goods, mostly machinery. Thus, if one thinks of the economy as having two sectors—one producing consumer goods, the other concerned with building new plant and equipment—the key substitution possibilities are domestic resources, both capital and labor, for imports in both sectors, rather than further substitution of home-produced consumer goods for imported final-consumer goods. And the analysis of these substitution possibilities must recognize that one of the domestic inputs—capital—has an import content.[9]

In order to build in these characteristics explicitly, I have been forced to make a key simplifying assumption—full competitive equilibrium both in the short and long run. Elsewhere I have argued that this is a fundamental misspecification of the development process (Nelson 1968*b*). A second simplifying assumption is that the capital-labor ratio does not differ in consumption and invest-

9 For a more detailed discussion and documentation, see Nelson (1967).

ment.[10] With these assumptions a quite general model can be worked out. In another paper, I have developed the Cobb-Douglas special case which admits of numerical estimation (Nelson 1968*a*).

Under these assumptions, domestic input of capital and labor can be viewed as producing domestic value added as follows:

$$V = V(L, K). \tag{1}$$

Consumption and investment goods are produced from input of domestic value added and imports:

$$C = C(M_c, V_c), \tag{2}$$

$$I = I(M_I, V_I). \tag{3}$$

All production functions are assumed to be linear homogeneous, with positive marginal products which are always positive within the range of relevant factor ratio variations. This last is a serious restriction on the shape of the isoquants[11] or the variation in factor ratios to which the model applies. In addition it is assumed that, for any set of factor prices, the import-value added ratio for investment is greater than for consumption. This further constrains the shapes of the production functions.

Let w be the going money-wage rate, i the short- and long-run rate of return on capital (possibly influenceable by policy), P_I the price of investment goods, and $r = P_I i$ the 'rental' rate for a unit of capital.[12] Then, the capital-labor ratio (in both consumption and investment activities) will be positively related to the wage-capital rental ratio.

$$\frac{K}{L} = R\left(\frac{W}{r}\right) \qquad R' > 0. \tag{4}$$

For later convenience it is useful to note here that equation (4) implies

$$\frac{K}{V} = S\left(\frac{W}{r}\right) \qquad S' > 0. \tag{5}$$

Let E be the exchange rate and P the price of domestic value added (to be specified shortly). The import, domestic input ratio in

10 Examination of capital-labor ratios in producer and consumer goods industries suggests this is not an unreasonable first approximation.

11 Ruling out, for example, less than unitary elasticity of substitution if all factor ratios are admitted.

12 Assuming no depreciation.

both investment and consumption will be positively related to P/E with (as one of our key assumptions) $(M_I)/(V_I) > (M_C)(V_C)$. This implies

$$\frac{M_I}{I} = U_I\left(\frac{P}{E}\right) \qquad U_I' > 0, \tag{6}$$

$$\frac{M_C}{C} = U_c\left(\frac{P}{E}\right) \qquad U_c' > 0, \tag{7}$$

and also

$$\frac{V_I}{I} = Z_I\left(\frac{P}{E}\right) \qquad Z_I' < 0, \tag{8}$$

$$\frac{V_C}{C} = Z_c\left(\frac{P}{E}\right) \qquad Z_c' < 0, \tag{9}$$

Finally, we need some price equations:

$$P = P(w, r), \tag{10}$$

$$P_I = P_I(P, E), \tag{11}$$

$$P_c = P_c(P, E). \tag{12}$$

All partial derivatives are positive.

The prices in the equations above are hybrids. These equations obviously can be rewritten in terms of the 'primitive' prices—the rate of return in capital, the wage rate, and the exchange rate. We, however, need not do this explicitly. For our purposes, it is sufficient simply to note the following. First, all the product prices have to be homogeneous of degree one in w and E. The linear homogeneity of the production functions implies that equations (10)–(12) are homogeneous of degree one in the variables on the right-hand side. Consideration of equations (10) and (11) simultaneously, and recalling that $r = P_I\, i$, shows that both P_I and P must be homogeneous of degree one in w and E, given i; then P_c must be also. Another way to see this is to recognize that a doubling of w and E will require a doubling of all product prices (including P_I) in order to keep i (the rate of return on capital) constant.

This implies that all factor proportions and input coefficients are homogeneous of degree zero in w and E. In equations (4) and (5) a doubling of w and E (hence $r = P_I i$) will preserve the w/r ratio. In equations (6)–(9) a doubling of w and E (hence P) similarly will preserve the price ratios on the right-hand side.

It now is possible to reexamine the consumption-investment choice set within a model that admits input substitution. Recall the following specification of input coefficients in the production of investment and consumer goods in a fixed coefficient two-gap model:

$$\frac{M_c}{I} = a_I \qquad \frac{M_c}{C} = a_c \qquad \frac{V_I}{I} = b_I \qquad \frac{V_c}{C} = b_c.$$

Assuming the same capital-labor ratios in both consumer and producer goods production:

$$\frac{K}{V} = F_1 \qquad \frac{L}{V} = F_2.$$

Ignoring the direct import activities the constraints of the two-gap model can be rewritten:[13]

$$M^* \geq a_I I + a_c C$$
$$K^* \geq F_1 b_I I + F_1 b_c C,$$

where M^* and K^* refer to maximum availability. Assuming that the labor-availability constraint never becomes binding before the capital constraint, the model is completed by the equation:

$$L = \frac{F_2}{F_1} K.$$

In our formulation the constants are turned into variables. The capital-labor ratio F_1/F_2 is determined by equation (4) which, given our conclusion that input ratios and coefficients are homogeneous of degree zero in w and E, can be written:

$$\frac{K}{L} = \frac{F_1}{F_2}\left(\frac{w}{E}, i\right). \tag{13}$$

Recalling the assumptions about equation (4), the capital-labor ratio can be seen to be positively related to w/E, and negatively related to i. An increase in w (given E and i) will not leave r unchanged. However, given that $r = P_I i$ is homogeneous of degree one in w and E, the percentage change in r will be less than the

13 The analysis will be focused on the region to the right of b in fig. 2; hence, there will not be any direct imports.

percentage change in w.[14] Thus w/r must increase and K/L must rise. An increase in E will affect P_I in the same direction, hence will decrease w/r. An increase in i will also increase the rental rate on capital.

The import coefficients likewise are a function of w/E and i,

$$\frac{M_c}{I} = a_I\left(\frac{w}{E}, i\right) \tag{14}$$

$$\frac{M_c}{C} = a_c\left(\frac{w}{E}, i\right). \tag{15}$$

Consideration of equations (7) and (8) shows that import intensity varies positively with both w/E and i, since an increase in either w or i increases P, and hence P/E.

The capital input coefficients are more complicated.

$$\frac{K}{I} = F_1\left(\frac{w}{E}, i\right)b_I\left(\frac{w}{E}, i\right), \tag{16}$$

$$\frac{K}{C} = F_1\left(\frac{w}{E}, i\right)b_c\left(\frac{w}{E}, i\right). \tag{17}$$

The first term in both equations, K/V, can be seen, from equations (5), to be positively related to w/E and negatively related to i. An increase in w (while affecting the price of machinery) will increase w/r, through the argument presented earlier. An increase in E or i will increase r.

The second terms of the equations, V_I/I and V_c/C, also are negatively related to i (which affects the price of domestic inputs), so the total effect of a change in i upon capital intensity is unambiguous (as should be intuitively obvious). However, V_I/I and V_c/C are negatively related to w/E, for obvious reasons. Thus the effect of a rise in w/E will be to increase K/V, but to reduce V_I/I and V_c/C. What happens on net depends on various elasticities of substitution. It is shown, in another paper, that for a Cobb-Douglas specification, K_I/I is independent of w/E—the two effects just offset each other—and K_c/C increases with w/E—the increased K/V effect outweighs the reduced V_c/C effect (Nelson 1968*a*).

But, whatever the direction of response of capital intensity to w/E, it is clear that for any given w/E and i, there is a set of linear constraints on C and I, just as in Section II. We can define both

14 Assuming both capital and labor are employed in the production of investment goods.

consumption and investment units as one peso or dollar's worth at some set of basic input prices, just as in Section II. Then, if we assume that capital goods are more import-intensive and less domestic input-intensive than consumer goods, the *M* constraint, and the *K* and *L* constraints will have the relative slopes shown in figure 3. The special form of equations (1)–(3), which together with cost minimization imply the same capital-labor ratio in both consumer and capital goods production, means that the labor and capital constraints have the same slope. The *V* constraint of Section II can be interpreted as the more binding of the *K* and *L* constraints in figure 3.

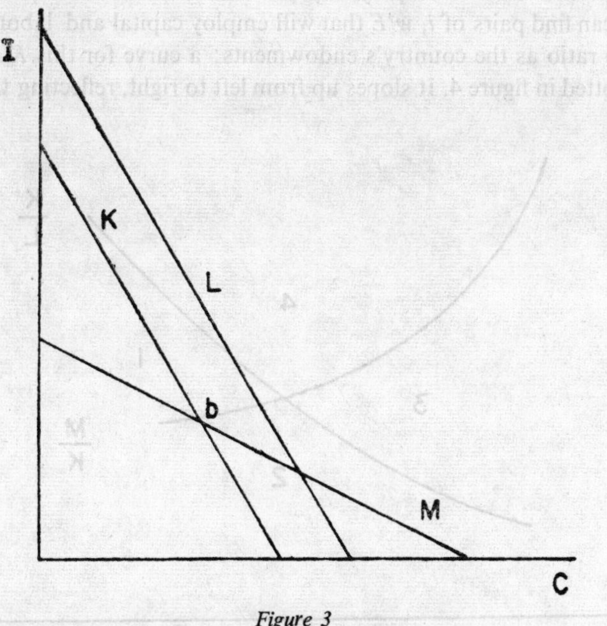

Figure 3

With two products, three inputs, and a given set of factor prices, in general, full employment of all inputs will be impossible. Thus in figure 3 there always will be unemployed labor.

But figure 3 assumes a given set of factor prices. We now are able to examine the effects of factor prices on the conclusions of the two-gap model. As factor prices change, the constraints will shift. As shown above, a decrease in W/E or i will reduce the imports utilized for a given output, and shift out the foreign exchange constraint.

Capital coefficients can be reduced and the constraint shifted out by an increase in *i*. (As we have seen, the effect of a change in w/E is ambiguous.) The labor constraint similarly can be shifted by a change in factor prices.

Under seemingly not unduly restrictive assumptions, there exists an *i*, W/E combination, so that, for any consumption-investment ratio, full employment of all three factors is possible. Further, if these factor prices obtain, the output of the economy, given its *M*, *K*, *L* endowments, is maximal along that *C*, *I* ray.

To see this, assume a given target ratio of I/C. Then, given the import constraint, one can plot alternative *i*, w/E combinations that will induce firms to employ any particular K/L ratio. In particular, one can find pairs of *i*, w/E that will employ capital and labor in the same ratio as the country's endowments; a curve for this K/L ratio is plotted in figure 4. It slopes up from left to right, reflecting that the

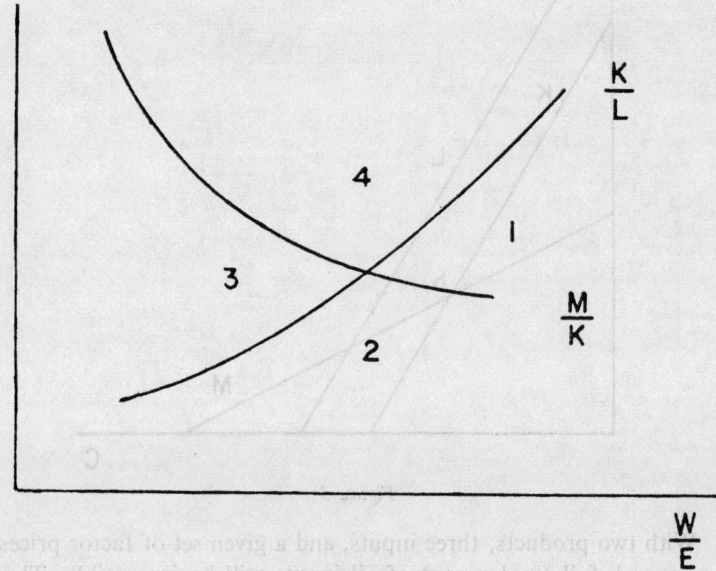

Figure 4

capital-labor ratio is positively related to w/E and negatively related to *i*. Thus a higher w/E, which would increase K/L, can be offset by a higher *i*, which would reduce it.

If the K/L curve of figure 4 reflects the country's relative endowments of *L* and *K*, full employment of *L* and *K* will be possible only if factor prices lie somewhere along the curve. In particular, if factor prices lie to the right of the curve—in region 1 or 2—full employment of labor will be impossible. The capital-labor ratio firms are motivated to employ will be higher than the country's endowments. Capital will become a constraint before labor. Thus, factor prices in regions 1 or 2 implies that the K constraint lies inside the L constraint in figure 3. A similar argument shows that, if factor prices are in region 3 or 4, the L constraint lies inside the K constraint. Factor prices along the K/L curve is the condition for the K and L constraints to coincide.

Similarly, if we ignore the L constraints, one can plot alternative pairs of w/E and i that will induce any given M/K ratio. There is some ambiguity with respect to the slope of the curve. In the Cobb-Douglas case, since M/K is positively related to both w/E and i, the curve slopes down from left to right. A higher w/E, which would increase M/K, must be offset by a lower i, which would reduce M/K. The M/K curve reflecting the country's relative availabilities of these two inputs has been drawn sloping down in figure 4. But, in general, nothing can be said (or is necessary to say for our purposes) about this slope.

Only if factor prices lie somewhere along the M/K curve will full employment on both K and M be possible. If factor prices lie above the curve—in region 1 or 4—firms will be induced to use an import-capital ratio larger than the country's endowment. Thus, the import constraint will not permit the capital stock to be fully employed. (Region 1, then, contains factor prices which cause unemployment of both capital and labor.) Conversely, in regions 3 and 2, at full employment of the capital stock, there is excess import capacity. Thus, for any C, I ray in figure 3, if factor prices are in region 1 or 4, the import constraint lies inside the capital constraint, if prices are in regions 2 and 3, the capital constraint lies inside the import constraint. If factor prices lie along the curve, the two constraints intersect at the ray.

In figure 4, the K/L and M/K curves intersect only once. Their intersection, of course, defines the set of factor prices at which full employment of all factors can be attained. Given our assumption that all factors have positive marginal productivity for all relevant factor ratios, this set of factor prices yields maximal output along the C, I ray, as well as full employment. Of course factor prices that will induce business firms to employ factors in the ratios reflecting availability is a necessary, but not sufficient, condition for general full employment and maximal output along the given ray. In addition the overall level of demand (given C, I proportions) must be 'right' so that not only the ratios of factor demanded, but total quantities, equal the country's endowments. But given that factor prices are 'right', this is a 'macro' question. Assuming that government fiscal and monetary policy can adjust the overall level of demand to equal capacity, the remaining condition is that of good fiscal-monetary policy.

There are some difficult questions regarding the conditions under which the curves will intersect, and under which they will intersect only once. The assumption that marginal products are positive within the range of relevant factor-proportion variation would appear sufficient to assure intersection. This implies, for example, that the nation's capital-labor ratio is not so low that the marginal productivity of labor at full employment is zero (as will happen at very low K/L if the elasticity of substitution is less than one). It also implies that imports are not so scarce that domestic inputs have zero marginal productivity in capital goods production (as could happen at high V/M ratios if the elasticity of substitution is less than one). Conditions for the intersection, if there is one, to be unique, are less clear to me.

The preceding analysis has taken the import constraint as fixed. Holding foreign aid constant, this implies that exports are not sensitive to factor prices. The model can easily be augmented to include factor-price-sensitive exports. If export earnings, in dollars, increase with a fall in domestic prices relative to the exchange rate, the implications of the model, developed in the next section of course, are strengthened.

IV The Policy Options Reconsidered

The introduction of factor substitution possibilities suggests that domestic policy may be far less helpless and much more potent in influencing employment and growth possibilities than the simple two-gap model of Section II suggests.

With factor substitution possibilities, it is possible to increase employment without reducing investment; indeed, it is possible to increase employment and achieve an increase in investment and consumption at the same time. With a given capital stock, an increase in employment (a higher labor-capital ratio) shifts the K/L

curve of figure 4 to the left, for, as equation (13) shows, to achieve a higher L/K requires a lower w/E for any i. The simplest case to analyze geometrically is one of no change in the C, I ratio, hence the M/K curve does not shift. The new equilibrium, with greater employment, more consumption and investment, the same capital stock, and the same level of imports requires, then, a lower w/E. (If the M/K curve slopes down from left to right, a higher i also will be required.)

The discussion above smacks of the possibility of getting something for nothing. This is both true and untrue. It is true in the sense that the option is open to get both more consumption and more investment. There are unemployed resources. It is untrue, in that real wages must fall for those employed. For, working through what happens to the price of consumption goods shows that an increase in E will increase Pc. (A decrease in w will cause a less-than-proportional full in Pc.) Thus there is a tension between higher employment and lower real wages for those employed. This is a classical tension, and a politically real one, in such countries as Colombia.

Given a level of employment, the costs of shifting the mix of output toward more investment and less consumption are clearly real. But in this model, this shift is at least possible to accomplish without the added costs of increasing unemployment. In this model, as in the fixed-coefficient model, investment is more import-intensive and less domestic resource-intensive than consumption. Thus an increase in investment relative to consumption will require a reduction in the import, intensity of both. This will require a decline in the price of domestic inputs relative to imports. In terms of figure 4, an increase in the investment-consumption ratio shifts the K/M curve downward.[15] The K, L curve does not change, reflecting the assumed equality of the capital-labor ratio in consumption and investment. (Note the symmetry to the analysis in the preceding paragraph.) Full employment of all factors in the post-shift situation thus require a decline in w/E and i.[16]

Putting both manoeuvers together indicates the wide range of policy options available in a situation where initially there is unemployed labor. It is clear that a given increase in employment can be used totally to increase investment, or totally to increase consumption, or

15 It is required that M/V increase in both activities; this requires a fall in P/E. To achieve this requires a fall in w/E, or i, or both.

16 That w/E and i must fall is required in order to preserve the K/L ratio.

any of a wide variety of combinations in between; the proportional increase in the C and I case is no magic. The frontier of possible increases in C and I from a given increase in employment must be concave (just as the C, I frontier in general must be concave)[17]. A greater than proportional increase in investment will require a greater decline in w/E than the proportional increase case; a greater than proportional increase in C will require a lesser decline in w/E.

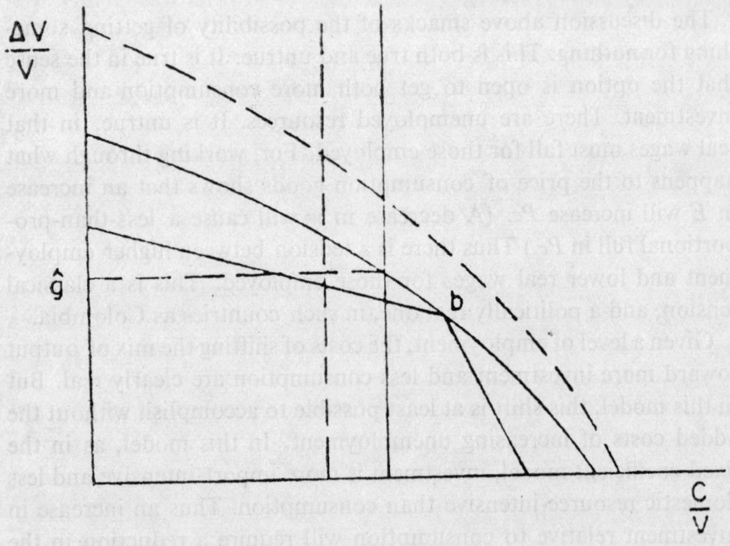

Figure 5

This makes good economic sense. The increase in employment relative to the capital stock calls for a decline in w/E relative to i, but any point along this new K, L schedule will sustain the new, higher labor-capital ratio. Since investment is more import-intensive than consumption, a high investment-consumption ratio requires a higher exchange rate relative to w and i than does a high consumption investment ratio.

Just as with the two-gap formulation, it is possible to translate the C, I choice set of the neoclassical model into a growth rate-consumption rate diagram. The 'inside' activity analysis frontier of figure 5

17 This is the well known implication of linear, homogeneous production functions, with one of the goods (investment) employing a different factor mix (a higher M/V) than the other. The formal proof will not be given here.

is drawn, assuming that factor prices generate full employment of all factors at point *b* and that they are fixed at that level. The 'outside' neoclassical frontier is drawn, assuming the factor prices adjust so as to generate full employment of all resources along any ray; in particular w/E is lower at the high investment (growth rate) end of the curve than at the higher consumption end.

In figure 5, if the target growth rate exceeds $\hat{g}$, there will be a foreign exchange gap. But if we are to the right of the savings constraint, say at point *b*, increases in savings can do more to close the gap than is implied by the fixed-coefficient model, assuming factor costs can be varied. Instead of the two-gap 'kink' there are smooth diminishing returns to both increased savings and increased aid alone, and complementarity between them. The diminishing returns to increased saving (reduced consumption) simply reflects the diminishing returns to domestic inputs, holding imports constant. Diminishing returns to aid reflects the same phenomenon the other way. That aid yields greater returns, in terms of growth at a high savings rate than at a low one, is retained in this model, reflecting the greater import-intensity of investment. But an increase in aid increases the marginal productivity, in terms of growth, of increased domestic savings.

Thus substitution possibilities mean that domestic policy can do more to increase employment, can have greater impact alone on growth, and is more important as a complement to foreign aid in influencing the growth rate, than the fixed coefficient two-gap model implies. However, achievement of these potentialities depends on the instruments of policy that a government can employ. In particular, their achievement requires, first, that the government have some ability to influence the C, I level and mix; and second that it be able to influence the effective exchange rate and the equilibrium rate of return on capital.

I shall not discuss here the assumption, implicit in the basic two-gap model as well as in the neoclassical variant, that government spending, taxing, and credit policy can move consumption and investment to any point within the constraint set. Similarly, I shall simply assume (naively) that the government can control the long-run rate of interest and the equilibrium rate of return on capital.

For what I want to focus on, and stress, is the role of the real effective exchange rate (in my model, E/w) as an instrument of employment and growth policy in a foreign exchange-constrained economy. The effective exchange rate, indeed all prices, are repressed in the conventional two-gap formulation. The preceding analysis suggests that, if there are substitution possibilities, increasing the effective exchange rate may provide the way out of the impasse of being able to increase neither employment nor investment (without reducing the other) because of the foreign exchange constraint.

An increase in E/w permits and stimulates import substitution, enabling an increase in the employment of domestic factors (principally labor) or a shift toward greater production of the more import-intensive good (investment), without causing an increase in pressure on balance of payments. What the exchange rate (or exchange rate structure) ought to be is clearly a function of objectives; the level of the effective exchange rate may be extremely important in determining the extent to which objectives can be met. If a higher growth rate and more employment is wanted than currently is being achieved, an increase in the effective exchange rate may be the key to enabling better performance. Of course, if higher wages for the employed rather than greater employment is the objective, or higher consumption rather than more investment, then the 'optimal' exchange rate would be lower.

To most people the idea that the optimal exchange rate is a function of policy objectives seems reasonable enough. Yet there seems some resistance to an implication that one cannot define, much less measure, the equilibrium exchange rate independent of policy objectives. I will not engage, here, in any exegesis of the conditions under which the optimal exchange rate also will be the rate that equilibrates supply and demand for foreign exchange in a competitive exchange market. Yet whether or not these conditions hold, it is obviously the case that the equilibrium exchange rate is not independent of a nation's objectives, or, more accurately, the policies employed to pursue them. If a country is willing to tolerate a high unemployment rate and a low growth rate, the equilibrium, as well as the 'optimal' exchange rate, will be lower than if policies are pursued to reduce unemployment and increase investment, The demand for foreign exchange obviously will be lower in the first case than in the second. So will its price be lower, as it ought to be.

Thus the equilibrium exchange rate certainly does reflect objectives and policies pursuing them, and it should. Let us consider the

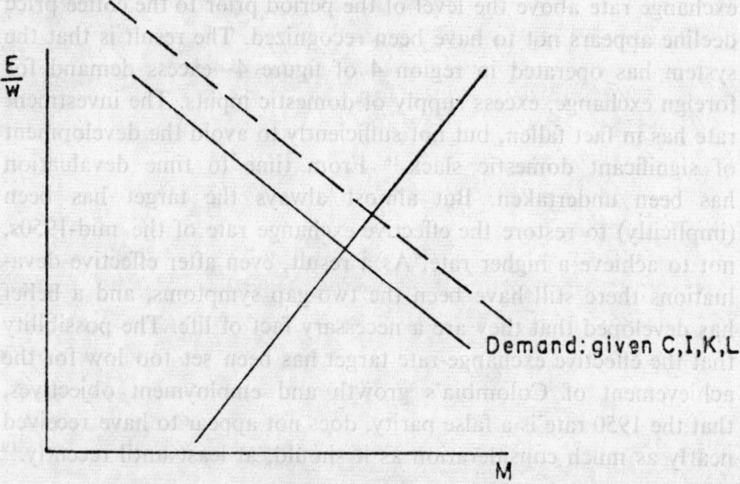

Figure 6

demand for and supply of foreign exchange. In figure 6, the supply of foreign exchange is shown as positively related to E/w; if one wishes one can draw the curve perfectly inelastic. The demand for imports, given any C, I ratio, is a decreasing function of E/w, reflecting the possibility to substitute domestic inputs for imports.

An increase in employment, with an associated rise in output of consumer or investor goods, obviously shifts the demand curve of foreign exchange to the right. Since investment is more import-intensive than consumption, an increase in I relative to C, holding K and L constant, also clearly shifts the demand curve to the right.

The diagram showing supply of and demand for foreign exchange permits us to interpret Colombia's recent economic malaise within the framework of the model. The falloff of coffee prices in the mid-1950s can be interpreted as a shift to the left in the supply of foreign exchange schedule facing Colombia (fig. 6), or as a downward shift in the M/K curve (fig. 4). For full employment equilibrium to be maintained, this required either an allocation of resources away from investment and toward consumption (which would conserve on foreign exchange) or an increase in E/w, which would both increase foreign exchange earnings and tend to diminish the import intensity of both investment and consumption.

The 1960 development plan calls, if anything, for an increase in the investment rate. The implication that this required an effective exchange rate above the level of the period prior to the coffee price decline appears not to have been recognized. The result is that the system has operated in region 4 of figure 4—excess demand for foreign exchange, excess supply of domestic inputs. The investment rate has in fact fallen, but not sufficiently to avoid the development of significant domestic slack.[18] From time to time devaluation has been undertaken. But almost always the target has been (implicitly) to restore the effective exchange rate of the mid-1950s, not to achieve a higher rate, As a result, even after effective devaluations there still have been the two-gap symptoms, and a belief has developed that they are a necessary fact of life. The possibility that the effective exchange-rate target has been set too low for the achievement of Colombia's growth and employment objectives, that the 1950 rate is a false parity, does not appear to have received nearly as much consideration as it should, at least until recently.[19]

REFERENCES

Chenery, H. and Bruno, M., 'Development Alternatives in an Open Economy: The Case of Israel.' *Econ. J.* 72 (March 1962): 79-1030.

Chenery, H. and Strout, A., 'Foreign Assistance and Economic Development.' A.E.R. 56 (September 1966): 679-732.

Cooper, R., 'The Balance of Payments.' in *Britain's Economic Prospects*, edited by R. Caves. Washington: Brookings Inst., 1968.

Curric, L., *Accelerating Development: The Necessity and the Means*. New York: McGraw-Hill, 1967.

McKinnon, R., 'Foreign Exchange Constraints on Economic Development.' *Econ. J.* 74 (June 1964): 388-409.

Nelson, R., 4 *Study of Industrialization in Colombia*: *Part I Analysis*. RM-5412-AID. Santa Monica, Calif: RAND Corporation, December 1967.

——, 'The Effective Exchange Rate. Employment and Growth on a Foreign Exchange Constrained Economy.' RM-5680-AID. Santa Monica, California: RAND Corporation, November 1968. (*a*)

——, 'A Diffusion Model of International Productivity Differences.' *A.E.R.* 58 (December 1968): 1219-48. (*b*)

Slighton, R., *Urban Unemployment in Colombia: Measurement, Characteristics, and Policy Issues*. RM-5393-AID. Santa Monica, Calif.: RAND Corporation, January 1968.

Vanek, J., *Estimating Resource Needs for Economic Development*. New York: McGraw-Hill, 1967.

18 The decline, of course, has not been deliberate.

19 The calculations, based on a Cobb-Douglas model, suggest that Colombia's problems would have been significantly fewer had the exchange rate been, say, 20 percent higher (see Nelson 1968*a*).

22

THE CHANGING TOLERANCE FOR INCOME INEQUALITY IN THE COURSE OF ECONOMIC DEVELOPMENT*

Albert O. Hirschman

WITH A MATHEMATICAL APPENDIX

Michael Rothschild

A DRASTIC TRANSVALUATION of values is in progress in the study of economic and political development. It has been forced upon us by a series of disasters that have occurred in countries in which development seemed to be vigorously under way. The civil war in Nigeria and the bloody falling apart of Pakistan are only the most spectacular instances of such 'development disasters'.

As a result, one reads with increasing frequency pronouncements about the bankruptcy of the 'old' development economics, with its accent on growth rates, industrialization, and international assistance, and about the need for a wholly new doctrine that would emphasize income distribution, employment, and self-reliance.[1]

The present paper is not written with the intention of stemming this tide, which surely represents a wholesome reaction and response to current problems. It is grounded, however, in the strong feeling and insistent recollection of one participant observer that the intellectual enthusiasm for development in the fifties and early sixties reflected elements of real hopefulness that were then actually present in many developing countries. What was not correctly perceived was the precarious and transitory nature of that early hopeful and even exuberant phase. This essay, then, is an effort to understand

*A preliminary version of this paper was presented as an invited lecture at the University of Puerto Rico at Rio Piedras in Feb. 1972. Discussions after that lecture and during subsequent seminars at Harvard and Yale led to a number of additions and reformulations. The author is grateful to Jorge Dominguez and Val Lorwin for detailed comments.

1 For a particularly forceful statement of this sort, see Mahbub ul Haq, 'Employment and Income Distribution in the 1970's: A New Perspective,' *International Development Review* (Dec. 1971), pp 9-13.

both where we were right and where we went wrong. It will proceed on a fairly abstract level, reach out into several fields other than economics, and stray, on occasion, from the immediate experience and concern that are at its origin.

I Gratification Over Advances of Others: The Tunnel Effect Introduced

I shall start by baldly stating my basic proposition. In the early stages of rapid economic development, when inequalities in the distribution of income among different classes, sectors, and regions are apt to increase sharply, it can happen that society's *tolerance* for such disparities will be substantial. To the extent that such tolerance comes into being, it accommodates, as it were, the increasing inequalities in an almost providential fashion. But this tolerance is like a credit that falls due at a certain date. It is extended in the expectation that eventually the disparities will narrow again. If this does not occur, there is bound to be trouble and, perhaps, disaster.

To make this proposition plausible, I shall first argue by analogy. Suppose that I drive through a two-lane tunnel, both lanes going in the same direction, and run into a serious traffic jam. No car moves in either lane as far as I can see (which is not very far). I am in the left lane and feel dejected. After a while the cars in the right lane begin to move. Naturally, my spirits lift considerably, for I know that the jam has been broken and that my lane's turn to move will surely come any moment now. Even though I still sit still, I feel much better off than before because of the expectation that I shall soon be on the move. But suppose that the expectation is disappointed and only the right lane keeps moving: in that case I, along with my left lane cosufferers, shall suspect foul play, and many of us will at some point become quite furious and ready to correct manifest injustice by taking direct action (such as illegally crossing the double line separating the two lanes).

It is easy to translate this situation into the language of welfare economics.[2] An individual's welfare depends on his present state of contentment (or, as a proxy, income), as well as on his expected future contentment (or income). Suppose that the individual has very little information about his future income, but at some point a few of his relatives, neighbors, or acquaintances improve their

2 See Mathematical Appendix for a more formal statement and development of the argument.

economic or social position. Now he has something to go on: expecting that his turn will come in due course, he will draw gratification from the advances of others—for a while. It will be helpful to refer to this initial gratification as the 'tunnel effect.'

This is a simple and, I believe, immediately persuasive proposition. While it has to be formulated with greater care so as to spell out the conditions under which it does or does not hold, perhaps I shall be allowed to dwell on it and to advertise its novelty. The tunnel effect operates because advances of other supply information about a more benign external environment; receipt of this information produces gratification; and this gratification overcomes, or at least suspends, *envy*. Though long noted as the most uninviting of the seven deadly sins because, unlike lust, gluttony, pride, etc., it does not provide any initial fun to its practitioners, envy is nevertheless a powerful human emotion. This is attested to by the writings of anthropologists, sociologists, and economists, who all have proclaimed, in general quite independently of one another, that if you advance in income or status while I remain where I was, I will actually feel worse off than before because my relative position has declined.

In economics this has been argued as the 'relative income hypothesis,' according to which the welfare of an individual varies inversely with the income or the consumption of those persons with whom he associates.[3] In sociology the topic has been profusely studied under the heading of 'relative deprivation.' While this term is sometimes used to denote any lag of real accomplishments behind expectations, its predominant meaning refers to the feelings experienced by a person or group of persons who are falling behind others or who see others catch up with them in regard to income,

3 James S. Duesenberry, *Income, Saving and Theory of Consumer Behavior* (Cambridge: Harvard University Press, 1949), Ch. III. A clear diagrammatical exposition is in Harvey Leibenstein, 'Notes on Welfare Economics and the Theory of Democracy,' *Economic Journal*, LXXII (June 1962) pp. 300-05. Leibenstein considers three possible ways in which individuals make comparisons between their income and that of others: '(1) *Pure* Pareto comparisons in which each individual takes into account his own income but no one else's; (2) the "share of the pie" comparisons in which each individual takes into account the income distribution from a relative point of view but not the absolute magnitude of his income; and (3) the "compromise Pareto comparison" in which individuals take into account both the absolute magnitude of their income and their relative income position' (p. 301).

The 'pure Pareto comparison', where an individual's utility is not decreased by the improving fortunes of his neighbor as long as his own income does not change, is a limiting case in this scheme. There is no room in it for the possibility of a positive interaction between my and my neighbor's utility.

influence, and status.[4] Finally, anthropologists, who are less given to using jargon, speak unabashedly of the envy caused by isolated advances of individuals in small, poor communities; they view many institutions, such as fiestas, gift giving, and appointment of the rich to financially burdensome honorary positions, as social mechanisms designed to lessen the potentially destructive impact of envy on personal bonds and social cohesion.[5]

This is no doubt an impressive body of converging writings, and massive data have been gathered in their support. But relentless pursuit of this line of reasoning and research may have led to a trained incapacity to perceive the tunnel effect and its importance in a number of contexts.

A preliminary way of rekindling perception is to reverse the signs of the phenomenon under study. Suppose my neighbor or acquaintance, far from improving his position, experiences a bad setback such as losing his job while I am keeping mine: Do I now experience the opposite of relative deprivation, that is, the satisfaction of relative enrichment? This is unlikely, for one thing, because envy, mortal sin though it may be, is an altogether gentle feeling if compared to *Schadenfreude*, the joy at someone else's injury, which is the emotion that would have to come into play to make me happy in this situation. The more important reason is the tunnel effect in reverse: once again I shall take what is happening to my neighbor as an indication of what the future might have in store for me, and hence I will be apprehensive and worried—less well off than before, just as he. This reaction is well-known from the onset and spread of depressions.[6]

The opposite reaction will surely take place when the economy

4 For an excellent survey and bibliography, see Thomas F. Pettigrew, 'Social Evaluation Theory: Convergences and Applications,' *Nebraska Symposium on Motivation, 1967* (Lincoln: University of Nebraska Press, 1967), particularly pp. 261-73. The concept was introduced by S. A. Stouffer and his associates in the well-known monumental study of the American soldier in World War II (*The American Soldier, Vol. 1, Adjustment During Army Life;* Princeton, N. J.: Princeton University Press. 1949). See below note 18, p. 528.

For a development of the concept in its narrower and more useful meaning, see W. G. Runciman, *Relative Deprivation and Social Justice* (London: Routledge and Kegan Paul, 1966). The wider meaning, which practically equates relative deprivation with any form of discontent is extensively used in Ted Robert Gurr, *Why Men Rebel* (Princeton, N. J.: Princeton University Press, 1970).

5 See Ch. 7 entitled 'The Fear of Envy' in George M. Foster, *Tzintzuntzan: Mexican Peasants in a Changing World* (Boston: Little, Brown, 1967); also Frank Cancian, *Economics and Prestige in a Maya Community* (Cambridge, Mass: Harvard University Press, 1963), p. 135 and *passim.*

6 See, however, note 24, p. 533.

experiences a cyclical upturn. Now the news that someone I know is getting his job back while I am still unemployed gives me a pleasure that overwhelms any possible envy, for the event is hailed as a confirmation that better times are under way for me also. This is close to the situation in countries that experience a vigorous surge of development.

As long as the tunnel effect lasts, everybody feels better off, both those who have become richer[7] and those who have not. It is therefore conceivable that some uneven distribution of the new incomes generated by growth will be preferred to an egalitarian distribution by all members of the society.[8] In this eventuality, the increase in income inequality would not only be politically tolerable; it would also be outright desirable from the point of view of social welfare.

II Some Evidence

But this possible consequence of the tunnel effect is a theoretical curiosum, whereas the effect itself definitely is not. In a number of countries its reality has impressed itself on careful observers. Interestingly enough, it was often stumbled upon by researchers who were looking for the opposite phenomenon, such as seething discontent and revolutionary fervor among the urban poor, and were surprised and sometimes not a little disappointed at what they actually found.

The following comments on a sample survey carried out over a decade ago in the *favelas* of Rio de Janeiro are a first case in point:

> One way of testing the favelado's sense of sharing in what goes on in the nation is to ascertain the extent to which he perceives national economic growth as producing real gains to himself. When asked in February of 1961 whether things had improved, had remained about the same, or had become worse for him during the last five years, nearly one out of two favelados replied that his present situation is worse. Another three out of ten found that their situation remained much the same.... The general sensation that things have not improved noticeably for themselves has not created any great disillusion among favelados with the idea of industrialization as a road to prosperity. The favelado does not deny that the nation's industrial growth has produced benefits for people like himself; he only states that his own situation has not changed

7 See, however, Section III below.
8 See, Mathematical Appendix for an exploration of this case.

appreciably. Thus, when asked immediately after the above question whether the growth of industry had benefited people like themselves, most answered affirmatively. Their explanation however, was almost entirely in terms of the expansion of job opportunities *for others*—friends, acquaintances, or simply other Brazilians.[9]

Writing also in the early sixties, a well-known Mexican political scientist coined the term 'hope factor' to explain what by then amounted to an astonishingly long record of political stability in his country.[10] Even after this record had been shattered by the events of 1968 and the Tlatelolco massacre, another observer wrote:

> Even though the perspectives of individual advance are limited, there is one reason for which one finds less disappointment with the development process among lower-class persons of all sectors than might be expected. With education spreading rapidly and with migration on the increase, there are a number of relatively easy ways of achieving personal advance. Thus even when an individual has been unable to get a new job or in general has not improved his income or position, it is nevertheless probable that *he knows one or several persons* who have been successful in these respects....[11]

The contrast between the objective situation of low incomes, poor working conditions, and general deprivation, on the one hand, and the subjective mood of hopefulness, on the other, were also found to be characteristic of the Puerto Rico of the late fifties:

> We suggest that Puerto Ricans feel far better off than the objective facts of incomes, education and occupations show....Puerto Ricans perceive the existing marked inequalities. Yet they do not feel particularly depreciated by them, and certainly not overwhelmed by them; indeed, on some counts, their views of life and how good it is have often seemed to ignore the objective situation...on every visible count, these people at all levels are full of hopes for the future.[12]

In an article dealing with the continent as a whole, two Latin American sociologists catch the essence of these situations by assert-

9 Frank Bonilla, 'Rio's Favelas: The Rural Slum within the City,' *The American Universities Field Staff Reports Service*, Vol. VIII, No. 3, New York, 1961, pp. 8-9.

10 Pablo González Casanova, *La democracia en México* (Mexico: Era, 1965, popular edition), p. 133.

11 David Barkin, 'La persistencia de la pobreza en Mexico: un análisis economico estructural,' *Comercio Exterio*, Banco Nacional de Comercio Exterior, Mexico, Aug. 1971, p. 673 (my translation and italics).

12 Melvin M. Tumin with Arnold Feldman, *Social Class and Social Change in Puerto Rico* (Princeton, N. J.: Princeton University Press, 1961), pp. 165-66.

ing that '...the patterns of deferred social mobility, even though somewhat mythical, are nonetheless effective.'[13]

Finally, we shall quote some revealing personal remarks about the general atmosphere of countries where mid-twentieth-century style, capitalist development suddenly 'broke out.' They come from an American anthropologist who reminisces about her stay in Venezuela, in an article in which she gives a sympathetic account of a recent trip to Cuba:

> I thought about what I had seen in Cuba, and about Venezuela, and about my own country....I thought about how when I went to Venezuela, I felt that for the first time I realized something about my own country which I had not previously seen there: the idealism which is inherent in what I had experienced (in the United States) as materialism and individual self-seeking I saw that for Venezuelans, for whom economic development had just begun...the democratizing of material consumption and the opening up of opportunities—for those able to seize them—was a truly exciting and liberating idea.[14]

This passage is of particular interest, first, because it sensitively renders the feeling of the early exuberant phase of development during which the tunnel effect operates; and, secondly, because it illustrates at the same time the considerable reluctance of social-justice-minded intellectuals to perceive the effect—it just goes too much against the grain of any but the most honest to speak of this deplorable 'false consciousness' or of that vulgar frontier atmosphere as an 'exciting and liberating idea'! Moreover, social scientists live in an intensely competitive atmosphere in which envy and 'relative deprivation' are far more prevalent than hopefulness caused by someone else's advance; and although one hesitates to make these ad homines points, they may help explain why the tunnel effect, though widely noted, has not been dealt with in a systematic way in either economic or sociological theory.

III Consequences for Integration and Revolution

A brief digression is in order. The various descriptions of the 'hope factor' reported in the previous section strongly suggest that the

13 Fernando Henrique Cardoso and Jorge Luis Reyna, 'Industrialization, Occupational Structure, and Social Stratification in Latin America,' in Cole Blasier, ed., *Constructive Change in Latin America* (Pittsburgh: University of Pittsburgh Press, 1968), p. 51.

14 Lisa Peattie, 'Cuban Notes', *Massachusetts Review* (Autumn 1969), pp. 673–74.

subject of this paper shades over into a topic familiar to political sociologists: the effect of social mobility on political stability and social integration. This relationship has usually been examined from the point of view of the reactions of the socially mobile themselves, while our focus has thus far been on those who are left behind. With respect to the upwardly mobile, the economist, with his touching simplicity, would tend to think that there is no problem: being better off than before, these people are also likely to be more content with the world around them. Social history has shown, however, that matters are far more complicated: as de Tocqueville already noted, the upwardly mobile do not necessarily turn into pillars of society all at once, but may on the contrary be disaffected and subversive for a considerable time. The principal reason for this surprising development is the phenomenon of partial and truncated mobility: the upwardly mobile who may have risen along one of the dimensions of social status, such as wealth, find that a number of obstacles, rigidities, and discriminatory practices still block their continued ascent particularly along other dimensions, as well as their all-round acceptance by the traditional elites, and consequently they feel that in spite of all their efforts and achievements, they are not really 'making it.'[15] Only as social mobility continues for a long period, and the traditional system of stratification is substantially eroded as a result, will the upwardly mobile become fully integrated—or 'coopted.'

Discrimination against *nouveaux riches* by the older elites is by no means the only reason for which the upwardly mobile may be critical of the society in which they live and advance. A more charitable interpretation would point to the possibility that convictions about social justice, once formed, acquire a life and staying power of their own so that they are not necessarily jettisoned when pressing personal problems of material welfare have been solved—not, in any way, until after a decent time interval.

This dynamic of the socially mobile is thus the reverse of the one that has been suggested here for those who are left behind: during a first and all-round paradoxical phase, frustration and continued

15 For an excellent survey with particular attention to this problem, see Gino Germani, 'Social and Political Consequences of Mobility,' in N. Smelser and S. M. Lipset, eds., *Social Structure and Mobility in Development* (Chicago: Aldine, 1966), pp. 371 ff. It is also possible, of course, that aspirations, once aroused, will outrun achievements, but this explanation of the discontent of the upwardly mobile is far less convincing than the one mentioned in the text.

alienation are the lot of the upward bound, while the nonmobile derive satisfaction from the anticipation that matters are bound to improve pretty soon. This earlier conclusion of ours can be maintained as the nonmobile see only the improvement in the fortunes of the mobile and remain totally unaware of the new problems being encountered by them. In a second phase there may then take place a symmetrical switch: the upwardly mobile become integrated, whereas the nonmobile lose their earlier hope of joining the upward surge and turn into enemies of the existing order. It is quite unlikely, however, that the beginning of the second phase will coincide for the two groups. Noncoincidence of these two changeovers will obviously be the norm. The upwardly mobile may become integrated while the left-behind ones are still experiencing the tunnel effect. Alternatively and more interestingly, the nonmobile may experience the turnaround from hopefulness to disenchantment, while the mobile are still disaffected. This last situation clearly contains much potential for social upheaval. Its possible occurrence might even qualify as a theory of revolution.[16] At this point, however, I shall abandon the matter to the historians for I must return to the tunnel effect and its reversal.

IV From Gratification to Indignation

As was pointed out, gratification at the advances of others arises under the tunnel effect not from benevolence or altruism, but strictly from an expectational calculus: I expect that my turn to move will soon come. Nonrealization of the expectation will at some point result in my 'becoming furious', that is, in my turning into an enemy of the established order. This change from supporter to enemy comes about purely as a result of the passage of time—no particular outward event sets off this dramatic turnaround. In this respect, the theory of social conflict here proposed is quite distinct from the '*J*-curve' hypothesis, which attributes revolutionary outbreaks to a sudden downturn in economic performance coming after a long upswing.[17] Such a downturn no doubt increases the likelihood of

16 It comes close to satisfying the criterion the French historian Ernest Labrousse has suggested for the arising of revolutionary situations: namely, that 'the vast majority of the country is united in a total rejection of existing society and of the reigning order of things.' Richard Cobb, *A Second Identity: Essays on France and on French History* (London: Oxford University Press, 1969), pp. 272–73.

17 James C. Davies, 'Toward a Theory of Revolution,' *American Sociological Review*, XXVII (Feb. 1962), pp. 5–19.

commotion, but it is by no means indispensable. Providential and tremendously helpful as the tunnel effect is in one respect (because it accommodates the inequalities almost inevitably arising in the course of development), it is also treacherous: the rulers are not necessarily given any advance notice about its decay and exhaustion, that is, about the time at which they ought to be on the lookout for a drastically different climate of public and popular opinion; on the contrary, they are lulled into complacency by the easy early stage when everybody seems to be enjoying the very process that will later be vehemently denounced and damned as one consisting essentially in 'the rich becoming richer.'[18]

Semantic inventions and inversions are perhaps the best portents of the turnaround. To give an example: in the fifties the term 'pôle de croissance' (growth pole), coined by François Perroux, was widely used for the growing industrializing cities of the developing countries. At some point during the next decade, this expression, which suggested irradiation of growth, gave way to a new term, 'internal colonialism,' which was now said to be practiced by these same cities with regard to their zones of economic influence.

V The Tunnel Effect: Social, Historical, Cultural, and Institutional Determinants of its Strength

In what kind of societies does the tunnel effect arise and gather strength? What are the conditions under which it will last for a substantial time period or, on the contrary, decay rapidly and turn

18 It is tempting to suggest a reinterpretation, along the foregoing lines, of the famous and paradoxical findings about the morale in the American armed forces during World War II. While wartime promotions had of course been much more prevalent in the Air Corps than in the Military Police, the survey conducted by Stouffer and his associates found more frustration over promotions in the former than in the latter. This finding has been the origin and one of the mainstays of the theory of relative deprivation. The study argued that Air Corps promotions, though frequent in comparison with those in the other branches, lagged in relation to expectations and aspirations aroused within the Corps by the actual promotions of those who made rapid careers. While other social scientists have later proposed different explanations, not enough attention has perhaps been devoted to the time dimension. The survey was taken rather late in the war, in 1944. Is it not likely that if a similar survey had been taken earlier, the finding would have confirmed the common-sense expectation that promotion morale was higher in the Air Corps than in the Military Police? Early in the war the rapid advances of some most probably reinforced morale in line with the tunnel effect; only later on, as the various members of the Air Corps reached their level and failed to achieve quite what they had been led to expect, did frustration take over. See S. A. Stouffer *et al., op. cit.*, pp. 250 ff.

into the opposite, namely disappointment, alienation, and outrage at social injustice? Answering this question is crucial for bringing our hypothesis down to earth and for ascertaining its empirical and heuristic usefulness.

For the tunnel effect to be strong (or even to exist), the group that does not advance must be able to empathize, at least for a while, with the group that does. In other words, the two groups must not be divided by barriers that are or are felt as impassable. Thus, the fluidity or rigidity of class lines will have an obvious bearing on the intensity of the tunnel effect.

But stratification according to social class is a distinction of limited usefulness for our purpose. However unevenly economic growth proceeds, any strong advance is likely to mean gains or new and better jobs for members of several different classes. One might therefore conclude that the tunnel effect will always come into being as, within each social class, those who are not advancing empathize initially with those who are. But this need not happen if each class is composed of ethnic or religious groups that are differentially involved in the growth process. Hence, the contrast between fairly unitary and highly segmented societies is particularly relevant for our topic. If, in segmented societies, economic advance becomes identified with one particular ethnic or language group or with the members of one particular religion or region, then those who are left out and behind are unlikely to experience the tunnel effect: they will be convinced almost from the start of the process that the advancing group is achieving an unfair exploitative advantage over them. The nonmobile group may thus make the prediction opposite to that implied in the tunnel effect: as a result of another group's advance, it will expect to be *worse* off. The possibility of this reaction will be discussed in the next section. In any event, it appears that highly segmented societies will or should eschew strategies of development that are politically feasible elsewhere because of the availability of the tunnel effect.

More concretely, the capitalist road to development appears to be particularly ill-suited for highly segmented societies; if it is followed there, it will require a far greater degree of coercion than it did in the fairly unitary countries in which capitalist development scored its historic successes. On the other hand, rejection of the capitalist road does not yield a ready proven alternative, for the centralized decision making typical of socialist systems is unlikely to function at all well in segmented societies.[19]

A variant of a segmented society in which economic progress becomes largely identified with one domestic segment is a society where most emerging economic opportunities are created or seized by foreigners. Once again, the tunnel effect will not prosper in such a situation. The greater the role of foreign capital and of foreign skilled personnel in the development process, the less expectation of eventual participation in it will there be on the part of the local population, including large parts of the local elites. Hence, tolerance for the emerging inequalities of income will be low, and the need for coercion to maintain social and political stability correspondingly high, even at an early stage of the process.

In passably homogeneous societies where resources are largely owned domestically, the tolerance for economic inequalities may be quite large as no language, ethnic, or other barrier keeps those who are left behind from empathizing with those who are 'making it.' It seems that, once again, 'to him who hath shall be given,' for the country that enjoys the manifold advantages of a nonsegmented citizenry gains thereby the additional latitude of being able to develop without having to impose the serious and perhaps crippling constraints arising from the need to make all portions of the community advance at a roughly even pace.

On the other hand, the greater tolerance of these more homogeneous countries for inequality has a real and possibly fearful price. As we know, the greater the tolerance, the greater is the *scope* for the reversal that comes once the tunnel effect wears off (unless the inequalities are corrected in time). In this fashion a somewhat counterintuitive conclusion is reached: the more homogeneous the country, the more prone will it be to violent social conflict in the course of development unless its leadership is uncommonly perceptive and able.[20] Once again I must leave it to the historians to ascertain whether any empirical sense can be made out of this purely

19 For a detailed argument, see the case study of centralized vs. decentralized decision making in a segmented society (rail vs. road in Nigeria) in my *Development Projects Observed* (Washington, D.C.: Brookings, 1967), pp. 139–48.

20 This point is similar to one that can be made about the economic consequences of the size of countries. While the literature of economic developments has—quite properly—stressed the advantages of size, particularly in connection with, import-substituting industrialization, large size also means that it is possible for a large backward region to fall cumulatively and hopelessly behind—as the progressive region absorbs for a long time virtually al

deductive proposition; it might be mentioned, however, that part of the evidence favoring the hypothesis could come not from actual revolution, or similar civil strife, but from protracted lower class alienation such as is found in Argentina, France, and Italy.

National homogeneity is ordinarily defined in terms of static characteristics such as unity of race, language, and religion. But the most effective homogenizing agent is perhaps an intensive historical experience that has been shared by all members of a group.[21] Wars and revolutions typically can be such experiences, and the tunnel effect is therefore frequently at its most potent in postwar and postrevolutionary societies. The result can be an irony-laden historical cycle: revolutions are often made to eradicate a certain kind of inequality, but after such a revolution and because of it, society will have acquired a specially high tolerance for new inequalities if and when they arise. A particularly apt illustration is the Mexican Revolution and its subsequent 'betrayal' through the sharply uneven development of recent decades. Similarly, the egalitarian or, rather, 'born equal' heritage of the United States—the collective leaving behind of Europe with its feudal shackles and class conflicts—may have set the stage for the prolonged acceptance by American society of huge economic disparities.

The more or less unitary character of a country is probably the most important single criterion for appraising the likely strength and duration of the tunnel effect. But other distinctions are of interest. It can be argued, for example, that the strength of family bonds has a direct bearing on these matters. In many cases, the advances of others will generate hope not so much for oneself as for one's children. The prediction that my children will have a better life than I did should improve my own welfare in any event, but it will do so with particular force if I expect my grown-up children to be living with me, to share in the expenses of the household, and eventually to support me in my old age. From this point of view, then, traditional family arrangements facilitate the operation of the tunnel effect and turn out to have some development-promoting potential.[22]

of the country's industrial growth and develops a modern agriculture to boot. So wide, protracted, and dangerous a cleavage cannot arise as easily in a small country, as, under most circumstances, economic growth there either has to spill over to the poorer regions or will come to a halt.

21 This important point was suggested to me by Katherine Auspitz.

22 For other arguments along this line, see my *A Bias for Hope: Essays on Development and Latin America*, (New Haven: Yale Unversity Press,

Provided it is not highly segmented, 'traditional' society is generally in a better position than its modern counterpart to take advantage of the tunnel effect. Members of traditional societies are typically tied to each other by a dense network of obligations that are both mutual and flexible: it is none too clear what it is that is owed nor when it falls due. Hence, when some members of such a society advance, their obligations are apt to expand, and many of those who remain behind expect to be benefited in due course and in some measure as a result of their pre-existing, if imprecise, claims on the former. La Rochefoucauld noted this effect in a maxim that in general is as fine a formulation of the tunnel effect as I have come across: 'The immediate feeling of joy we experience when our friends meet with luck . . . is an effect . . . of our hope to be lucky in turn or to gain some advantage from their good fortune.'[23]

Next, a distinction may be made between various 'theories of success' that typically prevail in different societies or cultures. If individual advances are attributed primarily to chance, the success of others will occasion the tunnel effect; for the next time fortune strikes, I may well be the lucky one. Hence, the belief that the world is governed by chance, ordinarily considered so harmful to sustained development, has something to recommend itself to the extent that the tunnel effect is considered a valuable, if somewhat volatile, resource for an economy attempting to achieve growth. If, on the other hand, success of others is likely to be attributed from the

1971), Ch. 14. The proposition about family arrangements that is put forward in the text is a special case of a more general proposition: the tunnel effect will be the stronger, the weaker is the time preference for present over future income, i.e., the lower is the discount rate. The Mathematical Appendix shows that the discount rate enters explicitly into the expression relating changes in *B's* income to *A's* utility. This is intuitively obvious: even a very strong positive effect of *B's* income increase on *A's* expected income will make little difference to *A's* present utility if *A* attaches a steep discount rate to his expected income.

23 *Maximes*, p. 582. The phenomenon in reverse was pointed out at about the same time by Thomas Hobbes: 'Griefe, for the Calamity of another, is PITTY; and ariseth from the imagination that the like calamity may befall himselfe; . . . therefore for Calamity arriving from great wickedness, the best men have the least Pitty; and for the same Calamity, those have least Pitty, that think themselves least obnoxious [= exposed] to the same.' *Leviathan*, Part I, Ch. 6. La Rochefoucauld and Hobbes both came upon these insights in the course of their search for a rigorous, if unpleasant, science of human nature. Unpleasantness of findings almost became a test of rigor and truth for them. Naturally enough, it did not occur to them that, in the situations at hand, self-centeredness has the virtue of overcoming envy and *Schadenfreude*, respectively.

outset to nepotism, favoritism, or similar unfair practices, then there will hardly be any initial feeling of anticipatory gratification among those who are not participating in the division of the spoils.

It is also conceivable, though perhaps not very likely, that success of others is attributed to their superior merit and qualities such as hard work. Those who are left out would then blame only themselves for their lack of advance. They could, as a result, either simply defer to the more successful members of their community, or they might envy them for being more richly endowed, or they could try to emulate them by redoubling their own effort. In this case, therefore, the result would be rather indeterminate, and one needs more information.[24]

A further possibility is that the success of others is attributed not to their qualities, but to their *defects*. One often rationalizes his own failure to do as well as others in the following terms: 'I would not want to get ahead by stooping to his (ruthless, unprincipled, servile, etc.) conduct.' This sort of attribution of success is not too dissimilar, in its consequences for the tunnel effect, from the one that concentrates on the merits of those who have risen. It makes it possible, of course, for those who are not advancing to rest content with their own station in life. But it could also happen that the next time around they will change their conduct and be a bit more ruthless, unprincipled, servile, etc., than hitherto. To the extent that it is easier to be servile and unprincipled than gifted and

24 Attribution theory, a relatively new branch of social psychology, has attempted to throw light on this area of human behavior. Experiments have been devised to study the extent to which onlookers pin the blame for accidents on those who have been involved rather than on ill fate. Apparently the onlooker typically resorts to what has been called 'defensive attribution': he looks for some good reason why the accident is one of the involved parties' own peculiar fault so as to gain the assurance that the mishap could not possibly happen to himself. (Only if no such good reason can be found, if in other words the person who might be blamed is and behaves very much like the onlooker, then and only then will the latter tend to exonerate the former and blame fate instead.) On the other hand, if another person, rather than being involved in an accident, experiences a lucky break, the onlooker will tend to credit chance rather than merit, thereby gaining some hope that a similar lucky break is in store for him. Besides being unflattering to human nature, these findings introduce an asymmetry into the operation of the tunnel effect: it will be stronger in the forward than in the backward direction; that is, the expectation to share eventually in the advances of others will be more pronounced than the expectation to follow them in their setbacks. For an experimental confirmation of this asymmetry and for references to other research in this area, see Jerry I. Shaw and Paul Skolnick, 'Attribution of Responsibility for a Happy Accident,' *Journal of Personality and Social Psychology*, XVIII (1971), pp. 380–83.

hardworking, attribution of success of others to their faults rather than to their qualities may actually facilitate the operation of the tunnel effect.

A distinction related to these theories of success is based on the various organizational ways in which individual advances are perceived to come about. Such perceptions depend fundamentally on the decision-making system. If decision making is perceived to be largely decentralized, individual advances are likely to be attributed to chance, or possibly to merit (or demerit). When decision making is known to be centralized, such advances will be attributed to unfair favoritism or, again, to merit. To the extent that merit is not a likely attribution, decentralized decision making, which permits success of others to be explained by chance, is therefore more conducive to giving full play to the tunnel effect. It is indeed characteristic of market economies. Centralized-decision-making economic systems have come typically into the world because of excessive inequalities existing in, or arising under, decentralized systems. It is interesting to note that they will strain to be more egalitarian not just because they want to, but also because they have to: centralization of decision making largely deprives them of the tolerance for inequality that is available to more decentralized systems.

Similar considerations apply as a *given* economic system evolves in the direction of greater centralization or decentralization. For example, the tolerance for inequality can be expected to decline when a capitalist economy becomes more oligopolized and bureaucratized. An upsurge in populist sentiment has usually been attributed to the greater concentration of wealth that has sometimes been characteristic of such a period. But the tolerance for inequality may decline even without such concentration, simply because those who are excluded from advances no longer perceive such exclusion as temporary bad luck, but as an inevitable or even calculated effect of the 'system.'

VI An Alternative Reaction: Apprehension over Advances of Others

It is a basic idea of this essay that changes in the income of *B* lead to changes in *A*'s welfare not only because *A*'s relative position in the income scale has changed, but because changes in *B*'s fortunes will affect *A*'s prediction of his own future income. The principal case that has been considered so far is the tunnel effect: *B* advances, and this leads *A* to predict an improvement in his own position as well. Mention has also been made of the diametrically opposite situation: a deterioration in *B*'s situation leads *A* to be apprehensive about his own, as is the case in a spreading depression. Is a mixed case conceivable? In other words, could *A* come to feel under certain circumstances that an advance on the part of *B* is likely to affect his own welfare *negatively*?[25] Actually this sort of prediction is not too farfetched: it is likely to be made in a society whose members are convinced that they are involved in a zero-sum game because resources are available in strictly limited amounts. This representation of social reality has been called the Image of Limited Good by George Foster, who claims it to be typical of many peasant societies around the world.[26] Assume the Image prevails in a community and that, at one point, a number of its citizens (group *B*) improve their position, while the income of the rest of the people (group *A*) remains unchanged. One conclusion to be drawn from such a development would of course be for both *A* and *B* to give up the Image. But suppose the community is strongly committed to it as a result of past experiences: one way of maintaining the Image is then to dismiss what has happened as purely transitory. And if the advance of group *B* appears to be irreversible, then the Image can be held on to only by the prediction that *A*'s fortunes will soon suffer decline.[27]

It is in fact possible that we have here come upon a better way of accounting for what has been described by Foster and others as the 'prevalence of envy' in peasant societies.[28] It may well be that when *B* advances, this makes *A* unhappy not because he is envious, but because he is worried; on the basis of his existing world view, he must expect to be worse off in short order. In other words, *A* is

25 This question arose as a result of Michael Rothschild's mathematical formulation of the tunnel effect. See Appendix.

26 *Tzintzuntzan*, Ch. 6.

27 One reason for this prediction could be *A's* feeling that *B*, as a result of his increased wealth, will also acquire more power, a good that is generally acquired at the expense of others, and that this redistribution of power, besides being in itself objectionable to *A*, will have in time an adverse effect on his economic position. Such a feeling is likely to arise particularly if *B* comes to be *substantially* better off than *A*. Oskar Morgenstern has pointed to this situation as one limitation to the doctrine of Pareto optimality. See his 'Pareto Optimum and Economic Organization,' in Norbert Kloten *et al.*, eds., *Systeme und Methoden in den Wirtschafts- und Sozialwissenschaften* (Tubingen: J. C. B. Mohr, 1964), p. 578.

28 *Tzintzuntzan*, pp. 153–55.

unhappy not because of the presence of relative deprivation, but because of the anticipation of absolute deprivation.

The reinterpretation of institutionalized envy, which is suggested here, can actually be seen to be closely related to the tunnel effect. In a society without the experience of sustained growth, an initially emerging situation in which one group of people is improving its economic position while another group remains stationary is probably felt as essentially unstable: either available resources have not increased, and in that case group *A* will necessarily suffer a decline to compensate for *B*'s rise; or some windfall gain has expanded total resources, and in this case group *A* will soon get its proper share of the windfall. Therefore, one or the other of these two outcomes is likely to be anticipated rather than the continuation of the current situation. Which one will be picked as most likely will of course make a great deal of difference to the course of social conflict in that society. The decision could often be narrowly balanced, as on a knife's edge, depending as it does on *A*'s perception of the causes of *B*'s initial advance. This perception will depend on the factors briefly reviewed in the preceding section. But it now appears that the alternative for those who are left behind is not merely between an expectation of sharing in the advances of others and the status quo, but between expectation of advance and anticipation of decline. This situation and the knife-edge character of the decision between these alternative expectations perhaps explain why the forecasting of social conflict is such hazardous business.

VII Concluding Remarks

The preceding argument suggests a few summary points and concluding remarks.

1. If growth and equity in income distribution are considered the two principal economic tasks facing a country, then these two tasks can be solved sequentially if the country is well supplied with the tunnel effect. If, because of existing social, political, or psychological structures, the tunnel effect is weak or nonexistent, then the two tasks will have to be solved simultaneously, a difficult enterprise and one that probably requires institutions wholly different from those appropriate to the sequential case.[29] To make matters worse,

29 Political scientists have described the difficulties facing the new states of the twentieth century in these terms. Whereas, so they point out, the countries of Western Europe had centuries to solve, one after the other, the

it may be impossible to tell in advance whether a given country is or is not adequately supplied with the tunnel effect: as was argued in the last section, it is conceivable that only development itself will tell.

2. On the basis of the distinction just made, it is possible to speak of two kinds of 'development disasters.' The first is characteristic of societies that have attempted to develop by means of a strategy implying the arising of new inequalities or the widening of old ones; but, in view of their structure, these societies should never have done so. Nigeria and Pakistan are probably cases in point. The other kind of development disaster occurs in countries in which the above strategy is nicely abetted for a while by the tunnel effect, but where ruling groups and policy makers fail to realize that the safety valve, which the effect implies, will cease to operate after some time. This situation has been increasingly typical of a number of Latin American countries: Brazil and Mexico have already experienced disasters, and there are numerous portents of more to come.

3. In contrast with most conventional representations, the development process is here viewed as being exposed to crisis, and perhaps disaster, even after lengthy periods of forward movement. The view here proposed necessarily allocates a decisive role to politics. Its implications for the political evolution of countries where the tunnel effect operates are obvious. As long as the effect is strong, the developing country will be relatively easy to govern. It may even exhibit a surprising aptitude for democratic forms, which, alas, is likely to be ephemeral; for, after a while the tunnel effect will decay and social injustice will no longer go unperceived and unresisted. As a first reaction, the coercive powers of the state will then be used to restrict participation and to quell protest and subversion. More constructive programs of responding to crisis are easy to conceive, but seem to be extraordinarily difficult to bring into the world.

---

various problems of modernization and nation building—territorial identity, authority, mass participation, etc.—the new nations are faced with all of them at once. See Samuel P. Huntington, *Political Order in Changing Societies* (New Haven: Yale University Press, 1968), Ch. 2; Stein Rokkan, 'Dimensions of State Formation and Nation Building,' in Charles Tilly, ed., *The Building of States in Western Europe* (Princeton, N. J,: Princeton University Press, forthcoming). Various alternative sequential paths are explored in Dankwar A. Rustow, *A World of Nations* (Washington: Brookings, 1967), Ch. 4.

Mathematical Appendix

Consider a society composed of two types of people, labeled *A* and *B*. We assume that utilities are interdependent in two distinct ways. The utility of people of type *A*, besides being determined by their own present income, $Y^A(t)$, is affected by the present income of people of type *B*, $Y^B(t)$, and by their expected future income, $E^A(t)$ which depends on *B*'s present income, among other things.[30] Hence we write

$$U^A(t) = V(Y^A(t),\ Y^B(t),\ E^A(t)). \tag{1}$$

It is natural to assume that *A*'s utility increases with his present and future income or that[31]

$$V_1 > 0; \qquad V_3 > 0. \tag{2}$$

The effect of *B*'s income on *A*'s utility is more complex. *A* evaluates it in two ways—first, according to whether *B*'s success (or failure) *considered by itself* pleases or displeases him and, second, depending on what he thinks *B*'s fate portends for him. Thus,

$$\frac{\partial U^A(t)}{\partial Y^B(t)} = V_2 + V_3 \frac{\partial E^A(t)}{\partial Y^B(t)} \tag{3}$$

In this expression V_2 is the pure effect of compassion or envy and $V_3 \partial E^A(t)/\partial Y^B(t)$ reflects *A*'s concern for *B*'s income as an indication of his own future prospects.

The text of this paper focused on the second term of (3). The first part of this term is essentially the rate at which *A* discounts future income.[32] The second part of the term, $\partial E^A(t)/\partial Y^B(t)$, has not been well studied. It is determined by the method that *A* uses to form expectations of his future income. Neither formal economic theory nor the weight of historical and econometric evidence indicates that there is any one preferred way to model the complex processes that people use to form expectations. We are thus free to

30 Symmetry and completeness would demand that $E^B(t)$, predicted future income of people of type *B*, be an argument of *A's* utility function. Rigor would require recognizing that the expectations of future income, which will occur over several periods, cannot always be faithfully represented by a single number. These (and other) fine points will be ignored here.

31 Subscripts denote partial differentiation.

32 From this observation it follows immediately that the greater the discount rate, the greater the tunnel effect, as observed on pp. 531–32, note 22 of the text.

speculate on the implications of different plausible specifications. Not only is the form of the expectations function not clearly prescribed, but also the signs of its first partial derivatives can conceivably be either positive or negative. If the tunnel effect is present, $\partial E^A(t)/\partial Y^B$ will be positive. But A could also feel that an increase in B's income does not augur well for him. In that case $\partial E^A(t)/\partial Y^B(t)<0$, and possibly $\partial U^A(t)/\partial Y^B(t)<0$, even though A is a perfectly decent benevolent fellow ($V_2>0$). Conversely, if A is subject to the tunnel effect but is mean spirited, then his hopes of future good fortune may swamp his envy. That is, it is quite conceivable that $\partial U^A(t)/\partial Y^B(t)$ should be positive even though V_2 is negative.

The rest of this appendix consists of explicit models of possibilities mentioned in the text. First, we give an example of a society in which everyone is made 'better off' by an unequal distribution of income. Then we show how an initial tolerance for income inequality may be reversed if the benefits of economic growth are not distributed equally.

1. *Preferences for Inequality*

Suppose that the utility function in (1) is linear,

$$V(Y^A(t),\ Y^B(t),\ E^A(t))= a_1 Y^A(t)+a_2 Y^B(t)+a_3 E^B(t), \tag{4}$$

and that A forms expectations by averaging his income with B's,[33] so that

$$E^A(t)=\lambda Y^A(t)+(1-\lambda)\ Y^B(t). \tag{5}$$

Society is composed of individuals of type A and type B in the ratio of N to 1. A sum of money is to be distributed among the populace. For political or administrative reasons, all people of each type must be treated exactly alike. Let us compare the utility accruing to persons of type A from a dollar spent on each of them,

$$\frac{\partial V}{\partial Y^A(t)}=a_1+a_3\lambda, \tag{6}$$

to that from the same N dollars spent on B,

33 Those who object to these simple forms are invited to think of them as approximations to whatever functional forms they find more plausible. Since the analysis is explicitly marginal this is appropriate. To the objection that the weights accorded $Y^A(t)$ and $Y^B(t)$ need not sum to one, it should be noted that any deviation from unity is absorbed in the parameter a_3.

$$N\frac{\partial V}{\partial Y^B(t)}=N(a_2+a_3(1-\lambda)). \tag{7}$$

If we presume that $a_2=0$, or that people of type A are indifferent to the well-being of B, then (7) becomes

$$N\frac{\partial Y}{\partial Y^B(t)}=Na_3(1-\lambda),$$

which will exceed (6) whenever

$$N>\frac{a_1+a_3\lambda}{a_3(1-\lambda)}. \tag{8}$$

So far we have not mentioned B's preferences. There is no reason to suppose that A's preferring that B get additional income should imply that B will not also be made better off by distributions of income to himself than by distributions to A.[34] Suppose B's utility and expectations function are of the same linear form as A's. Thus, if b_1 and b_3 are the weights B assigns to the utility of present and expected future income (b_2, the weight given to A's income, is presumed equal to zero for simplicity and symmetry) and μ and $1-\mu$ are the weights accorded B's and A's present income and in B's prediction of his own future income, then B will be made better off if he, rather than A, is given additional income whenever

$$\frac{1}{N}<\frac{b_1+b_3\mu}{b_3(1-\mu)}. \tag{9}$$

If both (8) and (9) hold, everybody will be happier if the benefits of growth are distributed noticeably and unevenly rather than equitably and imperceptibly. It is clear from (8) and (9) that this seemingly odd state of affairs is likely to obtain when N is large, λ small, and μ large. That is, the rich must be a relatively small segment of the population who themselves do not predicate their own good fortune on that of the masses (large N and μ). More crucially, the bulk of the population must find it sufficiently plausible that their fellow citizens' good fortune will spread to them (small λ).

It is interesting to speculate when λ is likely to be small. A plausible hypothesis is that people will be confident that their neighbors' good fortune will spread to them when (i) their neighbors

34 We do not consider the possibility that either A or B prefers an equal distribution to one in which A or B gets everything. Linearity precludes equality ever being preferred to inequality.

are not obviously different from them and (ii) the inequality has not persisted for long. This is, in part, the basis of the assertion in the text that the tunnel effect is more available to unitary than segmented societies and that relying on it for too long may lead to rising discontent, if not disaster. An example of such a reversal is given in the next section in which a more explicitly dynamic model is analyzed.

2. The Reversal from Tolerance for Inequality to Intolerance

In this section we discuss an example of the sort of process that could lead to a development disaster. As development takes place, all its benefits are distributed to B whose income grows steadily while that of A remains constant. Initially A's utility rises as he expects to share in B's bounty. As time goes on and his situation remains stationary, he becomes discouraged. Eventually his utility falls. A's utility function is log-linear so that

$$V(Y^A(t), Y^B(t), E^A(t)) = \alpha \log Y^A(t) + \beta \log Y^B(t) + \gamma \log E^A(t), \tag{10}$$

while predicted future income is a geometric average of $Y^A(t)$ and $Y^B(t)$,

$$E^A(t) = [Y^A(t)]^{(1-\eta(t))} [Y^B(t))]^{(\eta(t))}$$

or[35]

$$\log E^A(t) = (1-\eta(t)) \log Y^A(t) + \eta(t) \log Y^B(t). \tag{11}$$

A's utility as a function of $Y^A(t)$, $Y^B(t)$, and t may then be written

$$W^A(Y^A(t), Y^B(t),t) = (\alpha+\gamma(1-\eta(t))) \log Y^A(t) + (\beta+\gamma\eta(t)) \log Y^B(t). \tag{12}$$

We may plot the time profile of A's utility if we know the course of his income, of B's income, and of $\eta(t)$. Suppose that initially the income of A and B is equal,

$$Y^A(O) = Y^B(O) = Y, \tag{13}$$

and that B's income begins to grow at a constant rate g, while A's remains static,

35 Again we have chosen γ so that the weights on log $Y^A(t)$ and log $Y^B(t)$ sum to unity. Since we are about to examine how $\eta(t)$, but not γ, changes over time, more is implied than a harmless normalization.

$$Y^A(t) = Y;\ Y^B(t) = Y_e^{gt}. \tag{14}$$

Suppose further that A initially hopes to share in B's good fortune but grows more discouraged as time goes on. Symbolically this is $\eta'(t)<0$. A plausible specification is that

$$\eta(t) = \eta e^{-ht}. \tag{15}$$

Substituting (13), (14), and (15) into (12), we find that A's wellbeing at time t is given by

$$\begin{aligned} W^A(t) &= (\alpha+\gamma(1-\eta e^{-ht})) \log Y \\ &\quad +(\beta+\gamma\eta e^{-ht}) (\log Y+gt) \\ &=(\alpha+\beta+\gamma) \log Y+(\beta+\gamma\eta e^{-ht})\, gt. \end{aligned} \tag{16}$$

Differentiating (16), we have

$$W^{A\prime}(t)=g(\beta+\gamma\eta e^{-ht})gt-(h\gamma\eta e^{-ht}). \tag{17}$$

It follows that

$$W^{A\prime}(0)=g(\beta+\gamma\eta),$$

which will be positive whenever

$$\beta+\gamma\eta>0. \tag{18}$$

Thus, if there is not too much envy ($-\beta$ is not too large), A's utility will rise even though his own income remains static. It is easy to see that if A is malevolent or indifferent to B's fate ($\beta\leq 0$), then this state of affairs cannot persist. This conclusion follows from the calculation of the limiting value of A's utility. If $\beta=0$, then A eventually returns to a situation in which he was just as well off as he was initially,

$$(\lim_{t\to\infty} W^A(t)= W^A(0));$$

if A is envious, then he eventually becomes infinitely miserable,

$$(\lim_{t\to\infty} W^A(t)=-\infty).$$

If A is made better off by B's good fortune, then his asymptotic utility is infinite (as he accords a positive weight to B's infinite utility). However, even in this case it is possible that his fortunes will suffer a temporary reversal. If β is not too large and $\gamma\eta$ not too small, then the equation $W^{A\prime}(t)=0$ has a solution, say τ. When that τ is reached, *A*'s utility will begin to decline. Society's tolerance for inequality will reverse.

We hope these examples illustrate how easy it is to incorporate the tunnel effect into formal models. Many other variants are possible. It is not difficult to write down and analyze models in which the strength of the tunnel effect depends on the absolute size of *B*'s income or on the gap (absolute or relative) between the incomes of the two classes. Similarly, models with more than two classes of individuals are simple to construct. We are aware that the construction of formal models of the content of a theory is not equivalent to the detailing of testable empirical implications of that theory. However, it does seem a useful first step.

INDEX

LIMITED